# The Voice
# of the People

*John Doherty, 1798-1854*
*Trade unionist, radical*
*and factory reformer*

R G Kirby
A E Musson

Manchester University Press

© 1975 R. G. Kirby and A. E. Musson

Published by
Manchester University Press
Oxford Road, Manchester M13 9PL

ISBN 0 7190 0584 1

Printed by
John Sherratt and Son Ltd.,
Park Road, Altrincham,
Cheshire WA14 5QQ.

# Contents

# Preface

This book originated in researches started sporadically by myself some seventeen years ago, arising from general interest in early nineteenth-century trade unionism. John Doherty figures in all the textbooks and is recognised, indeed, as the most outstanding trade union leader of that period, but surprisingly little is actually known about him (and many of the statements made are erroneous). He therefore seemed an obvious subject for research, but since there are no surviving Doherty papers this would entail patient and prolonged combing of likely contemporary sources, such as local newspapers, trade union and radical journals, Home Office records, the Place papers, the Webb collection, the Oastler papers, and miscellaneous material (parliamentary reports, pamphlets, etc.), relating to trade unionism in the cotton and other industries, the factory reform movement, early co-operation, etc.

I had gradually accumulated a considerable file of notes when, in the late 1960s, Ray Kirby expressed a desire to carry out postgraduate research on Doherty at the University of Manchester. In view of his strong interest I agreed to hand over the material I had collected and to act as his supervisor, with an agreement on future joint publication. Since then he has very thoroughly and successfully continued exploration of the above sources and has produced a very substantial thesis, for which he has been awarded the degree of Ph.D. His researches were directed and his thesis was shaped in consultation with me, and I have subsequently revised it very extensively in content and interpretation and rewritten a great part of it. This book is thus a product of our joint research and writing, and we have agreed on its final published form, including this preface.

We have been able to throw much new light on Doherty and the various movements with which he was associated. In the first place, we have produced a great deal of new evidence about his role in the Manchester cotton spinners' society and the Grand General Union of Cotton Spinners of 1829–31, as well as about his wider trade union aims and activities, especially in the National Association for the Protection of Labour. Another of his major interests—indeed, the most long-lasting—was in the factory reform movement, and we have shown how this originated in Lancashire much earlier than the famous Yorkshire agitation initiated by Richard Oastler in 1830, and how Doherty persisted in his efforts to achieve the Ten Hours Bill long after he had ceased to play a direct and active role in trade unionism.

Concern with factory reform, of course, was a development from cotton spinners' trade unionism, but his activities extended much more widely, especially from 1829 onwards, firstly into general trades unionism and then into trade union and radical journalism, radical politics, co-operation and other areas, with the result that in 1832 he set up in Manchester as a radical bookseller, printer and publisher. To these interests we can add others, such as those in the Irish question, local Manchester politics, education, and temperance.

A picture emerges of a highly intelligent, self-educated, dedicated Irish trade unionist and radical reformer, passionate on some occasions, but usually very sane and well balanced, a good organiser and administrator, highly articulate in both the spoken and the written word, but generally pragmatic and non-revolutionary, believing in well organised constitutional action in both trade unionism and politics. Having spent two periods in gaol—one because of his trade union activities, the other on account of his outspoken journalism—he may be enrolled among Labour's 'martyrs', and no one, as Lord Shaftesbury commented on his death, was more 'faithful to a cause'. But he is not a figure to evoke sentimental regret, for he was ever combative, ever ebullient and fearless, ever hopeful of achieving a better, more just society.

Facts about Doherty's early activities in Manchester, from his arrival in 1816 until the late 1820s, are rather sparse, but we have felt it essential (in Chapter II) to place these in the trade union and radical background of those years, in which he clearly participated and from which he developed many of his later ideas. In fact it becomes evident that most of his subsequent schemes were less novel than is usually supposed and that their roots are to be traced in this earlier period.

Doherty's multifarious interests have necessitated division of his career into sections, under different subject headings. This makes possible more continuous and penetrating analysis of his ideas and activities in each of these fields. But this historical treatment is to some extent artificial, since these interests were never clearly differentiated, but were, in fact, closely interrelated; some repetition is therefore unavoidable. But we have tried to reduce this to a minimum by cross-referencing, though this, of course, creates another problem. Clearly, however, this sectional treatment is preferable to attempting a general chronicle of Doherty's life.

We are particularly grateful to Professor J. T. Ward, of Strathclyde University, both for valuable help on sources and for many suggested improvements in our text. Dr D. J. Rowe, of Newcastle-upon-Tyne University, also read our typescript and made extremely useful suggestions on numerous points. We are also, of course, greatly indebted to many libraries and record offices for unfailing courtesy and assistance in our researches.

Finally, we would like to take this opportunity of expressing our grateful appreciation of the many kindnesses of the late Mr T. L. Jones, former secretary of the Manchester University Press, and our regret at his sudden death. At the same time we also wish to thank his successor, Mr J. M. N. Spencer, for his subsequent helpfulness.

University of Manchester

A E Musson

# Abbreviations

| | |
|---|---|
| *Advertiser* | *Manchester and Salford Advertiser* |
| *Advocate* | *Poor Man's Advocate* |
| *Chronicle* | *Wheeler's Manchester Chronicle* |
| *Courier* | *Manchester Courier* |
| *Expositor* | *Workman's Expositor* |
| *Gazette* | *Manchester Gazette* |
| *Guardian* | *Manchester Guardian* |
| *Herald* | *Herald of the Rights of Industry* |
| *H.O.* | Home Office Papers |
| *Journal* | *United Trades' Co-operative Journal* |
| *Observer* | *Manchester Obesrver* |
| Parl. Papers | Parliamentary Papers |
| *Pilot* | *United Pilot and Co-operative Intelligencer* |
| *S.H.R.* | *Scottish Historical Review* |
| *Times* | *Manchester Times* |
| *Times and Gazette* | *Manchester Times and Gazette* |
| *T.L.C.A.S.* | *Transactions of the Lancashire and Cheshire Antiquarian Society* |
| *Voice* | *Voice of the People* |

# Introduction

Historians have frequently noted the importance of John Doherty in working-class movements of the early nineteenth century. S. and B. Webb recognised that he was 'a man of wide information, great natural shrewdness, and far-reaching aims', while J. L. and B. Hammond considered him to be 'the chief working-class leader of the time'; this opinion has been echoed by G. D. H. Cole, who referred to him as 'the most influential trade unionist of his time', and more recently by H. A. Turner, who has declared him to be 'one of the great figures of the early working-class movement'.[1] Contemporaries were equally aware of Doherty's contribution. Daniel O'Connell informed the House of Commons in 1838 that Doherty was 'as intelligent and as highly educated as any man could be expected to be, and a great agitator too, for a Ten Hours Bill. He was one of the leading men for many years amongst those who agitated on that subject. He was also secretary to his union.' A Scottish trade-union colleague, Patrick McGowan, wrote in 1832 that 'Mr Doherty's whole life has been devoted to promote the interests of that class to which he belongs, and . . . he has been the first public writer who has openly and manfully espoused the cause of the oppressed operatives, and fearlessly pleaded the cause of suffering humanity'. And Anthony Trollope, who met Doherty in 1839 in the course of his mother's research into factory conditions for her novel, *The Life and Adventures of Michael Armstrong, the Factory Boy*, remembered him as 'an Irishman, a Roman Catholic, and a furious radical, but a *very* clever man. He was thoroughly acquainted with all that had been done, all that it was hoped to do, and with all the means that were being taken for the advancement of their hopes, over the entire district.'[2]

In spite of this general recognition, only one attempt has been made to trace Doherty's career in any detail. R. Cassirer's thesis on 'The Irish influence on the liberal movement in England, 1798–1832', recognises Doherty as 'one of the most remarkable leaders of the early working-class struggles', and stresses his absolute insistence on the workers improving themselves by their own efforts, instead of relying on middle-class leadership; it also demonstrates his inter-linking of economic and political issues, and the Irish background to several of his ideas and tactics. However, wide omissions were inevitable because of the author's central theme, while even on that there is a serious error in the assertion that Doherty's work suffered virtually no difficulties because of anti-Irish prejudice.[3]

One reason why no biography of Doherty has heretofore been attempted is the lack of personal papers and records. Hence details of his early life and his family have to be gleaned from his publications, his evidence to the Select Committee on Combinations of Workmen in 1838, and other passing references. There is even confusion about the date of his birth. According to his son, Austin, who wrote to the *Manchester Notes and Queries* in 1888 in response to an enquiry about his father, Doherty 'was born at Buncrana, Inishowel, county Donegal, I believe in the year 1797'. But Doherty himself told the 1838 Committee that he was 39 years of age, while in the 1841 census his age is recorded as 40. Austin Doherty is, however, vague about his dates—he maintains that his father began business as a bookseller 'in the year of my nativity, 1830', when in fact he commenced in 1832—and the inattention to detailed accuracy in the census records of the period is notorious. Doherty's obituary in the *Manchester Courier* in 1854 gave his age as 56 years, as also did the certificate of his death, and so we can hesitatingly conclude that he was born in 1798.[4]

Doherty had little formal education. This he admitted during his speech in defence of a libel charge in 1832, when he pleaded the indulgence of the jury if he strayed from the usual forms and rules of the court, because 'at no period had he had for twelve months together the advantages of regular education'. Probably his early instruction depended upon his parents and the local parish priest, and there is no doubt that he remained conscious of its limitations. Thus, on the founding of the *United Trades' Co-operative Journal* in 1830, he felt it necessary to explain to his readers that, in common with most of the working classes,

> we have had but little time to spare for study. Those years which are usually devoted to learning, have been spent in toiling for a scanty subsistence. The slender stock of knowledge which we possess has been casually and, as it were, accidentally snatched from the common stock, during the usual and necessary periods of cessation from labour. Unfortunately for us, we have never tasted of the inspiring sweets of the pierian spring. We make no pretensions to classic lore. We cannot boast of an acquaintance with what is commonly called the learned languages; nor can we, at present, of course, aspire to a display of the beauties and elegances of composition. The only requisite qualifications which we believe we possess, to fit us for the task we have undertaken, is a moderate share of common sense and an accurate knowledge, from experience, of the wants, the wishes, the interests, and the *capacities* of the working classes.[5]

Nevertheless, the varied contents of Doherty's publications show that he had acquired much information, probably through reading and discussion in the evenings, and he made the imparting of knowledge to workpeople one of the chief items in his programme, through which they were to attain their rightful place in society.

Doherty was himself a child worker, starting at the age of ten in the cotton industry at Buncrana.[6] According to a nineteenth-century account, this consisted mainly of handloom weaving, with some calico printing, but there is no record of cotton spinning in that area, though it was the site of one of the earliest flax-spinning mills and an even earlier bleachworks.[7] It is impossible to discover in which of these works Doherty was employed. What is certain is that sometime in his youth he moved to Larne, in the county of Antrim, about fourteen miles north of Belfast, where he worked as a given special consideration in the Act of Union, the existing high protective duties being retained until 1808, after which they were gradually reduced to cotton spinner.[8] The Irish cotton industry was the one branch of manufacture the general level of 10 per cent by 1816. In 1801 this industry, which had been partly nurtured by the investment of Manchester manufacturers, employed about 13,500 people in the district around Belfast and progress continued in the next decade, during which the annual import of raw material trebled. In 1816, when the trade was placed on the same footing in regard to protection as other Irish industries, it was in a flourishing condition, which continued until the mid-1820s, when it suffered a rapid decline in the face of the competition of more technically progressive English firms, after the protective tariff had been abolished in 1821.[9]

As a cotton spinner, therefore, Doherty had less compelling economic reasons than most when he left Larne in 1816 and joined the flow of Irish immigrants into England and Scotland, which after the Napoleonic wars was fast becoming a flood. We can surmise that it was the high wages to be earned as a cotton spinner in Lancashire which formed the chief motivation for his moving to Manchester. There is a story that Doherty gained his first employment in a Manchester spinning mill by means of a forged certificate of character from Belfast. The first public reference to this charge was in 1828, when it was one of a series of accusations levelled against him by a faction within the Manchester spinners' union opposing his election to the secretaryship.[10] It is noteworthy that, although Doherty answered all the other charges against him in his first publication, the *Conciliator*, he did not explicitly rebut this one, merely promising to say more of it 'hereafter'. Perhaps he felt it unnecessary to recur to it, as the divisions which caused the paper's foundation were soon healed. Nevertheless, his failure to answer the accusation made it possible for later adversaries to repeat it on several occasions, usually to discredit the leaders of the ten hours movement. In 1833, in Tufnell's remarks on the evidence of Sadler's committee, given in the *Supplementary Report of the Central Board of Factory Commissioners*, he stated that Doherty was a man 'who (it is right that the characters of the leaders in this business should be known) originally came to Manchester with a forged character'. The allegation was repeated in the works of apologists for the factory system, like Andrew Ure's *Philosophy of Manufactures*, and again, as late as 1844, in *The Report of the Central Committee of Cotton Millowners and Manufacturers* opposed to the Ten Hours Bill. Thus Doherty was never able to eradicate this imputation against him, although the extended life of other stories, such as his being imprisoned 'for a gross assault upon a woman', should make one careful of accepting such propaganda at face value.[11]

Doherty worked as a cotton spinner in Manchester from 1816 at least until his election as secretary of the spinners' club in 1828. And he frequently recalled his experiences of life and work in a cotton factory in his later speeches and writing. In 1832, for example, in justifying his severity towards millowners, he declared:

> We have ourselves felt the full force and severity of the system in its worst days; we have been subject to all the petty tyranny and vulgar arrogance which insolence, ignorance and cupidity combined could practice or assume. We are practically acquanited with all the vexatious restrictions and illegal exactions which are constantly practised upon the poor, the feeble, and defenceless operative. We know what it is to be the victims of robbery which we have so feebly, we fear, attempted to describe and denounce. We

> have been shut up as prisoners in the 'hellish and stinking and health-
> destroying bastiles', to unremitting toil while our ears have been stunned
> and our understanding insulted by the fraudulent and empty boast of the
> 'blessings of free labour!' We have seen men so terrified at the casual
> approach of an employer, as to drop down speechless, and almost lifeless,
> and others stand motionless and petrified, lest they should incur his dis-
> pleasure. While all these things are fresh in our recollection, it is impossible
> we could speak with calmness and temper of the system. One thing, how-
> ever, we will say, we have not written one word from personal dislike. All
> that we have said has been merely with the view of reforming or of mitigat-
> ing the cruelties of the system.[12]

Certainly, then, his experiences as a cotton spinner coloured his attitude
towards the movements in which he became involved; but it is only possible
to name one of the actual factories where he worked. This was at the time
of the spinners' strike in Manchester in 1818, when he was working in the
New Mill of George Murray, who had migrated much earlier from Scotland
and become one of the biggest millowners in the town.[13]

Doherty was a leading figure in the Manchester spinners' union for two
decades. In 1819 he was imprisoned for two years for his part in their strike
of the previous year, and he was closely involved in their attempt to form a
federal union of their trade with other districts in 1824-5, and in their
efforts to oppose re-enactment of the Combination Laws in the latter year.
He was secretary of their club between 1828 and 1830, and again between
1834 and 1836, although he was by then himself a small bookseller. Later, his
connection with the spinners was still sufficiently close for him to give
evidence on their behalf to the 1838 Combinations Committee. Doherty led
the Manchester spinners in a six-month strike against a wages reduction in
1829. And immediately after the failure of this turn-out he initiated the two
projects for which he is now most famous—the Grand General Union of
Operative Cotton Spinners throughout the United Kingdom and, even more
ambitious, the National Association for the Protection of Labour, which was
the first substantial attempt to give practical effect to the idea of forming a
general union of workers in all trades, which had been widely discussed for
the previous decade. These bodies had faded into obscurity by 1831 and 1832
respectively, but in 1834 Doherty was involved in a stillborn attempt to convert the National Regeneration Society, founded to procure an eight-hour day
for the same wages, into a branch of Owen's Grand National Consolidated
Trades' Union. The Lancashire spinners also formed the basis of the factory
movement in the county from 1814 onwards, and under Doherty's influence
from the 1820s they organised several attempts to enforce existing legislation,
particularly between 1828 and 1830, and to secure new Acts of Parliament,
intermittently even considering direct action to win shorter hours. In addition, Doherty was a leading figure in political radicalism in Manchester for a
decade and a half after 1821, and in 1831 proposed a scheme for holding a
National Convention in London to persuade Parliament to extend the provisions of the Reform Bill to include household suffrage. He also participated
in attempts to secure radical control of Manchester local government in the
1830s, was for a short time between 1831 and 1834 involved in the co-operative movement, and was a lifelong supporter of Irish nationalism, temper-

ance and working-class education. Between 1828 and 1834, he edited a series of trade-union, factory reform and radical periodicals and was twice more in gaol during 1832, when a Stockport clergyman named Gilpin whom Doherty had accused of being implicated in 'body-snatching' sued him for libel. From 1832 to 1841 he was a small bookseller and printer, selling mostly radical, educational, temperance and religious literature, as well as popular fiction.[14] After 1841 his activities were confined almost exclusively to factory reform, and in the later 'forties he seems to have retired from public life.

Details of Doherty's private life in Manchester are far more scarce. He married an English girl, Laura, probably soon after his release from Lancaster Gaol in 1821. She is listed as a milliner in the *Manchester Directory* of 1828. According to the 1841 census, they had four children—Mary, born about 1823, Ambrose about 1825, Agnes about 1827, and Augustus about 1829. (In fact, we have already seen that the youngest child, called Austin, was born in 1830.) The family lived first at 6 Little Ormond Street, Chorlton Row, but had moved to 42 Port Street by 1828. In 1832 Doherty set himself up in business as a bookseller, stationer and printer at the offices of the *Poor Man's Advocate*, 37 Withy Grove. His wife helped to serve in the shop and in the following year he opened a reading room on the first floor. This closed down in 1834, but at the same time he moved to larger premises at 4 Withy Grove, becoming qualified to vote at both parliamentary and local elections. In the 1841 census Doherty was called a 'letter-press printer', but after that year his name disappeared from the directories and one 'Negretti Gaston, working optician', took over his shop. In 1842 he was living at 62 Devonshire Street, Hulme; but no further domestic reference has been found until his death in 1854, when the *Manchester Guardian* stated him to be an 'agent, of 83 New Bridge Street'. His death on Friday 14 April was sudden enough to call for a coroner's inquest on the following Monday, but the surgeon, Mr E. Thomas, having examined the body, reported that the deceased 'had died of disease of the heart, which was evidently of long duration from the great enlargement of the heart', and a verdict was returned in accordance with these findings. By this time his name was almost forgotten and he received only the briefest of obituaries in the local press. It seems possible, however, that the family interest in printing and bookselling may have been maintained, as is suggested by the name 'Caxton Villas' at which his son Austin was living at Urmston in the 1880s. Austin was by that time evidently a man of some substance, for in 1878 he had purchased land in this village near Manchester, on which he had built houses (including his own residence) and three small roads. The names of the latter form the only present-day memorial to his once famous father—Gilpin, Blincoe and Allen, the last named being a character in Harriet Martineau's *A Manchester Strike* reputedly based on Doherty himself.[15]

There is evidence to show that his married life was not uneventful. On the night of 8 July 1835 he returned home just before midnight to find that his wife had barred the door. Neither he nor his sister-in-law could prevail upon Laura to let him in and therefore he was about to go to the White Lion Inn to book a bed for the night when his wife rushed out, tore at his face, and stabbed him in the arm. The resulting disturbance attracted a police watchman, Joseph Robinson, who saw Doherty strike his wife to the ground. The watchman told him to calm down, but, his Irish temper clearly roused, Doherty began kicking at his own door and was thereupon arrested. Next morning he appeared at the New Bailey, charged with assaulting Laura, and Mr Davies, the superintendent of police, stated that there had been complaints about his conduct before; but Laura 'had been induced by a friend of the prisoner's' to leave the court, Doherty's explanation of the incident was accepted, and he was discharged, though covered in scars.[16] This incident was later twisted in another attempt to discredit him. When the government was considering the establishment of a Select Committee into Workmen's Combinations in 1838, following outrages by Glasgow and Dublin trade unionists, Edwin Chadwick wrote to Lord John Russell with some information he had received about combinations during his enquiries under the constabulary force commissioners in the previous autumn. 'The men of whom any account was given to me as their leaders were all notoriously bad characters. The Editor of their paper, *The Voice of the People*, was a man who had been imprisoned twelve months for a murderous assault upon his wife.'[17]

Laura probably considered that his wide-ranging activities caused him to neglect his domestic duties. In 1832, when he was appealing for financial support to fight Gilpin's libel action,[18] Doherty remarked on the notorious ingratitude of the working classes for their persecuted leaders; he believed from the assistance that he was receiving that this negligence was now being rectified, but mentioned in passing other problems which such leaders faced:

> What is perhaps not less painful and annoying, there is the almost incessant complaints, if not reproaches, of the wife at home. From the very nature of things, he who becomes a leader among his fellow-workmen must of necessity, be often out at a late hour. The same circumstances render it necessary that he should expend more money than others of his fellows, as all the meetings, or nearly all, are held in the public-house. Of this the wife soon becomes acquainted, and indeed, probably, as soon feels the effects. Her complaints, and too often reproaches, for what she chooses to call inattentions to her, follow almost as a matter of course; and every meal is embittered by her incessant and almost irresistible entreaties to quit a course which requires such a course of life, and causes her so much pain.[19]

Can we believe that such a heart-felt cry did not emanate from personal experience?

Of his appearance we know nothing, except that he did not have a beard and was sometimes referred to as the 'little Hibernian', though this comment did not necessarily apply to his stature. His personality is, however, clearly defined in his speeches and writing. He was a devout Catholic, often generous and sympathetic, a perpetual organiser, an eloquent orator, and marvellously resilient in the face of successive defeats. But on the debit side he had a fiery temper, was chronically unpunctual, was prone to inconsistency and sudden changes of policy, and was often somewhat dictatorial towards his colleagues, at least those who were themselves workmen.

We have outlined above the major landmarks of Doherty's public career, as well as a few details of his private life, suggesting how his early life in Ireland, his employment as a working spinner and his family relationships affected his attitudes and endeavours in working-class movements of Manchester, in which he was prominent for a quarter of a century. The following chapters will deal mainly with his contribution to the trade-union, factory reform and radical political movements, into all of which he enthusiastically joined almost immediately on coming from Ireland: his other activities in the fields of co-operation, Irish nationalism, temperance and education will also be recounted, and the philosophy which enabled him to span these various movements will be discussed. But first it is necessary to sketch the industrial urban background and the early development of cotton spinners' trade unionism in Manchester when Doherty arrived there as a youth in 1816.

NOTES TO INTRODUCTION

1 S. and B. Webb, *History of Trade Unionism* (1920), p. 117, n. 2; J. L. and B. Hammond, *The Town Labourer, 1760–1832* (1920), p. 249; G. D. H. Cole, *A Short History of the British Working-Class Movement* (1948), p. 70; H. A. Turner, *Trade Union Growth, Structure and Policy: A Comparative Study of the Cotton Unions* (1962), p. 69.

2 *Hansard's Parliamentary Debates*, 3rd Series, Vol. 44 (9 July–16 August 1838), p. 422; *Advocate*, June 30 1832; T. A. Trollope, *What I Remember* (1883), Vol. II, p. 7.

3 R. Cassirer, 'The Irish Influence on the Liberal Movement in England, 1798–1832', Unpub. Ph.D. thesis, University of London (1940), pp. 518–52. For examples of such prejudice, see below, pp. 52, 58, 355.

4 *Manchester Notes and Queries* (1888), Nos. 5062, 5063 and 5069; Parl. Papers, 1837–8, VIII, 3546–7; Census Returns, H.O. 107/572(2). According to the County Librarian of Donegal, there were 183 Doherty families in the Buncrana area in the 1790s, so there is no chance of tracing the actual record of his birth.

5 *Chronicle*, 1 September 1832; *Journal*, 6 March 1830.

6 Parl. Papers, 1837–8, VIII, 3152.

7 James A. Beck Collection, D 1286/2/6. We are indebted to Professor E. R. R. Green for this reference.

8 Parl. Papers, 1837–8, VIII, 3550. A. Redford, *Labour Migration in England, 1800–1850* (2nd edn., Manchester, 1964), p. 39, asserts that Doherty moved west in 1809, but he has apparently amalgamated testimony that he was born in 1799, started work at ten, and was employed as a cotton spinner at Larne.

9 G. O'Brien, *The Economic History of Ireland from the Union to the Famine* (1921), pp. 308–11.

10 See below, p. 51.

11 *Conciliator*, 29 November 1828; *Supplementary Report of the Central Board of Factory Commissioners*, Parl. Papers, 1834, Vol. 19, D2, p. 210; A. Ure, *The Philosophy of Manufactures* (1835), p. 282; *Factory Legislation—Report of the Central Committee . . . December 1844* (Manchester, 1845). The charge also occurred in R. H. Greg, *The Factory Question Considered . . .* (1837), p. 66. For the later 'smear', see below, p. 21.

12 *Advocate*, 21 April 1832.

13 *Conciliator*, 29 November 1828. For George Murray, see A. E. Musson and E. Robinson, *Science and Technology in the Industrial Revolution* (Manchester, 1969), pp. 440–1.

14 His publications included a reprint of the biography of Robert Blincoe, the factory apprentice, in 1832, together with other factory-reform literature.

15 H.O. 107/572 (2); Manchester Directories for 1824–5, 1828, 1829, 1833, 1836, 1838, 1840, 1841 and 1843; *Guardian*, 7 April 1842 and 22 April 1854; *Manchester Notes and Queries*, Vol. VII (1888); Urmston Borough Council Records, Planning Permissions for 1878; *A Penny Poor Man's Advocate*, 29 September 1832; H. Martineau, *A Manchester Strike* (1832). The significance of Blincoe and Gilpin will emerge in Chapters X and XI, in connection with Doherty's factory reform and radical journalistic activities.

[16] *Guardian*, 11 July 1835 .

[17] H.O. 44/31. We are indebted to Mr A. G. Rose for this reference. This garbled smear confused Doherty's two years' imprisonment for an alleged picketing offence in 1818 with this case involving his wife. See below, pp. 21–2, for the picketing affair.

[18] See below, pp. 435–8.

[19] *Advocate and Operative Reporter*, 20 November 1832.

# The rise of the factory system and early trade unionism among Manchester cotton spinners

The rise of the Lancashire cotton industry from a small-scale, domestic manu-facture in the eighteenth century into a great factory industry has been catalogued many times. This 'revolution' occurred following the famous series of inventions, firstly in spinning, with Hargreaves' jenny, Arkwright's water-frame, and Crompton's mule, and much later in weaving, after Cart-wright's original invention of the power loom. Imports of raw cotton into Britain rose astonishingly from 2·3 million lb in 1750 to 6·7 million lb in 1775, 56 million lb in 1800, and then to 228 million lb in 1825.[1] This expansion was at first accommodated within the domestic system, weaving being performed by the father, who taught his sons the art, while the mother was responsible for the preparatory processes, usually spinning herself and allo-cating the work of picking, cleaning, drying, carding, etc., among the children. But from the 1760s onwards dissatisfaction with the domestic system encouraged mechanisation and the growth of the factory system. The introduction of spinning jennies at first caused little reorganisation of labour; but as they increased in size and became too large for women and children to handle, it became common to group them together in factories, often with carding engines. More important was the introduction of the water frame, a water-powered factory machine which Arkwright patented in 1769. Two years after the patent was finally quashed in 1785, there were 143 factories of the water-frame type spinning warp thread, and Baines estimated the value of cotton goods manufactured to have risen from £600,000 in 1767 to £3,034,371 in 1787.[2]

Thus, the introduction of the factory system preceded the application of steam to the cotton industry in the 1780s. Moreover, in addition to the early water-frame factories, there was a tendency to group hand mules together in sheds, as earlier with jennies, and when power was employed it was often that of horses, as well as of water-wheels; such factories were often small and in rural areas. But the introduction of the steam engine greatly acceler-ated the trend towards large-scale factory organisation and urban concentra-tion. By 1800 at least ninety-three engines had been erected in Lancashire by two firms alone—Boulton & Watt and Bateman & Sherratt—and the great majority of these were in the cotton industry.[3] During the Napoleonic wars the cotton industry continued to expand, though less quickly than in the decades immediately before or after. Nevertheless, by 1812 the number of mule spindles in the cotton trade was over four million, compared with 310,000 water-frame and only 155,000 jenny spindles.[4] Therefore factory organisation dominated the spinning branch of the cotton industry by the time of John Doherty's arrival in Manchester, though jenny spinning in fact survived well into the nineteenth century.

Almost all the evils charged upon the factory system had been present under its predecessor. 'In many domestic industries the hours were long, the pay was poor, children worked from a tender age, there was overcrowding, and both home and workshop were rendered less desirable from the combination of the two under a single roof.'[5] Moreover, Smelser has shown how the family unit was in part perpetuated in the factories by the hiring of whole families together in early cotton mills and by adult male spinners hiring their own wives and children as assistants in town mills, thus allowing the father to retain control of his own family.[6] Nevertheless, the introduction of factory discipline did entail considerable changes for the worker who had been used to regulating his own hours at home. The new machines were only brought in amid great opposition, with outbreaks of machine-breaking and attacks on mills. Recruitment to the remote, water-powered mills proved exceptionally difficult, which problem the manufacturers attempted to remedy by the importation of labour, including Scottish and Irish. But adult males formed only a small proportion of the labour force and the chief difficulty was securing child labour in sufficient numbers. Apart from the isolation of many early mills, most parents were at first unwilling to place their children in them. Hence the early factory masters resorted to importing waggonloads of pauper apprentices from the big cities. Again, the abuse of the labour of parish apprentices did not begin with the factory system, but the rise of the latter certainly aggravated the evil, by greatly increasing the numbers so employed and congregating them together in large groups. One of the worst examples of such exploitation was that of Robert Blincoe, whose famous *Memoir*, first published in Richard Carlile's periodical *The Lion* in 1828, was reprinted and sold in pamphlet form by John Doherty in 1832, 'in order to give the most extensive publicity to the horrors of this infernal factory system'.[7]

It is now generally recognised that the worst excesses of the early factory system occurred in remote country mills. The application of steam power to the industry and its consequent movement to the towns, much more than the first ineffective factory legislation in 1802, led to the replacement of parish apprentices by 'free' child labour which was available in the northern towns; the use of parish apprentices had virtually disappeared from the cotton industry by the 1830s. But the rapid growth of urban factories brought new and more permanent problems.

Although water-powered mills continued to increase until about 1820, thereafter the more isolated factories declined and the already visible industrial concentration in Lancashire, Cheshire and parts of Scotland was confirmed. The number of mills in the Manchester area rose from two in 1782 to fifty-two in 1802, and to sixty-four in 1809. Expansion was then halted until after the end of the French wars, when there was a further increase to ninety-nine in 1830.[8] The immediate effect of this growth was a vast expansion of the population of Manchester, which Baines estimated to have risen from 41,000 in 1774 to 102,000 in 1801, and to 187,000 in 1821.[9] And there was a similarly startling increase in the smaller cotton towns in the area. Bolton rose from 18,000 in 1801 to 42,000 in 1831, Blackburn from 12,000 to 27,000 over the same period, Oldham from 12,000 to 32,000, and Stockport from 17,000 to 36,000.[10]

In spite of the efforts of its Improvement Commissioners, Manchester was unable to accommodate this rapidly growing population in any degree of comfort. The fall in the death rate, which had been an important factor in the growth of population, was checked and perhaps even reversed in the years after 1815. Manchester continued to grow apace through short-wave immigration and also the influx of great numbers of poor Irish labourers. The 1841 census gave the number of Irish in Manchester as 34,300, the great majority being unskilled labourers or hand-loom weavers.[11] Four years earlier Nassau Senior described the jerry-built houses and horribly insanitary, over-crowded conditions in the areas where the great mass of Irishmen lived.[12]

But the industrial revolution brought far more than physical and environmental changes. The rapid growth of the cotton industry was organised and effected by a new order of self-made men, who interpreted their success as justification for their belief in their own authority over their workers and in the non-interventionist role of the State as against its old paternalist functions.[13] The elaboration by Adam Smith and his successors, Malthus and Ricardo, of the alleged laws of political economy appeared to be proved by the rapid development of industrialisation. Against their own intention—for Ricardo actually supported some of Owen's early factory reform proposals and others favoured limited factory legislation—the political economists became the apologists of the new industrial society. Politicians, employers and writers endeavoured to use their 'laws' to demonstrate to the workers the blessings of machine production and the wage system and the futility of anything but acquiescence. Low wages, it was contended, were fixed by an iron law, and trade unions and legislation were alike powerless to amend working-class conditions. Middle-class radicals like Francis Place fully accepted this philosophy and maintained that the poor could only improve themselves by limiting their numbers and by education.[14]

However, the ideas of Adam Smith, Ricardo, Bentham and others could be given a different interpretation. Bentham's emphasis on efficiency and the 'greatest happiness for the greatest number' could be fashioned into acceptance of State interference and central control to remedy specific abuses. Smith and Ricardo held that the measure of the value of commodities was the quantity of labour incorporated in them, although neither questioned the right of the capitalist to share in the product of labour. But in the post-war years those who opposed the developing capitalist system combated the orthodox political economy of manufacturers and 'liberals' in the government by arguing that the labour which was the source of all value was exclusively the productive labour of the wage-earning worker. The consequent conclusion, stressed to varying degrees by such writers as Thomas Hodgskin, John Gray and William Thompson, that the labourer was being robbed of his rightful deserts, was a dominant motivating factor in Doherty's activities in trade unionism, factory reform and co-operation; and it was linked also to his political radicalism, for from Cobbett he learnt that the political system which sanctioned the workers' exploitation by their employers was causing him to be plundered too by idle pensioners, fundholders, bankers and aristocrats.

When Doherty arrived in Manchester in 1816 it was a time of social and political ferment in the town. The developments in spinning in the last quarter of the eighteenth century had meant years of prosperity for the hand-loom weavers, but their situation declined calamitously in the first decades of the nineteenth. The ease with which the trade was learnt and the growing influx of poor Irish immigrants caused a great expansion in their number, despite the gradual introduction of the power loom. G. H. Wood estimated that there were 184,000 hand-loom weavers in 1806 and about 240,000 in 1820, of whom perhaps 40,000 lived in Manchester. The number did not start to fall until after about 1830, even though they experienced unparalleled suffering as their wages fell from £1 in 1806 to 15s in 1813, to 8s 3d in 1820, and to 6s 3d in 1830.[15] Their distress drove them intermittently into food rioting and machine breaking, and also made them agitators for economic and political reform, especially in the years of post-war depression, when they undertook the desperate 'March of the Blanketeers' in 1817, and thronged to radical mass meetings, culminating in the 'Peterloo massacre' of 1819.[16]

It should not be forgotten, however, that by 1816 the industrial revolution had affected only a small number of trades. Most crafts retained their traditional methods, mechanisation not taking place until far into the nineteenth century. Even in the cotton industry, where the factory system was most advanced, there were almost twice as many hand-loom weavers (224,000) as factory operatives (117,000) in 1816, and the latter did not become the majority until 1834.[17] In the different handicraft trades there had long been organised clubs, with regulations governing entry to the trade, working conditions, friendly benefits, etc.[18] There was no great social distance between them and their masters, who generally worked on a small scale and were on comparatively friendly terms with their men. But in the cotton factories, as in the mines, the struggle between capital and labour became more acute. Both parties formed separate and mutually hostile organisations, backed, as we have seen, by opposing and conflicting philosophies. As the mills grew larger the estrangement between factory owners and factory workers grew wider. That this was realised and regretted by contemporary observers is clear from the comments of E. C. Tufnell, one of the Factory Commissioners, in a pamphlet published in 1834 attacking trade unions amongst the cotton spinners and other workers:

In those places where combinations have been most frequent and powerful, a complete separation of feeling seems to have taken place between masters and men. Each party looks on the other as an enemy, and suspicion and distrust have driven out the mutual sentiments of kindness and good-will, by which their intercourse was previously marked. A dispute between them is settled by no joint understanding; the two sides are not even allowed to discuss the matter but reference must be made to a junta, chosen by the workmen alone. Thus shackled in his operations, a master must either refuse all large orders for goods, or take them under the trembling apprehension, that should it so please the Union, his profit may be taken away, or even a loss incurred by the undertaking . . . Where a large capital is invested in machinery and buildings, the workmen are enabled to exercise a much greater control over their employers . . . It is not at all an unusual circumstance for 80,000*l.* to be invested in a cotton mill; the interest of this capital exceeds 75*l*. weekly, consequently that sum must be lost to the possessors of such a mill, every week that the men hold out.[19]

On the other hand, workmen like Doherty argued that the employer of a large labour force had the power to make a great number of men idle, and hence dependent on union funds, by a single stroke.[20]

The transformation of cotton spinning into a factory occupation performed by men from 1780 onwards was soon accompanied by the formation of combinations. As early as 1785 the Friendly Society of Cotton Spinners of Stockport was telling its adherents not to work 'below the usual prices'.[21] But this society must have comprised domestic or workshop operatives. The first unions of factory spinners were probably not formed until 1792. In that year a benefit club was founded by hand mule spinners at Stockport which lasted until 1802, when it was broken up by imprisonment of several of its members under the Combination Laws. Also in 1792 the first regular organisation was formed amongst the Manchester mule spinners. Apart from the usual benefits of a friendly society, the rules prohibited members from working in a shop where a strike had taken place and laid down that 'strangers', who had learnt to spin elsewhere, should pay 10*s* 6*d* to join the society.[22]

In 1795 the Manchester spinners conducted two strikes for wage increases, the second of which achieved success after one month. They defended their activities in an address 'to the Employers of Mule-Spinners, and the Public in general': they denied that they had any idea of combining against their employers, for

> Combination . . . is not in Question with us—the Nature of our Meeting, or Club, is not to encourage Idleness, or promote Disorder; but only to relieve our Fellow Labourers in Distress; and to say that Numbers of Industrious People have been dragged from their Places and menaced by the Members of our Club, until the Encrease of Wages demanded from their employers be granted—we deny.[23]

Nevertheless, when a fresh set of rules was registered with the magistrates a month later it was thought necessary to omit those articles dealing specifically with trade-society activities, while the benefit regulations were made more elaborate and comprehensive. In 1796, from which year the earliest rules of a Friendly Associated Cotton Spinners' Society at Oldham are extant, it was laid down among the list of offences that members who 'shall combine together to raise their wages contrary to law' should be fined.[24]

After the passing of the Combination Laws in 1799 and 1800 it became even more vital to cloak the activities of the unions under the guise of friendly societies. Nevertheless, during the brief period of peace and prosperity in 1801–02 the Manchester spinners struck successfully for a wage advance. But by 1803 and the renewal of warfare, a depression in trade induced the master spinners in the Manchester area to raise a fighting fund of £20,000 to defeat 'this dangerous and unjust combination'.[25] Thereafter the spinners were apparently kept quiet for a number of years, but in 1807 there was a turn-out from the Salford factory of George Lee, which was later occupied by Holland Hoole, a leading opponent of the Ten Hours Bill. The attitude of the men proved so obdurate that Lee decided to employ females as mule spinners, and females were still employed there in 1833.[26] This practice was repeated by at least one other firm, McConnell & Kennedy, who in 1810 took on a number of women as operative spinners, and continued their employment 'as a sort of check upon the combinations of the men'.[27]

The year 1810 also saw the formation of the first wider organisation among the cotton spinners of Lancashire. Taking advantage of a temporary surge in production—raw cotton consumption rose from 88 million lb in 1809 to 124 million lb in 1810, a level not again reached until 1821[28]—the Lancashire spinners formed a federation of their local unions and demanded that the piece prices in the country towns be brought up to those paid in Manchester. When the employers refused,

> all the spinners in all the mills in the neighbourhood of Manchester including Stockport, Macclesfield, Stalybridge, Ashton, Hyde, Oldham, Bolton, and as far north as Preston, simultaneously left their work, and had the strike continued a little longer, the whole of Scotland would have joined it. As it was, 30,000 persons were thrown out of employ; many of them paraded the streets of the above towns during the day, shouting and hooting at the residences of those persons, who, they supposed, were inimical to their cause. Attacks were frequently made on the factories, in defiance of the Police, who were utterly inefficient for protection; many masters were unable to leave their mills, for fear of their lives, and such workmen as were got to supply the place of the seceders, were held prisoners, in a state of almost continual siege, in the establishments where they worked. The *government* of this strike was carried on by a congress at Manchester, which was formed of delegates sent from all the principal mills. The chief leader in this congress, and, in fact, the chief leader and organizer of the turn-out, was a man named Joseph Shipley, who possessed the greatest influence over the workmen, and appears to have been a perfect Masaniello. This man, in the words of one of our informants, who, at that time, was a spinner and joined in the strike, was as 'a general in the army', the commander of thousands of willing agents, who performed his bidding with the utmost promptitude.[29]

According to Tufnell, the Union also demanded control of whom the masters should employ in their mills.

The strikers were supported by contributions of £1,000 to £1,500 per week by the spinners in work, of which about £600 came from the Manchester society itself. The 'congress at Manchester', which conducted the affairs of the union, in fact comprised forty or fifty people, some of whom were district delegates and others were the representatives of Manchester mills. Altogether £17,000 was distributed to the men on strike, but after four months the funds ran out, and with the onset of renewed depression the unemployed operatives, of whom about 3,000 or one-tenth were spinners, were forced to return to work at the old piece rates. The collapse of the strike caused great distress to those involved, which continued throughout 1811 and 1812, and according to Doherty, writing in 1834, 'the union was entirely abandoned. For many years there was not even a vestige of it remaining . . . [for] the odious combination laws were in full power to crush any attempt at organisation'.[30] However, Turner points out that mill strikes were already taking place in Manchester by the end of 1811 against wage reductions, while in the better trading years of 1813 and 1814 the first district wage list of which record survives appeared in Bolton, the Stockport spinners negotiated a compromise agreement with their employers, and the Preston society was reorganised.[31]

But when Doherty came to Manchester in 1816 the post-war depression was reaching its depths and the cotton spinners were involved in new difficulties. The Stockport spinners' wages were gradually eroded from the agreed level in 1814 until their net earnings were said to be only £1 in 1818.[32] And the Manchester spinners were forced to accept a large reduction in their wage rates, which they later claimed in some cases amounted to fully one-third.[33] The spinners stated that when they assented to this their employers promised to return to the former wage rates when trade revived. Their refusal to implement this pledge was to lead to further and more serious conflicts, in which John Doherty was an active participant.

Thus in 1816 the cotton spinners already had a history of active trade unionism spanning a quarter of a century. Because their labour involved strength and skill, unlike the majority of occupations in the cotton factories, it was performed mostly by men, who, with six or seven subsidiary workers in other processes dependent upon them, were therefore in a strong bargaining position with their employers, especially in times of good trade. They hired and paid their assistants themselves, and earned the highest wages in the whole industry. Although great variations existed, depending on whether the counts spun were coarse or fine, and on the number of spindles in the mule, Wood estimated that the average earnings for an ordinary week's work in Manchester and district ranged between 32s 6d and 36s 6d in 1804 for a fine spinner, and was 32s between 1814 and 1822; while a coarse spinner could earn between 20s and 28s throughout this period.[34] Despite rising war-time prices, these were high wages, especially when compared, as they frequently were by the employers and the hostile press, with the earnings of the hand-loom weavers.

Although mule spinning was a new occupation, created by the industrial revolution, the men sought to build up a trade club in the manner of the traditional skilled handicraftsmen. Thus the limiting of entry to the trade was included in the rules of the first Manchester society, while the Grand General Spinners' Union of 1829 sought to limit instruction, in the absence of traditional apprenticeship, to near relatives of members.[35] Weekly contributions were high. The Manchester society's acceptance fee for individual members was 10s, and its standard contribution was 7d per week, to which were added weekly 'levies' of 3d to 6d according to need.[36] Finally, a wide range of friendly society benefits were paid, including unemployment, sickness and funeral payments. From this period onwards, however, the status of the skilled journeymen cotton spinners was increasingly threatened by further technological developments, with the invention of the 'self-actor' mule, patented by Richard Roberts, the Manchester engineer, in 1825 and 1830, and the introduction of larger mules, with ever-increasing numbers of spindles. Both these developments reduced the demand for adult labour, while increasing the number of juvenile 'piecers', thus ultimately creating more spinners, increasing unemployment, and threatening to depress wages.

NOTES TO CHAPTER ONE

[1] B. R. Mitchell and P. Deane, *Abstract of British Historical Statistics* (Cambridge, 1962), pp. 177–80.

[2] N. J. Smelser, *Social Change in the Industrial Revolution, 1770–1840* (1959), pp. 54–5; E. Baines, *History of the Cotton Manufacture in Great Britain* (1835), pp. 217–18.

[3] Musson and Robinson, *op. cit.*, p. 423.

[4] Smelser, *op. cit.*, p. 121, quoting from G. W. Daniels, 'Samuel Crompton's Census of the Cotton Industry in 1812', *Economic Journal*, II (1930), pp. 108–11.

[5] J. L. and B. Hammond, *op. cit.*, p. 31.

[6] Smelser, *op. cit.*, pp. 185–93.

[7] J. Brown, *A Memoir of Robert Blincoe* (Manchester, 1832); *Gazette*, 2 November 1822; *Lion*, 25 June–22 February 1828; *Advocate*, 9 June 1832. For an assessment of Blincoe's *Memoir*, see A. E. Musson, 'Robert Blincoe and the Early Factory System', *Derbyshire Miscellany*, No. 8, February 1958, pp. 111–17, revised and reprinted in Musson, *Trade Union and Social History* (1974). See also below, pp. 375–6.

[8] G. W. Daniels, 'The Cotton Trade at the Close of the Napoleonic War', *Transactions of the Manchester Statistical Society* (1917–18), pp. 18–21; Manchester Chamber of Commerce, *Proceedings*, 27 April 1833.

[9] E. Baines, *History of the County of Lancaster* (1823). The official census figures for the town were 75,000 in 1801, 89,000 in 1811, 126,000 in 1821, and 182,000 in 1831.

[10] Mitchell and Deane, *op. cit.*, pp. 24–6.

[11] Redford, *op. cit.*, p. 155.

[12] Nassau W. Senior, *Letters on the Factory Act* (1837), pp. 24–5, quoted in F. Engels, *The Condition of the Working Class in England* (1844; English trans., 1958), pp. 75–6.

[13] For a workers' reaction to exploitation by these new men, see the address of 'A Journeyman Cotton Spinner' during the 1818 Manchester strike, quoted by E. P. Thompson, *The Making of the English Working Class* (1968), pp. 218–21.

[14] For the political economists and factory reform, see K. O. Walker, 'The Classical Economists and the Factory Acts', *Journal of Econ. Hist.*, I (November 1941); L. R. Sorenson, 'Some Classical Economists, Laissez Faire and the Factory Acts', *ibid.*, XII, 3 (Summer 1952); M. Blaug, 'The Classical Economists and the Factory Acts: A Re-examination', *Quarterly Journal of Economics*, LXXIII, 2 (May 1958). For a general survey, see A. W. Coats (ed.), *The Classical Economists and Economic Policy* (1972).

[15] G. H. Wood, *The History of Wages in the Cotton Trade during the past 100 years* (1910), p. 127. For a full account of the tragic decline of the hand-loom weavers, see D. Bythell, *The Handloom Weavers* (1969).

[16] D. Read, 'The Social and Economic Background to Peterloo', *T.L.C.A.S.*, Vol. XIV (1954), pp. 1–18.

[17] Wood, *op. cit.*, p. 127.

[18] A. E. Musson, *British Trade Unions, 1800–75* (1972), p. 21.

[19] E. C. Tufnell, *Character, Object and Effects of Trades' Unions* (1933 ed.), pp. 85–6. Workmen still occasionally became masters, however. James Frost, who was a member of the spinners' general union in 1810, had become a manager by the time of the 1818 strike, and was a master by 1824 when he gave evidence hostile to trade unions before the Select Committee on the Combination Laws.

[20] See his address 'To the Operative Spinners of England' in September 1829, Place Collection, Vol. 16, p. 96.

[21] G. Unwin, *Samuel Oldknow and the Arkwrights* (1924), p. 33.

[22] Webb Collection, Vol. XXXIV, ff, 116–17; Smelser, *op. cit.*, p. 319.

[23] Turner, *op. cit.*, p. 63; Smelser, *op. cit.*, p. 319.

[24] *Rules . . . of the Friendly Associated Cotton Spinners* (Manchester, 1795): Webb Collection, Vol. XXXVI, ff. 74–89.

[25] Turner, *op. cit.*, p. 63.

[26] *Advertiser*, 6 April 1833. See below, p. 379, for Doherty's argument with Hoole on this point.

[27] *Advocate*, 25 February 1832. Doherty wrongly stated in this article that this firm was the first to introduce the system.

[28] Mitchell and Deane, *op. cit.*, p. 179.

[29] Tufnell, *op. cit.*, pp. 25–6. This account was largely based on the evidence of James Frost to the 1824 committee on the Combination Laws: see Parl. Papers, 1824, Vol. 51, pp. 604–10. In fact, the strike began first at Stalybridge, but was intended to spread to each district in turn. In the event, the masters precipitated the crisis by locking out the men throughout the rest of the county.

[30] J. Doherty, *Quinquarticular System of Organisation* (Manchester, 1834), p. 2. This pamphlet was published anonymously, but circumstantial evidence indicates that Doherty was almost certainly the author. See below, p. 303.

[31] Turner, *op. cit.*, p. 67. In 1814 the Manchester spinners also established the first short-time committee. See below, p. 346.

[32] Webb Collection, Vol. xxxiv, f.120.

[33] *Observer*, 8 August 1818.

[34] Wood, *op. cit.*, p. 22.

[35] *Rules . . . 1792; Resolutions of the Delegates . . . December, 1829* (Manchester, 1830). See below, pp. 93–4.

[36] Turner, *op. cit.*, p. 85, quoting the *Cotton Factory Times*, 12 May 1933.

# II  Doherty and the cotton spinners' unions, 1818-27

Although the Manchester cotton spinners had been forced to accept a large wages reduction in 1816, they began to revive as trade recovered in 1818 and eventually made a concerted move for restoration of their former rates. The masters, however, combined in resistance, so that early in July all the operatives turned out and another prolonged and bitter struggle began,[1] in which Doherty was, for the first time, to achieve notoriety. Moreover, in this turmoil he acquired his earliest experience of wider working-class organisation—in projects for a general union of spinners, for a general union of all trades, for a 'general turn-out' or 'general strike', and for radical-political and trade-union collaboration to secure working-class rights, with demands not only for fair wages and working conditions (this was also a period of active agitation for Peel's factory bill), but also for democratic parliamentary representation. Though Doherty's participation in these movements is obscure, except for his militant trade-union role, they form an essential background to his later activities and ideas, which, in consequence, appear much less novel than they have usually been portrayed and can be seen, not as dramatically emerging in the late 1820s and early 1830s, in a sudden revolutionary upsurge, but as part of a more prolonged development of working-class organisation and ideology, evolving from earlier years.

Both sides in the Manchester spinners' strike were anxious to win the sympathy of the public. When the *Manchester Exchange Herald* criticised combinations 'as inconsistent with the spirit of the British Constitution, as contrary to the existing law of the land, and the true interests of the individuals',[2] the operatives held a general meeting and instructed Henry Swindells, one of their leaders, to reply on their behalf. He stated that 'the spinners ask no more than what was taken from them two years ago, when every necessary of life was low, or at a moderate price; they were then promised an advance whenever the state of the market would permit it'. Trade had now recovered and prices of foodstuffs had risen sharply, but the masters had repeatedly refused to fulfil their promise, so the men had no alternative but to strike.[3] In an 'Address to the Public' at the beginning of August, the operative spinners claimed that the widely publicised estimates of their high wages, amounting to 30s or 40s per week, ignored the fact that they were responsible for paying the piecers, generally about 7s 6d per week. Their average clear wages in 1816 had been about 24s, but were then reduced by 20 to 25 per cent, and had remained so ever since. It was also pointed out 'that Spinners relieve their own sick, as well as subscribe to other casualties'. Moreover, they worked very long hours, 'from five in the morning until seven in the evening (and in some mills longer) . . . in rooms heated from seventy to ninety degrees'.

They therefore believed that the public will say with us that no body of workmen receive so inadequate a compensation for their labour . . . All we ask is a fair and candid investigation into the ground of our complaints and we are confident that both justice and humanity will decide in our favour.'[4]

The masters showed no inclination to enter into public debate with their men, but their position was strongly supported in most of the Manchester and London papers. 'No class of people have had such constant and uniform employment, for the last twenty-eight years, as they [the cotton spinners] have had and this advantage the spinner enjoys at the risk and expense of his employer; for such is the nature of the trade, that when once a cotton mill is completed and fully set to work, it cannot be stopped or even interrupted without great loss to the proprietor (owing to the heavy overhead charges).' In addition, the spinners had higher earnings than all other sections in the trade, 'and we have ascertained that the net average weekly wages paid to men spinners, from the 1st of January last to the middle of June, when they turned out, was upwards of 31s; and for boys and girls, spinners, upwards of 17s, clear of all charges and deductions whatsoever'.[5]

The spinners organised the strike very efficiently. A delegate meeting comprising two men from each mill, was held and chose a committee of twelve from their own number to superintend the collection and distribution of funds and the appointment of 'piquets'; large numbers of operatives paraded regularly through the streets and around the mills, in a formidable 'system of intimidation'.[6] Support was organised from cotton spinners in other towns and from the different trades in Manchester and elsewhere. 'The system of support from one trade to another is carried on to an amazing extent, and they regularly send delegates out to the different towns who are in work to receive their subscriptions.'[7] There is no direct evidence of a formal federal organisation of the Lancashire cotton spinners, but that co-operation was widespread is clear from the fact that the Wigan spinners, also on strike, received a 'weekly stipend' from those in Stockport, who had already obtained an advance on their old prices but were to be reduced to their former scale if an advance was not made in Wigan.[8]

The extent of the support for the Manchester spinners is revealed by a series of letters in the Home Office papers.[9] Reports from local manufacturers and magistrates indicated, for example, that subscriptions were being raised on their behalf not only from cotton spinners in neighbouring towns, but also from many other trades, in London, following a visit by two delegates, Henry Swindells and William Jones,[10] as well as in the Potteries, Sheffield, Birmingham, and Scotland. In fact, the spinners went far beyond mere appeals for subscriptions in their efforts to secure trade-union support. It was reported on July 18 that a correspondence was afoot between the Manchester cotton spinners' committee and their counterparts in Scotland and Ireland in regard to 'an intended general rising or turn-out'.[11] This almost certainly referred to proposals for combined action by cotton spinners throughout the United Kingdom, but soon there were wider schemes for a general strike by all trades, to be organised by a projected general union.[12]

But the hollowness of these grandiose schemes was soon revealed by the inadequacy of the financial support received. In all, the spinners were reputed to have raised £4,500 in outside contributions,[13] but this was probably an overestimate, and with the large number of strikers involved, weekly payments were pitifully small, soon declining to a mere 9*d* or 10*d* per head for adult spinners, while piecers, like carders and all other workers in the factories made idle by the strike, got nothing from the spinners' funds.[14]

In these circumstances, the leaders of the strike restrained the passions of the distressed rank and file for longer than might have been expected. The strike began alarmingly, with a mob attack on a mill that was still working, and the military had to be called out and several rioters were arrested;[15] but thereafter only minor assaults connected with picketing of factories were reported, though the spinners' mass organisation continued to cause alarm. The Manchester authorities were seriously afraid that the strikers would be misled by radical agitators into violent disorders, schemes of 'a general rising' and 'rebellion', despite the spinners' explicit denial that their demands were connected with political agitation. It was reported that the spinners were training very early each morning 'in military manoeuvres', and that 'Johnson is their legal adviser and Bagguley is ascertained beyond doubt to be one of their advocates'.[16]

In this threatening situation, the tardiness of the Manchester magistrates in taking action against the spinners' leaders was a source of concern to the Home Secretary, Viscount Sidmouth. The magistrates considered it the duty of the masters to take action against their men under the Combination Act, but the masters complained of insufficient support from the authorities. On 1 August, therefore, Henry Hobhouse, Under-Secretary at the Home Office, urged that the magistrates should issue an address declaring their determination to uphold the peace and punish delinquents, and that they should encourage masters to prosecute offenders. The borough-reeve and constables immediately responded by issuing a public notice declaring that such workers as returned to their employment would be protected by the civil power, and the masters thereupon opened their mills.[17] But the strikers' resolution remained solid and on 12 August James Norris even reported that a few mills were working at two-thirds of the advance required, and it seemed possible that 'the masters generally—who meet regularly—will ultimately give a small advance'.[18] The Manchester magistrates, moreover, continued to hesitate about taking action against the spinners' leaders, fearing to exacerbate the situation.

This was the high point of the spinners' fortunes. Despite the widespread support from other trades, their funds continued to decrease, and the situation was aggravated towards the end of August when the treasurer, John Medcalfe, absconded with a reputed sum of £150 or £160, an event which caused great dissension within their ranks.[19] Not surprisingly, therefore, the discipline of the strike was now broken. When the masters again reopened their factories on August 24, a series of violent confrontations took place between those wishing to continue the strike and those willing to return to work. The military were called out several times, the riot act was read, and the 'knobsticks' ('blacklegs') were obliged to sleep in the factories for their own protection. Several rioters were arrested and finally, on August 29, under pressure from the Home Office, the Manchester authorities struck at the leadership, breaking into the spinners' meeting-room, in a public house, and apprehending several of the committee, who were then imprisoned to answer a charge of conspiracy at the next sessions.[20] Other leaders were subsequently arrested, including John

Brough, 'the captain of the pickets', on September 1.[21] The worst incident took place at the factory of Benjamin Gray, one of the most hostile masters, whose mill was daily besieged and eventually, on 2 September, violently attacked by the surrounding mob, who were repulsed by gunfire, resulting in the death of one spinner and injury to several others; further attacks were only quelled by military intervention.[22] Disturbances also continued at other mills, so on 4 September the magistrates placarded the town with a public warning that they would 'disperse and prevent such unlawful and dangerous assemblies', protect 'the well disposed and industrious', and 'bring to justice such as shall be found offending against the Laws'.[23]

The turn-out was now drawing to a close, as the hands gradually returned to work. James Norris reported that 'the breaking up of the *committee* of the spinners, the difficulty in consequence of getting new ones to act with vigour, the loss of support from other trades who will no longer contribute whilst the funds are misapplied or stolen, the want of confidence in each other, the miserable state to which the operatives are reduced by their neglect of work, the determination . . . to protect by all and every means those who are willing to go to work', all led him to believe that 'this serious combination is now broken'. By 8 September, the strike was reported to be practically over, 'many of the large mills being completely filled, and the rest filling as fast as can be reasonably expected'.[24]

The operatives finally had to accept their old rates unconditionally, and many were forced to sign a declaration that they were no longer concerned 'in any Combination among Journeymen Cotton Spinners for the purpose of opposing the interests of the masters, or for any illegal purposes', and that they would join no such society in future. About 250 spinners were turned away, being 'black-listed' for their active share in the turn-out. The masters had a very long memory: Brough, the 'great captain' of the 1818 strike, was reported in 1829 to have been reduced almost to beggary as a result of their proscription, earning a scanty living with a rag-and-bone cart.[25]

What was the part of John Doherty in these proceedings? It is clear that he played a militant role in the assembling and parading outside mills to prevent 'knobsticks' from going in to work. The spinners' committee had organised a system whereby mills were only picketed by turn-outs from other factories, so to combat this the masters agreed, at the instigation of Benjamin Gray, to gather together at certain factories to try to identify offenders. On 26 August, after the masters had reopened the mills for the second time, a crowd of several hundred assembled at Birley's factory and paraded round it. Peter Ewart, another millowner, was present, recognised Doherty among the crowd as 'a person who had obstructed two of his own hands on the 20 July last and as he seemed very forward he seized him and put him in the factory'.[26] A warrant was forthwith issued, but the crowd was incensed and tried to rescue Doherty out of custody. Nadin, the deputy constable, became a prisoner in the mill and it was necessary to send the head constable with assistance, backed by a company of the 95th regiment. The crowd round the mill swelled to about two thousand, who followed the soldiers as they escorted Doherty and six others who had been arrested in the subsequent disturbance, from Birley's mill to the New Bailey prison. The mob collected round the prison and many stones were thrown, and James Norris, the magistrate, was ultimately forced to read the riot act, before the rioters dispersed.[27]

What, then, can we say of the charge frequently levelled against Doherty, in an attempt to smear his moral character and reputation, that his crime was a 'gross assault upon a woman'?[28] It is noteworthy that neither the hostile Manchester newspapers nor the magistrates referred to any such incident at the time, nor did the indictment brought against Doherty at the Lancaster Quarter Sessions in January 1819 mention a specific case of assault. No female gave evidence against him at the trial. In 1828, at the time of the division in the Manchester cotton spinners' union, Doherty himself described his offence. 'I was convicted of doing that which is now perfectly legal. I was convicted of endeavour to maintain the price of your as well as my labour.' And in 1831 he gave a more detailed account,

> In 1818 we turned out, among the rest of our fellow-spinners of this town, for an advance of wages, which had been previously promised to us. During the continuance of the struggle, it pleased Mr Peter Ewart, and some of his minions, to charge us with being present at *but not taking part in*, an affray, when some 'knobsticks' were forcibly prevented from going to work in his mill at the reduced rate of wages; and on this charge, we were sentenced . . . under the late combination laws . . . for merely being present at a slight disturbance, in which not the slightest injury was done to any living creature.[29]

Thus, at the end of the strike, Doherty was one of many spinners awaiting trial, either for assault or for conspiracy. After his case had been initially heard at the New Bailey, he was sent for trial at the next Lancaster Quarter Sessions in October, together with the other accused spinners, fifteen in all. When the trials came on, however, their cases were traversed to the next Sessions. John Doherty's bail was £50 and it was paid by two sureties—John Zuel(?), an engraver of Cheetham Hill, and James Wroe, a bookseller of Great Ancoats Street, Manchester.[30] The latter was one of the most prominent political radicals in Manchester, which shows the importance attached to this case; here also was an early link between Doherty and radical journalism. Meanwhile, a widespread campaign was organised to raise a defence fund on behalf of the accused spinners, including a delegation to London, where an appeal for support was issued, emphasising the injustice of the laws against trade unions.[31]

At the next Quarter Sessions in January 1819, nine of the fifteen spinners who were committee-members again traversed their trials to the next Lancaster Assizes in March. But the cases of the other six spinners arrested for participation in disturbances during the strike was gone into. Doherty's indictment read as follows:

> Lancashire—The Jurors for our Lord the King upon their oath present that John Doherty late of Manchester in the said County, cotton spinner, together with divers other evil disposed persons to the Jurors aforesaid unknown to the number of 5000 and upwards being also cotton spinners on the 29th day of July in the 58th year of the reign of George the 3rd of the United Kingdom of Great Britain and Ireland King at Manchester aforesaid in the said county unlawfully did conspire combine and confederate and agree among themselves by force and violence and by strong hand and multitude of People to compel certain persons then and there carrying on the Trade and Business of Master Cotton Spinners to raise and advance the usual and accustomed wages

of the working cotton spinners then and there in the Employment of the said Masters and also by like force and violence to prevent hinder and deter the said working cotton spinners from exercising their said occupation as afore-said until their wages in their said employment should be raised and advanced as aforesaid to the great Terror and Damage of the said Masters and Employers and of the said working cotton spinners and against the peace of our said Lord the King his Crown and Dignity and the Jurors aforesaid upon their oath aforesaid do further present that the said John Doherty together with divers other evil disposed persons to the Jurors aforesaid unknown to the number of 100 and upwards on the said 29th day of July and on divers other days and times then next following in the year aforesaid at Manchester aforesaid in the said county with force and arms unlawfully riotously and [ . . . ? ] did assemble and gather together and being so assembled and met did assault beat and ill-treat divers working cotton spinners then and there, to wit on the said several days and times, in the peace of God and our said Lord the King being with intent by force and violence and by strong Hand and multitude of people to obstruct hinder and deter the said . . . Spinners from exercising and carrying on their said occupation in order and by means thereof to compel the masters in the said Trade and Business to advance the wages of the said confederates to the Great Terror and Damage of the said working Spinners and their said Employers and against the peace of our said Lord the King his crown and Dignity.[32]

Three witnesses gave evidence—Peter Ewart himself, Thomas Nicholl and John Reid. On 19 January Doherty was found guilty and sentenced to two years' imprisonment in Lancaster castle with hard labour (and for a further term of two years unless in the meantime he entered into a recognisance to keep the peace during that time, himself in the sum of £40 and two sufficient sureties in the sum of £20 each). The other spinners were also found guilty: three who had pleaded guilty were allowed to enter recognisances to appear for judgement when called, but the other two, James Gorton and David Crooks, were sentenced to terms of imprisonment of one and three years respectively. The sentences delighted the authorities. 'These verdicts,' wrote James Norris, 'are of great importance . . . to the future peace of this manu-facturing district and I trust will have the effect of deterring others from such offences.' Sidmouth was convinced that the verdicts would do more for the quietude of the Manchester area than any event for a considerable period.[33]

The severe sentences on Doherty and the others did, indeed, soon have the effect the authorities desired, especially as trades' subscriptions failed to cover the legal expenses involved. The spinners' committee, whose trial was still pending, abjectly submitted, acknowledging their crimes and expressing their repentance, whereupon the authorities—recognising that this submission would perhaps do more good than a trial and conviction—agreed to release them on sureties of £100 each.[34] Thus Doherty was one of only three cotton spinners ultimately punished and, since he was not one of the committee, his severe sentence appears to have been the result of his own obduracy on the one hand, and the desire of the authorities on the other to give out an exemplary punishment.

The alarm of the authorities in this period had been increased by an apparent connection between widespread strikes and reports of a general trades' union, anticipatory of Doherty's later schemes in 1825–6 and 1829–30.

B

It may seem surprising that the cotton spinners, whose internal trade policy was dominated by a desire to achieve an aristocratic position within the cotton industry, were so prominent in these early attempts to form organisations embracing different trades and industries.[35] But such schemes developed naturally from the traditional assistance given to each other by skilled trades when on strike : they were simply efforts at institutionalising well-established inter-union co-operation.

The plan of general union appears to have originated in Nottingham, according to James Norris, the Manchester magistrate, whose information was verified by other intelligence sent to Sidmouth.[36] The idea was being taken up in Manchester during the spinners' strike and caused considerable alarm because of its reputed connection with radical reformers or 'revolutionaries' such as Bagguley, Drummond and Johnson, who were said to be trying to utilise the strike to bring about public disorder and insurrection.[37] As early as 28 July the Home Office informed a Manchester magistrate of correspondence between the Spenceans in London and persons with influence over the 'malcontents' in Manchester, and that there was a 'projected assembly in Lancashire' for 10 August.[38] By the beginning of August the Manchester correspondent of the *London Courier* could state that the assistance given to the Manchester spinners proved that 'the whole mass of artificers through the country thus form a sort of *federative body*, united for the purposes of mutual support, whenever any of them choose to strike for increased wages'.[39]

These developments were regarded very seriously by the local authorities and Home Office. On 5 August James Norris reported the appearance on the streets of Manchester of an address 'To the Labourers of Manchester and its vicinity', stating that the only way for the workers to improve their distressed condition was to imitate the conduct of masters in every trade : 'every branch of labourers should immediately call district meetings, and appoint *delegates* to meet at some convenient place, to establish such a connexion as shall be deemed necessary for the good of the whole'. This handbill, reputedly written by either Bagguley or John Knight, was regarded by Norris as 'very dangerous and inflammatory'. He had information that a 'meeting of delegates of different trades from different towns in the area' was to meet in Manchester the following Monday (10 August), avowedly to consider the best mode of advancing wages but strongly presumed to be for worse purposes, viz. a 'general confederacy' or 'insurrection' against the government; he himself thought the labouring classes were discontented mainly about wages, but he feared that they might be misled by the 'machinations' of radical reformers.[40]

Similar reports came in from magistrates in neighbouring towns. From Oldham it was reported that a 'Central Committee' in Manchester had sent out circulars to local trades asking them to send delegates to the proposed general meeting, with the alleged object of establishing a 'general union for mutual support and general benefit', but really to organise 'rebellion'.[41] James Lloyd wrote from Stockport enclosing a circular signed by James Fielding, secretary of the Stalybridge spinners, and dated 7 August, which stated that the Manchester trades had asked him to solicit the workmen there 'to join their union of trades, as all trades in England are uniting in one body', and to send delegates to the Manchester meeting.[42] And on 10 August Norris was reported to have received an anonymous letter stating that the object of the 'revolutionaries' was to form 'a union of all trades, and turn out the work-men of all three kingdoms', so as to bring about anarchy and rebellion.[43]

It appears, however, from other correspondence, that the proposed delegate meeting did not take place on 10 August. But on 13 August a meeting of thirty-three delegates from each of the districts into which Manchester and Salford had been divided was held at the 'George Inn', St George's Road, and Henry Swindells, the spinners' delegate then in London, was appointed 'Grand Secretary for the United Trades of England' in his absence. Two representatives were appointed to attend a delegate meeting in Bury the following Monday.[44] Norris informed the Home Office that he believed the leaders intended 'ulti-mately to turn out as many trades as possible'; the Oldham colliers were intending to hold a meeting on Kersal Moor, following a deputation from the Manchester spinners to induce them to turn out, and he was afraid there might be widespread disorders.[45]

The projected trades' delegate meeting was eventually held in Manchester on 19 August, attended by representatives from Manchester, Stockport, Ashton, Oldham and Bury—including calico-printers, dyers and dressers, hatters, blacksmiths, jenny spinners, cotton weavers, bricklayers, fustian cutters, colliers, sawyers, shoemakers, slubbers, mule spinners and machine-makers. Ten resolutions were passed and publicised in a handbill, to form 'a Union of all Trades called the PHILANTHROPIC SOCIETY'. Government was to be by monthly delegate meetings in Manchester of all the trades enrolled, while the administration was to be in the hands of a committee of eleven persons chosen by ballot from the different trades, changing each month by rotation and completely every three months. Strikes against reductions and for advances had first to be approved by a general meeting of delegates so that the funds of the Society should not be overstretched. Auxiliary Societies were to be formed in each town to co-operate with the central Philanthropic Society. Finally, to avoid dissension, no member was to be allowed to intro-duce political or religious matters.[46]

Henry Hobhouse thought that 'probably no such meeting was held as is expressed in this paper', but about the continued reports of the intended formation of a general union of all trades he was seriously alarmed, and on 24 August he wrote round to several Lancashire magistrates asking for more information.[47] The Manchester borough-reeve considered that 'revolutionists are at the bottom of it', and that their aim was to organise a 'combination of trades' and a 'general turn-out', though he still thought there was 'no fixed national plan for any disturbance'. This view was shared by the Rev C. W. Ethelston, who blamed it on the inflammatory 'harangues and placards' of Bagguley, Drummond and Johnson. James Norris tempered alarmism with reality: 'I cannot think that the trades are at all organised for a general turn-out as no doubt calculated upon by the secret movers of these disturbances, but the idea necessarily acquires strength amongst the lower classes . . . and *some* no doubt are ripe for it at this moment.'[48]

There is no doubt that in late August and early September vigorous efforts were being made to organise a general union in Lancashire and elsewhere. Matthew Lauchlan, who replaced Jones as one of the spinners' delegates in London towards the end of August, reported that he had been very active in forming such a union in Lancashire, having visited Bolton, Bury and various other places, as a result of which he had been able to induce the weavers and colliers to strike on 1 September unless their wages were advanced by 7s in the £.[49] Norris was now convinced that there was 'indeed a simultaneous movement throughout the manufacturing district', and that 'the combination [is] very extensive and truly dangerous', under the influence of 'Bagguley Drummond and Co'.[50]

In the event, however, the general turn-out did not spread beyond the colliers and weavers, and most of these soon returned to work after wages concessions from employers, combined with arrest of the weavers' leaders.[51] In the second week of September delegates from Nottingham, Birmingham and Liverpool were in Manchester, to promote the 'General Union' and to bring financial aid for the spinners, but this came too late.[52] The general union was 'still much talked of', however, a committee was still sitting, and on 21 September another delegate meeting was held at Todmorden, which was intended to be the centre of the union because of its central, yet remote, situation between the manufacturing districts of Lancashire and Yorkshire. Numerous weavers' delegates attended, from as far afield as Somerset, together with printers and crofters from Bury, and also apparently shoemakers, tailors and other trades which had joined the union.

> The proposal was for each person to pay in 3d. per week, but in consequence of the great distrust each had of the other, the spinners having gone in, and the headmen of the spinners and weavers being in custody, they were alarmed, and the *clerks* . . . of the different divisions and townships who [had] collected the different contributions, were directed to divide the funds and return the money, amounting to about £40.

Thus, Norris considered, the union was now 'broken up'.[53] That it was languishing in the Manchester area was admitted by Henry Swindells, but he claimed that 'it was in a promising way in the country, and particularly at Nottingham'.[54] The Home Office also pointed out that although 'the project of effecting a Union of Trades' was 'possibly relinquished . . . as hopeless at Manchester and some other places', it was 'not entirely abandoned', but was still carried on in the metropolis.[55] It had been taken there originally by Swindells and Jones, the two spinners' delegates, who, soon after their arrival in London, had issued a circular, dated 12 August, soliciting the assistance of the metropolitan trades and their support 'in forming a Union of the operative Workmen, Mechanics and Artizans of the United Kingdom, to support each other in all Difficulties, which may occur between them and their employers, for the mutual benefit of the labouring people'. As a result, meetings of metropolitan trades' delegates and radicals were held later that month, at which John Gast, of the shipwrights' club, was a prominent speaker, together with Watson and other radical reformers.[56] These meetings continued throughout September, Gast being appointed chairman.[57] The eventual outcome was the formation of a defensive trades' association, called the 'Philanthropic Hercules', the rules of which were published on 2 December 1818. It was clearly based on the northern Philanthropic Society, with a subscription of a penny per week and a federal constitution comprising a central committee of trades' delegates and sub-committees for each particular trade.[58]

This metropolitan trades' union, however, appears to have had no longer an active existence than its parent body. It probably continued well into 1819, for when W. P. Washington sought aid in paying debts incurred in defence of the Manchester cotton spinners, his appeal was 'recommended' to the trades by John Gast and subscriptions were received at the 'Pewter Platter' public house, headquarters of the Philanthropic Hercules.[59] But, like the Manchester project, it proved ephemeral.

It is impossible to discover if John Doherty took any part in this transitory experiment in general unionism. There is no reference to him as being among the leaders, but he must have been strongly influenced by this early example of the spinners initiating institutional co-operation between the trades, and by the fact that he was one of the beneficiaries of an appeal to members of trade societies generally; he was also influenced, no doubt, by the associated radical-political agitation, as the link with James Wroe suggests.[60] He always retained this wider vision, and while never neglecting the sectional interests of the cotton spinners, he frequently associated those interests with the general advancement of the working classes.

These efforts at general union, however, were of little help to the Manchester cotton spinners after their complete defeat in the 1818 strike. Blacklisting, debts and internal dissensions, following the harsh sentences on Doherty, Crooks and Gorton and the submission of the spinners' committee, led James Norris to believe that 'there is no fear of their turning out again for some time to come, perhaps for years'.[61] Doherty himself stated later, in 1838, that the spinners' trade society was 'broken up' after the 1818 strike and that 'in the year or two following . . . the men contributed nothing to the funds of the Union', though they continued to contribute regularly for the purpose of securing a factory act.[62] In the slump and social distress of 1819, Manchester workmen generally turned to the political agitation that finally culminated in the notorious 'Peterloo' incident on 16 August. But despite Doherty's later statement, it seems likely that the spinners did, in fact, maintain some kind of organisation, even if only as a friendly society. During the dispute over his election in 1828,[63] his opponents asserted that after January 1819 the cotton spinners '*most generously* relieved him from most of the pains and penalties of his two years' imprisonment, by a *bounteous subscription* of 5s per week, together with useful books, newspapers, writing paper, pens etc.'. Doherty was deeply grateful for the assistance he received whilst in Lancaster Castle. 'I owe you a debt of gratitude, which, I am afraid I shall never be able to repay', he wrote in a letter dated 26 February 1828. 'The support which you so generously gave me, whilst inured in a dungeon for two long years, has made an impression on my heart, which nothing can erase while that heart remains warm. None of you can know, who have not experienced the same hardship, the value of that support, under such circumstances.' However, by November when the dispute had become more bitter, Doherty was tending to play down the generosity of this assistance. 'The "useful books, newspapers, writing paper, pens etc." were Cobbett's *Grammar* price 2s 6d, two quires of paper at 1s per quire and half a hundred of quills for which I paid 20s or what is much the same thing, it was stopped out of the "bounteous subscription", the first money I received.'[64]

Since the spinners' funds were dissipated by the 1818 strike, and the spinners' defence fund had finished heavily in debt,[65] this support for Doherty must have come from continued subscriptions, either to their society or to the relief fund organised in Manchester for the relief of imprisoned radicals and trade unionists.[66] Further evidence that trade society benefits continued to be paid, at least on a mill basis, can be found in another charge levelled against Doherty in 1828: 'No. 3 new mill allowed their men (when discharged for any thing not reflecting on their conduct) £7 10s 0d. At the expiration of his imprisonment, he [Doherty] came to Manchester, and with an impudent and bold effrontery demanded £7 10s 0d. He threatened them with an action at law for the recovery thereof, and actually sent them notice to that effect, together with the most abusive and offensive letters.'[67] Doherty completely denied this charge and challenged his accusers to produce his letter as proof. There is no other evidence for it, and it is perhaps a better illustration of the bitterness of the 1828 dispute than of the events of 1821.

There is no doubt, however, that Doherty's arrest and imprisonment had made him into a figure of some significance among the Manchester cotton spinners and radicals. While in Lancaster Castle he had sufficient importance to be entrusted with a petition from the Bridewell prisoners in the gaol, which he sent to John Cam Hobhouse in August 1820 for presentation to Parliament.[68] When he was released in January 1821, he was one of a number of political and trade-union prisoners to be given dinners of welcome in the different Lancashire towns. And he lost no time in making his mark on local reform affairs, by becoming one of the early Manchester leaders of Hunt's Great Northern Union.[69]

He appears to have been able to get work again as a spinner despite this reputation. With trade recovering, the spinners were already making plans for improving their conditions, and Doherty's ideas were among the most ambitious. About this time he appears to have proposed some scheme of co-operative production, anticipating developments in the late 'twenties and early 'thirties, but it was premature and the spinners continued to pursue traditional policies.[70] These years saw a revival of spinners' trade-union activity throughout the Lancashire cotton towns. In the spring of 1821, for example, there was a strike in Preston against a 10 per cent wage reduction, followed by another in Blackburn for an advance. But trade was still slack and the strikes were defeated, in Preston by a general lock-out, and in Blackburn by bringing in new hands and by use of the laws against combinations to secure imprisonment of some of the leaders.

By 1822 trade was distinctly reviving and the cotton spinners were anxious to share in the benefits. The Bolton spinners had a particularly active society, which dated continuously from 1811. By a series of 'rolling' strikes, at individual mills in turn, they now succeeded in forcing several firms to concede advances. Eventually, however, they were met, early in 1823, by a combination of all the Bolton master spinners, who issued a new list of prices, based on a principle that was to be at the heart of most of the spinners' disputes in the next decade—involving reduced piece prices on 'larger wheels', i.e. on new mules with a greater number of spindles than previously. The masters maintained that spinners on these larger mules would not have lower earnings, because of increased productivity—indeed earnings would rise—while the men argued that working the larger mules involved more arduous labour and payments to more piecers.[71] After a prolonged strike, the men were defeated, as the Manchester society had been, by the arrest of their committee, several of whom were sentenced to imprisonment. There was a similar ending, as the mills were filled with 'knobsticks', internal dissensions weakened the Bolton society, and, despite increasing violence, the new piece-list eventually had to be accepted.

The seized papers of the society showed that the Bolton men had received assistance from cotton spinners throughout Lancashire, as well as from other trades. Over twenty local spinners' societies as well as several individual mills had sent contributions, and the other trades which had subscribed included paper-makers, coalminers, bleachers, calico-printers, pin-makers, reed-makers, mechanics, sawyers, tailors, foundrymen, millwrights, slaters and butchers. The familiar pattern of 1818 was repeated. The informal links which the various districts of cotton spinners kept up through the delegate system were utilised to give financial backing to a particular region in difficulties. But unlike 1810 or 1829, no formal organisation of a federal nature appears to have existed. The Bolton spinners' committee simply sent out delegates to the different districts to explain the dispute and ask for support. Despite substantial contributions, however, the strike ended in complete defeat.

For the Manchester cotton spinners this was a period of quiet consolidation. It is clear that Doherty's assertion in 1834 that, 'from the latter end of 1818, up to the end of 1823, no union existed' was not strictly accurate. As we have seen, the functions of a friendly society probably continued to be carried on, and by the end of 1822 the Manchester spinners resumed their trade activities, by assisting the Bolton spinners in their strike. It was at this time that Thomas Foster began his active and distinguished career among them.[72] But the Manchester papers do not refer to any industrial action whatsoever taken by the Manchester spinners from the time of the 1818 defeat until 1824.

The repeal of the Combination Laws in June 1824, however, coinciding with boom conditions in trade, soon led to revived union activity in many trades and a series of strikes. At first the Manchester spinners used their new freedom to try to amend certain objectionable mill regulations and also in opposing employment of females, while in a few mills they began to seek wage advances. Several strikes occurred, with an alarming return to violence, including a case of vitriol-throwing against a 'knobstick'. The spinners' society denied responsibility and offered a £50 reward for discovery of the offender, but labour relations were clearly deteriorating.[73]

That the Manchester spinners were moving out of their quiet defensive mood is also indicated by their involvement in another attempt to form a general union of their trade, this time including not only all the Lancashire spinners but those of Scotland and Ireland as well.[74] This movement was stimulated by events in Glasgow, where the spinners were by this time formidably organised.[75] After a succession of strikes in various mills, with many acts of violent intimidation, a general confrontation occurred in the late summer of 1824, after the men had demanded the dismissal of a manager and the combined masters retaliated by proposing a reduction in wages equal to the weekly union subscription.[76] In the subsequent lock-out, the operatives at once set about organising assistance from other areas. Even before these events in Glasgow, however, it appears that the Manchester spinners had started to organise another general union of the Lancashire spinners. Now they widened their aim to try achieving a general union of the whole trade. In December they sent two delegates to Glasgow, who addressed a general meeting of the Glasgow spinners in the Circus, Dunlop Street.

> The delegates stated that the purport of their visit to this quarter was to establish a union of operative cotton spinners over all the three kingdoms, and to give mutual assistance in cases of general strikes such as the present. They also stated the determination of the English spinners to assist the Scottish ones while they stood out. There were 4,000 already associated in England and they expected that, by the end of next month, the number would increase to 16,000. As an earnest of their interest and kindness, they left £142 sterling to aid the Glasgow spinners in their strike, with a promise to support them to the last. They stated that on their return the most strenuous exertions would be made to raise more subscriptions in Manchester and the neighbourhood; and that they might speedily expect further remittances.[77]

Despite this apparent increase in co-operation between the spinning regions, their solidarity was soon shown to be illusory by the reappearance of differences between the leaders of the Manchester spinners and the rank and file. At a general meeting in the Manor Court House on 13 January 1825— according to the *Manchester Gazette* the first-ever meeting of the trade in public—it was made clear that the financial assistance to Glasgow had been sent by the committee against the wishes of the members generally, who considered that the Glasgow spinners had no right to dictate the appointment or dismissal of managers, which conduct would only reinforce demands for a re-enactment of the Combination Laws. No more aid was to be sent, but instead it was resolved 'that we, the Operative Cotton Spinners of Manchester, offer our mediation between the Operative Spinners of Glasgow and their employers, in the hope of putting a speedy termination to those unhappy differences which at present exist'.[78]

It is difficult to discover what part John Doherty played in these proceedings, since even after the 1824 repeal the workmen insisted on anonymity in newspaper reports, to avoid victimisation. However, at the above meeting, one of the speakers, who stated that he was twenty-five years old (Doherty's age) and had been a child worker, argued eloquently in favour of continued assistance to the Glasgow men in terms similar to those used by Doherty in 1829: that the oppressions of the factory masters had reduced the workmen to such degradation that it was positively their duty to resist; that if the Glasgow spinners were forced to submit, similar arbitrary actions would ensue against the Lancashire spinners; and that allowing one group of workers to be defeated would result in a general attack on workers in other areas and trades.[79] It is tempting to speculate that this was in fact Doherty speaking, since he was by now prominent among the spinners and probably an intermittent member of the committee, but it is impossible to assert this with any degree of certainty.[80]

At the end of January the Glasgow men unconditionally accepted the masters' terms and returned to work, though sporadic violence continued.[81] Nevertheless, the Lancashire spinners' attempt to form a federal organisation continued, in face of a concerted counter-attack. Their policy was to establish equalised wage rates throughout the region, while resisting reductions in prices on bigger mules, as at Bolton in 1823. To this the masters were implacably opposed, because of competitive factors such as differences in local costs of coal, transport, etc., and also in living costs, and the great variety in sizes of mules and counts of yarn, as well as in sizes of firms. The result was a succession of strikes in different areas, the most serious of which occurred early in 1825 at Hyde, where rates were notoriously low.[82] The masters combined, however, in resolute opposition, insisting on renunciation of the union, blacklisting strikers, and introducing new hands, while the operatives responded with attacks on 'knobsticks'.[83] Despite the reputed expenditure of £3–4,000 on the strike by the federal union, the men were eventually forced to return to work at the old rates.[84] Similar defeats were suffered in numerous other strikes. At Preston, the spinners at several factories turned out for an increase in January, claiming that their wages were up to 50 per cent less than those in Manchester.[85] But the union was very weak there since the defeat of 1821, and the masters virtually ignored the men's demands, quickly refilling their factories with new hands despite several cases of intimidation, and forcing those that returned to renounce the union. At Stockport, the hands in four mills had turned out as early as October 1824, to bring their prices up to the district average, but were defeated by the intro-duction of new hands and blacklisting.[86] In Oldham similarly, a prolonged strike against a wage-cutting firm also failed, amid a series of incidents between strikers and 'knobsticks'.[87]

Nevertheless, the federal union appears to have spread widely. The Glasgow spinners continued to support it, despite their defeat, and soon afterwards we find two of their delegates persuading the Carlisle spinners to join the general union: the men at several Carlisle mills struck for an advance and sent dele-gates to Manchester for assistance, though with disappointing results, according to the hostile *Carlisle Patriot*.[88] Even as late as February 1826, the Glasgow spinners were giving advice and financial assistance to the Belfast spinners, who were striking for an advance.[89]

It is very doubtful, however, whether the federal union had much reality outside Lancashire and Cheshire, and even there it soon disintegrated as a result of repeated strike defeats. That Doherty was intimately involved in it is indicated by his later analysis of its failure, at the spinners' delegate meeting in the Isle of Man in December 1829.[90] The main weakness, he declared, was lack of central control:

> . . . the one great error of the former union which had been established in England was, that all were at liberty to turn out, if a reduction was offered to them. It certainly must be mortifying to men to be obliged to submit to a reduction, more especially while they were in the act of subscribing to uphold others against the same evil. But, painful as it would be, he was well convinced that if men were to come out, district after district, even against reductions, they would soon be overwhelmed with the number they would have to support. This was precisely the case with the district union in England. Preston was attempted to be reduced, and they turned out; Hyde was attempted to be reduced, and they also turned out, though great numbers were out before. The result was, that contributions became heavy, and men fell off, till there were nearly as many receivers as payers. Thus

B*

the burden was intolerable for those who continued to pay, and yet there was no adequate support for the men who were struggling against the reductions. The consequence was, as in all such cases, the weak men began to run in, confidence was lost, and with it all hopes of success. Now had there been a law to keep men to their work, when the income was not equal to the outgo, had they suffered no more to turn out than just as many as they could support with the stipulated sum, 10s a week, the men could have subsisted on it; they would have had no fear of receiving less, and they would have continued in the spirit of resistance, until their object was accomplished. Then we could have turned to those who had been reduced, and said to them, 'now we can support you with 10s a week, now you may come out.

Doherty concluded that it was essential to have a specific rule that none should strike on any account without first obtaining the consent of a majority of the trade, if the new federal union was to be any more successful than that of 1824–5.[91]

The consequences of that defeat, however, proved of lasting significance. Above all, the widespread strikes had strengthened the master spinners' combined resistance and also stimulated them to technological innovation in an effort to break trade-union control. The long strike at Hyde and the inclination of the operative spinners generally to exploit their powerful position in cotton factories, induced Thomas Ashton and other masters to make a series of visits to Richard Roberts, of the machine-making firm Sharp, Roberts & Co., which resulted in the first successful invention of the 'self-acting' mule. This was advertised, in November 1825, as 'destined to work a complete revolution in the trade of spinning cotton'.[92] But it was only from the mid-1830s onwards that the self-actor spread rapidly through the industry, and the conflicts in which Doherty played a leading part were concerned mostly with 'hand-mule' spinners. [93]

More immediately damaging to the operatives was the spate of recriminations that followed the failures of 1824–5. Not only were there differences within the Manchester society, but also between some of the societies which had formed the federal union. Quarrels between the Manchester and Bolton spinners, for example, so damaging to Doherty's later schemes,[94] originated to some extent in this period. Thus Jonathan Hodgins, one of the Manchester spinners' leaders, not only incurred unpopularity by speaking favourably of the self-acting mule, but was also said to have 'in 1824 run away with the union in a coach and four . . . [and] the enormous expense of that journey created distrust and suspicion which had never yet been allayed'.[95] It is impossible to elucidate this vague accusation, but it seems to have reflected dislike of Manchester policy and control. This antipathy Doherty excited to a much greater degree, and in his case, too, its roots seem to have reached back into this earlier period.

Not only in Bolton, but also in Manchester, Doherty acquired a reputation for militancy.[96] This probably derived originally from his involvement in the 1818 strike, and he seems also to have been an outspoken activist in 1824–5, especially in the agitation against the Combination Laws.[97] But though a staunch advocate of workmen's rights, he was strongly opposed to violence, advocating moderation, respect for employers and compliance with the laws.[98] It is probable, therefore, that he was among those in the Manchester spinners' society who favoured trying to form a closer relationship with their masters and to end the situation—caused, they felt, by the Combination Laws—whereby any difference between them could only be settled by direct action and open warfare, harmful to both sides. Thus, on 15 November 1824, the Manchester spinners' committee sent a circular to each of their employers, proposing a meeting between them because 'we think it essentially necessary, that the Operatives and their Employers should occasionally meet, for the purpose of adjusting any real or supposed grievance that may arise'.[99] But co-operation of this kind in trade affairs was out of the question in view of the current conflict over piece prices.

The Manchester spinners did, however, make progress with another proposal in their circular of 15 November—that the employers and workmen should co-operate in regard to factory legislation. Early in 1825 they obtained a declaration from thirty-two of the leading spinning firms in Manchester in favour of a new bill introduced into Parliament by John Cam Hobhouse, and in the ensuing campaign they even agreed that their petition against re-enactment of the Combination Laws should not be presented so that the masters' co-operation would not be jeopardised.[100] But there were clearly divisions within the spinners' ranks between those who were vehemently opposed to employers on the issue of the Combination Laws and those who preferred to moderate this hostility to preserve co-operation on factory reform.

Doherty was probably among the more militant group on this issue, having himself suffered imprisonment. The Combination Laws and the common law of conspiracy had frequently been used to break spinners' strikes—in Manchester and Stockport in 1818, Blackburn in 1821, and Bolton in 1823—while the authorities winked at the co-existence of masters' associations, often held together by heavy penalties for breaking ranks. 'The sufferings of persons employed in the cotton manufacture were beyond credibility: they were drawn into combinations, betrayed, prosecuted, convicted, sentenced and monstrously severe punishments were inflicted on them: they were reduced to and kept in the most wretched state of existence.'[101] It is true, as Dorothy George and Daphne Simon have pointed out, that the older laws of conspiracy and of master and servant provided a more repressive instrument with heavier penalties than the Combination Laws, which carried a maximum sentence of three months' imprisonment; Doherty's case itself provides evidence to support this view.[102] But workmen tended to regard all these collectively as the 'Combination Laws', and as all unjustly oppressive, not being particularly concerned with the niceties as to which particular legal instrument was being used against them.[103] In his periodicals Doherty frequently recalled these oppressions. In 1828 he wrote that, 'when the odious and oppressive combination laws were in existence, the honest workman had no alternative, but either submit to whatever terms the greedy, avaricious and unprincipled adventurers might think proper to propose to him, or violate the laws. For it was a violation of the laws if only three of them should leave their work at once, whatever might be the oppressions that were imposed upon them.' And in 1830 he asserted that the Combination Laws 'taught the masters that the workmen were slaves . . . and prohibited the workmen openly combining to protect themselves, forced them to have recourse to secret plots, not to redress but avenge their wrongs. The most revolting outrages were committed [by workmen], which even the perpetrators did not pretend to justify, except because [there was] no other way of redress.'[104]

In such circumstances, it is surprising that it has generally been accepted that agitation by working men played little or no part in obtaining the repeal of the Combination Laws in 1824. This view has largely depended on the statements of Francis Place, the neglect of the question by most contemporary newspapers, and the remarkable apathy in Parliament as the repeal went through its various stages. Typical of Place's interpretation is his letter in the *Bolton Chronicle* in 1827:

> Notwithstanding the credit which has been taken by many classes of work-men for their exertions in obtaining the repeal of the combination laws, . . . the repeal was effected not by the concurrence, much less the assistance of the workpeople in a body, than in despight of them . . . It was the labour of several years by those who had no personal interest in the matter, absolutely unassisted in any way by those bodies of workmen who were the most oppressed, and not one of which bodies even ever condescended to notice any one of the several letters which were sent to them from time to time, for the purpose of collecting the information necessary to enable them who wished to serve them, to make a case on which to ground an application to the House of Commons for a committee to enquire respecting the operation of these laws.[105]

Yet Doherty later claimed that the repeal had been achieved through pressure by combined workmen. In 1829, for example, he stated that 'the repeal of the combination and arbitration laws were [*sic*] a proof of the efficacy of union. Who could obtain an act of parliament by his own individual exertions?' He asserted that the repeal was 'obtained by the united efforts of weavers, spinners, shoemakers etc'.[106] And investigation of local newspapers certainly shows that the various actions against the spinners, in 1818, 1821 and 1823, did produce severe strictures against the Combination Laws in the men's addresses. Moreover, Cobbett, who was turning his appeal to the industrial worker from 1816 onwards, twice used proceedings taken by the authorities and master spinners to end cotton spinners' strikes as examples of the oppressive system of government in action. On 30 September 1818, he wrote an eloquent address 'To the Cotton Spinners of Manchester, and to the Journeymen of all trades in England, on their turning out for a rise of wages, and on the ill-treatment which they have received from the Borough Press', which defended the spinners' rights to combine and strike to fix the price of their own property and attacked the Combination Laws. And again, in 1823, criticising the oppression of the Preston master spinners, he repeated these denunciations.[107]

For some years there had been strong feeling among workmen themselves against the Combination Laws. John Gast's 'Address to Mechanics' in November 1818, pointed out their injustice, while the *Gorgon* advised all members of the 'Philanthropic Hercules' in January 1819, to sign petitions for the repeal of the Combination Act. Later, on 22 June, Hume presented a petition from a number of journeymen, tradesmen and mechanics in London and West-minster in favour of repeal, and spoke of his intentions to introduce such a measure. Meanwhile, in Manchester during the radical activities leading up to

Peterloo in August, the workmen did not forget that 'the oppressors have got possession of the great part of the property of the nation, through the operation of the Corn Bill, and the Combination Acts'.[108]

In the early 1820s Place's efforts to obtain support among members of parliament and influential journalists at last began to bear fruit. Using information sent to Place by several trade societies in the north, Hume reintroduced the question of repeal into the House of Commons in 1822, and McCulloch wrote an important article on the subject for the *Edinburgh Review* (though it did not appear till 1824). But their careful calculations were upset by an independent move to achieve repeal by a bill introduced by Peter Moore on 3 March 1823. Though the bill was described by Place as a 'mass of absurdities', support was organised among workers at Coventry and Nottingham by Gravenor Henson, while in Manchester, William Longson, a weaver who played a leading role in agitation on this issue, began mobilising opinion with a letter in the *Gazette*, recommending all the labouring classes to unite to petition the legislature in favour of Moore's bill.[109] In November Cobbett told London mechanics that, 'an institution to get the Combination Act repealed could, I fancy, be the most advantageous that you could at this time establish'.[110] Parliament had in the meantime persuaded Moore to postpone his bill until the next session, but in September he asked artisans and labourers 'in every corner of the country' to petition in favour of repeal when the bill was reintroduced. In pursuit of this policy Longson wrote a letter in December on 'The Impolicy, Injustice, Oppression and Commercial Evils Resulting from the Combination Law, Exposed, with a view of Obtaining its Repeal', which was published in the *Manchester Gazette* and also as a separate handbill. Trades in other towns such as Sheffield also supported Moore's bill.[111]

By the beginning of 1824, therefore, a considerable body of working-class support had grown up in favour of repeal, largely independent of Place's prompting. He set about not to raise the workmen from their apathy but to channel their efforts in the direction he desired. On 14 January he inserted in the *Black Dwarf* the form of a petition which all bodies of workmen should send up to Parliament: attention was carefully shifted from complaints against the Combination Laws allowing employers to oppress workers to assertions that the Laws themselves were responsible for the existence of combinations and any interference between masters and men was injurious to all parties. In February Hume successfully moved for the appointment of a Select Committee into the effects of the laws relating to the emigration of artisans, the export of machinery and combination of workmen. As chairman of the Committee, he immediately sent out a circular to various towns asking for information. Notable among opponents to any changes in the law were the Manchester and Stockport employers.[112] On 5 February, however, Place sent out a circular to trade societies acquainting them with the appointment of the Committee, and as a result a steady stream of petitions was sent up to the Commons from various parts of the country. Among the Lancashire trades which sent delegates to give evidence to the Committee were the Manchester, Stockport and Bolton weavers and the Stockport spinners.[113] Place found, however, that their hopes from repeal of the Combination Laws were rather different from his: they had 'false notions' that it would lead to a rise in wages, not seeing that maintenance of wages depended on restriction of population, but blaming their distress on machinery, grinding masters, the combination laws, etc.[114] Later, in 1829, he recalled to Doherty that when he talked to the cotton spinners and weavers on this subject in 1824–5, emphasising the laws of political economy, and 'told them they were considered by their employers as so many machines or parts of machines by means of which their business was accomplished, then they revolted at the idea this suggested'.[115] No doubt Doherty himself, always so insistent on the dignity and independence of working men, was among those so 'revolted' by this philosophy.

Place undoubtedly played a vital role in securing the Select Committee's appointment, in rousing opinion and mobilising witnesses. On the basis of the evidence produced, a repealing bill was introduced by Hume and passed easily through Parliament, almost without debate. Thus one can conclude that although there was persistent complaint from trade unions on this issue, it was Place's 'wire-pulling' at the centre which was crucial in effecting the actual abolition. Indeed Doherty himself later recognised that Place had, 'perhaps, contributed more towards the repeal of the odious combination laws than *all* others put together'.[116]

The coincidence of repeal with a period of flourishing trade, high employment and increasing prices, however, upset Place's calculations. Freed from their legal restrictions, workmen in various trades throughout the country brought their unions into the open and struck for wage advances. The Manchester papers from July to December 1824 reported turn-outs there among spinners, dyers, shoemakers, foundry workers and calico printers. The cotton spinners, as we have seen, were very active in Manchester and other Lancashire towns, and also joined with those in Glasgow in efforts to establish a national union. Widespread alarm was aroused among employers generally. When Parliament reassembled in January 1825, therefore, deputations from the master shipbuilders and spinners were prominent in demanding that the government take action, while the *Times* and most other newspapers condemned trade-union activities. Huskisson threatened that if the workmen's conduct continued the Combination Laws would be re-enacted.[117]

The main argument of those in favour of re-enactment was that, since the repeal, trade unions had terrorised both masters and 'loyal' workers into obedience with their dictates, so much so that if their power was not broken the trade of the country would collapse. Joseph Hume, therefore, writing to the Manchester spinners on 27 December 1824, in approval of their condemnation of vitriol-throwing,[118] begged them to forsake tactics of secrecy and violence which had grown up because of the Combination Laws, but which he feared would, if continued, lead to an attempt at reimposing them. As a result, the spinners issued a second handbill reiterating their condemnation of violence and advising the Manchester trades generally to co-operate with Hume in his efforts at preserving the benefits of repeal.[119]

As a further earnest of their determination to appear peaceable, the Manchester spinners reversed their policy of aiding the Glasgow men and meetings of spinners were held at Manchester, Preston, Stockport, Hyde and elsewhere to pass identically worded resolutions, denying any desire to 'dictate' to their employers how their factories should be organised, regretting (where strikes had occurred) the differences with their masters, and asserting that 'our only object in associating [is] to bury our dead, support each other in time of sickness and when out of employment, and to obtain a fair and reasonable remuneration for our labour and skill, and just and equitable rules by which our conduct, as workmen, are to be regulated'.[120] Allegations that the spinners were bound by oaths were also refuted, while accusations of secrecy were shown up by extensive reports of their activities in the *Gazette;* oaths and secrecy, they maintained, were products of the Combination Laws, not of their repeal.

Pressure from employers was so strong, however, that on 29 March Huskisson secured the appointment of a Select Committee to enquire into the effects of Hume's Act and 'respecting the conduct of workmen throughout the United Kingdom'. He criticised the proceedings of workers' unions which he feared would ultimately destroy the country's trade and hinted at the existence of a confederation with republican ideals throughout the manufacturing, mining and shipping branches. Place forthwith issued a pamphlet exposing the errors in this speech, showing how repeal had actually reduced the incidence of violence, though it had not yet had time to eradicate all the harm caused by the old system, and proving that masters had still the power to defeat the workmen by themselves combining, as the Glasgow and Lancashire millowners had demonstrated.[121] Moreover, the Select Committee's terms of reference gave Place and Hume the chance to defend 'the conduct of workmen'. Hence, Place helped John Gast to form a committee of London trades' delegates to organise opposition to re-enactment of the Combination Laws,[122] and at the same time he urged provincial workmen to take similar defensive measures. Thus he wrote to Foster and McWilliams, the Manchester spinners' delegates whom he had already assisted over the short-time question,[123] and they immediately organised a meeting of the local trades on 14 April, which appointed a 'Manchester Artisans' General Committee' to co-operate with the one in London.[124] After a further trades' meeting on 3 May, petitions were drawn up by the cotton spinners, fustian cutters and weavers, opposing reimposition of the Combination Laws, which, they asserted, had brought frequent wage reductions and caused violence and secrecy, while repeal had benefited both workmen and fair masters by decreasing such evils. These trades also elected delegates to London in the hope of procuring a hearing before the Select Committee—Thomas Foster and Robert Hyde for the spinners, William Baxter and Robert Middleton, president of the General Committee, for the fustian cutters, and William Longson, secretary of the General Committee, for the weavers, though he was too ill in the event to make the trip.[125]

John Doherty was clearly one of the leaders of the spinners' agitation on this question and also a member of the Manchester Artisans' General Committee. On 16 May he wrote to Place,

> for the purpose of assertaining [*sic*] your opinion as to whether I am likely to be called before the Committee to give evidence relative to the effects of the repeal of the laws against combinations of workmen; and if so, how soon you think I am likely to be wanted? . . . One of our Deputies, Robert Hyde, whom you may have seen, and who is now returned from London has stated . . . that your opinion is that I shall not be wanted at all; but in a matter of so much moment, at least to me, I thought it best, as there is a gentleman on whose opinion I would implicitly rely, to depend on no

other. I have seen your very eloquent and able pamphlet on Mr Huskisson's speech. After reading that production, I should think, the Right Honourable gentleman would be almost out of concert with himself as to speech-making.[126]

In the event, Place and Hume could not secure a hearing for Doherty, although it is unlikely that Doherty's views on the independence of the working classes and the importance of unions in securing their rightful place in society would have fitted neatly into the pattern which they were trying to present to the Select Committee. Nevertheless, Doherty remained active at the local level in the Manchester General Committee.

The Place papers show that similar trades' committees were formed in other manufacturing towns like Birmingham and Sheffield, and that scores of petitions were submitted, but it was only with great difficulty that Place and Hume were able to persuade the Select Committee to call any workmen as witnesses.[127] The only evidence from the north-western cotton area was given by Thomas Worsley, the Stockport delegate to London, who repeated many of his arguments to the 1824 Committee.[128] Nevertheless, when the Committee reported and Wallace's Bill was introduced, based on its recommendations, it was specifically stated that there was no intention to revive the old act. Combinations of workmen for dealing with questions of wages and hours were still to be legal, but the concession was circumscribed by penalties against 'intimidation', 'molestation', or 'obstruction' and against any effort to 'coerce' employers or fellow-workmen, and thus it would be very difficult for unions to take effective action without incurring penalties under statute or common law.

The reaction of Lancashire workmen was almost immediately hostile. Longson published some observations on the new bill on behalf of the 'Manchester Committee of Artisans', in which he criticised its vague phraseology and its partial application to workers and not masters, who were clearly far more powerful than united workmen, as events at Glasgow and Hyde had shown; the few acts of violence since the repeal had not been committed by unions but 'by ignorant and obstinate individuals, whom no committee could control or restrain'.[129] Doherty at once set about organising opposition in the Manchester Committee, for when the bill passed the Commons he wrote to Place on 1 July in the following terms:

Last night I saw your very important letter to our friend McWilliam [sic], and was equally astonished and mortified at its contents. Mr McWilliams put it into my hands and desired me to lay it before the committee, which I did and was assured that it will promptly be attended to. I also showed it to Mr Prentice,[130] for which he was very thankful, and promised to make the subject his editorial article in tomorrow's paper. I expect we will have a petition ready for signature by tomorrow night, and if parliament is not to be immediately prorogued, in London by Monday or Tuesday night . . . I shall be very glad to furnish you with any information you may require, on this subject, that is within my power. No exertion that I can make shall be wanting.[131]

But despite further petitions from various towns the Bill passed quickly through the Lords and received the royal assent on 5 July. This was regarded by the organised workmen as a serious setback,[132] and throughout Doherty's life, in fact, trade unions were to remain under legal repression. But, as we shall see, they were not thereby prevented from making further advances, nor deterred from fighting for their rights.

This agitation against the Combination Laws appears to have given rise to another attempt at general union. Most labour historians have been content to repeat Doherty's later reference to it as evidence of its existence: 'In 1826 a Trades' Union was formed in Manchester, which extended, slightly, to some of the surrounding districts, and embraced several trades in each; but it expired before it was so much as known to a large majority of the operatives in the neighbourhood.'[133] G. D. H. Cole concluded that, though little is known of this general trades' union, 'we can hardly be wrong in putting this down largely to Doherty's influence'.[134] The outbreak of strikes following repeal of the Combination Laws soon aroused rumours of a widespread general union, as in 1818. Greville wrote that 'the whole body of mechanics in the kingdom are combined in the general resolution to impose terms on their employers'.[135] William Longson told Place as early as September 1824 'that several Trades are now forming themselves into one Union' and taking secret oaths, under the influence of the Glasgow spinners,[136] but the institutional basis for a general union does not appear to have been established until somewhat later, with the formation of trades' committees in different towns to co-operate in opposing re-enactment of the Combination Laws. Some of these, moreover, proposed to exercise control over trade disputes, as did the Manchester committee in their inaugural address in April 1825: 'Every misunderstanding which hereafter may take place, between Employers and Workmen, will be minutely investigated by this Committee, and a decision given whether any proposed strike against an individual employer be reasonable, just, or consistent with the sound policy of the leading principles of political economy.' The Committee hoped to 'prevent men from injuring themselves by unnecessary strikes, where an advance of wages may be impossible', while in cases where action was justified, the Committee's 'combined talents' would be better able to organise operations.[137]

When these various trades' committees sent deputies to London in May, they were immediately added to the London Artisans' Committee, and discussions covered a far wider field than the tactics of frustrating the intention to reimpose the Combination Laws. Questions such as entry to the trades, including apprenticeship, and the related problems of employment and wages were discussed.[138] Moreover, this collaboration between metropolitan and provincial delegates (including Worsley and Foster) led to the establishment of *The Trades' Newspaper and Mechanics' Weekly Journal*, starting in July 1825, and appealing to trade unionists throughout the country. Place, whose views on economic questions differed considerably from those of most working-class leaders, supported a rival publication, *The Journeyman and Artisan's London and Provincial Chronicle*, started the previous month.[139]

These trade-union ventures into journalism aroused considerable debate in Manchester and, despite some personal recriminations, doubtless helped to stimulate trades' co-operation there.[140] Indeed, under Doherty's influence, the movement soon became more extensive. On 1 July he wrote to Place on hearing that the House of Commons had passed Wallace's bill:

If they leave us to ourselves, some few outrages may be committed, but the only contention will be between the more violent and foolish, and the more intelligent and discreet part of the labouring classes; the one side is advocating, the other is depricating [*sic*] all violent and improper measures, until ultimately, all shall be convinced that the line of conduct best calculated to promote their interests would be reasonableness in their demands, submission to the laws, and obedience to and respect for their employers. But if they oppress us, if they make a law that will place us under the control of our employers, they will *force* all to *unite* in one great combination, not only against our employers, but against *themselves* and they will find us more troublesome than they expect.[141]

When the new Combination bill became law, there is evidence that Doherty's idea was put into practice, for in August we learn that 'the potters of Staffordshire intend to join the *Grand Union of England*, a body which at least has an imposing name, and if it have correspondent force, may be capable of paralysing the whole manufacturing industry of the country'. The potters stated that 'two *Delegates* waited upon us from Manchester yesterday, requesting us to join their Union : the same Delegates are gone to Birmingham, and so on throughout England'. By October the ultra-Tory *Stockport Advertiser* was demanding strong measures to reverse the evils caused by listening to the Broughams and Humes, the Whigs and the Radicals. 'The manufacturing interests of the country are in fact, at this moment, under the immediate control of the grand union of Trades, formed by a committee of delegates from each trade, and it is in their power to destroy, whenever they are pleased to do so, any branch of manufactures; and there is no power in the country to restrain them.' The workers were supported in idleness from a 'general fund', and because of 'the ravings of liberality' the law was unable to prevent the tyrannical measures of 'such a powerful body', or to protect the masters, 'whose capital is as the life-blood of the state'.[142]

Although this was clearly an exaggeration, large and widespread financial support was given to the Bradford woolcombers and stuff-weavers, in demanding an advance of 3s per week in June from their employers, who promptly locked out all those workers who would not renounce their union and circularised masters in neighbouring towns to ensure that they could not get alternative employment. The Manchester trades, including the spinners, contributed £402 out of a total of more than £15,800.[143] The full-time secretary of the Bradford union, John Tester, made constant appeals and tours for assistance, on the ground that the struggle would decide if all the trades would be able to combine to regulate their own wages or be enslaved by their masters. At the end of September he came to Manchester, issued a public address 'to the Mechanics, Artisans and Labourers of Manchester', and spoke at a public meeting of the working classes in the Manor Court Room in favour of forming 'an Union of Unions'. Many of the Manchester workmen who had been prominent in the Artisans' Committee also spoke, while Longson wrote a letter to the Leeds press quoting the Bradford turn-out as an example of the 'utility of trades' union'.[144]

But in November the Bradford workmen were forced to accept defeat and those who could find work returned on the masters' terms. The Lancashire spinners' federation was also breaking up after a series of defeats. By the

end of 1825 the cyclical boom was collapsing, to be followed by deepening
commercial and industrial depression, which seriously weakened trade unions
generally. As a result, the *Stockport Advertiser* rejoiced in December that the
alarming appearances of just two months earlier were now disappearing and
the operatives were learning their lesson, in face of misery and distress.[145]
Any idea of forming a general union on the basis of the Manchester trades'
committee's address of April 1825 was submerged as the workers were driven
on the defensive, and during 1826 turned back to hopes of political amelioration and to hopeless rioting and destruction of machinery. That this union was
very limited both in extent and duration, as Doherty stated, is indicated also
by the comments of a speaker at a Rochdale meeting in February 1828, on the
subject of a general union of trades, who said that 'immediately after the
repeal of the Combination Laws, such an union had been thought of, but it
had afterwards been abandoned because they could not agree about the
necessary arrangements'.[146]

Nevertheless, co-operation between the Manchester trades continued in
1826, if not for trade-union purposes. On 24 January about 1,500–2,000 working men attended a meeting at the Manor Court Room to petition Parliament
for repeal of the Corn Laws, when most of the leaders of the old Artisans'
Committee, including Doherty, were conspicuous.[147] The Corn Laws were
denounced as ruinous to English commerce and the major cause of dear food
and unemployment, and trades' committees in other towns were urged to
appoint representatives 'to act in concert' on this issue.[148]. This meeting was
the first of a series held in all the large manufacturing towns. A concerted
campaign against the Corn Laws developed, and John Gast's letters to the
*Trades' Newspaper* urging that the formation of a general union of the trades
for mutual protection would be of more benefit to the working classes than
repeal, were largely ignored. [149]

As the depression deepened, however, and reports accumulated of increasing
unemployment and wages reductions, especially among handloom weavers,
social distress became so severe that workmen turned to more desperate
measures. The handloom weavers could not be convinced that their suffering,
which was now unprecedented, was not caused by the introduction of the
power loom, which had spread rapidly during the previous years of prosperity,
following the first really successful steam-powered iron loom being put on
the market in 1822 by Roberts & Sharp. The storm broke at Blackburn, where
in April the weavers indulged in an orgy of rioting and machine-breaking,
with the result that 'not a single power-loom was left standing in Blackburn
or within six miles of it'. The outbreak spread swiftly through the East Lancashire towns and was soon raging in Manchester.[150] Not only were there attacks
on several power-loom factories there, but also on 'knobstick' spinners working in mills where wages had been reduced.[151] Relief funds were organised in
many towns, but were inadequate to relieve the profound and widespread
distress.

The spinners' leaders were now seriously alarmed that control of events
had been taken out of their hands. Although the spinners' suffering was much
less severe than that of the weavers, and hence their participation in rioting
comparatively rare, many of them had been put on short time or laid off, and
there were strikes against wage reductions in several factories. On 5 May

Foster, Hodgins and Doherty placarded the town with handbills addressed 'To the Unemployed Cotton Spinners of Manchester and its neighbourhood' at the order of a general meeting of the trade. While sympathising with their distress and supporting any measure to alleviate it, the handbill insisted that the destruction of machinery could never help matters, but must increase their misery, by augmenting the number of unemployed to be relieved by throwing more men out of work, by allowing foreign competitors with similar machinery to undersell them, and by giving hard-hearted capitalists an excuse for not contributing to the relief fund. Instead, workers were urged to 'join in one unanimous and earnest prayer to both Houses of Parliament for the TOTAL AND IMMEDIATE REPEAL OF THE CORN LAWS', as well as for regulation of the currency and reduction of public expenditure.[152]

But by the time this appeal was issued, the worst of the violence was already over. Quiet was restored by bringing in army reinforcements and by arrest of the ringleaders by the civil authorities. At the Lancaster Assizes in August, forty-six individuals were convicted and sentenced to transportation or various terms of imprisonment.[153] The rioting appears to have been wholly spontaneous, being the ultimate response to sheer economic hardship for which there seemed no solution. However, over the following weeks Byng's military reports to the Home Office began to make frequent references to the influence and numbers of delegates travelling about the Manchester and Blackburn districts. One of his informants was George Bradbury, prominent among the Manchester cotton spinners, who made constant allusions to arming and drilling at nocturnal meetings and to speakers urging rebellion, in a manner reminiscent of 1817–19. In June the *Morning Herald* reported a meeting of delegates from thirty-six places, which issued an address 'to all classes' in favour of a general union to obtain parliamentary reform, for only then could the necessary measures to alleviate distress be obtained.[154]

By July all the Manchester papers were concerned at the occurrence of torchlight meetings harangued by violent delegates. Abraham Whitaker, a Manchester operative spinner, reported to James Norris on secret meetings in Manchester, which were planning simultaneous risings in the manufacturing towns, then being prepared for action by the travelling delegates. A letter of James Foster on 26 July spoke of a 'Committee formed for Manchester, who are in the habit of meeting frequently and receiving deputations from other places, and carrying on a correspondence with them'. This 'Central Committee' was represented at a delegate meeting at Leeds on 28 July, which planned the organisation of classes and republican violence, according to a report of 'Alpha' to a Bolton magistrate.[155] But little more was heard of these activities after the sentences on the power-loom rioters in August. Political meetings continued to be held, addressed by the same workmen who had been prominent in the Artisans' Committee, but the proceedings were open and fully reported in the press,[156] while the weavers as a group turned to support organised demands to the government for the establishment of a Wages' Board to protect them, and the spinners continued their purely trade-union activities from which they were only temporarily diverted by the extreme distress of 1826.

By the end of 1825, as we have seen, the spinners' federal organisation had disintegrated, but most of their local unions were still intact. Among the

Manchester spinners, Thomas Foster, Jonathan Hodgins and John Doherty were now emerging as the dominant personalities. Their views, however, were not always representative of rank and file opinion. Foster and Hodgins seem to have concurred in Place's theories on the relationship between population and wages, while Hodgins' ready acceptance of mechanical progress and his reservations over the factory bill had earned him some unpopularity. Doherty was less conspicuous in public record than the other two, but seems to have shared their conviction of the hopelessness and futility of resistance to machinery, whilst emphasising the importance of union among the working classes. All of them were working spinners and probably members of the committee, elected from representatives of the different mills, but the only full-time official appears to have been Lee, who had been proscribed by the masters after the 1818 strike. All had figured in the movement for co-operation between the trades and in opposition to the Combination Laws; they had also collaborated in agitation for the 1825 factory bill, though Foster and McWilliams were more prominent at this stage than Doherty.[157]

The economic crisis and depression of 1826 placed the spinners on the defensive, and any consideration of trying to equalise wage rates throughout Lancashire was out of the question; in fact most of the factories were put on short time and there was a general attempt to reduce wages. The Manchester spinners were involved in a series of strikes against wages cuts in individual mills throughout the year.[158] In April the Ashton spinners were compelled to accept a reduction following a month's strike in seventeen mills, and in October the Stockport and Bolton operatives also submitted to a reduction on condition that the old rates would be restored when trade revived. But a long and violent struggle took place in Oldham, beginning early in September against a reduction of 15 per cent, which the men contended came on top of a previous decline of one-third over the previous sixteen months, but which the masters stated only brought them level with the rates paid in the surrounding districts of Hyde, Ashton and Bury. Such variations in local piece-rates, as we shall see, were to be a continual source of disputes. Another factor, equally perennial, was the question of rates on larger mules, for it was the more technically progressive firms which had made the reduction while a number of the other master spinners—presumably those with smaller mules—at first gave support to the strikers. A series of violent confrontations took place, in several of which the military were required and numerous arrests were made.[159] But these desperate proceedings were only a reflection of the hopelessness of the strikers' position, in the depths of winter and trade depression. By the end of January they were starved into submission, which was followed by sentences of imprisonment on the leaders.[160]

In Manchester, meanwhile, the situation was quieter and the spinners were consolidating their organisation, which had now acquired some degree of permanence, despite fluctuations in trade. In January 1827 one observer reported that, 'In Manchester the combination is organised to perfection—many of the Spinners pay as much as 5s or 6s per week to the general fund for supporting the "turn-outs" and no master can turn off a workman, unless such be approved of by the combination committee, without running a risque of all his work-people turning out.' A printed report of the money paid to the unemployed between 25 June and 15 December 1827 was sent to the Home Office in 1829, although it is not extant.[161] The spinners also retained their interest in wider working-class movements, as evidenced by their continued support of the *Trades' Newspaper*, though Thomas Foster expressed their disappointment at its lukewarm attitude towards strikes and its moderate line over political reform.[162]

The year 1827 was very quiet, relatively few disputes being mentioned in the Manchester papers. Wages were comparatively high, according to an advertisement for spinners in August, which stated that those on numbers from 110 to 200 could earn 'from 34s to 38s per week, clear of all expense'.[163] In 1828, however, more serious problems developed. At the very time when the lower piece prices in surrounding towns and the continued increase in the number of spindles per mule were causing masters to think of further reductions in piece rates, the Manchester spinners' union was split by a bitter controversy over the election of Doherty to the secretaryship.

NOTES TO CHAPTER TWO

[1] H.O. 42/178, James Norris to Viscount Simouth, 29 July 1818; *The Times* (London), 3 August, and *Courier* (London), 4 August 1818; *Cobbett's Weekly Register*, 19 December 1818; cuttings in Place Papers, Vol. XVI, Add. MSS 27,804.
[2] Typically, of course, the hostile press was critical only of *workmen's* combinations.
[3] *Gazette*, 18 July 1818.
[4] *Gorgon*, 15 August 1818; *Annual Register*, 1818, pp. 100–102.
[5] *Chronicle*, 15 August 1818.
[6] *Ibid.*, 14 November 1818; H.O. 42/178, Norris to Sidmouth, 29 July 1818.
[7] Norris, *loc. cit.*
[8] H.O. 42/178, letter from D. Lyon, of Wigan, attached to letter from F. Freeling to H. Hobhouse, 22 July 1818. Lyon also stated that the Wigan spinners had been addressed by a Stockport delegate 'who appeared to have some authority over them'. It seems unlikely, therefore, that the Wigan spinners struck 'out of turn, since this conflicted with the general tactic of the spinners' federations', as suggested by Turner, *op. cit.*, p. 68.
[9] H.O. 42/179, *passim*, but especially letter from the Rev. C. W. Ethelston, a Manchester magistrate, to Viscount Sidmouth, 24 August 1818, and Norris to Hobhouse, 10 August 1818. There are numerous extracts from the Home Office papers relating to this strike in A. Aspinall, *The Early English Trade Unions* (1949), Ch. VII.
[10] See below, p. 26.
[11] H.O. 42/178, Norris to Sidmouth, 29 July 1818, referring to a letter sent to Sidmouth by David Ramsay, a government agent in Stockport, 18 July 1818.
[12] See below, pp. 23–7.
[13] According to a report in the *Star*, 5 September 1818, quoted in Aspinall, *op. cit.*, p. 299, footnote.
[14] H.O. 42/179, W. R. Hay to Hobhouse, 1 August 1818, and Norris to Hobhouse, 13 August 1818.
[15] *Chronicle*, 11 July 1818. Seven of those arrested were sentenced to six months' imprisonment: *ibid.*, 8 August 1818, and H.O. 42/178, Hay to Hobhouse, 30 July 1818.
[16] H.O. 42/179, Norris to Sidmouth, 29 July 1818, and letter from Manchester borough-reeve and constables, 3 August 1818. Johnson and Bagguley were prominent local radicals.
[17] H.O. 79/3, ff. 203–5, Hobhouse to Hay, 1 August 1818, and H.O. 42/179, Norris to Sidmouth, 2 August 1818, enclosing copy of handbill.
[18] H.O. 42/179.
[19] *Ibid.*, Norris to Hobhouse, 26 August 1818; J. Lloyd to Hobhouse, 29 August 1818.

²⁰ *Ibid.*, Lloyd to Hobhouse, 29 August 1818; *Chronicle,* 5 September 1818. Doherty was not apparently a member of the spinners' committee at this time, but, as we shall see, he had been previously arrested (see below, pp. 21–2).

²¹ H.O. 42/180, Norris to R. H. Clive, 1 September 1818. The radical leaders, Drummond, Bagguley and Johnson, were also arrested a few days later. The Manchester magistrates' resolution was stiffened by the example of those in Stockport, where 15 spinners, including William Temple, the society's treasurer, had previously been arrested.

²² *Chronicle, Gazette,* and *Observer,* 5 September; *Mercury,* 8 September 1818. In the *Advocate,* 19 May 1832, Doherty claimed that the fatal shot was fired by James Frost, manager of Gray's mill, one-time trade unionist but later hostile opponent (see above, p. 16, n. 19). Such events burned deep into trade-union memories.

²³ *Chronicle,* 5 September 1818, *inter alia.*

²⁴ H.O. 42/180, Norris to Sidmouth, 7 and 8 September 1818, quoted in Aspinall, *op. cit.,* Nos. 292 and 294.

²⁵ *Observer,* 19 September; *Gorgon,* 26 September 1818; *A Penny Poor Man's Advocate,* 29 September 1832; *Report of the Proceedings . . . December 1829.*

²⁶ Doherty, as we have seen, had been working, prior to the strike, in Murray's New Mill (see above, p. 4).

²⁷ H.O. 42/179, Norris to Hobhouse, 26 August; Ethelston to Hobhouse, 28 August 1818. According to Ethelston, 'a man of the name of Dogherty was seized in an act of riot'. (In a summary note on the back his name is spelt 'Doherty'.)

²⁸ See, for example, Tufnell in the *Supplementary Report of the Central Board of Factory Commissioners,* Parl. Papers, 1834, Vol. xix, D2, p. 210; Ure, *op. cit.,* p. 282; Greg, *op. cit.,* p. 66. For further garbling of this false smear, see above, p. 6.

²⁹ *Conciliator,* 29 November 1828; *Voice,* 30 April 1831. See also *Guardian,* 18 June 1831, for another account of the incident by Doherty.

³⁰ Lancashire Quarter Sessions, Indictment Rolls, October 1818. Wroe was also appointed to receive subscriptions in Manchester for the spinners' defence fund.

³¹ H.O. 42/182, Clive to Norris, 6 November 1818; *Gorgon,* 9 January and 6 February 1819. An appeal was also issued on behalf of the spinners' mothers, wives and children, a copy of which is preserved among the Broadsides in Manchester Central Reference Library, P 3309. See also the *Black Dwarf,* 30 September 1818, for a denunciation by 'a Journeyman Cotton Spinner' of the inequality of laws which oppressed the workmen but ignored the 'abominable combination' among millowners.

³² Lancashire Quarter Sessions, Indictment Rolls, October 1818. (The rolls for January 1819 are missing.) The indictment, therefore, did not mention a *specific* assault by Doherty, only his participation in a crowd attacking the 'knobsticks' in general. There is a discrepancy between the date of the offence stated here, 29th July, and that in Norris's letter, 20th July, referred to above, p. 21 and n. 27.

³³ *Ibid.,* Order Book, January 1819; H.O. 42/183, Norris to Sidmouth, 29 January 1819, and H.O. 41/4, f. 247, Hobhouse to Norris, 1 February 1819. Norris stated that 'Dogherty' was 'indicted for conspiring with others to intimidate persons from working at Messrs Ewart & Co's cotton factory, &c'.

³⁴ H.O. 42/184 and 185, Norris to Sidmouth, 3 February and 8 March 1819, quoted in Aspinall, *op. cit.,* Nos. 321 and 326.

³⁵ Turner, *op. cit.,* pp. 99–100.

³⁶ H.O. 42/181, Norris to Sidmouth, 11 October and 18 November 1818; H.O. 79/3, ff. 334 and 340–1, Hobhouse to Norris, 23 November 1818, and 1 January 1819 (Aspinall, *op. cit.,* Nos. 308, 351, 316 and 318). In the last letter Hobhouse named two delegates who had previously been sent from Nottingham 'to abet the General Union of Trades at Manchester'. There appear to have been vague plans for a 'general insurrection' in the midland textile areas in the spring of 1817, and according to the Hammonds, Jeremiah Brandreth was reported in May to have talked about widespread preparations for a 'general strike', just prior to the 'Pentridge Rising'. J. L. and B. Hammond, *The Skilled Labourer* (1919), p. 358, referring to H.O. 42/165. But the relevant Home Office papers

appear to refer only to schemes for a political insurrection or 'day of rising', with attacks on barracks, seizure of arms, release of prisoners, etc. It is not at all unlikely, however, that trade unionists may have become involved in these schemes, as they were in Manchester in 1818 (though to what extent is uncertain), and it seems probable that the idea of a 'general turn-out' or 'general strike', to be organised by a 'General Union of Trades', did originate in Nottingham. See also below, p. 249.

[37] There are numerous such references in H.O. 42/179 and 180, several of which are quoted in Aspinall, *op. cit.* See also above, p. 20.

[38] The correspondent in Manchester was Longbottom, one of the spinners' leaders, and in London, W. P. Washington, originally from Manchester and now prominent in metropolitan radical circles, who later helped organise assistance for the arrested cotton spinners. Sidmouth had ordered the Postmaster-General to intercept Longbottom's correspondence. H.O. 79/3, ff. 96 and 186–92; Place Papers, Vol. XI, Add. MSS 27,799. Norris had also heard of the projected meeting on 10 August (H.O. 42/179, letter dated 2 August 1818).

[39] *London Courier*, 4 August 1818.

[40] H.O. 42/179, Norris to Sidmouth, 5 August 1818; *Sherwin's Political Register*, 8 August 1818. T. S. Withington, the Manchester borough-reeve, also linked the 'revolutionaries (formerly reformers)' with the spinners. H.O. 42/179, letter of 8 August 1818.

[41] H.O. 42/179, W. Chippendale to Hobhouse, 5 August 1818.

[42] *Ibid.*, J. Lloyd to Hobhouse, 22 August 1818.

[43] *Ibid.*, letter from W. Marriott, 17 August 1818.

[44] One being a secret agent, who immediately informed the Manchester authorities of all these proceedings. H.O. 42/179, Withington to Hobhouse, 14 August 1818.

[45] *Ibid.*, Norris to Hobhouse, 13 and 14 August 1818.

[46] Handbill forwarded to the Home Office by W. Marriott, reprinted in Aspinall, *op. cit.*, No. 260.

[47] See Aspinall, *op. cit.*, Nos. 263–6.

[48] H.O. 42/179, letters from Withington and Ethelston, 24 August, and from Norris, 26 August 1818.

[49] *Ibid.*, letter from James Hanley, a government spy, 31 August 1818.

[50] H.O. 42/180, Norris to Clive, 1 September 1818 (Aspinall, *op. cit.*, No. 280).

[51] See Aspinall, *op. cit.*, pp. 281–302. Pilkington, Kay and Ellison, the weavers' leaders, were tried and sentenced with Doherty in January 1819 (*ibid.*, No. 319).

[52] H.O. 42/180 and 181, Norris to Sidmouth, 11 September and 11 October 1818 (Aspinall, *op. cit.*, Nos. 298 and 308).

[53] *Ibid.*

[54] H.O. 42/182, Norris to Sidmouth, 18 November 1818 (Aspinall, *op. cit.*, No. 315. See also No. 316). The Manchester weavers continued to urge the idea in an 'Address to the Labouring Classes', *Sherwin's Political Register*, 3 October 1818.

[55] But the meetings to promote it there were 'not numerously attended' and the subscriptions were 'inconsiderable'. H.O. 41/4, ff. 204–6, Clive to Norris, 14 October 1818 (Aspinall, *op. cit.*, No. 309).

[56] H.O. 42/179, reports dated 17, 24 and 31 August 1818, by Home Office agent James Hanley. The spinners' delegates stayed in London for over a month, later visiting other towns, e.g. Norwich, to solicit subscriptions for the union of trades. H.O. 41/4, f. 181.

[57] As reported by H.O. spies, Perry, 4 September 1818, and Hanley, 8, 16, and 21 September, H.O. 42/180.

[58] *Gorgon*, 5 December 1818; Place Papers, Vol. XI. Add. MSS 27,799; G. D. H. Cole, *Attempts at General Union* (1953), p. 10.

[59] Place Papers, Vol. XI, Add. MSS 27,799. According to the *Chronicle*, 30 January 1819, quoting a London paper, it had 60,000 members, but this was doubtless a great exaggeration.

[60] See above, p. 22. Wroe was among the radical reformers denounced by local magistrates for circulating inflammatory publications. H.O. 42/182, Norris to Sidmouth, 18 November 1818.

[61] H.O. 42/181 and 182, Norris to Sidmouth, 11 October and 18 November 1818 (Aspinall, *op. cit.*, Nos. 308 and 315).

[62] Parl. Papers, 1837–8, VIII, 3460. See below, p. 347.

[63] See below, pp. 51–3.

[64] *Conciliator*, 29 November and 6 December 1828.

[65] James Norris discounted a story that the spinners' fund amounted to £600 in November 1818, in a letter to Sidmouth in H.O. 42/182, quoted in Aspinall, *op. cit.*, No. 315. If such funds had existed, they would presumably have been used to pay off the defence fund's debts.

[66] See below, p. 415.

[67] *Conciliator*, 29 November 1828.

[68] Broughton Papers, Add. MSS 36,458, f. 427. We are indebted to Dr I. Prothero for this reference. See below, pp. 414–5.

[69] *Observer*, 3 March 1821. See below, pp. 415–7.

[70] See below, p. 323.

[71] Numerous reports appeared in the Bolton and Manchester newspapers in the early months of 1823. See also H.O. 40/18, quoted in Aspinall, *op. cit.*, Nos. 391 and 393. The Bolton spinners had apparently been earning high wages, from 30s to 40s per week, clear of deductions. The strike also involved other matters, such as long hours and bad working conditions, harsh fines, truck, and tied cottages.

[72] *Quinquarticular System*, p. 3; *Voice*, 12 February 1831.

[73] Reports of these events are to be found in the local press in the later months of 1824 and early 1825. See also the Place Papers, Vol. XIII, Add. MSS 27,801, f. 255. (Joseph Hume was afraid that such outrages might lead to reimposition of the Combination Laws: see below, p. 36.) The Manchester spinners' secretary at this time appears as 'Abraham Noel', but this may have been a pseudonym for their 'corresponding secretary', a proscribed spinner named D. Lee (see below, p. 43).

[74] During the 1818 strike, as we have seen, there had been correspondence between the English, Scottish and Irish spinning districts and vague rumours of a general 'turn-out'. See above, p. 19.

[75] Turner, *op. cit.*, pp. 90–1.

[76] The conflicting statements of the masters and men appeared in the Glasgow papers in November. They were summarised in the *Gazette*, 11 December 1824, and also in a separate pamphlet (Glasgow, 1825), preserved among the Broadsides in Manchester Central Reference Library, P2185. See also the letter of a Glasgow spinner, P. McDougal, to Francis Place, dated 8 September 1824, in Place Papers, Vol. XII, Add. MSS 27,800, f. 238.

[77] *Gazette*, 25 December 1824, quoting the *Glasgow Chronicle*.

[78] *Ibid.*, 15 January 1825. See below, pp. 33 and 41–2, for the Manchester spinners' conciliatory policy at this time.

[79] *Ibid.*

[80] For evidence of Doherty's prominence by this time in the Manchester trade-union and radical movements, see below, pp. 31–2, 37–43, 417–8, 448–50.

[81] *Mercury*, 8 February, and *Gazette*, 9 July 1825, both quoting from the *Glasgow Chronicle*.

[82] *Chronicle*, 29 January; *Gazette*, 19 and 26 February 1825. Tufnell, *op. cit.*, p. 29, stated that the average Hyde price for No. 40s was 3s 7d, compared with 4s 7d 'in other places'. The operatives published detailed figures in the *Gazette*, showing how much lower piece-prices were in Hyde than in Stalybridge; they claimed that Hyde spinners' wages averaged only 23–25s per week, but the masters replied in the *Manchester Guardian* and other papers that, because of increased productivity on larger mules, weekly wages averaged 28–32s.

[83] Reports in local newspapers, February–May 1825.

[84] Tufnell, *loc. cit.*

[85] *Mercury*, 25 January, quoting *Preston Pilot*; *Gazette*, 14 May 1825.

[86] Place Papers, Vol. XV, Add. MSS 27,803, Part I, ff. 259–60.

[87] *Gazette*, 26 March and 9 April 1825.

[88] *Stockport Advertiser*, 11 March and 10 June 1825, quoting the *Carlisle Patriot*.

[89] *Ibid.*, 10 February 1826.

[90] See below, pp. 87–96. Doherty was hoping, of course, that in the Grand General Union of Cotton Spinners set up in 1829 he would be able to avoid these earlier mistakes.

[91] *Report of the Proceedings . . . December 1829.* Historians such as S. and B. Webb, G. D. H. Cole, S. J. Chapman, and H. A. Turner have wrongly concluded that Doherty was here referring to the general trades' union of 1825–6, for which see below, pp. 39–41.

[92] S. Smiles, *Industrial Biography* (1876), pp. 264–73; H. Rose, *Manual Labour Versus Brass and Iron* (Manchester, 1825).

[93] 'Hand mules', though power-driven, were not fully 'self-acting' or 'automatic', still requiring manual operation of the 'wheel-carriage' on which the spindles were fixed; the threads were stretched and twisted as the carriage was drawn out, and then wound upon the cops as the carriage was pushed in.

[94] See below, pp. 191–2 especially.

[95] *Mercury,* 23 November 1830.

[96] See below, pp. 51–2.

[97] See above, p. 21, and below, pp. 37–9.

[98] See below, p. 42. We shall see that this was generally his line, throughout his career, despite occasionally violent language.

[99] *Stockport Advertiser,* 10 December 1824. For a similar conciliatory policy by Stockport and Blackburn spinners, see Place Papers, Vol. XIII, Add. MSS 27,803, Part I, f. 261, and *Gazette,* 19 February 1825.

[100] See below, pp. 350–2.

[101] Place Papers, Vol. X, Add. MSS 27,798, f. 11.

[102] M. D. George, 'The Combination Laws Reconsidered', *Economic History* (supplement to *Econ. Journ.*), No. 2, May 1927, and 'The Combination Laws', *Econ. Hist. Rev.*, Vol. VI (1936); D. Simon, 'Master and Servant', in J. Saville (ed.), *Democracy and the Labour Movement* (1954), Ch. 6.

[103] Musson, *British Trade Unions, 1800–75*, pp. 25–6.

[104] *Conciliator,* 13 December 1828; *Journal,* 25 September 1830.

[105] *Bolton Chronicle,* 6 January 1827.

[106] *Courier,* 5 December; *Bolton Chronicle,* 5 December 1829.

[107] *Cobbett's Weekly Register,* 19 December 1818 and 30 August 1823.

[108] *Gorgon,* 5 December 1818, 23 January and 6 February 1819; *Mercury,* 29 June; *Chronicle,* 24 July 1819.

[109] Place Papers, Vol. X, Add. MSS 27,798, ff. 13–15; *Gazette,* 9 August 1823. For Moore's Bill see Thompson, *op. cit.*, pp. 566–7, who rightly emphasises that Place was not conducting a single-handed campaign and that his views on political economy were distrusted by many trade unionists.

[110] *Cobbett's Weekly Register,* 15 November 1823, quoted in D. C. Morris, 'The History of the Labour Movement in England, 1825–32' (unpublished Ph.D. thesis, London, 1952), p. 15.

[111] *Gazette,* 18 October and 27 December 1823; Place Papers, Vol. XII, Add. MSS 27,800, ff. 46 and 48.

[112] *Gazette,* 6 March; *Chronicle,* 20 March; *Stockport Advertiser,* 27 February 1824; H.O. 40/18.

[113] William Longson, William Temple, William Salt, and Thomas Worsley gave evidence on behalf of the Lancashire cotton operatives, Peter McDougal and William Smith for the Glasgow spinners. They denounced the Combination Laws, in Longson's words, as 'oppressive, partial and unjust', while master spinners' representatives deplored the violence and illegalities of trade unions. Doherty, of course, was listed among those who had suffered imprisonment. Parl. Papers, 1824, Vol. V.

[114] Place Papers, Vol. X, Add. MSS 27,798, f. 22.

[115] Place Collection, Vol. 16, Part II, f. 92.

[116] *Voice,* 5 March 1831.

[117] Place Papers, Vol. X, Add. MSS 27,798, ff. 26–8.

[118] See above, p. 29.

[119] Place Papers, Vol. XIII, Add. MSS 27,801, f. 255; *Gazette,* 8 and 15 January 1825.

120 *Gazette*, 15 and 22 January 1825.

121 F. Place, *Observations on Mr Huskisson's Speech* . . . (23 April 1825).

122 Place Papers, Vol. x, Add. MSS 27,798, ff. 31–2.

123 See below, pp. 350–2.

124 Place Papers, Vol. xv, Add. MSS 27,803, Part I, ff. 271 and 279; *Gazette*, 16 April 1825. For an earlier trades' committee formed in Stockport, with Thomas Worsley as president, see *Gazette*, 5 February and 12 March; *Stockport Advertiser*, 25 February and 4 March 1825.

125 Place Papers, Vol. xv, Add. MSS 27,803, Part I, ff. 231, 267, 276, 279, and 286. The spinners' brief also included the factory bill (see below, p. 350). None of these delegates was in fact called before the Select Committee, but they joined with the metropolitan and other provincial delegates in assisting Place to prepare information for Hume to use during the investigations. *Ibid.*, f. 275.

126 *Ibid.*, f. 283.

127 *Ibid.*, f. 297, and Vol. xiv, Add. MSS 27,802, f. 66.

128 Parl. Papers, 1825, Vol. iv, pp. 160–3. It was at this time that the Manchester spinners surprisingly agreed that their petition against reimposition of the Combination Laws should not be presented, lest it should militate against the passing of Hobhouse's factory bill. See above, p. 33, and below, p. 352.

129 *Gazette*, 2 July 1825.

130 Editor of the *Gazette*, which was reporting the workmen's campaign at length. Doherty later paid a warm tribute to Prentice's services: *Voice*, 18 June 1831.

131 Place Papers, Vol. xv, Add. MSS 27,803, Part II, ff, 298–9.

132 *Gazette*, 9, 16 and 30 July 1825. For Doherty's reactions, see below, p. 40.

133 *Herald*, 6 April 1834.

134 G. D. H. Cole, *A Short History of the British Working-Class Movement* (1948), p. 71. See also G. D. H. Cole and R. Postgate, *The Common People, 1746–1946* (1968), p. 237: 'Doherty had already made in 1826 an attempt to create an all inclusive Union of trades'.

135 C. C. F. Greville, *Memoirs* (1888), quoted by Morris, *op. cit.*, p. 19.

136 Place Papers, Vol. xii, Add. MSS 27,800, f. 235. Longson feared that 'this foolish measure' might lead to reimposition of the Combination Laws.

137 Place Papers, Vol. xv, Add. MSS 27,803, Part I, f. 279.

138 *Gazette*, 11 June 1825.

139 Place Papers, Vol. xv, Add. MSS 27,803, ff. 396–419.

140 *Ibid.*, Part II, ff. 314–6, 321.

141 *Ibid.*, f. 298.

142 *Stockport Advertiser*, 19 August and 14 October 1825.

143 Place Papers, Vol. xv, Add. MSS 27,803, Part II, f. 493.

144 *Gazette*, 24 September and 1 October; *Mercury*, 4 October; *Trades' Newspaper*, 30 October 1825.

145 *Stockport Advertiser*, 30 December 1825.

146 *Gazette*, 23 February 1828.

147 See below, p. 417–8.

148 *Trades' Newspaper*, 29 January; *Mercury*, 31 January; *Gazette*, 28 January 1826.

149 *Trades' Newspaper*, 1, 8 *et seq.*, January 1826.

150 *Mercury*, 7 and 21 March, 21 and 25 April 1826.

151 *Chronicle*, 29 April and 6 May 1826.

152 *Gazette*, 6 May 1826; Place Collection, Vol. 16, Part I, f. 129; H.O. 44/16.

153 *Chronicle*, 26 August 1826.

154 H.O. 40/20; *Morning Herald*, 10 June 1826. Bradbury had previously been very vocal in the agitation against the Combination Laws and in other spinners' movements.

155 H.O. 44/16 and 40/20.

156 See below, pp. 417–8.

157 See below, pp. 350–2. Doherty was also active in radical politics and in agitation on the Irish question: see below, Ch. xi. For Lee, see n. 73.

158 *Chronicle*, 15 and 22 April; *Gazette*, 10 and 17 June, and 16 September 1826.

159 *Mercury,* 14 March; Gazette, 22 April; *Trades' Newspaper,* 24 September, 8 and 15 October; *Bolton Chronicle,* 30 September; *Gazette* and *Chronicle,* 18 November 1826; Place Collection, Vol. 16, Part I, f. 241; H.O. 40/21 and 22.
160 *Mercury,* 30 January and 16 May; *Chronicle,* 2 June 1827.
161 H.O. 40/22 and 23.
162 *Trades' Newspaper,* 1 and 8 April 1827.
163 *Gazette,* 1 September 1827.

# Secretary of the Manchester  **III**
## cotton spinners, 1828–9

The Manchester cotton spinners' union at the beginning of 1828 had a history of almost continuous trade-union activity since the late eighteenth century. It has been shown that the usual textbook reference to them as 'Doherty's cotton spinners' overlooks the important contribution of several lesser-known figures in the union. In fact, Doherty was not elected to the secretaryship of the union until 1828, and the event caused a serious internal rift within the organisation, which lasted for almost the whole year.

Differences among the Manchester spinners have previously been noticed, in the aftermath of the 1818 strike, over aid to the Glasgow spinners in 1824–5, and in regard to Hobhouse's factory bill and the campaign against reimposition of the Combination Laws. Their leaders' attitude towards violence and destruction of machinery in 1826 also seems to have been unpopular in some quarters. In February 1827 Doherty admitted that he had incurred 'the distrust of my fellow-workmen and acquaintances, by exerting myself to prevent disturbances', though he would 'never . . . shrink from coming forward to express the strong indignation I feel at the unmanly conduct of the oppressors of the industrious poor'.[1] It was for an entirely opposite reason, however, that his critics objected to his becoming secretary of the Manchester spinners' union.

Doherty's censors were the members of the Imperial Lodge of the union, which comprised the 146 spinners working in the Old and New Mills of George Murray. They alleged that he had first obtained work in Manchester by presenting a forged character reference and that he had been so ungrateful for the support he received while in gaol from 1819 to 1821 that he had even tried to sue them for non-payment of dismissal benefit;[2] but his chief disqualification was his 'violent and unruly conduct' at the general turn-out, in contrast to 'the steady, manly and persevering manners of the Manchester spinners'.[3] On 26 February 1828, while the election to the secretaryship was pending, Doherty wrote an open letter to his accusers daring them to prove any of the charges which they had 'many a time and oft' made against him in the past, at a general meeting specially convened (which he preferred), or at a private meeting with him, or by the decision of impartial judges. 'I am not only willing, but anxious to have a full and fair investigation of my whole conduct, as connected with this society. I will do more; I will submit to the closest examination of my entire conduct, private as well as public, during my whole life. I will refer you to every place in which I have worked, since I was able to work, and to every family with whom I have lived, since I first left my parental roof.' But they would not be reconciled: the publicity of the dispute, and Doherty's successful candidature for the post, induced the dissidents to break away and form a separate Imperial Union.[4]

Doherty explicitly denied the charges against him as to his conduct towards his fellow-workmen at Murray's, and while he was sincerely grateful for the financial assistance he had received in Lancaster Castle, he asked why—if his behaviour in the strike had been so despicable—had they thus assisted in relieving him. Moreover, he had not in fact been convicted of violence during the strike, but of doing that which was now perfectly legal, i.e. peaceful picketing.[5] Already, however, Doherty's interests were considered to be too wide for the benefit of the union—the Imperials called him a 'plotting, mischievous fellow' who meddled with 'state affairs, town's affairs, trade affairs, and church affairs'—but in reply Doherty referred to 'What I have done and suffered for the body (you among the rest)' as evidence of his sincerity.[6]

The secession from the union was thus mainly the result of personal dislike of Doherty, but there is evidence that this aversion was based on more than just a fear that he would lead the union into too aggressive policies. This is found in some remarks by Gustave d'Eichtal, a French traveller who investigated the conditions of the English working population in 1828, concerning his conversation with William Smith, proprietor of the *Bolton Chronicle*: 'There are few Irish in Bolton in comparison with the rest of Lancashire, because they used to be too badly treated there. The main reason for this was their Roman Catholicism. These prejudices are less strong today, but when ordinary English working folk speak among themselves about an Irishman, it is still usually with expressions of strong distaste. When Dorthé [*sic*] was appointed Secretary of the Manchester Spinners' Committee it caused a great scandal.'[7] It is clear that this prejudice also existed in Manchester, for the Imperial Unionists constantly referred to 'O'Daugherty' in their addresses against him, and their repugnance is illustrated by their assertion that his conduct 'outstepped the bounds of moderation and decency'.[8] The force of this argument is increased by the fact that in most factories the immigrant Irish supplied the lower grades of labour, and there were thousands of Irish weavers; but they were rarely employed in the most highly-paid processes, like spinning. According to one contemporary source, there were less than a hundred Irish spinners in the whole of Lancashire in the early 1830s.[9]

Prejudice or not, the Manchester spinners were now in a hazardous situation. Throughout the 1820s the master spinners had been increasing the number of spindles on the hand mules, and the spinners' wages rose with the consequent improvement in productivity. But Doherty was aware that, as at Bolton in 1823 and Hyde in 1825, the Manchester employers were now anxious to reduce piece-rates again, and this was not the time for division. 'The times portend evil! Danger seems to impend over us,' he wrote in August in an address 'To the members of the Imperial Union,'

> and who amongst us can prophecy [*sic*] when it may burst on our devoted heads? or who can stem the torrent of its fury? Reduction after reduction has already been proposed to some of our body, with unexampled and unprecedented rapidity! If this baleful practice were to extend itself amongst the more respectable masters; if a reduction were to become general, that mind must be hardened indeed, with more than philosophical indifference,

that could survey the consequence with any other feelings than those of horror and dismay . . . should circumstances force a general turn-out upon us, what assurance have we that we should come out of the contest triumphant? It is true we have some money to assist us, but it would not amount to more than about 30s a man. And if that were gone, where should we turn for more? . . . But . . . if we should be defeated, if we should be broken up, and our confidence destroyed, what should be our condition!! . . . I protest my heart sickens with merely glancing at the scenes and sufferings which would inevitably follow! I turn with horror from the description! The recollection of the past rushes upon my memory, with all the force and terrors of reality! Our own intestine divisions cannot avert these calamities, but may hasten their approach.[10]

In this letter, Doherty asserted that he would resign, despite the resulting distress for himself and his family, but his resignation would only increase their divisions. Finally in November he took a remarkable and unprecedented step. He began a small eight-page publication, called *The Conciliator or Cotton Spinners' Weekly Journal*, which, as the title suggests, was intended to settle the 'unhappy differences' in their union, which had existed for nine months. The statements of both sides were to be included in the paper, but Doherty hoped that personal rancour would cease. Nevertheless, he did accuse his assailants of 'a malignity of disposition, and a deadliness of purpose', and criticised their anonymous accusations of him.[11]

Doherty himself was aware of the novelty of his policy. In the first number he stated that, 'although it may be a new feature in the history of the working-classes, in the adjustment of their disputes, to appeal to reason, *through the medium of the press*, yet if that powerful, and as to its effects on the public mind, stupendous engine, be of any utility in improving the condition of society, it cannot be injurious to us, but on the contrary, may ultimately produce much good'. Doherty's letters, which are quoted above, were copied into the journal, which in fact forms the only record of the schism, since none of the original letters, or the addresses of the Imperials, are extant. Within one month, Doherty was able to announce that 'the disputes which gave rise to the *Conciliator*, are likely to be brought to an amicable termination'.[12] This was in fact effected, the Imperial Lodge resumed its payments to the union, and £2 3s 3d was expended in the new year on a 'Reconciliation Dinner' in celebration.[13] Nevertheless, Doherty decided to continue the paper and turn it to 'more useful subjects'. From the fifth number it appears that he hoped to develop it rather along the lines of his later *Poor Man's Advocate*: it contained an exposure of oppression by an individual master which had caused a strike, a long report of one of the first cases brought by the 'Society for the Enforcement of the Factory Act' which had been formed by Doherty and the Manchester spinners' union in November, and miscellaneous information of an entertaining and educative nature.[14] But a considerable loss had already been sustained on the first three numbers, for which there seems to have been no charge, and although a price of 2d was then fixed, the fifth edition appears to have been the last, despite a promise of more information the following week.

Immediately on reuniting the union, Doherty led the Manchester spinners on a series of 'rolling' strikes to bring masters who were underpaying up to what the union considered the average town rate and to forestall the reductions he had feared. But the *Manchester Guardian* claimed that the rate of 2½d per lb. of No. 40's which the striking spinners demanded from Messrs Williams & Co. at the beginning of December was a 25 per cent advance on the average piece rate paid previously, which had varied between 1⅞d and 2⅛d per lb. of No. 40's.[15] Nevertheless, the spinners turned out the following week from Messrs Peter Ewart & Co. and from the Salford mills of Messrs Darbishire & Co. and Messrs Jenkinson and Bow, after similar demands had been rejected.[16] Reports that the operatives were intending to secure a general increase of wages, despite the trade depression, induced them to hold a general meeting at the 'Prince's Tavern' on 18 December. As a result, a resolution was advertised in several of the Manchester papers, signed by David McWilliams, Chairman, and John Doherty, Secretary, on behalf of the Society of Friendly Associated Cotton Spinners of Manchester, that there was no desire to seek advanced prices from the best and most respectable masters, of whom a list of thirteen was given. The following week McWilliams and Doherty had to admit that this resolution was hastily drawn up, and to insert another advertisement with the names of five more firms from whom increases would not be required.[17] Moreover, at the end of December, the spinners turned out from the factory of Messrs Thomas Ogden & Co., one of the firms from whom it was claimed no advance would be demanded.

The series of strikes led to considerable litigation. One of Darbishire's men was ordered to find bail to keep the peace on 10 December for being among a party who had surrounded the mill each night and annoyed those still at work. On 15 December six of Ewart & Co's spinners were ordered to return to work because they had left without giving the necessary fortnight's notice, but James Foster, the stipendiary magistrate decided that the rule whereby no two men could hand in their notice in any one week, by which the firm hoped to make a general strike of their hands impossible, did not apply in this case, although it was permissible in principle. Doherty, perhaps recollecting his own suffering at the hands of this firm, bitterly attacked such oppressive regulations in the *Conciliator*: Peter Ewart, junr., 'a youth, scarcely out of leading strings', had devised rules to keep his workmen in his service an almost unlimited time, and then came into Court, 'with the most unblushing impudence', to demand that the magistrate 'send back to his service, the wretched men whom he had duped, cajoled, and terrified into a compliance with his illegal contract'.[18] The following week, a case of assault on William Gibson, whom Messrs Ewart had hired after the spinners had turned out, was dismissed, when Gibson withdrew his identification of the offender—after being 'tampered with' by the spinners' committee, according to the local papers, although Gibson denied that any person from the Grand Lodge had seen him.[19]

On 24 December eleven of the striking spinners of Messrs Jenkinson & Bow were sentenced to three months' hard labour for leaving their work without the regular fortnight's notice; the men stated that they had quitted their employment on the orders of the club. However, a letter signed 'O' in the *Manchester Gazette* asserted that the committee had instructed the men to work out their notice, but that they had left of their own accord because their employers had themselves frequently discharged workers without notice.[20] Over the next weeks the firm's premises were continually picketed and on 15 January six men were taken into custody by the police at the request of Bow. None of them were strikers from the mill and there was no evidence of intimidation towards those at work; consequently all the men were discharged at the New Bailey the same morning, after promising, unwillingly, not to continue their proceedings. Doherty was in court and tried to open negotiations with Bow regarding possible commutation of the sentences of the men previously convicted, but 'Mr Bow declined to have anything whatever to say to Mr Doherty'.[21]

It was clear from these proceedings that a new spirit was abroad among the Manchester spinners, and this was not at all welcome to the authorities. Lt. Col. Shaw wrote from Manchester to Major-General Bouverie, military commander of the north, that the Spinners' Association, which had existed some years, had recently become very active. The committee, as part of a plan to raise wages generally, had directed that individual masters should be solicited for a 20–25 per cent wage increase, and that their factories should be picketed if the demand was refused. The funds of the association were understood to amount to £1,700, and large sums could be raised weekly. 'The leading person in the Association is a man named James [*sic*] Doherty. This association of the Workpeople has caused the masters to form themselves into an Association.' On 26 December Foster informed Peel of the progress of the strikes—two mills had granted an increase rather than face a turn-out—and wrote of his fears of the strike and picketing system extending generally, as the masters were not averse to shutting their mills in the present state of trade. As every striking spinner made six or seven other workers unemployed, Foster feared that a general discharge would endanger the public peace. In reply, Peel observed that it was essential that either the military or civil authorities should take effective measures to enforce the law against the parties so proceeding, to check them 'at the commencement of their career'.[22]

The Society of Friendly Associated Cotton Spinners of Manchester at this time encompassed ninety-one firms (including three at Bollington) and a total of 106 mills. The union's *Returns* for 17 January 1829, record that the total number of paying members that week was 1,705, as well as an unspecified number 'on pay', who were involved in the current series of strikes. By April the total number of spinners in the Club was 2,379, including 980 fine, 967 coarse, and 436 spinners 'on pay'.[23] The union had therefore nearly established a closed shop at this time; for instance, of seventy spinners employed at Murray's New Mill in January, sixty-one were members of the Club. Contributions were high: of these sixty-one spinners, for the week ending 17 January, five had subscribed 2s 7d, thirty-three 1s 7d, nineteen 1s 4d, three 1s 1d, and one 10d for three days. The total union receipts for that week were £123 4s 6½d, making an average of almost 1s 6d for the 1,705 payers. For collecting the subscriptions, the union was divided into seventeen lodges, according to numbers in, and locality of, the different factories: Fancy, Mountpleasant, Beehive, Comet, Industry, Reasoning, Caledonian, Benevolent, Temple, Philanthropic, Concord, Albion, Impartial, Integrity, Pilot, Imperial and Cheshire.

The largest item of expenditure in the January *Return* was £112 2s 4d paid to the men on strike. From the detailed list of payments, it is clear that strike allowance could vary, but the *Manchester Gazette* reported on 27 December

C

that the 'club allowance to the turn-outs' was 8s per week, and had just been increased to 8s 6d. Friendly society benefits continued (e.g., 'To funeral of Evan Evan's wife, 17 shop—£5'), and other expenses included the sending of delegates to Bollington and Stockport, and the entertaining of two men from Ashton, as well as the secretary's salary. However, expenditure that week was greatly swelled by a gift of £100 to the striking Stockport spinners. Because of this, the total expenditure was £238 8s 11d, and the balance in hand was reduced from £1,136 8s 1d to £1,021 9s 2½d; but in a normal week the receipts would virtually have covered the expenses, even though at least five mills and nearly three hundred spinners were on strike, so it is clear that the union was not as yet overstretched.

The government of the society was in the hands of a Grand Lodge of 16-18 members, representing the different Lodges and meeting once a week to discuss business. Each member received 6s 8d for attending each meeting, which was often paid in liquor when they met at a public house. In addition, special committee meetings could be called in emergencies, regular meetings of each separate Lodge were held to collect subscriptions and ensure the rank and file were kept informed of their proceedings, and general meetings of the whole body were assembled to discuss important policy decisions. John Doherty was the only permanent officer of the union and his salary as secretary was £1 13s per week, out of which he had to pay his subscription of 1s 4d.[24] On his election to the office, about March 1828, he ceased to be employed as a working spinner, for in August he told the members of the Imperial Union that he would resign from his post if it would end their divisions, 'even though I would have been reduced to the necessity of gathering cinders in the streets'.[25] Immediately, Doherty brought a more assertive tone into the spinners' union. His first task was to reverse the secession of the members of the Imperial Union, but at the same time he was hard at work organising the foundation of a Society for enforcing the Factory Act, which was established in November 1828, as virtually another arm of the spinners' union.[26] And to improve the organisation of the union, he instituted in August 1828 the first of the weekly *Returns of the Friendly Associated Cotton Spinners*, a weekly broadsheet, which was folded into quarters and thus conveyed eight small pages of intelligence to the members of the union. The weekly accounts of receipts and disbursements, mill by mill, were first set out, followed by a series of announcements, disclosing the dates of Lodge meetings, conveying information of the subscriptions to and proceedings of the society for protecting children employed in cotton factories, and publicising (or threatening to expose) the names of those members who had fallen into arrears in their payments, to 'encourage' a return to duty. Only a handful of these publications are extant—those that were sent to the Home Office by local magistrates. The last of these was dated 10 December 1830, by which time Peter Maddocks had replaced Doherty as secretary, but there is no evidence how long after this they continued to be published.[27]

The impressive organisation of the operatives' union was viewed with alarm by the master spinners. In December 1828 the latter were reported as having formed their own Association and held several interviews with local magistrates on the subject of the persistent parades near those mills on strike, which resulted in Foster's letter to the Home Secretary on the 26th[28]. On 5 January the Manchester master spinners met and passed a series of resolutions, that the prices paid in Manchester were already higher than in the surrounding towns, that the present strikes had been instigated by the spinners' union club, and that gross acts of intimidation were used against those willing to work. In retaliation, the masters appointed a committee to investigate strikes, to decide whether individual masters should be supported by the society, and a subscription was initiated to support those masters and pay the expenses of prosecutions.[29] More than fifty of the principal master spinners of the town and neighbourhood were soon reported as having joined the Masters' Association, although it should be stressed that their combined opinions had previously been expressed through the Chamber of Commerce and Mr George Evans Aubrey was the secretary of both organisations. On 21 January the Masters' Association met again and agreed that at the end of that week they would give their spinners notice to reduce their wages by 5 per cent (or about the amount of their union subscription) every succeeding fortnight until the workpeople of Messrs Williams & Messrs Jenkinson and Bow returned to their employment.[30]

These proceedings of the masters were clearly calculated to break the authority of the spinners' union, which held several meetings to discuss the subject. It was eventually decided that this was not tactically the best time for resistance in Manchester and the strikers were ordered to return to work, Doherty later claiming that £2 was awarded to each man for the sacrifice and inconvenience caused.[31] This decision appears to have been dictated mainly by the development of a critical situation in Stockport, which threatened to have serious repercussions in Manchester.

In December 1828, all the Stockport master spinners and manufacturers gave notice of a 10 per cent wage reduction to their spinners, dressers and power-loom weavers, claiming that it was made necessary by lower wages in neighbouring towns and by the depression in trade. This reduction was opposed by all the workmen, who turned out from each factory as the notice expired: by the end of the first week in January, fifteen establishments, employing 8,000 workers, were idle and two weeks later twice the number of factories were closed and over 10,000 unemployed.[32] Both sides immediately recognised that the dispute had more than local significance and that piece-rates throughout the region would depend upon the outcome.[33] Messrs Sharp, Roberts & Co., of Manchester, sent a circular to all the Stockport master spinners, informing them that they had now perfected the self-acting mule, the advantage of which included the entire saving of the operative spinners' wages. And the authorities prepared for trouble by sending 500 soldiers of the 76th Regiment to Stockport.[34] On the men's side, immediate measures were taken to organise financial support.

On 17 January the Stockport Associated Cotton Spinners received a deputation from the Manchester Spinners' Union, including Thomas Foster, John Lawton and Jonathan Hodgins, who presented them with £100 and emphasised their joint interest in resisting wages reductions; Stockport prices, it was argued, should not be reduced but brought up to the Manchester level. The strikers were urged to act peaceably and the threat of the self-actor was scoffed at.[35] On 27 January, however, when another Manchester spinners' deputation visited Stockport, this time including Doherty, his address showed a markedly more hostile tone. He urged the workers 'to resist, to the utmost, and not submit to be trodden upon by the tyrannical cotton lords, and brought down to the starvation point'. Since poor relief would be withheld from those who refused to work, they must send emissaries everywhere to appeal for funds. The Manchester Spinners' Union had determined to support them to the amount of £60 per week, for they were sure that the reduction, if effected, could only benefit foreigners and ruin this country. 'Labour must give value to everything, and they who would reduce the price of labour, were enemies to the country.' The other Manchester delegate spoke of the necessity of orderly conduct to achieve success and a resolution was passed in such terms, but Doherty, while advising them to behave with 'proper decorum' towards their masters, told them that the masters were only their 'superiors' in a monetary sense.[36]

Doherty's language did not match, however, the continuous stream of smears and vitriolic criticism against the strikers and their supporters in the ultra-Tory *Stockport Advertiser*. Wages being adequate, it was alleged, the strike could only be explained by the influence of evil and designing delegates, committees and unions over an otherwise contented body of workpeople. Outside interference by such as Doherty was particularly resented, and a correspondent was incensed by Doherty's allusions to Cobbett's writings in his Stockport speech, which was regarded as a 'taunt upon the authorities of the country by this impudent and conceited ape'. An editorial in the same paper also spoke contemptuously of Doherty—'we dare say the man's name is Dogherty, one letter probably smelling too strongly of the Emerald'—and of his officiousness as secretary of both the Manchester Spinners' Union and the Society for the Protection of Children employed in Cotton Factories.

> The poor creature may consider that talking of 'suspending the *commerce and economy* of an important district' is very fine, but our sincere advice to him on the occasion is that he betake himself with all speed to his former honest calling, and endeavour to comprehend that words do not necessarily convey ideas, and that Irish blarney is not the English language. If he would usefully employ himself, let him give us a statement of the salaries, eating, drinking and travelling charges of the Chairmen, Secretaries and Committees of the Clubs; and what is the amount they extract from the poor man's hard earnings.[37]

In fact, however, the efforts of these 'agitators' and their appeals to other trades and to the public produced considerable financial support, which enabled strike allowances of up to 4s per week to be paid to the spinners and power-loom weavers, and also provision of relief to ancillary workers.[38] Consequently the strike was conducted in a generally peaceful manner, with emphasis upon respect for the law.[39] Even the *Stockport Advertiser* conceded at the end of March that, although 10,000 persons had been out for twelve weeks, 'scarcely an indication of a breach of the peace has shown itself'.[40]

Despite the spinners' orderly conduct, however, the employers at Stockport and elsewhere were convinced that the extensive support given to the strikers urgently demanded an equally extensive counter-offensive. On 17 March a numerous meeting of the Master Cotton Spinners and Manufacturers of Manchester, Hyde, Stockport and the neighbourhood was held at the 'Star Inn' Manchester, with Thomas Ashton in the chair. Resolutions were adopted that

the 'widely-extended' combination of cotton operatives threatened the interests of trade, the property of the employers, the comforts of the lower classes,
and the peace of the State, and that immediate measures were essential to
counteract it, and 'that for this purpose an Association be formed of the
Master Cotton Spinners and Power-loom Manufacturers of Manchester and
its neighbourhood, and that a Committee be appointed to carry these resolutions into immediate effect, with power to add to their number, and to appoint
sub-committees in such places as they may think proper'. The meeting also
disclaimed any intention to reduce the value of labour, stating that their
efforts would be confined 'to the suppression of combination'.[41]

Despite this final disavowal, the Manchester master fine spinners at once
resolved that there should be a 15 per cent reduction in the prices paid for the
spinning of yarn at and above No. 80's. This the Manchester operative fine
spinners refused to accept and turned out at the beginning of April.[42] (The
power-loom weavers at several Manchester factories had already been
reduced to the Hyde standard following a short strike a month earlier.[43]) In
pursuance also of the above resolutions, a subordinate association of masters
was formed at Hyde, Stalybridge and Dukinfield, with the declared aim of
forcing their operatives to renounce membership of any combination and of
stopping their aid to the Stockport strikers, by means of threatened wages
deductions. And when the hands in three Hyde factories struck in refusal to
sign the employers' document, they were defeated within a week.[44]

These events at Hyde and the fine spinners' strike in Manchester reduced
support for the Stockport strikers, who now became increasingly violent.
Reports of intimidation and attacks on 'knobsticks' became more frequent,
including several cases of vitriol-throwing. The magistrates issued a public
warning against 'tumultuous assemblies' and other public support for the
strikers, while the masters sent further memorials to Peel expressing apprehension at the widespread union organisation with its terrible secret oath and
system of intimidation.[45]

After the arrest of six of the spinners' committee in late July, however, the
strikers were virtually leaderless,[46] and on 8 August the *Manchester Guardian*
prematurely reported that they had given in, using their predicament to
lecture the Manchester spinners on the injustice of resisting reductions in
piece rates on larger and more productive mules and on the ineffectiveness of
outrages perpetrated by combinations.[47] In fact it was not until the week
ending Saturday, 26 September, that the strike finally came to an end, the
men returning to work on the terms dictated by the masters.[48]

Whilst this contest was going on, an equally obdurate struggle developed
in Manchester. The masters' extensive combination and the threat of wages
reductions throughout the region clearly indicated that a crisis was at hand,
but Doherty—apparently far from certain the men could succeed in a head-on
conflict—made a valiant attempt to avert a calamity. On 24 February a
general meeting of the Society of Friendly Associated Cotton Spinners, held
at the 'Prince's Tavern', Princess Street, agreed to an address 'to the Master
Spinners of Manchester', which Doherty signed, as Secretary, and published
as a small hand-bill when it was refused insertion in the *Manchester and
Salford Advertiser*, although it did later appear in the *Manchester Times*. The
address fully admitted the slackness of the cotton trade and asserted that the

workmen were willing to share the misfortunes of the times. 'But this can [only] be done by reducing the time of labour by working a day or two a week less than is now done. We would submit to this. But do not, we solemnly ask you, attempt to reduce our wages. To that we will never submit unless starved into compliance.' Doherty believed that the desire to reduce wages was based on a false notion that 'we must sell cheap, or be supplanted by foreigners'. In fact, making exports cheaper by reducing wages only meant selling English skill and industry to foreigners at lower prices, while the amount of money circulating in the home market was proportionately reduced, but the same amount still had to be paid in taxes and for bread, because of the 'monstrous corn law'. Such a policy would destroy the workers' independence, create pauperism and lead ultimately to crime, debauchery and disorder. Yet not even the manufacturers would benefit, because price reductions would always keep pace with the fall in wages. In conclusion, 'we appeal to you as men, as husbands, as fathers, as friends and Christians, not to disturb that friendly feeling and good understanding which has hitherto subsisted amongst us, by adopting a measure that cannot be beneficial to you, and that must be ruinous not only to us, but ultimately to the whole community'.[49]

But it was now too late to divert the employers from their chosen course. Extending their Association from Manchester to the neighbouring cotton towns, they determined to take decisive measures to destroy the influence of what they saw as a combination including all the spinning operatives employed in the industry.[50] The Manchester master fine-spinners, desiring to end the system whereby virtually every mill had its own distinct price list, accepted a new district list of prices drawn up by Henry Houldsworth, one of their number, and presented it to the men on 21 March with notice that it would come into operation in a fortnight. The proposed reduction applied mainly to finer numbers of yarn: on No. 80's it was only about 5 per cent, but thereafter it gradually increased to 25–30 per cent on No. 250's. Moreover, the list introduced as a general principle a regulation that had previously been applied at only a few individual mills: a reduction on large mules of $1\frac{1}{2}$ per cent for every twelve spindles over 300.[51]

The masters claimed that the reduction was absolutely necessary because their rates were from 15 to 40 per cent higher than those paid in the surrounding districts, because the increase in the size of mules had raised the operatives' take-home pay, and because of the slump in trade which made continued competition with the country masters impossible.[52] The men did not dispute the fact that wages in Manchester were higher, but they were aware that the Ashton master spinners had resolved to lower their prices by 25 per cent whenever any reduction was effected in Manchester, hence reduction might follow reduction in this manner until the spinners were as helpless as the hand-loom weavers. Consequently, they held a series of shop meetings culminating in a general meeting which appointed a deputation to see the masters to induce them to postpone the application of the new list for three months, while the union ascertained if it was practicable to get the masters in the country districts to raise their rates to the Manchester level. If such an advance could not be obtained, the men would submit to the March list. But the masters refused to consider such a delay.[53]

Even so, Doherty later claimed that the union leaders, including himself, were still opposed to the strike taking place at this time. They had enough funds to last four months out of work, but presumably would have preferred to have concentrated their efforts on preventing the reduction at Stockport. Since open opposition to turning-out would inevitably have caused a division among the workmen, which the masters could have exploited, the leaders attempted to show up the difficulties of resistance by asking every prospective striker to send in a written statement of the number of weeks he could do without pay, and any possessions they could sell for support. It was expected that the response would be so poor that the rank and file would realise the impracticability of effecting their object. But in the event £300 was promised and instead of determining the men not to strike it had the contrary effect, and a meeting of deputies from the various factories on 26 March resolved to resist the proposed reduction.[54] On 4 April the fine spinners, to the number of 1,100, turned out from more than twenty Manchester factories, but, because of the number of subsidiary occupations dependent on the continuation of spinning, almost 10,000 individuals were thrown out of employment thereby.[55]

Despite the leaders' apparent reluctance to commit the body to a strike, it was organised in a meticulous manner. From the beginning there was talk of establishing a soup kitchen and adopting various means to economise their reserves (of which one was the above appeal!). A large room over the workshop of a builder, in David Street, was engaged for the purpose of holding their meetings, and some time was spent in propping and securing the floor to make it capable of supporting large numbers of people, so that no repetition of the Hyde tragedy could take place. In the first of the union's weekly addresses to the public, which Doherty wrote, it was stated that, 'as the present contest bears every appearance of being of long duration', the room was also intended to be used as a school, 'where reading, writing, arithmetic, and English grammar will be taught, and where the better informed will improve themselves by assisting in improving those who are behind them in intellectual attainment'. An appeal was launched for benches and for funds towards building up a library; Doherty's interest in education was clearly behind this novel scheme.[56]

But the main concern at a series of general meetings in the first weeks of the strike was the preparation of the men's own list of prices. On this there were considerable differences of opinion, one meeting on 10 April lasting nearly five hours. It was now widely recognised that some abatement was inevitable, on account of the trade depression, the lower piece-rates in the country, and the over-supply of hands (600 spinners were reported unemployed even before the strike). But the masters' proposals were considered excessive; indeed so strong was the opposition among the rank and file that even moderate proposals were unpopular. When the *Manchester and Salford Advertiser* of 11 April reported that the spinners' meeting of the previous day had agreed to submit to a reduction of from 5 to 10 per cent, a handbill was immediately posted on the walls of the town, signed by Doherty, stating that 'such a statement is WHOLLY WITHOUT FOUNDATION, no such proposition having been put to the meeting'.[57] And when Jonathan Hodgins proposed a scale by which the men would have offered about a third of the masters' proposed reduction, he was threatened with being thrown out of the window, called a number of offensive names, and forced to withdraw from their meetings.[58]

Another source of controversy was the reduction in piece-rates according to the number of spindles per mule. As at previous disputes in Bolton, Hyde and Oldham, the workers claimed that they deserved higher wages on more productive machines, because these were heavier and required more physical effort; while if they accepted the principle of the reduction, it would encourage masters to make constant additions to the size of mules, which would lead to repeated reductions and more technological unemployment. Doherty even stated—two years later, to be sure, when the men were seeking an alliance with the small-mule masters—that when the masters' list was presented, they had entreated their employers to join with the men in an effort to bring up the prices paid on large 'wheels' (mules) to those on small; if the attempt did not succeed within six months, the men would submit to the reduction without a strike—but 'this most reasonable request was violently rejected'.[59] Presumably this was the reason why the spinners agreed that one mill should restart on Monday, 20 April, at a slight reduction for Nos. 140 to 260 on mules of 300 spindles, 'in consequence of the great advantage which those masters possess, whose mules are from 400 to 500 spindles, over those of the smaller size'.[60] When the men did produce their own equalised list towards the end of April, the local papers reported that it envisaged only a reduction of the piece-rates paid on most counts before the strike, e.g. about $\frac{1}{2}d$ per pound on 80's, and about $3d$ on 200's, without reference to any regulations concerning the size of mules. This list was sent to the masters' meeting on 24 April, but although they acknowledged its receipt, they attempted no negotiations upon it.[61] However, when the spinners produced another list on 29 May, it followed the principle of the masters' list, quoting the prices to be given from Nos. 80 to 250 on mules of from 300 to 400 spindles. This accepted a $1\frac{1}{2}$ per cent reduction for every additional twelve spindles from 300 to 420, but of only 1 per cent thereafter. The reduction the men proposed was twice as great as in their April list, but still fell far short of the employers' proposals. For example, for No. 200's on mules of 300 spindles, the old price was 5s 4d per lb., the men now proposed 4s 10d and the March list specified a price of 4s 1d.[62] On Doherty's calculation that a spinner could spin 12 lb. a week, these prices meant weekly wages of 64s, 58s and 49s respectively, before deductions for piecers' wages, etc. Again, no negotiations were reported as having taken place following the men's second compromise offer in May.

Even before the masters' peremptory refusal of the men's April list, the men were anticipating a protracted struggle. On 25 April one local newspaper reported that they had agreed to reduce the strike pay from the regulation 8s to 2s 6d per week, and that deputies had been sent out to various parts of the United Kingdom to collect subscriptions. The following week, they were reported as being active in Liverpool and other places, and ultimately in the middle of May it was stated that their visits to several of the largest towns in the country 'have met with great success, and liberal promises of support have been received from other quarters'.[63] In his notes on the 1838 Select Committee, Francis Place states that David McWilliams 'was one of a deputation to London during the strike in 1829. The deputation came to beg money and were convinced that if they could obtain some money they could defeat the masters.' It is not clear, however, if the time here referred to was in April or when Doherty himself visited London later in the strike on spinners' business.[64] Early in May, a shopkeeper friendly to the strikers' cause placarded Manchester with 'A Plan', whereby the spinners were to divide the northern counties into 1,000 districts and send a delegate to each to collect a weekly subscription of 1d from every family; but this impractical scheme does not appear to have been seriously considered until the strikers were in desperate straits in September.[65]

In January the Manchester spinners had had a fund of more than £1,000 in hand, but presumably this was considerably eroded over the following two months by their weekly contributions of £60 towards the Stockport spinners. Hence the chief support for the fine spinners was the continued contributions to the union of the coarse spinners, who were still at work and whose subscriptions were at one time as high as 2s 9d per week.[66] Despite this sacrifice, by the end of May the allowance had fallen to 2s, and at the end of the strike Doherty revealed that 'the [total] support which had been rendered by the spinners' union amounted to no more than £2 16s 6d to each man'. He repeated this calculation to the 1838 Select Committee, when he praised the orderly behaviour of the strikers despite having to support their families for twenty-six weeks on an average of 2s to 2s 0¼d per week.[67] A further complication was the demands of the other classes of workers made idle by the strike. At the beginning, the Manchester card grinders' and strippers' association requested to be included in a combined appeal for subscriptions, but, unlike at Stockport where funds were at first more plentiful, they were told that they must seek assistance 'as a separate and distinct body'. Hence, at intermittent intervals throughout the dispute, appeals for support appeared from the card grinders and strippers, who also appointed their own collectors.[68]

Those on strike were generally refused poor relief. Thus at the New Bailey on 30 April, 'a very worn looking man' applied to the magistrates for relief, having been refused by the overseer of Chorlton Row, but he was again turned down because he had an offer to go and spin for Messrs Norris & Hodgson at guaranteed wages of 25s a week.[69] In these circumstances, it was vital for the spinners to retain the support of those sections of the community, like small shopkeepers and other trades, who would normally be disposed to favour them, and the result was a continuous propaganda war from both sides throughout the strike to win the support of public opinion.

As secretary of the men's union, Doherty issued weekly addresses on the state of the strike, many of which were noticed in the newspapers and several are preserved in the Place Collection. On 6 May a handbill appeared on the walls of Manchester and neighbouring towns stating that the fine spinners had turned out against a reduction of 30 per cent, and that they were entirely dependent upon 'an enlightened and sympathetic public for such support as may eventually enable us to maintain the price of our only property our labour, at such a rate as will maintain ourselves and our families in decency, without requiring parochial aid to eke out a scanty pittance, which is already the case with many descriptions of labourers in this once free and happy country'. As an earnest of their entitlement to

c*

receive assistance, Doherty stated that 'the Spinners of Manchester have paid, during the last six years, to their Union, for the support of the various trades, to the amount of £70,000,[70] and have supported by an allowance of 2s 6d to 8s a week, about 300 men'. He added that 'two men have been appointed, with proper credentials, to solicit the support of the general public of this town and neighbourhood'.[71]

A fortnight later, on 20 May, the five members of the committee of Manchester master spinners issued a reply to this statement, signed by their secretary, G. E. Aubrey. It was pointed out that a continual decline had taken place in the prices of all articles of manufacture, yet there had been no change in the wages of the Manchester fine spinners for more than twelve years; hence their wages of 28s to 70s per week were 15 to 40 per cent higher than elsewhere. Their prosperous condition was proved by the amount of aid they claimed to have given to other trades, while the wages they would still be able to earn, clear of all deductions, at the new prices, estimated on the average quantity produced before the turn-out, were calculated as 25–30s on Nos. 80 to 160, 30–40s on Nos. 170 to 210, and 40–60s on higher numbers.[72] The men's response warned the public against putting too much trust in their employers' computations. 'There are about 2,400 spinners in Manchester and its immediate vicinity, twenty-five, or may be thirty of these could, before the reduction was proposed, have earned 60s, 250, or perhaps 300, could have earned 40s, 600 25s, and 1,500 about 16s, some being as low as 12s, and others as high as 20s; this statement is rather over than under the mark.'[73]

The weekly addresses in the Place collection, all headed by the date, the week of the strike and the words 'To the Public', reveal that Doherty was anxious to bring forward all manner of political and social issues to justify the spinners' case. In his communication of 27 June, the twelfth week of the strike, he admitted that the average wage of the four classes of spinners which he had detailed the previous week, about 22s per week, was more than that of many other workers, but that was no reason for the spinners to be reduced; and moreover the nature of their employment—the heat, the long hours, the smell and the regular dismissals at the age of forty—made even the earnings quoted by the masters not excessive. However, the principal argument was that reducing wages would not benefit the country, because the welfare of the shopkeeper, publican and every description of tradesman was dependent upon that of the labourer, and 'the landowner only keeps up his income by the operation of an infamous and monstrous Corn Law'. Instead of passing all the burden of the £60 millions of taxes per year onto the labourers, their employers should join with them in demanding from the legislature 'the repeal of those odious and oppressive laws that are destructive alike to us both—the corn laws, and such a retrenchment of public expenditure as would enable them successfully to compete with foreigners, without entailing beggary and pauperism on our native country'.[74]

In the following week Doherty returned to matters of trade, but assumed an aggressive tone rather than trying to defend the spinners from the constant newspaper attacks. On 4 July he calculated that at the abatement the masters were proposing on No. 200's, those that employed 140 spinners would gain a yearly increase of profits of almost £5,500. They wished the masters to make good profits, but not at the expense of a decent living for their workers. And on 10 July, the fourteenth week of the strike, together with quotations from McCulloch on the national benefits from high wages, he extended his calculations to show the amount of money withdrawn from circulation by reducing workmen's wages and the consequent hardships for middle-class shopkeepers and tradesmen. 'Every man therefore,' Doherty concluded, 'who values his independence, who wishes to see labour justly and adequately rewarded, and who is anxious to see crime, pauperism and poverty banished from the land, is called upon as well by interest as duty, to support us against this unnecessary and unjustifiable reduction.'[75]

The wide circulation of Doherty's statements forced the master spinners' committee to publish another 'Address to the Public' on 14 July, repeating their arguments as to the reduction in the price of cotton yarn and the lower wage-rates in other districts making the abatement necessary, but moderating the more extreme of their claims by stating that the average earnings of the majority of fine spinners before the strike were 28s to 50s per week, and after the reduction they would guarantee clear wages of 24s to 40s. The employers also tried to undermine support for the strikers by declaring that the strike had prevented the circulation of £100,000 and impoverished about 9,000 workers in dependent occupations, whilst adding that 'were it generally known that these men were refusing wages which would average above 30s per week, and that for every spinner who remains idle from eight to ten individuals are kept out of employment and deprived of means of subsistence, few persons . . . would contribute to prolong so unnecessary a state of misery'.[76] To reinforce this address, several masters reopened their mills on Monday, 20 July, and offered to pay any spinners who were willing to work the wages guaranteed in it.

The workmen's response denied that the reduction was necessary when a few masters were still able to work at the old prices; but if the masters could convince them of the necessity, they would immediately submit, and for that purpose Doherty entreated them 'to name a time and place when a deputation from each body may meet to discuss the point in dispute'.[77] When the masters ignored this offer, Doherty produced his most radical publication during the strike, dated 25 July or the sixteenth week of the turn-out. A quotation from Goldsmith at the head, contrasting 'a bold peasantry, their country's pride' with the transitory significance of 'princes and lords', set the tone. The intention of the masters' address, which had been published in forty-eight newspapers, to check financial aid to the spinners, was recognised. It also criticised the tendency, readily shown by masters and newspapers, and even by workmen, to take the lowest wages paid as the standard, rather than the highest. If the operative spinners could be de-nominated well-off because they did not have to subsist on a few pence a day like the hand-loom weavers, could they not equally be said to be poorly rewarded compared with their masters, and should they consent to be reduced to similar destitution to enable 'a handful of cotton masters . . . to . . . wallow in luxury?' Did not the labourer produce all and therefore deserve an adequate supply of food, clothing and lodgings in return?

To answer the question of just what would be fair wages for a 12-hour day, Doherty drew up a table of the quantities of the necessaries of life, which every labourer should possess, and their value at current prices. Significantly he called it 'a calculation from *experience* . . . of the Weekly Expenditure of a Husband, Wife and Four Children, at the Present Prices of the Various Articles Consumed'. Twenty-two items were included, ranging from a catalogue of various foods and clothing to rent, rates and coal, together with incidentals such as medicine, school and books for three children, and an allowance for old age and sickness. The total weekly bill was estimated at £2 7s 6¼d, or nearly £111 a year. Doherty was aware that some people might ridicule the folly of supposing that workmen, 'mere *labourers*', should ever expect to receive 'such *enormous* sums'. But were they *exorbitant* for a man and his family after toiling twelve hours a day for six days a week, when a bishop received £384 per week, or £20,000 a year, 'for reading, or it may be writing, an hour's discourse once a week'?

Finally, in view of the extreme distress of the strikers and the masters' determination to reopen the mills, Doherty counselled the workmen not to be provoked into a breach of the peace, but to continue the orderly behaviour which had so far characterised the dispute. 'If, unfortunately, any disturbance should ensue, in which you may be concerned, you only will be the sufferers. Submit cheerfully, as we know you will, to the laws of the country. Obey the authorities of the town, who feel for and pity your sufferings. Shun, we beseech you, as your deadliest foe, all appearance of tumult.'[78]

The last address preserved in the Place Collection is dated 1 August, the seventeenth week of the strike. Doherty reverted to the minutiae of the strike, criticising the masters' refusal to negotiate with the workmen on the basis of the latter's May list. He declared that the masters' assertion that the 15 to 40 per cent lower rates paid in the country areas made the Manchester reduction essential, was not only exaggerated but hypocritical, considering that the masters' own list gave an employer with wheels of 468 spindles a 21 per cent advantage over another with mules of 300 spindles. A concluding paragraph in this address gives an insight into the reason for Doherty's later efforts to institutionalise the traditional aid given by different trade clubs to each other during strikes. He gave the spinners' heartfelt thanks to the Manchester dressers and dyers' society for their 'generous, liberal and undeviating support' throughout the strike. This Doherty contrasted with one or two other trades, who had waited 'to calculate the amount in £ *s* and *d*, of immediate gain or loss to themselves which their support to us might occasion them', and 'to ransack the records of half a Century, to ascertain whether every penny which our predecessors might have received or given, exactly balanced'. If every body of workmen followed the example of the dressers and dyers, not only would the spinners be well supported, but there would be some grounds for hope that the condition of thousands of honest but impoverished workmen could be improved.[79]

In addition to these weekly addresses, Doherty was also busy with a plethora of other correspondence in the spinners' cause. After the masters had presented their new list, he wrote on 28 March to Francis Place, with whom he had made contact during the agitation against the re-enactment of the Combination Laws. He informed Place that the masters' proceedings were likely to lead to an extensive and protracted strike, and opined that the resolution of the Hyde masters to abate their hands fortnightly until they ceased to contribute towards the Stockport strikers showed 'of what materials these men were made'. But Doherty also expressed another fear of the employers' machinations.

> The masters have formed amongst them a most extensive combination, and from their proceedings and movements, as well as their declarations, we are led to believe that they are applying, or are about to apply to Parliament for the renewal of the Combination Laws. In such an application I am persuaded that they cannot succeed. Yet it behoves us not to be idle if such be their hopes or intentions. You could easily inform us whether anything has been in motion amongst the members, relative to that subject. Perhaps you would be kind enough to drop me a letter on the subject, if you should find that they have been at work for the purpose already stated. We are anxious to know their movements as speedily as possible.[80]

In his reply of 27 April Place stated that he knew of no application being made by the masters for re-enactment of the Combination Laws and he did not believe that such a request would be attended to.[81] But he then proceeded to deliver a lecture to Doherty on his erroneous notions of the economic organisation of society. 'It is to be expected that people so distressed or so generally ill-used, should impute all the evils they endure to their employers, and should speak of them generally as cold blooded tyrants towards those who are dependent on them. True enough and lamentable enough it is, that generally speaking they are regardless of the very miserable condition of their workpeople; but this is the inevitable consequence of their situation.' Because the only motive for embarking on trade or manufacture is the love of gain, 'a really humane man will not be a practical cotton manufacturer . . . the scenes of wretchedness which . . . he would be compelled to witness . . . the images those would raise in his imagination, would be continually present, and make him unhappy'. Hence much of the spinners' printed address to their employers on 24 February, which entreated them to reduce hours rather than wages as the latter would lead to suffering and harm the long-term interests of trade, 'is worse than useless, inasmuch as it is an appeal to the humanity of the masters, against their interest. . . . Depend upon it the working people never will, or they never have, obtained anything by such appeals. The struggle is a struggle of strength, and "the weakest must go to the wall". Whatever the people gain, or even retain, is gained or retained, and must always be gained or retained by power.' Place concluded with a long explanation of the principle governing the rate of wages, sending Doherty a pamphlet by McCulloch on the subject, and affirmed that the notorious over-supply of hands in the cotton trade was the only reason for the reduction, and therefore the only remedy was not appeal to the government or clamour about the 'Grinding System' but to reduce the number of hands.[82]

Undeterred by this advice that the strike was a hopeless proposition from the start, Doherty engaged in a lengthy disputation during the turn-out with two individual employers in the correspondence columns of the local press. Towards the end of April several manufacturers, including Thomas Harbottle of Pollard Street, succeeded in reducing the wages of their hand-loom shirting weavers by 3d per piece after a short strike. Thereupon, Messrs J. & T. Parker gave notice to their shirting weavers of a similar reduction. When the

workmen turned out, the serious rioting then occurring at Rochdale, Macclesfield and elsewhere spread to Manchester and many power-looms were
destroyed and shops looted during the first week of May.[83] On 8 May Thomas
Harbottle wrote to the Manchester papers, denying reports which were
circulating that his initial reduction had caused the present disturbances, and
adding a rider on his prices for spinning, which, over a six-week period, had
averaged over £3 per week gross, and £2 after payments to piecers.[84]

The following week Doherty replied that Harbottle had not stated the
particular six-week period he had chosen, but his spinners' wages for the
*last* six weeks had averaged 50s 1d, from which each spinner must pay out
3d for tea, 3d to 1s for their sick, and 2s for gas in winter, as well as the
piecers' wages. Doherty admitted that summer wages of about 29s were as
high as any other coarse spinner in the town paid, considering the size and
quality of Harbottle's machinery, but what was the relevance of quoting the
earnings of a contented body of workmen, when it was notorious that it was
the hand-loom weavers who had been reduced by one-eighth and had participated in the attacks on the factories? 'It could avail nothing to Mr
Harbottle's ostensible object, to publish the earnings of those who have
never yet taken, *and I trust never will take*, any share in such lawless and
reprehensible proceedings as have lately disgraced the town.'[85]

Harbottle would not have thought it necessary 'to reply to any statement
from such a quarter', had not Doherty's letter contained figures which were
'palpably incorrect'. Therefore on 23 May he affirmed that interruptions had
taken place in the working of his establishment during the previous six
weeks, but the spinners who had worked full time during six succeeding
weeks had earned 63s 9½d even on the coarsest numbers, while the average
weekly earnings of all his spinners in the same period was 54s 6½d. He alleged
that Doherty feared the effects of publicising the huge earnings of the
spinners in comparison with the weavers, and that it was only the 'interference of the club' that prevented the fine spinners from returning to work.
Finally he ridiculed Doherty's claim that the spinners had always acted
peaceably, 'when it is too notorious that the barbarous and inhuman conduct
of the spinners has more frequently disturbed the peace of, and disgraced
the town, than any other class of operatives'.[86]

Doherty's short rejoinder on 30 May ended the controversy. While noticing
that his adversary had avoided replying to the statement of the workmen's
wages in the last six weeks, Doherty charged that, during the period Harbottle had chosen, the hands had been kept at the mill till nine or ten
o'clock at night, and had been paying 25s to 30s a week for piecers. Of any
violent proceedings by the spinners, Doherty repeated that he knew nothing;
and in answer to the contemptuous reference to himself, Doherty declared
that Harbottle 'should remember that it is not me alone, that is concerned in
this affair, but from two to three thousand men, who collectively, at least,
should be as much entitled to consideration as Mr Harbottle'.[87]

The other employer with whom Doherty publicly debated was David Holt,
who was generally considered as being especially sympathetic towards the
welfare of his workmen. Even before the strike had begun, Holt had written
to the *Manchester Gazette* that the masters' reduction was reasonable because
of the lower prices paid by home competitors. But since he considered that

employers were the natural guardians of their employees and had a duty to pay sufficient wages to give their workmen a comfortable subsistence with moderate exertion, he suggested that legislation should be enacted to invest the power of fixing and enforcing a minimum rate of wages for each trade in a committee or board of humane and liberal manufacturers engaged in the particular trade concerned.[88] At the end of May, Holt composed a further letter, repeating his arguments concerning the necessity of the Manchester masters' reduction and castigating the 'thoughtless, as well as unreasonable' conduct of the men in opposing it. If the workmen accepted the masters' offer, they would thus secure protection and defence against the continual deterioration in their wages caused by the proceedings of a few unprincipled country employers.[89]

Doherty's riposte comprised a more general defence of the operatives' position than his replies to Harbottle's specific accusations. Doherty commented that, as a master spinner, Holt was *'deeply interested'* in the success of the employers' project of abating wages, and this should be remembered when calculating the impartiality of his condemnation of the resistance of the workmen to a reduction of about one-quarter in the value of their property. As in his addresses, Doherty admitted that country prices were lower, but that the extent of the difference had been exaggerated was proved by the fact of two masters having profitably reopened their mills at the old prices. Moreover, if the reductions by the country manufacturers were denominated 'unprincipled', how could the attempt to copy it in Manchester be vindicated? It was not true that the journeymen spinners had been offered the choice of either bringing up the country rates or submitting to the reduction. Such an offer would have been gladly accepted, and even now the men would be willing to co-operate with their employers over a period of three months, at the end of which either the district rates would be raised or the Manchester prices diminished. In conclusion, Doherty ridiculed Holt's advice that the strikers should accede to the March list and then rely on the protection of their employers.[90]

On the same day as this epistle was published, another letter from David Holt appeared in the *Manchester Guardian*. He repeated that the employers were 'the best guardians of their servants' interests', and reminded the operatives that because of the increased productivity of mules, the reduced prices would give them net earnings 'equal to what they were when many of the articles in common use were 20, 30 and even 50 per cent higher than they now are'. Since the strike could only harm the workmen themselves and their dependants, its continuation could only be explained by 'the dictum of a few men amongst you', who sought only 'to perpetuate that feeling of hostility which can never lead to amicable adjustment of their differences but must, if persisted in, bring about that depression in their circumstances, which it is their professed object to avoid'.[91]

Doherty was naturally concerned to rebut the inference that he and a minority of militants were leading an otherwise contented majority into resistance against their wishes and interests. Untypically he chose a local tory newspaper, *Wheeler's Manchester Chronicle*, as the vehicle for his reply. Doherty insisted that the operatives' strike was by no means the result of undue influence by the union leaders, but had resulted solely from the masters' new list of prices. Similarly the thousands of dependent workers who were unemployed and in distress because of the turn-out should be on the conscience of the master spinners, not of the strikers who were struggling to retain a decent subsistence for their families. In addition, it was not the workmen's union which was dominated by the directives of a few functionaries, but the masters' association. 'If you know anything of our proceedings you must be aware that two of those men who usually took a leading part in our affairs have been driven from our meetings on account of their exertions to prevail upon us to surrender a part of our wages, to satisfy your association.' This Doherty contrasted with the action of the masters' association in preventing the reopening of a factory by a firm which had twice made compromise arrangements with its men.[92] Finally, Doherty challenged Holt to persuade the other masters to agree to the three months' truce, if he really desired to end what he called the 'unmeaning contest'; but Holt made no further communication on the subject.[93]

Along with this almost continuous stream of propaganda, the organisation and discipline of the Manchester cotton spinners' union was reflected in their orderly conduct throughout the first twenty weeks of the strike, which was conceded even by the most hostile commentators. Despite the large number of spinners unemployed, only one was reported to be among those arrested during the disturbances in May, and a local magistrate reassured the Home Office that there was not 'at present any indication of intended violence on the part of the Spinners out of work'.[94] Nevertheless, the mutual antagonism of capital and labour in the cotton industry was demonstrated by the complete absence of face-to-face dialogue between the two sides, although the *Morning Chronicle* did refer to the frequent addresses of employers and strikers as negotiations 'at a sort of arm's length'.[95] The increasing alarm of the authorities was reflected in a letter of Major-General Bouverie to the Home Office on 19 July, which suggested a government enquiry to settle the dispute. 'The minds of the operatives are worked up to a state of fresh excitement by the weekly Tracts or Pamphlets issued by the Club, and stuck up in the streets, written by a man of the name of Doherty who is their Secretary. He is stated to be a clever man and is decidedly a very mischievous one.'[96]

As we have seen, the announcement at the end of July that the masters intended to reopen their factories at guaranteed wages of 24–40s made Doherty seriously alarmed that the orderly proceedings of the spinners might be brought to an end.[97] Not a single workman was reported as having accepted the masters' offer, while the operatives' suggestion of a negotiated settlement was ignored by their employers,[98] but from this time on the tempo of the strike was considerably raised. In an advertisement dated 6 August, seventeen Manchester fine-spinning firms stated that they would again reopen their mills on 12 August and employ competent spinners 'on the terms of the printed list issued by us in March last'. This was inserted in all the local papers of Manchester and a great number of placards were also posted in neighbouring towns.[99] For a second time the strikers demonstrated complete solidarity. Several conferences were held between individual spinners and their former employers, but no agreement was come to, and during the course of 13 and 14 August shop meetings convened to consider the masters' proposal resolved to accept no other prices than those paid before the strike. The growing bitterness of the dispute was shown by the masters' committee engaging a corps of thirty-two men at wages of one guinea a week each, sworn in before the magistrates as special constables and daily stationed in the different fine-spinning factories, for the purpose of protecting any workmen who might return to their employment. The regular police officers were also directed to patrol the factory districts of the town, and both the cavalry and infantry placed under orders to muster in a few minutes if necessary. All these precautions were taken, although it was universally acknowledged that no spinner had gone into work and the turn-outs had 'behaved throughout the week with order and propriety, and without the slightest disposition towards tumult or violence'.[100]

However, the employers kept up a constant pressure. On 20 August fourteen firms issued a further set of placards asserting that they were in need of fine spinners who would be paid guaranteed wages varying from 25s to 45s net, according to the fineness of the counts, for a working week of 69 hours. A deputation was sent to Bolton (and presumably other local cotton towns) to try and engage new hands in place of the turn-outs.[101] As soon as the placards appeared on the walls of Manchester, Doherty retaliated with an address 'to the Master Fine Mule Spinners of Manchester', which showed that his patience had now been stretched beyond its limit. He began with a broad hint that the employers' offer could not be what it seemed. 'We can scarcely believe that when you have been endeavouring for twenty weeks to reduce us 30 per cent, you will turn round all at once and advance many of us from 10–15 per cent unasked by us.' Nevertheless, if such wages were genuine, the men would unhesitatingly accept them, only making two conditions: that an average weekly sum of 35s between the two extremes advertised be guaranteed to all the spinners, and that every master who proposed the reduction should receive back all his workmen together and pay that rate. In a final paragraph, Doherty derided the recent proceedings of the masters with withering scorn:

> We are sorry that you should have incurred any unnecessary expense in these hard times. Had you been as short of money as we are of meat, you would have saved the £110 a week which you pay to your Special Constables which you have employed. Give us the odd £10 and we will protect all the mills in town. If you will pay this sum in the shape of extra poor-rates, to meet the demands of those you are bringing from the country to spin for you, you will oblige many poor honest rate-payers.

And in a derisive postcript, Doherty recommended one gentleman, who had advertised for female spinners, to seek them in 'the purlieus of St George's', an area notorious for prostitutes.[102]

Doherty's outspoken sarcasm contrasts sharply with his careful cultivation of the spinners' cause over the previous four and a half months. Yet however cynical he was of the sincerity of the masters' offer, he cannot have believed his suggestion of an average guaranteed wage for all spinners on all counts, regardless of age and skill, was a viable alternative. Although, as we have seen, allegations that the strike was only perpetuated by the influence of the spinners' committee were made as early as June by David Holt, and were repeated with particular emphasis in the *Manchester Guardian* on 8 August,[103] Doherty's ill-timed address gave the local newspapers a real opportunity at last to castigate the spinners' proceedings in general. Typical was the following editorial in *Wheeler's Manchester Chronicle*:

> If it could be supposed for an instant that an obscure individual, acting in the capacity of their secretary, could presume to take upon himself the responsibility of publishing such a letter, we should give the entire credit to one, Mr John Doherty. But whilst we admit that the vulgarity of it may be perfectly characteristic of the journeymen's secretary, the tone of insolent defiance which it breathes must surely be in accordance with the sentiments of the whole body . . . The spirit that could dictate such a letter richly merits to be repressed and punished, . . . , we are decidedly hostile to concession, in whatever instance it is attempted to be extorted by insolence and intimidation. It can only tend to the subversion of all well-regulated society . . . It is not a question relating merely to the journeymen spinners of Manchester . . . It is a struggle between right and wrong—between a just and temperate union on the one hand, and a sturdy and turbulent faction on the other . . . Should the journeymen be successful, their conduct will form a precedent, and we shall shortly hear of similar practices in every commercial district of the Kingdom. We warn the masters of their danger but we have little hope of inculating any lesson of discretion in the men.[104]

As a result of the employers' placards, the factories were reopened on Monday, 24 August, but at only two mills—those of David Holt and Messrs Sandford & Green—were any spinners taken on (from Glasgow and elsewhere). Around both these establishments, crowds of strikers congregated during the evenings of the following week. As a precaution, the 'knobsticks' were permanently lodged inside the factories, while the police, accompanied by small detachments of soldiers, dispersed the assemblages as soon as they gathered.[105] The first small signs of a weakening in the total solidarity of the strike induced Doherty to make serious efforts at conciliation. He first appealed to the Manchester magistrates in an address dated 28 August. He emphasised that the dispute was now approaching its crisis point and feared that the longer continuation of the appalling distress, for which the employers were considered to be solely responsible, would make it impossible for the union to restrain its more turbulent spirits. 'We feel we are a mass of material which a spark may ignite, and the conflagration might be terrible.' He recalled that the workmen had made a series of attempts to negotiate with their masters, finally agreeing to accept the average wages the employers' offer would produce; consequently, the employers, and not the union, must bear responsibility for any outrages that might ensue. Doherty repeated his regular arguments concerning the evils of wage reductions and the operatives' contribution towards amassing great fortunes for many manufacturers over the previous forty years, and concluded by requesting the magistrates to act as arbitrators to settle the dispute; and in their mediation they were asked to give as much consideration to the blood and bones of the workmen as they had given to the inanimate property of their masters, in allowing them to parade an armed force through the streets to overcome the strikers and 'protect' the few old men, thieves and pickpockets who were at work. In another postscript, Doherty answered the criticism of his remarks on the individual who had advertised for women.

> All that we meant was, if he could not find in his heart to employ, and *pay* men for doing his work, he should look out for women whose morals are already corrupted, instead of those whose lives are yet pure and spotless. For everyone will admit, that to place persons of both sexes, of 15 or 16 years, indiscriminately together, and put them in receipt of 12s to 16s a week, which is entirely at their own disposal, without education and before their habits are fixed, and their reason sufficiently mature to controul [sic] their passions and restrain their appetites, . . . such persons will [not] grow up as chaste, moral and obedient to their parents, as if they had still not remained under the salutary restraint of parental controul [sic]. If the practice were to become general, of employing girls and boys instead of men, it could place the son and daughter of fifteen, at the head of the family, to whose whims and caprices the father must bend and succumb, or in many cases starve.[106]

Before Doherty's address could have any effect, the Manchester fine masters inflicted the decisive blow, by allying with their coarse-spinning colleagues. There had been hints of such a policy beforehand. Early in July one master coarse-spinner, Pooley, gave notice to his men that their wages would be reduced unless they discontinued paying towards the fund by which the striking fine spinners were supported.[107] The following week the *Manchester Guardian* alleged that all the master coarse-spinners had undertaken to discharge their hands who were similarly contributing, but this promise was not immediately carried out.[108] However, on Wednesday, 2 September, following a meeting of the master spinners' committee, seventeen coarse-spinning firms gave notice to their men that from 12 September their wages would be reduced by 5 per cent every fortnight, unless they signed a document pledging not to support in any way the striking fine spinners; and in case of their being discovered to do so, they would forfeit a fortnight's wages. The workmen concerned immediately held a meeting, resolved unanimously not to sign the document, and those of Messrs Birley & Co. actually turned out before the expiration of their notice.[109] William Arrowsmith, then employed as a coarse spinner by Messrs Fernley and Swindells, and later the secretary of the spinners' union, told the 1838 Select Committee on Combinations that his wages in 1829 amounted to about 18s per week, of which he was paying about 3s a week towards the strikers.[110]

The threatened elimination of the great bulk of the financial support which was enabling the fine spinners to continue their turn-out forced Doherty to step up his efforts towards securing a compromise agreement. On 3 September he wrote a letter to a local magistrate, Ralph Wright, enclosing by order of the union the address of 28 August in favour of arbitration, and adding that subsequently the coarse-spinning masters had proposed to abate their men by 5 per cent per fortnight, unless they abandoned their union. 'Thus they seem determined to exercise a right, by the use of which they mean to deprive us of the same privilege, nothwithstanding that the legislature intended to place us both on precisely the same footing in that respect.'[111] On 7 September James Foster informed the Home Office that he had received a similar letter from Doherty, enclosing the above address, which Foster thought was 'very artfully written', though he considered that to settle the dispute by arbitration, as proposed, would be 'utterly impracticable'. The principal objection to the proposal, however, seems to have been that it came from Doherty; for, later in the same letter, Foster stated that, if it was considered that the mediation of a third party might lessen the difference, he would be happy to make the experiment. The possibility of violence was thought to be so great at this stage that Foster's letter was 'Read by the Cabinet',[112] while on 12 September Wright stressed that the magistrates' power to shut inns and public houses in cases of actual or expected riot should be extended to retail breweries.[113]

Peel's reply acknowledging the information sent by Foster provides another interesting insight into the variety of efforts made by Doherty in the operatives' cause. The Home Secretary maintained that an important evil of the strikes and combinations was the extension of

> the mysteries by which a few able and artful men can exercise influence over numbers engaged in a common cause, and can apply them to very mischievous purposes, without any actual infraction of the law. Some short time since a Deputy from the Spinners (the workmen) made his appearance and solicited an interview with me. I was unwilling to have any personal communication with him on the particular subject on which he wished to see me, the difference between the Master Manufacturers and the Spinners relating to the rate of wages, fearing the misrepresentations to which a communication might be liable when reported by him in Manchester. I desired him to make it in writing but he declined. If I mistake not the Deputy . . . was John Doherty whose name is attached to the insiduous hand-bill which was enclosed in your letter. I certainly wish that this dispute could be terminated in any manner that would not encourage that sort of dangerous confederacy into which the labouring classes are prone to enter.

Peel concluded by applauding the masters' offer of fair wages varying according to the workman's ability as more rational than the men's demand of 35s for all.[114] There is no other reference to Doherty's visit to London, but we can speculate that it was made early in August when he was increasing his efforts towards obtaining a compromise and there was also a brief intermission in the succession of addresses which he issued.

The stillborn attempt to secure the local magistrates' mediation was only one of a series of efforts which persisted throughout September. During the first week a requisition signed by more than 100 'respectable manufacturers and shopkeepers' was presented to the churchwardens, calling upon them as guardians of the poor to act as mediators between the parties; but on 10 September they refused to do so, unless they were asked by the masters themselves.[115] Immediately following this failure, a similar independent group transmitted an identical declaration to G. E. Aubrey, secretary of the masters' association, and to John Doherty. After lamenting the extreme depression in business in the town, caused partly by the strike, the signatories suggested that, to restore activity to commerce and dispel the daily increasing danger of unpleasant disturbances, 'there may be a meeting of any given number of each [masters and men], in order that, by reasoning with each other, you may affect [sic] an amicable arrangement'.[116]

But by this time the master spinners were so certain they were about to succeed that they did not even reply to the initiative. On the other hand, the workmen were placed in such straits by the removal of the coarse spinners' supporting contributions, that Doherty was anxious to clutch at any straw that would allow the strike to end in anything but complete defeat and would clear the field for his ambitious ventures.[117] Consequently Doherty's response, accepting the idea of mutual deputations to settle their differences, either before the magistrates or the churchwardens, was expressed in remarkably submissive language compared with the sarcastic tone less than one month earlier. 'Our only fears are that our employers will consider that such a meeting would have a tendency to create too great a familiarity on our parts, and thereby lessen the respect and deference to which they are entitled. We beg to say, however, that should they condescend to meet us, we will endeavour to avoid everything that may be in the least degree offensive to them or any of the parties concerned. We hope we shall not forget that we are servants.'[118]

Although this statement again elicited no encouraging response from the employers, Doherty proceeded to make one final attempt at negotiation. He addressed an application to the churchwardens of Manchester, detailing the privations of the journeymen spinners, which rendered them eager to secure a satisfactory conclusion to the twenty-three week old dispute. 'They feel that as servants they are bound, as becomes them, to make the first friendly offer to their employers; and as you have kindly signified your readiness to become mediators between the contending parties, they most respectfully request that you will use your influence to procure a meeting of any given number of masters before you, with an equal number of the workmen.' The workmen were also ready to follow any alternative course of action which either the churchwardens or the masters considered better calculated to settle the dispute.[119] Doherty here clearly overstated the inclination of the churchwardens to take the initiative, and there was no immediate response to his application. Consequently, on 17 September, the spinners held a general meeting at their room in David Street and resolved to return to their employment, at a list of prices (for 300 spindles) half-way between Murray's late list and the masters' March list, 'but that a different system of percentage be adopted'. Thus the workmen were now prepared to accept a fairly large abatement, but hoped to moderate the rapidity with which their prices fell as the size of the mules increased. The resolution was communicated to the churchwardens, who replied on 21 September that they had sent it to the masters, who in turn had categorically refused to make any deviation from the March list. 'Under these circumstances, the Churchwardens are of opinion that the only proper course is, that every person shall, individually hire himself to the best advantage in his power, neither interfering with others, nor allowing himself to be interfered with.'[120]

Thus ended Doherty's final effort to salvage any concession in the operatives' desperate situation. The declaration of the coarse-spinning masters had forced him to make a virtue out of necessity. By 12 September *Wheeler's Manchester Chronicle* reported that more than twenty coarse-spinning mills were idle and an additional 15,000 had been thrown out of employment, in addition to the fine spinners and their dependants.[121] However, it was far easier for masters to engage new hands as coarse spinners, and the latter's turnout was less than one week old when two firms—Messrs Birley & Kirk and the Oxford Road Twist Company—were able to employ female spinners on the whole of their smaller wheels. And on 26 September the *Manchester Guardian* reported the strike of coarse spinners to be virtually at an end. Many factories had received fresh hands from Stockport (where the strike had just terminated) and elsewhere, who had agreed to renounce the club, and the old hands were therefore desirous of accepting the masters' terms.[122]

Meanwhile the fine spinners who had been engaged by Messrs Sandford & Green and David Holt towards the end of August[123] had continued to work. There was a series of minor incidents in the first two weeks of September, as crowds of strikers assembled around the factories, but on only two occasions did hooting and hissing escalate into actual physical assault[124] and no arrests were made. Nevertheless, Messrs Sandford & Green were induced to discharge their 'knobsticks', who were replaced on 7 September by six of their original spinners, more of whom trickled back to work on the employers' terms over the succeeding days. On the evening of 18 September, Doherty became involved in an argument outside this mill with one of the special constables, who ultimately conveyed him to the lock-up. He was soon released, however, and next morning applied at the New Bailey for a summons against the constable for assault, declaring that he had been grossly ill-treated and wished to have the man bound over to keep the peace. The defending attorney, Milne, observed that 'it would be much more proper if Mr Doherty would keep away from that neighbourhood', but the magistrate, Foster, was more sympathetic and eventually persuaded Doherty to drop the matter. But the incident did give Doherty an opportunity to state publicly that 'he did not wish to create any more ill-blood; there was plenty of that already. He had always done his utmost to preserve order, and should continue to do so.'[125]

Whilst thus engaged in these desperate endeavours to avert complete surrender, Doherty was striving behind the scenes to secure more widespread co-operation among the various districts of cotton spinners and among the trades in general, which would in the short term provide the Manchester spinners with resources to replace the subscriptions of the coarse spinners, but more importantly in the long run, would ensure that they, and other bodies of workmen, would never again be in a position of such comparative weakness against their masters and have to endure heavy wages reductions. On Sunday, 20 September, he convened a spinners' delegate meeting at the Manchester committee room in David Street, when it was resolved 'that a Grand General Union of Cotton Spinners, throughout the United Kingdom, should be formed, for the protection of their trade, the maintenance of their privileges, and to uphold the value of their labour'.[126] In fact, the delegates at the meeting represented only the Lancashire and Cheshire cotton-spinning districts, but Doherty was temporarily appointed secretary of the newly-formed general union until the next delegate meeting on 18 October. In an address which he issued on 22 September, he clearly recognised that defeat in the Manchester strike was imminent, but used this as an example of how the establishment of a general fund could avert similar disasters in future. 'Will any man say', he asked rhetorically, 'that with two or three years' savings in this way, masters at either Manchester or Stockport would have attempted the reductions, which they have now unfortunately succeeded in effecting?'[127]

The day after this address was published, an even more portentous meeting was held in the Spinners' Room. It was attended by delegates from thirteen Manchester trades—dressers and dyers, iron founders, card grinders and strippers, stretchers, machine-makers, whitesmiths, sawyers, smallware weavers, cotton yarn dressers, plasterers and painters, joiners and fustian cutters—and the idea was first publicy mooted that all the Manchester trades should form themselves into a union, to prevent any reduction of their wages. It was agreed that another meeting should be convened in the same room one week later, on 30 September, to discuss the measure further,[128] but in regard to the immediate crisis—the spinners' strike—a printed address was placarded on the walls of the town, headed 'Turn Out Spinners—Address from the Trades of Manchester and the Neighbourhood to the Public'. This condemned both the efforts of the master fine-spinners to force their men to surrender, by hiring 'unprincipled mercenaries', or special constables, to parade the streets, and bribing 'unprincipled wretches' to work, and also those of the master coarse-spinners to reduce their hands because they would not sign an infamous agreement, which would nullify the benefits from the repeal of the Combination Laws. Every friend of freedom, the address concluded, should assist those who were resisting a decline into slavery.[129]

Although these meetings can be seen as last-minute attempts to save the spinners from humiliation, in fact their importance in shaping the future development of Doherty's trade-union aspirations was of far greater significance, for there were already signs of open disagreement among the turn-outs on the policy of continuing the strike. Doherty's endeavours were therefore directed towards securing an orderly retreat, rather than the men drifting back to work piecemeal and thus abrogating the authority of the union. On Saturday, 26 September, a report became prevalent in the town that the old hands of Houldsworth's mill had offered to return to their wheels on the masters' terms, which rumour caused a great sensation among the spinners. A meeting was held the following evening to ascertain the correctness of the statement and it was decided to convene a general meeting on the Monday afternoon to learn the sentiments of the turn-outs generally. About 2,000 spinners attended—virtually the whole union membership—and it was found necessary to adjourn from their room to the builders' yard below.

Doherty informed his audience that the meeting had been called to test the truth of the story, prevalent in the town, that the majority of the men were willing to accede to the masters' terms after twenty-five weeks of resistance, but were prevented from doing so by himself and other leaders of the spinners' union. He did not believe it, but was willing to try his belief by putting the question immediately to the vote without speaking further. Thereupon the whole assemblage voted unanimously against accepting the March list, not a single hand being raised in approval. The meeting was then addressed by a spinner named Wood, who reprobated the 'base document' which the masters required them to sign on being readmitted to their mills. And Thomas Foster delivered a lengthy oration, exhorting all present to behave peaceably towards persons and property, and concluding by moving 'that the prices of the masters be taken into consideration that day six months', which was carried by acclamation. At the end of the meeting

Doherty announced that the trades generally were coming forward in their support and that the sawyers had sent them £50.[130]

Despite this hopeful information and Doherty's statement to the second general meeting of Manchester trades' delegates that 'letters had been received from different towns offering contributions to the fund', the true situation of the spinners was revealed by the desperate expedient of resolving to send out 500 deputies from their own body to solicit subscriptions from the different trades throughout the country.[131] Moreover, notwithstanding the unanimity of the determination to continue the strike on 28 September, it was evident at that meeting, and even more strongly at others on 1 and 2 October, that a growing number of the men, especially those who had been earning the highest wages, were willing to go back on the best terms they could get, provided that the employers would withdraw their document.[132]

The strike leaders were now convinced that, despite the continued intransigence of many of the rank and file, defeat was inevitable, and a serious outbreak of violence almost equally certain if the strike was allowed to drag on. Alarmed for their own legal position if such a situation should develop, and anxious that the union should not lose credibility and their ambitious future projects be nipped in the bud,[133] they called another general meeting for the morning of 3 October to settle the question. It was decided that the hands of each mill should vote separately and by secret ballot. The result, according to most of the local press, was that 767 men supported a return to work and 760 favoured remaining out, which numbers were in line with the large attendances generally recorded at these meetings; but one local paper reported the figures as being 307 and 300 respectively, and Doherty later testified to the 1838 Select Committee that the total number of votes cast was just over 700. He also disclosed that the actual voting had shown a majority of three in favour of continuing the strike, but he had been so certain that no benefit could result from protracting their miseries, that he had consulted the leading members of the committee and eventually decided to announce the verdict as being against continuance.[134]

What was indisputable was that the strike was now officially over after exactly six months. In the evening following the men's decision, the masters' association met and agreed to withdraw their document, but it was left to individual masters to determine whom to re-employ. Several employers stated that they intended to hire as spinners none but females and the older piecers. This system had previously only been acted upon at a few coarse-spinning establishments, but was now to be extended to fine-spinning factories.[135] Because of the manufacturers' selectivity in not hiring those who had been most active in the dispute, a great number of spinners—according to one estimate, about 400—were unable to find employment and therefore remained as an extra drag on an already over-stocked labour market.[136] Even those who were taken on had continued problems. The men's fear that the principle of reductions according to the sizes of mules would lead to perpetual abatements was reinforced immediately, for it was reported on 17 October that two fine masters were trying to reduce their hands by five hanks below the March list. Moreover, several masters introduced an anti-strike regulation like that which had caused disagreement at Ewart's factory in 1828, by which their workmen engaged to give a fortnight's notice of quitting, and only one hand in each room could give notice to leave in any one period of fourteen days.[137]

Nevertheless, although the strike had ended in complete failure, the Manchester spinners continued to maintain the discipline they had shown throughout the long dispute, and there is no evidence of any internal recriminations. That the quarrelling within the union that had occurred in 1818 and intermittently throughout the 1820's was not re-enacted must be put to Doherty's credit. And he succeeded in maintaining this control in spite of a bitter attack upon himself and the union, led by the *Manchester Guardian*. At the termination of the strike, the newspaper pointed out that the spinners' piece-rates had not been reduced for more than a decade, yet the selling price of yarn and piece-goods had considerably declined, lower wage rates had long been paid in the country districts, and the productivity of the mules had been greatly increased. Consequently, the spinners' wages were still higher, even after the reduction, than those of any equally numerous body of labourers in the kingdom, and only improper practices could have prevented the spinners, and particularly the older piecers who did not receive the union allowance, from accepting work on the mules. The article mentioned reports 'that the hands had been bound by oath to obey the rules of the committee', and asked if these could be 'authoritatively con-tradicted'. The journeymen's subscriptions would have been better placed in a savings bank, for their money had only benefited union officials and committee men, 'who must at least have a certain private interest different from, if not actually adverse to that of the great body of spinners; for in proportion as the latter are on good terms with their employers, must be the facility of dispensing with the services of committee men, and rendering it necessary for the latter to work for their own living'.[138]

Doherty's rejoinder was dated 16 October and was published in the follow-ing day's paper. He challenged the editor to name the 'functionaries' who had gained by the strike and show what they had got. Furthermore, he unequivocally denied that a binding oath 'either is, or ever has been, administered among the Spinners of Manchester'. Of the paper's other allega-tions, he promised to reply 'at a more convenient season'. The *Guardian* offered no comment on this letter, but printed beneath it a letter signed 'Q', which asserted that on the very day the spinners returned to work, 5 October, 'the secretary and several other persons, who we supposed to be members of the committee, were seen in the Legs of Man public-house in Portland Street, regaling themselves with *wine*'. It went on to infer that these men, 'who felt so warmly and talked so loudly of the distress of their fellow workmen', were actually buying wine with the aid of the funds entrusted to them, 'when their associates could not obtain bread'.[139] This report, however, may have been a cheap smear, in view of Doherty's strong support of the temperance movement.[140]

The Manchester cotton spinners' union not only survived this prolonged struggle, but was able, after the strike had ended, to pay off every penny owed to each turn-out in unpaid allowances.[141] In addition, Doherty had also set in train the two ambitious ventures for which his name is justly renowned in trade-union history. Early in October he released an 'Address to the Public' which maintained that the producers of the nation's wealth must learn a 'lesson of instruction' from the confessedly complete victory of the master spinners and join together in general union:

Had the various trades poured in their pence in time, for their support, a different result must have followed. It is not, however, too late to learn wisdom. It would be absurd to suppose that spinners were the only body that will be reduced, or at least attempted to be reduced, and it is to be feared, that unless there be a more general and effective co-operation amongst the working-classes themselves, these attempts will be, as in the case of the spinners, but too successful . . . The defeat of the spinners, instead of being looked upon as a discouraging incident, should be viewed as one of those occurrences which sometimes happen to show men their weakness and errors. Had a union of all the trades been formed six months ago, it might have saved the spinners from the reduction, and the country from feeling the effect of it. The formation of such a union is now too late to save them this time, but it may be in time to save them and others from the next.[142]

Thus the origins of the future National Association for the Protection of Labour were considerably earlier than is generally recognised, as G. D. H. Cole has at least hinted.[143] Over the succeeding months, Doherty worked persistently to extend the idea, which was well established by the time of the generally accepted starting-point of the Association in February 1830.[144] At the same time, he was pursuing his other grand project, which must be regarded as an integral part of the first, even if it is here discussed separately : this was the organisation and maintenance of a Grand General Union of Operative Cotton Spinners throughout the whole of Great Britain and Ireland.

NOTES TO CHAPTER THREE

[1] *Trades Newspaper*, 25 February 1827.
[2] See above, pp. 3 and 27–8.
[3] *Conciliator*, 29 November 1828.
[4] *Ibid.*, 6 December 1828.
[5] *Ibid.*, 29 November 1828.
[6] *Ibid.*, and 6 December 1828.
[7] 'Condition de la classe ouvrière en Angleterre (1828). Notes prises par Gustave d'Eichtal', *Revue Historique*, Vol. 79 (May–August 1902), p. 69. We are indebted to Dr W. H. Chaloner for this reference.
[8] *Conciliator*, 29 November 1828.
[9] *First Annual Report of the Poor Law Commissioners* (1835), App. B. No. 11, pp. 185–6, 197; Redford, *op. cit.*, p. 151; J. H. Treble, 'The Attitude of the Roman Catholic Church towards Trade Unionism in the North of England, 1833–1842', *Northern History*, Vol. v (1970), p. 97.
[10] *Conciliator*, 6 December 1828.
[11] *Ibid.*, 22 November 1828. None of the names of the Imperials was ever disclosed, but Mr R. Dyson, who is studying the Manchester Cotton Spinners Amalgamation, believes that they were led by William Fair, the treasurer of the union. The *Conciliator* was printed by J. A. Robinson, Star Street.
[12] *Ibid.*, 13 December 1828.
[13] *Returns of the Friendly Associated Cotton Spinners*, 17 January 1829, in H.O. 40/23, hereafter referred to as *Returns*.
[14] *Conciliator*, 20 December 1818.
[15] Spinners' piece-rates were based on the 'numbers' or 'counts' of the yarns, i.e. they varied according to fineness or coarseness, as measured by the number of hanks to the lb.—No. 40s, for example, being 40 hanks to the lb. These rates were also often expressed 'per 1,000 hanks': thus No. 40s might be $2\frac{1}{2}d$ per lb. or $5s\ 2\frac{1}{2}d$ per 1,000 hanks. A further complication was the introduction of varying rates according to the numbers of spindles on mules, in addition to the different prices based on yarn counts.

[16] *Guardian*, 13 and 20 December 1828.

[17] *Ibid.*, 20 and 27 December; *Gazette*, 20 and 27 December 1828.

[18] *Gazette*, 13 and 20 December; *Conciliator*, 20 December 1828.

[19] *Mercury*, 30 December 1828.

[20] *Ibid.*; *Gazette*, 10 January 1829.

[21] *Guardian*, 17 January 1829.

[22] H.O. 40/22. Foster estimated that the spinners had funds of £900–£1,700.

[23] *Returns*, 17 January 1829, in H.O. 40/23. The information that follows is taken from this source and also from a detailed analysis of the Manchester spinners' union on 4 April by the Manchester magistrate, J. F. Foster: see H.O. 40/23.

[24] Parl. Papers, 1837–8, VIII, 3502–12.

[25] *Conciliator*, 6 December 1828.

[26] For this important Society, almost ignored by historians, see below, pp. 353–64.

[27] H.O. 40/26.

[28] *Gazette*, 20 December 1828.

[29] *Guardian*, 10 January 1829.

[30] *Gazette*, 24 January 1829.

[31] Parl. Papers, 1837–8, VIII, 3417.

[32] *Stockport Advertiser*, 2 and 9 January; *Gazette*, 17 January 1829.

[33] The operatives alleged that Stockport rates were already 25 per cent below those in Manchester, but the masters maintained that they had long paid well above those in surrounding districts.

[34] *Stockport Advertiser*, 23 January; *Bolton Chronicle*, 17 January 1829.

[35] *Times*, 24 January 1829.

[36] *Chronicle* and *Gazette*, 31 January 1829.

[37] *Stockport Advertiser*, 19 February 1829.

[38] Doherty later claimed that the Stockport men received 7s per week, but he was perhaps exaggerating to enhance by contrast the pittance on which the Manchester strikers were subsequently forced to survive. *Journal*, 13 March 1830.

[39] Regular reports appeared in the *Stockport Advertiser* and in Manchester, Bolton and other local papers in the early months of 1829.

[40] *Stockport Advertiser*, 27 March 1829. There had, however, been reports of intimidation against 'knobsticks', and the Stockport magistrates had declared their determination to stop such behaviour, for which purpose 600 special constables were sworn in (*ibid.*, 13 March 1829). Even earlier, at the beginning of the strike, the Stockport masters had complained in a memorial to Home Secretary Peel of intimidation against hands willing to work. H.O. 40/23.

[41] *Gazette*, 28 March 1829.

[42] See below, p. 61.

[43] *Chronicle*, 28 February and 7 March 1829.

[44] *Mercury*, 7 April; *Guardian*, 4 April and 2 May 1829. Feelings in that area were embittered by a disaster which occurred at Hyde when the floor of the spinners' meeting-room in the 'Norfolk Arms'—overcrowded with operatives attending in response to the masters' threat—collapsed with heavy loss of life and many injuries. *Chronicle* and *Times*, 4 April 1829.

[45] *Stockport Advertiser*, 8 and 22 May 1829; H.O. 40/23 and 24.

[46] *Stockport Advertiser*, 24 July 1829. The committee-men were, however, eventually acquitted at the Cheshire Quarter Sessions in October, no evidence being presented to link them with specific acts of intimidation or violence (*ibid.*, 16 and 23 October 1829).

[47] *Guardian*, 8 August 1829. Cole, *Attempts at General Union*, p. 15, and J. L. and B. Hammond, *The Skilled Labourer, 1760–1832* (1919), p. 129, wrongly state that the strike ended in June.

[48] *Mercury*, 29 September 1829.

[49] Place Collection, Vol. 16, Part II, f. 66; *Times*, 14 March 1829.

[50] See above, p. 59.

[51] *Voice*, 26 March 1831; *Guardian*, 28 March 1829. According to David McWilliams' evidence to the 1838 Combinations Committee, Parl. Papers, 1837–8,

VIII, 3671, the reduction began at 336 spindles, and this has often been repeated; but all the calculations in 1829 referred to 300 spindles.

[52] *Chronicle*, 4 April 1829.

[53] *Times*, 28 March 1829; Parl. Papers, 1837–8, VIII, 3625.

[54] Parl. Papers, 1837–8, VIII, 3625. According to the *Guardian*, 28 March 1829, 'a considerable number declared that they could maintain themselves for six months without assistance'.

[55] *Guardian*, 11 April 1829.

[56] *Mercury*, 14 April 1829. See below, pp. 333–42.

[57] *Stockport Advertiser*, 17 April 1829.

[58] *Voice*, 13 August 1831.

[59] *Ibid.*, 26 March 1831. In contemporary terminology, mules were frequently referred to as 'wheels', because of the wheeled carriage, the length of which depended on the number of spindles.

[60] *Guardian*, 18 April 1829.

[61] *Ibid.*, 25 April 1829. This list would have entailed an across-the-board decrease of about 5 per cent.

[62] Both the employers' list of 21 March and the men's of 29 May are preserved in the Place Collection, Vol. 16, Part II, ff. 61–2 (sent, no doubt, by Doherty).

[63] *Chronicle*, 25 April, 2 and 16 May. These towns included London, Dublin and Glasgow, according to the *Courier*, 2 May 1829.

[64] Place Collection, Vol. 54, ff. 276–7. See below, p. 74.

[65] H.O. 40/23. See below, p. 78.

[66] Tufnell, *op. cit.*, p. 30.

[67] *Chronicle*, 23 May and 3 October 1829; Parl. Papers, 1837–8, VIII, 3419–22.

[68] *Times*, 18 April; *Times and Gazette*, 13 June, 18 July and 10 October 1829.

[69] *Mercury*, 5 May 1829.

[70] A misprint for £20,000.

[71] *Morning Herald*, 9 May 1829.

[72] *Guardian*, 23 May 1829.

[73] *Ibid.*, 20 June 1829.

[74] Place Collection, Vol. 16, Part II, f. 66.

[75] *Ibid.*, ff. 66 and 69.

[76] *Guardian*, 18 July 1829.

[77] *Times and Gazette*, 18 July 1829.

[78] Place Collection, Vol. 16, Part II, ff. 71–2.

[79] *Ibid.*, ff. 73–4.

[80] *Ibid.*, f. 89.

[81] In fact, the memorial of the cotton manufacturers and master spinners of Stockport to Peel, undated, but sent soon after the start of the Stockport strike in January, had pronounced that a general union existed throughout the cotton trade, which would ultimately destroy it unless the Combination Laws were re-enacted. See above, n. 40.

[82] Place Collection, Vol. 16, Part II, f. 92.

[83] *Mercury*, 5 and 12 May 1829.

[84] *Guardian*, 9 May 1829.

[85] *Times*, 16 May 1829.

[86] *Guardian*, 23 May 1829.

[87] *Times and Gazette*, 30 May 1829.

[88] *Gazette*, 3 April 1829.

[89] *Courier*, 30 May 1829.

[90] *Times and Gazette*, 6 June 1829.

[91] *Guardian*, 6 June 1829.

[92] On the one hand, Doherty was presumably referring to Hodgins' attempt to persuade the men to compromise; and on the other, to an occurrence described by McWilliams in his 1838 evidence, when the firm for which he worked, Sandford & Green, agreed to take back their workmen at a slight reduction from the old prices, but later withdrew their offer stating that they would forfeit £500 to the Masters' Association if they deviated from the March list.

[93] *Chronicle*, 13 June 1829.

94 *Mercury*, 12 May 1829; H.O. 40/23. Doherty must take some credit for this: contrast the violence of the simultaneous strike of Stockport spinners.

95 *Morning Chronicle*, 20 July 1829.

96 H.O. 40/24.

97 Place Collection, Vol. 16, Part II, ff. 71–2.

98 *Times and Gazette*, 25 July; *Guardian*, 18 July 1829.

99 *Guardian*, 8 August 1829, *inter alia*.

100 *Mercury*, 18 August; *Chronicle*, 15 August 1829.

101 *Guardian*, 22 August 1829, *inter alia*.

102 *Ibid*. The firm referred to in the postscript owned the Piccadilly Mill in London Road.

103 *Guardian*, 8 August 1829: 'these committee-men . . ., in the termination of a quarrel about wages, see the arrival of a period when, instead of living upon the fruits of other people's labour, they must work for themselves.'

104 *Chronicle*, 29 August 1829.

105 *Guardian*, 29 August 1829.

106 *Times and Gazette*, 29 August 1829. See Smelser, *op. cit.*, for the spinners' fear of being ultimately undermined as heads of their families by technological change within the factories; but see also below, pp. 147–8.

107 *Times and Gazette*, 11 July 1829.

108 *Guardian*, 18 July 1829. The alliance was reported to the Home Office as an 'important development' and the strikers were said to be aware of it (H.O. 40/24). J. L. and B. Hammond, *The Skilled Labourer*, p. 130, wrongly state that the coarse-spinning reduction *was* made in July.

109 *Guardian*, 5 September 1829; Parl. Papers, 1837–8, VIII, 3633.

110 Parl. Papers, 1837–8, VIII, 3778.

111 H.O. 40/24.

112 *Ibid*.

113 *Ibid*.

114 H.O. 41/6, ff. 487–9.

115 *Guardian*, 5 September; *Times and Gazette*, 12 September 1829.

116 *Guardian*, 12 September 1829.

117 See below, pp. 76–7.

118 *Times and Gazette*, 19 September 1829.

119 *Ibid.*, 26 September 1829; Parl. Papers, 1837–8, VIII, 3634.

120 *Times and Gazette*, 26 September 1829.

121 *Chronicle*, 12 September 1829.

122 *Chronicle*, 19 September; *Guardian*, 26 September 1829.

123 See above, p. 72.

124 *Mercury*, 8 September 1829.

125 *Ibid.*, 22 September 1829.

126 See below, pp. 85–6.

127 Place Collection, Vol. 16, Part II, f. 96.

128 See below, pp. 155–7.

129 H.O. 40/24. This address, dated 22 September, is included in a letter of 26 September from the Manchester borough-reeve and constables to Home Secretary Peel.

130 *Guardian*, 3 October 1829.

131 A 'considerable number' were actually despatched, furnished with credentials from the spinners' committee. *Courier*, 3 October; *Guardian*, 3 October 1829. For the origins of this plan, see above, p. 63.

132 *Ibid*.

133 A more hostile version appeared in the *Chronicle*, 10 October 1829, intimating that it was evident to Doherty and Foster, 'The Castor and Pollux of the Union', that the majority of the men favoured a return to work at the masters' prices, and so, to sustain their reputation for generalship, they concluded that it would be preferable that the desire to return should seem the voluntary expression of a majority of the spinners at a public meeting, instead of a discontented minority, with the leaders at their head, being forced to accept the employers' terms by a gradual collapse of the strike.

134 *Guardian*, 10 October 1829, *inter alia;* Parl. Papers, 1837–8, VIII, 3625.

[135] *Courier*, 10 October 1829.

[136] Nevertheless, according to the *Guardian*, 10 October 1829, Thomas Foster, 'who was undoubtedly the ablest and the most influential man amongst them', had secured work in one of the leading Manchester mills.

[137] *Times and Gazette*, 17 and 24 October 1829.

[138] *Guardian*, 10 October 1829.

[139] *Ibid.*, 17 October 1829. For the probability that new members of the union *did* swear an oath, however, see below, p. 305.

[140] See below, pp. 336–9.

[141] Parl. Papers, 1837–8, VIII, 3625.

[142] *Times and Gazette*, 14 October 1829; Place Collection, Vol. 16, Part II, f. 96.

[143] Cole, *Attempts at General Union*, pp. 16–17.

[144] For an even later date, see J. L. and B. Hammond, *The Town Labourer*, p. 295. For the National Association, see below Chapters VI and VII.

# The Grand General Union of   **IV**
## cotton spinners, 1829–30

We have seen that the earliest associations of mule spinners were established as purely local societies in particular towns such as Stockport, Manchester, Bolton and Oldham. Trade unionism in the cotton industry long retained these deeply-rooted local characteristics, but as spinning mills became increasingly concentrated in Lancashire communication between the different societies easily developed, assisted by the improvement of turnpike roads and the growth of coaching firms which the expansion of the cotton industry promoted throughout the area. Individual societies regularly sent out delegates to canvass support from other towns during strikes. The chief defect of this system was the unreliability of financial support, because of the absolute autonomy of each local association; delegates from a striking union could arrive in another town to find a turn-out also in progress there, or funds dissipated by previous disputes. A further disadvantage was the absence of an overall policy in regard to the disparate piece rates paid in the various districts.

As a remedy for these weaknesses, the spinners made intermittent attempts to establish federations—or at any rate some kind of agreed co-operation—as in 1810, 1818 and 1824–5, with the main aim of supporting individual societies in efforts to equalise piece prices.[1] But these were very loose organisations, unable to overcome the tendency towards sporadic local strikes, which soon caused the federations to disintegrate, as Doherty had observed.[2]

The strikes in Stockport and Manchester in 1829 revived such co-operation, but it was only when it became apparent that neither strike could succeed, and consequently that wage reductions might spread to every cotton-spinning district in turn if left unchecked, that Doherty was able to make progress in persuading the trade generally that spontaneous but independent support, however generous, was inadequate. He therefore embarked on another attempt to federate the local spinners' societies which was remarkable for the extent to which it tried to formalise the relationship between district unions, as well as for the excellent records it has left of its constitution and the debates that moulded it.

Nevertheless, an extremely cautious start was made, showing that Doherty was conscious of the danger of ruining the venture before it had begun, by offending the spinners' regional sensibilities. On Sunday, 20 September 1829, he called together a meeting of delegates from all the cotton-spinning centres of Lancashire and Cheshire, and it was agreed that a Grand General Union of Cotton Spinners throughout the United Kingdom 'be considered as now formed'.[3] This 'Grand Confederation' was to comprise districts of 100 or more spinners, smaller places having to join the nearest district. Doherty was appointed secretary until the next meeting of the districts in a month's time and was instructed meanwhile to prepare an address for general distribution. Preparatory to a wages equalisation policy, every district was to make 'a return of the number of men, in and out of employment, the size of the wheels and the prices paid for spinning'. A balance between the societies' sectional interests and Doherty's desire to avoid the lack of central direction on which the 1825 federation foundered was struck in the wording of another resolution, which stated that 'each district shall have the entire controul [*sic*] and management of its own affairs, subject to no other authority, but that in cases of a strike against a reduction, or for an advance of wages, every district shall contribute as much as they can individually afford, and as the circumstances of the case may appear to require, until a general meeting of districts shall otherwise decide'.[4]

Pursuant to his instructions, Doherty issued an address 'To the Operative Spinners of England' on 22 September. He began by stating that their own experience proved the impossibility of the labouring man, 'isolated and alone', maintaining the value of his labour against the fearful odds opposed to him. Not only were the laws of the land made by the rich and powerful to promote the interests of the employers, but they were administered also by the same classes. Moreover, the poor man became totally destitute by losing his labour, whereas the employer could dismiss any number of hands and still secure new ones because of the over-supply of spinners and the want of total unanimity and organisation amongst them. Wages reductions could thus be effected because of this lack of union. The power of one employer was only balanced when *all* his workmen were united and could leave his employ together. Even then the master had the advantages of wealth, education and influence to support him, and could not suffer, as an individual, from the mutual divisions and jealousies common among large bodies of workmen.

However, their situation was not yet hopeless. It could be redeemed by 'one vigorous and determined effort'. Although the Manchester and Stockport workmen had suffered a reduction, no masters would attempt a similar abatement after 20,000 spinners (including piecers who could spin) had accumulated a fund over two or three years by subscribing just 1d a week, which would produce £83 a week and £4,233 a year. Perfect security would be ensured for such a fund by depositing it in the Bank of England or in government securities, in sums of £80 each, dividing each cheque and depositing one half in the box of the central committee and the other in the boxes of each district in turn; a mutual check would thus be placed on unnecessary expenditure at either the centre or in the regions. Finally, Doherty reaffirmed that such a union would not in any way interfere with the local affairs and management of any district. The only effect on any district union would be to support and strengthen it, while the general union would bind the trade together and guarantee their faith in achieving independence and a comfortable standard of living. It was the duty of every man, therefore, to use his utmost exertions to promote such an important institution.[5]

The next delegate meeting of the English districts was scheduled to be held on Sunday, 18 October. No record of it has survived, but it is clear that Doherty was confirmed as secretary, and the original intention that the union should extend 'throughout the United Kingdom' was endorsed by the sanctioning of correspondence on the subject with their Scottish and Irish fellow-workmen. The outcome was the assembling of a representative conference of delegates from the whole trade of cotton spinning in the United Kingdom on the Isle of Man from Saturday, 5 December, until the following Wednesday evening. The publication of a 56-page report of the proceedings of this meeting, written by Doherty, ensures the survival of a remarkable memoir not only of the constitution of the spinners' general union, but of the discussions which led to its formulation.[6]

Seventeen individuals are mentioned in the report as having attended the meeting, representing, according to the figures they gave in, a total of 12–13,000 spinners in the United Kingdom. The majority came from England, eleven in all, including three from Manchester, two from Bolton, and one each from Oldham, Preston, Warrington, Wigan, Leeds and Carlisle. Five deputies represented Scotland, of whom three were from Glasgow and two from Johnstone, while the poorly-organised Irish spinners were limited to one delegate from Belfast. All the speakers are referred to by the names of the places which they represented, except for Doherty himself, who dominated the proceedings (at least according to his own account), Thomas Foster, and one Macvicker. Foster 'came at his own expence' from Manchester, 'for the purpose of aiding in the discussions, and it is but justice to say, that his superior talents contributed very materially to facilitate the . . . business of the meeting'. He was not, however, a middle-class interloper, as the Webbs alleged, but a working cotton spinner from Manchester who had been prominent in the spinners' union since its resurgence in 1822 and was probably even more influential than Doherty within it, at least until Doherty's election to the secretaryship in 1828.[7] Macvicker was one of the Glasgow delegates, usually referred to in the report as 'Glasgow 2'.[8] We can also deduce that the unnamed Manchester delegate was David Crooks, for Doherty referred to him as a worker who, at the Manchester strike in 1818, had been 'arrested and imprisoned five months before trial, and at his trial sentenced by an old and reverend hypocrite, to three years in Lancaster Castle'.[9]

The Isle of Man was chosen as the meeting-place because of its neutral, yet at the same time central situation. The conference was intended to be held at Douglas, but when the English delegates arrived on the Saturday morning, having sailed from Liverpool overnight, they found the Scottish and Irish deputies already in residence in Ramsey, and therefore decided to stay there, at the inn of a Mr and Mrs Heelis, because of transport difficulties. The deliberations began at midday, when Doherty proposed the first motion 'that the proceedings of that meeting, together with a brief sketch of the discussions that might ensue, should be printed, for the satisfaction of the body whom they represented, as well as to prevent misunderstandings, and accidental and involuntary misrepresentations, to which the proceedings would be exposed, if every representative were to give his own version of them'. He explained that the proposed publication would not be advertised in the newspapers, but produced as a pamphlet for distribution among their members in the various districts.

This proposition led to immediate controversy. A Glasgow delegate (2) stated that the spinners there were opposed to all publicity because it

D

enabled the masters to anticipate and counter their proceedings. He considered 'that the spinners of Manchester made their affairs too public; and on
that very ground, an objection had been raised to their journey, or their
uniting with Manchester at all'. Another Glasgow delegate (3) moved as an
amendment that a manuscript report be sent to every district, and not
printed. He was seconded by one of the Bolton representatives, who asserted
that 'it had long been the opinion in Bolton, that Manchester published too
much of their concerns', and this view was also supported by deputies from
Belfast and Johnstone. Doherty replied that the masters could always discover their intentions through 'pimps and spies' in any case. Moreover, it
would be beneficial for the respectable employers to know exactly what the
operatives planned, for when they realised that no hostility was intended
towards them, they would join with the men in preventing the abatements
by unprincipled country masters, who were notoriously the origin of all
general reductions and against whom the general union was in fact being
formed. He further declared that publicity was essential if an effective and
general union of spinners through the three kingdoms was to be formed, and
in conclusion asserted that the amendment was impractical, because it would
take far too long to write out fifty, or even a hundred copies, and misguided, because the masters could as easily get hold of a manuscript as a
printed copy. The other delegate from Manchester favoured a printed report
to satisfy his constituents that the considerable expense incurred in sending
men there—according to the Manchester *Returns* for 30 November this
amounted to £8 for 'two delegates to the Isle of Man'[10]—had been justified.
Eventually Doherty's proposal was carried by a majority of only two, after
three hours' argument. It was later decided that he should remain on the
island after the meeting to prepare the report and get 500 copies printed, so
that it might be circulated as soon as possible; he was to receive a fee of £3
for his services, he having protested that other suggestions ranging from £5
to £10 were excessive.

This wrangle was instantly followed by another. The Scottish delegates
insisted that no business should be transacted the following day, since to
work on the Sabbath towards the establishment of the Union would
immediately discredit it in the eyes of many of their colleagues at home.
Doherty replied that he also wished Sundays to be kept holy, but he could
not see how they were profaning that day in debating matters which would
save themselves and their families from that poverty, ignorance and crime
which repeated wage-reductions were so calculated to produce. He suggested
that they should all attend their respective places of worship and afterwards
resume their deliberations, so that no unnecessary expense was occasioned
their constituents. At this, Macvicker exclaimed heatedly that 'if the English
delegates are determined to press the question, and out-vote us again,
we shall have no chance with them, [and] we had better give up at
once'.[11] Doherty immediately denied that the English spinners had any
such intentions and prudently withdrew his opposition to the motion to
avert further dissension, it being agreed on his proposal that they should
meet an hour earlier than planned on the Monday. On the Sunday, when
Foster also arrived from Manchester, informal consultations did take place
between the deputies, which, according to Doherty, removed all feelings of

jealousy between them and inspired all to consider only the 'common cause'.

The conference at last got down to discussing the constitution of the proposed general union on Monday, 7 December. There was no argument on the basic proposition, moved by the Preston and seconded by the Manchester delegate, 'that one grand general union of all the operative spinners, in the United Kingdom be now formed, for the mutual support and protection of all'. But the principal point of dissension centred upon whether it would be better to have three national committees in charge of their own affairs and money, or one governing committee to supervise all. Thomas Foster, supported by the Bolton and Glasgow deputies, took his stance for the former arrangement, while John Doherty argued eloquently in favour of the latter, sustained by the representatives of Johnstone, Oldham, Manchester and Belfast.

Doherty maintained that three committees might temporarily remove petty jealousies as to precedency, but they had met together to establish one union and not three. Foster countered by contrasting Doherty's opposition to decentralisation to the policy he advocated at home. Their union of English spinners gave each district equal control over the affairs of the union, and no district was allowed to interfere with another;[12] Manchester and Bolton had no more to do with each other than 'any two separate things'. But according to Foster's plan for the grand general union, each nation would form but one district, so that if any of the three was in need of financial assistance, it would only be necessary to write to the other national committees, instead of sending out delegates, which often cost more money than the product of their missions.

Doherty replied that Foster's plan would not avoid giving more power to one town than another, for each national committee would have to sit somewhere, and the town in which it met was bound to have more power than the others, since it would be impossible for remote places to send representatives to every committee meeting. Moreover, national committees would entail much inconvenience: if a dispute occurred in one town, the local society would have to write first to its national committee; the latter must then communicate with the other countries, which in turn would have to consult with their respective *territories*, before the original town would be able to take action. This 'roundabout writing' would be saved by the adoption of one general committee; but with national committees they would experience all the evils Foster and the others feared in raising one district above others, without securing the advantage of one head to consult and direct. All that was necessary was to extend the principle of the district union in England, to embrace every district in the United Kingdom. 'They were but one trade, and he could not see why they should attempt to create, or perpetuate distinctions as to nations, while they were all bound by the same laws, injured by the same means, or benefited by the same cause.'

Thereupon Foster repeated his arguments concerning the dangers of making one district more powerful than the others. He asked if Doherty had forgotten that he could not form a union based on that principle even in England, and alleged that their last district union in 1825 was broken up principally because one district had been given the controlling power over the rest. 'The union which they had lately formed in England, would not allow either Mr Doherty or Manchester to have the ruling power. They had formed a committee from the various districts. And was it likely, that they should suffer Manchester, or Glasgow, or Belfast, or any other place to assume the power there, at the Isle of Man, which they had already refused them at home.' The one head that was necessary would be found in the annual meetings, which would make the laws. 'Really, the ambition of Mr Doherty, was equal to his arguments. He was to have one grand committee to manage the affairs of the whole union, and he would sit at the front of the table (as he then did), as secretary for the three kingdoms.'

Doherty at once rose to defend himself. Few men knew him better than Mr Foster, he declared, and he would ask him directly if he ever knew him to support any measure to promote his own interests or gratify his own vanity. When Foster vehemently retracted his insinuation, Doherty returned to the question of where the central committee should be established. 'He would say, then, that Manchester, from its numbers, its importance, and its situation as the first and most central spinning district in the United Kingdom, but not from any superiority, in the intellectual attainments of its people, should be the place where the seat of government ought to be held, and the district from which the materials to compose such a government should be taken. (Hear! hear! from Glasgow).' He added that if the annual meetings were to be attended by representatives from each district, as at the present conference, the high-sounding national committees would be 'mere nonentities', and if the annual meetings were to be the only head, then for fifty-one weeks a year 'they would have a body without a head'. His own plan of one general committee, obtaining its authority from the annual meetings, would be much more practical.

Although Doherty had the better of the theoretical argument, he could not overcome the sectional inclinations of the spinners. After some further debate, during which the Bolton delegates said that 'Bolton would not allow Manchester to govern them, as had been proved in the case of the union already established in England', the question was put and the motion 'that each nation shall manage its own affairs', although always subject to the decisions of an annual general meeting, was carried by a majority of four.[13] Nevertheless, such was the importance of this subject that Doherty tried later to revive discussion upon it on several occasions, but was unable to make any progress.[14]

The next question, of how the general union should raise the necessary funds, was settled without such controversy. Doherty suggested that the system adopted in the English union, of every member paying a penny a week to the general fund, over and above the local subscription in each district, be extended; and after Foster had explained that the fund so raised in England was only intended to be applied in emergencies, the regulation was carried unanimously. In connection with this subject, Doherty referred to the problem of 'big piecers' and the large numbers of men made redundant by the baneful practice of allowing piecers to spin. Unless they copied the entry controls of other bodies, they must continue to sink, but at this point in their discussion he only wished to propose that 'big piecers' should be enrolled as members of the union, paying the penny a week subscription and receiving the same strike allowance to 'prevent them from doing mischief'.

Doherty's views were warmly supported by the other delegates, and his proposal was unanimously adopted, he and a deputy from Johnstone being appointed to prepare an entrance ceremony for admitting piecers as members, distinct from that which they would receive on becoming spinners.

The remainder of Monday, 7 December, was spent in debating the whole issue of strikes and strike payments. There was general agreement with the proposal, made by the Preston delegate, that the allowance to strikers should be 10s per week, but a suggestion of paying an additional 5s for every two children was rejected as being extravagant. The Scottish deputies proposed that, in cases of a partial strike, the district where they occurred should support their own men as long as they could, by levying 1s 6d from each man in addition to his local subscription; only when the amount received was insufficient to pay the strike allowances, should they call on the other districts to make up the deficiency. Several English delegates protested; one of the Bolton men believed it would be difficult to get the rank and file to pay the levy, when the local subscription could already amount to 1s or 1s 6d, and David Crooks observed that the rule would impose a crippling financial burden in large districts, where partial strikes were frequent—'in Manchester, they had scarcely been free from them for two or three years'. Ultimately, the extra levy was reduced to 1s and the proposition of the Scottish delegates was adopted in its amended form.

A long discussion ensued on the crucial question of whether strikes for advances of wages, as well as against reductions, were to be supported from the general fund. The Glasgow delegates considered it essential that this should be done, because their employers had made the lower rates paid in the west of Scotland a constant pretext for offering wage reductions. They should take one district at a time and bring those out that were being underpaid, until they had one regulated list of prices throughout the country. However, a large fund should be accumulated before this policy was implemented, hence they suggested that a specified period should be laid down before strikes for advances be allowed. This proposal was supported by Crooks, who thought six months was a reasonable limit, and also by Foster and the other Scottish delegates. But one deputy from Bolton feared that too many districts would turn out together, unless a resolution was passed to prevent excessive strikes. And Doherty asserted that they should be very cautious about talking of increasing wages, for nothing was more calculated to alarm both employers and the public. Nevertheless he admitted that it was unfair that one master be allowed to pay less than others, and that to prevent serious reductions being offered it might sometimes be necessary to seek an advance. It would therefore be unwise to outlaw the seeking of advances for any given period. It was quite sufficient to say that strikers for increases should receive the same allowance as those against reductions, but no district, or part of any district, be allowed to turn out for an advance without the consent of the other districts. The meeting was satisfied that Doherty's proposal safeguarded the general good and again adopted it unanimously.

In fact, this resolution was made superfluous by a proposition subsequently adopted regarding authorisation for any district to go on strike for any cause. Doherty was anxious to avoid the 'one great error' of the federal union established in 1825, which allowed all to turn out if a reduction was offered to them. 'It certainly must be mortifying to men to be obliged to submit to a reduction, more especially while they were in the act of subscribing to uphold others against the same evil. But, painful as it would be, he was well convinced that if men were to come out, district after district, even against reductions, they would soon be overwhelmed with the number they would have to support.' In 1825 the proliferation of strikes first at Preston, and then at Hyde and elsewhere, had destroyed the district union.[15] If the present attempt was not to fail for a similar reason, 'they must have a specific resolution, stating that none should turn out, on any account whatever, without having first obtained the consent of the trade, or a majority of the entire body, and that *on no account whatever* should more men be brought out, than could be supported with the stipulated sum, during the whole strike'. Again, the force of Doherty's arguments provoked no serious disagreement from the other delegates. However, when he stated, in reply to a question about what should be the exact procedure if any district wished to strike, that this would entail a 'round about rigmarole' of writing to the various national committees and their districts, Foster accused him of raising unnecessary obstacles to the plan of three committees because of his opposition to it. Doherty stubbornly repeated his criticism of cliques of committeemen in Manchester, Glasgow or Belfast being able to determine on suspending the trade of a whole district, whose members might then have to subscribe 2s per week to support men perhaps imprudently brought out. Such a despotic system could not continue one month. But Macvicker, the Glasgow deputy, showed he was more worried about Scottish and Irish opinion being invariably outvoted by the English majority if the opinions of every small district were required. 'Glasgow had done very well by herself', he asserted, and the resolution as finally carried laid down that the particular national committee should take the decision, after consulting their own districts and the other two national committees on the propriety of a strike.

With these discussions, the Monday's business terminated. At the start of the first session on the next day, one of the Johnstone delegates moved that a distinctive union card be prepared, which would permit the holder to travel freely between all the districts of the Grand Confederation, and at the same time put a check on 'bad characters' who could then be prevented from getting employment.[16] The speaker complained that there had previously been a good deal of exclusiveness in some districts, with the object of keeping up employment and wages; if one union was to be formed, all must submerge their separate interests in the common cause. The Glasgow spinners were clearly being referred to, for two of their representatives strongly opposed this proposition, claiming that, when the Glasgow men had expended thousands of pounds to keep up their prices, it would be unfair to expect them to allow the west-country spinners, who had suffered their wages to sink so low, to come and share those benefits. Doherty deplored this exclusive spirit, for free mobility was one of the regulations essential to the existence of the general union: it was equally in the interests of strongly-organised urban districts and of weak and oppressed country areas. The greatest evil in the trade had been 'the continual and mischievous practice of unprincipled employers, in remote parts of the country, to reduce wages', which had forced the more honourable masters to follow their example, as in the case of the recent abatement in Manchester. Foster agreed that 'village tyrants were always the worst . . . like [in] that degraded hole in England, Hyde', and hence it was vital to give such districts every support to bring up their prices, and not exclude them until they could do so themselves, which was not feasible. Ultimately, with some technical amendments in the wording suggested by Doherty to placate the Glasgow men, the resolution was passed unanimously.

It was also agreed that some special payments, 'either weekly or in one separate sum', should be made to men who were 'proscribed' by the masters for their activity in union affairs. Many examples were given by both English and Scottish delegates of such victimisation. Foster stated the case of a strike leader in 1818, who had never been re-employed and was now a street-seller.[17] This was one of numerous instances, yet there was one among them who had 'nobly and boldly bid defiance to all consequences, and defended the spinners of Manchester throughout their late most important struggle, in a way which did credit to them and honour to himself, . . . his friend Doherty (applause)'. Doherty himself referred to the case of Crooks, the Manchester deputy, who had not only been imprisoned for three years following the 1818 strike but recently blacklisted for his part in the late turn-out of fine spinners. The delegate from Carlisle maintained that the men who suffered in this way were generally the cleverest and boldest among them, hence it would be preferable to employ them as full-time officials in their respective societies. Macvicker deflated this idea by showing that the number of proscribed men was far greater than the possible situations available, while Doherty asserted it would place the most independently-minded individuals among them in an invidious position in relation to their fellow-workmen. In view of his subsequent establishment in business as a bookseller, he did, however, make an interesting alternative suggestion to either subsidising persecuted workmen in office or giving them money to move to another district. This was to make such men 'a present of something handsome to begin some little way of business, and let their friends deal with them, and thus you will put them in a situation which will enable them, eventually by industry and frugality to acquire, perhaps, an independence, under the very noses of the men who sought to crush them'.

At this stage Doherty reverted to the question of piecers spinning and moved a resolution that no spinner should allow or teach a piecer to spin, after the first Monday in February 1830, 'except the son, brother, or orphan nephew of spinners, and the poor relations of the proprietors of the mills', and then only when they had reached the age of fifteen years and under the personal supervision of the spinner. There was general recognition that free entry to their trade, and the consequent over-supply of hands, was one of their most serious handicaps. The Preston delegate recollected that their local union had previously resolved not to allow a spinner to be more than ten minutes from their wheel-handles, and that the wheels were to stand during that time, but their employers had forced them to abandon the practice after a general lock-out.[18] Thomas Foster condemned the custom, common in Manchester, whereby indulgent overlookers allowed the spinners an extra half-hour for breakfast, while their piecers spun for them. He believed that in

Manchester alone five hundred spinners at least were produced annually.
Eventually he hoped that cotton spinners would have to serve a seven years'
apprenticeship before they were regular workmen, as in other trades. The
Bolton deputies concurred in the motion, but considered that more time was
needed before it should be put into effect, since it was essential, if the union
was to be effective, that all spinners should be members. Because at this time
in Bolton, for instance, there were between 700 and 800 spinners and less
than 500 payers to the local club, they proposed that the time of starting
should be 5 April 1830. A Glasgow delegate then moved that any person
breaking this rule should be fined half a guinea for the first offence, a guinea
for the second, and be expelled from the society for the third. Doherty's
resolution was then adopted along with the two suggested additions.

The deliberations on the Tuesday ended after a recommendation by the
Carlisle representative that an allowance be paid to persons 'on tramp' was
rejected by virtually all the other delegates. Doherty's report of the events
on Wednesday, 9 December, is far less detailed, recounting mainly the bare
bones of the resolutions that were passed. It was agreed that any person
taking work as a spinner at below what was considered the fair price, should
be fined £5 and be made to subscribe for a full year before becoming entitled
again to union benefits. The entrance fee to the general union was fixed at
10s per member after the first Saturday in February, £1 after the first Saturday in March, and £2 after April 5. All fines and entrance fees were to go
to the district where they occurred. Doherty's influence and concern for
central authority were more apparent in the following propositions, that 'the
national committees should have the power to inspect the books of any
district which they may suspect of any attempt to defraud the association,
by paying for less members than they really had, or by paying less than 1s
[each] in cases of strikes', and that a 'monthly correspondence' be kept up,
through the secretary, with each district, in which the offenders against the
interests of the trade should be exposed for general detestation. His belief in the
importance of the workmen having their own press for propaganda and communication purposes was also reflected in the decision that each district should
ascertain how many members would support a monthly publication exclusively
in their interest, which would cost from 2d to 3d per number and be entitled,
'The Operative Spinners' Monthly Advocate, or Register of their Affairs'.

Other resolutions laid down that female spinners be encouraged to form
their own association, with their own entrance ceremony, but to be supported
by the whole confederation in any effort to obtain prices comparable with
the rates of male spinners; that each district should petition Parliament in
favour of an amended act relative to the hours of labour of young persons in
cotton factories, and of extending the existing laws to persons of twenty-one
years;[19] that the next 'annual' meeting of the union be held on the Isle of
Man on Whit Monday, 1830, that Doherty be appointed secretary to the association, that he receive the best of thanks of the meeting 'for his exertions to
promote the well-being of the working classes generally, but of the operative
spinners in particular', and that he prepare an address to the spinners of the
United Kingdom, exhorting them to support their general union. Finally it was
specifically resolved that the grand general union was in no way directed
against the interests of the honourable employers:

It is not the intention of this Association either directly or indirectly to interfere with, or in any way to injure the rights and property of employers or to assume or exercise any control or authority over the management of any mill or mills, but, on the contrary, will endeavour as far as in us lies to uphold the just rights and reasonable authority of every master, and compel all the members of this association to pay a due obedience and respect to their respective masters, and all their confidential servants in authority under them, our only object being to uphold the best interests of our common country by averting all the horrid train of direful calamities, which have already made too much progress amongst us and which are inseparable from cruel poverty, ignorance, degredation, pauperism and crime, and to obtain for our families the common comforts and conveniences of life.[20]

As instructed by the conference, Doherty published an address 'To the Operative Spinners of the United Kingdom', of which 2,000 copies were issued, in addition to those appended to the Report. He first argued that the country was now facing a dangerous crisis, because of the continued depression in trade and the enormous load of taxation imposed 'to uphold in affluence and profusion, a greedy, hypocritical, and arrogant aristocracy'. Although these factors were causing hardships to both the working and middle classes of society, 'the experience of every age and nation' showed that the labouring, or really useful and productive classes would be *forced* to bear more than their fair proportion of the burdens which they had no part in creating. Doherty went on to repeat his arguments of the September address to the English spinners, that only by a complete union of the trade could they hope to resist reductions successfully, for only when the whole of the hands at one factory were combined could they equal the power of their master; and moreover when the honourable masters had finally forgotten those feelings of superiority engendered by the late and odious Combination Laws, they would welcome a *general* combination to prevent reductions, which harmed fair masters and the trade of the country generally as well as the workmen.

On the subject of the specific regulations agreed to at the Isle of Man, Doherty could not resist saying that 'they are, perhaps not such as may be found to give complete satisfaction to all districts and all parties'. However, 'it should be remembered, that the persons who framed these regulations, had no experience to guide them in the foundation of such a system', and any defects could be remedied at the next annual meeting. Meanwhile, it was essential that all workmen should forget 'squabbles about trifles' and make every effort to render their general union successful, for the benefit of both themselves and fair employers, so as to prevent 'the best prices from being reduced, and obtain better for the worst', which was 'all the most sanguine amongst us have looked for'. Doherty concluded by wishing success to 'this our first attempt to form a general and *effective* union'.[21]

Apart from being a remarkable and virtually unique document in recording the deliberations of obscure workmen in forming the constitution of an early trade union, the *Report* is also interesting in showing the compromise worked out between Doherty's hopes of a centralised union and the sectional feelings of the local spinners' clubs. The district committees retained most of their independence in financial matters, collecting their own subscriptions and

D*

distributing their various friendly society benefits; but the federated national committees had some theoretical control over decisions to strike and the keeping of accounts. Two critical factors in the attainment of skilled club status were accepted in principle—strict entry controls into the trade and unrestricted mobility between the various districts. But the adoption of three national committees made it unlikely that one central policy could emerge as a counterweight to the interests of individual districts. Doherty's position itself was equivocal: as secretary to the whole union, he could only be responsible to the annual meeting, but his authority was indeterminate, and in any case, since most spinners' clubs continued to act independently, his activities were still mainly among the Manchester spinners.

Although transport and communication difficulties did make the establishment of a national union throughout a particular trade a formidable task, national organisations in other trades were successfully launched and firmly established in this period, such as the Journeymen Steam Engine Makers in 1826 and the Carpenters and Joiners at a London meeting of delegates in July 1827.[22] Very little notice was taken by the authorities at first of the spinners' experiment in national trade unionism. There is no contemporary reference to the December conference in the Home Office papers, and in the provincial press it was merely recorded that 'a meeting of delegates from the Spinners' Union took place at the Isle of Man last week. The council or convention was composed of two members from every district in England, Scotland and Ireland, where cotton manufacture is carried on. A string of resolutions was adopted, and they separated to meet again as early as expedient.'[23] Doherty's statement to the 1838 Select Committee on Combinations that a copy of his report of the Isle of Man conference was sent to Sir Robert Peel, the Home Secretary, 'in order that there might be no doubt as to the tendency and objects of the combinations', must therefore be questioned, at least for the period immediately after the meeting.[24]

It was not until Major-General Bouverie, the commander of military forces in the north of England, wrote to Phillips, an under-secretary at the Home Office, at the time of a strike by Ashton spinners in May 1830, that the authorities began to take an interest in the spinners' proceedings. Bouverie believed that Peel probably knew of the existence of a 'grand General Union of all the Operative Spinners of the United Kingdom', which had met the previous year in the Isle of Man; but if this was not so, he enclosed a copy of the December resolutions that he had received from Lt. Col. Shaw, of Manchester, and added that it would be for Peel to judge if the nearly simultaneous turn-outs of spinners at Bolton and Ashton were not under the direction of the leaders of this Association and part of a 'widely-organised plan'.[25] On receiving this letter, Peel instructed his under-secretary to write to Lieutenant-Governor Smelt of the Isle of Man for all the information he possessed of the December meeting, including the names of those who proposed the resolutions, the numbers who attended, etc., and of the intended meeting later in the year; and Phillips transmitted a letter as directed on 20 May.[26] Smelt's reply was dated 23 May and was a remarkable illustration of the lack of interest shown by the governing classes in the spinners' activities at this time. 'I have to state that no such meeting took place in this Island to my knowledge, nor do I believe it possible that any such meeting could have taken place without my knowledge, nor have I the least intimation except that conveyed in your letter that a meeting of this kind is to be held this year. I am not aware of any circumstances which could have given rise to the statement made to Sir Robert Peel on this subject.'[27]

Confirmation of at least the effects of the spinners' delegate conference was received at this time in a letter to Peel from the borough-reeve and constables of Manchester, dated 26 May.[28] They stated that the combinations of workmen, long acknowledged in this district as an evil difficult to counteract, were now so systematic that it was necessary to report their most alarming features. A committee of delegates of the operative spinners of the three kingdoms had established an annual assembly in the Isle of Man to direct the proceedings of the general body towards their employers; orders were sent to the respective districts and sub-committees, by private circulars previously agreed upon. The 'most implicit obedience' was shown to these orders, and a weekly levy of 1d per head 'cheerfully paid', by which a great sum was raised and chiefly used to support strikers with 10s per week. General strikes were eschewed as impolitic, and instead they attacked individuals or districts singly, which were powerless to resist because of the amount of capital at risk. Although they professed that their only means was persuasion, in fact their plan was pursued by organised intimidation and assaults on those who desired to work. Yet the laws were unable to touch them, while their organisation was so good that the perpetrators of damage to property had usually dispersed before assistance arrived. The letter concluded with a warning that the 'general union' of all trades then being formed for mutual assistance in strikes necessitated decisive measures, or peace and prosperity would be destroyed; an identical letter had been written to the Prime Minister, Wellington.

Despite the alarm of his correspondents, Peel directed Phillips to reply on 28 May in terms which betrayed considerable scepticism. They were asked to send up any evidence of an 'annual assembly of a Committee of Delegates in the Isle of Man', including when it took place and the names of attenders, and also a copy of the printed circular issued by this assembly, promulgating orders to the districts and sub-committees.[29] One of the constables, Robert Sharp, patiently answered that the principal evidence for the meeting was Doherty's report as secretary, which had been published in the form of a book, a copy of which he now enclosed. 'Doherty and Foster', he wrote, 'are well known in this town', but added erroneously that Macvicker was also from Manchester. However, other verifications of the meeting could be found in the references to it in the *Returns of the Friendly Associated Cotton Spinners*, a weekly paper containing the receipts, disbursements and other information about the Manchester spinners' union, and, also, since December 1829, notices concerning the spinners' grand general union. The expenditure for the week ending 30 November included £8 for the deputation to the Isle of Man, while on 16 January 1830, it was announced that the printing of the report of the proceedings in the Isle of Man would be paid 'from the District Fund', or fund formed by the penny subscriptions. As late as 8 May 1830, a regular sum was still being charged 'to the Districts' for printing these reports. In one of the *Returns*, the date of which Sharp did not mention, the application of the penny subscriptions was described as being to 'a common fund, by which the value of Labour, or rather, the prices of spinning may be kept up throughout the whole of the three Kingdoms'. Sharp also regarded the establishment by Doherty in March of the *United Trades Co-operative Journal*, organ of the general trades' union, as a continuation of the policy originally laid down for the spinners to start their own newspaper, and concluded by avowing that there was 'strong reason to believe' that the meeting, advertised at the first spinners' conference to take place at the Isle of Man on Whit Monday, had in fact been held.[30] Final corroboration came from Lt. Col. Shaw, to whom the Manchester authorities in their first letter of 26 May had advised the Home Office to apply for information. Shaw wrote on 9 June that the Cotton Spinners' Union, formed at the Isle of Man, was becoming only a branch of the 'United Trades General Union', but that if the latter became fully established, its rules would probably be very similar, 'as the same leaders influence both'.[31]

The following day, Phillips wrote to Smelt that Peel had learnt that the spinners' delegate conference had met at the inn of Mr and Mrs Heelis, in Ramsey, on 5–9 December 1829, and therefore again desired that all information concerning that meeting and its intended successor on Whit Monday, 1830, should be sent.[32] On 12 June Smelt replied that the High Bailiff of Ramsey 'had ascertained from an innkeeper in that town that fifteen persons who had arrived in the Island during the course of the last week had assembled every morning for five or six days in a room in his house to transact some business; that he understood they were operative spinners from Manchester, Bolton, Oldham, Glasgow and Belfast'. They had departed on 9 or 10 June, but as none of the innkeeper's family attended the meetings, the nature of the proceedings was unknown. However, in the same letter, a later report from the High Bailiff disclosed that 'he had had an interview with one of these men who is still in the Island. He describes himself to be "John Doherty of Manchester, official secretary to the delegates of the operative spinners", and avowed their object in meeting to be the preventing of a reduction in wages . . . he also stated that they had entered into resolutions but that no political subject was allowed to be discussed at their meetings . . . that they had a similar meeting in this Island in December and that resolutions were then entered into, 500 copies of which were printed and published—that the resolutions which they had entered into this year should also be printed and that when printed he intended to transmit a copy to Sir Robert Peel'.[33]

Further information about the spinners' second conference is found in a similar correspondence towards the end of 1830, after Phillips had asked for Lt. Governor Smelt's comments on intelligence made to Peel 'that there is an unusual concourse of strangers at Ramsey in the Isle of Man and that they are there as it is supposed as a sort of central committee to promote sedition in the three portions of the United Kingdom'.[34] Smelt replied on 4 November that he had sent two investigators to Ramsey, who had found the town 'unusually free from the presence of strangers of any description'. However, they had lodged at the inn of Josiah Heelis, where the spinners' meeting had been held in June, and on interrogating him, 'they found that he did not expect a meeting to take place at this time, but that if any such meeting was in contemplation he expected to receive as he had on a former occasion a letter from John Doherty of Manchester to prepare accommodation for the persons who were to meet'. Mr Heelis, who had been a factory overseer at Bolton and seemed well-acquainted with the nature of workmen's meetings, also told the investigators that the June meeting was to have been held at Carlisle,[35] but the Isle of Man was preferred because it provided an easier and cheaper communication with the Glasgow and Belfast spinners.

> Mr Heelis also stated that the same individuals did not assemble in June last (with the exception of Doherty) who had met the year before—and that Doherty himself did not appear to know the names of the persons when they first met, but enquired for them by the names of the town from whence they were expected, viz. Is Bolton here? Is Glasgow here? etc. Mr Heelis did not now appear to know the names of any of these men excepting Doherty and another whom they called Mr James of Glasgow. They assembled in a room in his house during four or five hours every morning in private, dined together, drank a pint of beer and a glass of spirits each, the expense of which was defrayed by Doherty, any additional expense was paid by them individually. Heelis . . . expressed his belief . . . that the object of the meetings was to effect an assimilation of wages.

He showed the investigators the letter which he had received from Doherty previous to the June meeting, and promised to inform the authorities if he was given a similar notice in the future. Smelt concluded by asking if he should act to prevent any such conference taking place, to which the Home Office replied on 10 November that he should allow it to meet and try 'to discover the real objects which the individuals assembled have in view'.[36]

The accounts of the spinners' conferences of December 1829 and June 1830, together with apparently concrete evidence of the influence of their grand general union in the form of spinners' strikes at Bolton and Ashton, and the even more alarming prospect of a general union of the trades being established, induced the authorities to consider seriously taking counter-measures in the summer of 1830. On 21 and 22 June Phillips wrote to the borough-reeve and constables of Manchester and to Major-General Bouverie respectively, detailing the information received from the Lieutenant-Governor of the Isle of Man on the recent spinners' delegate assembly at Ramsey, of which the Home Office had first been given intimation in Bouverie's letter of 26 May and Sharp's of 7 June. On 22 June Phillips informed the Manchester officers that Peel had referred these letters to the opinion of the Law Officers, who had pronounced, 'that the Conspiracy detailed in your communications and in the documents which accompanied them, is an offence at Common Law, and is not within the protection of the Statute 6 Geo. IV c. 129, and that any act of insult or injury to deter workmen who are not members of the Union, or who are disposed to renounce its authority, from their employment, is liable to be prosecuted as misdemeanour at Common Law, notwithstanding the Statute gives to J.P.'s a summary power of conviction, and of imprisonment for three months in such cases'. However, it would not be possible to convict the Isle of Man delegates of a conspiracy in this country, without satisfactory evidence of some overt acts by them of carrying the conspiracy into effect in England. The practice of 'piquetting' might be a sufficient act, but to connect it with a conspiracy in the Isle of Man, it would be necessary to prove that it was either directed or approved by the delegates, that some agent authorised by them was employed in it, and that some payment was made by their order to maintain the persons who practised it. The Law Officers therefore concluded that 'it does not appear at present, that sufficient evidence had been found'.[37]

Of the actual discussions at the June conference, no record has survived. In fact, it was later alleged by certain Bolton leaders of the National Association opposed to the establishment of the *Voice of the People* that Doherty had been ordered to draw up a report of the proceedings of the spinners' meeting and been paid 10s per day for his trouble, but that no report had appeared four months' later, in spite of persistent complaints from the country districts.[38] However, from the report of spies employed by the Manchester police to attend a meeting of trades' delegates at the end of June to finalise the constitution of the National Association, it is clear that at the meeting of spinners' delegates in the Isle of Man, 'all was settled for the formation of the National Association'.[39] In addition, the current turn-outs of spinners at Bolton and Ashton were discussed, to both of which the official backing of the Spinners' Grand General Union was given. And Foster and McGowan were appointed to organise support for the union.[40]

The chief policy of the spinners' general union was the equalisation of wages as far as possible in every district, to remove the masters' pretext for making repeated reductions; but it is difficult to see what authority the federal body had over its constituents, whose actions appear still to have been influenced mainly by local considerations and circumstances. 'It was regarded as the function of the district to keep individual employers up to the district level, and that of the amalgamation to prevent district reductions and bring districts into line.'[41]

The first district in which the influence of the new spinners' federation was tested was Bolton, where a dispute arose as a direct consequence of the enforcement of the new list of prices at Manchester in October 1829. After compromise reductions had been agreed with one or two masters,[42] serious strikes broke out in March against the two large firms of Bollings and Ashworths, each owning several mills, which were insistent upon reducing piece prices from the level of 1823 to that of the new Manchester list, except that, whereas Ashworths were determined to make the Manchester reduction of $1\frac{1}{2}$ per cent for every twelve spindles above 300, Bollings were prepared to continue the 1 per cent which had been the practice in Bolton since 1823. Overall, piece prices would be reduced by 10 to 25 per cent.[43]

In the first week of the strike, both firms brought complaints at the local petty sessions against their apprentices or 'young spinners', who had been hired for terms of up to three years at prices 10 to 15 per cent less than those paid to the regular spinners and had left their work before the expiration of their contracts. It is clear from the legal proceedings that the resolution passed at the Isle of Man on the question of piecers spinning was already having some effect, in that the 'young spinners' concerned were members of the union and had been instructed 'to stand up for wages'. Moreover, the custom of allowing piecers to spin while the spinner was away from his wheels had now 'been forbidden by the union', which was endeavouring to stop the training and recruitment of such cheap juvenile spinners.[44]

Both firms were soon enabled to restart their mills with spinners from other districts, but particularly from among those Manchester fine spinners who had been unable to find employment after the end of their 1829 strike. In consequence, there were numerous violent attacks on 'knobsticks' and a plethora of assault charges; in one case a large gang almost destroyed the house of a 'knobstick', who was seriously injured. Special constables had to be sworn in and military forces were held in readiness.[45]

Meanwhile, support was organised for the turn-outs by the Bolton branch of the general union of trades, which had been launched by Doherty to resist wages reductions after the defeat of the Manchester spinners' strike in October 1829. On the evening of 14 April a meeting of members was convened at the 'Church Tavern', attended by 'several delegates from the country'.[46] Marshall, the secretary of the Bolton district of the general union, spoke of the progress that their association was making, especially among bleachers and calico-printers, and asserted that the striking spinners should be supported in their present contest. Resolutions were eventually carried expressing their 'indignation and alarm' at the 'cruel and unnecessary attempts of the masters to reduce earnings to starvation point', and determining that, while the funds of the general union could not yet be opened, a voluntary weekly subscription be entered into by members to support the present turn-out spinners. An appeal 'To the Working-Classes of Bolton' was issued by Marshall, pursuant to the orders of the meeting, together with an address to the general public by the spinners' club.[47]

These activities were too late, however, to prevent Ashworths' spinners submitting to defeat, towards the end of April. The firm had succeeded in getting many new hands and forced all their employees to sign a document renouncing trade unionism.[48] But the turn-out at Bollings continued amid unabated violence. Strikers were reported as attacking special constables defending the mills, throwing explosive canisters into the houses of overlookers, and 'walking in military order with sticks . . . and parading' round Bollings' factories. On this occasion at least, the *Manchester Guardian* was scarcely exaggerating when it condemned 'the outrages which the turn-outs are almost daily committing, for the purpose of preventing people from following their employment'.[49]

The strikers were encouraged by continued assistance from other trades. On 26 May Marshall told a meeting at Ashton-under-Lyne, convened to form a branch of the National Association for the Protection of Labour, that he was proud of the spirit of union fast spreading among the Bolton trades, as exemplified by contributions from the bleachers, block printers and many other trades. And early in June, when the strike had lasted fourteen weeks, the men were reported to be 'in high spirits' after hearing that 'all England, Ireland and Scotland'—presumably a reference to the second general delegate meeting of the cotton spinners recently held at Ramsey—'have pledged themselves to support the contest'.[50]

Unfortunately, by this time disputes were tending to spread to other areas, with further outbreaks of violence. At Chorley, where the spinners of Messrs Lightoller and Co. came out on strike against wages-undercutting, a can of gunpowder was exploded by night down the house chimney of an overlooker, with whom several 'knobsticks' were staying. And at Ashton a parcel of gunpowder was sent to the home of a master spinner, but fortunately failed to detonate.[51] The *Manchester Guardian*, reporting these 'diabolical' incidents, blamed them on the union :

> . . . we fear the inference must be, that these diabolical attempts were not the acts of isolated individuals, but that they were known beforehand to some of the parties by whom the proceedings of the combined Spinners in different parts of the country have been directed . . . At all events, there is no doubt that many of the outrages committed by turn-outs in different parts of the country have been known to, and approved of by their committees; and we have been credibly informed, that there is every reason to believe that the outrageous attack upon the houses and persons of some of the spinners of Messrs Ashworth, of Turton, a few weeks ago, was deliberately planned and organised by a committee sitting at Bolton and, that sums of money were paid by the Union fund to those who were engaged in it.[52]

Doherty replied with a leading article the following week in the *United Trades' Co-operative Journal*. The allegations, he asserted, were not made to assist in bringing the perpetrators of the crime to justice, but as a vicious attack on the Association of Journeymen Cotton Spinners, which the paper had long pursued 'like a prey', to ingratiate itself with the party who desired to crush the Association and every other means the workmen had of defending and improving themselves. He challenged the editor to publish any items of proof he possessed and the names of his 'credible informants', and concluded by declaring that he knew nothing of the incidents; if there had been any 'plot' their opponents, who wished to discredit the workmen, were the more likely participants.[53] Doherty's views were reinforced by protests from the Bolton spinners' committee, who vehemently denied that they had ever sanctioned or encouraged such outrages, pointing out that in the rules of their union, ever since its establishment in 1795, they had discountenanced acts of violence or wrongful insubordination; they, like Doherty, blamed such incidents on spies and 'designing' employers who wished to secure the re-enactment of the Combination Laws.[54]

The *Guardian*, not surprisingly, remained unimpressed. In another leading article, the paper repeated its charges that the spinners' combination was responsible for the recent outrages in Bolton, and condemned generally 'the beatings and vitriolisings, and barbarities of different kinds, which, at different times and in different parts of the country, have been brought home to parties of turn-out spinners'. In response, on 10 July the Bolton spinners' union declared that 'having been maligned' by the paper, they intended 'in a short time to submit their case to his Majesty's Government'. But the *Guardian* regarded this as a 'whimsical' gesture and threatened in return 'some disclosures' about these outrages.[55]

By this time, however, the strike was drawing to a close. Throughout June there were reports of intermittent assaults on 'knobsticks' working for Bollings, followed by further arrests, but by the end of the month a spinners' deputation was trying to negotiate a settlement. The strike finally ended on 21 July, after lasting nineteen weeks, when the men returned to work, having been forced to submit fully to the Manchester list, apparently extended to include the coarse numbers.[56]

This defeat was a considerable blow to the expectations of the cotton spinners, who had been led to believe that the formation of their Grand General Union would put an end to humiliations such as those suffered at Stockport and Manchester in 1829. Although the administrative details of the strike were organised by the local Bolton spinners' society, close contact was maintained with the national committee of the spinners' general union in Manchester. In fact, the Bolton branch of the National Association made Doherty's alleged neglect of his duties as secretary of the spinners' union at this time one of the reasons for their subsequent opposition to the establishment of *The Voice of the People*, with Doherty as editor. At a protest meeting in the Queen Anne Assembly Room, Bolton, on 16 November, one of the speakers, H. Rothwell, asserted that:

> The Bolton district [of the spinners' union] expected letters from him [Doherty] in the early part of every week, during a certain troublesome period [the spinners' strike]; but they generally were from four or five days earlier dated than the *Post Office mark*, and frequently never came to hand. He scarcely ever attended the delegates at the time appointed, and on one occasion he, the speaker, recollected that Mr Doherty only came to Bolton at one o'clock in the afternoon instead of nine o'clock in the morning, and the consequence was, that the country delegates had to return home before half the business was done . . . [On another occasion] he, Mr Rothwell, went over to Manchester on a Friday, and he found that Mr Doherty was absent on other business (for they must bear in mind that he held a plurality of livings) and there was his assistant, who knew not how to act, for want of Mr Doherty's instructions.[57]

But Doherty could not fairly be blamed for failure of the Bolton strike, which was mainly attributable to the employers' determination and their ability to recruit new hands, because of the trade depression and surplus of spinners. Nevertheless, it was a serious blow to his schemes and he admitted that it led to recriminations and despair. 'Many persons therefore began to despond, and consider that unions to protect wages were useless; this was another example added to an already great number, where such unions had failed to accomplish their intended object.' It was amid this mood of despondency that the Grand General Union of Cotton Spinners appointed two of their ablest men—Patrick McGowan of Glasgow and Thomas Foster of Manchester—to visit every constituent district to remove the considerable mutual suspicion between them, and try to establish the full and generous spirit of union and confidence among them, which was essential for the districts to co-operate towards the equalisation of prices.[58]

At the same time as the strike at Bolton, there was a series of disputes in the Hyde, Ashton and Stalybridge districts, with individual masters whom the men alleged were paying wages less than the average rates in that neighbourhood. Strikes in Hyde during February and March 1830 were notable for the fact that many masters gave support to the workmen in their efforts to prevent undercutting—co-operation of a kind which Doherty applauded as a model for future action.[59] A similar campaign was started at Ashton-under-Lyne, particularly against William Heginbottom, but his opposition was more resolute, feelings ran high, and in addition to the usual assaults on 'knobsticks', Heginbottom's house was attacked with stones and he and his family narrowly escaped death from a 'gunpowder plot'.[60] This, coinciding with a similar incident at Chorley, increased the public outcry,[61] and large rewards for information were offered by Heginbottom himself, the local masters, and the Home Office. Newspapers generally put the blame on the spinners' union, though the local operatives' society, like that at Bolton, indignantly denied the accusations and itself offered a £250 reward. Doherty also reacted angrily in the *Journal*, while the Manchester spinners' union held an extraordinary general meeting, which issued a resolution, signed by Doherty as secretary, expressing their outrage at the allegations of the *Guardian* and suggesting that the Ashton outrage was 'a deep laid and deadly plot against the character and *liberties* of the working-classes', perhaps even concocted in the *Guardian* office.[62]

Despite the large rewards, the guilty parties were never discovered, and therefore the complicity of either invidual spinners or their local club was never examined in a court of law. Events in the Ashton spinners' strike of December 1830 to February 1831 suggest that there was a militant faction within the spinners' union there disposed to use violence,[63] but no definite conclusion can be reached in this case. The strike itself appears to have petered out, when Heginbottom refused to take back his old workmen, but agreed to give the new hands an increase equal to that for which the former had left their employment.[64] It had been the concern mainly of the local spinners' society, the Grand General Union being involved only indirectly, despite Major-General Bouverie's fears that the simultaneous strikes at Bolton and Ashton were the result of a conspiracy initiated in the Isle of Man in December 1829.[65]

No doubt local societies were strongly influenced by the general union's policy of wages equalisation, but they were mostly responding to attempts by local employers to bring down piece-rates, on account of trade depression and competition from low-wage areas. For many years master spinners at Stalybridge, for example, had been paying rates considerably below those of their neighbours: whilst rates there were about 3s 0d to 3s 5d per 1,000 hanks of No. 40s, many Ashton masters were paying 4s 2d. During 1830, therefore, the Ashton millowners made repeated attempts to bring down their prices. On 21 April they met to discuss a general reduction, but could not agree on a mutually satisfactory offer.[66] Several individual firms, however, tried to enforce reductions—hence the strikes of the following months. In July, therefore, the Ashton masters assembled again and determined to reduce their prices to 3s 9d per 1,000 hanks for No. 40s and other prices accordingly.

This general threat, which, if successfully carried through, would inevitably have widespread repercussions, caused the general union to become more directly involved. It was agreed by 'the committee of the different districts'[67] to convene a meeting on Ashton Moss on 24 July, when about 4,000 spinners from Ashton, Dukinfield, Stalybridge, Mossley, Lees, Oldham, and Crompton attended; Doherty and Foster came from Manchester, and two delegates were also expected from Scotland, but did not arrive in time. Betts, the local spinners' secretary, moved the first resolution, attributing the proposed reduction not to the state of the market, but to 'a principle of avarice'. Doherty then submitted that 'to reduce the price of labour in any town, when the price in such towns is under the average prices paid in the United Kingdom, is a direct robbery of the comforts of the working-classes'. And finally Foster moved that the late reductions in Stockport and Manchester were 'entirely owing' to the low rates in Hyde, Stalybridge and Ashton, and a further abatement in the latter districts would cause similar results. All three resolutions were passed unanimously.[68]

The 'committee of the different districts' subsequently appointed a deputation, comprising Betts of Ashton, Foster of Manchester, and McGowan of Glasgow, to visit those masters who intended to reduce wages. Their visits, on Monday, 26 July, were followed by lengthy negotiations between the two sides in Manchester the following day, as a result of which the masters agreed temporarily to withdraw the proposed reduction, in order to give the union an opportunity of carrying out its policy of wages equalisation, particularly in the Stalybridge area.[69]

Prospects there did not initially look very favourable. According to Doherty, Stalybridge had long been noted as one of the lowest paid districts in the country, the workmen there were 'besotted and enslaved', and very weak in their support of trade unionism.[70] But they were now stimulated into action. Even before the notice of the reduction at Ashton was given, Betts had addressed a letter 'To the Spinners and Rovers of Stalybridge and its vicinity' on 13 July, urging them to end their state of vassalage, under which their wages were as much as 30 or 40 per cent less than the average rates in the country.[71] On the evening of Saturday, 7 August, a meeting of 5 to 7,000 spinners and rovers of Stalybridge and the neighbouring districts was held on high ground at the edge of the township. The leaders of the local spinners' society, together with the agents of the spinners' general union, McGowan and Foster, had chosen the factories of two firms, Orrell and Lees, as the first to be turned-out.[72] After Betts had taken the chair, McGowan stated that it was time the Stalybridge workmen took action to equalise their prices with other districts, and that the whole union would support them in their contest. Doherty then reiterated this encouragement and urged them to acquire knowledge, to be temperate, and to insist on having such a remuneration for their labour as would enable them to get plenty of good food, decent clothing, comfortable lodging and education for their children. Finally, Foster spoke in a similar fashion and concluded by declaring that he also intended to bring some Stalybridge masters to justice for infringing the Factory Act.[73]

Orrell's spinners turned out on Monday, 16 August, on the expiration of their notice, and those of Lees a week later.[74] The authorities were immediately alarmed at the strength of the workmen's position. During the summer, military forces were deployed in the Manchester area to deal with the increasing threat from spreading trade-union organisation and 'turn-outs', and on 24 August Lt. Col. Shaw wrote from Manchester to Major-General Bouverie informing him of the danger of a general turn-out in the Ashton-Stalybridge-Hyde area; he considered that the spinners' union was so strong that the use of force was ultimately inevitable if new hands were introduced. He was impressed by the workers' unity and militancy, and added anxiously: 'The excitement caused by the Revolution in France is greater than I should have anticipated: they talk a great deal of their power of putting down the military and constables.' Two days later Bouverie transmitted this letter to the Home Office, adding that he hoped these fears would prove without foundation, 'but as it appears to be in the power of the leaders of the working-classes to turn out at any time any number of them, it is impossible not to feel the necessity of being prepared'. Consequently he had asked Lt. Col. Shaw to interview the local magistrates, and through them to try and impress the masters with the impolicy of any hasty measures, like the sudden introduction of new hands, which would lead to violence by the strikers.[75] The Stalybridge authorities were clearly convinced, either by this interview or by appearances, that disturbances were about to take place, as they gave notice to a great number of householders to attend on 27 August to be sworn in as special constables.[76] Peel, for his part, agreed that precipitate action by the masters must be avoided, but also informed Bouverie that no weakness should be shown in face of the demands of the combined men, or the use of physical force and the influence of combination through fear would be confirmed.[77]

Because the same individuals were frequently prominent in the spinners' union and the general trades' union at both local and national levels, it was virtually impossible to resolve in what particular capacity a person was acting on every occasion, and the authorities were inclined to ascribe any action by the workers to the increasing influence of the National Association for the Protection of Labour, the rules of which had been formally ratified at a general delegate meeting in Manchester in June, 1830.[78] On 29 August Lt. Col. Shaw again wrote to Bouverie, stating that the position in Ashton and Stalybridge was still unfavourable because of the 'complete domination' of the working-classes by the 'leaders of the union of trades'. He had been able to discuss the situation with leading manufacturers and magistrates and to counsel prudence, but he feared that a crisis was in the end unavoidable because the union was taking mills two-by-two and demanding 4s 2d. When Bouverie sent on this letter to Peel on 1 September, he declared that he did not expect open violence, as it was decidedly in the interests of the union leaders to avoid it; they were more likely to try and gain their ends by intimidating any new hands taken on, which the police would find more difficult to counteract.[79] In his reply on 6 September, Peel urged that the authorities should seek a chance to enforce the law against picketing, or persuade the employers to indict individuals for conspiracy to obstruct the free employment of labour.[80]

But by this time the strike was already over. The spinners who had turned out were supported for three weeks with 10s per week from their union and half-wages to each of their piecers.[81] On 4 September both firms offered to concede about half the men's demands by advancing their prices to 3s 11d per 1,000 hanks. This the spinners accepted and returned to their work on Monday, 6 September. Lt. Col. Shaw wrote to Peel that he considered that the main reasons for the masters' agreeing to compromise were the strength of the union of trades, the picketing, and the state of excitement following the July Revolution in France, but the outcome was unfortunate for the encouragement it would give to the union of trades.[82] Certainly, in the *Journal*, Doherty rejoiced that the benefits of union had been demonstrated at Stalybridge of all places, for the advance obtained from Orrell and Lees had been taken by the other employers in the district as a model, and all had granted a similar increase without exception. In addition, he gave particular thanks to those Ashton masters who had consented to withdraw their proposed reduction of 14 July, to afford time to compel others to give an advance. This proved that, if the workmen had a strong union, employers would co-operate with them to enforce an equalisation of prices, which would remove the 'reprehensible spirit of ruinous competition', from which both honourable masters and workmen suffered. To ensure that the example of masters and men should be copied elsewhere, Doherty cautioned all workmen, while contending for their rights, not to forget that they were servants, or to assume a haughty tone inconsistent with the dignity and fair authority of employers.[83]

On 2 October, however, the *Manchester Guardian* reported that the spinners in the Ashton neighbourhood were continuing their forward policy. 'In consequence of the measures that have been taken by the spinners and the trades' unions,' it was stated, 'an advance has taken place in the wages of 600 spinners residing at Ashton, Dukinfield and Hyde amounting on an average, to 6s a week for each hand; the number benefited is likely soon to be increased. Meetings are held almost weekly, and a good understanding is said to exist between the workmen and their employers.'[84] But, with 'the spirit of combination' so rife in the district,[85] the 'good understanding' between employers and men rapidly evaporated and by November the master spinners of Ashton, Stalybridge and Dukinfield were ready to join together to enforce a general reduction of wages.[86]

Although the most serious strikes by the spinners in the summer of 1830 were in Bolton and Ashton, there were also stoppages in several other districts, in which the Grand General Union or the National Association were involved to varying degrees. There was a bitter dispute with Samuel Stocks, of Heaton Mersey, near Stockport, over an alleged reduction of his spinners' piece prices.[87] At a meeting of the working classes of Stockport at the 'Bull's Head' on 14 July to form a branch of the National Association, addressed by Foster, Doherty, and Longson, Thomas Worsley denounced Stocks as an 'oppressor and plunderer of the poor', who, in addition to reducing wages, also operated an atrocious system of truck.[88] In a letter to the *Stockport Advertiser,* however, Stocks rejected the charges against him and condemned the 'impudent, busy meddling' of 'such men as Worsley and Doherty' between himself and his workpeople; no combination of masters or men had ever done good, 'and the sooner Mr Doherty, Mr Worsley and Mr Foster, and all other *Misters* begin to work with their own hands, and *produce* something of use to their fellow-creatures, the better . . ., for *they only add to the number of those who do not work'*, and would continue to be a burden, 'as long as they can amuse you with fine speeches, and get their *salaries*'.[89]

Stocks also sent his letter to the *United Trades' Co-operative Journal,* and Doherty inserted the majority of it in the editions of 31 July and 7 August, declaring that he wished to see all disputes between masters and men settled by reason and argument. However, he interspersed his own comments to demonstrate that Stocks was, in fact, making unjustifiable reductions. Of the aspersions against himself, Doherty denied that he had even alluded to Stocks in his Stockport speech. Nevertheless, the conduct of an employer in reducing his workmen's wages was perfectly open to comment or animadversion, and the workers had every right to employ one of their fellows to contend for their privileges before a person confessedly much their superior in knowledge and ingenuity. 'We by no means wish to see the working-classes rely for assistance, on any other person or thing than themselves', but they were frequently worsted in interviews with their employers simply because of the latter's greater debating skill. Hence, Stocks' real opposition to what he called 'impudent, busy, meddling interference' was based on a fear that, if confronted by men of equal intelligence, he would be obliged, from the rottenness of his cause, to cower before them.[90] Unfortunately, the outcome of this dispute was not recorded, but the men did succeed in securing convictions and fines against Stocks for paying wages in goods.[91]

The Grand General Union also took an active role in a strike at Carlisle which began in September 1830. The Carlisle spinners had been represented at the Isle of Man conference in December 1829, the town had been considered as a possible location for the second delegate meeting in June 1830, and the local club had kept up a correspondence with their Glasgow and Manchester colleagues since the formation of the Grand General Union. This strike was of spinners in the mills of Jacob Cowen & Sons, either in an effort to bring up piece prices, or in resistance to a reduction. It is not clear whether it was initiated by the general union, in accordance with the policy of equalising prices, or whether it originated in local action. At any rate, Patrick McGowan and Thomas Foster visited the town toward the end of their 'missionary' tour of the district, addressing a meeting there on 20 September, on the eve of the strike, and Doherty gave support to the men in the *Journal*, threatening to use 'the whole force of their extensive union' against these 'selfish and unprincipled violators of the workmen's rights' if the alleged reductions were not withdrawn.[92] On the other side, the *Carlisle Patriot* followed the common line of trying to discredit Doherty and other agitators, who 'travel about at the expense of their fellow-workmen, creating ill-blood wherever they go between masters and men'; these men 'will work no more . . . so long as they can prey upon the industry of any portion of their fellow-workmen'.[93] Despite the support of the general union, however, the strike ultimately ended in defeat in mid-November, following the arrest of nine ringleaders.[94]

At the same time as the start of the Carlisle turn-out, it was reported in the *Journal* that the spinners employed by three Macclesfield firms were expected to strike during the following week, because of a recent reduction. In fact, this strike was also in line with the Grand General Union's policy of wages equalisation, for a fortnight later the Macclesfield spinners were said to have gained an advance in their prices from 3s 9d to 4s 2d per 1,000 hanks, which price it had been the aim both of the negotiations with the Ashton masters in July to preserve, and of the Stalybridge strike at the end of August to achieve.[95]

Amid all this activity in the other spinning districts and the exciting developments of the Grand General Union and the general trades' union, the Manchester cotton spinners were engaged in a period of consolidation following their defeat in 1829, which had provided Doherty with the pretext for his enlarged projects. He continued to be their secretary despite holding the same office in the spinners' general union and in the National Association, as well as editing the *Journal*, most of 1830, during the first ten months of which there were no reported turn-outs by the Manchester spinners. Nevertheless, they continued to meet regularly, to maintain their subscriptions and publish the weekly *Returns*, and to hold intermittent communications with their masters. A proposed reduction by Messrs Faulkner & Co. in February 1830 was averted by a threatened strike and by support from some of the biggest master spinners, who preferred to work short-time rather than reduce wages further.[96] But the spinners continued to suffer from the employment of females and from progressive piece-rate abatements as the size of mules increased, both of which practices the 1829 strike had failed to check.

In the first number of the *Journal*, on 6 March, a letter was printed from 'a poor man, a spinner with a wife and five children', who had lost his employment at 25 to 30s per week to a female spinner, who would be paid 12 to 14s per week. Doherty commented that this practice was harmful both to the females, who must perform fatiguing labour in unwholesome conditions which made even male spinners old men by forty, and also to the workmen who were thereby supplanted. Thus their natural roles were reversed, through the avarice of greedy employers, and 'the miserable father has to take the place of the mother', looking after the children at home instead of providing for them at work.[97]

Respecting the distress caused by this system, therefore, and by the further reductions that were being made on large mules, the Manchester fine spinners held a general meeting at the beginning of April and agreed to an 'Address to the Master Fine Mule Spinners of Manchester', which was written and signed by Doherty as secretary. It began by hoping that the operatives' 'respectful representations' would receive more attention than during the strike of the previous year, and that the proposals of employers like David Holt at that time, that masters and men should co-operate to prevent reductions once the March list was accepted, should not be forgotten.[98] The chief complaint was that several members of the employers' association had adopted 'the practice of employing boys and women spinners in the place of men . . . at a reduction of from five to ten hanks in the lb'. In addition, the men's warnings about the March list, which made a reduction of $1\frac{1}{2}$ per cent for every additional twelve spindles above 300 per mule, were proving justified. 'It gives an advantage to one class of employers over another, which cannot fail eventually to be ruinous to the oldest, the largest, and most expensive establishments in the town.' In fact the percentage ought to go the other way, for the larger mules required more manual strength from the worker and afforded greater profit for the master. Before the old firms were driven from the trade by new capitalists employing the largest possible machines, Doherty urged the masters to co-operate with the men in enforcing the same prices for all sizes of wheels, as at Glasgow, and suggested that they should meet together to discuss the question.[99]

This address was sent to G. E. Aubrey, the secretary of the Masters' Association, who returned a peremptory reply to Doherty on 8 April. He had no instructions to call a meeting of the Association, but had always understood its principle to be that 'no third party, whether of workmen or masters, has a right to interfere between a master and workman'. Doherty commented on this letter that the fine masters had not followed this rule during the late strike, when they had persuaded the master coarse-spinners to turn their men out, unless they withdrew support from their brethren who were on strike against an 'enormous wage reduction'. Because of this failure to persuade the masters to negotiate and the weakness of the Manchester spinners' union after their defeat, Doherty later estimated that there were between three and five reductions in the wages of the fine spinners during the two years after the end of the 1829 strike.[100]

Another matter that roused the spinners' society was Littleton's Anti-Truck Bill. The truck system, as we have noticed, was frequently a source of complaint, so the operatives were naturally incensed by a petition presented to Parliament against this Bill, allegedly from the master cotton-spinners of Manchester and their workmen, but in fact drawn up by one Manchester manufacturer, Hugh Birley, and the Hyde masters, probably led by the oppressive Thomas [Samuel?] Ashton. A general meeting of the Manchester spinners' union therefore authorised Doherty to issue a declaration disclaiming any connection with this petition.[101]

It is evident, however, that the Manchester society remained rather weak and dispirited after the failure of the 1829 strike. There are signs also of the reappearance of internal differences, this time over the decision to become members of the National Association. In the *Journal* of 14 August, Doherty felt compelled to write an open letter from the National Association 'To the Operative Spinners of Manchester', stressing that their unconditional surrender after six months on strike, the continued proscription of part of their body, and their replacement by women and boys, should not induce them to abandon their union as useless, but quite the reverse. They were defeated because their masters were aware that their union was confined to less than 2,000 spinners in Manchester alone; but had it comprised the whole of the labouring population of the United Kingdom, the masters could not possibly have effected their reduction, and in all probability would not even have attempted it.[102] But, as we shall see, Doherty was unable to create much enthusiasm for the Association in Manchester.

Sometime in the second half of 1830, however, Doherty ceased to be secretary of the Manchester spinners' society, being succeeded by Peter Maddocks, who had been a working spinner in the town for several years.[103] Precisely when Doherty gave up this office is unclear, but it is possible that it may have been as early as the end of July, when he wrote that, 'Having freed ourselves from some engagements which occupied much of our time before, we shall now be able to devote our attention almost wholly to the management of the *Journal*.'[104] But J. F. Foster's letters of December 1830 appear to indicate that it was not until about that time that Maddocks succeeded Doherty, who had 'left that situation in order to become the editor of a public paper which is intended to be established for the purpose of the Union, and to be supported from their funds; and the Union look forward to this paper as a powerful means of increasing and strengthening their influence'. This must be a reference to the *Voice of the People*, then about to be launched by the National Association, and it is probable that Doherty did not relinquish the secretaryship of the local spinners' society until after the Association's delegate meeting in November, when this decision was taken and when he also ceased to be secretary of that body, in order to concentrate on his editorial duties; a month later, moreover, he was relieved of the secretaryship of the spinners' Grand General Union.[105]

Long before that time, indeed, it had obviously become impossible for him efficiently to combine all the various offices he held—hence, no doubt, the complaints about his delays and unpunctuality.[106] Moreover, he clearly preferred to withdraw from direct participation in the spinners' union at the local level in order to concentrate on his wider schemes and on trade-union and radical journalism. Nevertheless, as the leading figure in the spinners' general union and in the National Association, he was still actively involved in Manchester trade unionism, and with the cotton spinners in particular, and kept constantly appearing on the local scene.

He did not leave the Manchester spinners in a very strong position. Not only were they dispirited by the failure in 1829, but their finances were much weaker.[107] It is significant that Maddocks' salary was reduced to £1 8s per week, 5s less than Doherty's had been. The society still had members in 87 mills, but the number of lodges had been reduced to fifteen: total contributions in the *Returns* for that week were £102 8s, total disbursements £91 16s 5½d (including £39 12s to 'Men out' and £35 to 'District'), and at the end of the week the balance in hand had risen from £15 8s 10d to £26 5s 4½d, a paltry sum compared with the funds before the strike.

But this situation can hardly be attributed to Doherty's rash leadership. On the contrary, he had tried to restrain strike action, to settle disputes by negotiation, and to restrict the use of the strike weapon to particular mills, in an endeavour to bring up undercutting firms; and the general union, in the establishment of which he played such an important part, was intended as a defensive bulwark against wages reductions, not as an aggressive body for gaining advances. The times, however, were not in his favour: in the years 1828–30 the economy was sliding to the bottom of a slump, and the master spinners, faced by falling prices and bankruptcies, were caught in the same situation and naturally sought to cut labour costs by use of more productive machinery and by piece-rate reductions (which did not, in fact, reduce actual earnings all that much, while prices generally were falling). In an overstocked labour market, with heavy unemployment, the spinners' unions were inevitably defeated, though their strong rearguard actions probably prevented wages from falling as far as they might otherwise have done.[108]

Doherty, as we have seen, had been subjected during these years to the most vicious personal attacks and smears by most of the local press and by some of the masters, but this campaign against him does not appear to have weakened his position among the trade-union membership—indeed it may well have strengthened it, adding to his 1818 martyrdom. He almost certainly resigned in 1830 and was not dismissed. At the same time, it is clear that he was by no means the spinners' sole leader: others such as Thomas Foster, David McWilliams and Jonathan Hodgins appear to have been almost equally influential. Nor did his going result in any change in the policy or methods of the local spinners' society. Thus in the later months of 1830 we find men turning-out at various Manchester mills to bring up piece-rates or to restrict the employment of women and 'stout lads' as spinners at lower wages, and the masters complaining to local magistrates and Government as loudly as ever about picketing, intimidation, secret oaths, and vague sinister plans by 'the

Union', which, in their view, required reimposition of the Combination Laws and military repression.[109] Moreover, the Manchester spinners were still persisting in their unrealistic demand for equalisation of piece-rates on large and small mules; in December 1830, for example, they again proposed a general list of prices for all sizes of mules, 'containing a specific price per pound for each number'. Although they received support from some of the less progressive masters there was justification for the *Guardian*'s view of this demand as 'perfectly absurd, especially in the cotton trade, which owes almost its existence to the improvement of machinery'.[110]

On the other hand, as Rudé has rightly observed, the aims and methods of the cotton spinners under Doherty were 'more forward-looking' than those of 'pre-industrial' workers: instead of engaging in riots, machine-breaking, etc, like handloom weavers, miners, or agricultural labourers, they were adopting peaceful, legal methods in industrial relations.[111] They were often spurned by the masters, and their members frequently broke loose and took to violent 'direct action', but Doherty and the other leaders displayed great powers of organisation and control. He repeatedly emphasised his total opposition to violence and 'Luddism', which resulted only in repression, while inevitably failing to stop mechanical progress: instead, he believed in strong trade-union organisation and, as we shall see, in constitutional agitation for parliamentary reform, factory legislation, etc. In the industrial sphere, instead of futilely opposing machinery, he sought to maintain trade-union control by restricting entry to the trade and by operating, as far as possible, a 'closed-shop' policy, at the same time trying to maintain piece-rates, and thus to prevent the over-rapid introduction of machinery and technological unemployment, whilst striving to secure for the workers some share in the fruits of increased productivity. Seen in this light, the effort to maintain piece-rates on ever-larger mules, though irritatingly obstructionist in the eyes of the *Guardian* and manufacturers, did make some sense, and though piece-rates were gradually forced downwards earnings were fairly well maintained[112]—no mean achievement in the very unfavourable economic and social circumstances of the time.

It is doubtful how far the Grand General Union strengthened local spinners' societies. It certainly seems to have stiffened their resolve to resist wage-reductions and fight undercutting, though it clearly led to exaggerated hopes and consequent disillusionment when strikes failed. At the same time it produced equally exaggerated fears in the minds of employers, magistrates, and newspaper editors, and even in Government. The authorities could not differentiate between the actions of local societies, the Grand General Union of cotton spinners, and the National Association. This is not surprising in view of the fact that the same individuals—notably Doherty—held office in several of these bodies and did not always distinguish between their different roles. Thus the considerable alarm aroused by the strikes of 1830 was created largely by the all-pervasive power which 'the Union' and/or National Association seemed to exercise. In fact, however, the extent of the influence of the spinners' federation over its constituent bodies, and the support which it gave them, were greatly exaggerated. Tufnell was one of the few contemporary observers who discerned the realities of the situation. He likened the several delegate conferences of cotton spinners to '*Parliaments* [which] levied taxes on their constituents, passed laws, printed their speeches and proceedings, and performed all the functions of a legislative body with as much formality as the House of Commons', but observed that 'the institution of this assembly . . . does not appear to have had any marked effect on the trade; the strikes and other *offensive* business of the Union, were still for the most part decided on by the local committees'.[113] Certainly, the strikes in the first half of 1830 at Bolton and Ashton were directed by the branches in the localities concerned, although correspondence was kept up with Doherty in Manchester. There is no record of any financial support from the Grand General Union or of a national committee meeting with any frequency in Manchester. The Scottish and Irish spinners do not appear to have established national committees, but they continued to send delegates to later general conferences.

The cotton spinners' local autonomy was even less affected by the formation of the National Association for the Protection of Labour. They discussed final arrangements for the official formation of the Association at their second delegate assembly on the Isle of Man in June 1830, and although the Grand General Union itself did not become a constituent of the larger body, many individual societies in the different towns enrolled separately as members. G. D. H. Cole listed fourteen spinners' clubs which contributed to the funds of the Association, but his calculations of their respective donations were made erroneous by several omissions, as we shall see. In fact, their subscriptions to the Association between July 1830 and March 1831, when they were one of its most generous financial supporters, amounted to £240 18s 1d, about one-sixth of the total contributions where the trade was specified. The largest sums came from Ashton (over £90) and Stalybridge and Dukinfield (£31), contributed in the period before the spinners' strike in those districts, but there were also substantial amounts from Oldham (£31), Manchester (£26), Rochdale (£22), Lees (£14) and Mossley (£12), and small donations from Chorley, Stockport, Clitheroe, Rossendale, Preston and Hyde.[114] The National Association, however, had no direct interest in any of the spinners' strikes until the great Ashton turn-out in December,[115] although local branches of the Association were vaguely connected with them and in some cases, as at Bolton, gave support.

After the second Isle of Man conference in June 1830, the Grand General Union did begin to play a more active role. The Bolton strike was officially recognised, although too late to prevent defeat. More important, Thomas Foster, of Manchester, and Patrick McGowan of Glasgow, were appointed to visit the various districts in an effort to raise enthusiasm and secure co-operation in the policy of equalising prices between the districts. They were immediately active in assisting Doherty and the Ashton spinners' leaders to persuade the local masters there to abandon their proposed reduction in piece prices, and they also played a part in the subsequent successful strike in Staly-bridge. Their influence was similarly significant, though less effective, in the Carlisle strike.[116] Doherty later declared that their mission had been 'eminently successful . . . Almost every spinning district, of any consequence, was enrolled in the union . . . and a number of the worst-paying employers were compelled to advance the wages of the spinners to something like the average rate.'[117]

On their tour McGowan and Foster spoke at several meetings with Doherty in favour of the National Association, but Doherty was anxious to show that the Grand General Union was distinct from the latter. 'A report . . . has been put into circulation, that Messrs McGowan and Foster, the Spinners' Deputies, are paid from this Society [the National Association]. This we beg to contradict as neither of them have ever received a farthing from the funds, for their able and efficient services.'[118] Nevertheless, the links between these trade-union organisations, and their growing strength and militancy, continued to alarm the authorities. The strikes, violence and intimidation of spinners, colliers and other trades in the autumn of 1830, generally attributed to the machinations of 'the Union' and/or National Association, caused employers, magistrates and Home Secretary Peel not only to consider possible prosecutions under the existing law or reimposition of more coercive legislation, but also to take further civil and military precautions. Thus on 25 October Peel recommended that a secret meeting should be held between Foster, the Manchester magistrate, Major-General Bouverie, Lt. Col. Shaw and other authorities to arrange precautions in case of a general disturbance; he suggested the possibility of raising 'a volunteer force of respectable folk and loyal workmen'.[119] Such a meeting was held, but the use of force against strikers was rejected, because of the influence of the general union and possible repercussions; legal action was preferred, but it was difficult to get evidence and witnesses.[120] Bouverie was particularly impressed by the spinners' organisation and their 'rolling-strike' tactics, under Doherty's leadership, though he confused their activities with those of the National Association.[121]

However, the real strengths of both the Grand General Union and the National Association were about to be tested, by the resolution of fifty-two combined firms in Ashton, Stalybridge and Dukinfield to enforce a general reduction in wages. This was not a reaction to the November Manchester spinners' strikes, as Cole states, for these were more concerned with the practice of employing females and boys as spinners.[122] Nor was it simply an attempt to challenge the power of the Grand General Union; but rather it was the culmination of a year's events in the localities concerned, in which the employers had sought to repeat the success of the Bolton masters in extending the principle of the Manchester list of prices of 1829.

NOTES TO CHAPTER FOUR

[1] See above, pp. 14–15, 19, 24, 29–32.
[2] See above, pp. 31–2.
[3] See above, p. 76.
[4] Place Collection, Vol. 16, Part II, f. 96.
[5] *Ibid.*
[6] *Report . . . December 1829.* The following section is based on this document, which is preserved among the Political Tracts in Manchester Central Reference Library, P.2410. For the thirty-two resolutions passed at the meeting, see G. D. H. Cole and A. W. Filson, *British Working-Class Movements: Select Documents, 1789–1875* (1967 ed.), pp. 247–51.
[7] S. and B. Webb, *op. cit.*, p. 118, based on Tufnell, *op. cit.*, p. 16. This is correctly doubted by Cole, *Attempts at General Union*, p. 18. Turner, *op. cit.*, p. 83, refers to evidence that Foster began life as a working spinner, but then repeats the Webbs' error and even asserts that it was because of middle-class sympathisers like Foster that the spinners temporarily deserted their simple and 'natural' associations for the more complex institution of 1829.

[8] Robert C. Sharp, a Manchester constable, was therefore in error when he wrote to Peel on 7 June 1830, that Macvicker was from Manchester: H.O. 40/27, f. 284.

[9] Another spinner, James Gorton, had been sentenced at the same time, but had died of gaol fever three weeks before his sentence expired: *Observer*, 2 February 1822. The 'old and reverend hypocrite' was the magistrate who sentenced Doherty—Parson Hay.

[10] *Returns*, 30 November 1829, quoted in H.O. 40/27, f. 284. The 'two delegates' were Doherty and Crooks; Foster paid his own expenses.

[11] Of this argument, Tufnell, *op. cit.*, pp. 81–2, later wrote that it was 'a curious comment on the atrocious violence' of Scottish trade unionists in particular 'that men, who do not hesitate to . . . take oaths binding to murder . . . can consider it a pollution of the Sabbath, to discuss on that day what concerns (in their opinion) the saving of themselves and [their] families from "poverty, degradation, and crime" '.

[12] See above, p. 86.

[13] Cole, *Attempts at General Union*, pp. 17–18, rightly states that this was a 'confusing discussion', but unfortunately concludes erroneously out of the muddle that the majority of four was in favour of Doherty's plan and that the Grand General Union was founded as a unitary body, subject to a single governing committee with its seat in Manchester.

[14] The union cannot therefore be attributed solely to Doherty's influence: his views were frequently disputed.

[15] See above, pp. 31–2.

[16] As a further check upon 'bad characters' getting work, it was later decided that a return of the names of the spinners and piecers paying in each district be made, so that Doherty could compile a list of all the spinners in the kingdom, attaching a number to every name; a copy of the list was to be sent to every district.

[17] See above, p. 21.

[18] Probably a reference to the 1825 Preston strike.

[19] See below, p. 362.

[20] This resolution was merely repeated at the third congress of the union in Manchester in December 1830. It could not therefore represent, as Cole, *Attempts at General Union*, pp. 27–8, asserts, a rejection of Doherty's over-ambitious schemes by the delegates at that meeting. See below, p. 138.

[21] The 1810 union was solely, and the 1825 federation principally, confined to England.

[22] R. W. Postgate, *The Builders' History* (1923), pp. 47–53.

[23] *Chronicle*, 23 January; *Stockport Advertiser*, 22 January 1830.

[24] Parl. Papers, 1837–8, VIII, 3639. See below, n. 33.

[25] H.O. 40/27, f. 268. For another discussion of the correspondence which ensued, see W. R. Serjeant, 'An Early Trade Union Episode at Ramsey', *Journal of the Manx Museum*, Vol. VII, No. 87 (1971). For the Bolton and Ashton strikes, see below, pp. 100–4.

[26] Isle of Man Government, Letter Books, Vol. III (August 1817–September 1832).

[27] *Ibid.*

[28] H.O. 40/27, f. 274.

[29] H.O. 41/6, f. 512.

[30] H.O. 40/27, f. 284. The 'general trades' union' was Doherty's National Association, dealt with in Chapters VI and VII.

[31] *Ibid.*, f. 291.

[32] Isle of Man Government, *op. cit.*

[33] *Ibid.* See also H.O. 41/6, ff. 515–7. Doherty presumably mixed up the two conferences when he told the 1838 Committee that it was the 1829 report which he sent to Peel. See above, p. 96.

[34] *Ibid.* The original information was contained in a letter from Colonel G. Murray to Peel on 29 October, H.O. 40/25: the correspondent thought that the 'strangers' might be political refugees from France or Belgium.

35 According to *Report . . . December 1829*, Doherty had proposed that the next congress be at Carlisle, but was outvoted.
36 Isle of Man Government, *op. cit.*
37 H.O. 41/6, ff. 515–20.
38 *Guardian*, 20 November 1830.
39 H.O. 40/27, f. 293.
40 See below, pp. 113–4.
41 S. J. Chapman, *The Lancashire Cotton Industry* (1904), p. 202.
42 *Bolton Chronicle*, 30 January, 6 and 20 February; *Journal*, 20 March 1830.
43 *Guardian, Chronicle,* and *Stockport Advertiser*, 13 and 20 March 1830; R. Boyson, *The Ashworth Cotton Enterprise* (Oxford, 1970). Ashworth stated in an advertisement for new hands on 19 March that the clear weekly wages of their spinners over the previous year had varied from £1 8s 11d to £1 15s 3½d, and of their apprentices from £1 1s 7d to £1 7s 9d. The firms argued, as in 1823, that increased productivity from larger and more efficient mules would maintain earnings, but the men feared that earnings would be reduced, while the work would be more laborious and there would be more technological unemployment.
44 *Bolton Chronicle*, 20 and 27 March; *Mercury*, 30 March 1830. The young spinners concerned were committed to gaol for a month.
45 *Bolton Chronicle*, 27 March and 17 April 1830; Boyson, *op. cit.*, pp. 145–7.
46 These probably included Doherty, who was present in Bolton that week to support his charges against a local manufacturer for trucking: see below, p. 361. Articles in the *Journal*, 20 and 27 March 1830, supported the strikers.
47 *Bolton Chronicle*, 17 April 1830; Place Collection, Vol. 16, Part II, f. 98.
48 *Mercury*, 27 April 1830.
49 *Ibid.*, 4 and 11 May; *Guardian*, 15 and 22 May 1830.
50 *Journal*, 29 May; *Bolton Chronicle*, 22 June 1830.
51 *Guardian*, 12 June 1830. For the Ashton strike, see below, pp. 103–4.
52 *Ibid.*
53 *Journal*, 19 June 1830.
54 *Bolton Chronicle*, 19 and 26 June 1830.
55 *Guardian*, 26 June and 10 July 1830. Here the controversy rested, but an interesting comment upon it appeared in the *Guardian*, 17 January 1838, during the arguments over the Glasgow spinners' sentences (see below, p. 309): 'In a turn out in Bolton in . . . 1830, some very serious outrages were committed; and it was then ascertained that a secret committee, called a "destruction committee", had been appointed by the turn outs for the purpose of planning and superintending the execution of these outrages. In 1831, not long after the murder of Mr Thomas Ashton, an attempt was made to throw a quantity of gunpowder into the dwelling house of a master spinner near Blackburn; and it was afterwards proved in a court of justice, that the parties engaged in the diabolical work, five in number, had been employed by the Bolton union committee, and had been promised £2 each for it.'
56 *Mercury*, 22 June, 6 and 13 July; *Chronicle*, 24 July 1829.
57 *Guardian*, 20 November; *Bolton Chronicle*, 20 November 1830. See below, pp. 190–1.
58 *Bolton Chronicle*, 7 August; *Journal*, 11 September 1830. For Foster and McGowan's mission, see below, pp. 113–4.
59 *Times and Gazette*, 3 April; *Journal*, 3 April 1830.
60 These incidents were reported in all the local papers in May and June 1830. Heginbottom was said to be paying only 1¾d per lb. for No. 40s, compared with 2d per lb., or 4s 2d per 1,000 hanks, paid by the other Ashton masters. There were also grievances in regard to fines, truck, and tied cottages.
61 See above, p. 101.
62 *Journal*, 19 June; *Times and Gazette*, 19 June 1830.
63 See below, Ch. v.
64 *Mercury*, 22 June 1830.
65 See above, p. 96.
66 According to later statements, all the employers were agreed on 3s 7d, except Charles Hindley, of Dukinfield, who proposed 3s 5d. Hindley, who played a very equivocal role throughout this whole affair, claimed that he was merely

'testing reactions', and subsequently encouraged the Ashton spinners' union in their resistance, asserting to Doherty that the masters could afford 4s 2d. *Chronicle*, 19 January 1833.

[67] Presumably an English national committee, in accordance with the rules agreed on in the Isle of Man, but which had probably met intermittently since the formation of the English spinners' federation in September 1829.

[68] *Times and Gazette*, 31 July 1830.

[69] *Ibid.; Journal*, 11 September 1830. It appears that Charles Hindley was mainly responsible for securing the masters' agreement to this proposal. But this, and his encouragement of workers to join the union and fight reductions, contrasted strangely with his previous proposals to the Ashton masters' association, and also with his refusal to allow his own men to subscribe towards the Stockport strikers in 1829. Hence, when Hindley stood as Whig candidate in the first election at Ashton in December 1832, he was not surprisingly accused of equivocation. *Chronicle*, 12, 19 and 26 January 1833.

[70] *Journal*, 11 September 1830.

[71] *Ibid.*, 24 July 1830.

[72] According to a later statement by a member of the Ashton spinners' committee, these firms had been selected after consultation with Charles Hindley, who informed them that the former was in such poor circumstances that it must yield or face bankruptcy, while the latter had just received a large order which must be executed within a specified time. *Chronicle*, 19 January 1833.

[73] *Journal*, 14 August 1830. The Stalybridge spinners agreed at this meeting to join the National Association. See below, pp. 181–2.

[74] *Times and Gazette*, 21 August 1830.

[75] H.O. 40/27, f. 305, and 40/26, f. 28. See also Rudé, *op. cit.*, pp. 92–3.

[76] *Times and Gazette*, 28 August 1830

[77] H.O. 40/26, f. 34.

[78] See below, pp. 167–71.

[79] H.O. 40/26, f. 42.

[80] *Ibid.*, f. 68.

[81] This money must have come from the local spinners' fund, supported by the grand general union; it would have been unconstitutional for the National Association to have supported a strike for an increase.

[82] H.O. 40/26, f. 63.

[83] *Journal*, 11 September 1830.

[84] *Guardian*, 2 October 1830.

[85] *Mercury*, 2 and 9 November 1830.

[86] See below, Ch. v.

[87] *Stockport Advertiser*, 9, 16, 23 and 30 July; *Journal*, 17 and 31 July, 7 and 14 August 1830.

[88] *Journal*, 17 July 1830. Worsley was then secretary of the Stockport spinners and of the local branch of the National Association.

[89] *Stockport Advertiser*, 23 July 1830.

[90] *Journal*, 31 July and 7 August 1830.

[91] *Journal*, 21 August; *Mercury*, 16 November 1830.

[92] *Journal*, 18 and 25 September 1830.

[93] *Chronicle*, 25 September 1830, quoting the *Carlisle Patriot*.

[94] *Stockport Advertiser*, 19 November 1830, quoting the *Carlisle Patriot*.

[95] *Journal*, 18 September and 2 October 1830.

[96] *Times and Gazette*, 20 February 1830.

[97] *Journal*, 6 March 1830.

[98] See above, pp. 68–9.

[99] *Journal*, 3 April 1830.

[100] *Ibid.*, 25 April 1830; *Voice*, 24 September 1831.

[101] *Journal*, 22 May 1830. See below, p. 363.

[102] *Journal*, 14 August 1830.

[103] Letters from J. F. Foster, the Manchester magistrate, to Lord Melbourne, the Home Secretary, dated 22 and 23 December, H.O. 40/26.

[104] *Journal*, 24 July 1830.

[105] See below, pp. 149, n. 32, and 190.

106 See above, p. 103.

107 *Returns*, 10 December 1830, in H.O. 40/26, f. 264. Cf. above, pp. 55–6.

108 See below, pp. 146–7.

109 In addition to the local papers, see H.O. 40/27, ff. 163, 312, 331, 366; H.O. 41/8, ff. 10–18; H.O. 43/39, f. 247; and Parl. Papers, 1833, XXI, D.2, pp. 38–40 (evidence to Factory Commission).

110 *Guardian*, 11 and 18 December 1830. Nothing came of this proposal at this time, because of the Ashton–Stalybridge strike and lack of funds, but it was revived a few months later; see below, pp. 142–4.

111 Rudé, *op. cit.*, pp. 92–3.

112 See below, pp. 146–7.

113 Tufnell, *op. cit.*, p. 16.

114 Cole, *Attempts at General Union*, Appendix 4, p. 180. For the errors in his figures, see below, p. 205, n. 233. The subscriptions of other spinners' societies, like the important branch at Bolton, were paid directly to the local district committees of the Association and hence not recorded separately.

115 See below, Ch. V and p. 182.

116 See above, pp. 104–5 and 108.

117 *Advocate*, 23 June 1832.

118 *Journal*, 25 September 1830.

119 H.O. 41/8, ff. 10–18.

120 H.O. 40/27, ff. 322, 340; H.O. 43/39, f. 247.

121 H.O. 40/26, ff. 104–9. See below, p. 185.

122 Cole, *Attempts at General Union*, p. 26. See above, p. 111.

# The Ashton–Stalybridge strike    V
# and decline of the
# Grand General Union

The Ashton master spinners had agreed, at the end of July 1830, to withdraw their proposed reduction in piece-rates, pending an attempt by the spinners' union to bring up employers in neighbouring Stalybridge.[1] In this, however, the union had been only partially successful, while in Hyde, where it had few members, rates were even lower. Moreover, the competitive position of the whole district had been altered by the recent reductions in Stockport, Manchester and Bolton. At the same time, the growing power of the union and of the National Association, which was said to be in 'great vogue' in the Ashton area,[2] caused increasing alarm and appeared to threaten the masters' authority. These factors finally induced virtually all the master spinners of Ashton, Stalybridge, Mossley and Dukinfield to combine at the beginning of November to offer a reduced list of prices to their men, who were told that they must either accept or be locked out. By the new list, the price per 1,000 hanks of No. 40s declined from 4s 2d to 3s 9d, and every associated master bound himself to forfeit £500 if he paid any other rate.[3] This abatement was identical to the one previously attempted in July. It was not, therefore, as Turner states, a newly concerted effort 'to provoke a battle with the spinners' combination';[4] the activities of the local spinners' club and the Grand General Union had merely delayed the employers of the district in effecting their earlier proposals. Nevertheless, the anti-union press was quick to attribute the reduction to the previous forward policy of the operatives; even the moderate local magistrate, J. F. Foster, informed the Home Office that the 'masters at Ashton, Stalybridge etc. have joined together to resist the union, and a collision now seems inevitable',[5] and as the struggle developed it increasingly came to be interpreted by both sides as a test of the authority of the Grand General Union over its constituents, and ultimately of the power of the National Association, and united workmen generally, to resist reductions in their wages.

The new list was to apply to fifty-two firms in the district, only an insignificant number of small firms not participating. On the masters announcing their intention, Doherty, in his capacity as secretary of the spinners' Grand General Union,[6] made a communication to the masters, through one of their number, Hindley, requesting that representatives from both sides should meet to settle the dispute amicably. The masters thereupon held a meeting and towards the end of the second week of November replied that seven of their number would confer with an equal number of representatives from their workmen, with a view to formulating a new list.[7] The meeting took place at the 'Commercial Inn', Ashton, when at the end of a lengthy and apparently friendly discussion the men proposed that time

E

should be given to procure lists from all the spinning districts in England, in order that an average list could be drawn up; when both sides had obtained the requisite information, another meeting should be held to reach agreement. The men requested a delay of only one month for this purpose, and, according to Doherty, the masters' deputation promised to recommend it to their association and to communicate their answer, through Doherty, on the following Tuesday, 16 November.

In fact, more than a week elapsed before the following brief letter was sent to Doherty, signed by three of the masters' deputation. Samuel Robinson, James Adshead and Charles Hindley:

> Sir—According to our promise, we take the earliest opportunity of inform-ing you that it has been resolved, at a general meeting of master cotton-spinners, that the list of prices appearing to them perfectly reasonable, [it] will be acted upon by them, from 11 December next; the notice having been put off for one week longer.

As the letter did not even allude to the men's proposal, Doherty regarded it as proof that the masters did not want to adopt a fair average list, but to have lower prices than other districts.[8]

Over the next fortnight, the situation deteriorated rapidly. On 25 Novem-ber, Hindley, whom the workmen later claimed had privately told both Doherty and Betts that he considered 4s 2d to be a price the market could bear, discharged all the hands from his Dukinfield works for attending a meeting of the National Association in Ashton on 19 November, which had been addressed by Doherty, Hodgins, Betts, Brookes and others.[9] And on 27 November the *Manchester Times and Gazette* reported that the conduct of the Stalybridge masters, in inducing the trustees of the Wesleyan Methodist Sunday School to cancel a meeting which was to have been held in their room to form a branch of the National Association, had engendered 'the worst feelings . . . in the bosoms of the men towards many of their employers'.[10]

At the beginning of December the Ashton spinners posted large placards on the walls of the town and nearby villages, signed by their secretary, Betts, and headed 'Labour and Wages'. They stated that 'In consequence of a determination on the part of the *renowned 52* to effect irretrievable *ruin* amongst the operative spinners of Ashton, Dukinfield, Stalybridge and Mossley, we deem it requisite that the whole of the working-classes of the above places should hold a public meeting to consult and devise on some legal means, by which the nefarious intentions of the master spinners may be fully defeated'. The assembly was called for the afternoon of Saturday, 4 December, to be held in a field near the 'Buck Inn', Dukinfield, 'when deputies from Manchester and the neighbouring districts, will address the meeting, and exhibit the fallacy of the master spinners' reasons for proposing the reduction they now offer'.[11]

A copy of this placard was immediately transmitted to the Home Secretary, Melbourne, by J. F. Foster. In his accompanying letter the magistrate alleged that 'the Committee' were supervising the negotiations with the masters and that the workmen appeared to know little about the proceedings.[12] In fact, there could be no doubt about the enthusiasm for a strike, at least in Ashton, if not in Stalybridge, but there was a certain lack of candour between the local spinners' committee and the rank and file. Doherty told the Ashton leaders that the funds of the National Association could not be opened, in view of a resolution previously agreed that a sum of £3,000 should be amassed before operations commenced, although a separate appeal would be launched in all the local branches of the Association to relieve the strikers; but this was not fully acknowledged to the men. Indeed, as in the case of the Manchester strike in 1829, Doherty was in favour of a compromise agreement with the masters, from tactical considerations and a belief that the turn-out could not succeed. When the Ashton leaders later accused Charles Hindley of having caused the strike, Joseph Mellor, one of the strikers, wrote to *Wheeler's Manchester Chronicle* that the members of the Ashton committee themselves were responsible, because they had misled the work-men and refused to listen to advice. 'Even Mr Doherty, for advising them not to turn out but to agree to an adjustment, was calumniated and accused of being a traitor to our cause, and although there was no sign of support they told us we should be well supported, and the men came out under the impression that they would receive 10s per week from the Spinners' Union, and 8s from the Trades' Union . . . Now let the public judge who in that affair proved themselves to be the worst enemies of the working classes.'[13]

An estimated 15–20,000 persons attended the meeting in Dukinfield, after marching in procession from each of the townships affected by the dispute, 'headed by bands, and carrying the *tricolour flag*'.[14] Samuel Powers, an opera-tive spinner, was called to the chair, and after warning the crowd against the firing of pistols and conduct which would form an excuse for the reimposition of the odious Combination Laws, introduced the first speaker, Betts. The latter condemned the masters' talk of equalising wages, when in fact they were bringing them down to the lowest scale, and criticised the Ashton employers for coalescing with their habitually more oppressive Stalybridge colleagues. He concluded by moving that the reduction from 4s 2d to 3s 9d, 'which will be as much as 5s weekly out of the labourer's pocket', was not prompted by necessity, but by 'a spirit of avarice', which resolution was seconded by Grundy and supported by Doherty in a long speech. Doherty began by describing the negotiations which they had undertaken with the masters' deputation, and declared that the employers' disregard of the men's proposal for ascertaining the average rates in the country had finally forced the deputies to admit that, 'it was not the prices they cared about . . . it was the growing power of the workmen which drew their attention'. Doherty maintained that it was unjust to have separate price lists in each district, because they gave excuse for continual reductions, as experienced in Man-chester. He accused 'the 52' of trying to provoke outrages, and called on the upper classes in the district to memorialise the government against their actions, which endangered the public peace. Nevertheless he cautioned the crowd to forswear violence.

> Many a well meaning person might suppose, (and be thereby encouraged to outrage), that this large assemblage might upset a whole world; but let me tell you, that you would be as nothing when opposed to the power which the government of this country possesses. Let not your passions hurry

you into contact with the force of government and the laws, but collect your moral force, that moral power which is of far more effect than *any* power which can oppress you. If you are only as united as the catholics of Ireland were, you will be blessed with similar success.

Notwithstanding this warning, Doherty concluded with a rallying cry 'that the operatives shall no longer be the slaves of masters and tyrants', and the resolution was then passed unanimously amid 'loud shouting'.

Jonathan Hodgins went further, in supporting the next resolution, for a regulated list of prices, when he made a veiled threat to the associated masters. 'He did not mean to say it was their duty to riot, but he did mean to say that . . . there was an evident boundary beyond which oppression could not be borne; and when it had reached that point, those who were the cause of that oppression were the first to suffer.' At this juncture, Betts secured a hearing for Hindley, one of the masters, who stated his desire to act as a peacemaker. He reminded the audience that the masters' association, far from wishing to destroy the operatives' club, had recognised it and even entered into negotiations on the question of postponement, a concession which had not been made by either the Stockport or Manchester employers before the strikes there. He considered that the masters' committee genuinely believed that no more than 3s 9d could be offered, 'as things now stand', but promised to do his utmost to procure a reconsideration of the men's claims. However, this speech did nothing to sway the resolve of the meeting, which went on to hear further addresses from Hodgins, Doherty, Foster, Brookes and Betts, and to pass a third resolution in favour of presenting a petition to the King, 'stating the grievances of the working-classes, and requesting that military aid be not granted in order to enable the masters to effect the reduction'. The assembly then dispersed and marched to their homes chanting '4s 2d or "swing"!', an ominous reference to the contemporary riots in the agricultural districts. And when, on the following Monday, a few employers in the district locked out their men for having attended this meeting, angry scenes occurred and factory windows were smashed, for which three men were arrested and eventually sentenced to terms of imprisonment.[15]

The *Manchester Guardian* maintained that the new list offered by the Ashton masters was not so much a reduction as a partial reversal of the advances forced by the union over the previous few months; 3s 9d per 1,000 hanks of No. 40s was as much as the market could afford, in the current lack of confidence arising from the political disturbances in Europe, and if that rate was nominally less than in some districts, the larger and more modern machinery in the Ashton area would ensure greater actual earnings. By Betts' own calculation that a 10 per cent reduction in piece-rates entailed a fall in wages of 5s per week, the gross wages of the Ashton spinners must previously have been 50s per week, and take-home pay must have amounted to 38s, and would therefore be 33s after the abatement; in fact the spinners earned better and more regular wages than any equivalent class of workman. Although their leaders gave verbal exhortations to the people to be peaceable, their real hope was to win their demands by intimidation, as shown by the resolution concerning the exclusion of the military and by the appearance of 4,000 persons at the Dukinfield meeting armed with 'short clubs, pistols, blunderbusses, and small hatchets'.[16]

Certainly, both the civil and military authorities were more concerned about the threat of violence accompanying this labour dispute than any other similar disturbance in the north-west since the hand-loom weavers' riots in 1826. On 2 December J. F. Foster informed Melbourne that the magistrates were prepared to use the military to disperse the Dukinfield meetings, if necessary. He had asked the Ashton magistrates to consider if the expected presence of men with pistols at the meeting did not make it illegal and give sufficient grounds for legal proceedings against the principal actors who had called and were to conduct it. Foster did not know if sufficient evidence existed to warrant such arrests, and in the event the meeting was allowed to take place and was carried off virtually without incident, save for a later attack upon two mills to turn the workers out.[17] Melbourne, for his part, considered that the carrying of arms and tricolours did make the meeting illegal, and replied to Foster on 9 December that a meeting between the civil authorities and Major-General Bouverie should be held to arrange measures for the dispersal of any such assembly in the future.[18]

On that very day, Bouverie did visit Ashton and Stalybridge, and as a result of his consultations with the civil authorities there, Colonel Shaw, the commanding officer of the district, offered to send two regiments into the neighbourhood. One of the Ashton magistrates, Astley, had already sworn in between 200 and 300 special constables,[19] but despite these extensive precautions an urgent correspondence was continued on the necessity of repression. On 13 December Bouverie wrote to the Under-Secretary at the Home Office that, 'I understand that Mr Foster has yesterday given it as his opinion that there is a good case for the apprehension of both Betts and Doherty, as well as some others in consequence of the part which they took on the 4th inst., connected also with their other transactions'. On the next day Melbourne wrote to Foster, urging expedition in the magistrates' organisation of the prosecutions, and adding that if it was found necessary to disperse any assemblies in future, the most important consideration was that the use of force must be shown to be legal, by a prior announcement of the magistrates that such meeting was contrary to law and would be prohibited.[20]

Most of this correspondence, therefore, was concerned with incidents before the strike became general on 11 December. The number of spinners involved in the turn-out was about 2,000, and the total of workers made unemployed thereby was estimated at 18,000.[21] During the first few days of the dispute, there was considerable unrest in the area. Large crowds assembled daily and marched about the different townships, carrying tricolour flags and banners inscribed with such slogans as 'Liberty or Death', 'Bread or Blood'; on Monday, 13 December, they gathered round several of the mills chanting '4s 2d or swing', on the next day they hooted at the masters in the streets as they passed on the way to the Manchester market; on Wednesday they paraded to Hyde in the vain hope that they could persuade the workmen there, few of whom were members of either the spinners' or the general union, to quit their employment; and on Thursday, 16 December, a crowd of strikers marched to Oldham, in the hope of raising support there.[22]

At the end of the first week of the strike, on 17 December, the magistrates in the Ashton neighbourhood posted a public notice, pointing out that parades and exhibitions of firearms for the purposes of intimidation and tumult were illegal and that they were determined to preserve the public peace. Notwithstanding the orderly state of Manchester at that time, the magistrates there issued a public warning against similar proceedings, because of their fear of the disturbances spreading to Manchester either through the operative spinners joining the strike in sympathy or through an 'invasion' from the Ashton district.[23] On 18 December Lord Melbourne sent identical letters to three magistrates in Ashton and Dukinfield, instructing them to consult with Bouverie on the dispersal of illegal meetings and processions, and to send spies to the meetings of the union to procure accurate reports of their intentions, so that the information could be used for prosecutions of the leaders.[24] Such persons were appointed, and three days later the rumours that the Ashton strikers were about to march on Manchester to turn out the mills there were so strong that a great number of special constables were sworn in. But in the event the threatened invasion did not materialise: in fact all the civil and military authorities' reports to the Home Office, and the accounts in local newspapers, agreed that from the issuing of the magistrates' notice on 17 December, which coincided with the arrival of troops in the area, until the beginning of January 1831, the Ashton district was generally peaceful, except for occasional instances of shopkeepers and other tradesmen being intimidated into subscribing or expressing support for the strike, by the local union threatening to bar members from doing business with them.[25]

Because of the wide publicity given to the statements of the union leaders at the Dukinfield meeting on 4 December, that the associated masters were trying to force upon their workmen a spinning price list lower than that paid in the surrounding districts, the combined master spinners and manufacturers of the district held a general meeting at the 'White Bear Inn', Manchester, on 14 December, and passed the following resolution, which was inserted in all the local newspapers:

> That the association have formed their price list from the best information they could obtain, and believe it to be a fair average of the price[s] paid in the immediate surrounding districts which they have to meet in the same market, and that disclaiming all idea of obtaining their labour below that of the spinners and manufacturers similarly situated, they are willing to submit it to a public examination and abide by the result.[26]

But the men made no immediate response to their masters' challenge,[27] the only effort at settling the dispute by arbitration, after the break-down of negotiations between master and men in November, being made by a group of local shopkeepers, who held fruitless consultations with both sides in the week before the strike became general.[28]

It was amid these circumstances that the third general delegate meeting of the Grand General Union of Operative Spinners of the United Kingdom met according to schedule in Manchester on Friday, 17 December.[29] Discussion of the Ashton strike was naturally high on the agenda. Since the Ashton masters had declined to co-operate in the project of calculating the average spinning prices in the region, the delegates determined to take action alone to implement the policy of equalised wage lists, which had been the main reason (along with the better organisation of assistance for strikers) for the formation of the Grand General Union and had motivated much of its policy. Early in the proceedings, a sub-committee of five persons was appointed 'to draw up a List of prices for coarse and fine numbers'. They made use of the lists of prices paid in the different districts, which were handed in by the respective delegates and revealed a variation in Lancashire from 3s 4d to 5s per 1,000 hanks of No. 40s. By Monday, 20 December, they had completed their efforts, determining upon the median rate of 4s 2d, the price which the union had been trying to achieve or maintain for the previous six months and for which the striking Ashton spinners were contending. The sub-committee prepared a list for all other numbers in proportion, which the conference adopted, directing that 2,000 copies of it should be printed for distribution to the several districts and thence to individual masters for their agreement; the prices to apply to mules of all sizes. A spy for the local authorities who was present at the meeting soon obtained a copy, which was passed on to Melbourne by J. F. Foster.[30]

To effect their policy, the delegates resolved to take militant action:

> We, the deputies appointed by the general body of operative spinners, being fully invested by our constituents with such power, do determine that a general strike of all those spinners who are receiving less than 4s 2d per 1,000 hanks for No. 40s (and other numbers in proportion) on all sizes of wheels, shall take place on Monday, the 27th instant: not one of whom shall return to work until the full price be given.[31]

This resolution was signed by Peter Maddocks, who had succeeded Doherty as secretary of the Manchester spinners and presided at the delegate meeting.[32]

The authorities were initially very alarmed about the effect this would have on the peace of the area, and extensive military preparations were made by Major-General Bouverie.[33] On 22 December J. F. Foster informed Melbourne that the spy at the delegate meeting had reported a statement that the union had 'a fund of £10,000 to spend and that the General Trades' Union had offered them further assistance when that was spent'. Foster believed that the sum was overstated, but added that if the funds were not 'very ample', the proposed measures would lead to iniquitous consequences.[34] However, on the following day, the magistrate repeated a conversation of which he had been told between a local manufacturer and Peter Maddocks, in which the latter had denied that the turn-out would extend to Ireland and Scotland and had admitted that, although the union hoped the strike would be general in England, they were not certain of many places, such as Preston, to which delegates had been sent to persuade them to join in.[35] By Friday, 24 December, the Manchester borough-reeve was able to report that his alarm had disappeared, following an interview with Maddocks. 'The Scotch and Irish delegates have protested against going out on the 27th wishing to see what turn the Manchester affair takes before they involve themselves. I learn also the important fact that Preston, Stockport, Bolton and Lancaster do not join the turn-out.'[36]

In Manchester, it soon became obvious that the general strike call was an empty threat. Already several disputes were going on there, not very successfully, against low piece-rates and employment of cheap female and juvenile labour; there was also a possibility of renewed action for equalisation of prices on large and small mules, though it soon became apparent that 'the general trades' union has at present, too much upon its hands to venture upon another turn-out'.[37] Moreover, the funds of the local spinners' society were almost completely depleted after the 1829 strike.[38] It appears that the local committee informed the general delegate meeting that they would be unable to pay any allowances to spinners on general strike; the call for such a strike, therefore, was merely intimidatory.[39] In the event, however, 27 December passed off without the slightest disturbance of the peace in Manchester. Only three additional factories turned out there, and legal action against some of the spinners for leaving work without notice soon had a sobering effect. In fact, all the disputes in the town fizzled out early in the new year.[40]

Other cotton towns were even less responsive than Manchester. At Stockport, Bolton, Preston and Carlisle the orders of the union were totally disregarded and the men continued to work at their old prices. At Hyde a meeting had been called for early in the morning of the appointed day, but the attendance was negligible; while a similar assembly of Blackburn spinners on Christmas Day agreed that they should all remain at work, since they were not unanimously in favour of striking. Only in the Longdendale–Glossop valleys, east of Stalybridge, was obedience paid to the grand union's mandate, when the hands of thirty-two factories left their employment on 27 December and declared their intention of not returning to their work until the masters consented to give 4s 2d per 1,000 hanks for 40s twist. But the lack of any general response caused them to 'complain bitterly of being unsupported by their brethren in other districts'.[41]

To the fiasco of the spinners' general strike failure was added the disappointment of the first pay-out from the strike funds for the Ashton and Stalybridge workmen on the very same day, Monday, 27 December. Instead of obtaining the expected benefits from either the Grand General Union or the National Association, only 5s was paid to the married and 3s to the single men, and some did not even collect so much. The money came entirely from sums raised in the neighbourhood, and apparently for the first time the strikers realised that they were not to be supported from the funds of the National Association. As a result the hostile press alleged that there was resentment among the Ashton men over the expenditure of Association funds on the establishment of the *Voice of the People*, that a minority were already willing to accept 3s 11d and some even 3s 9d; and such was the anger among the turn-outs in Ashton that disorders broke out and magistrates were forced to read the riot act. Their distress was increased further by the refusal of the overseers of the poor to relieve any of the spinners, although benefits were paid to piecers, carders and other dependent workers.[42]

In response to this sense of disillusionment, the National Association was at last seen to play a more active role, after the establishment of the *Voice of the People*. In the first number, mention was made of a communication from the Oldham district of the Association, requesting a vigorous effort by every member to aid their oppressed Ashton brethren, though 'without interfering with the association's funds'. On 8 January the same committee inserted another appeal for support, under the signature of their branch secretary, the old radical, John Knight. Meanwhile, in an address to the 'members of the National Association and Public at Large', on 3 January, John Hynes, the general secretary, urged the necessity of preventing another wave of reductions being initiated through leaving the Ashton men to their fate. 'Though the majority are members of the Association, they have, like genuine patriots, *resigned their claims upon it, rather than weaken the common stock.* Let not this sacrifice go unrewarded.' Hynes revealed that subscriptions had begun in various districts already, and that contributions in support of the striking spinners would in future be received at the *Voice* Office, 1 Spring Gardens, Manchester, and by the secretaries in the different districts of the Association. Although the funds of the Association were therefore to be kept separate from the Ashton appeal, it was felt that the masters had attempted the reduction largely to destroy confidence in the National Association, 'the growing power and importance of which seems to alarm those who have so long been accustomed to lord it over their unhappy dependants'.[43]

Appended to this address was the first acknowledgement of money received by the Ashton and Stalybridge spinners, and in the following weeks these contributions increased, the Nottingham trades being notably generous. By 12 March the total sum collected through the agency of the National Association had reached £595 9s 11d,[44] a fairly large sum considering the depressed state of trade, but plainly quite inadequate to relieve the estimated 18,000 workmen made unemployed by the dispute. Moreover, it is impossible to know how much even of these insufficient funds was ever distributed to the turn-outs, because of the eventual flight of Hynes with £160 of subscriptions in the middle of February, and his unsatisfactory keeping of the accounts beforehand.[45]

The *Voice* also gave publicity to the tour undertaken by Slater, as delegate of the Ashton strikers, to raise support for their cause. At the end of December and beginning of the new year he addressed meetings of the Leicester and Nottingham trades, together with Jonathan Hodgins, now a full-time salaried propagandist for the National Association.[46] Further encouragement was given by a meeting on 6 January of about seven hundred Manchester operatives in the Mechanics' Institution, Cooper Street, to consider 'the best means of raising additional support' for the strikers. A delegate from the Stalybridge spinners stated that the local committee had managed to relieve some families with 4s or 5s, according to their numbers and need, but their funds were now exhausted. They were upset by not receiving any assistance from the Manchester spinners, who thus showed themselves blind to the fact that if the present reduction was effected, the spinners in all the other cotton towns would be similarly reduced. This short-sighted policy was also condemned by John Hynes, who therefore proposed that the workmen of Manchester generally should 'enter into an immediate weekly subscription in support of those now struggling and suffering in defence of that natural, just and inalienable right—a fair remuneration for their labour'. John Betts, secretary of the Ashton spinners' union, seconding the motion, described the privation of the strikers resulting from the oppression of the '52 masters', and repeated his criticism of the *Guardian*'s statement that the new list was only equalising prices with other districts, showing how it would reduce earnings,

E*

already averaging no more than 21*s* per week, clear of deductions, through-out the year.[47] Doherty also supported the motion, detailing the November negotiations between the employers and the union and the ultimate rejection by 'the 52' of his suggestions for obtaining a regulated and equalised list of prices, which had initially been favourably received by the masters' deputa-tion. 'Thus, it would be evident, that the object of the masters was not to come to a fair rate of wages. One master . . . had said, in his (Mr Doherty's) presence, and this was acquiesced in by other masters, that they did not want a reduction for the sake of gain—a penny or two-pence per 1,000 was no object—but because they disliked the growing power of the working classes.' By turning such a great number out in the depth of winter, 'he could not but consider that they had incurred an awful responsibility, for there was no saying what might be done by half-starved people at a moment of excitement, and meeting under a sense of wrong'. After Doherty had revealed that letters had been received from Leicester, Nottingham and other places, stating that subscriptions from 1*d* to 1*s* per man were being raised in those quarters, the resolution was carried, it being explained that relief would be given to dependent workers affected by the strike as well as to the spinners. The meet-ing also agreed with Archibald Prentice's view that wages reductions resulted from trade depression caused by 'the accursed corn laws', and passed a resolu-tion accordingly.[48]

Doherty's first editorial comment on the dispute, in the *Voice* on 8 January, largely echoed his speech at the recent meeting, in recalling the efforts of the spinners throughout 1830 to bring up the Stalybridge prices and the masters' retreat from a negotiated settlement in November. Again, he sought to lay the blame for any violence at the door of the employers, who had proposed their scandalous reduction not only in mid-winter, but at a time 'when men's minds were unusually excited by recent events in France and Belgium . . . We are sure that every feeling man will reprobate such conduct, and tremble for the results, if the struggle be protracted'.[49] Unfortunately, the increasing distress of the strikers, the failure of the spinners' general strike, and the disappointing volume of relief obtained, had already provoked, during the previous week, a recurrence of the turbulent conduct which had marked the first days of the turn-out. A party of about five hundred strikers had attacked country mills near Stalybridge, in order to turn out the 'knobsticks', for which six of them had been arrested; brought before Ashton Petty Sessions, they were committed to Chester Castle for trial on charges of riot, assault, and machine-breaking. To Doherty's credit, the *Voice* devoted a column to evidence at the hearing, most of which reflected very badly upon the strikers.[50]

A far more shocking event, however, had occurred on the evening before this outrage. As Thomas Ashton, the eldest son of the leading manufacturer of Hyde, Samuel Ashton, was on his way to his father's mill at Apethorn on 3 January, he was shot dead by three strangers to the area, it was thought in mistake for his younger brother, James, who was manager of that factory but did not go in that day because of an indisposition. Suspicion originally fell upon two men whom James Ashton had recently dismissed on account of their having joined the spinners' union, but they accounted satisfactorily for their time on the night of the murder and were therefore discharged. At the inquest on 5 January, several witnesses were examined, but nothing was heard to incriminate anyone and the jury returned a verdict of 'wilful murder against three persons at present unknown'. But the hostile press had no doubt where the real guilt lay. The *Manchester Guardian* pronounced that, 'public opinion will connect the offence with the turn-out of spinners in the neighbourhood. It is well known that the spinners at Hyde have refused to turn-out; and the turn-outs at Ashton and Stalybridge have consequently been induced to look upon the employers at Hyde (who refused to allow their men to join the union) as the great obstacles to the success of their schemes. A very general opinion, therefore, prevails, (how correctly we cannot undertake to say) that the murder of Mr Ashton has been resorted to with the view of terrifying them into a compliance with the wishes of the workmen.' And *Wheeler's Manchester Chronicle* agreed with the prevailing conviction that the murder was committed 'at least with the connivance, if not the immediate direction of one of the secret committee by which the great body of workpeople are being directed', the motive being to make an example of one of Samuel Ashton's sons.[51]

When news of the crime reached the government, a royal proclamation was issued on 6 January, offering a pardon to any of the parties concerned (except the person who actually fired the shot), for information leading to the arrest and conviction of his accomplices. A reward of £1,500 was also put forward, comprising £500 from Samuel Ashton, £500 from other relatives, and £500 from the master spinners of the neighbourhood. Anyone giving such information was guaranteed protection by the police from the risk of personal violence.[52] Melbourne sent two London police officers to assist in the investigations and they immediately began to interrogate the strike leaders.[53] Doherty protested vehemently when they broke into the houses of several operative spinners and arrested them without producing a warrant; from one house they had taken a tricolour flag and some firearms.[54]

The reckless militancy existing in Ashton was expressed in written placards which appeared on the walls of the town on 6 January after Samuel Ashton's offer of a reward, inscribed 'Whe don't want £500, whe onely want 4s 2d'.[55] But that the body of Ashton spinners wished to be divorced from such sentiments was clear from the following resolution, passed at a general meeting and inserted in the *Voice* by Betts:

> That this meeting views with disgust the malignant aspersions cast upon the character of the operatives (who are now turned out against a reduction in their wages) by the *Manchester Guardian*, in insinuating that the late murder of Mr T. Ashton, of Hyde, may be imputed to the turn-outs in Ashton and neighbourhood.[56]

Meanwhile, however, in Manchester, on 8 January, a general meeting of master spinners, convened by the borough-reeve and constables, agreed to present the government with an account of 'the present disturbed state of this town and neighbourhood more especially as connected with the late atrocious murder at Hyde'.[57] This was supposedly directed against the violence and intimidation of the spinners' union, but was interpreted by middle-class reformers in Manchester as an attempt to discredit the emerging political agitation in the area. Dissatisfied by personal assurances from the borough-reeve that the proceedings related only to the activities of the operative spinners, whose violence had been displayed not only at Hyde and Ashton but in the picketing of at least a dozen Manchester mills, the reformers called a public meeting for the same evening, and after Archibald Prentice, Richard Potter, Thomas Fielden and James Whittle had denounced the 'infamous libel' on the town's inhabitants, and David McWilliams, one of the leaders of the Manchester spinners, had defended the conduct of the striking workmen as 'peaceable and orderly', it was decided to forward resolutions to the Government, proclaiming the tranquil state of the town and the necessity of 'a thorough reformation of the representative system'.[58]

In the *Voice*, Doherty supported this censure on the town's municipal officers and castigated the borough-reeve for taking the side of the master spinners in the dispute against 'the poor, uneducated and defenceless workmen', whose case had not even been heard. Such buttressing of the wealthy was symptomatic of all in 'authority', with the honourable exception of Mr Foster, 'our excellent stipendiary magistrate', but Doherty believed that the time was approaching when public officers would be forced to bend to the 'supreme power of the people', which was increasing daily and would soon eliminate all abuses and ensure equal protection for the poor workmen as for the rich employer.[59] *The Manchester and Salford Advertiser* also condemned the meetings of the master spinners as part of a 'miserable plot' hatched by Tory reactionaries. Among the wild rumours that had been circulating was one that Doherty had been arrested on a charge of seditious practices. But the story was as far from the truth as the invention that Manchester was threatened with disorder.[60]

While this controversy was raging, no progress was made in the investigations towards discovering the murderers, and after the London police officers had left the area the affair gradually faded out of the headlines. The incident was, however, regularly alluded to in anti-union publications, such as the *Character, Object and Effects of Trades' Unions*, whose author, while mistakenly asserting that the crime took place during the Manchester spinners' strike of 1829, had no doubt who were the guilty parties. 'In addition to the common outrages, which always accompany strikes, this was sullied with the crime of assassination. Many masters were shot at, but these villainous attempts were unsuccessful, except in the instance of Mr T. Ashton, one of the most respected of the manufacturers, whose yet unpunished murder attests the excess to which the workmen are capable of proceeding, when impelled by the spirit of combination.'[61] However, in April 1834, one James Garside, then serving a sentence in Derby gaol for theft, confessed to having committed the murder together with two brothers, Joseph and William Mosley.[62] The three men were bound over until the subsequent Chester Assizes and their trial took place on 6 August, when Garside and Joseph Mosley were convicted and sentenced to death, but William Mosley turned King's evidence and was pardoned. During the proceedings, the accused were questioned about their relationship with the Ashton spinners' leaders, and Garside stated that he knew John Joseph Betts, but not Samuel Downes, and that neither had anything to do with the crime; but William Mosley alleged that they had been hired to commit the offence by the spinners' union and had been paid £10 afterwards by Samuel Scholefield on 5 January 1831, at a meeting near the seventh lock on the Marple Canal.[63]

These disclosures naturally caused a great sensation. On 13 August a correspondent of the *Morning Herald* in Stockport reported that the magistrates had arrested Scholefield, an active agitator among the unions in the cotton trade in the period 1829–31 (although a joiner by trade according to the *Stockport Advertiser*), and charged him with having paid £3 6s 8d to each assassin; it was expected that the whole of the 1831 spinners' committee would be charged with instructing him to pay the money.[64] On 16 August, Thomas Platt, the spinner who had been discharged from the Apethorn Mill just before the murder and whom William Mosley had also implicated in the negotiations leading to the murder, was brought up before the magistrates, but released from lack of corroborative evidence. Another suspect, John Leigh, who had been arrested following some wild talk in an Ashton public-house, was also liberated, but Samuel Scholefield was again identified by the informant and committed to Chester Castle.[65] But despite another offer of a £200 reward for information, no further arrests were ever made, nor a successful prosecution ever instituted against Scholefield.

The strongest defence of the unionists came from the unstamped press, particularly the *Poor Man's Guardian*, which called William Mosley 'as great a villain as ever breathed' and alleged that Garside's original confession had only been made in the vain hope of securing a pardon. The same paper later maintained that the accusations were part of a conspiracy between the government and the capitalists to calumniate and destroy the unions.[66]

James Garside and Joseph Mosley were finally executed on 25 November,[67] but the controversy over union participation has continued. J. F. Foster, the Manchester magistrate, who had already warned Melbourne that the failure of the spinners' general strike call was likely to increase the threat of violence, because the restraining influence of the union leaders over the more turbulent spirits would be removed,[68] testified to the 1838 Select Committee on Combinations that Ashton's murder was supposed to have arisen from the dispute between the masters and men, but he did not believe the unions had directly encouraged the violence.[69] In the first historical account of the Ashton strike in 1860, however, William A. Jevons found 'no reason to suspect' the evidence of Garside, William Mosley and James Ashton, incriminating the spinners' union, since it was given 'by the actual parties concerned'.[70] Later historians have also tended to express their opinions on this question arbitrarily, depending on whether or not they believed the confessions. On one side, for instance, S. J. Chapman stated, 'There is little doubt that Thomas Ashton was murdered in 1831 on the instructions of trade-union officials.'[71] On the other, the Hammonds replied that 'there seems very little basis for this charge. Lt. Col. Shaw, in his official report on 4 January, wrote "The turn-outs have lately been behaving peaceably and in a very subdued manner, nor is there the least proof that the murder was perpetrated by them" . . . The charge against the union rests on statements in the confessions of the murderers themselves, and in view of the circumstances under which they were obtained it is difficult to attach any value to these confessions.'[72]

The available information makes it impossible to reach a definite conclusion. The attempt to murder Samuel Heginbottom, an Ashton manufacturer, in June 1830,[73] suggests that there was a militant faction among the local workers who were not averse to extreme methods and may have been implicated in the later outrage. Moreover, the calamitous publicity following the murder of Thomas Ashton did not end the mischief. On 10 January and again the next day, crowds marched from Ashton and Stalybridge, armed with pistols, to attack a mill at Hayfield, near Glossop, for the purpose of turning out the knobstick hands. The military had been called out on the second occasion and nine individuals were arrested, who were bound over by the Glossop magistrates to appear at the next Derbyshire assizes on indictments for 'riot and tumultuous assembly'. On 12 January a shot was fired at, and slightly wounded, James Howard, a Stalybridge manufacturer, who offered £300 reward for the capture of the offender. And on 14 January six shots were fired at Charles Kershaw, of Mossley, while he was sitting in his kitchen, and further rewards of £100 from the victim and £200 from the master spinners' association were offered. In both cases the government added £100. But these atrocities occurred at a time when the local union leaders had temporarily lost their authority over the strikers, disappointed at the fiasco of the spinners' general strike and at the refusal of the National Association to open its funds to relieve them. Despite exhaustive enquiries, no charges were brought against any union officials, nor was there any evidence that they were not sincere in their frequent protestations that the use of physical force could only harm their cause. The only specific accusation against them was in a letter from James Platt, spinner, in January 1833, which said not only that Betts, Slater, Brookes and others were responsible for the strike, having misled the rank and file on the amount of support they would receive, but also that, 'These same men were on a Secret Committee, and amongst the number who went out in masks in the night for the purposes best known to themselves.'[74]

Amid this background of violence, several attempts were made by the spinners' union, moderate employers, and interested onlookers to settle the dispute by compromise. Early in January, 199 shopkeepers and publicans of the Ashton district, who had previously expressed support for the men, petitioned Lord Derby, the Lord Lieutenant, to act as mediator, but he refused to do so after consulting Lord Melbourne.[75] Charles Hindley, however, entered into negotiations with the union, with a view to getting the two sides to reach agreement, and on 13 January a general meeting of the working spinners of Ashton and Stalybridge expressed their willingness to discuss the masters' resolution of 14 December 1830, which had asserted that the new price list was 'a fair average' of the rates paid in neighbouring districts and had offered to submit it to public examination.[76] The employers at once agreed to meet a deputation on 20 January.[77] Doherty welcomed the decision to accept the masters' challenge, but stated that neither he nor the Ashton leaders had been aware of the December resolution until the previous week. The *Guardian*, not surprisingly, ridiculed this assertion, since the resolution had been reported in all the local papers.[78]

While these negotiations were proceeding and before the meeting took place, an event occurred which must have further weakened faith in the general union, when William Harding, a 'money-steward' of the Manchester cotton spinners' society, absconded with a sum estimated at £60 to £75, the district subscription of the grand general union towards the turn-out spinners of Ashton and neighbourhood. A detailed description of Harding was published in the *Voice* and persons were despatched to Liverpool and other towns to seek him out, but he was never found and it was supposed that he had escaped to America.[79]

On 20 January the majority of the associated masters and delegates from the workmen in all but five of the fifty-two mills involved in the dispute met together at the Ashton town hall. The masters reiterated their belief that their printed list of prices was an average of rates in the area, which in turn were as high as the trade generally could afford, considering the recent recession. But they were willing to establish a joint committee to ascertain the prices paid before the strike in the surrounding districts, 'both parties agreeing to abide by the result determined by the proportionate amount of spindles working at the respective prices'. The men objected to this method of drawing up an average list, and, in accordance with the policy of the Grand General Union, proposed that the list should be based simply on the average of prices paid in each district, as reported to the Manchester delegate meeting in December.[80]

At this impasse the masters adjourned to the 'Globe Inn', and the men to the 'Crown Inn', for separate discussions. The operatives tried to break the deadlock by sending a note to the employers, stating their opinion that 4s 2d was only a fair reward for their labour, 'yet anxious to end the present unhappy contest, they are willing, on behalf of themselves and the body they represent, to accept 4s 1d, provided the masters will use their influence to bring up the other districts to the same price'. Despite this evidence of flexibility from the Ashton spinners, the masters made a brief reply, regretting the operatives' rejection of their proposals and stating that the men could resume work 'at the list price whenever they are so disposed'. Thereupon they peremptorily broke up their meeting, leaving the workmen still sitting in the 'Crown Inn' and anxious to continue negotiations.[81]

The *Manchester Guardian* editorial on the meeting attributed the breakdown of the bargaining to the operatives' refusal to accept the number of spindles as a basis for determining the quantity spun at each price and thus the average of prices actually paid for spinning; the same fear that such an enquiry would prove the justice of the masters' case had caused the men to delay a month before answering the masters' resolution of 14 December. On the other hand, Doherty asserted that the masters' abrupt termination of discussions affecting 30,000 famishing people proved that their only motive for entering the negotiations was to see if the men had yet been starved into submission. The masters' resolution, as he had suspected, was vague, insincere, and *not intended* to lead to practical results. It would be impossible to calculate the average price by counting the number of spindles: in Manchester alone, he knew of one mill with five different sizes of wheels. The masters had rejected the proposals to take the average of prices in the various districts, because the only desire of their association was to undercut their neighbours and goad their distressed workmen into acts of violence. Yet the press said nothing of this conspiracy by rich masters, while continually denouncing the combinations of workmen, which were always defensive in character. Most important, the employers' emphasis on the spinners' high wages of 30s to 35s per week ignored the bad working conditions in 'cotton hells'. Spinners deserved higher wages than other workmen, because their working life was rarely more than fifteen years. In proof of this, Doherty published a table, furnished by the Ashton strikers, of the numbers, from fifteen years upwards, employed in fifty-two factories in Ashton, Stalybridge, Mossley and Dukinfield. Of 1,669 employed as spinners and stretchers in these mills, less than a quarter (338) exceeded thirty-five years and one in twenty exceeded forty-five years. Doherty concluded with a prayer that, 'if 30,000 Englishmen are to be thus treated by those whom their toil has raised', workmen in other trades should not neglect their interests, which were also in fact their own.[82]

The union leaders sought to prevent rank-and-file disappointment expressing itself in mindless violence, by keeping alive hopes of a peaceful solution. On the very next day, separate meetings of Stalybridge and Ashton spinners passed resolutions that a memorial should be sent to Lord Melbourne, stating their actual situation and the amount of the intended reduction, the number of fines and other restrictions they suffered while at work, and the probability of subsequent reductions and strikes throughout the whole cotton-manufacturing area if the new list was accepted in their district. Letters were also sent to several members of parliament in the hope of obtaining copies of the information sent to the Home Office by the masters, so that replies could be made. The men also stated that they were willing to accept the masters' proposition for establishment of a joint committee to ascertain the average rates in other districts.[83] Although none of these projects had any effect on the intransigence of the employers, who were now planning the re-opening of their factories from a position of strength, no further serious disturbances were reported in the district for the duration of the strike.

The collapse of negotiations also led to increased efforts by the Grand General Union and the National Association, in collaboration with the local leaders, to get subscriptions for the strikers, who were now reported to be subsisting on 2s per week each.[84] Delegates toured the industrial areas, urging trades to combine in financial support, and meetings were reported in Glasgow, Oldham, Derby, Leeds, Hanley, Liverpool, and Belfast, resulting in the appointment of local trades' committees to organise the collection of contributions. Although the Ashton–Stalybridge strikers received no aid directly from the funds of the National Association,[85] it is quite clear that delegates from that body played a prominent part in organising support, at the same time publicising the aims and often setting up local branches of the Association.[86]

Unfortunately, however, this campaign was marred by a bitter dispute between the Manchester and Bolton committees of the National Association. The latter district had broken away because of the establishment of the *Voice of the People*, mainly because they regarded this as an improper diversion of the Association's funds,[87] and they now started another dispute over £50 of their previously-paid subscriptions, which they demanded should be handed over to the Ashton and Stalybridge turn-outs, but which Doherty maintained he could not disburse without authorisation from the districts. Doherty's opponents, in addition to attacking his 'peremptory' and 'haughty' manner in this affair, contrasted the lavish expenditure on the *Voice* and on the handsome salaries for Doherty and Hodgins with the refusal of aid to the strikers: 'the Ashton people were indignant at seeing Doherty and others appropriate funds to any other than the original intention' of supporting strikes.[88] Nevertheless, the Bolton district continued with their efforts to collect subscriptions for the strikers and forwarded a handsome 'donation' on 10 February.[89]

The efforts of the Grand General Union, National Association, and local spinners' clubs were at last succeeding—though, unfortunately, as it turned out, too late—in getting funds to the Ashton district. When the masters determined to reopen their mills at the beginning of February, the men stated that they would continue to resist, as they were in a better condition than before because their funds had been swelled by subscriptions lately opened in various places and also by the mysterious 'transmission from an unknown source of a bill for £1,000': as a result, the pay on Monday, 1 February, had been 3s 9d, in some cases 4s 2d, for each man, and the allowances were expected to continue rising.[90] In such circumstances, the hostile press redoubled its efforts to discredit the local and general union leaders in the eyes of the rank and file.

Such attacks had, of course, been commonplace throughout the strike. The *Manchester Guardian*, for example, in denouncing the union's price-equalisation policy, blamed it on the dictatorial authority of agitators whose objects were mainly 'political'.[91] On 8 January a letter was published from 'An Operative Spinner and a Well-Wisher' in Ashton, complaining of the starving condition of the neighbourhood because of the lack of support from the National Association, while a great sum had been used to begin the *Voice of the People*. While the men on strike had received only 3s to 5s to support their families for three weeks, 'Others, called delegates, are receiving £2 to £6 per week. Now let us begin to open our eyes, and no longer suffer these men in ruffled shirts, new top coats and boots, to parade the streets at our expense. If they are wishful to do us good, let them work for less wages, such as we can support, while we are in such a distressed state, not to expend our money in coaches, but walk from place to place.'[92] Similarly, on 15 January, *Wheeler's Manchester Chronicle* asserted that, while the turn-outs were penniless, 'their servant, Betts, can afford to travel the country in a chaise and pair'.[93]

But it was after the National Association and Grand General Union intensified their efforts to raise funds following the failure of the negotiations with the employers, that by far the most vitriolic onslaughts appeared in the *Stockport Advertiser* in a series of editorials under the general heading, 'The Turn-Out not a free Act'. On 21 January the paper stated that not one in twenty of the men had turned out willingly and they were only prevented from returning by fear of the delegates and their 'gang of hired desperadoes, vitriol throwers and assassins'. These 'agitators' earned large weekly salaries, for which their only qualifications were 'the power of speech, a little learning and a preference for pocketing the money of others to earning their own subsistence'. Their ignorance was proved by the iniquitious resolution to try and equalise prices throughout the cotton trade, ignoring differences in the power of engines, size and age of machinery, and quality of cotton used.[94] In the course of the next week, a meeting of Ashton spinners passed a vote

of censure on the editor of the *Stockport Advertiser* for his repeated falsehoods and attacks on the character of the strike leaders, and clearly Doherty
himself was goaded into making a protest, because the next paper contained
the following notice: 'An anonymous letter has been sent to us in reference
to an article of ours in last week's paper. The Writer may consider himself
fortunate, if he escapes legal proceedings, for we have no doubt of his identity.
Look to your own conduct in the affair, Mr D., our's we can justify.'[95]

The strike was blamed on such 'agitators', who, it was further alleged,
encouraged acts of 'personal vengeance'. Their official organ, the *Voice of the
People*—really derived 'from the pockets of the people'—gave tacit approval
to such outrages by perpetually warning the masters that they must take the
consequences for their own actions.[96] Doherty angrily refuted the allegation
that he and others had forced the workmen to strike. 'It is notorious that the
leaders opposed the turn-out; and we ourselves stated that as a measure of
policy the reduction should be partially submitted to . . . Every man in
Ashton and Stalybridge knows the statements to be as false, as the writer
is contemptible.' The nadir of debate was now reached. Doherty described
the Stockport paper as a 'vile vehicle of falsehood . . . [an]) atrocious libeller
of honest industry . . . [a] mean, mercenary, sycophant . . . who licks the feet
of his profligate and heartless employers and urges them to new acts of
tyranny and plunder'. In reply, the editor described Doherty's abuse as the
'barking and snarling of his natural tongue. Anything proceeding from such
a source we shall treat as we should the cur that molests us in the streets.'[97]
Doherty continued to defend himself, but with the defeat of the Ashton
strike and the absconding of Hynes, criticism of the National Association
and its officers became a torrent which threatened to overwhelm the whole
structure.[98]

There were now ominous signs of impending defeat. The strike of spinners
in the Glossop district, which had begun on 27 December following the
resolution of the grand general union, collapsed at the end of January, the
operatives returning on the employers' terms, though many were not accepted
as their wheels had been taken by fresh hands.[99] Then, at a general meeting
of the associated master spinners of Ashton, Stalybridge, Dukinfield and
Mossley at the 'White Bear Inn', Manchester, on 1 February, it was unanimously resolved to re-open their mills on 3 February 'to such of their workmen who choose to resume . . . at the masters' list price, and all such who
do not return to their work, their places will be supplied by others'.[100] A
meeting of the operative spinners on 2 February again rejected the employers'
terms in view of the additional support they were now receiving, and in the
event few of the men returned to work the following morning;[101] but the end
was not to be long delayed.

In the *Voice*, Doherty remained outwardly optimistic. On 5 February he
published an advertisement, signed by John Hynes 'by order of the Ashton
etc. spinners', stating that two firms had resumed work on their workmen's
terms and that with the continuation of liberal assistance, 'we will soon have
a favourable result to the contest'.[102] In fact the two factories which had
recommenced both employed fine spinners, whose prices were of course
more than 3s 9d by the new list. And by the beginning of the succeeding
week, all the Stalybridge spinners returned to work on the employers' terms.

Doherty claimed that these men had been permitted to return by the union to conserve funds, and the *Voice* reported a meeting of Ashton spinners on 10 February which had resolved not to submit.[103] But this was no more than an attempt to salvage some consolation from what rapidly became a complete defeat. All the Ashton mills had restarted on the new list by Monday, 14 February, and over the next few days the turn-out was also abandoned at Dukinfield and Mossley. The *Manchester Guardian* spoke for almost all the local newspapers in rejoicing that the strike had 'utterly failed', and that the authority and reputation of the unionists had been discredited. 'The confident promises of success made by the DOHERTYS, the BETTS'S, and we know not whom besides, have been completely falsified; and the allowances which the men were given to understand they would have had, have not been forthcoming.'[104]

All the spinners involved in the dispute had suffered from the loss of nine or ten weeks' wages at the harshest season of the year. But an estimated three hundred of them, including the most militant, faced the prospect of permanent unemployment in consequence of their employers' refusal to take them back, their places having been supplied by fresh hands, while many were blacklisted. Various schemes were projected to help these men, including co-operative production and emigration to America.[105] Appeals for their relief also appeared in the *Voice*, and they were included among those 'now suffering in consequence of turn-outs for the protection of wages' on whose behalf a voluntary subscription was launched by the National Association delegate meeting at Nottingham on 14 March, though with pathetic results.[106]

At the end of the strike Doherty rather hopefully asserted that 'The short history of this struggle supplies the materials of a very useful lesson to the great mass of labouring men, which we shall not fail to make use of on a future occasion.' Certainly, over the next six months, the effects of the strike were not forgotten. On 2 April Doherty wrote a blistering editorial, headed the 'Barbarity of Wealth', in which he condemned the reckless resolution of 'the 52' not only to blacklist one fifth of their poor workmen, but to print a list of their names, in red ink, and send it round the country to prevent them getting work elsewhere. 'New hands are to be made without number, and the old ones to be turned adrift to perish in the streets and plunder in the highways. They are to be hunted down like beasts.' An article in the same paper reported a recent vestry meeting at Ashton, where the support of numerous cotton masters secured the election of their nominees as officers for the ensuing year, and also the payment of £400 for the erection of a temporary barracks. Doherty commented that, 'We should be glad if these cotton masters extended a similar sympathy towards the wages of their dependants, and remembered that the additional taxes to pay for the extra salaries is to be wrung from wretches with whom they have left little to pay.' In July another editorial on 'The notorious 52', referring to their recent discharge of more workmen for subscribing to support those men on the blacklist, likened the Ashton masters to 'the Spaniards who pursued the poor native South Americans *with their dogs*'. Finally, on 20 August, Doherty referred to 'The 52 Again', who had insisted on their 'slaves' withdrawing from their union at the end of the late strike, which 'disgraceful condition' was almost universally accepted, leaving a few men saddled with a debt of several hundred pounds incurred in defending those arrested during the strike. He also intended shortly to give 'a historical sketch' of these masters' rise to riches, but this project did not materialise.[107]

These editorials, however, concealed an acrimonious disagreement between the Ashton spinners and the National Association, which had frequently been suggested by the press during the strike. The strikers felt that they had been let down. One source of grievance was the absconding of John Hynes with money subscribed for their support, so when he was recaptured with £51 of his ill-gotten gains still in his possession, the Ashton workmen naturally laid claim to it. In the middle of May, therefore, they sent two delegates to the Manchester committee with a letter demanding that sum, and also £9 to which they were also said to be entitled. This started another wrangle, however, similar to that over the Bolton subscriptions, the new secretary, John Cheetham, maintaining that he had no authority to make such payment. He was supported by Doherty, who condemned the Ashton delegates for their abusive conduct.[108] The result was the resignation of the Ashton spinners from the Association. And subsequently we find Doherty condemning the abject surrender of the Ashton workmen in renouncing their union at the dictate of their despotic masters.[109]

The failure of the Ashton–Stalybridge strike was followed by the decline and disappearance of the spinners' Grand General Union, which had committed itself to outright support of the turn-out at its third delegate meeting, in Manchester, in December.[110] Labour historians have never adequately recounted the proceedings of this meeting.[111] Apart from the contemporary press references to the general strike resolution, the only record of the conference was contained in the pamphlet *On Combinations of Trades*, which included in an Appendix the 'Resolutions of a Delegate Meeting of the Operative Cotton Spinners of England, Ireland and Scotland assembled in Manchester, on the 16th, 17th, 18th and 20th days of December 1830'.[112] Of the twenty-eight resolutions in all that were adopted, nine repeated identically the wording of those passed at the Isle of Man assembly in December 1829, which established the Grand General Union. The contribution was to remain 1d a week to the general fund in addition to the local district subscription; each member up to date with his payments was to receive a union card to enable him to move between districts; partial strikes were to be supported for as long as possible by extra local contributions of 1s per week; the same restrictions were to apply to the teaching of piecers to spin—not even the date for putting the policy into effect was changed (5 April 1830); the monthly correspondence between the secretary and the districts, in which the names of dishonourable members were to be exposed, was to be continued; and the same declaration that the Grand General Union had no intention of interfering with the rights and property of employers, or with the reasonable authority of masters and overlookers in their factories, was also adopted. Since this resolution merely reaffirmed previous policy, G. D. H. Cole was completely mistaken in suggesting that it was a new conciliatory gesture to employers and represented a desire by the spinners to dissociate themselves from Doherty's ideas as 'an ardent Owenite who believed that the distinction between master and man was destined to be swept away by the advent of the Co-operative Commonwealth'.[113] It is true, as we shall see, that Doherty gave strong support to producer co-operation, but he attacked the more idealistic co-operative schemes of this time, and there is no evidence whatever that he endeavoured to divert the spinners' Grand General Union into such utopianism.[114]

The resolution that each nation should manage its own affairs, subject to decisions by a general meeting of delegates, was also re-enacted. But because of Cole's erroneous belief that the Grand General Union had been established at the Isle of Man with one governing committee at Manchester, as Doherty wanted,[115] he has depicted this resolution about national committees at the December 1830 meeting as a deliberate rejection of Doherty's policy of centralisation in favour of Thomas Foster's more particularist proposals of the previous year—this alleged reversal being accompanied by Foster's appointment to succeed Doherty as secretary of the union.[116] In fact the change was entirely in the opposite direction, for the conference passed the following motions :

> That a council, consisting of three respectable persons, be appointed by and from the Manchester body to receive and pay all monies, one of whom shall retire monthly—to be allowed 1s each for every attendance. Such persons to hold no office or situation connected with the trade, in the district to which they belong, during their councilship; this council to have power to appoint persons to examine the books of any district which they may suspect of attempting to impose upon the Union.
>
> That two persons be appointed from the neighbouring districts to attend the council on days of meeting, and to assist in receiving and paying money, and in conducting the affairs of the Union. Any district refusing to send a proper person when called upon, to be fined in the sum of £1.

These regulations embodied all the centralisation that Doherty had desired at the Isle of Man to overcome the spinners' regional exclusiveness.[117] By a further resolution, the supreme authority was still to lie with the general delegate meetings to be held twice a year, of which the next was to take place at Liverpool on Whit Monday. How the administrative power of the central council of five was to be reconciled with the independence of the national committees was unclear (unless the former was meant only to govern the English spinners). But in the event the Grand General Union rapidly declined into insignificance in 1831—following the fiasco of the general strike call, the failure of the Ashton turn-out and the death of Thomas Foster, and not because of the 'constitution-mongering' at the Manchester conference, which H. A. Turner condemns[118]—and there is no record of the Liverpool meeting ever taking place.

The alterations in the government of the union naturally affected the procedure regulating the calling of strikes, but the basic policy of the union remained the same. Turn-outs against reductions or to procure advances on those prices which were below the average were to be supported by an allowance of 10s per week, with the qualification that, 'in conformity with the existing laws', the number of strikers should never exceed the capability of the Union to relieve them. Exceptions to the rule could now be made 'in cases of great emergency'—a modification of the expression 'on any consideration whatever' used the previous year, but the possibility that some districts might temporarily have to submit to reductions while other strikes were taking place was explicitly stated for the first time.[119] It was presumably to assist in the administration of this rule that it was resolved that one strike should be considered as officially terminated 'when all the wheels are running', and that the spinners made unemployed by the fresh hands 'shall continue on ailment two months after such termination, but no longer, except the strike be renewed'. The conference also made the first formalisation of the spinners' 'rolling strike' technique:

> Should any one or more districts be receiving the same price, and the power of the union is unemployed, but not being sufficient to support all who are receiving the low rate, such districts shall ballot for the precedency of striking for an advance. This shall only be the case when no other part of the members of the Union are receiving a lower rate. The lowest in all cases to take precedency in obtaining advances when no reductions are to be opposed.

To facilitate this policy, every shop in the union was to send in their wage-lists, which would be used in the ballot for preference, following which the council would fix 'the time and place of the strike'. The limits of such a forward policy were thus closely circumscribed, but the Grand General Union never attained a position where it could be put into effect.

When the question of the hours of labour, or the 'short-time' (factory reform) movement, arose at the conference, it was determined that £45 owing to Bolton by the short-time committee should be paid back, but that the subject generally should not be further discussed 'at the present meeting'. Several minor administrative resolutions were also adopted. The 'district depot' was to remain in Manchester, and 'Id per dozen was to be levied for district contribution'. (Probably this was for the relief of the Ashton strikers —the resulting funds were stolen by William Harding, when he absconded on 8 January.[120])

Although the meeting represented a victory for Doherty's centralising ideas, there is some evidence of dissatisfaction with his performance as secretary during the previous year. Indeed, it would have been remarkable had this not been so, considering the violence with which the Bolton spinners were leading the attack on the establishment of the *Voice of the People* with Doherty as editor.[121] One of their accusations was that he had neglected to make out a report, according to instructions, of the Isle of Man conference in June.[122] As we have seen, they considered that his negligence as secretary was partly caused by his many other interests.[123] This dissatisfaction was perhaps reflected in the resolution appointing Thomas Foster as secretary at a weekly salary of 30s, with the direction 'that he devote the whole of his time to the duties in his office'. Nevertheless, it seems very unlikely that G. D. H. Cole is correct in his suggestion that Doherty's withdrawal from the Grand General Union—an important landmark in his career, for he now ceased to have an administrative position in the spinners' union—was actually a dismissal;[124] for, although he was undoubtedly unpopular in some quarters, the conference in fact *adopted* his constitutional proposals, contrary to Cole's belief. Other evidence also suggests that there was no personal rift. Doherty continued to have a warm regard for Foster, as shown by his obituary on the latter's death two months later.[125] The reports of the meeting were printed under Doherty's supervision—and, indeed, may have again been written by him—in the *Voice* office. And that Doherty remained on good terms with the cotton spinners is clearly indicated by subsequent events and by his becoming secretary of the Manchester society once more in 1834.[126] Almost certainly, therefore, Doherty voluntarily resigned as spinners' general secretary in December 1830, because his own inclinations were to concentrate on editing the *Voice* and assisting in the administration of the National Association.[127]

Much of this conference was taken up, as we have seen, with the Ashton–Stalybridge strike and with formulating a list of average piecework prices, to be enforced by a general turn-out. But the latter proved a fiasco, because Scotland, Ireland, and most English districts refused to participate. Thus, at the very time when the cotton spinners had on paper created the only unitary constitution in their early history, the reality of their sectional inclinations was clearly demonstrated. Nevertheless, the Grand General Union remained active in January 1831, raising funds for the Ashton strikers. Though the defalcation of Harding was a further setback, contact was maintained between the English and Scottish spinners despite their disagreements at the congress, and a valuable donation was sent to the Ashton men by the Glasgow spinners towards the end of January, following promptings from the Lancashire spinners.[128] Moreover, Doherty told the 1838 Combinations Committee that 'we were connected with the Belfast spinners in 1829, 1830 and up to 1831'.[129] However, though the Manchester conference had upheld Doherty's policies, his concentration on the affairs of the National Association and the *Voice* rapidly caused the progress of the Ashton strike to be associated with that body rather than with the Grand General Union, whose power was on the wane.

Whereas the defeat of the Manchester spinners in 1829 was the direct cause of the attempt to form a federal union in the trade, the collapse of the Ashton spinners' resistance in the second week of February 1831 resulted in the final disintegration of that attempt. It coincided with the death of Thomas Foster on 8 February at the age of 38 from an asthmatic disease. Doherty described him as 'one of the most consistent, energetic and uncompromising, as well as able, leaders among the working-classes which this quarter of the country has yet produced', adding that the workmen generally, and the spinners particularly, had lost 'an able and honest friend'.[130] His funeral at the Wesleyan Methodist burying-ground, Cheetham Hill, on 13 February was movingly described in the *Voice*. He had scarcely had time to take up his new duties as secretary of the Grand General Union, and unfortunately, at this same time, his colleague on the important autumn tour of the districts, Patrick McGowan, was forced, temporarily, to 'withdraw from public affairs', when he was accused by the Glasgow spinners of spending too much time on the business of the National Association during that mission.[131]

There were no further references to the Grand General Union or to any delegate meeting in Liverpool as projected. It does, however, appear to have retained some tenuous existence. Doherty paid a final allusion to it in the *Poor Man's Advocate* in June 1832. 'The Union, however, which Mr McGowan had mainly contributed to mature, has since, from distrust or weariness, sunk into comparative insignificance. Had it then been followed up, and matured as it ought, it would now have been one of the most powerful and influential confederacies in this country. To this remedy the workmen must come at last. Union is the only ladder by which they can hope to ascend to their proper place in society.'[132]

The decline of the Grand General Union after January 1831 did not, however, end the working spinners' resistance in the different districts to the employers' practices of introducing reduced wage-lists and making progressive reductions as the size of mules increased, both of which had followed the failure of the Manchester and Stockport strikes in 1829. In April 1830 and again in December, as we have seen, the Manchester spinners had proposed to the master fine-spinners the propriety of establishing a general list of prices for all sizes of mules, 'containing a specific price per pound for each number'.[133] The plan was of advantage to the operatives as it would prevent continual reductions by large-mule masters, and also the coupling of mules and the employment of women and lads as spinners below list prices by small-mule masters (against which the local spinners' club was holding a series of strikes in the winter of 1830). But it would also benefit the small-mule masters by halting undercutting by their competitors, while the larger-mule masters would still profit from their more productive machines and from employing the best workmen, attracted by the higher earnings.[134]

The operatives' proposal was ignored in April, but in December several small-mule masters were reportedly interested. However, the workmen proceeded to try imposing their policy by unilateral action, in accordance with the resolution of the grand delegate meeting of 17 December, and three Manchester factories came out on strike on 27 December. But all these turn-outs had terminated by the middle of January and the local spinners' club returned to its policy of persuasion. On 12 February the *Voice* reported that they were endeavouring to prevail on the masters to agree to 'a more equalised list' than that of 1829. Those employers with small mules were said to be anxious for the alteration, because of the 21 per cent advantage given to the large-mule masters; but the latter objected, as the March list had been agreed to by *all* employers. Doherty commented that he could not predict the outcome, 'but we do know, unless a speedy alteration in the list is made, the spinning business will be little better than weaving. Many able and active spinners cannot earn more than 12s or 14s a week: yet fresh reductions are talked of!'[135]

A notice and letter in the *Manchester Times and Gazette* showed that the report in the *Voice* was not without foundation. While several master spinners had given notice of a reduction of ten hanks in the pound, a correspondent, who signed himself 'One of the Master Fine Spinners', wrote that the operatives' 'sensible and moderate and respectful' proposal was entitled to consideration. He condemned 'the rage for gigantic machines' which had lately seized masters and forced those who owned mules of 300 spindles to introduce women into their establishments at reduced wages. Finally he called on the employers to abolish excessive 'home competition', and to form committees to enable operatives to gain 'an equality of prices, in all ordinary cases' and to resist successfully any reductions.[136] Over the next few weeks, the union appointed three or four deputies, including David

McWilliams, to visit the masters and try to persuade them to alter the list, and about twenty-four employers apparently agreed to do so.[137]

A meeting of masters and men was held towards the end of February at the 'Palace Inn' where a new list was agreed upon. The main features of this were, firstly, a reduction of about 10 to 12 per cent on the smallest mules, whilst those of larger size were reduced in a smaller degree and on the largest size there was an *increase* of 2 per cent; and secondly, the masters were to do away with the employment, as spinners, of both lads and females, and confine themselves to male spinners only. The proprietors of the larger mules, however, immediately complained that this list was negotiated without consulting them and that they had received no notice of the 'Palace Inn' meeting. A general meeting of all master fine-spinners was therefore held on 2 March, but the large-mule owners were then told that the list was already fixed and that the parties concerned would put it into effect the following Monday. Consequently, the large-mule owners gave notice to their hands on the succeeding Saturday, 5 March, that they would make a reduction corresponding in amount to that agreed upon by their competitors. In consequence, most of the workmen employed on large mules turned out on 14 March, particularly at the establishments of James Kennedy, T. & R. Barnes, Faulkner & Co., David Bellhouse & Sons, Benjamin Gray and one or two others.[138]

Doherty supported the strike in the *Voice*. In a long article he recalled the warnings given by the operatives in March 1829 of the impolicy of the new list, yet the small-mule masters had contemptuously refused their offer to co-operate in equalising the prices on all mules.[139] Now those same employers considered the 21 per cent advantage given to the large mules to be ruinous, but their practice of employing women and boys at reduced rates had only provoked answering reductions from their competitors. 'Almost incredible' reductions in spinners' wages had occurred over the eighteen months since the end of the strike: the 1829 list had reduced the price paid for 200s from 5s 4d to 4s 1d, but the rate now offered was only 2s 11d. Nevertheless, another struggle was now in progress, not so much between masters and men, as between rival groups of masters, each trying to achieve the lowest labour costs.[140]

Despite this situation, so many spinners were suffering unemployment because of previous strikes and advancing technology, that new hands offered to accept the employers' terms almost as soon as the turn-out commenced. The strikers made some attempts to prevent this influx, but were rapidly overwhelmed by the great quantity of applications from out-of-work spinners, and all the factories in question were either filled, or nearly so, with hands working at the reduced rates by 26 March. 'The only consequence of the attempts to alter the relative prices for large and small mules', commented the *Guardian*, 'has, therefore, been a general reduction of wages, amounting . . . on the average, to about 10 per cent.'[141] But another outcome was the arrest of Peter Maddocks, secretary of the spinners' union, who was charged at the New Bailey on 23 March with having assaulted one Thomas Houldsworth and endeavoured by threats to prevent him from working for David Bellhouse & Sons. Maddocks had apparently directed the pickets, who had stopped Houldsworth reaching the factory by forcing him to go with them to a public-house: they had not used any violence beyond threats and the occasional push. J. F. Foster, the magistrate, decided that there was sufficient evidence to support an indictment for conspiracy, and Maddocks was therefore bound over to answer the charge at the sessions.[142]

The defeat of the strike did not close the controversy. On 31 March David Holt, the proprietor of Chorlton Mills, sent a circular 'To the Master Mule Spinners of Manchester', stating that the late reduction by the large-mule owners would lead to inevitable misery for thousands of industrious and previously comfortable workmen, because the small-mule proprietors were bound to counter it by abating wages further or employing women or grown-up piecers in order to compete in the market. He proposed that the masters should cease to dispute and instead co-operate to keep up the price of labour. In the *Voice*, Doherty directed his readers' attention to this 'excellent letter of that really philanthropic and benevolent gentleman, Mr Holt'. He considered that the scheme should have been implemented years ago, when wages were worth preserving; but the establishment of a 'regulated and standard list of prices' would still be of advantage to both sides of industry, and Doherty hoped that the masters would co-operate with the men both in its formation and in its future amendment, if such was found necessary.[143]

But on 13 April 'A large Mule Owner' wrote an angry reply to Holt's circular, which was inserted in the local papers. The correspondent mocked his adversary's claim to humanity by stating that Holt had chaired the meeting of small-mule masters at the end of February, which had agreed to reduce their spinners' wages, and also later meetings at which the co-operation of the spinners' union had been gained to a new list of prices, reducing prices on small mules and raising them on some of the largest, by threatening to hire females and boys. This action had forced the owners of large mules, on which the workmen could still earn the highest wages despite the reduction, to make a similar abatement, which had provoked the late strike and disturbance organised by the spinners' club. The small-mule masters were behaving like opponents of improved machinery, forgetting how the owners of spinning jennies had accepted the introduction of the original mules, and how the owners of the first mules had acquiesced twenty years ago when Holt and others had begun to use the larger mules of 300 spindles, which were themselves now being superseded. In fact, the 1829 list had been calculated with the interests of both sets of masters equally in mind, and for the sake of unanimity some owners of larger mules submitted to a *reduction* of the advantages they had *previously* had. The proprietors of the improved mules had made the recent reduction unwillingly and in self-defence; they would retract it if their competitors would return to the March list.[144]

David Holt responded to this letter immediately, asserting that the negotiations of the small-mule masters in February and March had been at the request of, and not forced on, the spinners' union; their new list still gave a 7 per cent advantage to larger mules, yet the latter possessed no improvement in construction over the smaller mules, only causing the labourer to work harder for less reward and increasing unemployment.[145] However, nothing further was heard of this controversy, for by now the Manchester spinners' union was at a low ebb. This was openly admitted in partial explanation of the lapse in their subscriptions to the National Association during the early months of 1831; in May, however, they expressed hope of reviving again by the adoption of some new regulations. Doherty, speaking in their support, explained that they had been almost broken by the great 1829 turn-out.[146]

No revival in fact took place. On 17 September the *Voice* reported that a reduction of almost a quarter had been proposed in the wages of the coarse spinners at one factory, which the men could not resist because of 'their own folly, or want of union'. The following week, the fine masters proposed a further reduction, which Doherty claimed would be the third, or in some cases the fourth or even fifth, abatement since the end of the 1829 strike. These effects of a two-year period of disorganisation he contrasted with the years from 1816 to 1829, when the spinners were 'properly united' and not a single reduction was effected, though scores were proposed. He referred, however, to a plan of reconstructing their union discussed at a numerous meeting on 21 September, which was an interesting precursor of the National Regeneration scheme of 1833–4. The master and operative spinners were to be called on to work no more than eight hours a day; Doherty believed that limiting over-production and sharing the work could alone prevent the spinners from being reduced to the state of the weavers, and that the plan could be enforced 'even in defiance of the masters'. He emphasised that 'only three weeks elapsed from the final and formal breaking up of their union'. before the second reduction was proposed.[147]

Thus it appears that the Manchester spinners' society had been rapidly disintegrating during the early part of 1831 and had ceased to exist as a formally organised continuous body. Trade depression and unemployment, successive strike failures, falling-off in membership and weakened finances, accompanied by Doherty's resignation, Foster's death and Maddocks' arrest, account for this collapse. Nothing came of Doherty's scheme for reconstruction and during the next few years the Manchester spinners appear to have had no formal trade-union organisation. They continued, however, to support the short-time or factory-reform movement, in which Doherty played a leading role.[148] Turner therefore states that the spinners' union was debilitated not only by its strike defeats, but also by 'the diversion of its leaders' interest to the agitation for a ten-hour day'.[149] But he is unaware of the long-continued participation of the union in the factory reform movement, especially in 1818–19, 1825, and 1828–30. This agitation in regard to factory children had always, among the cotton operatives, had the important ulterior object of reducing the working hours and increasing the employment of adults—hence its common appellation of 'short-time' movement. Moreover, the reduction of working hours is a perfectly normal and sensible objective for trade unionists, especially in trade depression, and is in no sense a 'diversion' from trade-union activity.

When, however, short-time working was introduced, in 1833, in response to trade depression, it reflected the weakness rather than the strength of the spinners' union. Tufnell reported that 'the cotton-spinning trade . . . has not been flourishing during the last year, and the Manchester factories have only worked eight hours daily. Wages for a time were reduced to a third, and the combinations were unheard of.'[150] It is possible, however, that the Manchester spinners' society may have revived at that time, as indicated by a notice, signed by 'A Committee of Eighteen', of a meeting at the 'Prince's Tavern' in

June 1833, when it was unanimously agreed 'that the contribution should be sevenpence per week for a few weeks, viz: fourpence for men out of work; one penny for Time Bill, and twopence for the Grand Lodge expenses. All moneys to be paid at the Saint Peter's Tavern, as usual'.[151] This seems like the terminology of the Manchester spinners' union, although the fact that it was addressed 'To the Members of the Lancashire Trades' Unions' has generally been taken to show the existence of some kind of federal organisation in the trade in 1833.[152] But in any case the revival of the Manchester spinners' union to anything approaching its 1820s strength had to await the reorganisation of 1834, under Doherty's renewed leadership.[153]

Spinners' societies in other towns experienced similar setbacks during these years. The outcome of the Ashton–Stalybridge strike led to immediate fears of similar action in other towns, such as Oldham, where there were similar 'cotton despots', as Doherty remarked.[154] The Oldham employers finally proposed the expected reduction early in June 1831, and the inevitable strike ensued, the masters showing no inclination to negotiate because of the extreme depression of trade. Equally inevitably, under these circumstances, the strike failed and the men were forced to accept the Ashton–Stalybridge prices, which it was alleged, entailed a weekly wage reduction of 11s in some cases.[155] Doherty blamed this on the action of the Ashton spinners in submitting to the 'avaricious conduct of their employers', and later commented that another general reduction of spinning prices was likely, 'and such will always be the case, when any class of operatives is divided in opinions and actions'.[156]

The collapse of the spinners' Grand General Union thus left them weak and fragmented, and although the separate local societies had revived by the mid-1830s, there was little participation in the general strike wave of 1834, and an effective federation was not again formed until 1842, when the headquarters were established at Bolton.[157] Nevertheless, although the spinners' piece rates fell dramatically on the larger mules between 1829 and 1833, their net weekly earnings only decreased slightly, from an estimated average of about 26s–27s in the former year to about 20s–25s in the latter, despite an increase in the number of assistants required from two to three or four.[158] In 1833 they were still in a favourable position compared with other adult male factory hands—carders ranged from 14s 6d to 17s, power-loom weavers from 13s to 16s 10d and dyers and dressers from 15s to 20s—with skilled but depressed workers like tailors earning 18s and shoemakers 15s–16s, and with most skilled building workers such as bricklayers who earned 17s to 20s, plasterers who earned 19s to 21s, and carpenters who earned 24s; of the workmen covered in the detailed report to the Manchester Chamber of Commerce in April of that year, only the machine-makers (26s–30s), iron founders (28s to 30s), mechanics (24s–26s) and sawyers (24s–28s) earned better wages than most of the cotton spinners. But Tufnell claimed in the following year that the relatively high spinners' wages had attracted an excess of hands into the trade and that the most serious problem for the workmen was unemployment, especially as more productive machinery was introduced:

It may be thought they would be able to attain their object by limiting the number of those admitted to the business, but this they have never been able to do, for one especial reason among others that the last resort of their power, a strike, invariably introduces new workmen, and thus their end is defeated by the very means taken to gain it.[159]

Smelser has asserted that the spinners' money wages rose during the period 1829–33, basing this view on Andrew Ure's calculations in his *Philosophy of Manufactures* (1835), showing that although piece-rates fell, weekly earnings actually rose because of increased productivity on the larger mules.[160] But it must be remembered that Ure was a propagandist for the factory system and a strong opponent of trade unions, and his figures are contradicted by those of the master-manufacturers themselves in the Manchester Chamber of Commerce as well as by the trade-union figures. Smelser admits that Ure's figures require qualifications, e.g. the spinner had to pay an increased number of piecers on larger mules. Moreover, it must be pointed out that, although there was not a large decline in money earnings, the price of bread rose sharply at this time, so that real wages may have fallen more. Rudé has rightly emphasised the background of trade depression, unemployment, and high food prices behind the social disturbances of the early 1830s: 'for twenty-one consecutive months from January 1830, the quarter of wheat in the London Corn Exchange never fell below 70s (its average over the previous seventeen years had been 59s . . .)'.[161]

In the current state of the standard-of-living controversy, it is doubtful whether anyone can speak with confidence about real wages in Manchester at this time, since there is no reliable local cost-of-living index available, but when one bears in mind the evidence not only about bread prices, but also about the heavy unemployment and short time in the area (to which there are innumerable contemporary references), it seems likely that the spinners' strike defeats and wages reductions resulted in worsening real conditions for themselves and their families during these years of trade depression. But they were certainly not a depressed class, by comparison with other workers, and Rudé creates a very misleading impression in stating that their wages 'were depressed by the progressive reductions of piece rates and the massive influx of Irish poor'.[162] This statement ignores the fact, rightly emphasised by employers—and over-emphasised by Smelser—that earnings did not decline in proportion to piece-rate reductions, and although there certainly were surplus hands in cotton-spinning, there was not a 'massive influx of Irish poor' into this branch of the industry. In fact, there were very few Irish spinners[163]—Doherty was a rare bird in that respect—and Rudé has obviously confused the situation of these factory workers with that of the handloom weavers, compared with whom cotton spinners were affluent 'labour aristocrats'.

Equally doubtful is Smelser's assessment of the motives of the spinners' strikes of 1829–31, as an attempt by the operatives to resist the pressures of the improved machines on the family economy; for there is far more validity in the more obvious explanation that the spinners opposed piece-rate reductions—in general, as well as on larger machines—because these threatened their standard of living, at the same time as the larger mules threatened to create more unemployment.[164] The strikes resulted from the efforts of employers to cut labour costs in a period of intense depression and fierce competition, especially from low-wage areas. It is true that the larger mules required more piecers, while tending to displace adult labour, and that the union therefore tried to restrict entry to the trade to sons and relatives, but the aims of this policy were to make their union more effective and to restrict the creation of excess hands, which was leading to unemployment, reduced wage rates and strike failures. There is no need, therefore, to look for complicated theoretical sociological explanations of the spinners' motives. Turner, on the other hand, whose analysis of cotton trade unionism is generally more convincing, is also mistaken in asserting that these were years of trade recovery with the spinners demanding wage advances. He rightly recognises that their more regular, aggressive trade activity coincided with booms—in 1810, 1818, 1824–5, and 1836—but fails to realise that the strikes of 1829–31 were contra-cyclical, defensive campaigns against reductions.[165]

The Grand General Union of cotton spinners was not, in fact, an example of aggressive trade-union development, but was essentially defensive, with the aim of establishing a general list of piece-prices to prevent progressive undercutting within and between districts. In this, however, it failed completely. From an organisational point of view, Doherty's achievements were considerable, but he was never able to overcome the spinners' fundamental sectionalism, despite the resolutions in favour of centralisation at Manchester in December 1830. From its inception in September 1829, moreover, he had acknowledged that not even the union of a whole trade was sufficiently powerful to resist the employers. The Grand General Union of cotton spinners was only part of his plan to establish an all-embracing general union of trades, whereby, as a limited practical objective, no body of operatives would be forced to submit to a large reduction as the Manchester spinners had been, and as a larger ideal, working men would achieve their just place in society. Doherty became more and more involved in the affairs of this larger union, which became known as the National Association for the Protection of Labour, and by the time the spinners' Grand General Union had entered on its decline after January 1831, his main hopes were already centred elsewhere.

NOTES TO CHAPTER FIVE

[1] See above, p. 105.
[2] *Guardian*, 6 November 1830.
[3] *Ibid.*
[4] Turner, *op. cit.*, p. 74.
[5] H.O. 40/27, f. 340.
[6] *Guardian*, 13 November 1830, referred to him as 'the secretary of the Trades' Union' [i.e. N.A.P.L.], but it is probable that the negotiations were regarded as purely the spinners' concern at this time, though it is not clear how separate Doherty kept his two functions.
[7] *Ibid.*
[8] *Voice*, 8 January 1831. But see below, p. 133, for a fundamental difference between the two sides in regard to the method of calculating an average price.
[9] *Stockport Advertiser*, 26 November 1830.
[10] *Times and Gazette*, 27 November 1830.
[11] *Guardian*, 4 December 1830.
[12] H.O. 40/27, f. 349.
[13] *Chronicle*, 26 January 1833.

[14] H.O. 40/26, f. 160, letter from J. F. Foster to Melbourne. He also reported that some of the crowd were 'armed with pistols' and that there was 'great excitement' at the meeting.

[15] *Guardian*, 18 December 1830, and 15 January 1831; *Chronicle*, 11 and 18 December 1830.

[16] *Guardian*, 11 December 1830.

[17] H.O. 40/26, ff. 160 and 194.

[18] H.O. 40/26, f. 181 and 41/8, ff. 446–8.

[19] *Chronicle*, 11 December 1830.

[20] H.O. 40/26, ff. 200 and 203.

[21] *Guardian*, 18 December 1830. Including their families, the subsistence of at least 30,000 was said to have been removed.

[22] *Chronicle*, 18 December 1830.

[23] *Guardian*, 18 December 1830.

[24] H.O. 41/9, ff. 105–8.

[25] H.O. 40/26; *Guardian*, 25 December 1830.

[26] *Guardian*, 18 December 1830, *inter alia*.

[27] But see below, p. 132.

[28] *Ibid.*, 11 December 1830. They later condemned the masters' reduction and the prevalence of the truck system in that area: *Times and Gazette*, 1 January 1831.

[29] See also below, pp. 138–41.

[30] 'A General List of Prices to be paid for spinning on wheels of all sizes, agreed to at a General Delegate Meeting, held at Manchester, on Monday, 20 December 1830,' in H.O. 40/26, enclosed with Foster's letter of 22 December. The prices were arranged at regular intervals, according to the fineness of the yarn, and the following are extracts from the list:

No. 40 twist 0s 2d per lb.   No. 80 twist 0s 5½d per lb.   No. 120 twist 1s 0d
No. 60 twist 0s 3¾d per lb.   No. 100 twist 0s 8d per lb.   No. 140 twist 1s 7½d

[31] *Guardian*, 25 December 1830.

[32] At this meeting, moreover, Doherty was replaced by Thomas Foster as secretary of the Grand General Union. He had already relinquished his similar position in the National Association the previous month, being succeeded by John Hynes. He was now to become editor of the *Voice of the People*, but still played a leading role in both the spinners' union and the National Association. See above, pp. 110–1, and below, pp. 140–1 and 190.

[33] H.O. 40/26, f. 283.

[34] *Ibid.*, letter of J. F. Foster dated 22 December 1830.

[35] *Ibid.*, f. 264, letter dated 23 December 1830.

[36] H.O. 40/25, letter by J. B. Clarke, Manchester borough-reeve.

[37] See above, pp. 111–2; *Guardian*, 11 December 1830. This statement again illustrates, however, the confusion between the activities of the local spinners' society, the spinners' general union, and the National Association.

[38] See above, p. 111. Intimidation was having to be used to force reluctant members to contribute, e.g. by threatened exposure of names and by sending 'the piquet'. *Returns* for 10 December 1830 (H.O. 40/26, f. 264). Some workers also complained of being 'forced . . . to turn out'. Parl. Papers, 1833, xxi, D. 2, pp 38–40; *Guardian*, 18 December 1830.

[39] H.O. 40/25, letter from J. B. Clarke, Manchester borough-reeve, to Melbourne, 24 December 1830.

[40] H.O. 40/26, ff. 293 and 305, letters from J. F. Foster to Melbourne, 27 and 31 December 1830; *Guardian*, 1 January; *Advertiser*, 15 January 1831; Parl. Papers, 1833, xxi, D. 2, pp. 38–40.

[41] *Guardian*, 1 January; *Chronicle*, 1 January 1831; *Stockport Advertiser*, 31 December 1830.

[42] *Times and Gazette*, 1 January; *Chronicle*, 1 January 1831; *Guardian*, 25 December 1830.

[43] *Voice*, 1 and 8 January 1831.

[44] *Ibid.*, 8 January–12 March 1831.

[45] See below, p. 209.

[46] *Voice*, 8 January 1831. See below, pp. 208–9. The Nottingham trades, under the leadership of Thomas Matthews and H. N. Bullock, were particularly responsive to the cause of 'the brave spinners'.

[47] In an editorial reply on 8 January, the *Guardian* asserted that gross earnings before the strike had been 50s per week, and take-home pay, even according to Betts' exaggerated calculations, would still average £1 7s 9d after the reduction.

[48] *Guardian*, 8 and 22 January; *Voice*, 22 January 1831.

[49] *Voice*, 8 January 1831.

[50] *Guardian*, 8 and 22 January; *Voice*, 22 January 1831.

[51] *Guardian*, 8 January; *Chronicle*, 8 January 1831.

[52] *Voice*, 15 January 1831, *inter alia*.

[53] H.O. 41/9, f. 298. According to the *Guardian*, 15 January 1831, *three* London officers were sent.

[54] *Advertiser*, 15 January; *Voice*, 22 January 1831.

[55] *Times and Gazette*, 8 January 1831.

[56] *Voice*, 15 January 1831.

[57] *Guardian*, 15 January 1831.

[58] *Times and Gazette*, 15 January 1831.

[59] *Voice*, 22 January 1831.

[60] *Advertiser*, 8 January 1831. See below, p. 187.

[61] Tufnell, *op. cit.*, p. 30.

[62] *Guardian*, 19 and 26 April 1834.

[63] *Ibid.*, 9 August 1834.

[64] *Morning Herald*, 13 August; *Stockport Advertiser*, 22 August 1834.

[65] *Stockport Advertiser*, 22 August 1834.

[66] *Poor Man's Guardian*, 16 and 23 August, 8 November 1834.

[67] *Chronicle*, 29 November 1834.

[68] H.O. 40/26, f. 293.

[69] Parl. Papers, 1837–8, VIII, 3253–4.

[70] W. A. Jevons, *An Account of the Spinners' Strike at Ashton-under-Lyne in 1830* (1860), in Webb Collection, Vol. xxxv, ff. 155–7.

[71] Chapman, *op. cit.*, p. 199, n. 1.

[72] J. L. and B. Hammond, *The Skilled Labourer, 1760–1832* (1919), p. 135.

[73] See above, pp. 101–2 and 104.

[74] *Chronicle*, 15 and 22 January 1831, and 26 January 1833.

[75] J. R. M. Butler, *The Passing of the Great Reform Bill* (1914), p. 170, quoting from H.O. 40/27.

[76] See above, p. 124.

[77] *Guardian*, 15 January 1831.

[78] *Voice*, 15 January; *Guardian*, 22 January 1831.

[79] *Voice*, 15 January; *Times and Gazette*, 15 January 1831.

[80] See above, pp. 124–5.

[81] *Voice*, 22 January; *Guardian*, 22 January 1831.

[82] *Voice*, 22 and 29 January 1831.

[83] *Guardian*, 22 January 1831.

[84] *Ibid.*, 29 January 1831.

[85] See above, pp. 121 and 126–7, and below, pp. 182 and 204, n. 208.

[86] *Voice*, 29 January, 5, 12, and 19 February 1831.

[87] See below, pp. 190–3.

[88] *Bolton Chronicle*, 22 January; *Chronicle*, 29 January; *Voice*, 5 February 1831.

[89] *Bolton Chronicle*, 5 and 12 February 1831.

[90] *Chronicle*, 3 February 1831.

[91] *Guardian*, 25 December 1830.

[92] *Ibid.*, 8 January 1831.

[93] *Chronicle*, 15 January 1831.

[94] *Stockport Advertiser*, 21 January 1831.

[95] *Voice*, 29 January; *Stockport Advertiser*, 18 January 1831.

[96] *Stockport Advertiser*, 4 and 11 February 1831.

[97] *Voice*, 12 February; *Stockport Advertiser*, 18 February 1831.

[98] See below, pp. 210–6.

[99] *Voice*, 29 January; *Guardian*, 29 January 1831.

[100] *Guardian*, 5 February 1831.

[101] *Ibid.*

[102] *Voice*, 5 February 1831.

[103] *Ibid.*, 12 February 1831.

[104] *Guardian*, 12 February 1831.

[105] *Voice*, 19 February; *Times and Gazette*, 19 February and 23 April 1831. The latter paper also revealed on 30 July 1831 that Betts was no longer secretary of the Ashton spinners, but was selling goods on the market. Nothing appears to have come of the co-operative scheme but a few men were assisted in emigrating.

[106] *Voice*, 26 March 1831. Cole, *Attempts at General Union*, p. 34, wrongly presumes that this appeal was 'a last desperate attempt to save the Ashton strikers from collapse'. Only five small donations 'for the unfortunate men of Ashton . . . still out of employment' were acknowledged in the *Voice*, 26 March–16 April 1831.

[107] *Voice*, 19 February, 2 April, 2 July and 20 August 1831.

[108] *Ibid.*, 21 May 1831.

[109] *Ibid.*, 20 August 1831. Doherty made this statement to Nottingham workmen who, after having so generously supported the Ashton men, were cold-shouldered by the latter during the long strike in the Nottingham silk trade in the following summer. See below, pp. 228–30.

[110] See above, pp. 124–6.

[111] Moreover, Cole, *Attempts at General Union*, p. 25, and Turner, *op. cit.*, p. 74, believe that it was the second delegate meeting, ignoring the Isle of Man conference in June 1830.

[112] *On Combinations of Trades* (1831), Appendix II, pp. 76–9.

[113] Cole, *Attempts at General Union*, pp. 27–8. The extraordinary statement of D. C. Morris, *op. cit.*, p. 53, that 'Doherty's idea of establishing a Co-operative Community was repudiated' at this conference, is presumably based on Cole's suggestion and is equally without foundation. Thompson, Rudé and others have made similarly erroneous statements regarding Doherty's alleged conversion of the cotton spinners to Co-operation.

[114] See below, Ch. IX.

[115] See above, pp. 89–90.

[116] Cole, *Attempts at General Union*, p. 27.

[117] This was recognised by contemporary observers. On 23 December J. F. Foster, reporting to Melbourne the conversation between Maddocks and a large manufacturer on the effects of the intended general strike (see above, p. 125), added that Maddocks further stated that the affairs of the Grand General Union, instead of being run by the different committees of the several districts as before, were now in the hands of a meeting of delegates, one of whom was to be sent from each district, and that the resolutions of this meeting would be absolutely binding on the several district unions 'in the same way (in his words) as Acts of Parliament'. H.O. 40/26, f. 264.

[118] Turner, *op. cit.*, p. 83.

[119] Cole, *Attempts at General Union*, p. 27, rightly points out that this policy rejected the idea of a general strike; but he wrongly states, p. 26, that 'the abortive appeal for a general spinners' strike *led* [our italics] at the December conference, to substantial changes in the constitution of the Grand General Union'. In fact, the apparently conflicting decisions were made at the *same* conference. The disharmony can be reconciled either by believing the local magistrate's report to the Home Office that the Grand General Union did not intend to support those who struck for 4s 2d per 1,000 hanks out of the funds and that the general strike call was merely a threat to intimidate the employers (see above, pp. 124–6), or by accepting that the delegates considered the Ashton strike to be an exceptional case 'of great emergency'.

[120] See above, pp. 132–3.

[121] See below, pp. 190 *et seq.*

[122] See above, p. 100.

[123] See above, p. 103.

F

[124] Cole, *Attempts at General Union*, p. 27.
[125] See below, p. 141.
[126] See below, p. 303.
[127] Although he was no longer secretary of the Association, he continued to dominate the Manchester central committee: see below, p. 219.
[128] The Glasgow spinners appointed a committee, including Patrick McGowan, to organise an appeal to the local trades, whilst they themselves were reported at the end of January as having sent £60 already and having instituted a weekly subscription of 1s 6d in aid of the strikers. *Voice*, 29 January 1831.
[129] Parl. Papers, 1837–8, VIII, 3552. See also the *Voice*, 19 February 1831, for support given by Belfast trades to the Ashton strike.
[130] *Voice*, 12 February 1831.
[131] *Ibid.*, 19 February and 27 August 1831.
[132] *Advocate*, 23 June 1832.
[133] See above, pp. 109–10 and 112.
[134] *Guardian*, 18 December 1830.
[135] *Voice*, 12 February 1831.
[136] *Times and Gazette*, 12 February 1831.
[137] Parl. Papers, 1837–8, VIII, 3658.
[138] *Guardian*, 26 March 1831.
[139] See above, p. 60.
[140] *Voice*, 26 March 1831.
[141] *Guardian*, 26 March 1831. David McWilliams, however, told the 1838 Committee that the weekly abatement equalled 7s, which 'we sacrificed for the purpose of making the matter as comfortable as we could wish with our employers': Parl. Papers, 1837–8, VIII, 3658.
[142] *Guardian*, 26 March 1831.
[143] *Voice*, 9 April 1831.
[144] *Guardian*, 16 April 1831.
[145] *Voice*, 23 April 1831.
[146] *Ibid.*, 21 May 1831. In fact they contributed nothing further to the National Association. The lack of enthusiasm for the Association among the Manchester spinners was a regular source of embarrassment to Doherty. See below, pp. 177, 235 and 259–60.
[147] *Ibid.*, 17 and 24 September 1831.
[148] See below, Ch. x.
[149] Turner, *op. cit.*, p. 74.
[150] Tufnell, *op. cit.*, p. 80.
[151] This notice is copied into Tufnell's pamphlet, p. 34.
[152] As by Turner, *op. cit.*, p. 74.
[153] See below, p. 303 *et seq.*
[154] *Voice*, 5 March 1831.
[155] *Times and Gazette*, 11 June–20 August 1831.
[156] *Voice*, 11 June and 30 July 1831.
[157] For a short-lived attempt at federation in 1836, with the usual equalisation policy, see below, p. 308.
[158] Manchester Chamber of Commerce, *Proceedings*, 27 April 1833. Many of the most skilled spinners could still earn 28s–32s weekly.
[159] Tufnell, *op. cit.*, p. 35. It was primarily for this reason—to reduce unemployment and raise wages—that the spinners' trade societies were so active in the ten hours' movement (*ibid.*, pp. 35–6).
[160] Smelser, *op. cit.*, p. 197.
[161] Rudé, *op. cit.*, p. 88.
[162] *Ibid.*
[163] See above, p. 52.
[164] See Musson's review of Smelser's book in the *Journ. of Econ. Hist.*, Vol. 20 (1960).
[165] Turner, *op. cit.*, pp. 70–78. For further consideration of the trade cycle and union activity, see Musson, *British Trade Unions, 1800–1875*, pp. 38–43, and also below, pp. 259–60.

# The origins and growth of the VI
National Association for the
Protection of Labour, 1829–30

The plan to establish a general union of all trades was not the product of a supposed 'Owenite' explosion among working men between 1829 and 1834. The two best-known previous attempts, in Manchester and London in 1818 and 1825, have been noticed already,[1] but a series of other, even less well-documented efforts were also made, which show that the ideal of a comprehensive union was almost continually present amongst leaders of workmen in one branch of trade or another from the end of the French wars in 1815. Indeed at least one endeavour had been made to give such an idea a practical substance even earlier. During Nassau Senior's investigation into the effects of combinations in 1830–1, undertaken at the request of Lord Melbourne, he received the following information in a letter from 'W.G.' of Manchester :

> In the year 1809 a Congressional Meeting was held at Carlisle at which delegates assembled from the different trades of England, Scotland and Ireland. The avowed object was to establish a uniformity of system and communication with each other. Combinations at that time had become so alarming that deputations from Scotland and from this neighbourhood were sent to London to confer with Ministers and devise some remedy, but nothing was done.[2]

Suggestions for all-embracing associations sometimes originated as the last resort of trades which were in extreme distress, either because of being superseded by machinery or because of the effects of foreign competition, and whose individual unions were therefore in a very weak position. When the cotton hand-loom weavers of Bolton met in November 1829 to discuss the propriety of joining the Bolton branch of the general union of trades recently established by Doherty in Manchester, one of their number, Richard Starkie, stated that the weavers throughout England, Scotland and Ireland were united not many years before and had broached a similar plan, but the idea had been ridiculed by the trades, 'who never came forward to assist the weaver'.[3] And when, through the efforts of John Gast, a 'General Association' of the London trades was formed and a central committee appointed, in January 1827, to agitate for a law to protect agreements between masters and men over wages from unprincipled reductions, it was dominated by the suffering Spital-fields silk-weavers.[4]

But most frequently these schemes were attempts to formalise the traditional inter-union co-operation and assistance at times of important strikes. In 1818 the Manchester spinners led the way in organising the Philanthropic Society, in order to widen support for their strike. And in 1825 the general trades' committees, established in the different towns to fight against re-imposition of the Combination Laws, were continued to collect subscriptions to assist the Bradford woollen workers, whose leader, John Tester, was prominent among those advocating the propriety of a general union of trades.[5] Two years later, the woollen weavers of the Rochdale area, threatened with a reduction of their wages contrary to the terms of an agreement between masters and men in April 1826, held a meeting at nearby Bury, at which one speaker, Whitworth, 'recommended, in strong terms, a general union of the whole of the trades', and the gathering later adjourned to the 'Hare and Hounds' to draw up a plan of operation.[6]

Similarly, in the spring of 1828, when the Kidderminster carpet weavers struck against a wages reduction, Gast revived the meetings of London trades' delegates and secured the appointment of a provisional committee to organise a general trades' union and to devise measures for support of the Kidderminster strikers.[7] A trades' committee was also formed in Kidderminster itself, which urged 'all to come forward, not only for support of the Carpet Weavers, but in forming an Union of Unions, and raising a general fund for the protection of wages, as the only mode of saving the operatives of the country from irretrievable ruin'.[8] Meanwhile, delegates from the carpet weavers were touring the country to procure financial assistance. On 1 July they addressed a meeting of Manchester operatives, when Foster, the spinners' leader, was among the principal speakers, and it was decided to establish a local trades' committee to organise subscriptions. But the response appears to have been lukewarm and another Manchester meeting, on 9 August, addressed by the Kidderminster trades' secretary, only attracted an attendance of about a hundred.[9] In London likewise, Gast's continuing appeals for unity ended in failure.[10] The Kidderminster men therefore had to give in towards the end of August. Nevertheless, the *Trades' Newspaper* reported that a total of £2,137 13s 9¾d had been subscribed for the carpet weavers. And on 18 September Gast addressed another 'Letter to the Mechanics of England' asserting that trade societies throughout the country should learn the lessons of the Kidderminster defeat and appoint delegates to meet together to devise measures for their mutual benefit.[11]

Apart from these practical examples of inter-union co-operation, theoretical encouragement came in 1827 from the publication of William Thompson's *Labour Rewarded*, which probably circulated amongst the most literate working-class leaders, like Doherty. From the Benthamite concept of the greatest happiness for the greatest number, Thompson argued that this could best be ensured by forming 'a central union of all the general unions of all the trades of the country'; this would prevent underpaid workmen causing an over-supply of hands through applying for jobs in more prosperous trades, by fixing the wages of all artisans at such rates as provided an equalised reward, the 'Central Union fund being always ready to assist the unemployed in any particular branch, when their own local and general funds were exhausted; provided always their claim to support were by the Central Union deemed to be just'.[12]

Doherty experienced one of the earliest attempts to establish a general union in 1818, when his own trade, the cotton spinners, took the lead. By 1825 he was already writing to Place in terms that showed he was convinced that it was only by establishing an all-embracing union that the workers could procure their political as well as their economic rights. In that year he was a member of the committee of Manchester trades, which was established to agitate against re-enactment of the Combination Laws and which represented the most effective example of inter-union co-operation in the area before the National Association.[13] In the summer of 1828 several of his closest colleagues, including Thomas Foster and David McWilliams in Manchester, and Thomas Worsley and William Longson in Stockport, participated in meetings to form general committees of delegates from the friendly societies in their respective towns, to join in the nation-wide opposition to Courtenay's bill for the regulation of these associations.[14] And in the following November, Doherty himself included in his *Conciliator* an extract from 'A Narrative and Exposition of the Origin and Progress, Principles, Objects etc. of the General Association, established in London, for the purpose of bettering the condition of Manufacturing and Agricultural Labourers', which address he 'earnestly recommend[ed] to the perusal of every working man in the United Kingdom' —though, admittedly, mainly because of the criticisms in the address of 'the filthy and mischievous doctrines of the "check population" people, and of the schemes of Emigration Societies'.[15]

The problems caused by the turn-out of Manchester fine spinners in April 1829 thus provided Doherty with the opportunity of implementing the current idea of general union, rather than being the cause of the idea. As early as May, in his capacity as secretary of the local spinners' club, he wrote to acknowledge a gift of £10 from the Liverpool sailmakers to the strike funds, and expressed the hope 'that our joint effort may eventually lead to a Grand General Union of all trades throughout the United Kingdom'.[16] And the paltry financial assistance from many trades during the turn-out consolidated his conviction that it was necessary to formalise such support and co-operation in order to make it efficient.[17] By the end of September 1829, Doherty was certain that the spinners' strike could not succeed, but determined that this failure should not lead to a decline in union activity as in the past, rather that it should form the springboard for putting his wider schemes into effect, to ensure that this was the workers' last defeat.

On the evening of Wednesday, 23 September, he convened a meeting in the spinners' room in David Street, at which an idea was mooted that all the trades in Manchester should form themselves into a union to prevent any reduction in their wages.[18] As a result of these discussions, it was announced by handbills, posted about the walls of the town, that a meeting to consider the propriety of this measure, as well as to organise more general support from the trades for the striking spinners, would be held on 30 September. On this evening about a thousand individuals assembled, including delegates representing about twenty different trades—dressers and dyers, iron-founders, fustian cutters, card-grinders and strippers, stretchers, whitesmiths, machine-makers, sawyers, smallware weavers, cotton-yarn dressers, plasterers and painters, joiners, brass-moulders, coachmakers, trunkmakers, cordwainers and millwrights. One of the deputies from the dyers' and dressers' union, named Tattershall, was called to the chair and briefly spoke in favour of cementing together '*for the protection of their rights*', but the chief speakers were the local spinners' officials. Thomas Foster, 'who appeared on this, as on all other occasions where he is present, to take a very leading part in the proceedings', asserted that, despite the repeal of the combination laws, the rich masters could still overturn the legislature's intention by forcing their men to sign the document; the one constitutional course of resistance left open to them was to use the power of their numbers by forming 'a general co-operation and combination of all the working-classes of the kingdom'. Doherty himself pointed to the present condition of the Manchester spinners after six months on strike as a example to them all: the masters would never have attempted to make such a reduction, he considered, 'if an universal trades' union had existed'. Several common themes of his later speeches and writings on behalf of the National Association (as the general union came to be called) also emerged: O'Connell's catholic rent was instanced as an illustration of the efficacy of a general union,[19] and the press was attacked for its venality and total want of independence, as a result of which, for example, no comment was made when rich masters, on whom the newspapers relied for purchases and advertisements, reduced their workmen by 30 per cent, yet had the latter ventured to demand a similar advance, their leaders would have been denounced as dictators and conspirators.

The other speakers included two smallware weavers: the first, Richard Moore, recommended the plan as crucial to prevent reductions spreading through every branch of trade; but John Urquart asked if the weekly subscriptions were intended to be used to support strikers, or, as he preferred, to subscribe a capital to be invested in co-operative production in some trade or trades. Although Foster maintained that no definite plan had yet been decided upon, Doherty did state that two basic principles had already been laid down—that the weekly subscription be $1d$ per week and that the funds be applied only to prevent reductions. It was ultimately resolved that a general union of all trades should be formed and that a provisional committee, comprising one deputy from each trade elected at separate meetings of their members, should meet at the spinners' room on the following Wednesday to prepare rules and regulations for the government of the projected union, which would be submitted to another general meeting of the trades.[20]

This scheme was strongly condemned by the *Manchester Courier*, which regarded it as a last attempt by the working spinners to save themselves from defeat and denounced the proceedings as 'a more dangerous and desperate line of conduct than had ever been dreamt of or anticipated . . . Should the turn-out spinners succeed to any considerable extent in this project, it may lead to results, the nature or consequences of which are beyond the range of human prescience. One thing, however, is certain, that should such a confederation as is contemplated take place, the legislature will be called on to interpose their authority; and one of the most probable consequences of such interference will be the re-enactment of the obnoxious combination laws.'[21] The editorial in the *Manchester Chronicle* was more concerned with a personal attack on Doherty, who was considered to have singled out that paper for particular abuse in his speech. The editor admitted that

> we have not disguised our suspicions of the motives which actuate that individual, and we could only reasonably expect that he would take an early opportunity of giving some expression to his resentment. Heaven defend us

from all controversy with the man! We should never have thought of bringing a name before the public which has, however, long stood 'Rubric on the walls', were we not aware of the influence that the lowest of mankind may accidentally acquire over the sentiments and conduct of large societies; and we deemed it not improbable that the good sense of the journeymen spinners had submitted even to the insignificancy of Mr John Doherty. We have at present no intention of honouring him by any further notice.[22]

In fact, Doherty's plan of general union was intended less to support the spinners' strike, which he already believed to be doomed, than to erect a barrier against similar reductions in future. Thus, when the workmen returned to work, Doherty issued 'An Address to the Public' early in October, admitting the completeness of their defeat, but entreating the labouring classes to learn from it the necessity of establishing a general union to obtain both their economic and political rights. 'By uniting and co-operating with each other, we may yet be able, if not to improve our condition, at least to prevent ourselves from sinking yet lower. And when employers find that they cannot reduce wages any further, they will then have the spirit to speak out, and demand a reduction in the burthens of the country, to save themselves from ruin.'[23]

Over the following weeks Doherty was occupied in correspondence with other districts concerning the formation of the Grand General Union of Cotton Spinners of the United Kingdom,[24] but the general union of the Manchester trades was reported to be making progress on 24 October,[25] and the provisional committee formed on 30 September had completed the formulation of the rules and regulations by the beginning of November, as well as appointing Doherty secretary to the organisation at an unspecified salary. These rules do not survive in a comprehensive form before they appeared in the *United Trades' Co-operative Journal* in May 1830, but references to them at early meetings do not suggest any significant alterations in the intervening period. Only organised trades, whose own rules and officers had been sanctioned by the Manchester committee, could join the Association. The entrance fee for each trade was fixed at £1 and after twenty societies had enrolled subscriptions were to commence at the rate of 1d per member per week. The funds were first to be kept in a suitable box and then banked in sums of £50; and for security reasons each cheque was to be cut in half and divided between the Manchester committee and each district in turn. Only strikes against reductions were to be supported (although constituent trades were free to seek advances by their own efforts), and an allowance of 10s per week was to be paid through the agency of the officers of the trade concerned to those members who had been subscribing to the Association for a minimum of three months.[26]

On this organisational basis the intended expansion, district by district, until all the working classes in the country were included, could now begin, and the first town chosen for this purpose was Bolton. On 17 November a public trades' meeting was held in the Queen Anne Old Assembly Room, to discuss forming a general trades' union there, to co-operate with that already established in Manchester. Two delegates attended from the parent society, James Turner of the dyers' and dressers' union, and Thomas Foster, who was passing through Bolton on his way back from Preston and took the place of Doherty, who had been deputed to attend the meeting but was 'unavoidably absent'. Both speakers quoted the recent failures of the Manchester and Stockport spinners' strikes as proof that no trade could stand alone against their employers. Trade-union violence was deplored: what was required was 'an union characterised by mildness and intelligence and constructed in such a manner as would command respect, even from its enemies'. Doherty's assertion, that the masters would no longer be able to throw the increasing burden of taxation onto the workmen by reducing wages and that they would thus become radical reformers, was repeated. In conclusion, it was stated that the provisional committee of the Manchester Union had resolved that all workmen who had paid their weekly subscriptions of 1d should receive 10s per week when on strike against reductions in their wages.

These advantages meant little to the Bolton handloom weavers. Several of their leaders spoke out against the plan because of the failures of past unions, the previous refusal of other trades to join with the weavers in inter-union co-operation, and the irrelevance of an effort to prevent wage *reductions* to a trade already in the lowest possible state of degradation, as a result of the introduction of power-looms; a clash of interest with the spinners was also apparent in the weavers' desire to stop exports of yarn in order to bring prices down and thus make possible an increase in their wages—they were evidently jealous of the spinners' high earnings. The proposal, therefore, to form a trades' union in Bolton, 'to co-operate with the great national confederacy for the protection of labour', was lost amid great uproar, although it was agreed that such trades as wished to join the union should each send two delegates to another meeting in a fortnight's time, on 1 December.[27]

In the meantime, a concerted attempt was made to convert the Bolton weavers to the plan of general union. A public meeting of their body was convened for that purpose on 30 November, but the proceedings began inauspiciously with the presentation of a series of resolutions expressing the weavers' hostility to the project. In reply, however, Doherty made one of his most eloquent and effective speeches, lasting more than an hour. He began by ascribing the previous failures of unions to their being insufficiently general: where the trades had co-operated, they had succeeded, as was shown by the repeal of the Combination Laws. He denied that the weavers could benefit by the spinners' refusing to manufacture yarn for foreigners, who would merely proceed to produce it for themselves, or by all craftsmen being reduced to the condition of the weavers. He went on to explain the rules of the general union. The committee had rejected the idea of supporting strikes for advances because of its impracticability and the overall objective: 'what they proposed was, that every trade should be kept at the present rate of wages, not to make all equal';[28] but the same subscription and allowance was laid down for all, and every trade was free to strike for an increase through its own individual efforts. The union was to expand as a real federation, only organised trades being allowed to join. Doherty concluded by exhorting the working classes to cease looking to those above them for improvement, but to attend to their own interests through the formation of a general union, by which alone they could end the system of the government raising taxes and the masters making profits by reductions.

Doherty's views, which were supported by Robert Ellison, a long-time weavers' leader, 'had a very visible effect upon the meeting'. Opposition was disarmed and a motion carried, with only one dissentient voice, in favour of joining with the other trades. The *Manchester Courier* reported a comment that even 'John Wesley had never made so many converts at one time as Mr Doherty had done that evening'.[29]

On the following night, 1 December, delegates from about a dozen trades, including the weavers, met and agreed to organise themselves as soon as possible, preparatory to joining the general union. Notices were also received from several other trades approving of the plan and pledging support.[30] The effect of Doherty's oratory on the weavers, however, appears soon to have worn off, for by the beginning of 1830 it was reported that despite the 'sudden conversion' of their leaders, 'the great body decline to join the proposed union of trades, conceiving the plan to be futile and impracticable'.[31] Nevertheless, delegates from other Bolton trades continued to meet together and a powerful district of the general union ultimately emerged. Their first public action took place in April 1830 when meetings were called to express support and organise a voluntary weekly subscription on behalf of the Bolton spinners, then on strike against a reduction of their wages.[32]

Meanwhile, Doherty's time was fully occupied by the first spinners' delegate meeting in the Isle of Man in December 1829, and the subsequent writing of the report and other correspondence connected with the Grand General Union of Operative Cotton Spinners of the United Kingdom, of which he was secretary. Apart from strengthening their own trade, this organisation was also intended as part of the process by which individual trades should first organise themselves before joining the general federation. But such a method of expansion was extremely rare—only one nationally-organised trade, the National Associated Smiths, ever joined the National Association,[33] and even the cotton spinners themselves subscribed to the funds from their separate districts and not through their Grand General Union. In fact the actual way by which the general trades' union spread followed the precedent set at Bolton. Public meetings of the different trades were called in each town, at which local leaders and delegates from either Manchester or Bolton spoke, and local committees were formed to organise a district of the general union. At the beginning of 1830 Doherty was trying to extend the plan of general union among other Manchester trades—he wrote, for example, to the letter-press printers in January, but they rejected the idea at a general meeting.[34] It was no doubt to overcome such apathy or hostility that he now turned to the creation of a specifically working-class organ of communication and propaganda, on the necessity for which he had spoken forcibly at the Isle of Man conference.[35]

In his account of the origins of the National Association, G. D. H. Cole fails to realise that the Manchester and Bolton meetings were an integral part of its early development, and he mistakenly dates its commencement from early in 1830. He is forced to explain the inception of the *United Trades' Co-operative Journal* on 6 March by referring vaguely to developments in the previous month. 'In February 1830 he [Doherty] got together some sort of representative Trade Union Conference at which it was decided

F*

to start recruiting for the General Union of Trades, and to begin formal operations as soon as twenty trades had enrolled.'[36] In fact, however, no record of such a conference seems to be extant.[37] And, as we have seen, the provisional rules of the general union, which Cole ascribes to the deliberations at this meeting, were in reality formulated by the provisional committee of the Manchester trades established in September 1829. The decision to begin a weekly periodical was doubtless taken by the same committee on Doherty's advice.

On 20 February 1830, an advertisement in the *Manchester Times and Gazette* announced that the first number of *The United Trades and Co-operatives Journal* would appear on the first Saturday in March, conducted by 'a committee appointed by the trades' and adding its profits 'to the united trades' fund'. The prospectus further stated that:

> The objects of this little work will be, to defend the rights and advocate the cause of the labouring classes, and to offer such advice as may appear best calculated to enable them successfully to resist the mischievous attempts that are continually being made to deprive them of the means of honest subsistence, by unnecessary and ruinous reductions of their wages . . . In a word, the conductors will endeavour to make it a medium of instruction and amusement, to those whose means preclude the possibility of their attaining the same ends from any other source.[38]

Under its slightly amended title, the *United Trades' Co-operative Journal* made its first appearance on 6 March and thereafter continued weekly for seven months and thirty-one editions, until it was forced to close down in face of pressure from the government stamp commissioners on 2 October. In the first volume, consisting of numbers 1 to 26 from 6 March until 28 August, it was priced 2d and was printed by Mark Wardle. It was a small octavo paper, the first sixteen editions of which were each eight pages long, as Doherty's first paper the *Conciliator* had been, and the remaining numbers being enlarged to twelve pages. The publications in the second volume from 4 September until 2 October, were each sixteen pages in length, priced 2½d, and printed by Alexander Wilkinson at the office of the *Manchester and Salford Advertiser*. All communications were directed at first to be addressed 'to the Editor, at the printer's', but later to 'the Office, 26 Oldham Street', which was in effect the headquarters of the National Association. As the prospectus showed, it was published from the first on behalf of the general union of trades, but not until number 28 did it officially acknowledge in a sub-heading that it was printed 'for the Co-operative Society', and more explicitly in the following numbers, 'for the Association for the Protection of Labour'.[39] It was sold by agents who were enrolled in the different towns as the Association expanded.

As editor, although unpaid, Doherty's influence on the contents of the paper was all-pervasive. His editorials continually stressed the necessity of the working classes acting together to improve their condition, whilst many of the abuses he considered to be the most oppressive—the long hours of children employed in cotton factories, the truck system, the venal middle-class press, intemperance, etc.—were vehemently attacked. Politics was, of necessity, kept to a minimum, for this was one of the first unstamped papers, in which political comment was prohibited; nevertheless, Doherty's view that the Association would win political, as well as economic, rights for the workmen was never far from the surface and became increasingly overt in the later numbers.[40] The news columns devoted much space to reports of meetings in various towns to establish new branches of the National Association, and of the proceedings and decisions of delegate meetings and the Manchester committee. The details of current strikes were extensively reported and commented upon. In the correspondence columns, enquiries concerning the rules of the general union were dealt with, while publicity was also given to other projects for the improvement of the working classes. Despite its title, and the inclusion in several numbers of suggested rules for the founding of co-operative stores, the paper in fact reflected Doherty's opinion that it was essential first for the workers to win economic power through general union before the more high-flown schemes of the co-operators should be considered: unqualified approval was reserved only for attempts at producer co-operation by individual trades such as the Manchester dyers. In fact, the word 'co-operative' in the title was a continuation of its meaning as 'inter-union co-operation' as it had been used at the early meetings of the general union, rather than referring to contemporary 'Owenite' thinking. The only defence against successive wages reductions, Doherty emphasised, was *'co-operation*. Partial co-operation, or local unions have already done much in preventing reductions. Extend the principle; form one universal union . . .' Later he distinguished between 'co-operative trading societies' and the 'still more important and more immediately useful . . . co-operative societies for the protection of labour . . . What, we ask, are Trade Societies or Trade Unions but Co-operative Societies?'[41] The advocacy of such 'united trades' co-operation' was the prime object of the *Journal*, but it also had an educative, informative purpose. The promise in the prospectus to include selections 'from the popular and interesting works of the day' was implemented whenever possible, notably by printing weekly extracts from Burdon's 'Essay on Education', by occasional informative articles such as the 'Administration of Provincial Justice. The "Great Unpaid"' (copied from the *Westminster Review*),[42] and by the inclusion of poetry and 'miscellaneous intelligence'.

Doherty's editorial in the first number set the tone for the whole work. After apologising for his lack of formal education,[43] he promised to make up for his consequent deficiency in knowledge by 'zeal and industry'. He went on to declare that:

> The main object of our little work will be, to inspire the labouring classes with a due sense of their own importance; to arouse them to a diligent and faithful performance of their duty to themselves, by a vigorous and determined resistance to any further encroachments that may be attempted, on their only real property, their labour, in the shape of reductions of wages. We shall endeavour to show to both masters and men that their real interests are one and inseparable; that it is the interest of both, as well as their duty, to endeavour to uphold wages by every means which the law permits . . . We hope too, we shall be able to convince the working classes generally, and the Trade Societies in particular, of the absolute necessity of their acting on some fixed and common plan for their mutual protection and support . . . ,

by the instrumentality of a general Union of the different trades . . . While on the one hand we shall humbly but earnestly espouse the cause of the poor, defenceless, and unprotected labourer, we shall on the other endeavour to elevate his mind and restrain his passions. We shall on all occasions inculcate a due respect for the laws and constituted authorities of the country; and as we are forbidden by law to enter on political discussions, we shall set the example—much as we dislike the law, unjust and impolitic as we consider it—of submission to its dictates . . . In a word, we shall endeavour to make the *United Trades' Co-operative Journal* a vehicle of instruction, and an organ of communication to the different trades whose interests may be affected by its pages, and whose happiness it shall be the constant and undeviating object of its conductors to promote.[44]

Over the following weeks, Doherty pursued the above points in greater detail in further editorials and in a series of letters, signed 'A Friend to the Operatives' (from the style and contents, probably Doherty himself). On 13 March he explained that the establishment of the *Journal* was specifically made necessary by the perpetuation of prejudices against working men which had been generated by the Combination Laws. No counterweight previously existed to the continual falsehoods and misrepresentations in the public press against workmen who joined together in unions and engaged in strikes. As a result, successive wage reductions had been enforced, which had been facilitated by the fatal apathy of the workmen themselves. Partial unions had had some success, but only a general union of the trades could withstand the full might of combined employers. When told that such a plan was chimerical, they should remember that 'power lies in your numbers', and that 'Mr O'Connell was told the same thing, when he commenced his career of agitation, for the emancipation of his country—how far he has been successful we need not now be told. The same reward . . . awaits the same exertions in our cause.' On 20 March Doherty denounced those 'respectable' upper classes who invariably opposed the claims of the workers, and detailed more explicitly the advantages of forming a general union—an accession not only to their economic but also to their 'moral and political strength', through which the working class would cease to be 'at once the most useful and the most oppressed portion of society'. On 27 March, in reply to an article in the *Guardian* on the 'prosperity' of workers in the cotton industry, Doherty instanced the degradation of which he had written in previous weeks, by quoting figures to show that wages in many trades had fallen by 50 per cent or more since 1810, whereas the prices of provisions were only 40 per cent lower. When the general union was fully established, he added, it should issue correct monthly reports on the state of trade and wages, which would by their authoritativeness soon banish such spurious statements from the press.

The establishment of the *Journal* as an organ of both propaganda and communication opened the way for the expansion of the general union. Doherty was anxious that the original principle that only organised trades could join should not be forgotten. In the first number, those Manchester trade societies wishing to become members were requested to present their entrance fee of £1, together with a copy of their rules, to the United Trades' Committee, which had by this time removed its headquarters from the spinners' room in David Street to the 'Moulders' Arms' in Chorlton Street. At the same time, the establishment of new branch societies in different towns was stimulated by the attendance of delegates from either the Manchester or Bolton committee to explain the basic principles of the general union.

Expansion was initially confined to Lancashire, and specifically to the cotton towns around Manchester. The first town visited was Chorley, where about six hundred operatives attended a general meeting at the 'Gillibrands' Arms' on 17 March to consider the propriety of establishing a 'Union of Trades' there, to co-operate with that already established in Manchester and Bolton. The chief speaker was Marshall, secretary of the Bolton district, who referred to several previous attempts to organise the trades upon the present principle in London, all without success; but now the workmen of Lancashire had the honour of laying the foundation of an institution which would ultimately benefit every labourer in the kingdom. He then read out and commended the resolutions of the Manchester trades' committee for the government of the Association. His views were supported by John Hynes, who explained that he had been deputed from the Manchester committee to speak in place of 'that talented and deservedly popular character', Mr Doherty, who had been expected to attend; and he regretted that, as this was the first such gathering he had ever addressed, he was a less than adequate substitute. Nevertheless the resolution to form a local union of trades at Chorley was afterwards carried unanimously, and a future evening was appointed for a meeting of delegates from the different trades to settle the arrangements.[45]

The Chorley committee, however, at first met with some diffidence among the local workmen and consequently invited Doherty to a second meeting on 3 April to explain the constitution and objects of the general trades' union more fully. In a long address, Doherty informed his audience that 'the object they sought to obtain was that freedom and independence which had long been the characteristic of Englishmen, but of which at present [only] a small remnant was left'. Practically, this was not to be effected by direct political action—'they were not met to inquire what species of government would produce the greatest quantum of happiness'—but by erecting an efficient barrier against ruinous wage reductions through 'what had been called, a Trades' Union, but which would be much more fitly and adequately designated, "*The national association for the protection of labour*" '.[46] This became the recognised title of the trades' union, though similar terms had been used from the earliest meetings, so it was not quite the novelty that Cole asserts.[47]

From Chorley, where a branch was now successfully established, the Association turned its attention to Bury, where between three and four hundred workmen attended a public meeting on 26 April. The principal spokesmen were again Marshall and Doherty. The former powerfully described the declining condition of workmen generally and hence the necessity of a general remedy, called on his audience to support the Bolton spinners in their current struggle, and ascribed the recent *advance* in the wages of the Bolton bleachers to their being members of the general union. Doherty maintained that the meeting represented 'the really respectable portion of the community', because they were useful and productive: to be 'respectable', it was not sufficient merely to wear black coats or white handkerchiefs, nor was it a qualification for 'superiority' to be enabled to run up large debts without the capacity to satisfy the creditors. Yet the laws of the country were made for the protection of such individuals: 'the poor man's son was punished with imprisonment for taking an apple out of the rich man's orchard, while the rich man and friends could gallop, with impunity, over the fields and fences of his humble neighbour'; and similarly the laws were administered to the advantage of the educated and wealthy employer rather than the poor and ignorant workmen. Against such odds, Doherty concluded, the labourers' only possible hope was to make common cause. And resolutions were thereupon passed, declaring the meeting's desire to form a branch union in Bury and that a local committee comprising two delegates from each trade should be elected and hold its first meeting on 1 May.[48]

The next branch committee was established at Edenfield, a small village about six miles from Bury, at a meeting in the 'Pack Horse' on 3 May addressed as usual by Marshall and Doherty, and also by Thomas Oates and John Hynes from Manchester. The growing interest in the Association was reflected by Doherty's assertion that, 'so anxious were the trades to be enrolled members of the union, that he had no fewer than four different invitations to attend similar meetings at Preston, Blackburn, Oldham and Ashton'. And the same copy of the *Journal* which contained this account also reported that another branch society had been formed by the Bolton committee at Horwich.[49]

Branches were soon afterwards formed in towns already indicated by Doherty as showing interest—Preston, Ashton and Oldham,[50] where meetings were held according to the now established pattern. The first overt sign of official disapproval occurred at Preston, where the operatives were denied the use of the Theatre for their meeting, which was eventually held on open ground in Chadwick's orchard on 11 May. Despite their well-known political radicalism, the local workmen were particularly submissive to their employers, with the result that Thomas Worsley, of the Stockport spinners, was forced to chair the assembly, and Johnston, a master tailor, was the only speaker from Preston. Nevertheless, nearly 3,000 workmen attended the meeting called by a local committee of the trades, which had already been formed and appointed Johnston as their secretary. A pre-arranged set of resolutions was moved by Francis Marshall and supported by Doherty, who emphasised that it was essential for the working classes to act on the advice recently given them by Peel in the House of Commons, to take the management of their affairs into their own hands. After stating that masters who reduced wages unnecessarily were moral villains as great as highway robbers and that honest employers would have nothing to fear from the general union, he went on to clarify the anomaly in the rules whereby workers like weavers could earn only six shillings per week when at work, but receive ten shillings for turning-out; to remedy this, the money was to be paid to the officers of each trade society from the general funds, and they themselves were to decide what proportion of the ten shillings should be disbursed to their members and add the remainder to their own treasury. Following this explanation, the resolutions in favour of forming a branch at Preston were unanimously adopted.[51]

The Ashton meeting was convened at the 'Commercial Inn' on 26 May, following local initiative led by John Joseph Betts, the spinners' secretary, who was elected chairman of the assembly. An estimated eight hundred workmen heard typical orations from James Turner and Doherty, representing the Manchester committee, and from Marshall, who instanced the financial assistance given to the striking Bolton spinners from trades such as the bleachers and block printers as proof of the spirit of union there.[52] And the resolutions to form a branch at Ashton and establishing a local committee of two deputies from each trade to meet at the 'Stamford Arms', also included an explicit assurance 'that the large manufacturers, who are generally the most humane and honourable, [and] as much interested in keeping up a fair, remunerating price for labour, as the workmen themselves, may rest assured that the union of trades cannot, by any possibility, have in any way an injurious effect upon them'.[53]

The importance of Doherty's contributions to these meetings was perhaps shown by his absence from similar discussions at the 'Grapes Inn', Oldham, on 21 June. Here, the visiting speakers were Hynes and Marshall, who first of all read out and commended the rules drawn up by the Manchester committee. But thereafter the proceedings were sidetracked by an angry debate upon a remark by Hynes that the masters wished to keep their workmen ignorant. A local employer attempted to refute this allegation by pointing out the masters' liberal contributions towards Sunday and charitable schools; but in turn two lifelong radicals, John Knight and William Fitton, asserted that education at these institutions was confined to inculcating the doctrine of passive obedience. As a result of this digression, the Oldham delegate to the first general delegate meeting of the National Association one week later stated that the trades there were still 'wholly ignorant of the system on which the Association was established'. Nevertheless, a branch was formed at Oldham during the course of the proceedings and John Knight became its secretary.[54]

Between the assemblages at Ashton and Oldham, however, the first district outside Lancashire had been formed at a public meeting of about 4,000 persons in Macclesfield, Cheshire, on 7 June. Thomas Worsley, of Stockport, took the chair, and the main spokesmen were Thomas Foster, of Manchester, Francis Marshall, of Bolton, and Reuben Bullock, of Macclesfield. And in the *Journal* Doherty declared his conviction that, 'from the spirited conduct of the people of Macclesfield at this meeting they fully appreciate the importance of the Union, and will become a very valuable branch'.[55]

The final town included in this initial phase of expansion under the provisional rules of the Manchester committee was Rochdale. There the flannel weavers were engaged in an almost continuous struggle with their employers against wages reductions, and such was the enthusiasm for the National Association that on the evening of 24 June about 10,000 individuals waited on Cronkeyshaw Moor in drizzly rain for nearly an hour for the arrival of the deputation to address them. The meeting had been summoned by the Rochdale trades' committee, which had already been formed. The speakers included several local workmen as well as the delegates of the general union, Marshall (of Bolton), Hindes (of Stockport), and Renshaw and Doherty (of Manchester). Doherty's address was particularly eloquent and closely argued. He first congratulated his audience on being able to meet together to air their grievances without fear of being dispersed by an armed force. Support for the Association, he went on, would not interfere with their efforts as individuals to obtain radical reform, nor would it bring them into conflict with honourable employers: the latter, pressed down by excessive taxation and the corn laws, were the creatures of circumstances as much as the workmen. But working men must not hope to escape from their poverty by relying on parliament or the magistrates, who only reflected the aspirations of their own class. 'By uniting together in a general association the working-classes would soon strike terror into the hearts of tyrannical and grasping masters', and secure their modest aims, 'to procure suitable meat to eat, a second coat to their backs, and a trifle to give to a friend in need'. Thereupon, the Rochdale operatives voted unanimously to establish a branch association.[56]

Despite this impressive catalogue of progress, the Association naturally had initial teething troubles. The small size of early numbers of the *Journal* was a source of widespread irritation, but a proposal by the Bolton branch to publish a monthly journal of double the size and price was rejected by the governing Manchester committee on 5 May. Later in the same month Doherty complained that, whereas every party and faction in the country had established and supported their own newspaper, the workmen neglected the *Journal*, founded by the united trades in their interest, and regarded it 'as a mere trading speculation of an individual'. More support was therefore essential, and to obtain it the committee announced on 22 May their intention to make the first enlargement of the paper, which was effected on 19 June. Complaints thereafter seem to have lessened, although the circulation never exceeded more than about 1,000 at its height, despite a further increase in size on 4 September.[57]

A more serious problem to overcome was inertia among the workmen. Not only was this reflected in their slowness to buy the *Journal*, but Doherty pointed out on 27 March that it threatened the whole general union plan. 'The power of the labouring classes to protect themselves, lies in their numbers, and in proportion as they are numerous and united can that power be made available to their purpose.' Doherty therefore denounced those who merely watched and criticised, or adopted a policy of 'wait and see'. These selfish sentiments were 'the natural fruit of that stagnant apathy, that criminal indifference to their own welfare, which has long been the characteristic and curse of the labouring classes. They have always been taught to look up to others, for any amelioration of their condition. . . . They have little or no idea of depending on their own resources and exertions. Like children, they expect everything to be done for them, and like fools they are always betrayed.'[58] Doherty attempted to combat this passivity by a series of editorials urging the benefits of self-help and the advantages of a general union. And on 5 May a public meeting of the Manchester trades was held in the spinners' David Street room to determine the future of the *Journal* and report on the progress of the Association. Apart from orations by Turner, Hynes and Doherty, this gathering was also remarkable for the first appearance of Thomas Oates, an Irishman and future leader, despite 'not being of that class which entitled him to take a part in their proceedings'.[59] But it did not notably increase local activity. On 29 May a correspondent denounced the 'inexcusable apathy' of the Manchester operatives, as shown by their failure to support their own publication or to assist the local silk smallware weavers in their current strike for a wage increase.[60] And on 19 June another correspondent, 'T.W.'[61], lamented that, compared with the enthusiasm of artisans in the neighbouring towns, progress 'in Manchester at least, does not realise our expectations'; because of its limited circulation, the *Journal* had failed to dispel jealousy and indifference. The writer's solution was the organisation of public discussions and debates in the town on subjects vital to the working classes, to arouse interest in the Association, a suggestion which Doherty welcomed as 'laudable and beneficial' and later persuaded the Manchester committee to put into practice during August and September.[62] But along with apathy there was personal rancour. Thus, according to Doherty, the representative of the Manchester moulders on the provisional committee harboured 'some unworthy feelings' against the general union leaders and persuaded his constituents to secede; but a special meeting of their trade on 14 June decided to dismiss him and to rejoin the Association.[63]

While facing inertia on the one hand, Doherty was forced on the other to combat considerable impatience among those who had joined the Association for it to commence active operations. Those trades that had paid their entrance fees were anxious also to start paying their subscriptions and see the Association taking action to prevent reductions. As early as 27 March Doherty was compelled to reply to this grumbling. He pointed out that the Manchester committee had originally agreed that no subscriptions should be paid until twenty trades had enrolled, in which resolution he heartily concurred because a union of trades must of necessity be general to be effective, and hence the promoters should first consolidate and concentrate their power and not seek a trial of strength prematurely and perhaps disastrously. Moreover, remarkable progress *had* been made. 'We have made many workmen better acquainted with the principles and the power of union than they were before—we have excited a spirit of enquiry as to the practicability of a general union, which is every hour gaining ground—and we have done that, which has never before been even attempted, here at least—we have established an organ of communication for those whose whole power depends on their understanding each other.'[64]

Despite these difficulties, the growing interest in the Association was reflected in a succession of different trades enrolling. These included fustian weavers from Edenfield, at least nine districts of calico-printers,[65] spindle and fly-makers from Manchester, basket-makers from Ashton, Oldham and Sheffield,[66] jenny-spinners from Edenfield, flannel-weavers from Rochdale, rope-makers from Manchester, coal miners and engineers from Bolton, mule-spinners from Stockport, mechanics and tallow-chandlers from Manchester, and sizers from Bolton.[67] Doherty recognised that a permanent constitution for the Association was now necessary, and on 15 May the *Journal* carried an announcement that a general delegate meeting of all the districts was being planned, together with an address from the Manchester provisional committee, which concluded that well-paid as well as impoverished trades would benefit from membership, 'without at all interference with the inequalities of wages in the different trades'. The address was followed by a detailed list of the laws established by the Manchester committee, which the general meeting was to ratify or amend.[68] And on 12 June, in a gleeful editorial, Doherty rejoiced that 'the Association is SUCCEEDING beyond our most sanguine expectations', that twenty different trades had now paid their entrance fees, and that the Manchester committee was convening the first general delegate meeting, to fix a code of laws under which to begin operations, at the end of that month.[69] The delegates were asked to come armed with lists of the numbers in each trade, and of those that could be counted as regular payers to the general fund, which facts were necessary to amass data on which 'to found our calculations'.[70]

The first general delegate meeting of the National Association took place on the three days between 28 and 30 June at the spinners' headquarters in David Street—the advertised venue, the 'Moulders' Arms', Portland Street, presumably not being large enough. A total of twenty-eight delegates attended, representing nine of the districts already founded[71]—Manchester (Doherty, Turner, Foster, Hynes, Oates and Renshaw), Bolton (Marshall, Barrow and Turner of Horwich), Ashton (Betts and Lowe), Rochdale (Buckley), Chorley, Preston, Bury, Oldham and Edenfield—and also individual Manchester and country trades like the calico printers, the Stockport spinners (Worsley), and the Sheffield basket-workers. The duties as chairman were shared between Turner and Worsley, while Hynes acted as secretary.[72]

Preliminary discussions centred on three main points. Firstly Doherty insisted on the importance of only organised trades being allowed to join the Association, and their being obliged to provide representatives on their particular district committees. This rule, he claimed, had already caused 'several trades desirous of joining the Association, who had never before had a Union among themselves to exert themselves to effect their own organisations'. Secondly, an inquest was held into the partial failure of the Oldham meeting the previous week to effect its purpose.[73] And thirdly, it was agreed that a full report of their meeting should appear in the *Journal*. Several delegates objected to their names being published for fear of dismissal, but Doherty emphasised that, 'in order to be effective, it [the Association] must be general', and publicity was vital in the process of extension.

The main deliberations revolved round the provisional rules drawn up by the Manchester committee. Several regulations were unconditionally accepted, notably that the Association should only support strikes against reductions, and that the subscription be 1d per week. Since twenty trades were now enrolled, it was agreed that contributions should begin on 12 July; but a long debate resulted from a proposal that the first subscription should be 1s in order to amass a strike fund. This idea was first mooted in an anonymous letter in the *Journal* of 19 June (probably from Doherty). Betts and Marshall stated that the Ashton and Bolton spinners, both of whom had recently been defeated in strikes, would be unable to raise such a sum, and their views evoked considerable sympathy. Marshall moved an amendment that the subscription should be doubled for the first three months, but Doherty condemned this suggestion as it would wrongly lead trades to believe that the Association would have sufficient funds to support them against a reduction in this initial period. An initial failure would doom the whole project: 'if they attempted to try their strength too soon, they would be defeated, and all hopes of establishing a General Union would be lost for ever'. Recalling that he had experienced much difficulty in persuading those trades already entered to defer their weekly payments, he nevertheless repeated the need for continued caution and building up a considerable fund before risking a challenge. Doherty's proposal, which was ultimately adopted, was 'That each Member of every Trade shall pay 1s on 12 July 1830 and be entitled to benefit in three months after the payment of that sum; and that such Trades as did not think proper to pay their shilling, should continue paying their pence for six months, before they were entitled to any of the benefits arising from the Society.'[74]

The next major debate was on the proposed rule for safeguarding the Association funds. A delegate from the calico printers favoured putting the money into a co-operative scheme, but Doherty ridiculed the idea.[75] Thomas Foster approved of depositing the funds in a bank and dividing the cheques in half, for this division between central committee and union lodges had been used successfully by the Manchester spinners; but he suggested that banking in sums of £20 rather than £50 would provide better security. Ultimately this system was adopted, with a compromise figure of £25 proposed by Doherty. Careful arrangements were also made for the sending and receipt of parcels of money.

Only two other of the Manchester committee's rules faced opposition. During discussion on the rule governing donations from interested individuals, Doherty proposed that masters be admitted as honorary members. But Oates led strong hostility to the idea and the original rule was eventually adopted. A successful objection was, however, made to the fixing of strike relief at 10s, which Betts, Turner and others considered excessive, and ultimately the sum of 8s was agreed upon, again as a result of a compromise proposed by Doherty.

In addition to ratifying (or otherwise) the existing rules of the provisional committee, the delegates also had to decide on permanent arrangements for governing the affairs of the Association. They were again assisted by a list of propositions drawn up by the Manchester committee. Resolutions were firstly passed deprecating the state of extreme poverty to which the working people had declined because of repeated reductions of wages, and establishing 'The National Association for the Protection of Labour' to check the deterioration. Surprisingly, the election of a general secretary provoked 'spirited discussion', but it was at length decided to appoint Doherty at an (unspecified) salary.[76] The supreme government of the Association was to lie with a General Committee, comprising one delegate for every thousand members and meeting once every six months. Executive authority was to be vested in 'a Provisional Council, consisting of seven persons, returned from as many districts', meeting monthly at Manchester and empowered 'to watch over the interests of the Association between each meeting of the general Committee, one of such Council to retire every month, and another appointed in his stead from a different district'. The secretary could convene the Provisional Council at other times to decide policy in all cases of emergency.

Finally, a series of miscellaneous resolutions was adopted, one of which recommended districts to set up debating societies to discuss topics of interest to workmen, and another determined 'that an office be taken, and a press and types purchased as soon as the funds will permit', because of Doherty's warning that the continued publication of the *Journal* under the present arrangements would involve the Association in serious loss. In all, twenty-five resolutions were passed at the three-day conference and published in the *Journal* of 10 July.[77]

This first general delegate meeting was also notable for the first overt signs of official disapproval of the Association. The early developments had provoked little reaction from those in authority. The occasional meeting had been inconvenienced when the manager of the advertised venue withdrew his consent, and in May the *Journal* even reported that a firm in Edenfield had dismissed two of their men for attending the assemblage to establish a local branch of the Association. But the first official report to the Home Office was not made until 26 May, when the Manchester borough-reeve and constables wrote to the Home Office and the Prime Minister that the 'present exertions' being made to form a 'general union' of all classes of operatives 'for mutual aid in turn-outs' necessitated decisive measures to check the evil. Copies of the *Journal* for 1 and 8 May, containing Doherty's editorials on the benefits of 'general union', were enclosed and the local military commander, Lieutenant-Colonel Shaw, was recommended as a good source for additional information.[78] On 9 June Shaw wrote as requested, explaining that the Grand General Union of cotton spinners was being absorbed as a branch of the 'United Trades General Union', but that the two bodies shared similar rules and leaders; the latter union was expanding by the formation of trades' committees in different towns, which then sent their allegiance to Manchester.[79]

The growing official interest culminated in the employment by the Manchester police of a spy to attend the delegate conference, and his report was transmitted to the Home Office by Shaw on 3 July. The spy was unable to gain admission to the meeting as he had not been authorised to represent a trade, but he had met a deputy from Glasgow[80] in the street and discovered that he had a letter of identification from Doherty. The spy then tried to sneak in himself under its auspices, and even met Doherty, but was again shown the door. His information on the first day's proceedings was thus rather vague, although he gathered that it had been agreed to form the National Association, with the central committee in Manchester and branch committees in other districts throughout the kingdom, the subscription to be a 1d per week, to fight against reductions or where wages were unreasonably low; the fact was also recorded that the deputies had dined at the 'Moulders' Arms' and had 'plenty of Cathale, gin and brandy'. That evening he met two delegates, plied them with drink and learnt more of the organisation details. He stated that they calculated on 50,000 paying the 1s entrance and thereby raising £2,500. 'This and the weekly contributions will support two trades turned out for two years (except the weavers— these they don't care about being so poor) at the rate of 10s per week.' It was also revealed that the final details for the formation of the Association had been settled at the second delegate meeting of the spinners' Grand General Union on the Isle of Man during Whitsun.[81] The 'Resolutions and Laws' of the Association, as determined at the Manchester conference and printed in No. 19 of the *Journal* on 10 July, were also sent to the Home Office by Shaw on 11 July.[82]

The authorities' concern at the results of the meeting on the one side was more than matched on the other by Doherty's virtually apocalyptic reaction. This assembly, he jubilantly commented on 3 July, would 'form an epoch in the history of the working-classes of this country . . . [who] are now . . . entering on a new era'. The organisation thus formed would raise them from feebleness and insignificance much more effectively than any secret society or acts of violence.[83] And on 10 July he emphasised that by paying their subscriptions the workmen could demonstrate their enthusiasm for the common struggle against the common enemy of wealth and monopoly; their object was not 'our own aggrandisement at expense of any other class', but as the producers of all wealth they demanded a sufficient reward to support themselves and their families without having so many idlers 'quartered upon us'.[84]

Nevertheless, over the following two weeks the *Journal* only recorded the payment of entrance fees by a few additional trades, such as the hat-roughers of Oldham and Ashton, the cotton spinners of Rochdale and Ashton, and the shoemakers and tailors of Ashton.[85] The first weekly contributions were not announced until 31 July, when a total of £41 9s 11d was received from six different sources—the Rossendale printers (£7 18s), Ribblesdale printers (£11), Ashton basket-makers (£2 9s 11d), Ashton spinners (£10), Chorley spinners (£3), and Preston district (£6 2s).[86] These sums doubtless refer to the total subscriptions received since the funds opened on 12 July, not having been advertised before because of disagreement among the Manchester committee as to whether public acknowledgement was necessary: the first weekly total was therefore not exceeded until 28 August. The receipts on 7 August fell to £19 11s 11d, but thereafter the amounts increased almost every week—to £32 1s 3d on 21 August, £54 17s 7d on 28 August, £55 17s 1d on 4 September, £78 1s 9d on 11 September, £74 7s 1d on 18 September, £216 6s 9d on 25 September, £160 13s 10d on 2 October, £225 11s 1d on 9 October, and £302 5s on 16 October.[87] The removal at this time of the donations of the Rochdale flannel weavers—whose subscriptions had been by far the largest but who were now disillusioned by the Association's failure to support them[88]—resulted in a dramatic fall, to £33 19s 1d on 23 October and £59 10s on 30 October. Thereafter contributions continued at a fairly substantial if fluctuating level until near the end of the year—£135 16s 3d on 6 November, £108 11s 10d on 13 November, £70 4s 9d on 20 November.[89] Unfortunately, no separate figures are extant for each week in the succeeding month, but the total receipts in the last week of 1830 were £46 14s 7d, and the recorded subscriptions to the Association for the first five months of its active existence can be calculated as £1,969 7s 9d.[90]

The mounting subscriptions were not the only justification for Doherty's optimism in July, for the succeeding months also witnessed a considerable expansion in the number of districts established and a commensurate widening of the Association's sphere of influence. The first meetings in this period however, were to complete the circle of districts in the cotton towns around Manchester. On 5 July about four hundred persons assembled at Blackburn under the chairmanship of Marshall and determined to form a branch there after hearing speeches from Hynes and Doherty. A similar number met at Stockport on 14 July and were addressed by Turner, Foster, Doherty, Worsley and Longson, the old weavers' leader, who emphasised that honourable masters would gain from the Association's power to prevent undercutting by their competitors; again, the workmen voted to establish a branch.[91] On 26 July a public meeting of trades was convened at the 'Sheffield Arms', Middleton, at which Doherty made a long oration. His main target was the silk weavers, who formed a majority of the meeting; they were an unorganised trade and Doherty urged that it was necessary for them to unite to join the Association. But the *Guardian* reported that most 'sat silent as wooden blocks, without speaking, noting, nor, apparently, *thinking*', though a few intimated that they would try to organise their trade and the meeting resolved to appoint a trades' committee to arrange for the formation of a branch.[92] A similar meeting was called in the 'Bear's Paw Inn', Wigan, on 31 July, but after Turner and Doherty had enumerated the advantages of the Association, an argument developed with William Carson, one of the most ardent and active northern co-operators, who condemned the general union and argued in favour of co-operation. After Doherty had ridiculed his ideas, however, the meeting decided unanimously in favour of establishing an Association branch and appointed a trades' committee to effect it.[93]

This meeting virtually completed the process of organising the textile towns of Lancashire and Cheshire (although a fifteenth branch in this area was founded at Lees, near Oldham, following a meeting on 23 October at which Hodgins and Doherty spoke, and a sixteenth at Clitheroe, after a meeting addressed by Doherty on 27 November).[94] Doherty now turned to the crucial task of extending the Association to areas farther afield. The first such branch had already been formed in Newtown, Montgomeryshire, at a meeting on 14 July, but this was primarily an expression of support for the Rochdale flannel weavers, then on strike, and no subscriptions appear to have been sent from that quarter to Manchester.[95] The real expansion of the Association was associated with a propaganda tour of the Midlands undertaken by Doherty in August 1830. He was accompanied by Francis Marshall, the Bolton secretary, and the delegates of the spinners' grand general union, Foster and McGowan, also spoke at several of the meetings.

All these four leaders spoke at the first meeting of the tour on 10 August, at the 'Durham Ox' inn, Nottingham, where it was agreed to set up a branch. Sixteen trades were represented and they decided to depute two persons each to attend at the 'George and Dragon' on 23 August to make the necessary arrangements. The leading figures at the subsequent meeting were representatives of the smiths, moulders, fender-makers and plain silk-hose hands, and Thomas Matthews, a member of the Derby smiths' union, was unanimously elected secretary of the Nottingham branch of the Association.[96] This became a particularly thriving district. By 18 September nine trades had given in their entrance fees to the weekly meetings of the Nottingham committee, which was already influencing other towns in the area in favour of the plan. In response to a request from a deputation of the Mansfield plain silk-hose hands on 12 September, three delegates were appointed to convene and address meetings at the 'Black Swan', Mansfield, on 18 September, and at the 'White Swan', Sutton-in-Ashfield, on 20 September. As a result, the Mansfield trades agreed to form a division of the Nottingham district, and the Sutton workmen to send representatives to the Mansfield delegate committee.[97]

On the evening following the first Nottingham meeting, the same speakers spoke at the 'Nag's Head' inn, Derby, before two or three hundred persons. The usual resolutions were carried unanimously, and further arrangements for the organisation of a district were made at a subsequent delegate meeting on 7 September, at which the most prominent trades were the paper-makers, plain silk-hose hands, and fancy hose hands. At the latter assembly, several delegates proposed that a district with less than a thousand members should be allowed to send a representative to the half-yearly meetings, if his expenses were paid, and criticised the rule by which every trade paid the same entrance fee whatever the number of their members. But Doherty replied in the *Journal* that important financial decisions at general conferences must in fairness be taken by delegates equally representing the rank and file, while all trades were similarly represented on the district committees and hence should pay the same entrance.[98]

The third Midlands town visited by Doherty was Leicester, where a meeting of the trades was held under the chairmanship of a local printer and stationer, John Fowler, on 25 August,[99] and a committee of seven appointed to arrange the formation of a branch. They convened a further meeting on 7 September, which issued an address to every workman in the town and county of Leicester detailing the benefits that would accrue to them from joining a body which already comprised 'from 60 to 70,000 members'. As at Derby, however, some initial hesitancy among the workmen to become members can be deduced from a query sent by Fowler to Doherty asking if a small proportion of the men in a trade like framework-knitting would be allowed to join and receive payments from Association funds.[100]

Finally, a numerous assembly of the artisans of Birmingham was held in the last week of August at the 'Swan' tavern. The proceedings commenced by Marshall reading the laws of the Society and McGowan urging the necessity of general union among the working classes. Doherty then held forth in similar terms, emphasising the impotence of workmen as individuals, and adding a homily on the virtues of temperance and sobriety. The final speaker was the co-operative lecturer, William Pare, who paid a generous compliment to Doherty: 'The delegates were all strangers to him but Mr Doherty; and him he could recommend to them, from a slight acquaintance, as a sincere friend to the working-classes.' On reflection, he believed that the plan was calculated to do good, but that time was necessary to examine the rules fully; his suggestion that the deliberations should be adjourned till 8 September was therefore adopted.[101]

A very long report was published of the adjourned meeting, held in the Institution for Promoting the Fine Arts, Temple-Row, and attended by about five hundred persons. Two members of the provisional committee appointed at the first gathering, named Hetherington and Cox, opened the proceedings by commending the laws of the Association, the latter in particular lamenting the deteriorating condition of workmen because of their mutual jealousies, intemperance and the introduction of machines. But Morrison, a journeyman painter, opposed the formation of a branch in Birmingham for a number of reasons. Firstly, it would engender ill-feeling between employers and workmen, when in fact both were equally entrapped by the existing system of competition; secondly, their problems were more likely to be alleviated by two agencies already established in Birmingham—the Political Union and the Co-operative Societies; thirdly, the Association was too narrow in principle, entirely excluding as it did trades such as the agricultural labourers not yet organised in unions; and finally, Manchester was insufficiently central to be the seat of government, which would involve towns in heavy expense in sending a deputy up to 100 miles for the monthly deliberations of the provisional committee. He was succeeded by William Pare, who wished success to any plan of collaboration between trade unions to prevent unnecessary reductions; but the Association could only succeed in its wider aims if it adopted co-operative production during strikes, for they were otherwise powerless against the competition of machinery, unorganised labourers, and foreign workers who would undersell the English artisan if he temporarily succeeded in raising his wages and standard of living.[102]

In reply, the first two speakers forcibly defended the rules of the Association. Doherty had detailed how carefully these had been worked out and predicted that, once the benefits of union were apparent, mutual jealousies would disappear, and 'nothing could prevent even agriculturists organising themselves, as they must before they could help the nation in this great cause'. They pointed out, moreover, that Manchester was the logical centre at first, for it was also the birthplace, and claimed that 60,000 had already joined the Association, whose subscriptions were £250 per week. The meeting eventually agreed to resolutions recommending all local trade unions to join the Association and all disorganised trades to consider forming unions, requesting Pare to deliver a number of lectures on the state of the working classes, and re-electing the provisional committee with a mandate to form a branch.[103] Nevertheless, although this committee did continue to meet, few Birmingham trades came forward to join, and no subscriptions appear to have been sent from that town to Manchester.[104]

The results of Doherty's programme of planned expansion into the Midlands in August 1830 were thus somewhat mixed. But attempts to form new districts elsewhere continued apace up to the end of the year. On 18 September a branch was founded at Glossop, following a public meeting addressed by several of the Ashton spinners' leaders as well as by Doherty and Hynes.[105] And at a meeting at Leeds on 7 December, at which Jonathan Hodgins and Thomas Oates were the chief speakers, a resolution was carried that the remedy for their current distress was a national union to prevent reductions, although a branch association was not at this time established.[106] But the most significant advances in this period were made in respect to individual trades. On 2 October the *Journal* reported that the hatters were successfully adopting measures for reorganising their national body and had sent two delegates to the South 'to induce the hatters of that quarter to join the Association'.[107] More important was the sending of delegates into Staffordshire at about the same time to organise a union among the potters. On

18 October Hodgins and Thomas Foster attended a meeting officially convened by a local member of parliament to denounce the truck system, but they maintained that low wages were an even worse evil.[108] Foster's boast on his return to Manchester, that 'he and others had been in the Potterys and united 20,000 to the Union', was clearly exaggerated;[109] but the *Staffordshire Mercury* reflected local concern by recording the introduction, into that hitherto peaceful district, 'of tri-coloured flags, nobody knowing from whence or by whom—the distribution of inflammatory tracts by strangers, who avoid answering any questions as to their employers—and the appearance in the neighbourhood of persons bearing every characteristic of emissaries from a dangerous society'.[110] In the following month the two delegates returned to the area, accompanied by Doherty; they all spoke at an assembly of hatters, colliers and potters at Hanley on 15 November, in favour of joining the Association.[111] At the same meeting they persuaded the potters to form the China and Earthenware Turners' Society, which had affiliated to the Association by March 1831, and changed its title to the National Union of Operative Potters in August 1831.[112] At this same time approaches also appear to have been made to the colliers of several Lancashire towns, who, having formed a district union, were reported to the Home Office at the end of October as beginning to join with the general Trades' Union', and became involved in widespread strikes in November.[113]

This period of expansion after the first delegate conference in June was both reported and further encouraged by Doherty in the *Journal*. Accounts of meetings, as well as the numerous entrances of individual trades, continued to fill its columns. In July he inserted an ambitious two-part editorial on 'The Cause and Consequences of Reducing Wages', in which he argued that national wealth included only those articles which the people could buy and hence was diminished by lowering wages; this practice, therefore, far from being meritorious as the '*most learned*' men postulated, was the greatest national curse, nor was there any justice or 'necessity' in making workmen suffer for the masters' desire to maintain profits or to amass wealth faster than ordinary profits would allow. Moreover, cheapening British exports by abating wages could only benefit foreign consumers, while the quantity of imports must be equivalently depressed. 'Thus, in whatever light reductions are viewed', Doherty concluded, 'they necessarily impoverish and degrade the country and should be resisted by all lawful means. Indeed, if possible, the law should prohibit them.'[114] Having established this theoretical foundation, Doherty returned to more practical matters relating to the progress of the Association itself. This body, he proclaimed on 4 September, was 'now rapidly extending itself all over the country'; and thereafter estimates of the membership grew progressively more optimistic—60,000 on 18 September, 80,000 on 2 October, and almost 100,000 on 27 November.[115]

Doherty's ebullience reached new heights in the *Journal* of 2 October, when he inserted an 'Address of the National Association for the Protection of Labour to the Workmen of the United Kingdom'. Heading this eloquent rallying-cry for action was a quotation from Shakespeare's *Julius Caesar*, showing how there was a time for decision in the lives of all men, on which depended their future salvation or perpetual misery. The artisans of Britain were now at these crossroads. They had been degraded to the lowest levels of slavery and pauperism by, above all, the process of wage reductions. But now, as the producers of all wealth, they had an opportunity of reversing their fate, not by violence and hopeless destruction of machinery as resorted to by continental workmen, but by the more rational and legitimate method of forming a 'union of all the trades'. Already 80,000 men had joined the Association, numerous districts had been formed, and the *Journal* established. If they would only cease their divisions and mutual jealousies, if co-operators would realise that the success of their trading speculations depended upon keeping up wages, and that 'the interests of co-operation are closely connected with, and indeed, inseparable from the success or failure of this union', victory was assured; for one million workmen, subscribing 1d per week, would raise over £4,100 weekly, nearly £220,000 in a year, and over £1 million in five years. 'Depend upon it', he concluded, 'the great day of justice and retribution is at hand, when the workman will emerge from his present prostrate condition, to that higher rank and enjoyment justly due to his merits.'[116]

The problems facing the Association, however, were now multiplying. Some of these were administrative. Several of the regulations adopted on paper by the deputies at the June conference never came into practical operation. For instance, there is no evidence to show that the prescribed entrance fee of 1s per member was ever remitted by most trades (although 'entrance money' was occasionally included in the subscription lists). Similarly, but far more crucially, the executive powers of the Association remained in the hands of the Manchester Provisional Trades' Committee, in whose name orders were regularly inserted in the *Journal*,[117] and the intended Provisional Council, of delegates from seven alternating districts meeting monthly in Manchester, was not apparently established.[118] This tended to arouse objections to excessive Manchester control and necessitated the convening of general delegate meetings more frequently than at the six-monthly intervals originally envisaged.

Related to these problems of non-operation of rules were others concerned with their interpretation. The correspondence columns of the *Journal* were regularly filled with hypothetical or practical questions of application from different district committees, which Doherty endeavoured to answer.[119] More serious situations arose when individual branches independently placed their own constructions on particular regulations. Thus on 21 August Doherty heartily deplored 'a sort of exclusive spirit' displayed by some district committees in refusing admission to certain ill-paid trades on the grounds of poverty; this was contrary both to the laws, which covered all '*organised*' bodies, and to the spirit of the Association, whose ultimate object was 'a union of the whole body of working-classes'.[120] And three weeks later Doherty heaped equal abuse on 'certain persons, in a town not twelve miles from Manchester',[121] who were urging members to adopt the system of 'twisting in'. Secret societies, he went on, were unnecessary for British artisans, who could meet to debate their affairs openly. 'Those who urge secret tests or oaths are either very egregious fools or designing knaves; in either case their counsel is dangerous, and must carefully be avoided.'[122]

Inevitably the Association had to face problems of organisation and to overcome criticisms from 'snarling, carping harpies' in its early days. It was therefore necessary to recruit 'honest, intelligent, and persevering men, as officers, until the thing be fairly established'.[123] But it was not easy to find such men. Apathy and inertia were widespread among the working classes. Thus the reported foundation of a branch in any town did not necessarily mean the commencement of activity there: further visits and meetings were often required. For instance, in early September we find Marshall and Hynes addressing a meeting of workmen at Horwich on the advantages of the Association, though a branch had reportedly been formed there earlier. And about the same time a similarly renewed appeal had to be made to the workmen of Oldham by Foster, McGowan, and Doherty, who 'hoped the trades of Oldham would soon join the general union . . . [and] expatiated at some length on the necessity of radical reform, and the great benefit that would accrue from the recent revolution in France'.[124]

But Doherty's deepest embarrassment continued to be the indifference of large sections of Manchester workmen, despite his exhortations. These feelings were prevalent even among members of his own trade, the Manchester cotton spinners, who were engaged in the summer of 1830 in a debate as to whether their membership of the Association was beneficial. Consequently on 14 August Doherty published a long address to the trade to assist their conclusion. He declared that their strike defeat of the previous year, in spite of their club including all the spinners in Manchester, should have convinced them of the 'impotency [and] utter uselessness of partial unions in averting the evils of which you have been the victims'. Many of them had been blacklisted, or replaced by women and boys at even lower wages, 'yet, with all these things before you, you hesitate to co-operate with those whose aid you wanted in your difficulties, and *whose aid you may again want* under the same circumstances'. Their only hope to prevent further reductions, he concluded, was therefore wholehearted participation with other trades in the National Association.[125] In the following week, he extended his message to all the operatives of Manchester, whom he bluntly accused of 'cold indifference' towards the exertions of their fellow-workmen, and of stupidity in complaining of wage reductions at the same time as neglecting the one institution by which they could be counteracted. The Manchester workmen, Doherty asserted, should set an honourable example to the country in the struggle for independence. He therefore proposed that a public discussion should be held, at which all objections to the plan could be thoroughly aired and, he predicted, eliminated. All local workmen were invited to attend the debate at the Spinners' Room, David Street, on 23 August.[126]

A partial explanation for the Association's weakness in Manchester is that the trade societies were at that time also being earnestly proselytized by the exponents of co-operation, and there was by no means complete agreement between the two sets of propagandists.[127] Doherty was sympathetic towards co-operative principles, and the early numbers of the *Journal* contained much information about co-operative stores and extracts from the *Co-operative Magazine*; the experiment in co-operative production by the Manchester dyers and dressers' society at a workshop in Pendleton was particularly commended. But disputes soon broke out between the rival advocates of the two systems. Co-operators argued that trade unions had failed to maintain wages and that they had wasted their funds on futile strikes; it would be far more constructive, they maintained, to go in for co-operative retailing and manufacture, thus retaining for themselves the whole product of their labour, building up capital and eventually forming co-operative-socialist communities. Many trade unionists, on the other hand, tended to regard these co-operative schemes as impractical and idealistic, and pointed out that unless trade unions fought to maintain wages and employment, there would be no funds for co-operation, since the working classes would be reduced to abject poverty. These arguments caused bitter recriminations in Manchester, eventually boiling over in public debates on the rival merits of the National Association and the co-operative system during August and early September 1830. In other towns, too, such as Wigan and Birmingham, the Association also met with criticism from co-operators and there is little doubt that the preference of Birmingham artisans for co-operation and political reform partly explains why a thriving district never materialised there.[128] Doherty tried to secure friendly agreement, although at times he too became exasperated by what he regarded as the narrow-minded outlook of the co-operators, while he himself always emphasised the prime importance of trade unionism. The disagreements between trade unionists and co-operators should not be over-stressed—there was a good deal of basic sympathy and common endeavour—but they were certainly of some significance and have been neglected by labour historians, who have tended to view trade unionism and co-operation in this period as parts of a united working-class movement.

Of greater seriousness, however, than these internecine squabbles were the difficulties arising from the Association's growing involvement in trade disputes. Whereas, in the first half of 1830, assistance for the striking Bolton spinners—apart from publicity in the *Journal*—had been left to the Bolton branch committee,[129] and an appeal for support was considered sufficient for the turn-out Manchester silk-weavers (who were in any case seeking an advance),[130] Doherty recognised that in similar situations the Association had now to be seen to be involved.

The first trade which the Association had to support was the Rochdale woollen weavers, who had been involved in a series of disputes with their masters for more than a year over the progressive reduction of their 1824 wage-rates. After successive defeats, about 7,000 men turned-out in May 1830, demanding a full restoration, and though some manufacturers made concessions, about 5,000 strikers were still out at the beginning of July. Consequently the local union sent out delegates to solicit subscriptions for the strikers. One of their most successful missions was to Newtown, Montgomeryshire, where the local flannel weavers and spinners resolved to contribute to the support of their Rochdale colleagues at a meeting on 14 July, which also resulted in a decision to form a branch of the National Association.[131]

The position of the Association in these proceedings was complicated by the fact that the strike was not technically against a reduction. But the Rochdale workmen, who had joined the general union at an enthusiastic meeting on 24 June,[132] closely identified their cause with their hopes from the Association, and this feeling was shared by disinterested observers like the writer in the *Manchester Times and Gazette* of 17 July, who stated that, 'the union of trades . . . have now an opportunity of showing the practical utility of their association, by rendering timely assistance to the poor weavers of Rochdale'.[133] Accordingly, Doherty inserted in the *Journal* on 10 and 17 July appeals to the trades in favour of the strikers' claims.[134] A meeting of the working and other classes of Rochdale was also convened on 17 August on Cronkeyshaw Moor, 'for the purpose of more fully detailing the plan on which the national association for the preservation of labour is formed'. Torrential rain and the rival attractions of the annual wakes' week kept the attendance down to about a thousand, but, after listening to Hanson, the flannel weavers' secretary, Turner, Foster and Hynes from Manchester, and McGowan from Glasgow, they heard a far-reaching address from Doherty. He began with a lengthy calculation demonstrating how the workers were robbed of at least three-quarters of the produce of their labour by the government and the employers. But even more interesting to the Rochdale weavers was his unequivocal declaration that wage-reducing masters would not be allowed to take advantage of the three months 'probationary period' before the funds of the Association were opened, because the Association 'would support every trade to contend for the price which they had when they entered'.[135]

By this time almost all the Rochdale weavers had returned to work, the majority at their old prices, a few at the full 1824 rates. But they had now been given an assurance of Association support in any major strike in future, a fact that was recognised by at least one Manchester newspaper : 'In October, the flannel-weavers, who have already been admitted into the General Trades' Union, will be entitled to receive relief from that body, and will then be better able to resist their employers.'[136] Small wonder, therefore, that Doherty's announcement received cheers from the entire assembly and appeared to revive 'drooping spirits'.[137] Moreover, in the seven weeks between 4 September and 16 October advertised contributions from the Rochdale district to the Association amounted to a staggering £560, not far short of half the total volume of subscriptions during that period.[138] In the meantime, strike preparations continued apace. A meeting of flannel-weavers on Cronkeyshaw Moor in the first week of September resolved that, 'to secure to ourselves the statement price of 1824, it is absolutely necessary that every weaver and spinner do join the Weavers' Union and also the Trades' Union without loss of time. That as the Trades' Union commences its operation after the 12th October next, it is necessary that the weavers and spinners do adopt those measures that will secure to themselves, when that period arrives, the protection of the Union of Trades . . . [and] that every district, and every member in such district, do, as soon as possible, pay up their arrears both to our own and to the Trades' Union.' Regulations were also adopted appointing collectors and ensuring that no work was taken out that would have to be finished after 12 October.[139]

The National Association was now fully committed to the weavers' cause and a leading participant in the negotiations. On 17 September a special delegate meeting was held to discuss matters 'of a rather important nature', the details of which were not, however, disclosed.[140] Nonetheless, there can be no doubt that deliberations over tactics at Rochdale was the conference's *raison d'être*, for at the beginning of October circulars were sent to the leading woollen manufacturers in that area, inviting them to meet a deputation from the National Association for the purpose of 'ascertaining the manufacturers' intentions as to the prices they intend to pay', in order that the 'meeting of delegates sitting at Manchester' might take measures accordingly.[141]

The Association at this point took another noteworthy step forward, when it was recognised by the Rochdale woollen manufacturers as competent to negotiate on behalf of their workmen. The deputation, which included Doherty, had an interview with seven of the employers and the conference lasted about an hour and a half. The deputies insisted that the men would accept no less than 20s in the £ on the 1824 prices, but the masters declared that the state of trade made 18s in the £ the maximum possible offer. Indeed, one of them stated that, if the *present* wages of 16s in the £ were maintained (which afforded wages of 10–11s per week for the 'industrious weaver'[142]), there would only be work for two-thirds of the year. During this deadlock, about 4,000 workers attended a meeting on Cronkeyshaw on the afternoon of 13 October, to receive the report of the delegation and determine future actions. The principal speaker, Doherty, struck an immediately cautious note.

> He said they were assembled for the purpose of calling on the association for the protection of labour, to bring into operation those powers, which they had been concentrating for the defence of those now present. . . . They would allow him to say that the union was now in its infancy; they had power, wealth, and great discretion opposed to them; and all they had to defend themselves with, was their good sense, unanimity, and integrity. One false step in their proceedings would be a great injury, and it was become their duty to be very cautious that a false step did not take place, as, by such a circumstance, they might lose all the ground they had obtained.

After describing the interview with the employers, he therefore recommended that they should not attempt a general strike of the whole town, but should imitate the procedure of the spinners by bringing pressure on individual masters in turn, who would be disposed to give in rather than lose their orders to their competitors.

Further speeches were given by McGowan, Foster, Turner, and a few local leaders, after which the assembly agreed that the final decision should be made by their union committee, after consultation with the Association deputies at the 'Woodman' inn that evening. These deliberations, however, only resulted in further delay, a special committee of weavers being appointed to prepare a complete list of the prices paid by all manufacturers in the district.[143] This list was presumably intended to ensure that the first turn-outs were against the lowest paying masters; but, in the meantime, opinion rapidly turned against strike action. At the end of October the special committee issued a circular to the general committee of the weavers' union, inviting them 'to attend a meeting of the general committee at the Woodman, on 2 November, in consequence of some of the districts being of the opinion that a strike would not be advisable under present circumstances, and others that it would'. And on the evening in question, after lengthy deliberations, 'it was resolved to abandon for the present all thoughts of a turn-out, either partial or general'.[144]

Why were the months of careful preparations, which seemed to be leading inexorably to a general strike of Rochdale weavers, so peremptorily overturned in October? Firstly, the suppression of the *Journal* at that time by the authorities appears to have brought home to Doherty more clearly than ever the overwhelming strength of the forces opposed to the workmen.[145] Secondly, on a practical level, Doherty must have realised that the Association had got itself into an impossible position, for to support nearly 7,000 men with strike relief at a cost of more than £2,000 weekly was totally out of the question at this early stage in its existence; his support for 'rolling' strikes as an alternative was thus easily understandable. And finally, the enthusiasm among the Rochdale weavers themselves began to wane in the face of trade depression, the employers' resistance, and the lukewarmness of the Association's leaders. This anti-climax had serious repercussions. Not only was the deluge of subscriptions pouring into the central coffers from Rochdale suddenly and completely extinguished, but the somewhat chimerical power of the National Association was exposed and the tactical skill of Doherty and other leaders was, for the first time, found wanting.[146]

The participation of the Association in another major industrial dispute of this period—involving the Lancashire coal miners—is far less easy to trace. On 20 September all the colliers in the Bolton area turned out for a considerable *increase* in wages, which they had largely succeeded in obtaining by mid-October.[147] Meanwhile, similar strikes had occurred at coal-mining centres throughout the district, including Bury, Ashton, Oldham, Rochdale and Stockport. The disputes were also accompanied by some violence towards both persons and property : for instance, a steam-engine boiler was destroyed at a colliery at Radcliffe Bridge, near Bury, and some 'knobsticks' were thrown into the canal by strikers at Oldham.[148]

The Association should not have been concerned in this affair, since the workmen were indubitably asking for a wage increase. Yet *Wheeler's Manchester Chronicle* reported on 23 October that, 'it is understood that the colliers will be supported in their struggle by the General Trades' Union'. And, even more remarkable, the same paper revealed on 6 November that, 'we understand that the Trades' Union . . . last week advanced £1,000 to the colliers to support them in their struggle'.[149] Similarly, correspondence in the Home Office papers indicates that the colliers' union was short of funds and was beginning to combine with the general union during October.[150] The advertised receipts of the Association for that month, however, recorded only two districts of coal-miners paying their entrance deposits[151] and neither was directly involved in the strike. On 27 October, however, the Oldham colliers, who 'had expressed a desire of becoming members' of the general union, were addressed by John Hynes at a meeting to discuss the idea.[152] The actual role of the Association is therefore problematical, but there is no doubt that the rumours of its involvement led to a considerable increase in official interest in and disapproval of the National Association,[153] for many coal-owners were local magistrates, who were responsible for sending reports to the Home Office.

More crucial to the future of the Association, however, was its growing involvement in the complicated labour relations of the Ashton cotton-spinning district during 1830. A branch had been established there after a meeting on 26 May,[154] and the local spinners, after paying their entrance fee to the Association at the end of June,[155] became regular subscribers to the funds over the following weeks. On 7 August the Stalybridge spinners agreed to join the Association, at a meeting numerously attended by workmen from that and the surrounding neighbourhoods and addressed by Doherty, Foster, McGowan and Betts, and this was followed in September by a partially successful strike among the Stalybridge spinners.[156] But although one military observer was inclined to blame 'the strength of the union of trades' for the employers' willingness to compromise,[157] and the meeting to form a branch at Stalybridge on 7 August had certainly discussed 'the present prices paid for the spinning of cotton yarns',[158] in fact, as we have seen, this dispute arose mainly from the militancy of the local Ashton spinners and the equalisation-of-wages policy of the Grand General Union of cotton spinners.[159]

Nevertheless, contemporary commentators continued to regard the Association as being influential on the course of events. The *Manchester Guardian*, early in October, linked 'the trades' union' with that of the cotton spinners in the campaign to raise wages in Ashton, Dukinfield and Hyde, and a month later reported that the Association was 'in great vogue' in the Ashton district.[160] A general meeting of the working classes convened in Ashton market place on 19 November was dispersed by the police, but three days later about 4,000 operatives reassembled at another open space in the town and listened to orations by Doherty, Hodgins and Betts on the justice of working men obtaining their economic and political rights, and the necessity of establishing a periodical to replace the suppressed *Journal*.[161] On 27 November, however, the *Manchester Times and Gazette* revealed that a meeting to establish a branch at Stalybridge had been prevented by the interference of local cotton masters, which had greatly accentuated ill-feeling at a time when the masters had just issued their notice of a wages reduction.[162]

We have already seen that the motive behind this reduction was primarily economic—the altered relative position of the Ashton cotton-spinning district following the abatements at Stockport, Manchester and Bolton.[163] The existence of the Association certainly helped to increase obduracy on both sides, but the strike was by no means *caused* by the masters' desire to check the rise of that body, and the negotiations in the weeks preceding the actual closure of the mills were carried on by the leaders of the local and grand general spinners' unions. Moreover, despite the Ashton spinners' regular contributions and the turn-out being incontrovertibly against a reduction, the Association funds were not used to relieve the strikers, because of a recent amendment to the rules that a reserve of £3,000 should be amassed before payments were made.[164] It was only after the fiasco of the general strike call by the spinners' Grand General Union on 27 December and the consequent discredit of that organisation, that the National Association began to take a leading part in procuring subscriptions for the strikers and its fate came to be involved in the outcome of this struggle.[165]

Nevertheless, the Association came increasingly to be connected with this and other strikes, such as those of the coal miners, and in consequence became increasingly an object of press criticism and official concern. For more than a year after the first discussion of the idea of establishing a general union in Manchester at the end of September 1829, the local press was remarkably free from adverse comment regarding its activities. Indeed, for a period of seven weeks after the closure of the *Journal* on 2 October 1830, the *Manchester Times and Gazette* acted as the Association's unofficial organ of communication, inserting advertisements of the weekly subscriptions to the funds, editorials condemning the iniquities of restricting the freedom of the press, and lengthy reports of meetings.[166] But the escalating receipts advertised in the late summer and autumn, the progressively increased estimates of the Association's membership, and the widespread strikes among the Lancashire colliers, eventually produced its inevitable response. The first censure appeared in the *Macclesfield Courier* early in October. 'This pernicious society', the paper alleged, had now more than 80,000 members, and contributions of £500 weekly, both of which were increasing, and had reached 'such a formidable height, that it has claimed the attention of the executive'. One local manufacturer had complained to the Home Secretary because of a recent visit by a deputation to the cotton factories in Macclesfield; 'and we know that when the Duke of Wellington was at Manchester, he was made fully acquainted with the extent and danger likely to arise from the Union in that town and neighbourhood'.[167] The first editorial condemnation of the Association in the manufacturers' own paper, the *Manchester Guardian*, was as late as 23 October. 'Of this organisation, we believe, little is known, except by its effects; it is understood, however, that persons who become members of it bind themselves to obey the directions of some committee, and that work-people have repeatedly been called upon by such committee to engage in turn-outs, without being permitted . . . to exercise any discretion in the subject.' The article went on to describe the means by which the union made this power felt, by forcing masters to discharge non-members, prohibiting them from employing 'knobsticks', and regular 'gross and wanton outrages on property or person'. To counteract these evils, it recommended a general combination of masters or they 'will be vanquished in detail'; many employers were already demanding the re-enactment of the Combination Laws, but the paper believed that this should only be done as a last resort. In the same edition, a letter, signed 'Justus', attacked the proceedings of the Association at Bury, where the crofters threatened to apply the 'rolling strike' technique to the bleaching establishments, with the assistance of the miners, who were to force the master colliers to cease supplying coal to the offending works in turn. The writer concluded 'that no individual can withstand a power so vast', and urged the necessity of 'strong measures . . . to protect the trade of the country from the ruin with which it is menaced by this "Union" '.[168]

The allegation of secrecy, of course, ignored the deliberate publicity which Doherty had given the Association's affairs in the *Journal*, while that of intimidation neglected the fact that it had not taken direct control of the conduct of any trade dispute, though it may have encouraged a more truculent attitude. This did not, however, prevent the frequent repetition of such allegations over the succeeding months. And they were almost immediately supplemented by charges of venality and self-interest against the Association's leaders, after a general meeting had agreed on 26 October to the establishment of a new weekly newspaper, the *Voice of the People*, staffed by union officers, a decision which provoked a barrage of vituperation throughout the local press, as well as secession from the ranks of the Association.[169] And the wave of condemnation was prolonged and even extended by the outbreak of the Ashton spinners' strike in December, which was accompanied by widespread reports of arms being taken to meetings like that at Dukinfield on

G

4 December,[170] and was caused, according to the *Guardian*, not by genuine grievances, but 'by the artful and exaggerated representations of the trading manufacturers of combinations, who have an obvious and direct interest in getting them [strikes] up, because their own occupation would be totally destroyed, if there were a general good understanding between masters and their hands'.[171]

The increase in trades' disputes at this time not only aroused the dis-approval of the press but the fears of all classes of manufacturers. Their first really overt act of retaliation occurred in the middle of October, when some weavers turned out from the works of a Bolton bedquilt manufacturer, who was 'so fully convinced of the mischievous effects of the "Trades' Union", the cherished bantling of Messrs Doherty, Foster and Co., of Manchester, that he . . . determined not to employ, hereafter, a single individual who belongs to that confederacy'.[172] And a month later, during the manoeuvres leading up to the Ashton spinners' strike, Charles Hindley, of Dukinfield, dismissed all his hands for attending an Association meeting on 19 November.[173] Moreover, pressure mounted on the government for repressive action to be taken, because of a tendency to regard strikes by individual bodies of workmen as part of a general conspiracy. For instance, when G. R. Chappell and B. Gray, two Manchester master spinners whose operatives had turned out in October, wrote to Peel on 23 October and 6 November respectively, to demand the reimposition of the Combination Laws, they both emphasised the threat from the National Association, including the swearing of assassination oaths.[174] And an even wilder statement was contained in an undated and anonymous letter sent to the Home Secretary by a Mr Herries, which quoted a large Manchester manufacturer as stating that there were 180,000 people in the Association who were ready to take up arms to carry their ends and were paying a rent, like the Roman Catholic rent, of £500 per week—all through repealing the Combination Laws.[175]

These appeals found a willing response from the government, whose con-cern at the growth of the Association had been excited considerably earlier. After the partial success of the attempt to infiltrate the first grand delegate conference in June,[176] the Home Secretary, Peel, kept in close contact with trade-union affairs in the north by means of reports from the civil and military authorities. These communications seldom distinguished between the actions of separate bodies of workmen, and hence the Tory government, and its equally receptive Whig successor, was soon convinced of the existence of a widespread conspiracy. As early as August, as we have seen, Lieutenant-Colonel Shaw was writing that 'the union of trades' was so strong in the Ashton–Stalybridge district, and the workmen so excited by the French revo-lution, that he feared there would be outbreaks of violence. In reply, Peel counselled the employers to avoid precipitate action, while recommending to the military authorities that they 'must prepare for the worst, and not allow such use of physical force to triumph'.[177] By the end of September it was rumoured that 'the Duke of Wellington [Prime Minister] has his eye upon this association, which is now said to consist of upwards of 80,000 members, and that an agent of government will shortly be down amongst them'.[178]

Tension increased during October with strikes among the Manchester spinners and the Lancashire colliers, while the exaggerated claims by Doherty and others of the Association's membership and power were accepted and even elaborated upon. On 30 October General Bouverie sent in a more detailed analysis of the current situation in the north-west. The spinners and weavers, he alleged, were all bound by oath to the rules of the Association, which were admirably drawn up for their purpose, and, except for the oath, in no way illegal. 'The association numbers—the Trades' Union, of which Dogherty is the Secretary and Director—are variously stated, but amount certainly to many thousands, and their funds are very great.' When the colliers' union was fully integrated, Bouverie believed that the general union would be 'complete and irresistable'. The leaders planned to keep wages up to what *they* considered equitable, by rolling strikes in each trade; it was unlikely that a general strike would be called and the union's resources thus over-stretched, 'as the leaders are men of too much penetration, and have too much an interest in the continuance of their own power to allow matters to come to such a pass. Dogherty, for instance, besides the management of the Funds, has, I am told, £600 p.a.; the other officers are paid in proportion.' He understood that the Association's headquarters were in London, that it extended as far as Glasgow, and that it was mixed up with the rapidly increasing political feeling, 'excited by recent events in France and Belgium'. As a post-script to this tissue of facts, half-truths and falsehoods, Bouverie wrote again on 6 November, that the grand union had weekly receipts of about £330 and its early October membership of 80,000 had risen considerably since by the accessions of colliers and 'many of the smaller unions in Yorkshire, viz Bradford, Huddersfield'.[179]

It was at this time that a combined meeting of army leaders and Lancashire magistrates, convened on Peel's initiative to discuss the crisis, rejected the use of force against strikers, because it might lead to widespread disturbances through the influence of the Association;[180] and even J. F. Foster, the most moderate and objective of the local functionaries, feared that this influence could be used for political ends and recommended that legislation was essential for closer control of picketing, and that 'confidential persons' be utilised to collect detailed information for a prosecution against the union leaders.[181] The gravity with which the industrial situation was regarded is illustrated by the fact that, Wellington's Tory government having now fallen, Peel appended the following note to Foster's letter of 13 November: 'I take the liberty of recommending the subject of this letter—and the whole of my most confidential communications with Mr Foster regarding the Trades' Union at Manchester to the immediate and serious consideration of my successor in the Home Department.'[182]

Despite its commitment to parliamentary reform, the new Whig government shared the hostility of its predecessor towards the working classes. Of Lord Melbourne, the Home Secretary, this was particularly so, as he revealed in a private letter, dated in September of the following year, by which time the power of the Association was waning:

> When we first came into office in November last the union of trades in the North of England and in other parts of the country for the purpose of raising wages etc., and the general union for the same purpose,[183] were pointed out to me by Sir Robert Peel in a conversation I had with him on the then state of the country, as the most formidable difficulty and danger with which we

had to contend, and it struck me as well as His Majesty's Servants in the same light.

We considered much ourselves, and we consulted much with others, as to whether the arrangements of those unions, their meetings, their communications, or their pecuniary funds could be reached, or in any way prosecuted by any new legal provisions, but it appeared upon the whole impossible to do anything effectual, unless we proposed such measures as would have been a serious infringement upon the constitutional liberties of the country, and to which it would have been impossible to have obtained the consent of Parliament.[184]

Melbourne's response to this situation was immediately more positive than that of the cautious Peel. 'In November 1830', wrote Nassau Senior, the political economist, 'a few days after he had received the Seals of the Home Office, Lord Melbourne requested me to inquire into the state of combinations and strikes.'[185] Over the following weeks, Senior, with the assistance of a lawyer named Tomlinson, collected much information on this subject, exclusively from the authorities and manufacturers rather than from workmen and tending, therefore, to be biased and exaggerated : for instance, one manufacturer informed them that the Association had 400,000 members, though Senior preferred to believe the evidence of the Manchester borough-reeve, who stated that it had 100,000 members and funds of £6,000. Hence, when the report was privately sent to Melbourne, it alleged that thousands of loyal and innocent workmen were being terrorised by an ignorant minority, because the 1824 repeal of the Combination Laws had failed to distinguish clearly enough betwen the legalising of trade unions and the continued illegality of violent methods, and the 1825 Act had made the procedure for prosecuting offenders too complex. The proposed legislative remedies included increased penalties for intimidation, soliciting union subscriptions, picketing and vitriol-throwing, the authorisation of masters or constables to seize delinquents without summons or warrant and to compel them to give their names and addresses to Justices of the Peace, distinctly delineated powers for magistrates to employ the military to disperse pickets and protect property and persons, very severe punishments for masters who encouraged combinations, and improved facilities to encourage offenders to inform against their companions. If these measures failed to discourage combinations after a fair trial, Senior and Tomlinson suggested that union funds deposited in Savings Banks should be liable to confiscation. 'Should this expedient also fail, the last measure must be to restore the rigour of the Common and former Statute law against combinations altogether, only making the Statute Law more effectual by taking away the power of appeal from summary convictions by Magistrates.'[186]

It was scarcely surprising that even Melbourne hesitated before introducing such a catalogue of repression into the Commons. Even so, the outbreak of the Ashton spinners' strike in December 1830, while Senior's investigations were yet proceeding, heightened his concern and a torrent of letters flowed between Whitehall and Lancashire, discussing the strategic movement of troops, arrangements for the prevention of illegal meetings such as that at Dukinfield on 4 December, and the possibility of arresting the leaders of the local strike and the Association.[187] Indeed, so alarmed was Melbourne that on

30 December he wrote to William Hulton that 'no military force' could prevail against the secret councils and funds of the Union: 'This combination, or rather conspiracy, is an evil of a different nature, and requires another remedy, which it is difficult to discover and apply, but to devising which I may say, being very desirous at the same time of not exciting very sanguine expectations, the best attention of the Government will be directed.'[188] Meanwhile, the other activities of the Association were closely watched. For instance, on 23 December Colonel H. Custance informed Melbourne that a general meeting of trades was to be held at Leicester, at which 'a man named Doherty from Manchester is to take the lead'. Whereupon the Home Office instructed the Mayor of Leicester to send reliable persons to the meeting and to take proceedings against any speaker who tried to excite riot or disaffection.[189]

During the last week of December 1830, rumours swept through Manchester that Doherty had been arrested under a state warrant for sedition or even high treason. One gentleman had 'seen' him, in the custody of Lieutenant-Colonel Shaw and a Bow Street officer, crossing the New Bailey bridge, en route to the New Bailey prison; and another 'witnessed' his boarding a stage coach between two London police-officers to be conveyed to the Secretary of State's office. Several local papers even reported definitively that 'Mr D——y, who had appeared conspicuously as one of the most forward in the dissensions between the employers and operatives in Manchester, was on Friday apprehended on a charge of being concerned in seditious practices'.[190] The story was not without some foundation, for the local magistrates, encouraged by the Home Office, were seriously considering the arrest of Doherty and other leaders at this time;[191] the *Manchester and Salford Advertiser* believed, indeed, that a warrant for Doherty's arrest *had* been applied for, 'on a charge that was not true, and which the [Home] Secretary did not believe to be true'.[192] In fact, neither Doherty nor any other Association leader was ever arrested, despite constant efforts to implicate them in violence. And Senior's suggestions, for legislation to ease the bringing of prosecutions against unionists and to curb the power of combinations generally, never came to fruition, largely because the gradual decline of the Association during 1831 eliminated the necessity for official action.

Despite the mounting hysteria, the only overt act of state repression against the Association during the second half of 1830 was the enforced closure of the *United Trades' Co-operative Journal*, the last edition of which appeared on 2 October. This had contained Doherty's challenging and optimistic address 'to the Workmen of the United Kingdom', in which he had claimed the establishment of the periodical as one of the main achievements of the Association.[193] But whilst pretending that the *Journal* was purely a trade-union periodical, he had increasingly been including political news and comment, which rendered it liable to the newspaper stamp duty. This provided the government with a convenient pretext for its closure, doubly desirable on account of the Association's growing strength and the rising political excitement, which Doherty was helping to stimulate. Thus the *Journal* was the first casualty in the official campaign against the unstamped press which began in the autumn of 1830.[194]

Its circulation never seems to have exceeded 1,000,[195] but its readership was perhaps ten times that figure because of its availability in public houses and reading rooms, and the range of its influence was commensurate with that of the Association, if the range of its sale was in fact reflected in its advertised list of agents—at Manchester (where it had seven outlets), Macclesfield, Rochdale, Stockport, Ashton, Lees, Crompton, Oldham, Stalybridge, Hyde, Blackburn, Preston, Glossop, Nottingham, Derby and Newcastle-under-Lyne by 2 October.[196] Considering the crucial importance which Doherty attributed to an organ of propaganda as a unifying force, the replacement of the *Journal* was now the first priority for the Association. For seven weeks, notices, advertisements and reports were inserted in the *Manchester Times and Gazette*. Indeed, this organ of the middle-class radicals briefly found common cause with the associated workmen in denouncing the restrictions on the press. A strongly-worded editorial on 9 October criticised the Stamp Office for giving no notice of the illegality of the *Journal* until a sum of £400 or £500 was due—or even of £500,000 if the penalties for printing on unstamped paper were enforced.

> This is a pure specimen of the liberty of the Press. A few humble workmen by extraordinary exertions and perseverance, succeed in establishing a small weekly publication, devoted almost exclusively to affairs of trade, and which they endeavour to make the vehicle of useful information, at a price which brings it within the reach of those for whom and by whom the work was established and conducted—the labouring classes; and in step, the officious and lynx-eyed 'Commissioners of Stamps', . . . lay their fiat upon it, thereby depriving the workmen of the information which its pages contained. This, I suppose, is one of the benefits for which the people are to be grateful to Lord Wilton's 'hereditary aristocracy'. Where is the difference, it may be asked between entirely prohibiting the spread of knowledge, and laying a tax upon its communication, which cannot be paid.[197]

The Association's use of the *Manchester Times and Gazette*, however, was no more than a temporary expedient, less because of a bitter disagreement that soon arose between Doherty and its editor, Archibald Prentice, than because of Doherty's basic insistence that workmen should control their own press, and because of the inadequacies of using a local paper to publicise a *national* body. As soon as the *Journal* disappeared, therefore, plans were immediately set in train for an even more ambitious successor, leading to the establishment of the *Voice of the People*, the most significant of the journalistic memorials to Doherty's ability and career.

The initial step in these events was the insertion of an advertisement in the *Manchester Times and Gazette*, convening a public meeting of the working classes of Manchester, Salford and district, in the Mechanics' Institution, Cooper Street, on 26 October, to discuss the foundation of an effective organ of communication, 'consistently with the laws of the country',[198] to replace the *Journal* and represent the interests of workmen throughout the United Kingdom.[199] James Turner took the chair and the principal speakers were Hodgins, Renshaw, Doherty and Hynes from Manchester, Sadler from Stockport and McGowan from Glasgow. They all denounced the bias and misrepresentation of the stamped press, which, Doherty pointed out, was part of the whole system of political control and economic exploitation. The establishment of an independent workmen's newspaper was therefore essential to redress this situation and ensure the success of the Association. Resolutions were unanimously passed expressing the necessity of political reform and determining upon the starting of subscriptions to establish 'a weekly newspaper, to be called "The Voice of the People", devoted exclusively to the interests of the working-classes'. At the same time it was agreed to petition Parliament for abolition of all restrictions on the press.[200]

The suppression of the *Journal* by the authorities thus unintentionally contributed towards an increasing identity of interest between the leaders of the Association and local radicals, which developed more clearly in 1831.[201] This was also visible in other towns which Doherty energetically visited at this time to gain support for the new journalistic venture. Thus at Chorley, where he addressed a meeting on 29 October on the importance of the Association and the necessity of establishing their own newspaper, his audience consisted mostly of members of the local political union; Doherty urged workmen, in fact, to unite and bury their differences 'on mere points of theory'.[202] Unanimous support was given to the project in this and other towns which he visited, including Lees,[203] Macclesfield, Bury, Stockport, etc., except—significantly—in Bolton, where the committee refused to call a general meeting.[204]

Doherty also wrote to Francis Place on 3 November, seeking his help and advice in a situation of renewed legal repression.[205] He first referred to 'the suppression of our little Journal' by the Stamp Commissioners, who had 'required the stamp duty to be paid on every copy that has been printed'. The result was that 'the printer became alarmed and refused to print even the number that was then in type'.

> The working-classes, however, seem determined not to be silenced, and we are now making arrangements for the establishment of a weekly newspaper, to be called the *Voice of the People*. The paper we intend to have out by the 1st of January at the latest. We are about to have a press and materials of our own to print with . . . [for] the paper is [to be] the property exclusively of the working-classes. We possess a fund of between one and two thousand pounds, raised entirely from the weekly pennies of the working classes. This is an important fact, and show [sic] you the spirit that is abroad amongst them.

Doherty enclosed a copy of the Association's 'laws', upon which he asked for Place's opinion, as well as on 'the establishment of a Newspaper'. And later in his letter he asked Place to let him know if he heard of 'a first rate press and types to be disposed of for ready money'. At the same time, he sought Place's views on the renewed threat of legal repression against trade unions.

> Many people here, alas, seem to entertain the opinion that an attempt will be made in the present session to renew the Combination Laws, or something like them. This I have no apprehension about. You will be better able, however, to judge of this matter than I can possibly be. I do know that many of the masters here have had meetings on the subject. If any thing of the kind should be attempted, perhaps you will sugest [sic] to us what should be done.

Doherty himself, however, was mainly concerned about 'the restrictions on the press', against which they were getting up petitions and writing to M.P.s, and it was primarily in this agitation that he sought Place's support.[206]

With this campaign already under way, the third general delegate meeting of the National Association was held in Manchester between 8 and 10 November, a month ahead of the six-monthly schedule adopted at the first conference in June.[207] A number of momentous decisions were made: the Association funds deposited in Messrs Heywood & Co.'s bank were to be withdrawn forthwith and used to set up the *Voice of the People*; every member was to be asked to pay 6d during the next three months, in weekly instalments of ½d over their usual contributions; John Doherty was to be the editor of the *Voice* at a salary of £3 per week (with an advance of 5s if the speculation succeeded), and Thomas Oates its reporter at a weekly salary of £2 (subject to an increase of 5s on the same conditions); J. Hampson was to be the printer and receive 2 guineas (rising to £2 5s if the paper succeeded), two trustees were to be entered at the Stamp Office as proprietors, petitions to Parliament were to be sent from every district in favour of the removal of restrictions on the press, and the first number of the *Voice* was to be published on 1 January 1831. John Hynes was appointed Association general secretary at a salary of 27s per week in place of Doherty, while Jonathan Hodgins was made an itinerant delegate to visit various parts of the country and set up additional districts, at a weekly salary of £4 10s, plus coach fares. To safeguard the Association's funds, additional levies were to be made whenever they fell below £2,000.[208]

These decisions marked an important turning-point in Doherty's career, a swing towards his becoming a full-time trade-union publicist, and ultimately an independent radical publisher, rather than a trade-union official and organiser. It would appear that his experiences in editing the *Conciliator* and *Journal*, and in issuing addresses to trade unionists and the general public, had given him a strong taste for working-class journalism, in which he would be able to find scope for expression of his wider views on politics, co-operation, factory reform, etc., as well as on trade unionism. Moreover, he was well aware of the precariousness of a trade-union official's position,[209] and may already have discerned the possibility of setting himself up independently in the publishing field, like several other working-class leaders, especially in London. Having now ceased to be general secretary of the National Association, he was soon afterwards also to relinquish his offices in the cotton spinners' union, both central and local, in order to concentrate on editing the *Voice*.[210] Nevertheless, he remained deeply involved in trade-union affairs: as editor of the *Voice*, he had a very influential position and he continued to play a direct and active, and not merely a propagandist, role.

Doherty's relinquishment of his secretarial offices might have been expected to reduce the complaints, notably in Bolton, against his multifarious activities and consequent inefficiency. But, in fact, the delegate meeting's decisions, especially the proposed establishment of the *Voice* with Doherty as editor, were strongly opposed by the Bolton delegates, Marshall and Meadows, who maintained that their constituents would not accept them: the split, which had grumbled beneath the surface for some time, now publicly burst wide open. Although Bolton men, especially Marshall, had frequently co-operated with Doherty in extending the Association, it appears that he was still disliked and distrusted in that town. There was a deep distaste of him as an Irish Roman Catholic immigrant, and also criticism of his performance as secretary of the cotton spinners' general union, combined with dislike of his centralising policies, while his insistence on publicity and his condemnation of secret oath-taking aroused further opposition.[211] The plan to establish the *Voice*, therefore, which was seen solely as Doherty's brainchild, opened the floodgates of resentment.

As soon as the Bolton delegates returned from the November conference, they called a branch meeting to present a report.[212] Marshall began the assault by deprecating the expense of an estimated £1,000 in a way contrary to the original purpose of the Association; Doherty, he added, was not worth 10s per day, and Oates had little experience as a reporter, yet their huge wages were to be paid by persons whose earnings might not exceed 6s weekly. He was followed by other speakers who all believed that the establishment of a newspaper under Doherty—a 'marked man' among the masters and hence vulnerable to a prosecution for libel—was an unnecessary risk, when other friendly newspapers were willing to publicise their proceedings.[213] Another spinner, H. Rothwell, declared that Doherty was the 'sole instigator' of the project, and explained at length his inadequacies as secretary of the spinners' general union, particularly his unpunctuality, neglect, dictation and 'plurality of livings'. But the most vitriolic criticism came from Finley Frazer, who observed that

> Doherty's plan of a trades' union was to have one million of members, and this immense mass to be governed by a single press; the idea was ridiculous; besides where was the use of paying sevenpence for a paper, when the same information could be had for 4d; and above all men in the world, Doherty was the most unfit to be an editor, his political and religious feelings were of too strong a cast for him to conduct a newspaper discreetly; besides he had no talent; he had already been connected with one publication which had done great injury to the working classes, by the injudicious manner in which he had placed trade matters before the public. . . . The editor of a trades' paper ought to be able to steer a judicious course between the imprudent workman and the tyrannical master. He ought instead of possessing an irritable and vindictive temper, to have a heart overflowing with the milk of human kindness . . . He was also too negligent to manage a paper suitable to the wants of the operatives . . .: in short, he cared for nothing else but pocketing his salary. Doherty had told his own version of the story to the districts, otherwise a very different result would have been the consequence.

Finally, Frazer added, Hodgins was equally unworthy of trust and responsibility because of his acceptance of work on a self-acting mule and his high-handed action in the spinners' union of 1824–5.[214]

The assemblage passed a number of resolutions in accordance with the spirit of these speeches, with which only C. Rothwell, who believed the working classes required a press of their own, disagreed. The establishment of the *Voice* was condemned as injudicious and liable to cause great loss, while the exorbitant salaries awakened 'just suspicions as to the motives of some of the leading advocates for the establishment of the Trades' Union'.

G*

And finally a motion was passed deploring the transmission of money from districts throughout the kingdom to Manchester, because of the resulting expense and dislike of one district's excessive power over the rest; and in consequence it was decided 'that no more money should be transmitted from this district of the General Trades' Union to Manchester, under existing circumstances'.

This meeting was not very numerously attended, the reason being, it was explained, that several trades only sent representatives. Doherty, on the other hand, regarded this as evidence that it was a 'hole and corner meeting' got up by his personal enemies and inspired by the proprietors of the middle-class radical press in the locality, who feared the competition of the *Voice*. And he succeeded in having a further meeting of the Bolton trades convened on 24 November to reconsider the newspaper question and discuss the conduct of those who had called the previous meeting to overturn measures of the Association fairly decided on. To a packed and turbulent audience that evening, Doherty put his case, adding that the salaries had been fixed independently by the trades' delegates, and accusing the *Bolton Chronicle* of fabricating Frazer's speech in the report of the first meeting—which charge was indignantly denied and Doherty was forced to withdraw.[215] All the prominent Manchester leaders—including Hodgins, Oates, Turner, and the ailing Foster—also attended, but their arguments were limited by a resolution passed at the commencement of business, confining each speaker to a quarter of an hour, a decision taken, according to the *Guardian*, from experience of the 'speechifying' of 'Messrs Doherty and Co'. At length an amendment was easily carried, 'that the funds of the Bolton Union be not appropriated to the establishment of a newspaper at present'.[216] And thus, although Doherty had braved the haunt of his bitterest detractors, his eloquence was this time insufficient and the wounding and weakening split within the Association was confirmed.

The announcement of the newspaper project stimulated a wave of criticism throughout the local press. Whereas recent comment about the Association had stressed the violence frequently associated with strikes,[217] emphasis now turned more insidiously to the questionable motives of its leaders. On 30 October, for instance, the *Guardian* warned the working classes against 'professional combinators', who provoked contests with the employers, in which the workmen were always the greatest sufferers:

> But what do the DOHERTYS and the other people of the same kind care for their sufferings so long as they can themselves obtain employment? What did they care for the hunger and nakedness of the spinners in this town during the turn-out of last year? Nothing. Being themselves well-clothed and well-fed out of the funds of the combination, they, when seated at a tavern over their wine, felt nothing of and cared nothing for the poor starving spinners and their families. . . . It is a fact, that, just at the conclusion of the turn-out, when the spinners were compelled by the pressure of hunger to accede to the terms of their masters, some of the leaders of the turn-out were seen comfortably seated over a bottle of wine at a public house.[218]

The revolt of the Bolton branch gave an added impetus and apparent justification for such vilification, and disparagement now transcended the political spectrum. The tory *Wheeler's Manchester Chronicle* entered the fray on 20 November, with a long editorial, headed 'The Trades' Union', and inserted, it was claimed, to protect the labouring classes 'from the artifices of designing pretenders' :

> At the establishment of the Union, it was natural to anticipate, knowing the character of its manager and agents, that the contributions of the working-people in the district would never be applied to any useful purpose, on their behalf; and that opinion . . . has already been shown to be somewhat prophetical by the measures modestly submitted to part of the general body by Mr John Doherty and his compatriots. A few weeks ago, Mr Doherty, not content with his rewards as Secretary of the Union, became ambitious, and manifested a great anxiety to add to his other graces a literary reputation. Forgetful of the design of the Association, he proposed the establishment of a newspaper, for the patriotic purpose of advocating the interests of the working-classes—the newspaper press in this district not being, in his opinion, able or pure enough for so immaculate a public man. The cloven-foot was apparent, but the unsophisticated operatives to whom the design was propounded did not 'smell a rat', and as it would seem ascribed the project to the disinterested feeling and kindness of Mr Doherty and his coadjutors.

The paper went on to rejoice, however, that workmen of greater experience at Bolton had recognised the ambition and self-interest of the 'agitators' and exposed the true nature of the scheme. In consequence, it concluded, 'the working-classes will have only themselves to blame if they submit to be duped any longer'.[219]

The whig *Manchester Guardian* and ultra-tory *Stockport Advertiser* similarly congratulated the Bolton men on their wisdom and understanding.[220] But the most devastating assault came from the radical *Manchester Times and Gazette*, which printed on 20 November, for the benefit of the 'contributors', a detailed profit and loss account for the 'Intended New Paper'. This estimated weekly expenditure on such items as stamped paper, rent and taxes, salaries, postage, etc., at £74 2s, while weekly receipts, assuming sales of 2,000 copies at 7d each and an average of twenty advertisements (which a working man's paper would find great difficulty in attracting), would not surpass £52 16s 8d. Thus weekly losses would be £21 5s 4d, while there would be an initial capital outlay of about £600 for type, presses and office furniture: thus the total cost to the Association at the end of two years would be £2,811 14s 8d, compared with the reported estimate of only £1,000 by the 'projectors'.[221]

Doherty immediately retaliated by stopping all Association notices and advertisements in the *Times and Gazette*,[222] and by despatching a letter in which he sarcastically questioned the disinterestedness of Prentice's motives and disputed his figures. By excluding Hodgins' salary, which was not connected with the cost of the paper, and by reducing the estimated expense on several items and adding receipts from jobbing printing, the weekly loss on the *Voice* would be no more than £1 5s 4d, even on Prentice's circulation and advertisement figures; Doherty reckoned, however, on selling 'another couple of thousands a week more'.[223] In a brief counter printed beneath this letter, Prentice declared that the working classes were being deliberately deceived :

'if before we were convinced that there was gross ignorance in the promoters of the scheme, we are now convinced that THEY KNOW they have been wrong, and will not confess it. They are cajoling poor people into a speculation in which £2 or £3,000 will be forever lost, as we are prepared to prove ON THEIR OWN CALCULATIONS, to any deputation from the Union, of persons not *interested* in getting up the thing for their own employment and emolument.'[224]

This wrangle with Archibald Prentice was further irritated by a dispute as to the circulation of the *Times and Gazette*, Doherty eventually having to make a public retraction.[225] This success stimulated Prentice to further attacks, notably the publication in the following week of a 'Lankeshur Letter' from 'Rachel Ritewell', which chided him for saying 'aught agen Mesthur Docherty. Donnot yo think ut if yo wur gettin sitch a noise living eawt o' th' poor foke, us he as bin dooin for this geit whoile, ut yod do your best to keep your shop. Yoi, awn shur yo wind;—un if he *dus* speik un speechify un print newses, un lose by em, wot has he to care abeawt tat, us long us he gets his celery?'[226]

The breach with the Bolton branch and the violent press campaign did not prevent Doherty pressing ahead with the scheme. Further meetings were held in different towns, ostensibly for strengthening and expanding the Association, but also to secure support for the proposed newspaper and to petition for removal of all press restrictions; many of these meetings were attended by Hodgins in his capacity as full-time organiser. Between four and five thousand workmen attended a meeting at Ashton, for instance, on 22 November, at which Hodgins opened the proceedings by eulogising the Association and stressing the necessity of a newspaper. When 'an old cobbler' criticised the use of funds, subscribed to protect themselves from reductions, for paying large salaries to editors, clerks, reporters, and itinerant speech-makers, he was answered by Doherty and a local spinner named Grundy. The former pointed to the growing thirst for knowledge throughout the population, which could only be satisfied by newspapers; but only the enemies of the working people had sufficient capital to establish them. The National Association, however, would soon have 100,000 members, which would ensure at least 15,000 sales for their own paper, a circulation which was more than any other provincial paper and would ensure advertisements, adding its profits to the Association funds. Grundy read out the 21st rule, which stated that, as soon as a sufficient fund could be raised, 'a printing press, types, etc. should be purchased' for the use of the operatives; this, said Grundy, adequately dealt with the allegation of the Bolton committee that funds were being diverted from their original purpose. At the close of the proceedings, the establishment of the *Voice* was sanctioned and a petition to Parliament approved, by all except about half-a-dozen in attendance.[227]

During December 1830 Hodgins spread the same message farther afield. He appeared together with Oates at a meeting in Leeds early in the month, which was one of few signs of interest in the Association in Yorkshire; three resolutions were passed, attributing the general distress among workmen to unnecessary wages reductions, asserting that the remedy lay in the Association, and agreeing that a new newspaper, devoted to their interests, was desirable. And at the end of December, Hodgins and Slater, the Ashton spinners' delegate, spoke at separate meetings of the Leicester woolcombers and tailors, which agreed to join the Association, support the Ashton turn-outs, and approve the *Voice*.[228] Further encouragement came in a letter from Thomas Matthews, secretary of the Nottingham district, dated 26 December, expressing the approbation of that branch for Doherty's plan and condemning the personal and conspiratorial opposition of Bolton leaders like Marshall, who was described as 'a disappointed man' of 'shallow abilities'. Meanwhile, a letter of Doherty's detailing the case for the paper was published in the *Manchester and Salford Advertiser* of 4 December. This provoked a rowdy confrontation at Horwich, where, on 12 December, the Bolton committee convened a public meeting of members of the Blackrod and Horwich districts of the Association, to explain their reasons for opposing the *Voice* and to protest at the alleged falsehoods in Doherty's letter. Frazer, Marshall, Lomax and H. Rothwell all spoke, but were outmanoeuvred by several addresses from Doherty, and the stormy debate terminated in the early hours of the following morning with the unanimous adoption of a motion regretting the hasty and inconsiderate steps taken by the Bolton district relative to the establishment of the *Voice*, and earnestly requesting them to reconsider the matter and re-unite themselves to the general body.[229]

At this time Doherty was making final arrangements for the publication of the *Voice*. On 11 December the 'Prospectus' of the new paper, which had appeared in *Carpenter's Political Letters* a week before, was published in several Manchester newspapers, which showed that it was a far more ambitious project than Doherty's previous attempts and recalled the *Trades' Newspaper* of 1825. It was to be priced 7d, stamped, and to contain copious reports of the activities of workmen throughout the country as well as the ordinary intelligence of newspapers. As the exclusive property of the working classes, it would espouse their interests, but since they were the producers of all wealth, this would benefit the whole nation. Moreover, the paper would expose the injustice of legally protecting all inanimate property, while neglecting that which gave value to all—LABOUR—and it would recommend all lawful methods for workmen to secure their due influence in the state. 'We shall prove, that in the present circumstances of this country, the idea of independence, in any shape, among the working-classes, without combination, is an utter absurdity. The great object then of our labours, shall be to unite the productive classes of the community in one common bond of unity for their mutual protection. We shall endeavour to collect their scattered energies into a common focus, to give them importance and consequence, by acquainting them with their own strength; to consolidate their power, by uniting their exertions.' Similarly, in the political sphere, the *Voice* would advocate the fullest measure of popular rights—including universal suffrage, short parliaments, and above all, the vote by ballot. Religious questions would be avoided, for, while 'satisfied of the soundness of our own religious opinions', the right of every person to worship his Creator, according to his own conscience, was recognised. Doherty realised that financial difficulties were likely because of the opposition of selfish capitalists, pampered aristocrats, innumerable tax-eaters, and apathetic workmen, as well as lack of experience in 'fine writing', but ultimate success was certain, given only an 'impartial hearing'.

On a practical level, orders and advertisements were to be sent to the agent, C. H. Lewis, of Market Street, or to Hynes at the Association head-quarters, 26 Oldham Street. All manner of printing would be undertaken at the office of the *Voice*, No. 1 Spring Gardens, where the paper was printed by J. Hampson on a press purchased by the committee of five in charge of the publication.[230] During the following week Doherty was relieved of his position as secretary of the grand general union of cotton spinners, in favour of Thomas Foster, and prepared to take up his new role.[231] The first number of the *Voice of the People* appeared, according to plan, at the end of 1830, amid mounting excitement among both workmen and their adversaries.

What was the real position of the National Association by the end of 1830? How sound were Doherty's claims to a membership approaching 100,000, how 'national' was its extension, and what power did it possess? The total receipts between 31 July 1830 and 1 January 1831, amounted as we have seen to £1,969 7s 9d.[232] But the full contributions for 1830 must also include thirty-six payments of £1 each as entrance fees from different trades paid before 31 July 1830, and therefore amounted in all to £2,005 7s 9d.[233] (It is impossible to discover how many Manchester and Bolton trades paid their entrance fees before the establishment of the *Journal*.) At the end of this chapter these subscriptions are tabulated according to their geographical origin and the particular trades concerned. It can be seen that the vast majority of contributions came from Lancashire and Cheshire, nearly a third, in fact, coming from Rochdale alone. Of the rest, the majority originated from Nottinghamshire, Derbyshire, and Leicestershire, with meagre receipts also from Cumberland and Yorkshire. Moreover, the range of trades which subscribed to any substantial amount was as limited as the Association's geographical extent. Almost half of the advertised contributions merely mentioned the particular district, but of the total donated by specified trades, over four-fifths came from the various textile manufactures. The most enthusiastic contributors were handworkers in these trades, suffering severely from commercial depression, an excess of hands, and mechanical competition : notably the Rochdale flannel-weavers,[234] much the most generous subscribers, for they must have sent in almost all the cash from that district, though only £151 of it was specifically recorded in their name;[235] the calico-printers, almost certainly hand-block printers mainly, were another group of workers suffering from the competition of machinery and looking hopefully to the Association for support; and various categories of Midlands silk workers, such as framework-knitters in the hosiery trade, formed another depressed section, with similar hopes, similarly doomed to failure.[236] There was also, however, strong support from cotton factory workers in the north-west, especially from the mule spinners, though the Manchester spinners, to Doherty's chagrin, were extremely lukewarm;[237] others included power-loom weavers, card-grinders and strippers, dyers and dressers. A wide range of other workers, employed in textile machine-making, hatting, and the building trades, as well as in many of the traditional urban handicrafts, had also contributed, but only in small amounts and in a few localities.[238] It is difficult to estimate the total paying membership, because there is no evidence as to what proportion of the subscriptions covered entrance payments, and because there were such sharp fluctuations in weekly receipts. At the first general delegate meeting, at the end of June 1830, it was agreed that trades need not pay the shilling entrance fees (to which there was strong opposition), but could simply pay their weekly pence for six months before becoming entitled to benefits.[239] If, as seems likely, most trades decided to do this, then the claims of 60–70,000 membership in September and October may not have been far from the truth: if the maximum weekly receipts of £302 5s announced on 16 October came entirely from penny subscriptions, then the paying membership would have been 72,540.[240] But the receipts for that week were exceptional—the average for September was £106 3s 2d, and for October £180 12s 3d—and probably included some entrance payments, so it is doubtful whether the Association membership rose above 50,000 even at its zenith in mid-October, and it may well have been substantially less. Moreover, contributions fell catastrophically thereafter and paying membership appears to have fallen to no more than 15,000, probably less, by the end of the year.

The Association thus ended 1830, strictly confined in both extent and numbers. It had serious problems to contend with, particularly the secession of a major branch, discontent with Manchester as the centre of government, and the strike of Ashton spinners, which was already causing rumblings of discontent among the turn-outs because of the Association's failure to give financial assistance.[241] On the other hand, the authorities were certainly convinced of the power and influence of the Association, and the establishment of the *Voice* as a powerful organ of publicity held out hope of widening that influence. In fact, when the crisis occurred early in 1831, the Association was found wanting, and the *Voice*, instead of being the organ of a vibrant and expanding general union, became mainly the forum for Doherty's own social and political aspirations for the working classes.

Contributions to the National Association, 31 July 1830 to 1 January 1831, by location

| Lancashire | £ | s | d |
|---|---|---|---|
| Ashton-under-Lyne | 170 | 13 | 5 |
| Aspinall Smithy | 14 | 0 | 0 |
| Blackburn | 131 | 0 | 0 |
| Blackrod | 3 | 0 | 0 |
| Bolton | 70 | 0 | 0 |
| Bury | 80 | 11 | 0 |
| Catterall | 1 | 0 | 0 |
| Chorley | 56 | 0 | 0 |
| Clitheroe | 15 | 18 | 0 |
| Denton | 1 | 10 | 0 |
| Droylsden | | 13 | 0 |
| Edenfield | 7 | 6 | 2 |
| Garstang | 1 | 0 | 0 |
| Gorton | | 12 | 0 |
| Haslingden | 2 | 5 | 0 |
| Henfield | 1 | 0 | 0 |
| Horwich | 40 | 19 | 9 |
| Irwell | 22 | 12 | 6 |
| Lees | 23 | 10 | 6 |
| Manchester | 195 | 5 | 5 |
| Middleton | 10 | 13 | 9 |
| Mossley | 15 | 15 | 10 |
| Oldham | 44 | 15 | 8 |
| Preston | 6 | 2 | 0 |
| Ramsbottom | 19 | 16 | 0 |
| Ribblesdale | 27 | 0 | 7 |
| Rochdale | 661 | 4 | 2 |
| Rossendale | 27 | 3 | 8 |
| Standish | 1 | 0 | 0 |
| Total | 1,652 | 8 | 5 |

| Cheshire | £ | s | d |
|---|---|---|---|
| Bollington | 1 | 3 | 1 |
| Hyde | 1 | 0 | 0 |
| Macclesfield | 21 | 16 | 8 |
| Stalybridge | 67 | 15 | 2 |
| Stockport | 7 | 0 | 0 |
| Total | 98 | 14 | 11 |

| Derbyshire | £ | s | d |
|---|---|---|---|
| Derby | 60 | 2 | 11 |
| 'Derbyshire' | 1 | 0 | 0 |
| Total | 61 | 2 | 11 |

| Leicestershire | £ | s | d |
|---|---|---|---|
| Leicester | 39 | 11 | 2 |
| Total | 39 | 11 | 2 |

| Cumberland | £ | s | d |
|---|---|---|---|
| Carlisle | 4 | 16 | 4 |
| Total | 4 | 16 | 4 |

| Yorkshire | £ | s | d |
|---|---|---|---|
| Sheffield | 1 | 0 | 0 |
| Shipley | 5 | 0 | 6 |
| Total | 6 | 0 | 6 |

| Nottinghamshire | £ | s | d |
|---|---|---|---|
| Mansfield | 14 | 13 | 4 |
| Nottingham | 113 | 6 | 11 |
| Old Basford | 1 | 0 | 0 |
| Sutton-in-Ashfield | 2 | 0 | 0 |
| Total | 131 | 0 | 3 |

| | £ | s | d |
|---|---|---|---|
| Total where location specified | £1,993 | 14s | 6d |
| Total contributions | £2,005 | 7s | 9d |

Contributions to the National Association, 31 July 1830 to 1 January 1831, by trade

|  | £ | s | d |
|---|---:|---:|---:|
| 1   Textile trades | | | |
| (a) Cotton and other textile workers, mainly in the north-west: | | | |
| Mule spinners | 217 | 3 | 1 |
| Calico printers | 170 | 8 | 10 |
| Power loom weavers | 65 | 12 | 3 |
| Card grinders and strippers | 26 | 15 | 7 |
| Cotton yarn dressers | 22 | 8 | 6 |
| Crofters (bleachers, etc.) | 12 | 13 | 9 |
| Silk twisters | 9 | 10 | 0 |
| Sizers | 3 | 11 | 6 |
| Stretchers | 3 | 1 | 11 |
| Wool combers | 1 | 16 | 8 |
| Dyers | 1 | 0 | 0 |
| Jenny spinners | 1 | 0 | 0 |
| Hand loom weavers: | | | |
| Flannel | 151 | 0 | 0 |
| Broad silk | 21 | 16 | 8 |
| Silk smallware | 3 | 1 | 8 |
| Woollen | 3 | 5 | 0 |
| Fustian | 1 | 0 | 0 |
| Nankeen | 1 | 0 | 0 |
| Total | 716 | 5 | 5 |
| (b) Framework knitters, mainly in the Midlands hosiery trades, etc. | 129 | 10 | 11 |
| 2   Textile machine-making, including spindle and fly makers, mechanics and machine hands, bobbin and carriage makers, engineers and needle makers | 54 | 6 | 8 |
| 3   Hatters | 45 | 8 | 8 |
| 4   Building trades, including sawyers, joiners and plasterers | 27 | 12 | 0 |
| 5   Miscellaneous skilled trades, including iron moulders, smiths, shoemakers, tallow chandlers, tobacco pipe makers, basket makers, farriers, miners, paper makers, ropers, fender makers, sinker makers and lock makers | 66 | 0 | 8 |
| 6   Unskilled trades, including quarrymen and labourers | 1 | 3 | 1 |
| Total contributions | 2,005 | 7 | 9 |
| Total where trade specified | 1,040 | 7 | 5 |

NOTES TO CHAPTER SIX

[1] See above, pp. 23–7 and 39–41.

[2] Webb Collection, Vol. I, f. 120.

[3] *Bolton Chronicle*, 21 November 1829. The speaker was presumably referring either to 1824, when a vain attempt was made to form a general union among the weavers, or to 1827, when they tried without success to re-establish it. See D. Bythell, *The Handloom Weavers* (Cambridge, 1969), p. 185.

[4] I. J. Prothero, 'London Working-Class Movements', Unpubl. Ph.D. thesis (Cambridge, 1966), p. 85. For the plan of the Manchester silk weavers to form a general association of united trades to support each other's strikes, see *Bolton Chronicle*, 12 January 1828.

[5] See above, pp. 23–6 and 40–1.

[6] *Bolton Chronicle*, 7 April 1827.

[7] *Gazette*, 3 May; *Trades' Newspaper*, 14 June 1828.

[8] *Gazette*, 26 July 1828.

[9] *Chronicle*, 5 July; *Mercury*, 5 August; *Courier*, 9 August 1828.

[10] Prothero, *op. cit.*, p. 86.

[11] *Trades' Newspaper*, 6 September and 4 October 1828.

[12] W. Thompson, *Labour Rewarded* (1827), pp. 87–9.

[13] See above, pp. 37–9.

[14] *Trades' Newspaper*, 19 April and 3 May 1828.

[15] *Conciliator*, 22 November 1828.

[16] S. and B. Webb, *op. cit.*, p. 106.

[17] See above, p. 80.

[18] See above, p. 77.

[19] Catholic Emancipation had been obtained that year.

[20] *Times and Gazette*, 3 October 1829, *inter alia*.

[21] *Courier*, 3 October 1829.

[22] *Chronicle*, 3 October 1829.

[23] *Times and Gazette*, 10 October 1829; *Place Collection*, Vol. 16, f. 96.

[24] See above, p. 87.

[25] *Times and Gazette*, 24 October 1829.

[26] *Journal*, 15 May 1830.

[27] *Bolton Chronicle*, 21 November 1829.

[28] Doherty did not desire to bring down even the aristocrats, but only that they should 'work for what they received of the public money'. He was clearly no egalitarian.

[29] *Bolton Chronicle*, 5 December; *Courier*, 5 December 1829.

[30] *Guardian*, 5 December 1829.

[31] *Ibid.*, 12 December 1829, and 2 January 1830.

[32] See above, p. 101. The role of the Bolton district secretary, Francis Marshall, in the expansion of the National Association in the summer of 1830 was second only to Doherty's.

[33] This society paid in only £1, presumably its entrance fee.

[34] A. E. Musson, *The Typographical Association* (1954), p. 70.

[35] Though he was then referring to the cotton spinners' concerns.

[36] Cole, *Attempts at General Union*, p. 18.

[37] Moreover, the important trades' conference in the following June was always reported as the first such meeting: see below, pp. 167–71.

[38] *Times and Gazette*, 20 February 1830.

[39] The periodical is preserved in the Manchester Central Reference Library.

[40] See below, pp. 207 and 421 *et seq.*

[41] *Journal*, 13 March and 17 April 1830. See below, Ch. IX, for Doherty's relationships with the Owenite co-operative movement.

[42] *Ibid.*, 4 September 1830.

[43] See above, p. 2.

[44] *Journal*, 6 March 1830.

[45] *Ibid.*, 20 March 1830; *Bolton Chronicle*, 20 March 1830.

[46] *Journal*, 10 April 1830.

47 See above, p. 155 and 158. Cole, *Attempts at General Union*, p. 20.

48 *Journal*, 1 May 1830.

49 *Ibid.*, 8 May 1830.

50 The Blackburn branch was not established till 5 July: see below, p. 172.

51 *Journal*, 15 and 22 May 1830. For the need to revive this branch in January 1831, see below, p. 218.

52 See above, p. 101.

53 *Journal*, 29 May 1830.

54 *Ibid.*, 3 July 1830.

55 *Ibid.*, 12 June 1830.

56 *Chronicle*, 26 June 1830.

57 *Journal*, 13 March, 8–29 May, 26 June 1830; *Voice*, 8 January 1831.

58 *Journal*, 27 March 1830.

59 *Ibid.*, 1 and 8 May 1830.

60 *Ibid.*, 29 May 1830. The strike was defeated after ten weeks.

61 Possibly Thomas Worsley, though the letter was sent from Manchester.

62 *Journal*, 19 June 1830. See below, pp. 177–8.

63 *Ibid.*

64 *Ibid.*, 27 March 1830.

65 Including 'Derbyshire' and Carlisle, the first successes outside Lancashire and Cheshire.

66 The first accession from Yorkshire.

67 *Journal*, 17 April–26 June 1830.

68 *Ibid.*, 15 May 1830.

69 *Ibid.*, 12 June 1830.

70 *Ibid.*, 26 June 1830.

71 No mention is made of a delegate attending from Macclesfield.

72 The report of the meeting appeared in the *Journal*, 3–24 July 1830.

73 See above, p. 165.

74 Marshall later obtained an amendment that trades in distress could pay their shillings in instalments.

75 See below, p. 324. For the calico printers' later interests in co-operative production, see below, pp. 239 and 330.

76 Whether the 'spirited discussion' comprised some opposition to Doherty was not reported. He probably resigned at this time as secretary of the Manchester district to fulfil his wider duties, although the first public reference to his successor, John Hynes, as 'Secretary to the Manchester District', was not until October: see *Times and Gazette*, 30 October 1830.

77 They are reprinted in Cole, *Attempts at General Union*, Appendix 3.

78 H.O. 40/27, f. 274.

79 *Ibid.*, f. 291. See also above, p. 98.

80 Presumably Philip McGowan from the spinners.

81 H.O. 40/27, f. 293.

82 *Ibid.*, f. 207. Shaw also enclosed No. 18 of the *Journal*.

83 *Journal*, 3 July 1830.

84 *Ibid.*, 10 July 1830.

85 *Ibid.*, 3–24 July 1830.

86 *Ibid.*, 31 July 1830.

87 *Ibid.*, 7 August–2 October; *Times and Gazette*, 9 and 16 October 1830.

88 See below, p. 181.

89 *Times and Gazette*, 23 October–20 November 1830.

90 *Voice*, 1 January 1831. But see below, p. 196, and for a detailed analysis, see pp. 198–9.

91 *Journal*, 10 and 17 July 1830.

92 *Guardian*, 31 July 1830.

93 *Journal*, 7 August 1830. See below, p. 325, for the argument with Carson.

94 *Guardian*, 30 October and 4 December 1830.

95 Previous labour historians, such as Cole, have exaggerated the importance of this branch. See below, p. 178.

96 *Journal*, 14 August and 4 September 1830.

97 *Ibid.*, 18 September; *Nottingham and Newark Mercury*, 25 September 1830.

[98] *Journal,* 14 August and 18 September 1830.

[99] In the meantime, Doherty had been back in Lancashire addressing various meetings.

[100] *Journal,* 28 August and 18 September 1830. Doherty replied in the affirmative.

[101] *Ibid.,* 28 August 1830.

[102] Doherty had apparently claimed at the previous meeting that the Association would give the workmen 'power to get three good meals a day, all of which should, if he pleased, consist of animal food'.

[103] *Ibid.,* 25 September and 2 October 1830.

[104] See below, p. 217.

[105] *Journal,* 25 September 1830.

[106] *Chronicle,* 11 December 1830.

[107] *Journal,* 2 October 1830.

[108] *Times and Gazette,* 30 October 1830.

[109] H.O. 40/27, f. 163, letter from G. R. Chappell, a Manchester millowner, 23 October 1830.

[110] Quoted in *Chronicle,* 30 October 1830.

[111] H.O. 40/27, f. 347.

[112] Cole, *Attempts at General Union,* pp. 22–3; W. H. Warburton, *History of Trade Union Organisation in the North Staffordshire Potteries* (1931), p. 53.

[113] H.O. 40/26, ff, 104–9. See below, p. 181. For the formation of the colliers' union in South Lancashire, see R. Challinor, *The Lancashire and Cheshire Miners* (1972), pp. 25–6.

[114] *Journal,* 24 and 31 July 1830.

[115] *Journal,* 4 and 18 September, 2 October; *Guardian,* 27 November 1830.

[116] *Journal,* 2 October 1831. Ironically, the periodical was closed down after this edition: see below, p. 187.

[117] See, for example, *Journal,* 17 July 1830.

[118] Delegates from other towns did 'sit in' on Manchester committee meetings, but on no regularised basis: see below, pp. 241–2 and 268–9, n. 202.

[119] See, for example, the enquiries of the Leicester and Derby trades, referred to above, p. 173.

[120] *Journal,* 21 August 1830.

[121] Probably Bolton, in view of later developments and the local leaders' attitude towards excessive publicity. (See above, p. 88, and below, p. 191.)

[122] *Journal,* 11 September 1830.

[123] *Ibid.,* 4 September 1830.

[124] *Ibid.,* 11 September; *Times and Gazette,* 11 September 1830. Both these towns had been visited before: see above, pp. 164–5.

[125] *Journal,* 14 August 1830. See also above, pp. 144–5, and below, pp. 235–6.

[126] *Ibid.,* 21 August 1830.

[127] See below, Ch. IX, for a more detailed examination of their disagreements.

[128] See above, pp. 172 and 173–4. Another factor in Birmingham was the lack of strongly marked class divisions. See below, p. 217.

[129] See above, p. 101.

[130] *Journal,* 29 May 1830. In this appeal Doherty also condemned the violence associated with this dispute as counter-productive.

[131] *Mercury,* 11 May, 13 June; *Journal,* 24 July 1830. See above, p. 172.

[132] See above, pp. 165–6.

[133] *Times and Gazette,* 17 July 1830.

[134] *Journal,* 10, 17, and 31 July 1830. But only a few small contributions from various trades were subsequently acknowledged.

[135] *Times and Gazette,* 21 August 1830.

[136] *Chronicle,* 14 August 1830.

[137] *Journal,* 21 August 1830.

[138] *Ibid.,* 4 September–2 October; *Times and Gazette,* 9 and 16 October 1830.

[139] *Chronicle,* 11 September 1830. During previous disputes, men had been prosecuted for leaving work unfinished.

[140] *Journal,* 25 September 1830.

[141] *Guardian,* 9 October 1830.

142 *Chronicle,* 9 October 1830.
143 *Guardian,* 16 October 1830.
144 *Mercury,* 2 and 9 November 1830.
145 See below, p. 187. Doherty referred to this warning of governmental power at the Rochdale meeting on 13 October.
146 Yet no labour historian has ever mentioned the Rochdale affair in connection with the Association.
147 *Mercury,* 19 October 1830.
148 *Ibid.,* 28 September and 12 October 1830.
149 *Chronicle,* 23 October and 6 November 1830. The latter report was almost certainly untrue.
150 H.O. 40/26, ff. 104-9. See above, p. 175.
151 *Times and Gazette,* 16 October 1830.
152 *Ibid.,* 30 October 1830.
153 See below, p. 185.
154 See above, pp. 164-5.
155 *Journal,* 3 July 1830.
156 *Guardian,* 14 August 1830. See above, pp. 105 and 106.
157 H.O. 40/26, f. 63, letter from Lt. Col. Shaw.
158 *Times and Gazette,* 14 August 1830.
159 See above, pp. 104-7.
160 *Guardian,* 2 October and 6 November 1830.
161 *Ibid.,* 27 November 1830. See below, p. 194.
162 *Times and Gazette,* 27 November 1830. See above, p. 120.
163 See above, pp. 104 and 119.
164 See above, pp. 121, 126-7 and 134, and below, p. 204, n. 208.
165 See above, pp. 126-8 and 134.
166 *Times and Gazette,* 2 October-20 November 1830.
167 Quoted in *Courier,* 13 November 1830.
168 *Guardian,* 23 October 1830.
169 See below, p. 188 *et seq.*
170 See above, pp. 120 and 123.
171 *Guardian,* 18 December 1830.
172 *Ibid.,* 16 October 1830.
173 *Stockport Advertiser,* 26 November 1830. See above, p. 120.
174 H.O. 40/27, ff. 163 and 331; see also f. 366.
175 *Ibid.,* f. 319.
176 See above, pp. 170-1.
177 H.O. 40/26, ff. 28-42, 68. See also above, p. 106.
178 *Guardian,* 2 October 1830. H.O. 40/25, f. 7.
179 H.O. 40/26, ff. 104-9, 119.
180 See above, p. 114.
181 H.O. 40/27, ff. 322 and 340, letters of 28 October and 13 November 1830.
182 *Ibid.,* f. 346. Peel's note was dated 19 November 1830.
183 Melbourne was apparently still blind to the fact that the Association was formed only to oppose reductions. It is not clear why he mentioned two separate general bodies, unless he made the sophisticated analysis possible for labour historians (unlikely in view of his other misconceptions) and distinguished between the twin manifestations in Lancashire and Yorkshire.
184 *Melbourne Papers,* Ch. v, p. 130, quoted in Webb Collection, Vol. I, f. 200.
185 N. W. Senior, *Historical and Philosophical Essays* (1865), Ch. 7, 'Combinations and Strikes', quoted in Webb Collection, Vol. I, f. 198.
186 MSS Report to Home Office in 1830 by Senior and Tomlinson, quoted in Webb Collection, Vol. I, ff. 187-96.
187 See above, pp. 123-4.
188 *Melbourne Papers,* ed. by L. C. Sanders (1889), p. 20, quoted by Morris, *op. cit.,* p. 56.
189 H.O. 40/27, f. 40, and 41/9, f. 191.
190 *Voice,* 1 January 1831.
191 See above, p. 123. See also pp. 129-30, for the local industrial and political circumstances in which this rumour developed.

192 *Advertiser*, 8 January 1831.

193 See above, pp. 175–6.

194 See below, pp. 421–2.

195 *Voice*, 8 January 1831. Although Bowring estimated it at 1,200: *ibid.*, 5 February 1831.

196 *Journal*, 2 October 1831.

197 *Times and Gazette*, 9 October 1830.

198 The plan was from the first, therefore, to establish a stamped newspaper.

199 *Times and Gazette*, 23 October 1830.

200 *Ibid.*, 30 October; *Chronicle*, 30 October 1830. For the petition, see the *Prompter*, 11 December 1830. See also below, pp. 422–3.

201 See below, pp. 236–8.

202 *Bolton Chronicle*, 13 November 1830.

203 *Guardian*, 30 October 1830. Doherty addressed a meeting at this town, near Oldham, on 23 October, before the Manchester meeting; an Association branch was formed.

204 *Voice*, 1 January 1831.

205 Place Papers, Add. MSS 37,950, ff. 96–7. Doherty had previously sent Place copies of the *Journal* up to the tenth number, and he now completed the set.

206 See below, pp. 422–3.

207 This explains why no delegate conference met in December, because of which Cole, *Attempts at General Union*, p. 26, erroneously suggests that it was postponed until the following March. The second conference met at the end of September to discuss the Rochdale crisis (see above, pp. 179–80).

208 *Guardian*, 20 November 1830. It was presumably at this conference that the resolution was passed that no strike relief should be paid until the funds reached £3,000 (i.e. £2,000 in reserve plus £1,000 for establishing the *Voice*).

209 See above, p. 93.

210 See above, pp. 110, 149, n. 32, and 140–1; also below, p. 196.

211 See above, pp. 52, 88, 90, 91, 100, 103, 176, and 189.

212 *Bolton Chronicle*, 20 November 1830, *inter alia*.

213 Meaning probably the *Manchester Times and Gazette* and the *Bolton Chronicle*, which seem to have provided the Bolton men with their estimated figures.

214 See above, p. 32. Hodgins was employed on self-actors after the 1829 Manchester strike.

215 The rapidity with which relations with the orthodox radical press had deteriorated can be gauged from the fact that only a month earlier, at the Chorley meeting, Doherty had praised the editor of the *Bolton Chronicle* as a man, 'who had always been ready to fight in the cause of the injured and oppressed workman'. *Bolton Chronicle*, 13 November 1830.

216 *Guardian*, 27 November; *Times and Gazette*, 27 November 1830.

217 See above, p. 183.

218 *Guardian*, 30 October 1830. See above, p. 79.

219 *Chronicle*, 20 November 1830.

220 *Guardian*, 20 November; *Stockport Advertiser*, 3 December 1830.

221 *Times and Gazette*, 20 November 1830.

222 The only extant reference, therefore, to the Association subscriptions in the last five weeks of 1830 is in the pamphlet *On Combinations of Trades* (1834 edn.), pp. 83–94. See below, p. 205, n. 233.

223 For the actual circulation, midway between the predictions of Prentice and Doherty, see below, pp. 206–7. Doherty's figures were based on consultations with James Whittle, editor of the *Manchester and Salford Advertiser*.

224 *Times and Gazette*, 27 November 1830.

225 *Ibid.*, and in several other local papers.

226 *Ibid.*, 4 December 1830.

227 *Guardian*, 27 November 1830.

228 *Chronicle*, 11 December 1830; *Voice*, 8 January 1831.

229 *Voice*, 1 January 1831; *Bolton Chronicle*, 18 December 1831.

230 *Carpenter's Political Letters*, 4 December; *Times and Gazette*, 11 December; *Courier*, 11 December 1830.

231 See above, pp. 140–1. According to a letter from J. F. Foster, the Manchester magistrate, to Melbourne on 22 December 1830 (H.O. 40/26), it was at this time also that Doherty gave up the secretaryship of the Manchester spinners' society, being succeeded by Maddocks, in order to concentrate on editing the *Voice* (see above, pp. 110). But Foster stated that the paper was established by the spinners' union, which he confused with the National Association.

232 See above, p. 171.

233 This figure is reached by combining the lists of subscriptions in the *Journal* between 31 July and 2 October, in the *Manchester Times and Gazette* between 9 October and 20 November, and in the pamphlet *On Combinations of Trades*, pp. 83–94. There are no advertised subscriptions in the newspapers between 27 November and 25 December. On the other hand, the pamphlet for some reason omitted the donations for 9, 16 and 23 October, and 20 November 1830 (and for 12 March 1831); hence the exclusive use of this source by Cole (*Attempts at General Union*, p. 30 and App. 4, pp. 176–86) and others has resulted in an underestimate of the total receipts, and also in the lack of awareness of the size of the Rochdale contributions. See below, p. 221.

234 Handloom weavers generally, however, had shown little interest. See above, pp. 158–9 and 172, for signs of hostility or apathy among them.

235 See below, p. 217.

236 As we shall see in the next chapter.

237 See above, pp. 110, 144–5, 177 and below, pp. 235–6 and 259–60.

238 For a more detailed discussion of the pattern of membership, see below, pp. 258–60.

239 See above, p. 169.

240 For the figures of weekly receipts, see above, p. 171.

241 See above, pp. 126 and 134–5.

# VII The National Association in decline, 1831–2

The first edition of the *Voice of the People* was published a day ahead of schedule on 31 December 1830, to avoid the New Year's festivities.[1] Thereafter, it appeared weekly on Saturdays, the numbers in the first volume, for the half-year ending 25 June 1831, each comprising eight quarto pages of four columns, and those in the second volume, from 2 July to 24 September, four folio pages of seven columns. The paper was far more ambitious than Doherty's previous publications in its size and inclusion of a much greater variety of information, covering items of foreign news, local and general intelligence, advertisements, miscellaneous extracts, births, marriages and deaths, and commercial and sporting reports, as well as the more usual editorials, correspondence and accounts of meetings on trade union and political subjects. And, in view of the recent fate of the *Journal*, it was stamped and priced 7d, an announcement at the head of each paper explaining that this was made up of 'Paper, Print etc.—3d' and 'Taxes on Knowledge—4d'.

The administration of the *Voice* was in the hands of a committee of five representatives from the Manchester committee of the National Association, who met together each Thursday to audit its accounts, and two proprietors, James Turner and Ellis Pigot, were registered at the Stamp office.[2] It was printed on its own press by John Hampson, at No. 1 Spring Gardens and published at first at the printer's, but from 16 April at No. 73 Market Street; after 9 July the publisher was Charles W. Wallis, of No. 63 Durham Street, Salford. Although various reports indicated that the Association had amassed a fund of two or three thousand pounds to start the paper, they probably originated in a misunderstanding of the resolution passed at the November delegate meeting concerning the raising of a reserve fund of £3,000 before any industrial action was supported.[3] In fact, the money must have come from the ordinary subscriptions to the Association, for the special appeal which was launched among the members for additional contributions of 6d each to support the *Voice* yielded only £35 4s 1d in the first seven weeks of 1831,[4] after which there were more pressing financial claims. The principal sources of revenue must therefore have been advertisements and sales. There were thirty-five advertisements in the first number, apparently confuting Prentice's forecast,[5] but that figure was never exceeded and the average soon declined to about fifteen per paper. The circulation figures, however, were much more successful: 16,200 copies were sold in the first six weeks, at the end of which weekly sales had reached 3,005.[6] By 5 March the circulation had risen to 3,359, 'and yet, notwithstanding this most extraordinary number, they have never yet been able to supply the whole of their orders'; in fact the *Voice* claimed a total readership of almost 40,000, since more than a thousand copies were sold to inns, public-houses and reading rooms.[7] Most copies were doubtless purchased in Manchester and the surrounding Lancashire towns, but the paper had agents in London, Dublin, Glasgow, Nottingham, Derby, Leicester, Leeds, Birmingham and elsewhere, and Doherty's repeated complaints of interference or negligence at coach-offices or post-offices show that sales cannot have been negligible at several of these places.[8] Circulation was adversely affected, however, when Doherty acquired some personal odium through his disagreement with Hunt over the Reform Bill,[9] and more than half the revenue from sales in any case disappeared in the stamp tax. Jobbing printing was also undertaken from the *Voice* office, but it is unlikely that this yielded much profit, and in fact the paper was never free from financial difficulties throughout its existence.

The circulation figures were not the only indication that the Bolton seceders from the Association were mistaken in their view that Doherty was unfit to be editor. The early numbers carried numerous letters from district secretaries throughout the north-west and midlands, congratulating him on the appearance and contents of the *Voice*, and many of the leading London radicals soon rallied to its support. Dr. Bowring, editor of the *Westminster Review*, referred at a public meeting in February to the establishment of the *Voice* as proof of the people's anxiety to get knowledge; Francis Place, despite his personal dislike of Doherty,[10] wrote that the paper 'is wholly got up by workmen, and is particularly well-conducted'; and Jeremy Bentham was among the paper's correspondents.[11] In general, S. and B. Webb have concluded that the *Voice* was 'an excellent weekly journal', revealing Doherty to be a man of 'wide information, great natural shrewdness and far-reaching aims'.[12]

Whereas his other publications were set up principally to publicise one particular cause or represent one particular organisation, Doherty envisaged the *Voice* as an equal rival and competitor with the orthodox press of Manchester. The latter had hitherto neglected the interests of the working classes and the new paper was intended to rectify this situation. Two bold mottoes stood at the head of each edition: 'The greatest happiness to the greatest number', and 'When the Condition of the Labourer is depressed, the Prosperity of the Other Classes can rest on no solid foundation'. And in his first editorial, Doherty claimed public support because of 'the merit of the principles we are pledged to advocate'. These were strongly political: the cause of liberty was progressing throughout Europe, and here in England the voice of the 'united people' should be heard in demanding democratic parliamentary reform.[13]

From the outset, therefore, Doherty was speaking of 'union' in political as well as trade terms. And although a further sub-heading was added from 2 July making clear that the paper was published 'by an Association of Working Men', the *Voice* in fact became progressively more dominated by political news and comment as the crisis over the Reform Bill grew more intense and the difficulties of the National Association increased.[14] In the first number, Doherty had to apologise for 'not adverting to that important subject [the National Association] this week', and with a detailed history of the origins of the Ashton spinners' dispute taking up much of the editorial space the following week, it was not until 15 January that he made his first detailed remarks about the body out of which the paper had been born. Even then, most of the article comprised criticism of various piecemeal or erroneous projects for improving the condition of the labouring classes—like the abolition of truck, cultivation of waste lands, distribution of bibles, mass emigration, or birth-control—all of which ignored the *real* cause of distress, which was the £60 millions per year paid in taxes, £12 millions paid in tithes, and £8 millions in poor rates, and would fail to reverse the process by which immense wealth constantly accumulated in the hands of a few capitalists to the ruin of the producers. Working men should ignore the schemes of their 'betters' and rely on their own efforts for improvement. Nevertheless, he concluded by denying rumours that the Association was in any way political, and after listing some of the most important regulations, invited the attention 'of every industrious man' to the National Association, through which alone they could match the strength of their employers.[15]

The wide spectrum covered in the *Voice* thus gives some validity to Turner's assertion that Doherty was by this time on the way to becoming a 'full-time publicist' rather than an active trade unionist.[16] But this assessment ignores the central role which he continued to play in the deliberations of the Manchester committee for most of 1831. Moreover, in every single edition of the paper there were advertisements of the weekly receipts of the Association, reports of district meetings or assemblies to form new branches, correspondence reflecting the state of the organisation and suggesting reforms, and accounts of the deliberations either of the Manchester committee or of the intermittent general delegate meetings, while the dominant topic in the early numbers was the Ashton–Stalybridge spinners' strike.

The National Association was not technically involved in this strike. Preliminary negotiations were carried on by Betts, the local club secretary, and Doherty in his capacity as secretary of the Grand General Union of cotton-spinners, and when the men turned out in December they did not qualify for the 8s per week strike relief from the Association, because of a recent resolution that £3,000 should be amassed as a reserve fund before the funds were opened. But the increasing distress and dissatisfaction of the rank-and-file workmen, who appear to have believed that they were to be supported by both the grand general union and the National Association, and the rapid decline of the former after the failure of the spinners' general strike call of 27 December 1830, forced the Association to take a more positive role. And the press came more and more to regard the central issue as being not so much the rate of wages as the masters' right to control their own property and to resist the encroaching power of the union. 'If the rate of wages had really been the only matter in dispute, the masters, we are inclined to think, would not have considered it so important to maintain the ground they have taken, as we know that they actually do.'[17]

At the beginning of 1831, the Association launched a special subscription for the men on strike, and an appeal for support, signed by John Hynes, the secretary, was published in the *Voice* of 8 January.[18] Throughout the first five weeks of the year, and especially after the failure of local negotiations to end the strike on 20 January, meetings were held in the different towns, including Leicester, Nottingham, Manchester, Derby, Leeds, Belfast, Hanley and Liverpool, to stimulate contributions for the men on strike, at which Jonathan Hodgins, full-time 'agitator' for the Association, and Slater, the Ashton spinners' delegate, were frequent speakers.[19] Meanwhile Doherty gave strong editorial support to the operatives' cause in the *Voice*, as well as defending them and the Association generally from allegations of being implicated in the murder of Thomas Ashton. During this period, a total of £595 9s 11½d was collected under the auspices of the National Association for the relief of the Ashton spinners. Nearly half of this, as might be expected, came from Lancashire, but there was generous support also from Nottinghamshire.[20] Yorkshire, where the Association had as yet made little progress, also responded, while smaller amounts were received from other counties where the Association had established branches, including Staffordshire, Leicestershire, Derbyshire and Cheshire; Glasgow also contributed and a tiny sum was sent from Belfast following a visit by Lancashire delegates early in February.[21]

Not all this money, however, was subscribed by Association members, and even in towns where there were branches the lists of contributions included sums from such sources as friendly societies, orange lodges and public-house collections as well as from trade unions. The existence of the National Association *did* assist in the process of collecting funds to support a trade against a reduction, as Doherty had hoped in October 1829, and the *Voice* certainly provided publicity, but the total amount received was far less than the sum of almost £16,000 raised for the Bradford workmen in 1825,[22] or indeed that of £1,835 raised independently by the Bolton mechanics during their 28-week strike later in 1831.[23] Doherty realised that it was impossible to support 20,000 made idle by the strike, and for that reason he had originally advised that the dispute be settled by compromise; but the Association was in part caught out by its own extravagant propaganda during the autumn of 1830. The Ashton workmen were especially disappointed by the miserable quantity of subscriptions obtained from Manchester, and the reputation of the Association was certainly not enhanced by the embarrassing confrontation between the Manchester and Bolton committees over the question of payments to the men on strike.[24] Arguments that the money expended on establishing the *Voice* was misapplied and that the salaries paid to officials were exorbitant were particularly persuasive among the Ashton operatives as their distress increased. But the most damning indictment of the Association was its ineffectiveness in providing assistance during the turn-out: indeed there is doubt as to how much of the money subscribed was actually paid out in strike relief, for when the general secretary, John Hynes, absconded with £160 in February, it was said to be part of the Ashton funds. And even if this was not true—for advertised subscriptions to the Association fell from £132 17s 11d on 29 January to £9 16s 9d on 5 February, whereas the Ashton donations remained relatively constant[25]—the fact that cash transmitted for the strikers was not ultimately distributed remains unaltered.

At the beginning of February there were reports that the volume of money reaching Ashton was at last allowing more adequate relief to be paid, and Doherty continued publicly to predict success. But, in fact, the strikers were exhausted and dispirited, and when the employers reopened their mills on 3 February resistance rapidly crumbled and all spinners whom the masters were willing to accept had returned to work by 14 February. This comprehensive defeat had calamitous effects on the Association. The frequent assertions in the orthodox press that the strike was caused by 'agitators', who had misled the workmen as to the ability of the union to support them, were apparently vindicated. And the faith of the Ashton spinners in the power of the Association was shown to be as mistaken as that of the Rochdale woollen weavers before them. Their resentment was not reduced by the negligible response to an appeal to Association members for further support, and they finally resigned altogether in May amid great bitterness, when the Manchester committee refused to give them the money seized from Hynes on his recapture and which was supposed to be theirs.[26]

Doherty's hopes from general union were not shattered by this crushing defeat,[27] but he now had to face another catastrophe. On Monday, 7 February, James Hanson, a Rochdale weaver who was also the seller of the *Voice of the People* in that town, paid over £6 of sales money to John Hynes. This sum should immediately have been handed over either to Doherty as the conductor of the publication or to William Keeling, the acting publisher;[28] in the unusual circumstances of both these men being absent, Hynes could have given it to any of the five members of the managing committee of the *Voice*. But when Hanson paid a further visit to the offices in Spring Gardens one week later, he found no reference to his payment in the account books. He challenged Hynes to explain and the secretary accepted that he had received the money, but forgotten to acknowledge it. Thereupon, Doherty and Keeling, who were present at this altercation, ordered Hynes to draw up a statement of accounts by the time of the next committee meeting on the Thursday night of that week, for this was not the first complaint of his inattention to his duties.[29]

On the following Thursday evening (17 February), however, Hynes pre-empted any further discussion by returning to his home in Gun Street, changing his coat, going out and promptly disappearing. He left behind a theatrically-worded suicide note for his wife, declaring that, 'Distrust may be excited—my character may be injured, but by the time you read this I shall be cold and indifferent to mortal censure'. But the information that, before leaving home, he had counted out a sum of money and asked his wife, 'Who would have thought that I should ever have been worth so much as £100,' and, moreover, that a man answering his description had been seen that evening at the 'Albion' coach-office boarding a coach for London, suggested that he had in fact absconded with a large amount of Association funds—later revealed to be about £160.[30] Consequently, posting-bills were forthwith distributed, describing Hynes and offering a £10 reward for his apprehension, and Doherty set out for London, Oates for Liverpool, and other workmen to Hull and elsewhere, in pursuit of the fugitive.[31]

The affair naturally caused a great sensation. The Manchester press, which had repeatedly attacked the leaders of the Association throughout the Ashton strike as being individuals who had a general financial interest in fomenting industrial discord and were disposed to stir up violence, now had the opportunity to continue the campaign after the strike was over with more pointed and direct accusations of corruption. And just as the murder of

Thomas Ashton had apparently justified the charges of intimidation made against the unionists, the defalcation of Hynes gave practical confirmation to previous hints in the press that the officers of the Association were abusing the workmen's trust. The *Stockport Advertiser* of 21 January, for instance, had advised the contributors to visit the homes of the 'agents of mischief' and see the comforts and luxuries which their offices supplied : 'let any competent man inspect the accounts of their stewardship, the receipts and payments, and call for *vouchers for every sum*, and the cause of their comfort will be apparent'. The paper repeated this assertion in an editorial printed before Hynes' flight but published the day afterwards.[32] And a correspondent of the *Guardian* on 12 February, who called himself 'A Payer to the Union', revealed that he had refused to pay his subscription during the past week, because of the leaders' consistent refusal to publish the accounts. 'I find that all the men that have been agitating are differently dressed than they were when they were at work. They are now gentlemen, with fine clothes and boots, and will go only into bar-parlours to smoke segars [sic] and drink wine and spirits.' After stating that he had heard that '[Hodgins] had charged £43 for four weeks' agitating', which was 'better than spinning', the writer went on to refer to Doherty's rise in the world, through his union activities : 'only think that a man should be transformed from a spinning wheel, to be the manager of a printing office, and an editor of a newspaper'. The union members were, he concluded, being 'diddled' in these ways out of their money.[33]

Since Hynes had disappeared towards the end of the week, these papers had little chance to comment in their editions published on the Saturday morning, although the *Guardian* did record the incident as another lesson for industrious workmen as to the uselessness of paying to unions, and the *Times and Gazette* remarked that 'we are not at all surprised that the association has been robbed'.[34] Nevertheless, the leaders of the Association recognised that the robbery, occurring less than a week after the Ashton spinners' final surrender, would radically shake the confidence of the rank and file and might destroy the Association completely if the newspaper attacks were not anticipated and replied to. On 19 February the Manchester committee transmitted to the different districts handbills signed, in Doherty's non-attendance and Hynes' absence, by one of their number, Thomas Atherton, and addressed 'To the Members of the NAPL'. Hynes' conduct was admitted to have caused 'serious injury' to the workmen's cause, for the oversight of the delegates to the Manchester meeting in November 1830, in not requiring adequate securities from Hynes on his appointment as secretary, had been shown up, and the enemies of the Association had been presented with a wonderful opportunity to castigate it. But if the workmen continued to be determined and zealous in the cause, as they had at the time of the defection of the 'Bolton faction', the blow would prove relatively harmless in the long run; for Hynes would be caught and punished, he would be shown to have been the only delinquent and the funds would be saved from further robbery by calling an immediate delegate meeting to make new financial arrangements.[35]

In his first editorial comment on the affair on 26 February, Doherty struck a similar note. The greatest injury was not the money stolen by

Hynes but the ammunition given to their foes. He emphasised 'that the fraud committed by Hynes was not a necessary consequence of the system upon which it [the Association] had been conducted, but arose merely from a want of attention to the regulations already laid down'; for had all districts sent their money to the committee at the 'Moulders' Arms' as instructed, Hynes would not have got his hands on it. He therefore counselled continued perseverance to make the Association a success.

Meanwhile, the Manchester committee quickly appointed a new secretary, John Cheetham, and tried to dampen further criticism by appointing auditors from different towns to check the Association accounts; within two weeks they reported 'that the result has proved much more favourable than they at first expected', and promised to give full details to another general delegate meeting, which was to assemble at Nottingham on 14 March. They had found that the accounts had not been kept 'in a manner calculated to give general satisfaction'; but a proper system would henceforth be established, security would be obtained from every officer, and thus the Association, 'by the misconduct of Hynes will be placed on a firmer and more respectable basis'. Finally, it had been discovered that nearly all the stolen money belonged to the Ashton men, for whose relief renewed subscriptions were now requested.[36]

Thus Doherty and the Manchester committee tried to reduce the effects of the robbery, by spreading the area of responsibility for it beyond the immediate leadership, minimising the financial loss to the Association, and stressing the improvements in the administration which this misfortune would stimulate. But the orthodox press of the district was in no mood to let the Association leaders off the hook, and the papers of the week ending 26 February contained even more column inches of abuse than after the murder of Thomas Ashton. The *Stockport Advertiser* revelled in this confirmation of its claims that the members of the Association were being robbed by their officers; no doubt there were other official plunderers. While Doherty had gone in quest of the secretary, the paper added, 'it is to be hoped that *he* may have a safe return, for *there are sundry accounts* which need *his* elucidation'. Doherty's vigorous denials in the *Voice* of the charges that the delegates had stirred up the Ashton strike for personal gain had blown up in his face; and an investigation should be carried out into the funds of the *Voice* itself, to see if 'Mr Doherty's own services' were in fact given to the public, as he asserted, 'from pure and disinterested motives, free from all influence of a pecuniary or selfish nature'.[37]

The *Guardian* similarly believed that there were other officials guilty of fraud, for Hynes was only himself following the example of the spinners' steward, William Harding, a few weeks earlier.[38] The extent of the workmen's loss was far greater than the actual sum Hynes had appropriated, because of the inadequacy of his accounting. Most serious of all, Doherty's pursuit to London was no more than a 'wild goose chase' and wastage of more money, for in the unlikely event of his discovering the delinquent, no prosecution could be brought, as Hynes had not, in the paper's opinion, broken any law. 'No person or persons had such a property in the money that a bill of indictment could be laid against him for stealing it. So that, if we are not mistaken in our opinion of the law, the fact is, that *anybody*

who can get hold of poor men's hard earned money under such circumstances . . . *may put it openly in their pockets, and laugh in the faces of their
dupes.'* Both editors concluded by advising the workmen to cease giving their
money to support useless trades' unions and strikes, the *Guardian* believing
that they would be better off if they behaved soberly and industriously, and
put their surplus money into savings banks instead.[39]

On the same day the *Manchester Times and Gazette* also published a
lengthy editorial, in which Prentice recollected that he had predicted the
previous November that the *Voice* would lose at least £15 a week; now he
challenged Doherty to prove by publication of the accounts that the paper
was losing less than £30 a week. He angrily rejected the claims of the Manchester committee that his paper had lost half its circulation to the *Voice*
—in fact the figure was nearer one-tenth, or 350 copies—and that he had
an interest in promoting the downfall of the Association, for he had in
reality repeatedly omitted letters critical of its management. But he now
printed a long and anonymous letter from 'A Working Man' highly critical
of the Association's management. The writer claimed that few trades in
Manchester would join the general union because of their dislike of the
provision that all the money should be sent to one town, instead of each
town keeping its own funds—for this provided excessive temptation for the
central officers to run off, especially since the resolution that nothing
should be paid out until £3,000 was amassed; there were also suspicions of
the leading conductors, who could appoint Hynes to a post of confidence
in charge of large amounts of cash, notwithstanding that he was a stranger
newly arrived in Manchester, an Irishman whose only talent was to 'tip
them the blarney', and without even the ownership of his own cottage. The
letter continued by doubting if the committee really desired to capture
Hynes, and concluded by pointing to the present distress of the Rochdale
flannel-weavers and Ashton spinners as proof of the conductors' betrayal of
the workmen's trust.[40]

Doherty considered the refutation of these attacks to be of first importance, for he took up nearly a whole page of the next issue of the *Voice* to
insert a reply, written in the first person and signed, since '*all* those who
have attacked the Association have attacked me personally, and seem
anxious to separate me from the cause of the workmen'. At the head of the
article, he copied extracts from the above three editorials and proceeded
to answer each in turn. To the editor of the *Stockport Advertiser* he promised
legal action, if he could raise the means, for the 'scandalous' imputations
that he himself was guilty of corruption; Doherty emphasised that he desired
no restriction on the free expression of opinion, but was solely guided by
considerations of 'TRUTH'. In reply to the editor of the *Guardian*, he made
a more detailed defence of trades' unions, which he considered to be the
workmen's only protection in face of the hostility of Parliament, press and
masters. He deplored that paper's talk of 'outrageous and illegal conduct' by
turn-outs, at the very time when several of them were in prison awaiting
trial, and while nothing was said of the victimisation of workmen by the
Ashton 'fifty-two'. The real motive was to preserve as large a share as
possible of wealth for the 'greedy capitalists', by undermining the labourers'
faith in unions and their leaders, and persuading them instead to support

savings banks, 'that last scheme of the Jews and jobbers to get possession of the little savings of the industrious millions'. Finally, Doherty pronounced the motives of the editor of the *Times and Gazette* to be equally suspect— the fear of competition from the *Voice*. Why else, Doherty asked, would a professing radical reformer so consistently decry the establishment of a working-man's paper, instead of rejoicing at its appearance, as both Bowring and Place had done, or at least offering constructive advice as to ways of improving it? As for publishing the accounts, Doherty pointed out that losses must inevitably occur in the early stages of any such venture.[41]

In reply, the *Times and Gazette* briefly noted that Doherty, in his 'long tirade', had taken special care to avoid all the questions that paper had posed, while the *Stockport Advertiser* contemptuously dismissed Doherty's threat of a libel prosecution; the editor rather ingenuously denied that he had meant Doherty by his hints of 'other official personages' involved in corruption, though 'Mr Doherty best knows if the character suited him'. As the 'writer of libels on all the master cotton spinners of this district and dealer out of every foul-mouthed epithet which the English language furnishes, . . . we treat his threats, CUR-LIKE as they are, with due disdain'. The same paper printed a particularly vicious letter, signed 'Amicus Humani Generi', which suggested that Hynes, as an Irishman, might have gone off on a pilgrimage to pray his grandmother's soul out of purgatory, and advised Doherty, his countryman, to ask a father-confessor for information. The correspondent concluded that the spinners had been deservedly punished for foolishness in placing their money at the disposal of 'a greedy, needy, rapacious gang of Irish adventurers, who prefer idleness to honest labour'.[42] But by this time new developments had taken place in the affair to replace the interest in the newspaper controversy.

Doherty's excursion to London had not been as futile as the Manchester papers had imagined. He had learnt that Hynes had travelled there under the name of Brown, representing himself to be a Manchester newspaper pro- prietor, and had moved on from there to Ireland where he was taking leave of his friends and relatives before embarking to America. On Doherty's return, the Manchester committee despatched Slater, one of the Ashton operatives, to Ireland forthwith. From Dublin, Slater was able to trace the miscreant across to Galway on the west coast, where he succeeded in having him lodged in the town gaol.[43] From there, on 9 March, Hynes sent a remarkable letter to the Manchester committee, entreating them not to waste more funds subscribed by poor workmen or divert the money from its original purpose by instituting a 'vindictive' prosecution against him, for he had taken the advice of a most eminent counsel and discovered that it would be 'morally impossible' to obtain a conviction, 'both for want of sufficient evidence, and the state of the law, upon the question'.[44] However, the Manchester committee confuted both the *Guardian*'s and Hynes' assess- ment of the legal niceties of the case, by preparing a prosecution against the defaulter, not for the money stolen from the Association, but for the £6 paid to Hynes by James Hanson on account of the *Voice of the People*, which, unlike the general union, had legally registered proprietors.[45] They obtained a warrant from the magistrates at the New Bailey, authorising the apprehension and detention of Hynes, and Worthington, the beadle, was sent to Galway at the Association's expense to serve the warrant. And on 17 March, exactly one month after his departure, Hynes was escorted back to Manchester and placed in confinement in the New Bailey prison. That same day he was brought up on an embezzlement charge before the magistrates, Ralph Wright and J. F. Foster. The prosecutors were represented by John Owen and Edward Foulkes, who called Hanson, Doherty, Keeling, Gulliver and Turner in turn to explain the circumstances of the case. The defending counsel, Stansfield, questioned whether Hynes, as the hired employee of the general union, had any responsibility to receive money for the *Voice* proprietors. But the magistrates determined that this point had been fully made out, for it had been a regular practice, and committed Hynes for trial at the subsequent Quarter Sessions.[46]

The following weeks saw a considerable amount of continued legal activity. The solicitors engaged by the Association were busy preparing a further indictment against Hynes, which charged him with stealing on 16 February a sum of £20 from his employers, 'Thomas Atherton and others' (the Manchester committee), £5 10s and three promissory notes to the value of £25 from Ellis Pigot (proprietor of the *Voice*), and the same £5 10s and promissory notes from Thomas Oates (reporter for the *Voice*).[47] They also decided to bring two indictments against Hynes for embezzling the £6 paid to him by Hanson, one in the names of 'Thomas Atherton and others', and the second in the names of Ellis Pigot and James Turner. At the Salford Easter Quarter Sessions on 17 April, the Grand Jury found true bills against Hynes on all three indictments, to which he had pleaded not guilty. At the same time, his attorney made application for part of the £51 found in his possession when taken into custody to be used to defray the defence expenses; and this request, which Doherty described as akin to returning 'the robber's plunder . . . to aid his escape from justice', was successful to the amount of £5.[48]

The case was eventually heard on 22 April. Evidence was taken only on the first indictment, charging the prisoner with stealing £6 from the Manchester committee. After hearing testimony from Doherty, Gulliver, Hanson and Atherton, the jury deliberated only two or three minutes before returning a verdict of guilty. The prosecutors then agreed to concede acquittals in the other two indictments, and the chairman sentenced Hynes to twelve months' imprisonment with hard labour in Lancaster Castle. And the proceedings closed with the court ordering that the money found upon Hynes should be restored to its rightful owners.[49]

In a long editorial upon the subject on 30 April, Doherty rejoiced that the prognostications in the local liberal press, that there was no way in which the Association could bring Hynes to justice, had been proved fallacious—especially as he had been convicted 'not for having taken away the money of the proprietors of the newspaper, entered at the stamp office, not by any legal technicality of this sort, but FOR HAVING STOLEN THE PROPERTY OF THE ASSOCIATION'. And the workmen's funds would be safe in future, so long as they ensured that all whom they entrusted with money were hired and paid for their services, and were not members or shareholders. All officers must therefore be obliged to renounce all share and interest in the funds which they administered; if any frauds were

H

then committed, the state would bear the expense of prosecution. But Doherty could not help commenting also upon the marked leniency of the punishment, compared with his own sentence of double that term for 'merely being present at a slight disturbance' during the 1818 strike of Manchester spinners. Apart from the fact that his own judge had been Parson Hay, who was still notorious for his part in the Peterloo massacre, 'the only way in which the gross disproportion can be accounted for is, that the one was an offence against the poor, and consequently unimportant; the other an offence against the rich, and therefore deserving of double punishment'.[50]

No editorial comment upon the trial appeared in the local tory or liberal papers. Only the radical *Manchester and Salford Advertiser* remarked upon it, in an article lampooning the *Guardian* for asserting that Hynes had broken no law and ridiculing that paper's apparent sympathy for the robber rather than the robbed.[51] But this small victory in the verbal debate was poor compensation for the general injury inflicted upon the Association by the Hynes affair, not only in the actual financial loss, but also psychologically in the loss of confidence among the rank and file and more practically in the secession of the Ashton spinners on being refused the money recovered from the villain, and in the generally chaotic state of the accounts for many weeks after the initial desertion. Moreover, the robbery stimulated increased demands for independent control by each district of its own funds, and the partial blocking of this proposal by Doherty at the general delegate meeting at Nottingham in March provoked the complete secession of the Bolton branch from the Association amid further recriminations.[52]

The most significant events for the Association in the early part of 1831 were, therefore, the successful establishment of the *Voice of the People*, the defeat of the Ashton spinners' strike, and the defalcation of John Hynes. There was, however, a continued effort to maintain the impetus towards expansion started during the autumn of 1830. With Doherty tied largely to Manchester by his editing duties, the principal agent of these activities was Jonathan Hodgins, who had been appointed as full-time propagandist for the Association by the November delegate conference at a salary of £4 10s per week plus coach fares. His initial function was to speak at meetings in support of the establishment of the new paper.[53] But from the turn of the year his main efforts were concentrated on extending the Association in the Midlands, where Doherty had made the preliminary advances in August 1830.[54] At the end of December and in January he toured Leicestershire, Derbyshire and Nottinghamshire, addressing meetings in numerous towns and villages, either of individual trades or of trades generally, and enjoyed some success, mainly among the textile workers—framework knitters, lacemakers, etc.—and especially in Nottingham, where twenty-four trades were reported to have enrolled in the district association. Nottingham, indeed, became at this period the most thriving of all the districts, under the leadership of Thomas Matthews, a smith, who was secretary, and H. N. Bullock, secretary of the plain silk trade workers and member of the district committee, who was later to become general secretary of the Association. Nottingham, as we have seen, was most generous in its support of the Ashton strikers and was chosen as the venue for the next general delegate meeting in March 1831.[55]

Hodgins had far less success, however, in Birmingham, which he visited early in February. There the committee appointed in the previous September[56] was still functioning, but had completely failed to interest the Birmingham trades in the general union project. Hodgins and other speakers now urged the audience to imitate the example of towns like Nottingham, Derby and Leicester in supporting the Association, and some progress was made in that William Pare, the co-operative lecturer, who had been sceptical of the scheme in the previous summer, seconded the motion that all the trades should join the Association. At the end of the proceedings, several trades promised to convene meetings immediately and the committee was enlarged,[57] but eventually this second attempt to organise the town proved as unsuccessful as the first. Birmingham never sent any subscriptions to Manchester either for the Association or for the special appeals launched to support individual groups on strike later in 1831. Unlike Manchester, the normal unit of production in the town was the small workshop, the gulf between capital and labour was not therefore great and there was a good deal of fluidity between the social classes. Hence the workmen there were not enthusiastic for an organisation whose militant working-class aims were constantly being stressed by Doherty in the *Voice*, whereas they were willing at that time to support Attwood's Political Union under middle-class control, and later produced their own peculiarly moderate brand of Chartism.[58] Nevertheless, the germ of the idea of inter-union co-operation lived on in the city, later to be exploited by the Builders' Union in 1832.[59] Hodgins was apparently no more successful at Wolverhampton, the last town he visited on his Midlands tour, where the local paper was able to rejoice that 'our fellow townsmen will not give money to artful demagogues, who live by going from place to place urging discontent and law-breaking'.[60]

This series of disappointing responses, coinciding with the shattering blow of Hynes' embezzlement, provoked widespread complaints that Hodgins was not providing value for his large salary and that he was over-charging on his expenses.[61] Discontent eventually became so great that he had to be dismissed. This step, together with the death of Thomas Foster early in February,[62] deprived Doherty of much-needed assistance and was partially responsible, so he later claimed, for the limited expansion of the Association in the following period.[63]

Nevertheless, some success was achieved in the early months of 1831, not only by Hodgins' missionary work, but also by local efforts, often roused, as we have seen, by the Ashton spinners' delegates. Early in the new year, there was a revival of activity at Rochdale, where a general meeting of the flannel-weavers passed a resolution regretting that, after having subscribed so enthusiastically to the Association funds there should now be such 'indifference' among them, and determining henceforth to renew their support. This revival was reflected in the reappearance of the flannel-weavers among the trades subscribing to the Association, though on nothing like the former scale, and also in small contributions to the Ashton strikers. But the continuation of the trade depression rapidly reduced them to a state of extreme distress, so that by the summer of 1831 they were begging the Association for support (again in vain) and in no position to contribute towards it.[64]

The following weeks saw an attempt to perfect the organisation of the Association in the north-west, by including those towns in Lancashire slightly farther afield from Manchester than those originally enrolled, and by rousing Cheshire. On 22 January the *Voice* reported that Preston was coming forward and seemed to be determined to be 'though last, not least' among the Lancashire districts.[65] Considerable effort was put into campaigns in Liverpool, where meetings on 11 February and 30 March were addressed by various speakers, including Hynes (just before he absconded), Oates and Doherty from Manchester, as well as delegates from other towns; a committee was appointed and Doherty hoped that an effective branch would soon be formed there.[66] Meetings were also held during this period at Hyde and Accrington, in order to bring these towns into the Association.[67]

The results of this activity, however, were disappointing. Preston did at last become a fairly active district, but interest lapsed in Liverpool and a fresh start had to be made there in July.[68] The meeting at Hyde proved a failure,[69] on account of the notoriously low support given to trade-unionism there, the recent murder of Thomas Ashton, and the depressing exhibition of defeat in nearby Ashton and Stalybridge. Nor was the Accrington branch at first a really integral part of the parent organisation, its main activity from mid-summer being connected with the calico-printers' long strike and schemes of co-operative production.[70]

Farther afield, some initial success was achieved in Belfast, through the efforts of the Ashton spinners. After their delegates had addressed a general meeting of the trades there on 2 February, not only was a small subscription sent for the turn-outs, but a district branch of the Association was started, including at first the cotton-spinners, warpers, cabinet-makers, carpenters, and tobacco-makers, with hopes of extending the organisation to include all towns within thirty miles of Belfast.[71] At the end of May, Doherty congratulated *Rushlight*, an Irish radical paper, for publicising the National Association and recommending Irish workmen to join it, and added, 'we long since held out the hand of fellowship to them, and we have now, in fact, a district in Belfast'.[72] Nevertheless, it is unlikely that this Belfast district had any closer connection with the Association headquarters at Manchester than did the Belfast spinners with Doherty's Grand General Union. Certainly, in view of the resolution passed at Nottingham that each district should hold its own funds, it never sent any money to the central coffers.

One important new adherent was, however, gained by the Association in this phase. In November 1830, as we have seen, Foster and Hodgins succeeded in persuading the Staffordshire potters to establish the China and Earthenware Turners' Union and in infusing them with interest in the plan of general union, but the workmen wisely desired time to get their union on its feet before formally joining the Association. Eventually, however, at the end of February, they unanimously decided to do so, on account of the weakness of isolated local societies.[73] This union was still attempting to get new members for the Association in October 1831,[74] revealing that its enthusiasm for the project was of rather longer duration than that of many other districts enrolled at this time.

Doherty's role during this period was noticeably less public than over the previous months. Editing the *Voice*, unlike the *Journal*, was a full-time occupation for which he was paid a salary of £3 a week. Consequently, he spoke at fewer meetings than before and was only out of Manchester for any length of time on one occasion—while in pursuit of Hynes to London. Nevertheless, he remained firmly in control of such central policy as there was, when affairs were not being dominated by the current emergency, and the reports of the Manchester committee meetings, when they began to be published later in the year, revealed that Doherty was still by far the leading personality in the Association. In the early numbers of the *Voice*, he began the task of building up a theoretical framework behind the Association's activities. Four papers contained extracts from an article sent in by a 'talented friend' discussing 'the present state of feeling between the Rich and the Poor'. These maintained that the gulf between the two classes had never been wider, for the aristocracy of title had been replaced by an aristocracy of wealth, which 'has established a slavery more hideous in its effects, and has ground down its victims to the extreme verge of poverty'. The legislature was criticised for framing its policy solely in the interests of the rich, and the increasing intelligence of the masses of workmen was pointed to as a factor which would eventually end this unjust situation.[75] Doherty himself carried on an increasingly bitter disputation with W.R. G.[reg], a prominent local master spinner, on the subject of machinery, which the latter claimed had brought unparalleled and general prosperity.[76] Doherty agreed that the introduction of labour-saving machinery *should* always benefit the workmen, for labour was always irksome and disagreeable—'the sentence on man's first transgression'—and only engaged in to satisfy wants. Its use had not brought general benefit, however, because the produce had not been applied for the public good, but had been appropriated by a few machine-owners: hence the condition of the labouring classes was in fact notoriously wretched everywhere. It was 'sheer folly' and counterproductive for workmen to oppose new machines, which could bring extra comforts into the cottages of the poor; instead, they should unite and ensure that they obtained for themselves 'a full share of the produce of every machine'. When Greg accused Doherty of a desire to influence artisans towards law-breaking, Doherty closed the correspondence by advising his adversary to adhere to the law himself by ceasing to cut short his workers' statutory dinner-hour, and to send his future letters to his 'kindred spirits' at the *Guardian*.[77] Finally, Doherty consistently urged his readers to abjure violence. When, for instance, several windows were broken at Rossendale and reports circulated blaming Association members, Doherty disputed the story, but added that, 'should any charge against a member be proved, we will pay the expenses from the district fund, and give up the offenders to justice'.[78]

These disquisitions had come to a sudden halt after Hynes' flight on 17 February, and were transformed, as we have seen, into vigorous defence of the integrity of the Association and its leaders. On a more practical level, the Manchester committee responded to the crisis by convening a general conference of delegates—the fourth of its kind within nine months—at Nottingham on 14 March. This assembly took the significant decision to instruct the branches in future to look after their own funds, thus fundamentally altering the original organisational basis of the Association.[79]

Thereafter the central accounts are no longer a reliable guide to the actual state of the Association and its paying membership. It would be useful, therefore, to examine the condition of the general union at the time of this conference, and see if the high hopes of progress at the end of 1830 were being fulfilled.

The advertised subscription lists for January show how far feelings of solidarity with the Ashton workmen were reflected in increased financial support for the Association. Receipts rose from £35 15s 7d for the week ending on 8 January to £167 15s 10½d on 15 January, £91 0s 0½d on 22 January, and £132 17s 4d on 29 January. Thereafter, however, there was a dramatic fall, to £9 16s 9d on 5 February and £25 1s 9d on 12 February, when Hynes admitted to some 'omissions'. No list was published on 19 February owing to the secretary's disappearance, but the following week a sum of £55 0s 3d was advertised as having been subscribed before that unfortunate episode 'and not previously acknowledged', as well as a mere £1 12s 6d sent in since. Only a partial recovery was visible in the two weeks before the Nottingham meeting, £18 13s 4d being donated on 5 March and £20 19s 8d on 12 March. Thus the total receipts of the National Association for this ten-week period (including a further £1 acknowledged from Wigan on 30 April), amounted to £559 13s 1d, a not insubstantial sum considering that this was a time of continued trade depression and that the workmen also contributed during this period over £620 to two groups of strikers and £35 4s 1d to the special fund for the *Voice of the People*.[80]

Estimates of the Association's total paying membership, based on these figures, must be even more tentative than for 1830. The sharp recovery in January may possibly have raised it to around 25,000 (the average weekly receipts for that month being £106 17s 2½d). The Ashton failure and the Hynes affair must have caused a substantial decline thereafter, but it is impossible to quantify the deterioration from the data available, since the totals were so distorted by Hynes' 'omissions' before his departure, and by the districts' reluctance afterwards to send money to Manchester because of the fear of theft and because they were anticipating the changed financial arrangements to be made at Nottingham. The geographical range of the Association had not extended beyond the counties involved by the close of 1830.[81] Lancashire was still by far the heaviest contributor,[82] but the proportion of subscriptions from Nottinghamshire, Leicestershire, and Derbyshire was rising. Contributions from Cheshire had virtually dried up and only a small sum had been sent from Yorkshire, while the Staffordshire potters had merely paid their £1 entrance fee. Textile workers continued to predominate, but the contributions of the mule spinners had fallen substantially as a result of the Ashton failure and decline of their general union. Larger contributions were made by the calico printers of Lancashire, cotton and silk dyers, the different branches of the Midlands silk operatives, and various groups of hand-loom weavers, including flannel, cotton and worsted smallware, woollen, nankeen and linen. Many individual societies of workmen in trades largely ancillary to textiles, as well as in the building industry and in the miscellaneous handicrafts listed at the end of the previous chapter, continued to subscribe, but their proportion of the whole was still insignificant.

Thus by the time of the Nottingham delegate conference, the Association had received a total of £2,565 0s 10d in subscriptions.[83] It had a number of strong branches in Lancashire and was expanding in the Midlands, but those were virtually the limits of its extension. Moreover, the shattering blows of the Ashton spinners' defeat and Hynes' disappearance had drastically reduced the confidence of the districts in the central leadership and abated the flow of money towards Manchester to a trickle. The view of the Association as an organisation in decline was reflected in the decrease of official interest in its activities from the high point at the end of 1830, when the government was considering the introduction of strong anti-union legislation to check it and was scheming to arrest Doherty.[84] After the metropolitan police officers, sent to Lancashire to hunt for the murderer of Thomas Ashton, had left the area, mention of the Association in the Home Office correspondence virtually ceased and the authorities turned their attention to the growing number of radical *political* societies.

It was in an effort to arrest this decline in the Association's fortunes that the general delegate meeting was convened on 14 March 1831. This conference was attended by twenty-four delegates from the various districts. The main topic of discussion was a resolution that each district should hold and manage its own money to prevent misappropriation, but that a contingent fund of £3,000 be lodged, with proper security, in Manchester for the disposal of the committee. This motion was moved by Francis Marshall on the instructions of the Bolton branch, whose members had agreed to rejoin the Association on condition that this financial reorganisation was made.[85] The proposal met with some sympathy—indeed Marshall later claimed that 'nearly the whole of the districts' had sent similar resolutions—but it was vigorously opposed by Doherty, who stated that making each district independent would overthrow the whole basis of the Association and render it no better regulated than 'any common club'. A full day's debate ensued and ultimately a new regulation was decided upon, which was a compromise between the previous arrangement of central control and the Bolton proposition. In future, small sums were no longer to be sent to Manchester, but each district would bank its own money in sums of £25, transmitting half-cheques to Manchester and retaining the other halves themselves. Thus separate banking was introduced, but the system of controls by which neither the Manchester committee nor the districts could expend money without the consent of the other was maintained. In addition, it was agreed that officers of the society should henceforth be elected by secret ballot; that a voluntary subscription be launched throughout the districts to relieve those men who were suffering because of turn-outs to protect wages—a reference to current disputes among the Nottingham and Derby silk-workers and the Lancashire calico-printers,[86] and also to those spinners blacklisted since the Ashton strike;[87] and, in view of the mounting excitement over the first Reform Bill, it was agreed that the Association should exclude all purely political subjects from its discussions. Finally, the delegates ordered that all arrears from the various districts should be paid up to that date, so that they might all start under the new system on an equal footing, and that the Association might be enabled to fulfil its engagements. The latter was no unnecessary addition to the wording; for such was the state of the finances that £30 had to be advanced from the Nottingham branch funds to pay for the delegates' expenses in returning to their respective homes.[88]

The results of the Nottingham conference were far less propitious than had been hoped. Far from re-establishing the right conditions for the Association to make progress after its recent disappointments, an increased number of difficulties proliferated over the succeeding months. The most serious of these was the state of the accounts. Certain safeguards *were* introduced, as recommended by the auditing committee in February and by Doherty in his editorial on 30 April.[89] Thus, when the *Voice* advertised on 5 March for a young man to fill the situation of canvasser, 'the most unexceptionable references, and security to the amount of £50' were demanded. And later, in August 1831, a public declaration was signed by Doherty, Wallis and Oates, respectively the editor, publisher and reporter of the *Voice*, by Bullock, then the general secretary of the Association,[90] and by all the journeymen who worked in the office, forfeiting any previous interest in the funds or property of the newspaper establishment or the Association, and acknowledging their liability at law for those funds or property. Doherty argued that this would remove all fear of embezzlement and prevent a plea of partnership being set up in future, as Hynes had attempted at his trial, and he recommended the members of every branch to insist on their officers signing a similar document.[91]

But the new financial arrangements introduced at Nottingham did not solve the problems of the Association accounts. Under the new system, each district managed its own funds and each branch secretary was supposed to make a monthly return of the receipts to the general secretary for publication in the *Voice*; and the general secretary was to produce a similar statement at monthly intervals for the Association generally. But this never worked out in practice and there were repeated complaints that these local and general returns were not being published, and that members were therefore falling into arrears with their subscriptions.[92] Connected with these complaints were continued suspicions that the real reason why these returns were not published was to mask extravagance by the leaders. Such suspicions, for example, were at the root of an acrimonious dispute between Doherty and the Oldham branch, which sent delegates demanding to inspect the books for themselves. The Manchester committee eventually agreed to permit such inspection by a single delegate from each trade.[93] But no further subscriptions were ever acknowledged from Oldham. Bolton, moreover, continued to refuse to transmit funds to Manchester.[94]

According to the revised financial arrangements, it depended upon the diligence of each district secretary whether any subscriptions were advertised. Consequently, over the following six months up to the last published list of donations on 10 September, the volume of the weekly receipts varied enormously, from nothing at all on several occasions to a maximum of £141 5s 2d on 21 May. As Doherty had feared, increasing the independence of the branches reduced the unity of the Association, which progressively came to speak with more than one voice and ultimately split up into its separate units. From the time of the Nottingham conference to 10 September, total subscriptions amounting to £466 5s 2¼d were advertised, which sum was rather less than had been subscribed in the previous ten weeks, and moreover included the receipts of a special appeal in the late summer in support of the

*Voice*.[95] It is impossible to know how much more was contributed in the different districts and never acknowledged. What is certain is that the donations which were published, inadequate as they were, no longer came to Manchester, with the result that the Manchester committee suffered from a chronic shortage of funds and was caught up in a series of embarrassing incidents in consequence.

During the week after the conference, for example, a delegate from the Nottingham pantaloon trade workers, who were on strike for a wage increase, came to Manchester to seek subscriptions for his fellows and to demand the return of the £30 advanced by the Nottingham district to subsidise the Association delegates. He was unable to obtain it, however, and later had to borrow £1 from the Bolton committee to relieve his own distress. When a letter of protest was sent from Nottingham in the following week, Doherty was forced to admit the validity of their claim at the Manchester committee meeting on 26 April, but asserted that 'the money must first come in' before it could be paid out, and he could not judge when this would be. He added, however, that it was never intended that the expenses of meetings should be defrayed from the ordinary subscriptions, but from extra contributions of 1d per quarter from each member, and it was the latter payments which the districts had not made.[96]

The Association's financial weakness, and lack of enthusiasm among its members, were also illustrated when the committee decided in April to expend £29 on a steel engraving for printing Association membership cards, for each of which a charge of 3d would have to be levied. But the response from the workmen was negligible, and in August the districts had to be urged to forward money as soon as possible to cover the expense.[97]

At the next delegate meeting, in Manchester, in June, there was a prolonged financial investigation, which passed the accounts both of the Association and of the *Voice*,[98] but by August renewed complaints induced the Manchester committee to appoint as auditors the secretaries of those trades which had expressed most dissatisfaction. At the same time, they were under increasing pressure of enquiries as to when the funds would finally be opened. Doherty's reply was, 'in a week, if you all contribute', but he pointed out that since March the districts had kept all the money contributed and only occasionally sent in returns. How, then, was it possible to open the funds, when the Manchester committee had no idea what these actually amounted to?[99]

Just as the attempt of the Nottingham delegate meeting to improve the state of the Association's accounts was counter-productive, so it failed to mend the split between the Bolton branch and the rest of the general union, and in certain respects exacerbated it. Just prior to the conference, the Bolton trades agreed to rejoin the Association if the finances of each district were made entirely independent of Manchester; but in the event of this condition not being accepted, they would form a completely separate organisation.[100] As we have seen, the Nottingham conference only partially accepted the Bolton proposition, although in practice the revised arrangements did have the effect which the Bolton men had desired and Doherty had feared, of reducing the central authority of Manchester. But the Bolton leaders chose to regard the Nottingham decision as further evidence of Doherty's all-embracing influence over the policy of the Association, and relations there-

H*

fore deteriorated even further over the next few months. Not only did Bolton refuse to co-operate in the new financial arrangements, but there was a resumption of the previous damaging controversy in regard to the *Voice* and the allegedly improper diversion of Association funds to its establishment, which was said to have been contrived by Doherty, Hynes and Hodgins, and was causing the Association to run increasingly into debt. There was also criticism of the waste of money on Hodgins' missionary tours. Moreover, Marshall pointed out that Hynes had originally been Doherty's protégé, while Frazer asserted that ever since he had known Doherty 'that person was always breeding factions', and that his articles in the *Voice* created dissensions between masters and men. The Bolton trades therefore decided on 29 March to form a separate association. Doherty defended himself against these allegations, securing support from leading trade unionists not only in Manchester but also in other towns, pointing out how all the proceedings had been sanctioned by Association delegate meetings, as well as by trades' meetings in many towns; but this controversy was very wounding.[101]

Thus the reforms of the Nottingham conference only succeeded in institutionalising the secession of the Bolton district. Relations between the 'Bolton Trades' Union' and the Manchester committee remained very strained. The Bolton committee objected, for example, to strike delegates (e.g. from Nottingham) and trade-union 'tramps' being sent to them for relief, and decided to refuse any further such assistance 'until the National Association is conducted upon those principles which originally formed the basis of the society'. Doherty condemned this action as revealing the Bolton secession in its truly selfish colours, and the Manchester committee passed a resolution emphasising that the Association *was* being conducted on its original principles and criticising the 'indifference' of the Bolton trades to the plight of other workers on strike or unemployed.[102]

Nevertheless, the formation of a separate association at Bolton showed that they had no objection to inter-union co-operation in principle, but were chiefly opposed to domination from Manchester at the centre and especially to the personal authority of Doherty. When it became apparent that the Nottingham changes *had* reduced the financial authority of Manchester, against Doherty's policy, there was no real reason to continue the division, for the *Voice* was by now an established fact. A more conciliatory spirit was apparent in June after talk of wage reductions being made by several Bolton master-spinners, and two delegates were sent to the Manchester committee with a proposal to end the long-standing dispute.[103] Thus when the next general delegate meeting was held in Manchester, towards the end of June, the Bolton Union sent a representative and the chairman was able to announce the surprising, but welcome, news 'that Bolton has again become an integral branch of the National Association'. This was made official on 12 July, when the Bolton committee passed a resolution, which was inserted in the *Voice* by Marshall, 'that all the trades commence paying on 9 August next; and it is expected that the trades of Bolton will be as forward in paying their just quantum as any district in the United Kingdom'. But the Bolton branch was by this time considerably reduced in strength, there is no record of any resumption of payments, and on 23 August Frazer admitted that they were in need of a meeting to effect a revival.[104]

By that time the financial weakness of the whole Association had become even more evident. The Nottingham conference's decision that each district should hold its own money reduced the possibility of the Association *ever* being in a position to open the funds for their fundamental purpose of relieving the members of constituent societies on strike against wages reductions. This necessitated continuance of the system, adopted during the Ashton dispute, of separate and voluntary appeals being launched on such occasions. Rather than directly financing strikes, the Association merely assisted the progress of the different delegates from the individual unions through the network of its contacts in the various districts, and provided publicity and encouragement in the *Voice*; thus, it was a supplement to the traditional system of inter-union assistance during turn-outs, rather than a replacement as Doherty had hoped. In this way, the Association became involved in a growing number of disputes during 1831, but was never capable of saving the workmen from their usual defeat.

One of the most significant and long-lasting of these disputes affected the Lancashire calico-printers. Different districts of calico-printers had been among the first to pay their entrance fees to the Association in 1830, and Ellis Pigot, the secretary of the Block Printers' Union, formed in July 1830 and covering most of the county, was one of the registered proprietors of the *Voice of the People*, and proprietor of the inn where the Manchester delegate conference met in June. Towards the end of 1830 and early in 1831 a serious dispute boiled up at the works of Messrs Butterworth & Brookes, at Sunnyside, near Haslingden, in Rossendale, in regard to the employment of apprentices, low wages, and truck payments.[105] Eventually, at the beginning of February the firm discharged their journeymen block-printers, making a total of six hundred men idle. The forces of capital and labour now lined up for another major confrontation. On 22 February a general meeting of the Associated Master Calico Printers was held in Manchester and a resolution adopted to assist Messrs Butterworth & Brookes in every way possible, even to the extent of stopping their own works and defraying the whole expenses of the dispute. Tension mounted in the area and a military force was lodged at the works to guard them.

On the other side, an appeal was launched for the workmen 'turned out to resist oppression', and lists of subscriptions were advertised intermittently in the *Voice* from 5 March onwards. Total donations of £289 18s 3¼d were published before the last mention of the Sunnyside strike as a separate dispute on 30 July.[106] The Block Printers' Union and the other trades involved appear to have been responsible for organising the appeal, and almost all the contributions originated from friendly societies, trade clubs and other 'friends' in the North Lancashire area. But Doherty gave the appeal the authoritative backing of the Association, by comparing the tyrannical behaviour of the master printers with that of the 'fifty-two' Ashton master spinners and recommending that the different trades should show the same unity and resolution as the masters by generously supporting the strikers. Certainly, the masters considered that the Association had a significant psychological effect, even if its influence was limited in terms of practical subscriptions. In early March the dispute spread when Messrs Turner & Co., of Mill Hill, near Blackburn, in proposing a 20% reduction in the wages of their block-printers, ordered them to sign a document relinquishing membership of the National Association. The men, having resisted and been dismissed, inserted a statement in the *Voice*, throwing themselves 'on the protection of the members of the Association throughout the United Kingdom', and Doherty appended a bitter attack on masters, who, while being united themselves against all their workmen, insisted on their hands forsaking their unions, and, while using the law to defend their own property, were content to despoil that of the workmen. Another appeal was launched for these men, but only small contributions came in, mostly from neighbouring areas, and although the *Voice* reported in April that the strike was still continuing and the men relying upon their fellow-workers for support, nothing further was heard of this particular dispute.[107]

Meanwhile, the unrest accompanying the Sunnyside strike was continuing, resulting in violence, military intervention, and sentences of imprisonment on several of the men.[108] On 10 May a delegate attended the Manchester committee meeting, seeking assistance, but all that could be done was to recommend the strikers to the various trades.[109] The whole affair received a massive escalation, however, on 14 June, when twenty members of the Association of Master Calico Printers met together again and resolved to commence paying from 1 July according to a graduated scale of prices, which they asserted would enable them to compete in the market with the prices of those goods printed in Ireland, Scotland and the South of England. The men claimed that the new prices would entail a reduction of 25 to 50 per cent on their already low wages, and on the date of the expiry of their masters' notice all the block and machine printers of those twenty firms turned out. Efforts at a negotiated settlement in Manchester on 19 July ended in failure and more violence followed, with attacks on men who refused to join the strike. There was also continued controversy regarding printers' wages, with even greater divergencies between the figures produced by masters and men.[110]

With 3,000 workmen out on strike against a large reduction, the National Association was bound to take a more active interest than when only one firm was involved. It attempted to assist the calico-printers in several different ways. Firstly, the efforts which were already being made to raise subscriptions for the Sunnyside men were redoubled. Shortly after the masters' notice was given, the fifth general delegate conference met in Manchester, on Monday, 21 June, lasting most of that week, during which a resolution was passed expressing regret at the 'great and scandalous' reduction proposed to the journeymen block-printers and the persistence generally of the ruinous reducing system, and calling on every member of the Association, and operatives generally, not only to resist this, but every other inroad on the workman's property. After the failure of the negotiations on 19 July, the *Voice* announced that deputies from the Lancashire calico-printers would be waiting upon the different trades of Manchester, and the closer involvement of the Association in this dispute, now it was more widespread, can also be seen from the fact that one of the places where subscriptions could be sent was the *Voice* office itself. But the total results of these activities were disappointing, only £90 7s 4½d being advertised altogether on behalf of the calico-printers, and again mainly from the neighbouring Lancashire towns.[111]

Another form of assistance was the publicity offered in the *Voice*, not only for the correspondence of the Block Printers' Union, but also in the shape of Doherty's strong editorial support. On 30 July, for example, he strongly appealed to the trades to support the fund for the striking calico-printers, the more especially since those workmen had been so generous in helping others and had been such early and consistent contributors to the National Association. Indeed, he added, had the other trades followed this example instead of being so apathetic, the general union would by now have been firmly established and the present reduction would never have been attempted. If the workmen did not now come forward and reveal the 'moral force of a great national union of their body', they could expect no mercy from their oppressors, and would deserve none. A week later, he ridiculed the associated masters' offer of a £300 reward for information regarding attacks on 'knobsticks', by stating that the money would be better spent on fair wages, instead of provoking 300 men 'of irreproachable character' to such violence by grinding reductions; at the same time, however, he urged them to desist from further outrages.[112]

Doherty's publicity achieved some success. On 2 July Pigot wrote that a general meeting of block printers' delegates had asked him to thank Doherty 'for the favours inserted in your extensively circulating journal'. His editorial of 30 July, calling on the working classes to unite to support the calico-printers and to obtain their rights, was copied into the *Register* by William Cobbett, who, after observing how greatly middle-class tradesmen and shop-keepers gained from higher wages being paid to labourers, commented that, 'I heartily agree with this article, and hope the precepts and advice of the able and spirited writer will be acted upon'. And this, in turn, brought the dispute to the attention of the metropolitan radical, John Cleave, who wrote to Doherty on 17 August that he intended to send him a hundred copies of his pamphlet giving a full report of Cobbett's trial for stirring up the 'Swing' riots; these could be sold at 1s each and the proceeds donated to the calico-printers' fund. Cleave ended his letter to Doherty by stating that 'I am greatly indebted to the labour you have already performed, in advocating high wages and the rights of workmen generally, and I sincerely pray that you will be long spared, to give lustre to the cause which you so efficiently serve'. The pamphlets were duly sent and advertised for sale in the *Voice* on 3 September.[113]

But the beginning of the calico-printers' strike coincided with the time when Doherty, disappointed with the state of lethargy into which the Association had fallen, was anxious to turn the general union in new directions to ensure ultimate success.[114] One of the schemes which he was anxious to promote was producer co-operation. Since the printers were themselves planning to open their own manufacturing premises, Doherty gave enthusiastic support to this project, which led eventually to their taking over a mill and estate at Birkacre, near Chorley, where they started what has been described as 'the most ambitious attempt at co-operative production during the early Owenite period'.[115]

The role of the National Association in the printers' scheme, however, was strictly a supporting one, as it was in the strikes of this period. At the same time, the Association was able to identify itself with the upsurge of feeling in north-east Lancashire during the calico-printers' strike, by holding a series

of meetings at which the aims of the Association *and* co-operation were publicised. At Great Harwood, Haslingden and Burnley thousands of workers
were addressed by delegates from the strikers and also by Thomas Oates,
resulting in resolutions not only in support of the printers and against the
grinding system of successive wages reductions, but also in favour of the
National Association, branches of which were consequently formed in that
area. A similar meeting at Blackburn was addressed by Bullock, general secretary of the Association, as well as by Oates and several local workmen, but
this ended in disorder, when two Blackburn radicals attempted to turn the
discussion to politics and deprecated the idea of the Association as impractical.[116]

Despite this enthusiasm which the Association helped to stimulate and the
encouraging start to the co-operative print-works at Chorley, the practical
problem of relieving a large body of workmen on strike proved too great for
the Lancashire calico-printers to surmount, as it had for the Ashton spinners.
In neither case was the Association capable of raising sufficient funds, while
the alternative of co-operative production could only employ a small proportion of the strikers. By the second week in September, all the works involved
had restarted with a full complement of hands on the masters' terms, and
even the *Voice* had to acknowledge another complete defeat.[117] Moreover,
although the co-operative venture at Chorley survived a little longer, it, too,
experienced increasing difficulties and eventually collapsed after about two
years.

If the calico-printers' disputes were the most long-lasting of those strikes
for which the Association launched special appeals, perhaps the most significant for the history of the Association during this period were those
involving the Midlands textile workers. At the beginning of March 1831, the
drawer, pantaloon, shirt, petticoat and cap workmen of Nottingham turned
out for an increase, claiming that their wages were only 8s per week for the
best workmen. They were soon joined by workers in the plain silk-hose branch
at both Nottingham and Derby, who demanded restoration of their rates of
1824, claiming that, as a result of repeated reductions, their average earnings
had been brought down to a similarly low level. Although the Association's
prime object was not to advance wages but to resist deductions, the
workmen believed that they merited special consideration, since the framework-knitting trade was among the worst paid in the whole of Great Britain,
and they therefore inserted appeals for subscriptions in the *Voice*.[118]

The framework knitters' confidence that their cause would be backed by
the Association seemed to be vindicated when Doherty declared their appeal
to be just and requested contributions to be forwarded to the *Voice* office.[119]
The 2,000 workmen on strike had enthusiastically supported the general
union, so Doherty apparently believed, as in the case of the Rochdale weavers,
that it was important for the Association to demonstrate its concern for their
plight, rather than insist on strict application of the rules. Moreover, the
Nottingham trades had previously given generous aid to the Ashton turn-outs,
despite the fact that their wages were far lower than those of the spinners.
In the event, however, the Association was again embarrassed by its failure
to produce what it promised.

To further their appeal, both groups of strikers sent delegates to Lancashire, but with unfortunate results. We have already seen how the Nottingham delegate was unable to obtain the £30 owing from the Manchester committee and later arrived in Bolton in a state of near destitution.[120] But G. Robinson, the Derby branch secretary, who came as the representative of the plain silk-hose trade, fared little better. On 9 April the *Voice* reported that he had visited a number of trade societies in the Manchester area and that, having received 'the warmest pledges of support for the unfortunate body of workmen he represents', he was hopeful that such promises were not in vain, as their distress was deplorable. The response, however, was most disappointing. On 2 and 9 April the *Voice* advertised total receipts for the two groups on strike of £70 5s 4½d, and all of this inadequate sum had been contributed from the Midlands with the solitary exception of £2 from the Lees spinners. By 16 April, therefore, the plain silk-hose hands had been forced to return to work on their old terms, and Doherty was driven into making excuses for Lancashire's indifference by referring to the present miseries of the whole community and also to the fact that the workmen had turned out for an advance, which, although just and fair, could be used as an argument against giving them Association support.[121]

Thus Doherty was forced into what was virtually a complete retraction of his words of only three weeks before, though he tried to disguise this with expressions of sympathy and regret, in response to bitter complaints from the Midlands.[122] But these recriminations ceased temporarily in view of the urgent task of collecting contributions for the Nottingham drawer, pantaloon, shirt and cap trade, whose strike had continued despite the return of the plain silk-hose hands. The support of the Association was re-emphasised on 23 April, when Cheetham, the new general secretary, appended a note to the advertised donations declaring that the turn-outs were 'contending for the just rights of every Englishman, viz a fair and adequate remuneration for labour', and hence the Association could recommend their case to 'the humane part of the community'.[123] In Nottingham the district committee of the Association identified itself even more closely with the strike, by sending a deputation to meet the masters on 9 May, and although these negotiations proved fruitless, a special meeting of local trades' delegates on 10 May reasserted their confidence in the Association. The strikers inserted a further appeal in the *Voice*, describing their privations, expressing hope that the Lancashire spinners would now fulfil their promises of reciprocal support, and announcing that a new delegate, Luke Pickburn, had been sent to the Manchester area.[124]

Pickburn's delegation proved even more disastrous, however, than the previous missions. When he attended a meeting of the Manchester committee on 17 May, Doherty was of opinion that he ought to call on the separate trades, but it was agreed instead to hold a general meeting two days later. This, however, was badly organised and only about fifty workmen turned up. Doherty spoke warmly in support of the Nottingham men and urged the working classes to unite to obtain a comfortable living wage,[125] but had again to make excuses for the lack of support. It was agreed to issue an appeal to the local trades, subscriptions to be sent to the *Voice* office, but the prospect was far from encouraging.[126] The *Manchester Guardian* eagerly pounced on the meagre attendance at this meeting as fulfilment of its predictions, at the time of the Ashton defeat and Hynes' flight, that the Association would decline and that 'the operatives of Manchester, who have normally swelled such assemblies, are regaining their senses'. Meanwhile, Pickburn met with a complete rebuff in Bolton, because of the differences with the Manchester committee, and—most bitter disappointment of all—when he called a meeting of the Ashton workmen, not more than twenty turned up and the business had to be abandoned.[127]

The last list of subscriptions for the cap and drawer branch workers was advertised on 11 June. A total of £42 14s 2¾d was acknowledged in the two months since collections for that trade alone had begun, and of this, almost all, as before, came from the Nottingham area. These workers consequently had to accept defeat, like the plain silk-hose hands previously. Both trades were thrown into a state of disorganisation and naturally disillusion with the Association was rife. Even so, the organisation of the Association in the Nottingham district did not entirely disintegrate, as had been the case at Ashton. Indeed, Bullock, the plain silk-hose branch secretary, succeeded Cheetham as general secretary in July, and as one of his first actions inserted an appeal in the *Voice* of 23 July addressed to the workers in the two defeated trades, advising them that membership of the Association would still be of benefit in preventing their employers from making further wages reductions. But after similar lack of support for another smaller strike in Nottingham that month, enthusiasm for the Association in that area rapidly evaporated.[128]

A total of £518 2s 11½d had been raised in special appeals, under the resolution passed at the March conference, to support the Lancashire calico-printers and the Midlands textile workers, but none of these strikes was successful. Nor did appeals from various other trades prove any more successful. The most important of these was from the Rochdale flannel-weavers, who had renewed their allegiance to the Association early in 1831.[129] By April they were again suffering from serious trade depression, heavy unemployment and further wages reductions, and so appealed despairingly to the Association. Doherty again advised them to adopt the 'rolling strike' technique, by selecting one or two of 'the most obnoxious grinders' for strike action, to bring them up to 16s in the £1 on their 1824 rates. Should they require aid, he was sure that 'the ready co-operation of the entire union will be afforded; for none have a better claim for the support of their fellow-workmen. They were the first and best supporters of it.'[130]

This advice they proceeded to follow, but fearing the effects of strike action and of being let down again, as in the previous October, they pressed for voluntary support from the Association, even though they were no longer able to pay their subscriptions and although they were actually striving to achieve a wages advance. Doherty continued for some time to support their cause warmly in the *Voice*, filling them once again with false hope, but eventually he had to recognise that their situation was, in fact, so hopeless that nothing could be achieved by strike action. He therefore changed his policy completely, recommending instead that the weavers should forward petitions to Parliament, describing their condition, weekly income, rent, etc., and asking for immediate relief in the first place, but also for a general enquiry into the condition of the English labouring classes.[131] Thus once more the Rochdale weavers were badly let down, all talk of strikes was soon abandoned and they finally and completely withdrew from the Association.

Despite the disarray in the accounts, the continuation of the dispute with Bolton, and the conspicuous lack of success in supporting strikes, the Webbs have characterised the period after the Nottingham conference as being one in which 'the Association was spreading'. G. D. H. Cole also believed that in these few months 'Doherty tried to extend the organisation', while pointing out that his success was strictly limited; and D. C. Morris commented similarly that, after the conference, 'Doherty's efforts were concentrated on recruiting new members'.[132] In fact, as we have seen, this was the very time when hopes of extending the Association in a logically planned way from the centre had to be abandoned, when complaints of the excessive expense incurred necessitated the dismissal of Jonathan Hodgins, and when the Association began to disintegrate as a result of strike failures. Consequently the very few accessions between the Nottingham conference in March and the Manchester conference at the end of June were either the product of local efforts to build on earlier initiatives from the centre, or were accessions in name only, affording little practical benefit to the Association.

The most important new involvement during this period was that of the coal miners, who had been tenuously connected with the Association in the autumn of 1830 when there were a number of strikes in Lancashire, but had never actually joined it in any strength.[133] At the end of April 1831, a general meeting at the 'Prince William', Bolton, of fifty delegates, representing 9,000 colliers in Lancashire, Staffordshire, Yorkshire, Cheshire, Wales and elsewhere, belonging to the Coal Miners' Union, recommended that they should all 'immediately join the Trades' Union' or National Association.[134] But no financial contribution from the Miners' Union was ever acknowledged and the connection between the two bodies remained vague.[135] It is possible that the North Staffordshire miners may have joined, for when they turned out for an increase of wages in May, the combined colliery masters issued a declaration that they would not re-employ any workman who was either a member of 'the trades' union' or had demanded the increase; and it was also reported that the operative potters were supporting the colliers. But the Association appears to have had no active part in the dispute, except for the insertion of one letter from the workmen's committee in the *Voice*.[136] In June there were fearful riots among the colliers and ironworkers of Merthyr Tydvil, after the former had struck against a wage reduction and forcibly stopped the ironworks. Fifteen workmen were shot dead by special constables and one of their leaders, Dic Penderyn, was later executed. But, despite hints that the rioters were organised by and 'in union with Birmingham and Manchester', and bold assertions from the local leaders 'that the insurrection would not be confined to Wales, but that arrangements had been made for a simultaneous rising in other manufacturing and mining districts of the kingdom', there is no evidence of any intervention by the Association, though Doherty demanded an investigation into the circumstances surrounding the fatalities, and also repeated his call on the government to institute a full enquiry into the condition of workmen in every branch of industry.[137]

For the Lancashire miners also, this was a time of industrial unrest. Colliers on strike in Oldham during June and July received some support in the *Voice*, but by the end of August they were forced back to work on the employers' terms and the colliers' union was reported to be 'on the point of dissolution on account of the paucity of its funds'.[138] The Association seems to have had a closer connection with miners in the Bolton area, for on 29 August a public warning was issued in that town that any tradesman or shopkeeper who purchased coal from a master who was trying to force his men to leave the Coal Miners' Society or 'the Trades National Association for the Protection of Labour', or to reduce their wages, would be boycotted by all the members of those two organisations, and that this system would apply 'in Lancashire, Yorkshire, Staffordshire, Wales, or any other Place, as far as the above Societies have extended'. This proposal outraged the *Guardian*, which asserted that such 'public threats', and such a 'system of proscription', demanded 'the immediate notice of the public authorities'.[139] But nothing further was heard of the matter, nor indeed of any further involvement of the miners in the Association.[140]

If the coal-miners seemed to be the most important *trade* to enter the Association during this period, the most significant new *area* of involvement apparently was Yorkshire. After some early signs of interest among the Sheffield basket-makers, Association activity in that county had completely lapsed, the only other subscriptions sent to the central coffers before the end of 1830 being from the Shipley printers.[141] The first attempt to remedy this situation occurred with the appointment of Hodgins as full-time 'agitator' for the Association. On 11 November, the day after he had taken up his post, it was reported that bills were posted in the streets of Halifax announcing a public meeting to be held on Skincourt Moor that afternoon, to consider the propriety of the workmen in that district becoming members of the National Association for the Protection of Labour, and revealing that 'deputies from this Association in Manchester and Glasgow will address the meeting'.[142] A month later, Hodgins and Oates spoke at a meeting of Leeds workmen, which passed a resolution in favour of the general union project.[143] At about that time also, the same two deputies visited Sheffield, but they met with some opposition at the meeting called to discuss the question of that town enrolling, and were particularly abused by the *Sheffield Iris*, which denounced the scheme as intended only for 'transferring the money from the pockets of the "abused operatives" of Sheffield, into the strong box of a certain Lancashire committee'. So successful was this campaign that the same paper could rejoice in the following May that 'not a penny was sent from Sheffield to the Manchester Council'.[144]

The response to the Association delegates in Yorkshire appears to have been generally insignificant, for in the first ten weeks of 1831 the only subscriptions from that county were some further small donations from Shipley and £1 each paid in entrance money by the Bradford wool-combers and the Knaresborough linen weavers, although the Yorkshire workmen were more generous in their assistance to the Ashton spinners.[145] After the Nottingham conference, however, there were more encouraging reports of progress in the *Voice*. On 26 March the blanket-weavers of Dewsbury paid their deposit fee after obtaining a wage increase, and the correspondent stated that 'the National Association is rapidly spreading in this district'. On 4 April Oates spoke at a meeting of about 5,000 Bradford workmen and resolutions were adopted approving of the Association and of using every means to establish it throughout the kingdom. At the Manchester committee meeting on 19 April, Cheetham read a letter from Leeds announcing that the Association was spreading rapidly in that quarter, that more than 9,000 were already enrolled, and that the number would probably reach 20,000 eventually. And later, on 19 July, a 'Well-Wisher' wrote to the paper on behalf of the Leeds committee, maintaining that the 5,000 woollen weavers in the area were only prevented from joining the Association by their current dispute with one of their masters, Messrs Gott & Sons, and that the cloth-dressers were also in favour of the plan. Since the committee intended in about a month's time to call a meeting of delegates from those trades which supported them, the correspondent added that 'the presence of Mr Doherty will shortly be of great avail in this town'. Knaresborough was also enrolled into the Association.[146]

But the reality was far different from these reports, for, apart from the deposit of the Dewsbury weavers, the only other subscription acknowledged from the whole of Yorkshire after the Nottingham conference was £2 for the *Voice* from Bradford in August.[147] Trade unionism was developing in the county, but as Cole has shown, it was fully independent of the Association, if stimulated by the Lancashire example.[148] At the Manchester delegate meeting in June, Knaresborough was the only Yorkshire town represented.[149]

Thus neither the miners nor the Yorkshire trades proved in practice to be strong supporters of the Association. On the other hand, this period did witness the formation of some new districts; but these were formed in towns where the trades had previously contributed separately to the Association and now found it necessary to amalgamate and elect branch committees, following the Nottingham resolution concerning the local retention of funds. On 5 April, for instance, a meeting of delegates from such trades as were joined to the Association at Macclesfield was held to form a district: this was still in existence in July, but no more contributions from the town were ever acknowledged.[150] More important was the recognition of Loughborough as a separate district of the Association on 2 April, following a meeting of the trades there.[151] This branch was so enterprising that it contributed more funds to the Association than any other in the last six months of advertised subscriptions. But even this did not prove entirely beneficial, as it was the cause of a brief disagreement between the Manchester and Nottingham committees. The latter deplored the formation of Loughborough as a separate district, because it would encourage other small towns and villages to set themselves up as branches and thus lead to excessive fragmentation. Instead, Nottingham argued that there should be only one district for each county or group of counties, and subscriptions should all be sent to the largest town at the head. This reorganisation was supported by Doherty, but he delayed an attempt to implement it until the following August, when it was already too late to arrest the Association's decline.[152]

Thus the Association gained few significant accessions during the spring and early summer of 1831, and Doherty's chief efforts at this time, far from being aimed at expansion, were directed towards overcoming the widespread apathy among the working classes. On 26 March, for instance, while repeating his belief that it was absurd for workmen to oppose the employment of machines, he deplored the fact that their 'indifference to their own welfare' had permitted their employers to seize the benefits of mechanisation, while they suffered from unemployment and reduced wages; the only remedy was to bestir themselves and 'unite for mutual protection, or sink into irretrievable woe'.[153] And later, on 4 and 11 June, he published a very significant address entitled 'An Appeal to the Producers of Wealth, as to the best means of securing the fruits of their own industry', which perfectly illustrated his thinking at this time. He began by comparing the poverty of the labourers with the luxurious conditions of their capital-owning industrial masters, who lived off their labour, and of their political masters and idlers, who lived off their taxes. Only by their own exertions could the workmen retain the fruits of their labour, but they were hampered by apathy and indifference on the one hand and by diversity of aims on the other. The first difficulty would be overcome if the workmen realised how easily a general union could be formed, first by each trade becoming united, then by the printers, spinners, weavers, agricultural workers,[154] etc. in each neighbourhood forming a district, and finally by the districts coalescing according to the general laws of the Association for the protection of labour. 'Their reward would be adequate wages, independence of mind, and the ready admission of political rights.' The second difficulty would be overcome with general agreement on the basic and fundamental point—that their poverty and helplessness must be alleviated. On this, 'both the opinion and the interests of the working classes are the same', hence every operative should strive first to build up the most efficient organ of alleviation—a 'UNION'. And only then should the debate begin as to whether to use the powers of such a union to secure further reforms from Parliament or the establishment of a fully co-operative system.[155]

Based on this remarkable synthesis of the currently diverse campaigns of the trade unionists, co-operators and political radicals, Doherty was already planning by June 1831, important new involvements for the Association to revive it from the malaise into which it had fallen.[156] For, while Doherty was setting grand proposals in train, one of the most serious and discouraging weaknesses in the Association was disaffection in Manchester itself. The complaints of disinterest and even hostility among the Manchester trades, which had been so frequent in the summer of 1830,[157] were revived after the Nottingham conference, which had abolished the position of Manchester as the central treasury of the Association. Initially, Doherty proposed the same solution as had been attempted in the previous year—the holding of weekly meetings at which working men could discuss any of their manifold grievances and oppressions, but where religious topics and 'anything upon which they might quarrel' would be excluded. On this occasion, however, nothing came of this idea, but instead all members of the Manchester committee were advised, on the recommendation of Doherty and Kirkham, to bring with them to the regular meeting on 19 April a colleague from their own trade in order that the Association principles might be explained more widely;[158] and various important topics were introduced at the Manchester committee meetings, such as a short-time or factory bill, a Wages' Protection Bill, and the Reform Bill, which were also given publicity in the *Voice*.[159]

Such measures, however, did little to stimulate a revival of interest. Particularly galling for Doherty must have been his having to plead on behalf of his own trade, the Manchester spinners, regarding their arrears of subscriptions.[160] He summed up his disappointment in an article entitled 'Prospects of the People' on 28 May. While his opinions in favour of a National Association were being taken up with enthusiasm by operatives as far afield as Ireland and London,[161] apathy and distrust prevailed nearer home. '*Here alone*, where the measure ·had its birth, and where, in fact, it was first taken up, is it now misunderstood and neglected.' He therefore exhorted the workmen of this and all other provincial districts, to take courage from the spirit displayed elsewhere and show what the masses could effect by uniting their small means.[162]

When a further delegate conference was convened in Manchester in June, advantage was taken of the presence in the city of many of the leading lights of the Association to convene a public meeting of operatives on St Peter's Field on the evening of 24 June, at the conclusion of the conference, 'for the purpose of explaining the principles and objects of the N.A.P.L., and for pointing out the general advantages of union to the productive classes'. Bullock, the Nottingham framework-knitter, who was appointed general secretary by the conference, took the chair, and there were many speakers from various other towns, but the longest speech came from Doherty, though he admitted that it was an 'ill-chosen time' to address them on that subject, when they were so involved in the reform question. But reform, although desirable, could not prevent wages reductions or other oppressions of the workmen, which were caused by the competitive system, and this system reform would not alter. Whether their aim was to co-operate, protect their wages, or assert their political rights, it could only be achieved by union, for 'union was the foundation of every improvement which could be made in their condition'. The assembly went on to adopt three resolutions, pointing out the great advantages of the Association to the working classes, advising all workmen to support the *Voice*, and recommending operatives throughout the country to petition Parliament to abolish all restrictions on the press.[163]

Yet even this meeting was counter-productive, for not only did it fail to re-invigorate the Manchester workmen, but it also provided the local press with renewed opportunity to assert that the Association was in decline. Although the *Voice* claimed that six or seven thousand operatives attended it, the *Guardian* alleged that less than half that number were present, and moreover that the speakers complained of the apathy of the workmen, who displayed little enthusiasm for the objects of the meetings.

> The fact is, the people have begun to discover the true value of the scheme of Messrs Doherty and Co.: they have begun to say to themselves, 'What has the union done for us, or for anybody, except the individuals who have been working it? It has certainly emptied our pockets, and filled those of Mr Doherty and his associates. But what did it do for the spinners at Ashton and Staley Bridge, when they attempted to raise their wages, or for the spinners of Manchester, when their wages were reduced? It did nothing, it can do nothing; and we will have nothing to do with it.'[164]

Despite the errors it contained,[165] this was a serious attack. And its tone was fully echoed in two lengthy editorials in *Wheeler's Manchester Chron-*

*icle* on 25 June and 2 July, which placed its estimate of the attendance at only a few hundred and asserted that this proved that the labouring classes of Manchester were at last realising the 'jugglery and fraud' to which they had been subjected so long. The editor was particularly struck with the apathetic reception of the orations.

> There were no tokens of approbation or recognition even for Mr Doherty, and the flattery with which his myrmidon, Oates, bespattered his great lord, passed unheeded: it might soothe the dignity of his master, offended by the silence of the crowd, but it did not restore the confidence of the men, whose money that master and his satellite had basely received for months. As one man said, 'the workmen of Manchester will not part with their money any more for the Union—they are tired'.[166]

These articles enabled Doherty to return to his old pursuit of attacking the orthodox press. The *Voice* on 9 July carried a particularly severe editorial upon 'The Doating Chronicle', which 'tiny vehicle of twaddle and small talk' had laboured for several weeks 'to provoke us to notice him'. How dare this 'apostate tory', who had for long supported all exactions from the poor and defended every kind of oppression by Castlereagh, Sidmouth, continental despots, and the 'butchers of Peterloo', and yet had recently been forced by the power of the people to accept a moderate measure of reform, now charge us with 'basely receiving hard-earned workmen's money'! Doherty agreed that he received 'from the voluntary offerings of the working classes, a respectable sum weekly', but he was proud to have their confidence and asserted that their willingness to pay this, despite great poverty, was proof of their unshakable desire to gain their rights.[167] But, despite this bravado, Doherty was acutely aware that the Association had stagnated ever since the disappointments of the previous February, and he was already proceeding with a number of projects, far more ambitious than the original and more limited intentions of October 1829.

One of the most important of these schemes attempted to combine the Association with political radicalism.[168] Although the original impetus behind the formation of the general union had been the need to curb wages reductions, and expansion had taken place on that basis, Doherty never hid the fact that he believed that, with a powerful trades' union established, the ruling classes could not long prevent working men obtaining their *political* rights; and, indeed, the government had been given the pretext for suppressing the *Journal* by Doherty's frequent excursions into the political arena. His position as editor of the *Voice* gave him the opportunity to develop his radical views more fully, and as the debates over the Reform Bill became more strident during 1831 Doherty devoted an increasing amount of space to it. Many of the trades' leaders, on the other hand, were anxious that the Association should not get side-tracked by the political controversy, and a rule was adopted at the Nottingham conference expressly prohibiting the introduction of political topics.[169] But Doherty proceeded as though this rule had never been passed. At the Manchester committee meeting on 26 April, some fears were expressed that the introduction of the 'cap of liberty' into the design of the Association membership card would encourage a belief that they were introducing political topics. Doherty explained that they had every intention to adhere strictly to the Nottingham resolution, though he could see no more objection to workmen discussing politics than any other subject.

> The only reason for introducing the 'cap of liberty' at all was merely to show, that in all their associations and proceedings, they never lost sight of the sacred cause of freedom. It was merely intended to remind the possessors of the plate or engraving, that while they were struggling for food, or endeavouring to uphold their wages, they should never lose sight of the freedom and happiness of their country.[170]

But Doherty had already adverted to politics at previous committee meetings, and he continued to do so. Whilst he recognised that the Reform Bill was not directly connected with the business of the Association, he emphasised that it inevitably affected working men in general and he therefore got the Association involved in the current political controversy. Thus he secured the backing of the Manchester committee for the point of view, which he shared with Francis Place, that the Reform Bill should be accepted and supported, as a first step, against the view of Henry Hunt and his more radical supporters who advocated outright rejection.[171] But Doherty's view on this issue was by no means generally acceptable and the controversy so adversely affected sales of the *Voice* that a special delegate conference had to be convened at the end of June to take measures to secure its continuance.[172]

Meanwhile, Doherty shifted his ground somewhat by proposing on 7 May that the working classes should hold meetings in every town to elect deputies to go to London simultaneously to present petitions to Parliament for the Preston or household suffrage.[173] He was hopeful that, in those towns where the Association was organised, the meetings might be arranged by the local branch committees, for his circulars describing the plan were despatched, where possible, to the district secretaries. His plan had a mixed reception, however, and Doherty had therefore to explain to the Manchester committee on 18 May that he did not regard it as the business of the Association, but as a general question in which any man, whether or not he was a member of the Association, might participate. It was wrong to suppose that the committee or the Association were at all committed by it. In fact, it was not a question for consideration by the Association at all.[174]

Thus although Doherty certainly emphasised the importance of political matters to trade unionists, although such topics figured prominently in the pages of the *Voice*, and although he involved the Association to some extent in political controversy, he certainly did not endeavour, as some writers have suggested, to transform the Association into a political body. His scheme for a national conference of labour delegates had a much wider basis; although he undoubtedly hoped that local trade unions would assist in organising it, he did not envisage it as a solely trade-union affair, but as involving the working classes generally. Beer was therefore greatly exaggerating in stating that Doherty 'dreamed of creating a political Labour Party with the trades unions for its units . . . all the unions should together form a National Association to undertake the emancipation of the working class by means of parliamentary and socialistic action'.[175] In fact, all that Doherty did was to try to use the Association's journal, and to a much more limited extent its organisation, to further his political reform ideas. And even in this he was in advance of most of the rank-and-file in the factory districts, who, as Rudé has observed, 'only stood at the threshold of a self-conscious working-class movement, and were not yet ready to play an independent political role'.[176] There were deep differences between them on the question of parliamentary reform, ranging from the politically apathetic, through supporters of the Reform Bill, to extreme democratic radicals, while a great many trade unionists were entirely against mixing political with trade affairs. Doherty was not, therefore, able to carry the Association membership with him in his political schemes.

Further proof that Doherty was aware of the Association's decline in the period after the Nottingham conference can be seen in another new policy proposal, which envisaged workmen applying to Parliament for measures to alleviate their distress. Previously, he had always insisted on workmen improving themselves by their own efforts, just as for long he believed that factory operatives did not need parliamentary help to reduce their hours of labour.[177] But on 12 April he told the Manchester committee not only that they should petition Parliament in favour of Hobhouse's Factory Bill, but also that he had been converted to the idea of soliciting Parliament for a Wages' Protection Bill, by the indifference of many workmen to their own interests, by the series of reductions suffered by the Manchester spinners, and by the fate of the Rochdale weavers. He tried, however, to conceal that such an application would, on his earlier view, be a sign of weakness, by asserting that Parliament would only be forced to grant the measure through the strength of their union.

> The government had yielded through fear in the revolution of 1688. It was fear that caused the Catholic emancipation bill to pass; fear that brought reform to what it was; and fear must wring from the legislature that protection they wanted. Their numbers and unanimity would create that fear, and the exercise of it would effect their object.[178]

At the same time, Doherty also asserted that, such was the generality of distress among the manufacturing and agricultural population, the government's failure to act could only proceed from ignorance. Hence it was essential that a committee of enquiry be established, to which witnesses should be called from all parts of the country. The operatives should remember that the agricultural labourers had succeeded in raising their wages through their late proceedings, and though he would deprecate any use of violence, yet they must use all legal and constitutional means to draw attention to their condition.[179] Doherty continued to advise the workmen to apply to Parliament for an enquiry throughout 1831. In June, as we have seen, he recommended it to the Rochdale flannel-weavers, whom the Association had proved incapable of helping. On 27 July Doherty spoke at a meeting of the National Union of the Working Classes at the Rotunda in London, and proposed as an additional clause in a parliamentary petition which that body was preparing, 'that a committee of enquiry be instituted to examine the real state of the working classes of this kingdom'. His proposal was opposed by John Cleave on the grounds that enquiries had previously been held but had always reported that the people were in 'a flourishing state', and it was eventually negatived by a large majority.[180] But Doherty continued to speak in favour of the idea, for instance at a 'meeting of the unemployed' of Manchester in St. George's Fields on 12 December.[181]

Thus Doherty's efforts to use the Association in the agitation for political reform only served to increase the divisions within it, while his advocacy of applications to Parliament for relief was in itself a sign of the Association's weakness. However, his third new departure in policy was totally in accord with his belief in independent action by the working classes, and entailed identifying the Association with the incipient movement for producer co-operation in Lancashire.[182] Throughout 1830, as we have seen, there was considerable disagreement between trade unionists and co-operators, and despite extensive public debate between supporters of each system, echoes of this controversy persisted into 1831. On 16 March, during a co-operative lecture in the dyers' room, Manchester, William Carson, a leading exponent of the system, from Pemberton, near Wigan, criticised the Association, 'which he considered to be founded on an unsound basis, and said that it would crumble before long. He also considered the *Voice of the People* to be a mill-stone about the Association's neck, which would definitely accelerate its downfall.' And at the adjourned Liverpool meeting on 30 March to publicise the Association in that city, opposition to the plan was voiced by members of the 'Friends' Co-operation' Society.[183] On the other side, Doherty continued to express objections to the impractical aspects of Owenite co-operation.[184] What he did support wholeheartedly, however, was 'co-operation by trades' to acquire machinery and produce goods for themselves. On 14 May, for example, he referred to the success of the dyers' workshop at Pendleton, begun the previous autumn, as a 'triumph of co-operation'; his enthusiastic support for similar efforts by the Lancashire calico-printers during the summer has already been described, and on 24 September the *Voice* reported that the operative sawyers had also opened a yard for the sawing and sale of timber.[185] Better relations ensued after the first co-operative congress in Manchester in May, which the *Voice* reported. Doherty saw possibilities of securing more support for the Association by alliance with the co-operators, who did, in fact, respond to his advances.[186] Even Carson inserted an advertisement in the *Voice* on 2 July, detailing the wares manufactured and sold by his co-operative society at Lamberhead Green, and the Liverpool co-operator, John Finch, published two long addresses to 'the Creators and Distributors of Wealth' on 31 August and 14 September advising them to join the Association so long as it abjured industrial strife in favour of co-operative production.[187] Doherty, for his part, publicly announced his complete conversion to the co-operative system on 11 June, when he also warmly welcomed the appearance of a local plan for establishing a community.[188] The improved understanding between the two parties was symbolised at the second co-operative delegate conference at Birmingham early in October, when the *Voice* was adopted as the official organ of the movement.[189]

In July and August, based on this alliance, Doherty launched a campaign to advance both the Association and co-operation, by holding meetings at several of the towns in the neighbourhood of the current calico-printers' dispute.[190] Many of these were well attended, and indeed a temporarily thriving branch was established at Accrington. But Doherty could not rebuild the Association on these new foundations: for, while producer co-operation might have been a viable proposition for small numbers of skilled trades anxious to protect their wage-rates by employing surplus hands, it could not assist groups like the Rochdale flannel-weavers who might have as many as 2,000 out of work in the trough of slumps. And sadly, by the time the *Voice* was recognised as the co-operators' publicity medium, its last number had already appeared.

Cole's description of Doherty as 'an ardent Owenite', intent on creating a 'Co-operative Commonwealth', has been repeated uncritically by Morris and also by Rudé, who has asserted that the leaders of the Association, 'being Owenites, tended to indulge in the millenarial fantasy of rapidly transforming society into a co-operative commonwealth'. E. P. Thompson similarly maintains that Doherty 'rightly saw, in the growing popularity of Owenite ideas, a means of bringing the organised workers of the country into a common movement'.[191] These statements, however, ignore the divisions between unionists and co-operators during most of the Association's existence, and the fact that they were only healed when the Association was disintegrating through strike failures and internal recriminations. Doherty's late 'conversion' was more of a desperate attempt to salvage the general union than an act of faith in Owenism; in fact, his basic trade-unionist, class outlook was quite different from Owen's, and his adoption of Owenism was limited, in practice, to supporting trade-union schemes of co-operative production, all of which, however, ultimately failed.[192]

Doherty's hopes of infusing new energy into the Association by combining unionists, political radicals and co-operators in a unity based on his 'Appeal to the Producers of Wealth' on 4 and 11 June,[193] thus proved abortive, an *institutional* alliance with the radicals being rejected by the unionists, and producer co-operation having an insufficiently wide practical appeal to be an adequate replacement for general support during strikes, which had originally induced workmen to join the Association. These failures did not, however, exhaust his innovatory zeal. His fourth new policy in the summer of 1831 was intended to transform the organisational structure of the Association. He aimed to do this through the establishment of a number of 'grand divisions', moving the central headquarters to London, and undertaking at the same time a massive and renewed campaign of 'agitation' for the purpose of consolidation and expansion. The 'grand division' plan originated with the Nottingham branch committee, who had intended to propose it to the March delegate conference in their town, but did not bring it forward until early April, after recognition of Loughborough as a separate branch.[194] Nottingham, as we have seen, considered that there was too great a proliferation of small branches and therefore proposed, in a letter to the *Voice*, that the whole country should be partitioned into ten grand divisions, each containing four counties and administering a certain number of sub-divisions, the contributions of which would all be deposited in one of the principal towns of the grand division; the secretary of each principal town to hold direct correspondence with Manchester, transmitting the information himself to each sub-district, whose respective secretaries would then in turn inform the different trades. The correspondent was convinced that the plan 'would save great expense in postage etc., and would increase the stability of the National Union of Trades'.[195]

Doherty, who himself believed that the Nottingham delegate conference had given excessive independence to each individual branch, apparently gave a favourable reception to this letter, for on 26 April he told the Manchester committee that, 'on that night fortnight he would endeavour to have a plan prepared of a division of the kingdom into districts or divisions, for the purpose of extending the association'.[196] However, a special meeting of delegates belonging to the Nottingham district subsequently pronounced itself 'fully satisfied with the present organised state of the association',[197] and Doherty himself found his time fully occupied with the 'simultaneous petitions' project, so nothing further was heard of the promised plan for a number of weeks.

The increasing malaise of the Association, however, caused it to be reconsidered at the fifth general delegate conference, held in Manchester on 20–24 June. This meeting was again convened in 'special' circumstances, only four months after its predecessor, and the number of delegates attending was reduced from twenty-four to twenty, representing Manchester, Nottingham, Birmingham, Derby, Mansfield, Sutton-in-Ashfield, Knaresborough, Rochdale, Oldham, Ashton, Macclesfield, Bury, Bolton, Blackrod, Chorley, Preston, Blackburn, Accrington, Clitheroe and Rossendale.[198] The main discussions were on the finances of the *Voice* and the Association generally, but a decision was taken in favour of the 'grand division' plan in principle and Doherty was set to work once more to prepare the details.[199]

At the subsequent meeting of the Manchester committee on 28 June, Doherty stated that he was still preparing the plan, but indicated that the leading towns in the various divisions might be Manchester, Leeds, Nottingham, Liverpool, Birmingham, Glasgow, etc. Each division should hold a half-yearly meeting, while the supreme government would be an annual general conference of all the divisions, 'either in London or any other place'. (Thus Doherty was already considering transfer of the Association's headquarters to London.) This scheme, he thought, would be the only means by which they could include all the productive classes in a strong national organisation.[200]

Consideration of it was deferred to the next meeting, but no report of this meeting was published and there was a further delay of two months before the project was referred to again, in a letter from Derby read to the committee by Doherty on 30 August, urging adoption of the plan as agreed on at the late delegate meeting.[201] The reason for these repeated postponements was the hostility of the Manchester committee to any further loss of their own power and also to proposals for an extensive campaign to expand the Association to cover the whole kingdom. And in arguments over these proposals they came increasingly to be at odds with Doherty.

The Manchester committee, as we have seen, had become the effective central executive of the Association, since the original scheme of having a Provisional Council of seven district representatives had never been put into operation.[202] But Manchester's preponderance had aroused resentment, especially in Bolton, and Hynes' defalcation had destroyed confidence in central financial control, which was therefore ended by the March conference in Nottingham. Manchester still remained the administrative centre, but was now placed in financial difficulties and the trades there began to murmur at having to meet the incidental expenses; the committee, moreover, tended to become more parochial in outlook and there were complaints of their neglecting general Association affairs, a view supported by the June delegate meeting held in Manchester. They seem to have remained satisfied with the Association's limited extension—or to have considered that this was all that was practicable—and were inimical to the grand divisional plan with its accompanying proposals for further expansion by agitational campaigns. Thus at the meeting on 28 June, when Doherty sketched his divisional scheme, differences arose over a request from William Bonner, of Liverpool, that delegates from Manchester should visit that city to help in organising the trades there. Several committee members wished to concentrate on their own affairs in the Manchester district—itself still inadequately organised—but Doherty spoke out strongly in favour of such 'missionary' work, emphasising that it was their duty to extend and consolidate the Association; the divisional plan he regarded as an essential basis for such expansion. It was eventually agreed that Oates should be sent to Liverpool, but that further consideration of the plan for 'extending the Association' should be postponed to the next meeting.[203]

For the next five weeks, however, the meetings of the Manchester committee were either not reported or mentioned only in very cursory fashion, a change so marked that it almost certainly masked continuing disagreement. Meanwhile, organisational activity was resumed in desultory fashion, with visits by Oates to Liverpool, Bolton and several north-east Lancashire towns, where, as we have seen, he urged the joint merits of the 'National Association and Co-operation'; contact was even made with trades in Bristol, though without any apparent outcome.[204] Eventually, Doherty's forward policy was adopted, after a 'long discussion' in the committee on 9 August on the necessity of visiting the different districts 'to revive and organise them'.[205] It was agreed that Oates should go to Nottingham, Chesterfield, Mansfield and Blackburn as soon as possible; but in the event, while Oates did go to Blackburn,[206] it was Doherty himself who undertook the preliminary part of the Midlands tour, a change of plan reflecting the seriousness with which the crisis in the affairs of the Association was regarded. Almost exactly a year after his original visit to Nottingham, which had helped to launch a flourishing district, Doherty now returned to try to revive the flagging enthusiasm there. There was a sparse attendance, however, at a public meeting on 15 August, and he had to face hostile criticism on account of the betrayal of the framework-knitters in their recent strike. But while Doherty sympathised with their feelings of disappointment, he pointed out that the Association leaders were not to blame, for they could not 'work miracles' or 'create money by magic'. 'It was quite clear that if men would not pay money into the union, it could not be paid out.' The difficulty, he explained, was that all the trades were so distressed, they hoped to be contributors *to* the Association for three months, and then to benefit *from* it to the amount of 8s a week. This was possible only if all workmen of the kingdom joined it, but he was not so naive as to expect a perfect national union to be built

up all at once; this would, in fact, take several years. They should not therefore delight their enemies by deserting the Association.

The note of caution in Doherty's remarks was in marked contrast to some
of his early propaganda on behalf of the Association, the extravagance of
which doubtless partly accounted for the depth of the operatives' disillusionment with its practical performance. Nevertheless, the eloquence of his
expression apparently moved the crowd in his favour, before heavy rain
caused the meeting to be adjourned for a week. In the meantime, Doherty
moved on to nearby Chesterfield, where he addressed another meeting of
operatives the following night. He began by attacking the publicans, who
had all refused them the use of their rooms, despite the labourers being
chiefly responsible for keeping them in business. The workmen should
retaliate by shunning public-houses altogether and using their spare pence
instead for the acquisition of knowledge. After referring also to the evils of
the truck system as practised in the town, Doherty proceeded to explain the
principles of the Association and the audience ultimately agreed that they
should become members.[207]

Doherty then returned to his editorial duties in Manchester, but his place
was immediately supplied by Thomas Oates. The latter's first task was to
attend the adjourned meeting at Nottingham,[208] which was followed by a
tour to other Midland towns, including Leicester, Loughborough, Coventry,
Kidderminster, Bromsgrove, and the Potteries, during the later part of August
and early September.[209] The reports of his campaign indicate that he succeeded
in stimulating existing branches and in promoting the establishment of
several new ones, but later evidence suggests that the impact of his visits
was superficial and temporary.

At this same time, an earlier suggestion from William Bonner, of Liverpool,
was adopted, that the Association should publish a series of cheap tracts,
explaining the advantages of general union to the working classes. Despite
the *Voice*, Bonner stated, the principles of the Association were not widely
known or understood: 'in Liverpool, not more than one out of two hundred
know even of the existence of the Association'.[210] Contemporaneously,
therefore, with this expansionary campaign, two 'Association Tracts' were
advertised for sale at a halfpenny each, though their contents were not
specified.[211]

While this campaign of agitation was being debated and then put into
practice, Doherty was also slowly advancing his scheme to make London the
centre-point of the 'grand divisions'. The relationship between the London
workmen and the Association had remained obscure throughout 1831. In
March the combined efforts of the British Association for the Promotion of
Co-operative Knowledge and the carpenters' trade club succeeded in forming
the 'Metropolitan Trades' Union' for the purposes of 'mutual assistance and
protection'. That the National Association may have had some influence
upon its formation is indicated by an article in *Carpenter's Political Magazine* in January 1832, on the 'National Union of the Working Classes and
Others' (as it had by then become). This traced the origins of that body back
to the Manchester delegate conference in June 1830, which was mistakenly
said to have established the National Association; but the zeal for the latter
had, the author maintained, soon abated as no workmen except those in

the immediate neighbourhood of Manchester could take a direct and active part in its proceedings. 'The consequence therefore was, that independent Unions, having the same object in view, but modified by local or political circumstances, sprung up in various parts of the country; and among others, the one whose denomination stands at the head of this article.' Hence Beer may well be correct in stating that the London joiners based their ideas for the Metropolitan Trades' Union on the National Association.[212]

But, as Beer and Oliver have shown, over the next few weeks the trade-union character of this organisation was gradually eliminated, by the decision to admit as members those who did not belong to trade societies and by the growing domination of political radicals as the controversy over the Reform Bill mounted, an ascendancy which was symbolised in an alteration of the title to the 'National Union of the Working Classes'.[213] There seems no evidence to back the assertion of G. D. H. Cole that the London workmen, after forming the Metropolitan Trades' Union, began 'entering into relations with Doherty and the NAPL'[214]—indeed the reports of their deliberations give no indication that they were even aware of its existence, although its activities had often been referred to in *Carpenter's Political Letters*,[215] while Doherty was slow to recognise the possibilities of this metropolitan development. His first public reference to it was not, in fact, until 28 May, when, as we have seen, he contrasted the apathy of the Manchester workmen with the 'zeal and determination' of the London operatives in what he considered to be the cause of 'National Association'.[216] But by this time the London organisation was set upon an exclusively political course.

After the Manchester delegate conference of 20–24 June had sanctioned the 'grand division' scheme in principle, Doherty began to pay more attention to events in the capital. The *Voice* for 25 June included a report of a meeting of the 'National Union of Working Classes, and Others' during the week, at which a Birmingham speaker stated that 'the *Voice of the People*, published at Manchester, was the result of union among the working classes; they subscribed their pence, started it, and now supported it by their mutual exertions'. This was greeted with loud applause and John Cleave averred that the paper 'had echoed the sentiments of this union, and congratulated the people of Lancashire on its formation'.[217] At the Manchester committee meeting on 28 June, Doherty expressed both his hopes for the future and disappointment at the past, with regard to the workmen of the metropolis:

> He deemed it important to know something of the principles of the association which had been established in London. He had watched their proceedings narrowly, which he found reported in that excellent paper, *The Ballot*; and he regretted to find, except one or two sidewind notices, they did not seem to know that such an association as this was in existence. He hoped the operatives in London did not intend to ride the high-horse, or carry all before them their own way, without consulting their fellow-workmen throughout the country. He did not make this observation from any ill-will, but merely because of the utter silence of the speakers at those meetings, who had never alluded to them; and he believed, indeed he had once had an occular [sic] proof of the fact, that some of the London trades considered themselves far superior to any of the country people, as they termed all out of London. No spirit of this sort, he hoped, would be per-

mitted to prevail either with the operatives of London or with them in Manchester. He could assure them, that any amendment or improvement that could be suggested, either by their friends in London, or elsewhere, he would most cheerfully adopt and give it all the support in his power. Their object was to raise and benefit the workman; he hoped all would labour earnestly and cordially for that great purpose.[218]

It was presumably in the hope of building a bridge between the two organisations that Doherty visited London at the end of July and spoke at the Rotunda to members of the National Union. He asserted that their only solution was in 'union', adding that 'the great work of shaking off our fetters is begun in London; and extensive arrangements are making in the north'.[219] But he was probably referring here to political reform, and in fact no publicity at all was accorded to this trip in the *Voice*, and it did little towards achieving wider union. In August, as we have seen, some assistance was given to the striking Lancashire calico-printers by John Cleave, while in return on 10 September the *Voice* advertised a collection of 28s in the newspaper office, including 10s from Doherty, on behalf of William Carpenter, the London radical, then in gaol for publishing his unstamped *Political Magazine*.[220] Doherty's main effort, however, came in response to 'The Address of the National Union of the Working-Classes', adopted at a meeting at the Rotunda on 31 August and aimed at 'our fellow workmen in Great Britain and Ireland . . . individually, or in each of your respective trade, benefit or co-operative societies'. This address detailed the manifold distresses of the operatives and recommended 'that a grand National Conference should be held on as early a day as may be deemed convenient, in order to devise the best means of obtaining the rights of the working classes, and securing them for the future'.[221]

In reply, Doherty immediately penned 'An Address from the Committee of the NAPL . . . to the Trades, Artisans, and other friends of the workmen's rights, happiness and independence, of London and its vicinity', which the committee adopted at their meeting on 7 September. He took the union, which the former address had advocated, to comprehend industrial as well as political terms of reference, and explained that the Manchester operatives 'have struggled long and arduously for the purpose of forming such a union', and regretted that hitherto 'the operatives of the metropolis, who from their local situation, their talents, numbers, and public spirit, were so well calculated to give an impulse to such an effort, should have so long remained inactive'. Hence their joy at perusing the address and hailing the accession of the London men to the cause was as great as their previous regret. Doherty went on to describe the vast power of the wealth producers if they could only unite, since they already maintained 'the nobility, the clergy, the merchants, manufacturers, shopkeepers, publicans, soldiers, the menials of all these, and the very dogs and horses of those who affect to depise us'. And this union could easily be formed, once the workmen realised the inefficiency of dividing their energies in partial associations, whether co-operative societies, sick clubs and benefit societies, oddfellows, foresters, political unions, and trade unions, and instead agreed 'to amalgamate the whole of these various societies into one grand and stupendous aggregate'. Doherty concluded by praying that they would forget past differences and jealousies, and lay the foundations at last of such a union, to obtain their rights, shield them from injustice, and secure the fruits of their industry.[222]

This address, recalling in its language Doherty's attempted alliance of political radicals and unionists in the summer, brought to an end the pre-liminary campaign of agitation, which was to precede the final adoption of the 'grand division' plan at another general delegate conference of the Association. It was highly questionable, however, how far the plethora of meetings, speeches and resolutions was reflected in increased practical sup-port for the Association. Moreover, they took place against a background of mounting dissension within the Manchester committee. The old complaints revived about the unfair financial burdens on Manchester and about arrears of subscriptions. From the branches, on the other hand, came grumbles about the continued closure of the funds, lack of support from the Association, and 'individuals' benefiting from it. Oates and Doherty also disagreed in regard to the Nottingham proposal for graduated subscriptions and benefits, the former arguing that it was necessary to boost the Association's finances and open the funds, in order to expand the Association, while Doherty clung to the uniform penny subscription, which even the poorest worker could afford and which would be sufficient if the union was made truly national by organising activity. He again stressed that the funds could not be opened if the districts did not send in their contributions. Ceaseless campaigning was necessary, but this would cost money. Numerous meetings were often necessary before a branch could be firmly established: even Manchester and Bolton had required repeated canvassing, while Leeds, Sheffield and other towns had been visited but not enrolled. Critics of expense had forced the Association to abandon attempts at expansion and to dismiss Hodgins,[223] with the result that, 'We are at present . . . confined in our exertions to a few towns in Nottingham, Lancashire and Derby. In all Yorkshire they had but one committee; we are but partially organised in four out of forty counties of England'. In regard to complaints about how the Association was run, Doherty pointed out that it was a democratic body—a 'little Republic'—in which every workman had a voice, through their delegates, and that the latter could dismiss the officers at a moment's notice if suspicions of improper conduct were well founded. As for the personal attacks on himself, Doherty observed that all through the ages, in all countries, reformers and patriots had been subjected to such calumny and accusations of self-interest. 'Even the Redeemer did not escape the revilings of those whom he came to save.' But this abuse would not deter him from his purpose. For it was the main aim of his life to destroy the system whereby those who produced all received least, and to see the workmen recognised as the equals of their so-called 'masters'.[224]

It was as a result of Doherty's persistence that the Manchester committee eventually agreed to send Oates on a 'missionary' tour in late August and early September.[225] Moreover, Doherty had even more ambitious plans for expanding the Association, producing a list of forty towns in England, four in Scotland, and four in Ireland, where he believed immediate visits would result in the formation of branches. He thought that for the next three or four months 'the whole force of the Association should be devoted to the extending of it in other places than those already enrolled'.[226] But the reality underlying this optimism was revealed by repeated complaints of the committee's neglect in organising the trades even in Manchester itself,[227] and, even more ominously, by the state of the finances, especially of the *Voice*, which necessitated yet another delegate conference, in Derby on 12 September.

An examination of the state of the Association at the time of this conference reveals decline rather than expansion. Total receipts of only £466 5s 2¼d were acknowledged in the six months since the Nottingham meeting in March, and even this sum included donations to a number of special appeals for different purposes that were launched in this period, adding to the confusion in the accounts.[228] Doherty's statement of the geographical limits of the Association also reflected realities, except for his unaccountable omission of Leicestershire, where the general union was still fairly strong. Lancashire still had the most districts, and contributed the majority of the cash, but its proportion of the whole was continuing to fall. The county had donated a total of £243 0s 3d during the period, followed by the three Midland counties, Leicestershire £126 15s 7d, Nottinghamshire £53 14s 2d, and Derbyshire £19 3s 10¼d. Yorkshire had contributed £11 and there were also smaller isolated contributions from places in Cumberland, Staffordshire and Cheshire. The range of trades contributing likewise remained about the same.

Apart from declining numbers and funds, the Association had further cause for concern in the condition of its literary offspring. After quickly amassing a circulation of 3,359, the *Voice* had, as we have seen, suffered a decline in both popularity and sales owing to Doherty's wrangling with Henry Hunt, while the number of advertisements declined drastically.[229] The special delegate conference convened in Manchester towards the end of June had spent much of its time investigating complaints against the conduct of the officers of the *Voice*, and the delegates declared unanimously that the calumnies heaped upon them had been undeserved 'and were the result of envy and jealousy, and not praiseworthy motives'. Nevertheless, this meeting did institute some alterations in the form of the paper. Volume II, which began on 2 July, was printed on folio-sized paper, with four pages in each edition. This arrangement, according to Doherty, would allow them to go to press with the latest news, 'a difficulty which we have laboured under from the start', and it would also enable them to include two extra columns of intelligence; it proved that they were determined to spare neither pains nor expense in rendering the *Voice* equal, if not superior, to any provincial paper. In addition, a new sub-heading was added to the title 'by an Association of Working Men', and Doherty's editorials were divided into political and industrial topics.[230] A further innovation was made in July, when the Association opened in Market Street the 'Operatives' General Printing Establishment', where, according to the advertisement inserted in future numbers of the *Voice*, every description of letterpress printing would be 'tastefully and expeditiously executed on the shortest notice', and a number of radical and educational works cheaply sold. In the same month, Doherty visited London in an effort to secure advertisements for the paper. And in August a reminder was sent out to the districts by Bullock that those members of the Association who had not paid their sixpences for the newspaper as originally

I

intended, were now desired to do so, which appeal realised the sum of £37 12s over the succeeding weeks.[231]

Despite all these measures, the paper continued to struggle financially, Doherty even having to contemplate stopping publication of a country edition; he had to deny rumours of the paper being insolvent, but admitted that, while they had property to the value of £900, their current debts amounted to £131, and even this did not take stamps into account.[232] Clearly some radical steps were now as necessary to save the *Voice* as were Doherty's 'grand division' and agitating plans to revitalise the Association.

The decline of the National Association did not pass unnoticed in other circles. Even the suspicious Melbourne could write on 26 September, in a letter explaining why none of the anti-union legislation, which the government were contemplating at the end of 1830, had been introduced, that, 'in the meantime these unions . . . in the north . . . began of themselves to slacken'.[233] But if the Association was previously in a state of slow degeneration, its sixth general delegate meeting within fifteen months, at the 'Pheasant Inn', Derby, on 12 September, hurled it into a condition of unmitigated crisis. After four days' deliberation, the delegates determined that the publication of the *Voice* should be transferred to London, as soon as a committee of the trades could be formed there and other necessary arrangements made. And it was also decided that in future the respective branch committees should be the agents for the sale of the paper to save expense. These intentions were announced in the *Voice* on 17 September, when the readers and agents were also warned that a suspension of publication for one or two weeks might be necessary to effect the transfer.[234] And on 24 September, in the last edition of the paper ever to appear, Doherty detailed the justification for the projected removal. Experience had shown that advertisements, by which alone a newspaper could make a profit because of the 'monstrous' taxes on the press, would not be sent to a workman's paper. Furthermore, its content needed to be general in character to attain a general circulation, but this was impossible with a provincial publication, which caused much of the news inserted from other districts to be out of date : London, by contrast, was the source of all news and the seat of Parliament. Finally, as the primary object in establishing the *Voice* had been to stimulate the workmen to form a general union, 'it is essential that such a paper should emanate from that place which will give it the greater facility for being read by the working classes *in all parts of the kingdom* . . . A paper established for such a purpose . . . instead of being confined to two or three thousand a week, should be, at least, fifty thousand.' Until the paper reappeared, Doherty added, important Association affairs would be publicised in the *Manchester and Salford Advertiser*, 'the only really honest and able paper now published . . . in any of the surrounding counties'.[235]

This statement was completely ignored by most of the local press, a reflection of the Association's declining significance, but Prentice, editor of the *Times and Gazette*, pointed out that his warnings of the previous November had now been fulfilled, especially in regard to the meagre number of advertisements sent in.[236] The *Voice*, as he had predicted, had finally failed, at a loss to the operatives, he calculated, of at least £1,500. To counterbalance this, they had not gained a farthing in additional wages from Doherty's fulminations against tyrants and oppressors, and his want of political knowledge had been well demonstrated by his oscillations over the Reform Bill.[237] On the other hand, James Whittle, editor of the *Manchester and Salford Advertiser*, paid a glowing tribute to Doherty's endeavours. 'The public know that we have never treated that paper with rivalry; and we say, with sincerity, that we have appreciated the ability and, better still, the perfect sincerity of purpose with which it has been conducted; and we regret that a necessity should have arisen for changing the scene of its publication; and that we hope it will soon reappear.' And while Doherty was perforce silenced, Whittle made a biting reply to Prentice's observations on his behalf, asserting that Prentice's own misfortune in the newspaper business gave him no right to proffer unsolicited advice on that score, and that his figures of losses on the *Voice* were exaggerated.[238]

For three weeks after the Derby conference, the Association was on the surface functioning normally. A new branch was even formed in early October at Lane End in the Potteries.[239] But that the situation was becoming increasingly desperate is suggested by Doherty's putting forward the idea of a general strike. It is not clear whether he originated it or whether he got it from William Benbow, who was urging such 'a grand national holiday' on the London trades about this same time.[240] Doherty's proposal was first mooted on 17 September, in comments on a prolonged dispute between the Yorkshire woollen weavers and Messrs Gott, but clearly had strong radical-political overtones. He suggested that the following plan would be simple but effectual, and would contrast their worth with that of their self-styled superiors :

> Let a day be fixed upon : let that day be well-known and fixed—say one month or six months hence; and when it arrives, *let every workman in the United Kingdom* REFUSE TO WORK ANOTHER STROKE *until his class are permitted to exercise their due share of influence in the affairs of their country, and the same justice is meeted [sic] out to them which has hitherto been dispensed to others.*

And on 19 September, when called upon to address a meeting of local handloom weavers convened to debate how they should try to bring up underpaying masters, he urged them to prepare to act upon his suggestion of refusing to work on a given day, till their grievances were redressed; and excited some laughter by depicting the consternation which such a determination would produce among those now considered their lords and masters.[241]

There is no evidence, however, that Doherty carried the idea any farther at this time.[242] This was no doubt because he soon became embroiled in serious disagreement with the Manchester committee, who were opposed to the new policy decided upon at Derby. As the executive of the Association, it was their duty to take immediate measures to effect the intended transfer to London. However, on 20 September, at their first meeting after the Derby conference, their first resolution was that the two officers, Oates and Doherty, should 'withdraw' while they discussed the matter further—a command which Doherty obeyed only after strong protest. The result of these discussions was a circular sent out to the different districts on 22 September, stating that the committee had agreed to suspend the paper after the next edition, but that they believed that, 'to remove the paper to, and carry it on in London, . . . would require above £1,000', and hence they had decided that a monthly magazine, published in Manchester, would be more eligible, 'and would, instead of losing, pay well'. They asked that the opinion of the other districts should be discovered through public meetings and sent to Manchester without delay. The occurrences at the committee meeting were largely covered over in the official *Voice* report, but Doherty did express his strong disagreement with the committee's estimate of the expenses of removal, which, he maintained, could be done 'for less than £20, perhaps for less than £10'.[243]

Realising that the Manchester committee were hoping to overturn the decision of conference, Doherty immediately wrote letters revealing that intention to Derby, the district which had introduced the resolution regarding the *Voice*, and also to Nottingham, which he denominated 'the head of that division', a terminology which implied that the 'grand division' plan was implemented, at least on paper, at the Derby conference. The response to those letters and to the committee's circular, according to Doherty, was favourable to the removal, and the Midlands division even threatened to send men to Manchester to effect it, if the committee did not do so. And on 28 September Doherty informed Bullock, the secretary, that he intended to resign the editorship at the end of the week unless steps to arrange the transfer were initiated, for the last number had appeared on 24 September and his post was now a sinecure and a drain on the Association's resources. In reply to this ultimatum, a few members of the committee met on Saturday, 1 October, and appointed Doherty to go to London. Since, however, he was previously engaged to attend a meeting at Bradford on 3 October, he travelled there first that day, being ordered also to collect the considerable amount of cash owing from a number of Yorkshire towns, including Halifax, Bradford, Leeds, Huddersfield, Dewsbury and Barnsley, and pay it to their paper-maker in London, to whom they in turn owed over £100. In the event, Doherty could only collect something under £20 and it was not until 7 October that he finally arrived in London.

Doherty found his task of interesting the London workmen in the Association and the newspaper made considerably more difficult by the sensational developments surrounding the Reform Bill, which was rejected by the Lords on the day after his arrival. He became closely involved in the radical reaction to this event and spoke bitterly at the Rotunda on 17 October.[244] But he also applied himself to the job in hand, consulting Bowring, Cobbett, Place, Carpenter and Carlile among others, in regard to the possibility of re-establishing the *Voice*, and procuring estimates from several printers of the costs of all different sizes of printing paper, which he laid before the committee on his return. In addition, he met Robert Owen and other leading co-operators, who, having recently made the *Voice* their official journal at their Birmingham delegate meeting,[245] expressed warm support for moving the paper to London—indeed, according to Doherty, it was on that condition that they recognised it as their organ. He also cleared up certain matters with the Stamp Commissioners.[246] Less successful, however, were his endeavours to induce the London trades to form a district committee. Such was the state of political excitement that the most he could do was to issue a circular, convening a meeting of delegates from each trade, co-operative and benefit society for 10 November, by which time he hoped that he would himself be in the capital permanently, bringing out the new *Voice*.[247]

Doherty returned to Manchester on 23 October and on the following day appeared before a meeting of the 'Board of Directors', comprising one from Bolton, one from Blackburn and two from Manchester, and a few other members of the Manchester committee. He gave a detailed account of his mission, handed in the estimates which he had obtained, and claimed total expenses of £13 10s 1d for his three weeks' employment, during which he had travelled nearly 500 miles. This statement was constantly interrupted and at the end of it one of the Manchester committee, Lang, angrily shook his fist in Doherty's face and brought forward a number of charges against him which the committee had prepared in his absence. Firstly, he had stated that the *Voice* could be removed for £10–£20, yet over £13 had already been expended and nothing achieved. Secondly, he had secretly corresponded with Nottingham, Birmingham and Derby on the subject against the wishes of the committee. Thirdly, his trip to London was longer, and his expenses greater, than his authority warranted. Fourthly, his expenses generally were more than those of any other officer. Fifth, he had lost the confidence of the committee and of the Manchester trades generally, and hence should not hold any office connected with them. Sixth, he had persuaded the committee to send him to London in July to canvass for advertisements, and had got none. Seventh, he had overturned decisions of the committee, notably in regard to the arrears of the Manchester sawyers when they wanted to rejoin. And eighth, he had brought back from London books worth £4–£5 for sale in the shop without their authority. From the same meeting also emanated an 'Address of the Board of Directors of the Manchester Committee' to the members, setting out their side of the case concerning the *Voice*. They stated that none of Doherty's estimates for the cost of producing a paper in London was considered low enough to induce them to recommend 'the hazardous experiment of a removal', particularly when compared with the costs of printing on their own press in Manchester. A publication, printed in Manchester and edited by Thomas Oates (whose relations with Doherty had been strained since their disagreement over the sliding scale of payments plan and who had strongly supported the committee on the newspaper issue) might attain a circulation of 3,000; and by reducing its size, employing fewer printers, cutting the editor's salary, and abolishing the post of canvasser, it could be sold for 6d and still make a weekly profit of £5 10s. Moreover, it would be supported by the co-operators, who had agreed to a proposition submitted by Oates at their late congress that the various societies should become shareholders in it, by subscribing £1 each. For these reasons the Directors had agreed to re-establish the *Voice* in Manchester as soon as possible. And they concluded by ascribing the paper's previous failure to Doherty's personal unpopularity, alleging that

> the circulation . . . for several months prior to its suspension, was almost unaccountably trifling in Manchester. *The Voice of the People* was spoken of, the term was scouted, and the paper was cried down as '*Doherty's Voice*'

> . . . Notwithstanding, the Manchester Committee continued their support
> and respect to Mr Doherty; and it was not until a crisis approached—until
> the torrent of public feeling became irresistible—that they expressed their
> conviction, that the Association could never prosper—that the *Voice* would
> not succeed, whether it remained in Manchester or was removed to London,
> or Constantinople, so long as Mr Doherty remained in connexion with it.

During his wrangle with the committee, Doherty was promised that a
written statement of the charges against him would be drawn up. When this
had not been sent after a week, he tendered his resignation, which was
accepted by the committee on 1 November; they offered him his salary for
the last week and hoped, somewhat optimistically, that 'no further angry
feelings or unnecessary explanation be entered into'. Doherty was in no
mood to fulfil that hope. He peremptorily refused the proffered wages, which
he had not earned and therefore regarded as a bribe, and spent the next week
preparing *A Letter to the Members of the N.A.P.L.*, which was later issued as
a 24-page pamphlet.[248] This described the committee's unconstitutional
refusal to implement the decision of the Derby conference, followed by his
own delegation to London preparatory to the transfer of the newspaper, and
then went on to answer in minute detail the charges brought against him.
Many of these, he alleged, reflected more seriously on the committee
than himself. If the paper had not been removed, it was because of their
obstinacy and incompetence; part of the money already expended had been
employed in collecting debts, on their own instructions. If he had stayed too
long in London, he had no inkling that it was against the committee's wishes,
for on 17 October he had received a letter from Bullock relating to the
negotiations with the Stamp Office, saying 'do not return until you have
gained all the necessary information relating to the paper'. If his claims for
expenses had ever been excessive, which he denied, they as the paymasters
had power to refuse them, yet had never done so. If he had secretly corresponded with several districts in the last week of September, it was because
they had excluded him from their meeting and hence prevented him from
publicising his suspicions—that they were trying to overturn the decision of
the Association—through the normal channel of communication, the *Voice*.
In regard to his London visit in July, he had actually brought back goods
worth £25 for sale in the shop and ten advertisements for the paper. It was
ridiculous for them to complain of his having brought back a quantity of
books from his recent trip, for they were always lamenting the shortage of
stock in the shop. And he had only once tried to alter a decision of the
committee, when they erroneously tried to extort arrears from the Manchester sawyers as a condition of re-admittance, forgetting the original law
adopted in 1829 that any trade had only to pay for thirteen successive weeks
to qualify for benefit. But the gravest charge was that he had lost the confidence of the Manchester workmen, and Doherty recognised that the Manchester trades were hostile to the removal, the committee having used his
three weeks' absence to prejudice minds against him, assisted by the slanders
of Archibald Prentice and the abuse of 'inveterate Huntites'. He had therefore
determined to resign 'rather than be, even by pretence, an obstacle in the
way of that union which it has been the great object of the best part of my
life to create and consolidate'.

Doherty's conclusions were that the accusations had been concocted by the committee, because it was essential to get rid of him in order to prevent removal of the paper. He pointed out the difficulties in which he had been placed, considering the characters with whom he had had to deal—some zealously urging him on, others petulantly pulling him back, and all watching him with jealousy and suspicion; considering the prejudices of the workmen and the slanders of the non-producing aristocracy and hostile employers; considering that he stood 'almost, if not entirely alone' in the course which he had taken; and considering that his name was coupled, though accidentally, with the villainous plunderer Hynes.

> Taking all these into account, and the time that I have been connected with the Association, from its humble origin in October 1829, to October 1831, through its varying fortunes, from the nature of the charges at the end of all this, may I not congratulate myself on coming out of the furnace—and God knows a warm one it has been—with so little loss to either my honour or reputation.

Doherty next turned from defence to a criticism of the conduct of the committee, which, he said, had been motivated simply by a desire to prevent loss of their own power, at whatever hazard to the Association itself. The 'Address of the Board of Directors' had ignored his lowest estimate of publication costs in London, while grossly underestimating the expenses in Manchester and forgetting that the *Voice* had already failed there. No newspaper costing 6*d* had ever succeeded, and they were unlikely to achieve sales of 3,000 considering the abilities of Oates, who had never been a workman himself, and could never have learned sufficient of their feelings during his nine months' apprenticeship to allow him to edit a workman's paper. They had also omitted to mention that the co-operators' support was conditional on the paper being transferred to London. Finally, how could the committee reconcile their assertions of the unpopularity of '*Doherty's Voice*' in Manchester and of a 'crisis' enforcing them to dispense with his services, with their deputing him to collect debts and go to London? Moreover, Doherty had been thanked for his conduct at every delegate meeting since the formation of the society, including the latest at Derby, and his accusers themselves had stated at the head of their 'Address' that they had 'the most gratifying proofs of the *esteem* in which, though silent, the *Voice* is still held. Everywhere (and NOWHERE, MORE THAN IN MANCHESTER) the cry resounds, "When will the Voice come out?"'

To conclude this long communication, Doherty recalled his continuous efforts to improve the condition of working men by directing their energies towards a common object. He believed that the ground-work, at least, of such a union had been laid, and that, although a number of untoward circumstances had retarded its progress, it would still succeed, given judicious management. He had withdrawn so as not to do anything to hold back that success, though he denied that his conduct warranted the forfeit of their confidence. He therefore asked the members to choose whether his policies or those of the Manchester committee were most likely to promote the general interests of the operatives, adding that, whatever their decision, it would never lessen his determination to expose and overcome injustice.

But Doherty's letter, in fact, did no more than confirm that the Association had suffered the last of the series of setbacks which had beset it during 1831, and this blow was ultimately crippling in view of the already weak state of the organisation. What were no more than the remnants anyway of the two major areas where the general union had taken root now completely split apart, the Midlands supporting Doherty's plan to remove the centre of operations and the newspaper to London, and Lancashire backing the Manchester committee's determination to keep both in their hands. The first casualty was Doherty's hope of establishing a committee in London. The Manchester committee were naturally uninterested in following up his original circular, hence they sent no representative to the meeting of delegates from the trade, co-operative and benefit societies of the capital, convened at the 'Rose and Crown' on 10 November to hear more about the Association. The delegates waited impatiently for over an hour, and then resolved, 'That this meeting do separate under great disappointment at not meeting Mr Doherty or some competent person to explain the objects of the circular, and that the Chairman be instructed to write to Mr Doherty for an explanation'. Two days later J. Canham wrote to Doherty as directed, adding that some of the delegates had travelled three or four miles, 'and of course were not very well pleased'.[249]

For the following weeks, both sections of the Association continued with their respective newspaper ventures. On 9 November Doherty attended a delegate conference of the Nottingham, Derby and Leicester 'division' at Leicester. According to his account, the Manchester committee refused his request to send a representative, although it appears that Oates did attend. The delegates issued an address urging the restoration of unity and detailing their future plans for the newspaper. It was hoped that all societies of working men, including co-operative, trade, benefit and sick societies, political unions, and, if they chose, the separate branches of friendly societies such as the Odd Fellows or Druids, would become shareholders; a central committee was to be appointed in London and the paper would not be started until at least a thousand societies had notified deposit of shares. It is clear from this that Doherty was still hopeful of an alliance of trade unionists, radicals and co-operators, but he now had no official position as a base to further that ambition and could make no progress. When he did begin a new publication at the start of 1832, entitled the *Workman's Expositor* and later the *Poor Man's Advocate*, it was printed on small-sized paper along the lines of the *Conciliator* and *Journal* rather than the *Voice*, and was published in Manchester and devoted almost entirely to exposing the evils of the factory system.[250] Nevertheless, on 14 January 1832, in reply to an enquiry from a Bolton correspondent respecting the re-appearance of the *Voice*, he did assert that, although it was 'utterly impossible that the paper can ever appear again as a Manchester paper', and 'certain people' had tried to prevent its removal to the metropolis, 'efforts are still being made to establish it as a London paper'. And he warmly supported the Leicester plan, through which, 'instead of starting as the *Voice* did, at first, with a weekly circulation of 2,000, and limited, from its locality to a particular quarter', it would, by being at the 'very source of political intelligence and the hot-bed of corruption', probably commence with a 10,000 circulation in London, from which it would be able to exercise an influence over the whole kingdom.[251] But by this time he seems to have lost contact even with the Midland unionists, and the only signs of activity were from that rump of the Association in the north still giving allegiance to the Manchester committee.

Shortly after the Leicester conference, a delegate meeting of the 'Northern Districts of the National Association' was held in Manchester on 21 November, thus clearly exhibiting the split which had occurred. These Manchester and other delegates expressed their opinion 'that to remove the *Voice* to, and establish it in London, is impracticable, because of the heavy expense which must necessarily be incurred; and further, because the removal of it would be in opposition to the views and wishes of our districts'. They also pronounced 'their firm determination to promote a National Union, however opposed by designing or disappointed individuals'. These statements provoked an angry retaliation from Doherty, who pointed out that a majority of the districts had supported the transfer at Derby, and in regard to the insinuation against himself, asked who had heard of Oates or Bullock, or any of them, 'until my individual exertions called them into existence? . . . Yet they dare insinuate, that I am the enemy of the union, and this Association in particular. Why, I should be a most unnatural monster to destroy my own production.'[252]

The plans of the Manchester committee for the newspaper made no more progress at first than Doherty's, and there were increasing signs of restlessness at the delay.[253] On 14 January, however, the committee at last succeeded in launching their own journal, which they entitled the *Union Pilot and Co-operative Intelligencer*. It was edited by Oates and comprised eight octavo pages, resembling in size and style Doherty's *Poor Man's Advocate*, although including, according to their publicity, only '*authentic* cases of oppression'.[254] It was initially priced 2*d*, but copies of the publication are only extant from 10 March, from which date the price was reduced to 1*d*. Since Wallis, the printer of the *Voice*, had resigned his situation at the meeting of northern branches on 21 November, the new paper was first issued from the Operatives' Establishment in Market Street, but after 18 February, from new premises, which the committee took at 88 Oldham Street. All communications were then invited to be sent to Bullock at this shop, where a variety of books and stationery was also on sale and jobbing printing carried out.[255] Unfortunately, the conductors spent much of their energy in vicious disputation with Doherty. A particularly bitter controversy developed, for example, from an article published by Doherty on 18 February, accusing Messrs Crompton & Ditchfield, of Prestolee New Mill, near Bolton, of grossly overworking their hands and exacting unjust fines from their spinners. A complete denial of these charges, written by the masters and counter-signed by twenty-eight of their men, was accepted for insertion in the *Union Pilot*. This outraged Doherty, who lamented on 24 March that press and types, which were purchased for the publication of the late *Voice*, a paper originally established for the defence of the workpeople, were now employed to vindicate the characters of such men. He would never sink to such sickening 'impartiality' between masters and men. Most of the employees associated with the

1*

declaration, he added on 7 April, were overlookers, themselves responsible for discipline in the factory, and the whole document was a joint effort of the *Guardian* editor and

> that curious compound of treachery, malignity, falsehood, vulgarity, and assurance, Mr T. Oates, who, having discovered that the working-classes will no longer support his insufferable vanity, and the puerile or malicious emantions of his puny and imbecile brain, is endeavouring to recommend himself to the workmen's oppressors by abusing and calumniating us . . . and acting as a fitting excrement and legitimate offspring of those charnel-houses of all that is honest, virtuous and independent—Irish Charter Schools.

In the *Union Pilot* Oates replied in kind, avowing on 31 March that Doherty's writing was 'best fitted to mingle with the elements of the dunghill heap', and that his public rejection of impartiality made him the 'advocate of injustice' rather than the 'poor man', and adding on 14 April that his implication regarding the authorship of the declaration was no more than a 'wilful lie' by a 'pitiable aspirant for notoriety'.[256]

Amid these arguments, the Manchester branch of the Association actually seems to have ceased to function for the first two months of 1832. But on 10 March 'an address to the Trades of Manchester' was published, signed by Bullock on behalf of the committee, announcing that a meeting of delegates from all the local trades would be held at their office in Oldham Street on 21 March, when a new plan of union would be submitted, to be called a 'General Social Compact for the Protection of Labour'.[257] In the event, thirty delegates representing fourteen trades attended the meeting, and the causes which had led the Association to decline almost to the point of extinction in Manchester were discussed at length. After a proposal that the union should attempt the equalisation of wages had been firmly dealt with, the delegates agreed that the committee's plan would restore confidence by guaranteeing the faithful execution of the union laws and the safe investment of funds, and a provisional committee was appointed to bring the 'new plan of Association' formally before the respective Manchester trades. Weekly discussions ensued 'on the merits of the National Association and Co-operation', preparatory to a further general delegate meeting of the Manchester trades on 18 April, which resolved *'to have an Association'* and that if insufficient trades came forward to entitle Manchester to the honour of being the headquarters, they would vote for the town where most zeal was shown and send the money there in future.[258] But the *Union Pilot* ceased to appear after its seventeenth number on 5 May, the 'new plan' of the Manchester committee was never explained in detail, and the National Association then finally disappeared from the town where it had been born amid such high hopes over two and a half years earlier.

Even this did not signal the final end of the Association. Connected with the attempt to revive the Manchester trades in March, Bullock also sent out letters to other towns and on 24 March the *Union Pilot* reported favourable responses from a new area, the north-east, where unspecified groups of workmen at both Newcastle-upon-Tyne and Barnard Castle had resolved to join the National Association. Although no further reports of progress reached Manchester from that quarter, save for a single letter from Barnard Castle on 28 March stating that they had sent delegates to Bishop Auckland, there

was continued optimism in Yorkshire. As we have seen, contributions from
that county had been virtually non-existent right up to the last acknowledgement of receipts on 11 September, but Doherty was invited to attend a
meeting at Bradford on 3 October. Thereafter, he was too heavily involved
with his visit to London and dispute with the committee to continue the
expansionist policy he had previously envisaged,[259] and apart from this one
visit, Cole has rightly shown that the Webbs erred in believing that Doherty
attempted to build up the Yorkshire branches while editing the *Poor Man's
Advocate*.[260] Nevertheless, developments continued in Yorkshire despite the
lack of active encouragement from Manchester. On 28 January Doherty
reported the receipt of a letter from Bradford, asserting that the Association
was prospering there, and predicted that it would doubtless succeed 'eventually everywhere'. An 'adjourned meeting' of the Bradford branch was held
in April, and John Tester, the old leader of the woolcombers during their
strike in 1825, later reported that the Association was 'all the rage' in that
city during this period.[261] Towards the end of March, Peter Bussey, the secretary of the Bradford district, attended a public meeting in Wakefield, which
established a branch association in that town, appointed a committee, and
chose a treasurer, president and secretary.[262] And on 7 April the *Union Pilot*
published part of a letter from Leeds, which stated that their district was
prospering, some mechanics having just joined, the linen weavers being
expected soon to do so, and several other trades having expressed their
interest. Such was the activity in Yorkshire that Oates referred to it on 24
March as a stimulus for the attempted revival of the Manchester trades at
that time, and on 5 May Bullock claimed that they were beginning to alarm
the manufacturers of the county with their power.[263]

After the Association had disappeared in Manchester, Doherty began again
to refer to these developments. On 2 June he thanked the Bury branch of the
Association for the donation of 10s towards his legal expenses over the
Gilpin affair,[264] and took the opportunity to maintain that he had never
for a moment forgotten the interests of that important society, but had
abstained from speaking of it 'because our advice and counsel, given eight
months ago, was insolently rejected, and ourselves grossly and scandalously
calumniated'. Nothing could be more base than the conduct of the late
managers of that institution towards him, but the management had now
passed into the hands of the spirited and intelligent operatives of Leeds, and
it shall have 'our zealous and unceasing support'. And two weeks later, in
an article congratulating the Glasgow operatives for showing their enthusiasm
for union by establishing the *Glasgow Trades' Advocate*, Doherty urged the
English workmen to follow their example. They were reminded that the
National Association, which was first commenced at Manchester, still
existed, and the management had passed to the spirited Yorkshire operatives,
where, he hoped, that factional spirit, which had destroyed the Association
in Manchester, would be avoided. Doherty understood that the Association
intended to revive the *Voice* as soon as possible. However, he advised those
discussing the question in Leeds that it would be impossible for them to succeed with the paper anywhere but in London, where it could hardly fail, and referred them to his arguments on that subject in his letter of November 1831.[265]

But, in fact, Doherty never kept to his stated intention of adverting again to this subject, and the Leeds Clothiers' Union, with its emphasis on secret ceremonies and oaths, developed along entirely separate lines from the National Association.[266] The latter, which had been a declining force from February 1831, and little more than a shadow after the last advertised list of receipts and closure of the newspaper in September 1831, was finally laid to rest after the middle of 1832. Nevertheless, the name survived a little longer yet, as an appellation for some of the trades' committees which persisted in various cities after the wider organisation was broken up. The last reference was not indeed until 1833, in a pamphlet written by Reuben Bullock, of Macclesfield, which stated that the workmen must act together on their own behalf to keep up wages, and added that 'the association for the protection of labour is on the same principle'.[267]

Why had the National Association failed? A contemporary critic, the author of the pamphlet, *On Combinations of Trades*, detailed several of the reasons as early as the summer of 1831, for by that time the extravagant anticipations of its founders, of a million members subscribing over £4,000 a week and raising £1 million within five years, had already been shown up by the published list of subscriptions up to March 1831. The writer pointed to 'inconsistency and miscalculation in the principles and objects of the National Association' as the cause of this disappointment. Their invitation to *all* workmen to join was directly opposed to the regulation limiting admission to organised trades only, and to that assigning 8s a week as the strike allowance; but if the Association had separated those earning above 12s per week from the vast multitude subsisting on less, the wide differences between the interests of low and high paid labour would have been manifest. Well-rewarded workers, like spinners and calico-printers, were opposed to any influx of unskilled labour into their trades, although such crafts were easily learnt. Yet the low-paid labourers had been invited to join, since both groups had certain common grievances and interests, and hence the emphasis upon every *political* subject in the speeches of the leaders and their newspapers. 'By this means, the cause of the highly-paid artisan becomes, in some degree, identified with that of his poorer brethren, but the union can only be temporary', unless there was greater equalisation of wages. In addition, the writer continued, the Association also had weaknesses as an insurance society against loss of wages. Some trades were more prone to wages reductions and strikes than others, yet all paid the same penny contributions; and, moreover, all received the same strike pay, whether they had contributed for four months or four years. Co-operation between trades at times of strikes had probably become more common since this General Trades' Union was organised, but it had existed even before the repeal of the Combination Laws. And it did not appear 'that since the formation of the National Association, there has been any opposition to the reduction of wages, which might not previously have been offered'. One reason for this had been 'the almost invariable refusal to apply the funds to the support of turn-outs, . . . which has also increased the schism amongst the members of the Association'. On the other hand, a large portion of the funds had been applied to start a newspaper, which, though it was ably written and widely read, had induced the districts to demand control of their funds and led to the complete secession of the Bolton branch. The author's prediction, therefore, for the future of the Association was pessimistic, but in the event accurate: 'the laying aside of this unwieldy piece of mechanism, is probably not very remote'.[268]

Hindsight permits a more comprehensive assessment of the Association by the labour historian. The total subscriptions in the fourteen months of advertised lists between July 1830 and September 1831 amounted to £3,066 10s 1¼d.[269] Over two-thirds of this total came from Lancashire, with a much smaller contribution from neighbouring Cheshire. There had been a gradually growing response from the three Midland counties, Nottinghamshire, Leicestershire and Derbyshire, but only very small contributions from Yorkshire, Cumberland and Staffordshire. The Association was clearly never 'National'. Moreover, its membership was predominantly among textile workers: weavers (mainly hand-loom, but also power-loom), mule spinners, calico-printers, etc. in the north-west, and framework knitters, lacemakers, etc. in the Midlands, though there were also contributions from textile machine-makers, hatters, building trade workers, and a medley of other skilled craftsmen.

The receipts show that the claims for a membership of 100,000 were greatly inflated. The number of paying members probably never reached more than half that figure, possibly less, even at the peak in October 1830, and it declined rapidly thereafter. It is also clear that the most highly skilled and paid workers, like the letterpress-printers and engineers, held almost entirely aloof from the general union movement, preferring to rely on the strength of their sectional organisations; though a few textile machine-making trades did contribute, the number of skilled workers outside textiles who were attracted in was relatively small. As we have previously noted, the most enthusiastic support came from groups like the flannel-weavers, framework knitters and hand-block printers, whose condition was declining because of mechanisation and an overstocked labour market, and who supported schemes of general union since their own organisations were so weak, especially in times of their most desperate distress such as 1826 and 1829–31.[270] The Association did, however, also recruit some of the new skilled and semi-skilled workers in cotton factories. Although these tended to be most active during booms, when full employment and industrial prosperity provided favourable conditions for trade-union pressure, their industry suffered keenly from fluctuations in trade and hence they were sometimes called upon to fight defensive actions in slumps.[271] The regular failures of these strikes caused the cotton spinners in 1829–30 (as previously, to a lesser extent, in 1818 and 1826) to turn to the idea of general trades' union, as a means of organising more widespread financial support. It was out of the Manchester cotton spinners' failure in 1829 that there emerged not only the Grand General Union but also the National Association, and, as Turner has previously observed, the spinners were mainly instrumental in establishing the latter, with a constitution based on that of the spinners' general union, with the same penny weekly subscription and half-yearly delegate meetings.[272] Moreover, the extent of the spinners' support was even greater than is suggested by their recorded subscriptions, for it must be remembered that they were a comparatively small body of skilled workers, but only paid the same penny subscription as the much more numerous lower-paid workers.

On the other hand, it is clear that their support proved fairly short-lived : strike failures, especially the disastrous Ashton–Stalybridge defeat, rapidly destroyed their hopes from the Association and they virtually ceased to subscribe thereafter. Turner is therefore mistaken in stating that the Association remained 'largely under their dominance'.[273] In fact, the Manchester spinners, dispirited after the 1829 strike failure, never appear to have been enthusiastic supporters. The prominence of Doherty, Foster and Hodgins in the Association tends to create a misleading impression of enthusiasm for the general union idea among the local spinners, whereas Doherty repeatedly had to condemn or make embarrassed apologies for their persistent lukewarmness.[274] By early 1831 the Manchester spinners' society was very weak and had ceased to subscribe to the Association; altogether they contributed only £25 11s 4d.

The Association was thus the product of a temporary coincidence of interest among the declining handicraft trades and the new factory workers during the 1829–31 trade depression, in fighting against wages reductions. The more strongly organised and relatively well-off skilled workers, both handicraft and factory operatives, were, as we have just mentioned, generally most active in boom years, but for this brief period some of them, notably the cotton spinners, were enticed by Doherty, albeit somewhat reluctantly, into his scheme of general union. The events of 1829–31, however, convinced them of the futility of such schemes and hence they remained, for the most part, aloof from similar attempts in future, such as Owen's Grand National Consolidated Trades' Union in 1834 and the National Association of United Trades in 1845. The depressed handicraft trades, on the other hand, continued vainly to seek salvation in such schemes or in political radicalism and Chartism.[275]

The original aims of the Association were never actually put into practice. The Manchester Provisional Trades' Committee remained the executive throughout, while the intended supreme head of a general delegate meeting every six months was replaced by a series of crisis conferences assembled at much shorter intervals. More seriously, the funds were *never* used for their principal purpose of protecting constituent trades, a number of separate and additional appeals being launched instead. Apart from the administrative costs of running the Association, the only expenditure to which the funds were put was to purchase the equipment for the *Voice of the People* and finance the continued publication of that paper. And yet, after the twin catastrophes of the Ashton failure and the flight of Hynes in the second month of its existence, that paper was the organ of a declining institution, for all the eloquence and ability which Doherty displayed in his editorship. Between July 1830, and February 1831, the Association seemed to have great potential strength, even seriously to concern the government. But during that period it was only being carefully nurtured, and after the decision to decentralise control of the funds in March 1831, it rapidly declined as a unified organisation. It was only during this last period that Doherty attempted to institutionalise an alliance with political radicalism, that he was converted to support of co-operation, and that he contemplated the desperate expedient of a general strike. But none of these schemes could arrest the decline. And when he tried to broaden the Association and move the centre of operations to London, he found in the Manchester trades that same spirit of sectional provincialism which had weakened the spinners'

Grand General Union, and the Association in its turn faded away, though not without much noise and angry disputation.

But the Association was in some respects a glorious failure. It was far more than a mere precursor of the G.N.C.T.U., for it lasted longer, had a greater number of paying members, and was considerably less dominated by Manchester than was the latter organisation by London. It also introduced the principle of a federation of trade unions with a general meeting of delegates as the supreme head, which was later copied by the builders' union with its grand lodge, and through them the G.N.C.T.U. with its delegate conference.[276] Moreover, while trades like the cotton spinners and the iron-moulders[277] mostly held aloof from the G.N.C.T.U. because of their previous disappointment, the Association did leave behind several strongly organised trades like the potters, and traditions of inter-union co-operation in several towns, like Derby, which the G.N.C.T.U. was later able to exploit. And Doherty's ground-work in improving relations between unionists and co-operators also prepared the way for later developments in the builders' union and the Grand National. Finally, the National Association was important for its part in channelling workmen away from the ineffectual riots and machine-breaking, which was their past, towards united and non-violent action, which was their future. Its failure should be seen against the background of trade depression and heavy unemployment, which lasted throughout its existence; the price of bread was also high, and these were years of almost revolutionary political agitation;[278] and yet over the districts where the Association held sway, there were no disturbances to match those of the preceding slump in 1826, nor those in the agricultural areas and in South Wales during 1830 and 1831.

And what of Doherty's role in the National Association? Its successes and failures should be seen as his also, for his energy and drive had largely called it into existence in October 1829 and his determination and persistence were responsible for keeping it in being. On the other hand, his exaggerated statements of the Association's aims, membership and strength contributed to the disappointment and collapse when the realities of weak organisation, inadequate funds and strike failures became apparent. And whilst his personal dynamism initially created enthusiasm, some of his other characteristics contributed to its disintegration : his personal unpopularity was a major factor in the wounding Bolton secession, his intolerance of opposition as epitomised by his disregard of the rule prohibiting political discussion was another source of division, and his impatient treatment of colleagues left him short of friends when the Manchester committee finally broke free of his influence in September 1831. He would never recognise the separate interests of low and highly-paid workers, and hence consistently opposed any idea of introducing a sliding scale of payments and benefits; but the need of the worst-paid operatives for *advances* forced Doherty into a position of supporting such strikes despite the original intentions. His dream of including all workmen in a single, unified structure was shattered by strike defeats and Hynes' treachery on the one hand, and by local insistence on each district controlling its own funds on the other. Nevertheless, his resignation from the post of editor of the non-existent *Voice* on 1 November did not end his contribution to the trade-union movement, nor even his connection with the cherished idea of a general union of all workmen.

*Total contributions to the National Association, 31 July 1830 to 10 September 1831, by location*

### Lancashire

| | £ | s | d |
|---|---|---|---|
| Accrington | 27 | 14 | 0 |
| Ashton-under-Lyne | 180 | 16 | 11½ |
| Aspinall Smithy | 14 | 0 | 0 |
| Aspull | 1 | 8 | 0 |
| Blackburn | 196 | 10 | 0 |
| Blackrod | 30 | 7 | 10 |
| Bolton | 70 | 0 | 0 |
| Bury | 195 | 8 | 11 |
| Catterall | 7 | 0 | 0 |
| Chorley | 81 | 10 | 6 |
| Clitheroe | 70 | 12 | 2 |
| Denton | 4 | 2 | 9 |
| Droylsden | 1 | 3 | 0 |
| Edenfield | 7 | 6 | 2 |
| Garstang | 1 | 0 | 0 |
| Gorton | | 12 | 0 |
| Haslingden | 11 | 15 | 0 |
| Henfield | 1 | 0 | 0 |
| Hollinwood | 1 | 10 | 0 |
| Horwich | 53 | 19 | 9 |
| Irwell | 22 | 12 | 6 |
| Lees | 31 | 0 | 2 |
| Liverpool | | 13 | 6 |
| Manchester | 327 | 5 | 8 |
| Middleton | 10 | 13 | 9 |
| Mossley | 15 | 15 | 10 |
| Newton-le-Willows | 1 | 0 | 0 |
| Oldham | 67 | 8 | 6 |
| Preston | 40 | 5 | 11 |
| Radcliffe | 2 | 17 | 6 |
| Ramsbottom | 19 | 16 | 0 |
| Ribblesdale | 27 | 0 | 7 |
| Rochdale | 703 | 3 | 2 |
| Rossendale | 67 | 13 | 6½ |
| Standish | 1 | 0 | 0 |
| Stubbins | 1 | 0 | 0 |
| Wigan | 3 | 1 | 9 |
| Total | 2,300 | 6 | 3 |

### Nottinghamshire

| | £ | s | d |
|---|---|---|---|
| Arnold | 1 | 0 | 0 |
| Bulwell | 1 | 0 | 0 |
| Kirkby-in-Ashfield | 1 | 5 | 0 |
| Mansfield | 28 | 18 | 0 |
| Nottingham | 228 | 10 | 10 |
| Old Basford | 6 | 4 | 2 |
| Sutton-in-Ashfield | 23 | 4 | 8 |
| Total | 290 | 2 | 8 |

### Cheshire

| | £ | s | d |
|---|---|---|---|
| Bollington | 2 | 18 | 5 |
| Hyde | 1 | 0 | 0 |
| Macclesfield | 22 | 16 | 8 |
| Stalybridge | 67 | 15 | 2 |
| Stockport | 9 | 0 | 0 |
| Total | 103 | 10 | 3 |

### Derbyshire

| | £ | s | d |
|---|---|---|---|
| Belper | 2 | 6 | 8 |
| Derby | 105 | 0 | 7¼ |
| 'Derbyshire' | 7 | 10 | 0 |
| Total | 114 | 17 | 3¼ |

### Leicestershire

| | £ | s | d |
|---|---|---|---|
| Leicester | 119 | 2 | 0 |
| Loughborough | 71 | 18 | 0 |
| Shepshed | 6 | 17 | 7 |
| Total | 197 | 17 | 7 |

### Cumberland

| | £ | s | d |
|---|---|---|---|
| Carlisle | 12 | 3 | 4 |
| Total | 12 | 3 | 4 |

### Yorkshire

| | £ | s | d |
|---|---|---|---|
| Bradford | 3 | 0 | 0 |
| Dewsbury | 1 | 0 | 0 |
| Knaresborough | 1 | 0 | 0 |
| Sheffield | 1 | 0 | 0 |
| Shipley | 8 | 12 | 9 |
| Total | 14 | 12 | 9 |

### Staffordshire

| | £ | s | d |
|---|---|---|---|
| 'Potteries' | 1 | 0 | 0 |
| Shelton | 8 | 0 | 0 |
| 'Turners' union' | 1 | 10 | 0 |
| Total | 10 | 10 | 0 |

| | £ | s | d |
|---|---|---|---|
| Total where location specified | £3,044 | 0s | 1½d |
| Total contributions | £3,066 | 10s | 1½d |

*Total contributions to the National Association, 31 July 1830 to 10 September 1831, by trade*

|  | £ | s | d |
|---|---|---|---|
| 1 *Textile trades* | | | |
| (a) Cotton and other textile workers, mainly in the north-west: | | | |
| Calico printers | 252 | 6 | 6 |
| Mule spinners | 251 | 10 | 5 |
| Power loom weavers | 80 | 1 | 11 |
| Cotton and silk dyers | 69 | 1 | 5 |
| Card grinders and strippers | 31 | 0 | 7 |
| Cotton yarn dressers | 28 | 11 | 2 |
| Crofters (bleachers, etc.) | 18 | 7 | 9 |
| Silk twisters | 15 | 11 | 4 |
| Wool combers | 8 | 15 | 4 |
| Sizers | 6 | 5 | 0 |
| Stretchers | 4 | 1 | 11 |
| Flax dressers | 1 | 13 | 9 |
| Jenny spinners | 1 | 0 | 0 |
| Hand loom weavers: | | | |
| Flannel | 171 | 0 | 0 |
| Cotton, worsted and smallware | 44 | 10 | 11 |
| Broad silk | 21 | 16 | 8 |
| Nankeen | 11 | 11 | 6 |
| Woollen | 10 | 15 | 0 |
| Silk smallware | 3 | 1 | 8 |
| Blanket | 1 | 0 | 0 |
| Fustian | 1 | 0 | 0 |
| Linen | 1 | 0 | 0 |
| Total | 1,034 | 2 | 10 |
| (b) Framework knitters, mainly in the Midlands hosiery trades, etc. | 350 | 12 | 6¼ |
| 2 *Textile machine-making*, including spindle and fly makers, mechanics and machine hands, bobbin and carriage makers, engineers, frame smiths and needle makers | 67 | 6 | 7 |
| 3 *Hatters* | 60 | 14 | 3 |
| 4 *Building trades*, including sawyers, joiners, carpenters and plasterers | 36 | 17 | 11 |
| 5 *Miscellaneous skilled trades*, including iron moulders, smiths, shoemakers, tallow chandlers, tobacco pipe makers, basket makers, farriers, miners, paper makers, fender makers, sinker makers, lock makers, engravers, potters and cabinet makers | 114 | 10 | 1 |
| 6 *Unskilled trades*, including quarrymen and labourers | 12 | 19 | 7 |
| Total where trade specified | 1,677 | 3 | 9¼ |
| Total contributions | 3,066 | 10 | 1¼ |

NOTES TO CHAPTER SEVEN

<sup>1</sup> It was, however, dated 1 January 1831.

<sup>2</sup> *Guardian*, 12 March 1831. Turner, a cotton-yarn dresser, we have previously noticed as very active among the Manchester leaders of the Association; Pigot was secretary of the block-printers' union.

<sup>3</sup> See above, p. 204, n. 208. For the reports, see *Carpenter's Political Letters*, 31 December 1831.

<sup>4</sup> *Voice*, 1 January–12 February 1831. There may have been some subscriptions before the end of 1830. For the renewal of this special appeal, see below, pp. 247–8.

<sup>5</sup> See above, p. 193.

<sup>6</sup> *Guardian*, 12 February 1831, *inter alia*.

<sup>7</sup> *Voice*, 26 March and 9 April 1831. The mistaken belief of S. and B. Webb, *op. cit.*, p. 123, repeated by Butler, *op. cit.*, p. 170, and by Cole, *A Short History of the British Working-Class Movement*, p. 72, that the *circulation* surpassed 30,000 has been shown by Cole, *Attempts at General Union*, p. 39, to be based on a misunderstanding of this estimate of *readership*.

<sup>8</sup> *Voice*, 5 February 1831, for example.

<sup>9</sup> See below, pp. 237 and 424–6.

<sup>10</sup> See below, pp. 430–1.

<sup>11</sup> *Voice*, 8–22 January, 5 March 1831; F. Place, *Letter to a Minister of State on Taxes on Knowledge* (1831), quoted in Webb Collection, Vol. I, f. 202. As early as the second number, Doherty was rejoicing that 'nothing can exceed the interest excited by the publication of our paper. From every quarter of the kingdom, we are daily receiving orders and assurances of support, and one common feeling in its favour seems to pervade all classes.'

<sup>12</sup> S. and B. Webb, *op. cit.*, pp. 117, n. 2, and 122.

<sup>13</sup> *Voice*, 1 January 1831.

<sup>14</sup> See below, pp. 422 *et seq.*

<sup>15</sup> *Voice*, 15 January 1831.

<sup>16</sup> Turner, *op. cit.*, p. 84.

<sup>17</sup> *Guardian*, 15 January 1831.

<sup>18</sup> *Voice*, 8 January 1831.

<sup>19</sup> See above, p. 127.

<sup>20</sup> Nottingham subscribed over £51, while Manchester's contribution was only about £6.

<sup>21</sup> *Voice*, 8 January–11 March 1831.

<sup>22</sup> See above, p. 40.

<sup>23</sup> M. Tylecote, *The Mechanics' Institutes of Lancashire and Yorkshire before 1851* (Manchester, 1951), p. 32. It should be remembered, however, that both these disputes lasted far longer, and that the Ashton receipts do not include sums collected at, or sent direct to, that town and therefore not advertised in the *Voice*.

<sup>24</sup> See above, pp. 134–5.

<sup>25</sup> *Voice*, 29 January and 5 February 1831.

<sup>26</sup> See above, p. 138.

<sup>27</sup> See above, p. 137.

<sup>28</sup> According to the note at the foot of each page, John Hampson continued to be both printer and publisher until April, but clearly this was not quite accurate.

<sup>29</sup> *Voice*, 19 February 1831. Most of these details, however, were not made public until his later trial.

<sup>30</sup> The statement of Cole, *Attempts at General Union*, p. 30, that Hynes absconded with only £100 is doubtless based on Hynes' rhetorical question to his wife. For the true amount, see *Stockport Advertiser*, 29 April 1831.

<sup>31</sup> *Voice*, 19 February, *Times and Gazette*, 19 February 1831.

<sup>32</sup> *Stockport Advertiser*, 21 January and 18 February 1831.

<sup>33</sup> *Guardian*, 12 February 1831.

<sup>34</sup> *Ibid.*, 19 February; *Times and Gazette*, 19 February 1831.

<sup>35</sup> *Voice*, 26 February 1831. In a postscript the address warned members against Archibald Prentice's threatened exposure in the *Times and Gazette*; his real motive was fear of the *Voice*, which had halved the circulation of his newspaper.

36 *Ibid.*, and 5 March 1831. It has already been shown, however, that the money stolen was far more likely to have originated in ordinary subscriptions rather than the special Ashton donations.

37 *Stockport Advertiser*, 25 February and 4 March 1831.

38 See above, pp. 132–3.

39 *Guardian*, 26 February 1831.

40 *Times and Gazette*, 26 February 1831.

41 *Voice*, 5 March 1831.

42 *Times and Gazette*, 12 March; *Stockport Advertiser*, 11 March 1831.

43 *Guardian*, 12 March 1831.

44 *Advertiser*, 19 March 1831, which described the letter as 'a curious specimen of cool impudence and arrogance'.

45 *Guardian*, 12 March 1831, Hynes was, however, eventually convicted for robbing the Association.

46 *Chronicle*, 19 March; *Times and Gazette*, 19 March 1831.

47 Salford Quarter Sessions, Indictment Rolls, April 1831. The *Guardian*, 16 April 1831, erroneously calculated the total theft at £26 6s.

48 *Guardian*, 16 April; *Voice*, 16 April 1831.

49 *Chronicle*, 23 April 1831, *inter alia*.

50 *Voice*, 30 April 1831. The declaration by the officers which Doherty recommended was eventually carried out in August. See below, p. 222.

51 *Advertiser*, 23 April 1831.

52 See below, pp. 223–4.

53 See above, p. 194.

54 See above, pp. 172–4.

55 *Voice*, January 1831.

56 See above, pp. 173–4.

57 *Voice*, 12 February 1831.

58 See A. Briggs, 'The Background of the Parliamentary Reform Movement in Three English Cities', *Cambridge Hist. Journ.*, Vol. x (1952), and 'The Local Background of Chartism', in *Chartist Studies* (1959); and A. Fox, 'Industrial Relations in Nineteenth Century Birmingham', in *Oxford Econ. Papers*, N.S., Vol. 7 (1955).

59 For this organisation, see R. W. Postgate, *The Builders' History* (1923).

60 *Stockport Advertiser*, 25 February 1831, quoting the *Wolverhampton Chronicle*.

61 *Voice*, 26 March; *Times and Gazette*, 2 April 1831.

62 See above, p. 141.

63 *Voice*, 27 August 1831. See below, p. 246.

64 *Ibid.*, 8 and 15 January 1831. See below, p. 230.

65 *Ibid.*, 22 January 1831. For the report of a branch first being formed there, see above, p. 164.

66 *Ibid.*, 19 February and 2 April 1831.

67 *Guardian*, 12 February; *Voice*, 5 March 1831.

68 See below, p. 239.

69 *Guardian*, 19 February 1831.

70 See below, pp. 225–8.

71 *Voice*, 19 February and 30 April 1831.

72 *Ibid.*, 28 May 1831.

73 *Ibid.*, 5 March 1831.

74 See below, p. 249.

75 *Voice*, 8–22 January, 12 February 1831.

76 For W. R. Greg's pamphlet in that year, however, which was sympathetic towards factory reform, see below, p. 364.

77 *Voice*, 15 January–5 February 1831.

78 *Ibid.*, 12 February 1831.

79 See below, p. 221.

80 *Voice*, 8 January–12 March 1831. The last of these papers is missing from the British Museum file, but there is a cutting of the advertised list of subscriptions in Place Collection, Vol. 51, f. 7. The two groups of workers were the Ashton

spinners (£595 11s 1¼d) and Sunnyside Calico Printers (£24 13s 6¼d, on 5 and 12 March).

81 Indeed, the toehold in Cumberland, at Carlisle, had apparently been lost.

82 And Manchester had now considerably improved its performance, with total contributions of over £75.

83 This figure should be compared with that of £1,866 12s 3d for the same period, erroneously copied by Cole, *Attempts at General Union*, p. 30 and Appendix 4, pp. 176–86, from *On Combinations of Trades*, pp. 83–94. See above, p. 205, n. 233.

84 See above, pp. 184–6.

85 *Guardian*, 12 March 1831. See below, pp. 223–4.

86 See below, pp. 225–30.

87 But not, as Cole, *Attempts at General Union*, p. 34, mistakenly suggests, a last attempt to save the Ashon spinners from defeat.

88 No report of this conference has survived, since the *Voice* for 19 March is missing; these resolutions are referred to in the *Voice*, 26 March and 30 April, and *Times and Gazette*, 2 April 1831.

89 See above, p. 215.

90 Bullock (see above, p. 216) took over from Cheetham in July.

91 *Voice*, 5 March and 20 August 1831. The Hynes affair continued to have repercussions, e.g. there was a row when Cheetham refused to hand over to the Ashton spinners the money confiscated from Hynes (see above, pp. 138 and 209), and again when it was discovered that a number of missing cheques were held by Hynes, and the Association had to bargain with his wife to recover them (*Voice*, 21 May 1831).

92 *Voice*, 14 May and 18 July 1831.

93 *Ibid.*, 14 May 1831.

94 See below, pp. 223–4.

95 *Voice*, 26 March–10 September 1831. But special appeals for strikers are not included. See below, p. 230.

96 *Times and Gazette*, 2 April; *Voice*, 30 April 1831.

97 *Voice*, 30 April, 21 May and 20 August 1831.

98 See below, pp. 241 and 247–8.

99 *Voice*, 27 August 1831.

100 *Bolton Chronicle*, 12 March 1831. See above, p. 221.

101 *Ibid.*, 26 March; *Times and Gazette*, 2 April; *Voice*, 26 March, 2 and 9 April 1831. The controversy continued thereafter: see, for example, Frazer's letter in the *Bolton Chronicle*, 23 April 1831.

102 *Times and Gazette*, 21 May; *Voice*, 28 May 1831.

103 *Chronicle*, 11 and 18 June 1831.

104 *Voice*, 25 June, 23 July and 27 August 1831.

105 *Mercury*, 21 December 1831; *Voice*, 1 and 22 January, 26 February and 5 March; *Chronicle*, 5 March 1831. The masters alleged that the earnings of their hand-block and machine printers had averaged 27s and 31s per week respectively over the past year, but the block-printers' union estimated average weekly earnings of block printers in Lancashire as only 10s. The firm's actions were directed particularly against the block-printers, who were, of course, most vulnerable.

106 *Voice*, 5 March–30 July 1831. The figure may possibly be an over-estimate, due to double-counting.

107 *Ibid.*, 5 and 26 March, 2, 16 and 30 April 1831.

108 *Chronicle*, 30 April and 16 July 1831.

109 *Voice*, 14 May 1831.

110 *Chronicle*, 9 and 30 July; *Times and Gazette*, 6 August; *Voice*, 13 August and 3 September; *Guardian*, 13 August 1831.

111 *Voice*, 25 June, 23 July, 13 and 20 August, and 3 September 1831.

112 *Ibid.*, 30 July and 6 August 1831.

113 *Ibid.*, 2 July, 13 and 20 August, 3 September 1831.

114 See below, pp. 233–4 and 236.

115 A. E. Musson, 'The Ideology of Early Co-operation in Lancashire and

Cheshire', *T.L.C.A.S.*, Vol. LXVIII (1958-9), reprinted in *Trade Union and Social History* (1974). For more details, see below, p. 330.

116 *Times and Gazette*, 16 July; *Voice*, 6 and 27 August 1831.

117 *Chronicle* and *Voice*, 17 September 1831.

118 *Voice*, 26 March and 2 April 1831.

119 *Ibid.*, 26 March 1831.

120 See above, p. 223.

121 *Voice*, 2, 9 and 16 April 1831.

122 *Ibid.*, and 30 April 1831.

123 *Ibid.*, 23 April 1831.

124 *Ibid.*, 14 and 21 May 1831. Thomas Matthews expressed similar hopes of financial support in a letter to the *Nottingham Review*, 13 May 1831, referring apparently to a Nottingham proposal for a graduated scale of contributions and strike payments, according to wages, by which it was hoped that the Association funds might soon be opened. See below, p. 246.

125 See below, p. 457.

126 *Voice* and *Guardian*, 21 May 1831.

127 *Voice*, 21 and 28 May; *Times and Gazette*, 28 May 1831.

128 *Voice*, June–July 1831. See below, p. 242.

129 See above, p. 217.

130 *Voice*, April 1831.

131 *Ibid.*, 14 and 28 May, 25 June, and 2 July 1831. For Doherty's proposal for a committee of enquiry, see below, pp. 238–9.

132 S. and B. Webb, *op. cit.*, p. 123; Cole, *Attempts at General Union*, pp. 34–5; Morris, *op. cit.*, p. 55.

133 See above, p. 181.

134 *Voice*, 30 April 1831.

135 The Blackrod miners contributed £2 7s in June (*ibid.*, 18 June 1831).

136 *Ibid.*, 14 May; *Guardian*, 18 June 1831.

137 *Voice*, 11 and 18 June 1831. See also G. D. H. Cole, *Chartist Portraits* (1965 ed.), pp. 152–3.

138 *Voice*, 18 June; *Guardian*, 16 July and 27 August 1831.

139 *Bolton Chronicle*, 3 September; *Guardian*, 10 September 1831.

140 Recruitment of miners into the Association has been greatly exaggerated by S. and B. Webb, *op. cit.*, p. 123, Challinor, *op. cit.*, pp. 26–8, and J. E. Williams, *The Derbshire Miners* (1962), p. 88.

141 See above, p. 198. The name was spelt 'Shepley'.

142 *Carpenter's Political Letters*, 11 November 1830.

143 *Chronicle*, 11 December 1830. See above, p. 194.

144 *Guardian*, 28 May 1831, quoting the *Sheffield Iris*. S. Pollard, *A History of Labour in Sheffield* (Liverpool, 1959), refers to the existence of a 'Trades' General Union' in Sheffield in 1830–1, but its policy was to promote co-operation between masters and men.

145 See above, p. 209.

146 *Voice*, 26 March, 16 and 23 April, 23 July and 21 May 1831.

147 *Ibid.*, 27 August 1831.

148 Cole, *Attempts at General Union*, p. 42.

149 *Voice*, 25 June 1831.

150 *Ibid.*, 9 April and 30 July 1831.

151 *Ibid.*, 2 April 1831.

152 *Ibid.*, 19 April 1831. See below, pp. 240–1.

153 *Ibid.*, 26 March 1831.

154 A notable inclusion at a time when trade unions were composed predominantly of skilled industrial workers.

155 *Voice*, 4 and 11 June 1831.

156 Doherty's change in policy was probably not only the result of the Association's decline, but also a reflection of the general expansion of working-class aims and organisation in this period, which saw the first co-operative congress at Manchester in May and the reawakening of political radicalism.

157 See above, pp. 177–8.

[158] *Voice*, 9 and 16 April 1831.

[159] This was the sum of the Association's connection with the short-time movement. The assertion of S. and B. Webb, *op. cit.*, p. 123, that promotion of the short-time bill was the *only* activity of the Manchester committee at this time is based on a misunderstanding of Doherty's evidence in 1838 to the Select Committee on Combinations. See *Parl. Papers*, 1837–8, VIII, 3455, referring to the *spinners'* union.

[160] *Voice*, 23 April and 21 May 1831. See above, pp. 144–5 and 177.

[161] For Ireland, see above, p. 218; for the Metropolitan Trades' Union, see below, pp. 243–4.

[162] *Voice*, 28 May 1831.

[163] *Ibid.*, 25 June 1831.

[164] *Guardian*, 25 June 1831.

[165] The Ashton strike was against a wages *reduction*, not for a rise, and the Association had not been established until *after* the 1829 Manchester strike.

[166] *Chronicle*, 25 June and 2 July 1831.

[167] *Voice*, 9 July 1831.

[168] For more detailed consideration of Doherty's political views and activites, see below, Ch. IX.

[169] See above, p. 221.

[170] *Voice*, 30 April 1831.

[171] See below, pp. 425–6.

[172] See below, pp. 241 and 247–8.

[173] See below, pp. 427–30.

[174] *Voice*, 14 May 1831. Moreover, it proved a complete failure.

[175] M. Beer, *A History of British Socialism* (1919), Vol. I, pp. 298–9.

[176] Rudé *op. cit.*, pp. 100–2.

[177] See below, pp. 367–8.

[178] *Voice*, 16 April 1831.

[179] *Ibid.*

[180] *Poor Man's Guardian*, 30 July 1831. For Doherty's visit to London, see below, pp. 245 and 247.

[181] *Guardian*, 17 December 1831.

[182] See below, pp. 327 *et seq.*

[183] *Times and Gazette*, 19 March; *Voice*, 2 April 1831.

[184] See below, p. 326.

[185] *Voice*, 24 September 1831.

[186] See below, p. 329 *et seq.*

[187] *Voice*, 28 May, 2 July, 3 and 17 September 1831.

[188] *Ibid.*, 11 June 1831. See below, p. 329.

[189] See below, p. 331.

[190] See above, pp. 227–8.

[191] Cole, *Attempts at General Union*, pp. 27–8; Morris, *op. cit.*, p. 53; Rudé, *op. cit.*, p. 92; Thompson, *op. cit.*, p. 876.

[192] For a fuller discussion, see below, Chapter XI.

[193] See above, p. 234.

[194] See above, p. 233.

[195] *Voice*, 9 April 1831. Cole, *Attempts at General Union*, p. 40, wrongly interprets this letter as early opposition to over-expansion by Doherty.

[196] *Ibid.*, 30 April 1831.

[197] *Ibid.*, 14 May 1831.

[198] Letters were read from other districts apologising for non-attendance 'because of the expense'.

[199] *Voice*, 25 June 1831.

[200] *Ibid.*, 2 July 1831.

[201] *Ibid.*, 3 September 1831.

[202] The Manchester committee was reinforced from time to time by delegates from other districts, e.g. in the *Voice*, 28 May 1831, Cheetham announced that a meeting of the 'Board of Directors' would be held on 6 June and that one

delegate would be required to attend from Bury, Oldham, Blackburn, Rochdale and Ashton districts, but this was not a regular procedure.

203 *Voice,* 2 July 1831. Doherty pointed out that the committee had similarly objected in 1829 to his initial proposals for visits to neighbouring towns, and that he had therefore been obliged to attend the earliest meetings in Bolton at his own expense. Bonner subsequently condemned those committee members who forgot that 'the Association will never become *National,* if delegates were not sent to all parts of the kingdom where it was not established'. *Ibid.,* 9 July 1831.

204 *Ibid.,* 9 and 23 July 1831. See above, pp. 227-8.

205 *Ibid.,* 13 August 1831.

206 See above, p. 228.

207 *Ibid.,* 20 August 1831. For Doherty and temperance, see below, pp. 336-9.

208 It was on this occasion that Thomas Matthews put forward the idea of graduated instead of uniform subscriptions and benefits. See below, p. 246.

209 *Voice,* 27 August, 3, 10 and 17 September 1831.

210 *Ibid.,* 2 July 1831.

211 *Ibid.,* 27 August and 3 September 1831.

212 *Carpenter's Political Magazine,* January 1832; Beer, *op. cit.,* p. 301.

213 W. H. Oliver, 'Organisations and Ideas behind the efforts to achieve a general union of the working classes in England in the early 1830s' (Unpub. D.Phil., Oxford, 1954), pp. 54-60.

214 Cole, *A Short History of the British Working-Class Movement,* p. 73.

215 See, for example, 11 November 1830, *inter alia.*

216 See above, p. 235.

217 *Voice,* 28 May 1831.

218 *Ibid.,* 2 July 1831. Doherty's 'occular proof' could have been obtained on visits to London either in 1829 during the Manchester spinners' strike or in February 1831 when he went there in search of Hynes. See above, pp. 74 and 210.

219 *Poor Man's Guardian,* 30 July 1831. The practical reason for the trip was to gain advertisements for the *Voice.* See below, pp. 247 and 250.

220 *Voice,* 10 September 1831. See above, p. 227.

221 *Poor Man's Guardian,* 3 September 1831.

222 *Voice,* 10 September 1831. The 'Address' was copied into the *Poor Man's Guardian,* but not until 12 November 1831.

223 See above, p. 217.

224 *Voice,* 13, 20 and 27 August 1831.

225 See above, pp. 242-3.

226 *Voice,* 3 September 1831.

227 *Ibid.,* 10 and 17 September 1831.

228 This does not include the £518 2s 11½d contributed for the various trades on strike under the special arrangements made at Nottingham. Cole's estimate, *Attempts at General Union,* p. 35, for the subscriptions in this period, of about £600, erroneously counted in some of this cash. The sum *does* incorporate the following amounts, however: £37 12s for the newspaper, after the original intention that each member should subscribe 6d towards the cost of establishing the *Voice* was reasserted in August 1831; £20 14s 2d in response to a printed circular sent out to the different districts on 8 August, the contents of which were not specified, but may have suggested extra donations to finance the agitation connected with the 'grand division' plan; £17 18s 7d to pay for the steel engraving and membership cards; 11s 7d in 'special subscriptions' for strikers under the Nottingham system, but not specifying a particular trade; and 5s 10d in 'quarterly pence'. All these calculations are based on the *Voice,* 26 March-10 September 1831. It must be remembered, however, that local districts were now holding their own funds and were very lax in reporting contributions (see above, pp. 221-3). It is impossible, therefore, to make any reliable estimate of total paying membership.

229 See above, p. 237, and below, pp. 248-9.

230 *Voice,* 25 June and 2 July 1831.

231 *Ibid.,* 16 July and 20 August; J. Doherty, *A Letter to the Members of the National Association for the Protection of Labour* (Manchester, 1831).

[232] *Voice*, 27 August 1831. Doherty was constantly complaining of delays, excessive charges, and robberies of newspaper parcels in coach offices, and pleading for agents to remit the balances of their accounts.

[233] *Melbourne Papers,* Chapter v, quoted in Webb Collection, Vol. i, f. 200.

[234] *Voice,* 17 September 1831.

[235] *Ibid.,* 24 September 1831.

[236] See above, p. 193. In fact, the number of advertisements per edition had fallen continuously throughout the first volume, from 24 in January, to 15 in February, 14 in March, 13 in April and May, and 9 in June. The new arrangements for the second volume caused a revival, to almost 15 in July, but thereafter the number fell again to 13 in August and 11 in September. The average number of advertisements for the nine months of its life was slightly less than 15 per paper.

[237] *Times and Gazette,* 1 October 1831.

[238] *Advertiser,* 1 and 8 October 1831. R. Detrosier later told the Factory Commissioners that the *Voice* lost about £2,000. *Stockport Advertiser,* 29 November 1833.

[239] *Ibid.,* 8 October 1831.

[240] Beer, *op. cit.,* pp. 314–8; N. Carpenter, 'William Benbow and the Origin of the General Strike', *Quarterly Journal of Economics,* Vol. xxxv (1920–1); A. Plummer, 'The General Strike during One Hundred Years', *Economic History (Econ. Journ. Supplt.),* No. 2, May 1927; A. J. C. Rüter, 'William Benbow's Grand National Holiday and Congress of the Productive Classes', *Int. Rev. for Soc. Hist.,* Vol. i (1936). The idea seems to have originated in the years 1817–18, first of all in Nottingham and then spreading to Manchester, where both Doherty and Benbow were active at that time, the latter as a radical shoemaker (see above, pp. 23–7).

[241] *Voice,* 17 and 24 September 1831.

[242] See below, p. 290, however, for his later advocacy of a 'general strike', in 1834.

[243] *Voice,* 24 September 1831. The account of these events given here relies largely on Doherty's own version of them in his *Letter to the Members of the N.A.P.L.* in November, which naturally reflected his own opinions.

[244] See below, p. 430.

[245] See above, p. 239, and below, p. 331.

[246] Treasury Papers, T 22/20, f. 153; Hollis, *op. cit.,* p. 51.

[247] It is noteworthy that Doherty did not consider the *political* National Union of the Working Classes to be the basis of an organisation in London.

[248] It may only have been circulated privately at first, for it was not advertised publicly for sale, price 3*d,* until the following March. See *Advocate,* 24 March 1832, and *Poor Man's Guardian,* 9 June 1832, for its subsequent advertisement in London.

[249] Doherty, *A Letter to the Members.*

[250] See below, p. 368.

[251] *Expositor,* 14 January 1832.

[252] Doherty, *A Letter to the Members.*

[253] An acrimonious correspondence developed, reaching a low-point with accusations and counter-accusations of forgery by Oates and Doherty. *Advertiser,* 24 and 31 December 1831; *Expositor,* 7 January; *Advocate,* 21 January and 11 February 1832.

[254] *Advertiser,* 17 March 1832. Our italics.

[255] *Ibid.,* 18 and 25 February 1832.

[256] *Advocate,* 18 February, 24 March, and 7 April; *Pilot,* 31 March and 14 April 1832.

[257] *Pilot,* 10 March 1832.

[258] *Ibid.,* 24 March, 7 and 21 April 1832.

[259] See above, p. 246.

[260] Cole, *Attempts at General Union,* p. 42, referring to S. and B. Webb, *op. cit.,* p. 124.

[261] *Advocate,* 28 January 1831; Cole, *Attempts at General Union,* p. 43.

[262] *Pilot*, 31 March 1832, quoting the *Wakefield and Halifax Guardian*.

[263] *Ibid.*, 24 March, 7 April and 5 May 1832.

[264] The Bury district had been one of the few to flourish throughout 1831. Its secretary, Howarth, was publicly thanked for his efforts by the Manchester committee on 7 September (*Voice*, 10 September 1831), and as late as January 1832 it was reported that almost all the workers in an extensive bleaching works at nearby Radcliffe still supported the Association (*Chronicle*, 21 January 1832).

[265] *Advocate*, 2 and 16 June 1832.

[266] Cole, *Attempts at General Union*, pp. 56–69.

[267] R. Bullock, *On Mending the Times* (Macclesfield, 1833), p. 6, in White Slavery Collection, Vol. 10, No. 16.

[268] *On Combinations of Trades*, pp. 46, 65–71.

[269] Including £72 16s 1d contributed for the *Voice* and other special appeals, but excluding all the subscriptions for the strikes of Ashton spinners, Midlands framework knitters, and Lancashire calico-printers, for whom assistance was by no means confined to Association members. The total receipts are tabulated according to location and trade on pp. 262–3.

[270] See above, p. 196.

[271] For the effects of the trade cycle on trade unions, see Musson, *British Trade Unions, 1800–1875*, Chapter 5. Hobsbawm, *Labouring Men* (1964), pp. 126–57, errs in stating that during the first half of the nineteenth century trade unions were generally more active in slumps.

[272] Turner, *op. cit.*, p. 101. Indeed, the Association rules may well have been drawn up at the second congress of the spinners' grand general union. See above, p. 100.

[273] *Ibid.*

[274] See above, pp. 144–5, 177, 235–6.

[275] See, for example, Oliver, *op. cit.*, and I. Prothero, 'London Chartism and the Trades', *Econ. Hist. Rev.*, 2nd ser., Vol. xxiv, no. 2, May 1971.

[276] Oliver, *op. cit.*, p. 189.

[277] See H. J. Fyrth and H. Collins, *The Foundry Workers: A Trade Union History* (Manchester, 1959), p. 27.

[278] Rudé, *op. cit.*

# VIII Doherty's role in trade unionism after 1832

The final collapse of the National Association in 1832 did not mark any falling-off in trade-union activity. Trades whose initial organisation had been influenced by the Association, like the potters, continued to be strongly associated, while an ambitious federated union was established among the building trades, determined to eliminate the system of 'sub-contracting'. Co-operation between the Scottish trades increased under the direction of Alexander Campbell, a Glasgow spinner, and the Leeds Clothiers' Union, taking in both woollen and worsted workers from the leading Yorkshire towns, pursued a policy of mounting aggression.[1] With trade becoming more prosperous during 1833, strikes and lock-outs were more widespread than in any year since the twelve-month period which succeeded the repeal of the Combination Laws in 1824. Anguished and exaggerated cries proliferated in the stamped press regarding the existence of some secret conspiracy linking these various bodies. 'The working classes throughout the kingdom are just now more than ordinarily active in some important, though secret, undertaking. A new trades' union has been formed, the objects and laws of which are strictly confined to the initiated, and we are credibly informed that the number of members already exceeds 900,000.'[2]

This period also witnessed constant propaganda and lecture tours by Robert Owen, popularising his co-operative and labour-exchange ideas. In August 1833 he issued an 'Address to the Productive Classes of Great Britain and Ireland', including both masters and men, whom he advised to work together to eliminate the basic cause of distress, the competitive system. Instead of wasting so much effort in strikes, the producers should show their power by producing only for themselves, which would force the non-producers either to participate or starve, and thus society would be 're-generated', based on unity and co-operation instead of commercial cupidity and class rivalries.[3] On 24 September he attended the 'Builders' Parliament' in Manchester, along with 275 delegates from all over the country, and persuaded them to adopt his grandiose scheme for a 'Grand National Guild of Builders' to take over the whole building industry from the general contractors.[4] And on 9 October he convened in London a congress of co-operative and trade-union delegates from all over the country, which sanctioned the establishment of the 'National Moral Union of the Productive Classes' as the organ through which society was to be 'regenerated', and at the close of the deliberations Owen announced his determination to undertake a further tour of the midlands and the north to proselytise his plan among the workmen there.[5]

One trade remained surprisingly free from this turmoil. Even Tufnell, bitter critic of the unions, reported in March 1834, that 'the cotton-spinning trade . . . has been undisturbed by strikes' : because of trade depression, short-time working had been introduced, wages had been reduced, and 'combinations were unheard of'.[6] After the break-up of the Grand General Union, the operatives had been unable to resist piece-rate reductions and the increasing employment of cheap female and juvenile labour, and the Manchester spinners' society appears to have collapsed.[7] Doherty had ceased, by the end of 1830, to hold any official position in either the local or the general union, and he never returned to his old occupation; after the collapse of the National Association, he set himself up as a printer and bookseller in Withy Grove early in 1832.[8] Nevertheless, his relations with his old colleagues remained close, especially in the factory reform or ten hours' movement, in which he played a leading role.[9]

This movement, of course, was ostensibly on behalf of factory children, but an important ulterior motive among the operative spinners was the desire to reduce their own working hours. And at times when there seemed little hope of securing favourable legislation, Doherty emphasised the desirability of independent trade-union action to achieve this objective. Thus in September 1831, he warmly supported a determination of the Manchester spinners to reconstitute their union and unilaterally introduce an eight-hour day.[10] Nothing came of this proposal, but Doherty returned to the subject in an article in the *Poor Man's Advocate* in June 1832, lamenting the decline of the Grand General Union into 'comparative insignificance'. The workmen had forgotten, he feared, that union was the only ladder by which they could ascend to their proper place in society. And he quoted the answer of Hobhouse, who had introduced the Factory Acts of 1825 and 1831, but was now a Whig minister, to a recent deputation of operatives, that they must not trust to acts of parliament to improve their condition, but must take on the management of their own affairs, unite, and defend themselves. To this, Doherty added that if the workmen were too selfish or indolent to do so, they were 'too worthless to deserve help, and too contemptible to excite pity'.[11] Doherty's preference for direct action was reinforced in the summer of 1833, when he went with John Fielden, John Wood and other delegates to protest to Lord Althorp at the government's intention to introduce a bill to reduce the hours of children under thirteen to eight, rather than of *all* workers to ten. In reply, so Doherty testified to the Select Committee on Combinations in 1838, 'he [Althorp] gave us a lecture about combinations; he asked us why we did not combine, for that purpose, or rather he asked us whether we had ever combined against it. He said, "There are many combinations and strikes; have you ever combined against long hours?" I said I could not say we ever struck for it, though we had a great dislike of it. He said "I am sure you can do it better in that way than we can do it in Parliament"; and I have since given the workmen Lord Althorp's authority that they could do it better for themselves.'[12] Doherty's opportunity to implement this advice arose as early as the following October, when Owen arrived in the north to publicise his National Moral Union project.

John Fielden, a large-scale cotton manufacturer at Todmorden, radical member of parliament for Oldham, and Doherty's colleague on the short-time delegation, was also interested by Owen's visit. He had become the centre of considerable controversy during the previous year because of his efforts to make known what he considered to be the terrible condition of the working classes of Lancashire, especially the hand-loom weavers. In October 1833, he invited Owen to stay with him at Todmorden during his northern tour.[13] Over the next fortnight, Owen spoke at several Yorkshire towns in favour of 'the Trades' Union and Labour Banks and Stores', culminating in a particularly successful meeting at Huddersfield 'to forward the measures proposed . . . and to enlist in our cause some leading men who had taken an active part in promoting the Ten Hours Bill'.[14] From there he travelled to Todmorden at the end of the first week in November and stayed for three days in earnest conversation. Although Fielden believed that Owen had some 'peculiar notions' and that some of his schemes were impracticable, he was persuaded by his guest's account of the ferment of activity organised by co-operative and trade societies in each town, that they were on the eve of very important changes. Fielden therefore suggested that to atone for their disappointment over the ten hours' bill and to obviate the necessity of further legislation, the adult factory workers should insist on 1 March 1834, when the eight-hour limit for children under eleven was scheduled to be intro-duced, that their working-day should be similarly reduced, but their present wages as for a 69-hour week maintained. If this regulation were adopted throughout industry and agriculture, prices would rise in proportion, but they should ignore the bugbear of foreign competition, since the vast increase in production over recent years had only succeeded in cheapening their goods for foreigners; the biggest sufferers at home would be the non-pro-ducers on fixed incomes, the workers having the advantage of more time for education and home-life to compensate for dearer goods. So convinced was he of the utility of this plan that he had determined to set the example in his own factory at the appointed date.[15]

Owen believed that Fielden's plan was the 'best he had ever heard', a typically Owenite title of the 'National Regeneration Society' was adopted for the project, and a 'Catechism' was prepared, explaining in a series of questions and answers how eight hours' labour was sufficient to satisfy all wants and would make more general education and improvement possible, and preaching in messianic language how the abolition of the system of individual competition would lead to perfect happiness in human society.[16] Owen then returned into Yorkshire, reading extracts from the 'Catechism' at Leeds on 18 November and asserting to both masters and men that they could ameliorate the present distress within a few weeks by 'a union of skill, of labour, and of capital'.[17] His efforts to interest the leading factory reformers, however, were disappointing. Oastler wrote to him on 11 and 22 November that he supported an eight-hour day, but was committed to the Factory Reformation Society formed at Birstall so recently as 28 October to continue the ten hours' agitation; moreover, he was opposed to the slogan of 'twelve hours' wages for eight hours' work', which was like asking for '12d for 8d', and concluded definitively that 'it is impossible any of us can meet at Bradford and it seems altogether unnecessary—we have said all we can say'. Bull was a little more sympathetic and suggested some Christian amend-ments to the Catechism, but he wrote on 30 November that his time would be much taken up in future by family and parochial duties. Only from Pitkeithley on 3 December did Owen receive whole-hearted support, in a letter revealing that the Huddersfield short-time committee would meet to discuss the question on 26 December and predicting that 'the Regeneration system will be firmly established on that day over the West Riding for we are to have delegates from every town . . . and as many as we can from the Lancashire Regeneration Societies'.[18]

Meanwhile, Fielden was making similar efforts to gain support in Lancashire. In the week after his meeting with Owen, he discussed the project widely in Manchester, as a result of which he communicated to William Cobbett, his parliamentary colleague at Oldham, on 16 November, that several master spinners had promised to adopt the system if the others would, that the local short-time committee was taking the matter up, and that George Condy, the radical barrister, whose taking over the *Manchester and Salford Advertiser* from James Whittle had little affected its political stance, had promised to advocate the measure in his paper. Cobbett endorsed the scheme in a public letter of reply on 11 December, in which he traced the ancestry of the eight-hour working day back to the 'good old days' of King Alfred, criticised the emigration schemes of the 'feelosofers', and asserted that the scheme would end the iniquity of three million labourers keeping five million 'tax-eaters' in idleness.[19] Condy began his campaign on 16 November with an open letter to Charles Wood, the government whip, in the course of which he stated that there was an 'extensive confederacy of manufacturers and their men already formed in Yorkshire, and expanding rapidly into this district', with the object of obtaining 'Eight Hours' Work for Twelve Hours' Wages' from 1 March next.[20]

One member of the short-time committee who was particularly enthusiastic for the venture was John Doherty, for it well fitted his desire that the labourers should reduce their hours themselves, and it would also serve to get work for the unemployed cotton spinners, whose mounting numbers so weakened the spinners' union. In addition, he was already concerned at the growing signs of a country-wide counter-attack against the unions, for the Leeds woollen workers and Lancashire builders were at that time involved in hopeless resistance to the signing of their masters' 'document', and the practice was shortly to be copied at both Leicester and Derby. On 8 November he composed an address 'To the Operative Calico-Printers and Others of England', written on behalf of the Scottish printers, who were on strike against a wage reduction. Their masters had advertised for new hands in England, but Doherty prayed that operative printers would not be deluded, for, as he had asserted in 1829, once one reduction was effected it would spread through the whole body. It was their duty and interest to subsidise the men on strike.

> The cause of the operatives is the same throughout the United Kingdom. Whatever evil injures one, if not successfully opposed, must eventually injure all. Every individual operative is therefore bound to support, by every means in his power, the whole body of his fellow-labourers. The war between 'Capital' and Labour still rages with unabated fury. 'Capital' is struggling to strip Labour of even the shadow of remuneration. 'Capital' is supported by government and law. Labour has nothing to sustain it but the energies, wisdom, and virtue of its owners. These, properly directed, are

much more than sufficient to do all that the workmen require. These neglected, the unhappy workmen are at the mercy of every speculative adventurer in the country.[21]

Doherty also shared Fielden's opinion concerning the state of the working classes of the district. On 12 November, Colonel Evans, the member of parliament for Westminster, who had been touring Lancashire with Richard Potter, the member for Wigan, to gain first-hand knowledge of conditions there, and had visited several works in Manchester, told a meeting of Salford electors that 'he had been extremely gratified by the splendid appearance and progressive state (as it appeared to him) of things here'.[22] This remark so outraged the members of the working-class Political Union in Manchester that they appointed a deputation, headed by Condy, Doherty and James Turner, and comprising also a number of local workers, to apprise Colonel Evans of the real condition of the manufacturing operatives in the area. An interview lasting two hours took place at the Royal Hotel on 26 November, when the workmen began by detailing the state of their respective trades. Doherty then stated the results of a personal survey which he had made into the circumstances of the families of twenty-five weavers, spinners, house-painters and labourers living near St Michael's Church, comprising ninety-eight individuals in all. Their aggregate earnings for one week amounted to £10 17s 3d, but after deductions for rent and other incidentals, they had only 1s 6d per head for food and clothing weekly. He mentioned many instances of entire families working, eating and sleeping in one room, of poor weavers unable to leave their homes for want of shoes and clothing, and of fathers compelled to lie in bed until their 'tattered and torn' linen was washed and dried by their unhappy wives and daughters. One man whom he had visited, Doherty concluded, could not rise from his bed because of excessive labour and lack of food, and another, with his wife and sick child, had no bed but a sack of straw, with no covering save what they wore during the day. Colonel Evans replied that he had read of such cases in Dr Kay's pamphlet,[23] but believed that they had escaped the notice of master manu-facturers, who were so engrossed in managing their immense establishments. The wages question involved a variety of considerations, over many of which the masters had no control; but he had seen Birley's and Fieldens' wages-books, and the weekly earnings of their employees (male, female and child) averaged 10s 9½d and 10s 0½d respectively. Doherty bluntly countered that the masters were well aware of the existence of the scenes described, 'but they coolly declared their ignorance as to a remedy, except by the people dying off'; the statement of Birley's work-force had falsely omitted many children, whose wages would reduce the average to about 7s per week, Doherty stated, referring to the report of the Select Committee on Commerce and Manufacturs for confirmation. The discussion ended with some allusions to trades' unions, the member of parliament asserting that unions of trades might do some good if they behaved peaceably, but that agitation for the repeal of the corn laws and reduced taxation would be more efficacious. After this observation, Doherty escorted Colonel Evans around 'some of the habitations of misery' apparently amicably enough, but according to the *Guardian* account the meeting did not finish without some violent language;

for the deputies stated that 'they were tired of petitioning; and one of them went so far as to say that the next time they did so it should be with arms in their hands (one account we have heard, describes the phrase used as *"with steel dipped in blood!"*)'. The same declamation was reported to the government by the military commander in the north, General Bouverie, who added a statement by the deputies 'that March next was the time when they meant to enforce their claims'.[24]

The culmination of these activities was a meeting of workmen and others at the 'Prince's Tavern', Princess Street, Manchester, on 25 November, to consider 'the strange anomaly' of overwork for some co-existing with low wages, unemployment and starvation for others. Nineteen resolutions were adopted, formerly constituting 'The Society for Promoting National Regeneration' and appealing to the workmen throughout the country to apply to their employers in the first week of January 1834, for their concurrence in the adoption of the regulation of 'eight hours' work for the present full day's wages' from 1 March; 'missionaries' were to be appointed to visit the workmen and masters in every trade and district to propagate those resolutions, and were to report their progress to a further meeting on 17 December; any masters willing to comply were asked to communicate their intention to the Society's office in 48 Pall Mall, King Street; it was hoped that local schoolrooms might be opened for two hours extra daily after 1 March to provide free education for the workmen; and subscriptions were to be collected to defray the expenses of the 'missionaries' and of the education provision. Messrs Oastler, Wood, Bull and Sadler were thanked for their efforts to obtain a ten hours' bill, but requested now to agitate for the new limitation; Owen was deputed to establish branch committees of the Society in every district which he visited, especially the Potteries, Birmingham, Worcester, Gloucester, Nottingham, Leicester, Derby and London; and the workmen throughout Europe and America were asked 'for their support and co-operation in this effort to improve the condition of the labourer in all parts of the world'. Finally, a committee of twenty-two individuals was appointed to implement these propositions, including Joshua Milne, who chaired the meeting, John, Joshua and Thomas Fielden, William Clegg, George Condy, George Marshall, an advocate of labour exchanges in Manchester, John Doherty, George Higginbottom, James Turner and Philip Grant from the short-time committee, and Robert Owen. These resolutions were advertised throughout the local and national stamped and unstamped press, along with an address detailing the system of education to which the Regenerators subscribed. Both men and women were to be taught all branches of useful knowledge, thrift, temperance, etc., but the former were to be particularly instructed in the techniques of their respective trades, and the latter in domestic duties; a similar bias was to hold in children's education.[25]

The Society, with its emphasis on co-operation between masters and men, education, and a thorough and swift reorganisation of society, was of course completely different from Doherty's earlier Association, which was a federation of trade societies for strictly trade-union purposes. As such, the new scheme excited ridicule rather than fear in the orthodox press. The *Guardian* called it 'one more added to the numerous matters of moonshine, with which, for many years past, the wrong-headed, however well-meaning,

Mr Robert Owen, has been deluding himself, and failing to delude the public'. The editor asked, 'from a society of which John Fielden Esq. M.P., is the *Alpha*, Robert Owen Esq., the *Omega*, . . . and John Doherty the *Iota*, what practical good can any living man expect? Granting to some of them the merit of *meaning* well, they have vexed the dull ears of the public with their senseless conundrums as to the mode of doing good long enough already.' And the writer concluded that, although some brief excitement might be produced among the lowest class of labourers, if trade were prosperous in the spring, the more intelligent operatives would realise that the proposition threatened both their means of existence and the public peace. *Wheeler's Manchester Chronicle* was equally derisive, calling Owen a 'dreaming vision-ary' and urging the working classes not to be 'entrapped by the "disinterested" oratory of Mr John Doherty'. More seriously, the writer expressed surprise at the name of John Fielden, an English member of parliament, being asso-ciated with the appeal to foreign workers, which was no more than a 'traitorous call to revolution'. This rather extreme reaction was echoed further afield in London by the *Morning Chronicle*.[26] And criticism was not confined to the hostile press. William Fitton, the Oldham radical, addressed a particularly deprecatory letter to Fielden on 11 December, asserting that the competitive spirit was so universal and basic in society that years of moral education would be necessary to eliminate it; in the meantime, united exertions towards further political reform and reduced taxation would be more useful than wasting their strength on 'an impractical project'.[27]

In reply, the brunt of the propaganda battle was borne at first by Condy, who published a series of editorials from 30 November under the heading of 'Rights of Industry', the slogan chosen to represent all the Society's pub-licity. Extensive use was made of Fielden's figures to demonstrate how far over-production had adversely affected both the labourers, who had been so brutalised by low wages, unemployment and long hours that 14,000 men were now needed to keep order in London, and also the employers, whose profits were constantly being eroded and who would consequently do better to join with their workmen in introducing the new system rather than oppos-ing the unions with the 'document' as in Yorkshire, Leicester and Derby. To Fitton's objections, Fielden replied in person. Agricultural workers, dock-labourers, etc. already worked an eight-hour day, taking the average for the whole year. It was in manufactures like silk, cotton and flax that the worst excesses of overwork existed; there had been a threefold increase in cotton production between 1815 and 1832, yet the standard of living had fallen. The Regeneration Society did not wish to encourage strikes, and hence had recom-mended the labourers to ask their masters to effect the regulation voluntarily. Only if the employers generally proved blind to their own interests would the Society 'devise such a legal and peaceable mode of proceeding as they may consider proper to obtain the adoption of the regulation'.[28] Finally, the Society published a series of tracts towards the end of December, the first extracting evidence from the Select Committee on Commerce and Manufac-tures to show how eight hours' labour daily would benefit operatives and employers, and containing fourteen tables to demonstrate the decline in the value of goods, profits and wages, the second comprising the Catechism of the Society, and the third the letters of Cobbett and Fielden on the subject from the *Register* of 14 December 1833. All these could be purchased at Doherty's bookshop in Withy Grove, as well as at other booksellers.[29]

Meanwhile, arrangements proceeded for the appointment of missionaries, at meetings of trades' delegates in Manchester early in December,[30] while Doherty was dispatched to Derby to explain the project to the men on strike there, and with instructions to proceed also to other towns in that area where he was well known through his activities in the National Association. There was some objection to this decision, for Condy stated that the Derby meeting was, for some reason, held 'against our advice', but William Clegg informed Owen that it was 'a special appointment', which it was thought best not to delay, in view of the existing situation there.[31] At a public meeting of Derby operatives, convened at the 'Nag's Head' on 12 December, Doherty described the present wretched state of the employees in all the great branches of manufacturing, quoting Fielden's figures to show that over-production was the cause. Something must be done, he contended, to distribute the produce of machinery more fairly among the people; and the remedy was to reduce the quantity produced by one-third, by working eight hours, and to continue the same wages. The consequent rise in prices would strike home against the non-producers, whose hoards of wealth would be got at and distributed more justly among the community; and given fair play, the English workmen could still outstrip all their foreign rivals. Doherty admitted there would be difficulties in fulfilling the project, but these could be overcome by tireless persistence. He concluded with a description of the rewards which they would receive for their efforts, the language of which suggests that he had not remained unaffected by his closer proximity to Owen over the previous weeks:

> Heaven will smile upon us; our own consciences must approve, and posterity will applaud us; and when our hour comes to quit this vale of tears, and go to our great account, we shall look back with feelings of consolation and delight to the struggles we have made in this glorious cause of justice, peace and kindness. Our last moments will be cheered by the reflection that we have contributed something to chase vice, injustice and oppression from the earth, and we shall go down to the grave with peace and satisfaction, knowing that we have bequeathed a brighter and happier inheritance to our children than it was our lot to be born to.

After Doherty had sat down amid loud applause, the scheme was put to the vote and unanimously agreed to, a committee then being appointed to effect it.[32]

But Doherty's words failed to impress Francis Place. When James Turner, one of the Manchester missionaries, wrote to him on 11 December, asserting that 'the feeling is growing very strong in favour of the project' for eight hours a day at the same wages, which the writer described as the operatives' reaction to Althorp's Factory Act, Place replied four days later that while he believed eight hours were enough for any man, many years must pass before the working classes were wise or honest enough as a body to establish themselves in respectable circumstances. As for the regenerators' scheme in particular, Place went on,

K

*you will not succeed* in your endeavour. . . . You would not succeed even if the attempt was to reduce the time to eight hours for eight hours wages. It is absurd in the extreme to suppose that with a redundancy of hands, many at all times having no employment, there will be a general concurrence in the proposal. Doherty has I see been at Derby, has been shouted at and applauded for a speech like all his speeches, a curious mixture of sense and nonsense of reason and folly. *I* have no doubt *he* thinks he shall succeed, and he is one of those who learns nothing from repeated failures. He is so doggedly sure that he is right, that nothing can convince him he is wrong, so I have no hopes of making a convert to reason of him. I do not however think he will do any harm, and sure I am that the proposed agitation will lead to much reasoning, and thus elicit much truth, and this will be serviceable to the people.

When this project had inevitably failed, Place hoped that all concerned would be disposed to enquire diligently into the causes of the failure, 'and not to cheat themselves with false informers which can do them nothing but evil'; and that, having discovered the causes, they would seek the true remedy in the right way.[33]

Unaware of this censure, Doherty continued his delegation over the next three weeks. After Derby, he addressed a meeting of about five hundred Nottingham operatives on the following night, and on 16 December he spoke at a similar gathering at the 'Boot Inn', Loughborough. Both assemblies adopted resolutions in favour of the plan and appointed committees to further that determination. On the two subsequent evenings he attended public meetings at Leicester, both of which were poorly attended because, according to Doherty, they were inadequately publicised; two meetings were also necessary at Mansfield on 19 and 20 December, and on the following day he spoke at a meeting of 'a few intelligent operatives' at Chesterfield, before travelling on to Sheffield. In that town he shared the platform with Robert Owen and they 'satisfactorily answered' several questions, before a motion was passed approving the measure; the audience expressed a desire for further discussion of the question and a second meeting was held on 30 December, when Doherty and Owen were again the main speakers but were heard by 'slender numbers'.[34] In the meantime, Doherty attended a meeting at Oldham on Christmas Day, where slightly more enthusiasm was shown, probably owing to the spinners becoming involved in strikes.[35] James Mills, the local spinners' secretary, took the chair, and the first speakers were Knight and Lomax, two prominent radicals, and James Turner. Doherty then entered into his usual detail of the mounting distress of the people, asserted that the remedy was to make labour more scarce and hence more valuable, and explained that 'the possessions of the people were amassed in a heap to keep idlers; that heap was strongly guarded; now they were not proposing to break upon this heap, but to stop all supplies from going into it in future'. And he disputed any objection that their previous efforts at union had failed, for 'such attempts prepared the way for greater changes'. After an adjournment to 30 December, a committee was appointed, comprising delegates from each workshop or factory, with Knight as its secretary, to carry the Manchester resolutions of 25 November into effect.[36]

Thus Doherty had succeeded in forming branch committees at a number of towns, but the enthusiasm which had greeted his visits to the same places on Association business was notably absent. While these efforts were being made, Owen was involved in similar activity in pursuance of the directive of the Manchester committee. On his return to London, he immediately convened a meeting of operatives and masters from all the metropolitan trades at the National Equitable Labour Exchange on 9 December. This meeting, which was attended by a number of leading radicals, co-operators and unionists, including Cleave, Hetherington and others, expressed support for the venture and passed resolutions establishing an auxiliary society in London in connection with the parent body in Manchester. It was hoped to link this closely with the metropolitan trade societies, but there was some strong feeling against Owen's ideas of class-collaboration, several trade unionists advocating instead collective action for a minimum wage. There was also objection to Owen's interference with trade union affairs, his 'despotic authority', and the impracticability of his schemes for a 'new world'.[37]

On the other hand, the regeneration plan was warmly supported by the *Crisis* and the *Pioneer,* while Hetherington gave it his blessing also in the *Poor Man's Guardian,* although he believed that the unions of workmen would not achieve the redistribution of wealth, which they all desired, unless they first obtained universal suffrage.[38] The first action of the London Auxiliary Regeneration Society was the convening of a public meeting of trade unionists and others on 23 December to consider the best means of supporting the Derby men. This assembly adopted a series of resolutions recommending the Derby strikers to follow the regenerators' policy and propose to their masters only to return if they agreed to pay the present wages for eight hours' labour, and that if this was refused they should be helped to start manufacturing on their own account, for which purpose the London trade societies were asked to make subscriptions.[39]

Meanwhile, Owen had left the capital once again to continue his tour of agitation. On 19 December he reported back to the *Crisis* office from Worcester, that he had established branch committees of the Regeneration Society in that town and previously at Birmingham and in the Potteries. During the next fortnight he attended meetings of operatives at Sheffield, where Doherty also spoke as we have seen, and at Barnsley, Leeds and Huddersfield, finding a new spirit of 'union, kindness and forbearance' among them, but being generally disappointed in his discussions with the masters. Finally, on 2 January he spoke at a meeting of the Derby trades' union. Owen hoped that the current disputation between masters and men would soon end, since both were the creatures of circumstances; the means of reconciliation was in the auxiliary society of regeneration recently established in Derby. Within a week, he predicted, delegates of masters and men would be conferring together to establish that system, from which time might date 'the millenium of the world'. Regrettably, however, the masters showed no disposition to hasten the advent of this happy state when Owen met them next day.[40] Nevertheless, on his return to London, he inserted in the *Pioneer* of 11 January 'An Address to the Trades' Unions and to all the Producers of wealth and knowledge throughout Great Britain and Ireland', advocating a union of masters and men for mutual happiness, which was the 'real object' of the National Regeneration Society.[41]

The formation of new branch committees was also continued by the Manchester committee in the new year. As early as 5 January, Bouverie had informed the Home Office that the Regeneration Society was 'gaining ground in Manchester' and 'might be dangerous'.[42] Progress continued after that date, the establishment of branches being reported at Chorlton-on-Medlock, Blackburn, Bolton, and Warrington in January and early February, following visits by delegates from Manchester.[43] On 22 February Doherty reported that by his own and Owen's efforts and by those of the missionaries, almost thirty branches had been established, not only at those towns where accounts of meetings had been printed, but also at Rochdale, Heywood, Bury, Burnley, Preston, Chorley, Wigan, Stockport, Ashton, Stalybridge, New Mills, Macclesfield and Congleton.[44]

The Society continued, however, to attract critics. At the end of January 1834 Colonel Torrens, the political economist and member of parliament for Bolton, published a pamphlet entitled 'Wages and Combinations', exposing the fallacies of 'Fielden's "Rights of Industry" phantom', and warning the labourers against pressing upon profits, on which their wages depended. And at the same time, some members of the Sheffield Regeneration Society, led by Ebenezer Elliot, the author of the 'Corn Law Rhymes', led a rebellion against its 'founder', Owen, to whom they published an open letter asserting that machinery had already brought great benefits to the population generally, and that the true reason for the existence of distress was the Corn Laws, and concluding that 'your plan is already a failure, even in theory'.[45] Condy replied to both detractors in the *Manchester and Salford Advertiser*. Torrens was reminded that profits and wages were already falling, despite the self-congratulation of political economists and placemen, while Elliot should recollect that 'we sent Mr Doherty into your town. He saw you, argued with you, and proved these and a hundred assertions, connected with the subject, and having the same bearing upon it, to your refutation, if not to your conviction'. Owen also published his own rejoinder to the Sheffield criticisms, denying that he wished the corn laws, or any other monopoly, to remain; but he repeated that individual competition was the basic defect in society, and that the Regeneration Society, which Fielden, and not he, had inaugurated, was destined to counteract it.[46]

Although Condy's paper was devoting much of its space to the question, it was at this time that the Manchester committee decided that the Society needed an organ of publicity exclusively in its interest. And on 8 February appeared the prospectus for Doherty's fifth periodical, the first number of which was to be published that day, entitled *The Herald of the Rights of Industry, and General Trades' Union Advocate*. It was chiefly to publicise the aims, and report the progress, of the National Regeneration Society, but would also generally attempt to stimulate the working classes to cease their apathy and join one unified movement to break the power of the 'money-changers, the vile and vulgar aristocracy of wealth', and thereby to attain that station of happiness and independence to which they were entitled. Original articles of a moral, social and educational nature were also to be included occasionally, and the paper was to be published simultaneously in London, Manchester, Edinburgh and Dublin.[47]

The *Herald* in fact appeared without the trade-union reference in its title, but carried the sub-heading, 'Published by the Society for Promoting National Regeneration'. It was edited by Doherty, comprised eight octavo pages, and cost 1d. Manchester was the sole place of publication, but it had agents eventually in Manchester, Stockport, Bolton, Preston, Macclesfield, Leeds, Bradford, Huddersfield, Keighley, Featherstone, the Potteries, Nottingham, Derby, Leicester, Birmingham, London, and Glasgow; its circulation in Manchester and Salford was estimated by Bouverie in March at about eight hundred.[48]

In the early numbers Doherty preserved a rigid orthodoxy on the ideals of the Regeneration Society. His opening address declared its advocacy of 'a revolution, co-extensive with society itself'. This was made necessary by the unparalleled distress affecting every branch of manufacturing industry, which was caused by the fact that the workers were having to support a large number of idlers, who had gained possession of the vast increase in production which improved machinery had made possible. Their remedy was, by preference, a union of masters and men to institute an eight-hour day for the same wages from 1 March, but if the employers refused to co-operate, the operatives would bring the regulation into force on their own. And he proceeded over subsequent weeks to follow up these points in detail. In each paper from 15 February to 8 March, the attention of 'the Creators of Wealth in Great Britain and Ireland' was drawn to extracts from the Select Committee on Manufactures, Commerce and Shipping in proof of the state of adversity in the hand-loom weaving, woollen, iron, cotton-spinning and manufacturing, and shop-keeping trades, which should be compared with the prosperity of loan-mongers, money-changers, and bankers. And that this impoverishment was matched among the agricultural workers was demonstrated by the reports of the Poor Law Commissioners, parts of which Doherty printed on 15 March. A copy of a petition to the Commons from 'the Manchester Society for Promoting and Protecting the Rights of Industry', recently forwarded to Fielden for presentation, was included on 22 February: this described the unexampled privations of the labourers, contrary to accounts of affluence and comfort prevalent in Parliament, and demanded an impartial enquiry into the real state of the country, after which measures of relief should be instituted, and particularly a shift in the burden of taxation from necessities to luxuries. And on 22 March Doherty published a 'Memorial' sent to the King from the Regeneration Society, respectfully protesting at the statement in the speech from the throne at the opening of Parliament, 'that Commerce and Manufactures afford the most encouraging prospect of success', and apprising him of the true facts. The remedy for this misery was, of course, that proposed by the regenerators, and in the first two editions Doherty inserted appeals to the operatives and master manufacturers respectively, explaining the mutual advantages to be obtained from adopting the system. The workmen should realise from their exclusion from the Reform Bill that they could rely only on their own efforts, and from the fact that the employers were now attacking not only wage rates but also their right to form unions, that united action was more urgent than ever; if they would struggle together for the 'rights of industry', their 'physical redemption' could be achieved 'in a single day'. And the masters would be weaned from dependence upon the 'Infernal Philosophy' of the 'High Priest

Malthus' and of McCulloch, who taught them that distress was the result of over-population and monopolies rather than the enormous taxation, paper money, and excessive individual competition; by ceasing to over-produce, they could increase their profits, ensure regular trade without the present fluctuations, and above all restore the affections of the workmen.[49]

Consequently, although the first week in January passed off without the intended approaches of the workmen to their masters to implement the new regulation on 1 March—in fact the only such action taken in the whole of January was by deputations to the master spinners and manufacturers of Stockport—the regenerators could point to some progress in the first two months of 1834. On 8 January Turner wrote to Place that, despite the latter's scepticism, 'we are gaining ground very fast; whether we succeed or not we shall do an immense deal of good', and he asked to be informed if Place heard any rumours about a government intention to act against them.[50] And on 8 February Fielden informed Owen that 'the Regeneration Society in Manchester is going on as well as could be expected for the time, they hold Committee Meetings twice a week, the Missionaries are pursuing their plans of diffusing information on the subject. A weekly publication "The Rights of Industry" comes out today . . . and will be sold here and throughout the Kingdom.' But Fielden added that little had yet been done in Yorkshire, and the apathy shown there, in consequence of the bitter recriminations surrounding Sadler's election defeat at Huddersfield on 8 January,[51] would make it necessary to postpone the period for commencement beyond 1 March. A notice would be required to this effect, but they could discuss the matter further when they met in London the following morning.[52]

While this new policy was being discussed by Owen and Fielden in London, some workmen in the north were at least attempting to put the original determination into practice. On 21 February about fifty of the leading Manchester master cotton spinners were served with a printed notice from the Regeneration Society, signed by their working spinners, calling upon them to begin working eight hours a day and paying the same wages, and setting forth Fielden's calculations to show why it was in their interest.[53] The *Guardian* commented that 'the regenerators, and their dupes, the workmen, must have a strange opinion of the misunderstandings of the employers, if they suppose the latter can be imposed upon by such nonsense'. It pointed out that profits had previously been high in the cotton trade because foreign countries demanded all that could be produced; but now that they manufactured extensively themselves, it was essential to keep our prices low to make our exports competitive. Consequently, the masters would ignore the request, the writer opined, while the workmen would surely not wish to repeat their sufferings during the last strike for such a 'visionary scheme'. On the other hand, the *Herald* reported that the masters' reactions to the applications were 'much more favourable than we were disposed to hope for', revealed that similar measures had been taken at Oldham and several other towns with a like result, and counselled all who had not yet presented their applications to 'do so without delay'.[54]

Considerable confusion clearly prevailed among the directors of the Society, for on the very day that these petitions were handed to the master spinners, a meeting of branch delegates in Manchester decided, after hearing reports from the various localities, that in compliance with letters received from Yorkshire and Scotland and to ensure simultaneous co-operation, they should recommend postponement of the date for commencing the eight-hour day from 1 March to 2 June, unless at the next delegate meeting on 16 April it was decided that it was practicable to effect it earlier. It was also resolved that Condy, Clegg, Seed and Doherty be appointed to prepare a circular to all the branch committees, announcing this postponement and the reasons for it; and all committees were asked to work towards forming new branches in their neighbourhoods. Symbolic of the lack of co-ordination in the management of the Society at the time of this crucial, but inevitable, change of plan, was the fact that when James Lowe, the secretary, inserted the notices of the deferment in the *Manchester and Salford Advertiser*, the date for the commencement of the new world was unfortunately misprinted as 24 June.[55]

The debacle delighted the critics of the project. On 25 February J. F. Foster reported that an informant had gone round the country manufacturers asking about the progress of the Society and the probability of a general commotion among the workmen. From the information received, he concluded that nothing formidable would occur for some time, especially as the threatened turn-out had been postponed until June. The notices had been most generally served at Oldham, but elsewhere the masters were sure that no strike would take place, even in Manchester where the affair seemed to have gained most ground.[56] The *Guardian* was typically more direct and scathing, observing on 1 March that,

> we understand that the promoters of the hopeful scheme of national regeneration . . . have graciously condescended to defer the commencement of the new era of happiness on earth. . . . We imagine this will turn out to be what the ancients were wont to call a postponement of the Greek Kalends. . . . The fact, we believe is, that the working classes are not such egregious fools as they were supposed to be. They have no inclination to throw themselves out of employment, merely that certain persons may fish in troubled waters, and profit or try to profit by general confusion.[57]

In reply, Doherty could only assert rather lamely that the original projectors of the scheme had never hoped that they would be prepared all over the country within three months, but had believed that they would work with greater urgency if a time was fixed upon rather than left indefinite. Manchester and its neighbourhood were 'perfectly ready' and the only difficulty would be in keeping them back. But as it now seemed certain that the employers would not voluntarily check their 'pernicious power', it was essential that all workmen should act together, and 'Yorkshire is not quite ready to join us; Scotland, though in motion, is not prepared for this day; and Ireland, we can hardly say, as yet fairly moving'. Nevertheless, the great progress of their principles over the previous period, Doherty concluded, 'affords a glorious earnest of what another three months will enable us to do'.[58]

Efforts to spread the ideals of the Society did continue. On 8 March Doherty appealed 'To the Members of the Trade Unions of England, Ireland and Scotland', submitting that their partial societies had succeeded in checking wages reductions, but had failed to secure increases because of a 'want of union between the unions themselves', because they acted 'in apparent hostility to the masters' and excluded them, and because they made no attempt to shorten their hours of labour and in fact had suffered them to be lengthened. Instead of increasing their production to subsidise idle drones, they should rally round the Regeneration Society as a common centre, send delegates to the meetings, and by 2 June the whole kingdom would be prepared, and they could gain all with 'no turn-out, no strike, no more sacrifices, but one great moral effort'. And that Union, too, would be the 'parliament of the people', for the people would elect its members and benefit by its acts.[59] At the same time, a serious attempt was made to develop the initial interest which Owen had aroused in Yorkshire. Already on 4 February a branch had been formed at Keighley, following a visit by two missionaries. On 20 February Grant attended a similar meeting at Leeds, and the Leeds Factory Reformation Society eventually voted to transform itself into a Regeneration branch. And on 26 February Pitkeithley wrote to Owen from Huddersfield that 'we have had a regeneration missionary and formed a committee, and hope things will move on in the good way'.[60] A branch was also established in Bradford, with Peter Bussey as secretary, after a series of meetings addressed by Condy, Grant, Clegg and Fielden; but Oastler and Bull remained very lukewarm, the latter writing an open letter 'To the Friends of the National Regeneration Society', in which, while declaring his support for the Society's ideals, he expressed his opinion that it could not succeed because of disunity, intemperance and other moral failings of the working classes.[61]

Coincidental with Bull's letter, Doherty was inserting in the *Herald* between 15 March and 5 April a series of replies to supposed 'Objections' that might be raised to the Regeneration scheme. The first argument was that the workmen were too immoral and dissipated to co-operate and effect it: he denied that this was so, for the operatives had selflessly agitated for the Reform Bill, which expressly excluded them; and was not the best antidote to such vice as did exist, he countered, to give the people time for moral and scientific instruction? Secondly, it was said that the labourers on piece-rates would counteract it by working over-time: if this was so, Doherty replied, it would be better to abolish piece-rates for a more regular income, but in any case all workmen would ultimately realise the evil of over-producing. Thirdly, the employers' co-operation was necessary and could not be obtained: but Doherty asserted that, once the workmen recognised the utility of ignoring the advice of Parson Malthus to reduce their numbers by ceasing to beget children and instead followed that of the regenerators to reduce their hours, making enough work for all and *better* wages, they would stand together pledged to start the new regulation on 1 June [*sic*] and the masters would be powerless to resist. Fourthly, the individual labourer's condition would be worsened by the increase in prices: this had been the most serious concern of all for the workmen, Doherty admitted, but the retention of the same wages was only a temporary expedient until the value of labour naturally increased, and the workers would also gain from no longer having to pay to clubs and the parish to relieve the unemployed, and from the inevitable recognition of their political rights. Finally, the employers feared the loss of foreign markets: but this ignored, Doherty observed, that other countries fixed the rate of their customs duties according to the amount by which English goods undersold their own.[62]

Thus Doherty was by this time stretching credulity to promise a wage *increase* if the operatives would support the Society. But despite his arguments and reports of new branches being formed, the regenerators continued to be the butt of the local press. On 22 March an editorial in *Wheeler's Manchester Chronicle* declared that, despite the issue of enormous numbers of placards, circulars and cheap periodicals, and the zealous efforts of five operative missionaries receiving 26s a week each, the Regeneration Society had been numbered 'among the things that were'. The missionaries had been discharged and the meetings had ceased, thus proving the increasing good sense of the working classes, who would no longer be 'deluded by the high-sounding professions of itinerant orators'. In reply, the *Manchester and Salford Advertiser* asserted on 29 March that the Society was in fact more active than ever and was planning simultaneous meetings throughout Lancashire and the West Riding on 14 April during the approaching Easter, and went on to defend the integrity of the operative missionaries compared with the materialism of many politicians and churchmen. And on the same day Doherty in the *Herald* maintained that the Society's prospects were never more favourable, for now many employers, for instance at Bury, were anxious for its success, the additional committees established in Yorkshire had raised the total of branches to over forty, and the paper had established itself as an efficient organ of communication. 'Never did any cause progress so rapidly', and if the operatives would but contribute a halfpenny per week the missionaries would be sent out to other districts and the measure would be completed.[63]

But in fact the course of events during 1834 was moving strongly against any project which sought to foster co-operation between masters and men. The attitude of employers towards the unions was clearly demonstrated by their widespread determination to force their workmen to sign the document, and the Derby dispute in particular became increasingly another test case of the respective strengths of capital and labour. In the early part of the strike, both Doherty and Owen visited Derby in vain attempts to induce the contestants to adopt the eight-hours system, and as we have seen, the London Auxiliary Regeneration Society was instrumental in initiating the metropolitan subscriptions for the strikers.[64] But the major part in organising these country-wide collections was played by the Derby Committee at Birmingham and subsequently by the executive of the Grand National Consolidated Trades' Union, one of whose first decisions was to establish a levy of a shilling per member to set the men up in business.

In Manchester, leaders of the Regeneration Society joined with others in efforts to raise support for the Derby workmen. Early in January 1834, a meeting of the operatives of Manchester and Salford in the Salford Co-operative Institute appointed a committee to organise a general subscription, and weekly committee meetings were held there each Tuesday evening, when 'all persons desirous in helping the novel project attempted by the Turn-Outs and their Friends, of uniting Capital and Labour in the same hands', were invited to hand in their donations.[65] On Sunday, 2 February, another local group, the 'Friends of Civil and Religious Liberty', held a similar meeting at the Temple of Liberty in Manchester, with George Hadfield, a working spinner, in the chair. The first two speakers were the radicals, Edward Curran and Nathan Broadhurst, who chastised the people of Manchester for coming forward so late in such a vital cause, and successfully moved resolutions bitterly condemning the 'tyrannical' combinations of masters, which were left untouched while the labourers were persecuted merely for uniting to defend themselves, and commencing a subscription for 'the brave 1,800 men, women and children of Derby'. They were succeeded by Doherty, who stated that he did not object to such a meeting as this on a Sunday as it was for benevolent purposes, but the workman had the greatest interest in keeping the Sabbath sacred at it was his only free day. He then detailed the absurdity of the workers calling men 'masters', who were mere traders in the labour of others, and compared the rights and privileges of black slaves, who were protected by law, with the condition of the 'white slaves'. After outlining the course of the Derby dispute, he declared 'that the rod was preparing for the people of Manchester, and that it would fall heavily and deservedly on their backs if they did not bestir themselves', and he concluded by moving that books be left with friendly shopkeepers, so that subscriptions might be raised more effectually 'for the oppressed and suffering turn-outs of Derby'. This was seconded by Sharrocks, the missionary, who had just returned from Derby and stated that 'there were 1,800,000 men in secret Trade Unions', determined to become capitalists themselves. The meeting unanimously adopted this resolution and then adjourned for a week.[66]

Doherty appears to have been made responsible for co-ordinating and transmitting the subscriptions to London, but the amount of pecuniary assistance from Manchester was derisory. On 15 March the *Pioneer* advertised the first donations from the city—a total of £1 10s, 'received by Mr Doherty'—and two weeks later further sums of £1 6s 2½d from the Manchester silk and cotton dyers and 6d from one James Whittaker, 'by John Doherty', were acknowledged.[67] In fact, of the total receipts of over £4,783 for the Derby strikers, only £5 9s 2½d originated from Manchester. And, despite extensive efforts elsewhere, the G.N.C.T.U. proved no more successful on its testing-ground at Derby than had the National Association at Ashton, for the workmen were forced to return on their employers' terms towards the end of April.[68]

The language at the meeting for the Derby workmen on 2 February hardly accorded with Doherty's role in the Regeneration Society. A further sign of the times was, of course, the appearance of the G.N.C.T.U. itself. The London Auxiliary Society continued to be mentioned briefly in the metropolitan unstamped early in 1834, and as late as April Owen was still endeavouring to forward the aims of the Regeneration Society, which he believed was still widely supported in the provinces.[69] But it was massively overshadowed by the formation of the G.N.C.T.U. at a grand meeting of trade-union delegates in London on 13–19 February, likened by the *Crisis* to a 'Trades' Parliament', which was far greater in importance, and would in time be more influential, than its equivalent at Westminster.[70] Although its paying membership only amounted to about 15,000, there was talk, as with the National Association, of far greater numbers and of even more far-reaching aims. The Grand

National, however, made little progress in the north-west, and a spy reported to the Home Office in April that its delegates, George Petrie of the London tailors and one Thomas, had met with 'but a cool reception from several places in Lancashire'.[71] Presumably the recollection of their previous disappointment in the National Association was a sufficient disincentive to prevent the trades generally in that district embarking on another general-union venture. But branches were established at Oldham, Macclesfield, and Congleton, and signs of interest in the G.N.C.T.U. among the Manchester trades produced a significantly more militant tone from the Regeneration Society. Moreover, the apparent fulfilment of Doherty's long-standing general-union hopes caused him to resume his former emphasis upon independent action by the workmen.[72]

Another major incident affecting the situation was the savage sentence of the six Tolpuddle agricultural labourers to seven years' transportation, at the Dorchester Assizes on 19 March, for administering unlawful oaths. This threw trade unionists into ferment throughout the country, widespread meetings were held to adopt petitions against the sentences, and the G.N.C.T.U. was provided with a new rallying cause to atone for the disappointment at Derby, while the Regeneration Society was driven farther into hostility against employers. Manchester played its part in this agitation. On 29 March Doherty wrote in the *Herald* that the punishment was 'in reality, for being members of Trade Unions', and was further proof of the heartless and cruel determination of the Whigs to crush the efforts of the workpeople, and of the necessity for the unions to prepare for the approaching crisis.[73] And in the following week he added bitterly that the sentences were part of a 'War' being carried on by the governing classes against the whole working population, in succession to Peterloo, the Six Acts, and the Special Commission which had tried the agricultural labourers in 1831. The edition for 5 April also carried an address 'To the Members of Trades' Unions', exhorting them not to be deterred by this 'perversion of the law' and insisting that the tyrants could not now resist their united power. As proof of this belief, Doherty proclaimed that each succeeding effort made by the operatives over the previous ten years had been more successful than the previous one. A Trades' Union had been formed in Manchester in 1826, but had not extended far and soon collapsed.[74] 'In 1829, another was formed which speedily extended itself throughout Lancashire, Derbyshire, Cheshire, Nottinghamshire, Leicestershire, and parts of Yorkshire, and several other counties. This soon established the Newspaper called the *Voice of the People*. That, like its predecessor, failed, but out of its ruins sprung the present Trades' Unions, still more extensive and powerful.' Now, they were strong enough to force the government to pardon the victims if they launched a united agitation. And they should also decide upon their wider tactics in the approaching confrontation. Doherty urged that they should 'STRIKE! not against some handful of greedy and wretched employers, as we have heretofore done, but against the whole tribe of idlers of every grade, class or condition'.

Doherty considered that a 'crisis' had now developed and that, unless they took immediate action, the sentences on the Dorchester labourers would soon be followed by 'a ferocious act to destroy the Trades' Unions', which the ruling classes would enforce with 'their standing army and their Bourbon police'. The working people should realise that they were the creators of all wealth and that by united strike action they could overcome 'the idlers' who exploited and despised them—the landowning aristocracy, 'capitalists', and all the 'Jews, bankers, usurers, traffickers, fund-holders, loan-mongers, and borough-mongers'. It was in this context that Doherty referred to the possibility of a 'general strike'.[75] But he raised it only to deprecate the idea, for his urgent call to 'STRIKE'—repeatedly emphasised—took a very peculiar form:

> We do not advise you to strike against all work, for that might prove as fatal to us in the end, as the existing state of things. If a strike against all labour should take place, it is just possible that we might be beaten by it . . . All men are not prepared to subsist a week without work; many might be pinched . . . and they might be induced to help themselves by violence. That, we all know would, in such an event as a general strike against the idle, be hailed as a god-send. They would immediately call out their hired legions and butcher us by wholesale. One instance of this kind would prove fatal to us, for the others would be terrified.

The answer was for all trade unionists to join the Regeneration Society and resolve from 2 June to work an eight-hour day for the present wages—though they would soon have much more. This single step would secure them for ever, as no judges dare hang, or soldiers shoot, men for ceasing to work when they were tired. By acting in this way they would provide for their own subsistence, but not create surplus wealth for their exploiters, and they would make it impossible for the government to get the necessary taxes to maintain 'the immense gang of soldiers, policemen, parsons and others, all of whom are in some way or other employed in keeping us down'. And if eight hours did not achieve their ends they could 'easily come down to six hours, and even lower than that'.

The first public meeting in Manchester on behalf of the 'Dorchester convicts' took place on 7 April at a chapel in Every Street, Ancoats, where Rev J. Scholfield, a well-known radical, was the minister. Philip Grant took the chair and the speakers included James Rigby, Elijah Dixon, R. J. Richardson, Petrie from London, and Fleming from Edinburgh, who all condemned the partial administration of the law against secret oaths, when the Duke of Sussex was suffered to preside over a lodge of freemasons and the late Duke of York over the Orange lodges. Doherty also made a long speech, in which he began by attacking 'the crafty, base and cruel Whigs', who, like the Tories before them, 'now sought to trample them under foot'. 'The condition of these unfortunate men [the Tolpuddle labourers] might be that of any individual there present, for they were all members of Trades' Unions—he had been so himself, and was proud of it, and that man who would not support his union, under whatever circumstances, was a traitor to the common cause of industry.' He also denounced the use of an obsolete statute passed to counteract the naval mutinies of 1797, and trusted that the whole country would rise up to halt such oppression, although he advised strict observance of the law; reducing their working hours was the surest means for the operatives to defeat their enemies. He ended his remarks by moving a resolution demonstrating their fear that the sentences would be part of more general government repression of trade unions. This expressed the meeting's opinion that any legislation resembling the late 'odious' combination laws, designed to keep down the work-people of this country and thereby continue the present monstrous system of pillage of the creators of all wealth, would be the most certain means of disturbing the peace of society and would eventually lead to open outrage and violence, 'which may prove too strong even for an English military government, for it cannot be supposed that the working people can much longer submit to be treated like bullocks or hogs, but as rational beings, holding valuable rights, which they now know, and knowing dare maintain'. The meeting unanimously passed this motion and also agreed to initiate a subscription for the six victims and to petition both Parliament and King for a remission of the sentences. After deciding to request John Fielden to present their petition to the Commons, the business closed with a vote of thanks to Scholfield for the use of his premises, which Doherty accompanied with the suggestion of the propriety of erecting a building for the purpose of holding public meetings of the working classes of Manchester, for which a trifling donation from every workman would suffice.[76]

The furore only induced the government to hurry the unfortunate labourers onto the convict ship all the faster. On 12 April Doherty censured the haste, 'indecent as heartless', with which the 'vindictive judgement' had been carried out, but equally rejoiced that the whole event had failed in its intention of cowing the unions into submission. Instead, workmen throughout the kingdom were pouring in petitions to the government to reverse their policy, and if they would but show the same unity in striking the blow on 2 June, their oppressors, now staggering, would totally collapse.[77] Despite the departure of the convicts, protest meetings continued to be held over the following weeks, especially in the Yorkshire towns, where one of the assemblies, in Huddersfield on 19 April, was organised by the local committee of the Regeneration Society and also discussed the demand for an eight-hour day.[78] This phase of the campaign culminated in the monster procession in London on 21 April and Melbourne's refusal to receive their petition.[79] But the question continued to be agitated in trade union and radical circles, until the remainder of the sentence was finally remitted in 1836, though Loveless and the others did not return for another two years. Meanwhile, in 1834, there was little more talk among the operative supporters of the Regeneration Society of attempting to implement their policy with the co-operation of the employers.

The effect of the sentences at the Dorchester assizes was soon reinforced by other sensational developments nearer Manchester. For some time, there had been unrest among the trade unionists at Oldham, who appear to have had some connection with the Yorkshire Trades' Union and shared that body's regard for secrecy and oath-taking; one of the few active branches of the Regeneration Society was formed at a meeting there on Christmas Day, 1833, and Oldham was the only town in Lancashire to join the G.N.C.T.U. in any strength. The impetus behind this activity came from the local cotton spinners, who, unlike their colleagues in other towns during this period, were not kept quiet by their mills being worked on short time. Towards the end of 1833 spinners in several mills came out on strike, either against wages reductions or the coupling of mules, while the Regeneration

Society's campaign for reduced hours also appears to have had some influence. By 22 February, according to *Wheeler's Manchester Chronicle*, the disputes had spread to more mills and to 'several trades'.[80] Although the Oldham branch of the Regeneration Society obeyed the central decision not to attempt the introduction of the eight-hour system on 1 March, it was reported on 12 April that 'scarcely a day passes but the hands of one mill or another leave their work for a day or so, and then return again, when they have brought the masters to their terms'. Almost a dozen Oldham factories had been affected in such fashion in previous weeks.[81]

On 14 April the authorities reacted strongly to this situation, when three police-beadles broke into a meeting of the spinners' union in a public house, arrested two of the committee, Brierley and Taylor, and seized books and papers. The following day, however, as the two prisoners were being taken for examination before a magistrate, the police were attacked and serious rioting ensued, in the course of which one of the rioters, named Bentley, was shot by armed 'knobsticks' from one of the beleaguered mills; order was only restored by calling the military from Manchester and arresting many of the rioters. On 16 April, when the two committee-men were examined, it became evident that the Oldham union *had* been involved in secret oath-taking in connection with the Yorkshire Trades' Union, and they were held to bail to appear at the next Salford Quarter Sessions.

A very tense atmosphere persisted in the town. On 16 April a meeting of all the union lodges was held on Oldham Edge and although a series of speakers recommended cessation of violence, it was resolved 'that all the trades incorporated in the union'[82] should work no more until Brierley and Taylor were released, until justice was done to the workmen of England, and particularly until the 'murderer' of Bentley was brought to account. The crowds in the town seemed so threatening that the riot act was eventually read and many special constables were sworn in. On the following morning a much larger meeting was held at the same place, attended by a crowd variously estimated at from twenty to thirty thousand persons, who were addressed by Doherty, Rigby and Curran, from Manchester, on the subject of the National Regeneration scheme, and also by a delegate from the Yorkshire trade-unionists in Bradford. Doherty read extracts from the London papers containing accounts of the proceedings of the workmen at Lyons and Paris, where there had been disturbances because of a government edict against trades' associations, and he assured them that before the sun set, every man in France would have his rights and a democracy would be established. One of the other speakers stated that if the Oldham men held out for a few days longer, the whole of the trades in the union would join them. Resolutions were then passed, confirming those adopted on the previous day, but adding that even if those conditions were met, they would still only work in future for eight hours a day; the destruction of property was also deprecated, although it was denied that this was done under the authority of the union, and the conduct of the police was reprobated for having entered the union-room in what was alleged to be a 'drunken state'.[83]

Both the authorities and the workmen regarded the situation as extremely serious. An editorial in the *Manchester and Salford Advertiser* on 19 April alleged that the 'Whig reign of terror, exemplified by the Dorchester prosecution, . . . has now appeared in Oldham', with a drunken police attack on an unoffending lodge of unionists. On the same day Doherty adopted a similar line in an address in the *Herald* 'To the Members of Trade Unions' : their crisis had now arrived and neither Parliament nor the courts would help them. Therefore for the next month he advised them to prohibit the introduction into their lodges of every topic except the eight-hour day, and then they would resolve to adopt it on 2 June, 'and your oppressors must scream like half-strangled rats, but none will help them'.[84] On 16 April James Turner wrote to Place detailing the union version of the course of events at Oldham, and asserting that the workmen had refused to work any more until they had their grievances redressed; 'what they will do I cannot tell, [but] we have some awful forebodings. . . . There is not a mill going, there is not an individual working and what will be the end god only knows.'[85] On the other side, the Oldham magistrates wrote to Major Doran, the officer commanding the troops in the town, on 17 April, giving an account of the numerously-attended meeting that morning addressed by Doherty and others, whose advice to remain on strike and to persuade others to follow their example was 'listened to with great attention'; they also reported that the 'Committee of the Trades' Union' was extending the strike to Saddleworth, Crompton, and Mossley and calling another meeting of the whole body on the following morning, the day of the coroner's inquest on the death of Bentley, and they therefore feared that the military force in Oldham would be insufficient to protect the public peace.[86]

This ugly situation was prevented from developing into further tragedy by a verdict of manslaughter against two of the 'knobsticks', who were consequently committed to Lancaster gaol. This outcome did not please the more reactionary sections of the local press. *Wheeler's Manchester Chronicle* greeted it with 'astonishment' and maintained that the evidence of intimidatory conduct by the unionists and the damage to property warranted a verdict of 'justifiable homicide'.[87] But its instant effect was to moderate the sense of outrage felt by the Oldham workmen. And this tendency was reinforced by the establishment of an official inquiry into the action of the police in forcibly entering the union lodge, which eventually resulted in the dismissal of two of the officers concerned on 14 May.[88]

For a few days after the death of the turn-out spinner, there was a general strike in Oldham, certainly as far as the cotton trade was concerned, and 12,000 operatives were involved.[89] But the reduction in tension was accompanied by a decline in enthusiasm for the strike. Despite the exhortation of the Manchester regenerators at the meeting on 17 April, all the mills at Mossley, Royton and Shaw had restarted four days later and deputations of workmen from each mill in Oldham approached their masters during the subsequent week asking to be taken back, so that virtually every factory in the district was again at work by 26 April. On that day, the *Guardian* rejoiced that the men had surrendered without any of their conditions relating to the liberation of Brierley and Taylor, the restoration of their papers, and twelve hours' wages for eight hours' work being fulfilled, 'so that the turn-out which was to produce such important consequences has come to a very lame and impotent conclusion'. One beneficial result was to destroy any chance of the agitators for 'national regeneration' creating the mischief which they desired, for 'the shallow dreamers who have propounded that absurd scheme' had placed their principal reliance on the Oldham workmen to effect the plan. 'We will venture to predict that very little more will be heard of "national regeneration".'[90]

In fact, the writer was a little premature in his assessment of both the Oldham situation and the general state of the Society. A dispute still persisted between the Oldham hatters and their masters, and there were continued troubles at several cotton mills. Indeed, the *Stockport Advertiser* stated that another general strike was expected in the town, notices having been served on every millowner that after 1 June the operatives would work only eight hours for full wages.[91] That day passed off without incident, however, for the workmen were anxiously awaiting the results of the trials at the Salford Sessions the following day of the cases arising from the disturbances of the previous April. In the event, several of the rioters were sentenced to terms of imprisonment of up to eighteen months, but Brierley and Taylor, charged with conspiracy to administer an illegal oath, escaped the fate of the Tol-puddle labourers by pleading guilty and were discharged. Long quotations from this oath were printed in the local papers along with suitably outraged comments,[92] but in fact trade unions generally were taking the warning and following the example of the G.N.C.T.U. in giving up oaths. In the week after these hearings, it was reported that the Oldham trade unionists were burning their books and intended to make every member memorise the rules. On 27 June the Oldham 'Trades' Union' convened a public meeting to organise a public subscription to defray the expenses connected with the recent court cases, as well as for the eight men still in Lancaster Castle awaiting trial at the Assizes.[93] But thereafter support for general unionism abated in Oldham as elsewhere, and even the sentences of death recorded against six of the workmen for machine-breaking seems to have aroused more sorrow than anger.[94]

The events in Oldham, coinciding with the sentences on the Dorchester labourers, led to a significant change in the policy of the Regeneration Society, with Doherty and the operative members of the Manchester committee attempting to move the Society towards alliance with the trade unions and adoption of a more militant programme. Until the Oldham arrests and fatality, plans to implement the original intent were proceeding, despite the Derby strike, the rise of the G.N.C.T.U., and the Dorchester sentences. As late as 12 April Doherty wrote that support for the eight-hour measure was every day increasing, the districts near Manchester and in the West Riding being especially enthusiastic, and that more and more towns were asking for missionaries to be sent. The factory workers in Manchester were continuing their applications to employers, but were meeting with opposition even from such generally sympathetic millowners as David Holt and Thomas Brookes, whose objections Doherty answered at length in the *Herald*. Whilst recognising the humanity and fair-mindedness of these employers, Doherty was now driven by the current attacks on trade unions into using very outspoken hostile language towards government, employers and capitalists in general, denouncing exploitation and repression, arousing class feeling, and appealing for trade-union solidarity in strike action to secure the eight-hour day.[95]

At the delegate meeting held as planned in Manchester on 16 April,[96] most of the reports indicated that slow progress was being made with applications, but trade-union interest was said to be growing. Doherty therefore urged that 'the society must change its tactics' and 'join the unions, which were becoming all-powerful'. He advocated a conference with union leaders, to try to get their co-operation in the eight-hour scheme. The Oldham affair clearly exercised an influence,[97] though some delegates were opposed to co-operation with the unions. Doherty's proposal was eventually accepted, and the Society also agreed to send a deputation to a general meeting of delegates from the trades of Lancashire and Yorkshire to be held in Oldham in May.[98]

The altered tactics of the Regeneration Society coincided with a renewed attempt by the executive of the G.N.C.T.U. in London to make general union a reality. On 15 April they issued an official notice inviting the largest unions in the country, including those of the builders, cotton spinners, potters and clothiers, who had hitherto held aloof, to send delegates to represent their interests on the council in London.[99] It would appear, however, that both Doherty and the metropolitan leaders greatly exaggerated the strength of the trade unions in this period of excitement. The authorities made a cooler, more realistic appraisal of the situation. The Manchester magistrate, J. F. Foster, who made detailed enquiries into the state of union funds and membership in Manchester at this time at the request of the Home Office, reported on 15 April that he did not believe that their situation was immediately threatening, though they could be potentially dangerous in the long run. 'The Spinners' Union, which has long been the most powerful, is indubitably much reduced in its resources and others are in the same condition.' But he warned that they had so improved their organisation and inter-communication that they could become 'more formidable than ever, if the state of trade or any other circumstances induced them to put forth their strength'.[100]

Doherty was determined that this potential, which he had been endeavouring to develop over the previous years, should be realised at last. Consultations between unionists and regenerators took place in private and on 22 April Doherty published a strongly-worded address, entitled 'The Struggle for Existence—To the Workmen of Manchester', which was placarded over the walls of the town. The battle between rich and poor, between capital and labour, was now at its crisis, he asserted, for their enemies were resolved to destroy their unions, which were their only strength; first the Dorchester men had been carried off and prayers for redress spurned, and more recently a lodge of their Oldham neighbours had been feloniously broken into, books and papers seized, members arrested, and a workman shot dead in open day. Would they yield the right to get their own terms for their labour, and hence their very right of existence, without one great peaceful effort towards emancipation? Oldham had struck the first blow against the oppressors, by ceasing work to a man until justice was done and they obtained the present wages for eight hours' work. The men of London, Birmingham and everywhere were ready to stand. Doherty implored the Manchester men to second their efforts and resolve to reduce their hours, make their labour scarce and more valuable, and their enemies must then either starve or work themselves; but if they delayed one week, the unions might be hunted down, Habeas

Corpus Act suspended, and their leaders arrested. Blood had been shed, the law violated, and power raised to crush the Unions, Doherty concluded, but in return they should 'rise in moral might, and STAND STILL, and you will immediately triumph against all foes'.

A copy of this placard was sent to the Home Secretary, Melbourne, on the following day by Foster, who still did not believe that the population was ripe for a general strike or tumult and was encouraged by the fact that all mills were still at work despite the address. But the publication of such 'a very violent and mischievous placard . . . could not but give us cause for anxiety', he added, as it made clear that the Union would exert itself to the utmost to effect its objects, 'and we know they have had many secret meetings to determine proceedings'.[101] Later, another Manchester correspondent informed Melbourne that the address 'was written and printed by . . . Doherty of Hyde's Cross in this town; he is one of the travelling agents of the National Regeneration Society and has rendered himself notorious by his seditious and inflammatory addresses to the working classes at Nottingham, Derby, Oldham etc.'.[102] Doherty's plan received a setback, however, when the events in Oldham were discussed again at an adjourned delegate meeting of the Regeneration Society on 24 April. Some deputies argued that an attempt should be made to effect the eight-hour plan immediately in co-operation with the Oldham unionists. But others replied that all their arrangements had been taken with a view to enforce the scheme on 2 June and immediate adoption was a fitter topic for consideration by the trade unions rather than by the Regeneration Society. They preferred the mutual co-operation of employers and employed to ensure ultimate success, instead of endangering its final adoption by risking an instant movement. The latter view won the day and a series of resolutions was adopted, that an address to the operatives of England be prepared, that subscriptions be started to pay the expenses of an itinerant missionary, and that the various branches make efforts to extend the circulation of the *Herald*. After hearing from Rigby and Grant of meetings on the two previous nights, at Ashton and of the Manchester spinners, both of which pledged to support the plan, the delegates adjourned their meeting for a further month.[103]

Nevertheless, the 'Address of the Regeneration Society to the Labourers of Great Britain', which Doherty printed in the *Herald* on 26 April, scarcely moderated the militant tone of recent pronouncements. The events at Oldham were again described at length up to the funeral of James Bentley the previous Sunday, and their general strike was called an 'example of heroic courage'; but nothing less than a *general* determination could effect the great change which they desired.[104] There was no mention of waiting for 2 June, but in fact the regenerators were soon driven back to this policy by the rapid return to work at Oldham.[105] It was at this time that a renewed link was forged with the Grand National in London, when the 'Friends of Civil and Religious Liberty' in Manchester, who were continuing to meet for weekly discussions each Sunday and whose topic for debate for the four weeks after 20 April was introduced by members of the Regeneration Society, formed themselves into a Miscellaneous Lodge of the Consolidated Trades' Union, according to an announcement by their secretary, Edward Curran, on 3 May.[106] Meanwhile, the Manchester committee sent out circulars to about forty associated trades in the district, requesting them to send delegates to a conference at the Society's office on 2 May to ascertain the feelings of each trade on the objects of the regenerators. On that day twelve trades sent representatives and another five sent written replies, but most stated that they could not give the authorised opinion of their constituents, since they had not had sufficient time to convene general meetings of their respective bodies to decide the question. But provisionally, the joiners, masons, cotton-yarn dressers, glass-cutters, fustian-cutters, smiths, farriers, cabinet-makers, iron-moulders, woollen spinners, tailors, and hand-loom weavers expressed approval for the plan in principle, although several still required more information, and the last two groups had no longer any organisation of their own. The brickmakers expressed no opinion, but promised to hold a general meeting, and only the bakers and the sawyers believed the idea impracticable because of their dependence upon piece-work.[107]

This response from the Manchester trades must have disappointed Doherty, more than half having failed even to reply to the circular, and no particular urgency being shown by those that did. Nevertheless, in the succeeding day's *Herald* Doherty inserted an appeal 'To the Operatives of Lancashire and Yorkshire', emphasising once more the necessity of adopting the plan in face of the mounting government offensive. This was clearly addressed to a meeting of more than fifty trade-union delegates from the two counties, which met at Oldham that day. Pursuant to the resolution passed on 16 April,[108] a representative of the Regeneration Society attended this meeting to explain its objects, and the delegates eventually agreed that 'the scheme of eight hours' work per day for the present amount of wages, is a question of paramount importance to any other object which the trades' unions have in view. We, therefore, pledge ourselves to advocate the plan in our respective lodges, and urge the necessity of carrying it into effect by the time proposed.' Subscriptions were to be started to pay the expenses of agitating the question in each district, and each lodge was to inform the Manchester society as to their opinion of the best means to secure the system's final adoption.[109]

By this time there was established in Manchester a body called the 'General Trades' Union of Manchester and Salford', which had presumably been formed after the G.N.C.T.U. delegate, George Petrie, had visited the city and spoken at the meeting in defence of the Tolpuddle labourers on 7 April,[110] although it never formally affiliated to the metropolitan body. This local trades' federation, which probably had links with the Regeneration Society, organised a public meeting on 5 May to consider 'the present critical situation of TRADES' UNIONS, in consequence of the threatening interference of the Legislature, and to devise the best and speediest means of securing themselves from future molestation'.[111] The Manchester unionists had only held back from convening the meeting earlier, a correspondent informed the Home Office, 'in order that the results of the meeting of the Trades' Unions in London might be known'. Over the following week, large placards headed 'Unions' Crisis' appeared on the walls of the town, stressing the importance of the working classes attending this gathering, the venue of which had been fixed for Granby Row Fields.[112] In the event, representatives from about two dozen local trades attended and a series of resolutions was adopted, declaring that, as labour was the only capital of the working classes and as they were not protected in the enjoyment of their capital like their employers, they had a right to protect themselves by unions; the sentence on the Dorchester men was denounced and all attempts by the government to interfere with the unions were deprecated; and a petition to the Commons, embodying these resolutions, was adopted.

In fact, however, this meeting was a further sign of the unionists' weakness. Although the *Poor Man's Guardian* reported that 20,000 persons had taken part in the procession to the place of meeting, the local press exultantly told a different story. The *Manchester Herald* called it a 'miserable failure', and *Wheeler's Manchester Chronicle* agreed, estimating the attendance at nearer 6,000 and hoping that this would prevent repetition of the 'Regeneration-mania' in Manchester, for it showed that the workmen were thinking for themselves and were unlikely to wish to lose even a day's earnings on the advice of these interested 'frothers'. The authorities were equally relieved. The local army commander wrote to the Home Office that they had made extensive military preparations, as the meeting was clearly meant to be intimidatory, but in fact it had not succeeded, not more than 2,000 having assembled and a few hundred spectators: this was, he added, 'a great blow to the prestige of the union leaders'. And Foster reported that only 4,000 had attended the meeting, and asserted that 'they still plan a general turn-out for 2 June, but I am satisfied such a call must fail'. Even the *Manchester and Salford Advertiser* commented that it had expected more than 4,000 to turn up, and could not explain whether the disappointment resulted from a lack of interest or because only an imperfect union had as yet been formed among the Manchester workmen.[113]

Doherty did not for some reason attend this meeting, but he did not allow its failure to daunt him. On 8 May the conference between the Manchester trades and the Regeneration Society, adjourned on 2 May, was resumed in the Society's office, though even fewer delegates appear to have attended. The cotton dressers expressed strong support for the plan and invited missionaries to attend their next general election. The hand-loom weavers reported that, by great effort, they had managed to get up some form of organisation among themselves since the previous meeting, with the intention of enrolling themselves as a branch of the general consolidated union, and believed that the eight-hour plan was well suited to their needs. The tailors were also to meet representatives of the consolidated union on 13 and 14 May, when they promised to bring up the objects of the Regeneration Society; their delegate added that a number of trades were about to join the consolidated union, all oaths and useless ceremonies were to be abolished, and the requirements were in future to be such as the most timid might readily subscribe to. The bricklayers promised to make every effort to have the eight-hours plan adopted by the general union comprising 20,000 members to which they belonged. And the bakers asserted that it was to be considered at a general meeting of their body during Whitsun. The conference was also informed that the delegates who had recently met at Oldham had signified the intention of their respective lodges to join the G.N.C.T.U.[114]

Further discussion on 'the soundness of regeneration principles' took place on 15 May. But a more realistic attitude at last prevailed at the adjourned delegate meeting of the different districts of the Regeneration Society, which took place in Manchester the following day. Few towns appear to have sent personal representatives, but letters were received from Liverpool, Chorley, Halifax, Huddersfield, Bolton, and Ashton relating the progress of the plan in those localities. The chief topic was the time for commencement of the scheme, the amended date of 2 June now looming large before them. A resolution to throw in their lot with the general unionists, a policy which Doherty had been following in practice for the previous month, was finally agreed in principle: it was determined 'that as soon as the consolidated union had been fairly organised, arrangements should be made for the adoption of the plan'. Since the establishment of the G.N.C.T.U. on a solid basis was believed to be imminent, it was also felt that a specific time should still be set, and that the intervening period should be used for zealous and active promulgation of their views among trade unionists. It was consequently resolved in the end 'that the period for carrying the eight-hour plan into effect be further extended to Monday, the 1st of September next', and the delegate meeting was then adjourned to 15 August.[115]

Doherty kept up the pretence till the end. In an article on 'Trade Unions' on 10 May, he praised the London operatives for their peaceable conduct in their procession on 21 April, which gave the government no pretext for repression. He went on to praise the London tailors, who were currently on strike and had demanded, among other improvements, the adoption of the eight-hour plan for eight months of the year; but he condemned the 'dastardly stratagem' of their employers in hiring female labour to replace the men, which practice had been widely adopted throughout cotton manufacturing, and which it should be one of their first tasks to end. The antidote was again in their hands, however, for their labour could not be undercut in such a way were they merely 'to acknowledge the natural equality of women; include them in all your schemes of improvement, and raise them as high in the scale of sense and independence as yourselves'. The two final editions of the *Herald*, on 17 and 24 May, included addresses under the heading of 'Union is Strength', which described the anomaly of labour providing all the wealth of the country and yet being the least rewarded, and again urged the necessity of the labourers ceasing to be apathetic and uniting to make labour scarcer as the remedy.[116]

After lasting for a mere sixteen numbers the *Herald* ceased to appear, without warning, after 24 May. Notwithstanding a despairing effort to secure the adoption of the plan at Oldham,[117] the Regeneration Society thereafter slipped rapidly into oblivion, along with the movement for general union with which it had striven to ally at the last. On 6 June the 'Leeds Sub-Committee' of the Manchester and Salford Trades' Union issued an appeal to the various Manchester trades to send deputations to a meeting on 9 June to arrange support for the distressed workmen of Leeds on strike against their masters' document, and to discuss how best to oppose Rotch's bill. Twenty individuals attended and it was agreed to begin subscriptions for the striking workmen. But almost immediately it was reported that the strike had collapsed, the woollen workers being forced back to work on their masters' terms, and the Leeds' Trade Union entirely dissolved.[118] In London the tailors shared the same fate and the G.N.C.T.U. faded into obscurity under the weight of secession and defeat. Meanwhile, in Manchester on 21 June, the *Manchester and*

*Salford Advertiser* bravely reported that the 'Regeneration Society . . . is very steadily pursuing its object', an interview having taken place at the Society's room two nights earlier with a deputation of hand-loom weavers, in reference to the recently-appointed parliamentary committee of enquiry into their condition, and a determination being come to that the matter be resumed on 26 June. But the *Guardian* also referred to 'National Regeneration' on the same day, asking sarcastically if anyone knew what had became of that scheme 'which had made so much news' a few months before. 'After having been announced for the 1st of March, its commencement was postponed . . . to the 2nd June; but that day has long since passed over, without our hearing or reading a word on the subject in any quarter; so that we suppose the scheme must have been forgotten by its promoters as completely as it certainly was by us at the time.'[119]

This scathing allusion to the Society was its obituary, for there was no reference to any adjourned delegate meeting on 15 August, and certainly no action taken on 1 September. Personal contact continued between the Manchester and London Owenites, however, in the following period. On 2 April 1835, James Lowe, who had been secretary of the Regeneration Society, issued a notice in his capacity as secretary of the 'Manchester Association for the Promotion of Social Happiness'—presumably the renamed remnants of the regenerators—convening a meeting of the advocates of Owen's new social system to discuss the formation of a branch of the 'Association of all Classes of all Nations', which was about to be formed at a London congress.[120] But Doherty's own connection with the Owenites ceased completely after June 1834.

The National Regeneration Society was harshly dealt with by contemporaries of all shades of opinion. From the employers' viewpoint, R. H. Greg recalled in 1837 that the Society had been formed in November 1833, by the chief agitators for a ten-hour bill in Manchester, to establish an eight-hour day for the present wages; it was clear, therefore, that since the members of the short-time committee only lived through 'agitation', they would not be satisfied with a ten-hour bill, but simply go on arguing for an 'eight-hour bill', and indeed Owen had recently been lecturing in Manchester for a two-hour day. From the viewpoint of the middle-class radical, Place wrote, in an 1834 essay 'for the people', that he supported trade clubs, 'but I do not approve of Trades' Unions for absurd and unpracticable purposes, such for instance as endeavouring to promote a general strike for twelve hours' pay for eight hours' work, at a time when powers did not exist . . . to prevent an actual fall of wages'. And from the operatives' viewpoint, William Arrowsmith, secretary of the Manchester spinners from 1836, when asked by the 1838 Combinations Committee what became of Doherty's suggestion to follow Althorp's advice and win shorter hours for themselves, could only remember that 'there was some mention of applying to give over all in one day, to strike all over the town, and there were some meetings about it, but somehow or other it fell to the ground'.[121]

Historians have scarcely been more charitable. J. T. Ward has called it a 'fatuous' scheme and blames Owen's intervention for killing Oastler's Factory Reformation Society and the remnants of the short-time movement. N. J. Smelser accuses the Society of 'scapegoating and Utopian idealisation of the past', rightly showing that the spinners were now involved in 'regressive' activities against new machinery, although his explanation of their desire to shorten hours as an endeavour to re-link the labour of adult and child in the factory is surely less convincing than the more obvious one that they hoped thereby to share out the work and thus reduce the number of excess hands in the trade.[122]

Certainly, the Society had a completely impractical policy and was riddled with conflicting aims. Its initial hopes of building up a union with the employers was out of tune with the spirit of the times, and conflicted with its later phase when there was hope of cementing links with the G.N.C.T.U. and talk of a general strike; this change of emphasis during the Society's short life has not previously been noted. The early stress on the domestic role of women also contrasted with Doherty's talk of equality at the last. The only serious attempt to implement the policy was at Oldham, and then mainly as a reaction to local events. The Manchester trades largely held aloof—the spinners do not appear to have gone beyond the stage of discussing the project—and upon this lack of enthusiasm, which was also displayed towards the G.N.C.T.U., the Society finally foundered.

John Foster's recent book, concerned predominantly with demonstrating the rise and fall of 'a revolutionary class consciousness' in Oldham during this period,[123] rightly emphasises the Regeneration Society's origins in the factory reform movement, but ignores its original class-collaborationist basis and also greatly exaggerates the extent to which it became a 'mass movement', uniting 'the various [working-class] industrial and political organisations'.[124] It is ludicrous to assert that the Society's prime aim was to utilise the factory reform issue 'as a lever for fundamental political mobilisation';[125] its direction was never in the hands of revolutionary radicals, and it was certainly not 'the political wing of Doherty's union'.[126] It is true that Doherty and others did eventually make some strong socio-political declamations in their speeches and writings, denouncing both employers and government, but that was after the Tolpuddle case and the Oldham incidents, when trade unionism was so seriously threatened. Yet even then, Doherty never advocated revolutionary violence, but simply refusal to work more than eight hours a day. In Oldham there was a more tumultous movement, but that arose primarily out of the cotton spinners' strike and arrest of their leaders; becoming linked with the Regenerators' eight-hour movement, it had an almost entirely industrial motivation and was certainly not a 'political general strike'. Even there, moreover, the movement soon collapsed and united trades' action fizzled out. The historical evidence we have produced demonstrates overwhelmingly, in fact, that there was *not* a united, sustained, widespread, and thoroughly class-conscious 'mass movement' in the early 1830s, but that the Regeneration Society, like the National Association for the Protection of Labour, never became very widespread, that it was weakened by divisions, that trade societies generally never gave their support, and that it soon, therefore, collapsed in utter failure.

Doherty's ideal of co-operation between the trades did not, however, disappear completely with the failure of the Grand National in London and the Regeneration Society in Manchester. A Trades' Committee was formed in Manchester at the end of 1836 during a strike of fustian cutters, and a similar, if not the same, body was functioning over the next two years, co-ordinating local opposition to the introduction of the New Poor Law, and co-operating during 1838 with similar committees formed in London and other towns to prepare evidence for the Select Committee on Combinations of Workmen.[127] And in 1845 a conference organised by the Sheffield trades actually succeeded in establishing the National Association of United Trades for the Protection of Labour, a general union, whose title clearly showed that Doherty's efforts between 1829–31 had not been forgotten : its insistence on action being taken against reductions only, with advances being left to individual societies, recalled the policy of Doherty's Association, and support for producer co-operation by the trades resembled Doherty's efforts during the second half of 1831 and also the ambitions of the G.N.C.T.U. But few of the larger unions joined the later Association, and although it lasted until the 1860s, its history only confirmed that the spirit of general unionism of the years between 1829 and 1834, which, as we have seen, only marginally touched the most skilled and strongly organised trades even during the so-called 'revolutionary' period, was still extremely weak.[128] Nevertheless, trades' co-operation still continued sporadically, as it had done since 1817–19 : there were further attempts to organise a 'Mass Movement' and 'Labour Parliament' in the Lancashire strikes of 1853–4; further collaboration occurred in the builders' strike of 1859, and in various other movements in the 1860s, leading to the formation of the United Kingdom Alliance of Organised Trades in 1866 and the Trades Union Congress in 1868.[129] Thus there was no watershed or discontinuity in this respect at mid-century and Doherty's efforts were part of a continuing trend in trades-union organisation. But after 1850, as before, the strongly sectionalist aspects of trade unionism continued to predominate.[130]

The failure of the National Regeneration Society caused Doherty to restrict his aims and turn his attention back to that body which had formed the basis of his introduction to the wider trade-union world, the Manchester cotton spinners. Hardly a single dispute had disturbed that trade since their unsuccessful resistance to the employment of women and the continued reduction of piece-rates during 1830–1.[131] But these grievances remained, for the introduction of ever-larger mules resulted not only in lower piece prices but also in redundancies, which both reduced the number of contributors to the union and added to the excess of hands in the trade. The appearance of the *Herald* gave them an outlet for such grievances, and letters from 'An Operative Cotton Spinner', dated 20 January, 16 February, and 2 May 1834, were printed in that publication. The first two communications demonstrated, with the help of tables, how greatly piece-rates had fallen for the finer counts between 1828 and 1833; he revealed that some masters were already employing mules of 816 spindles in Manchester, and calculated that the average reduction in price for the different counts on these machines, compared with those on mules of 300 spindles in 1828, was about 60 per cent. And although an operative on the newer machine could turn off the work of nearly three men on the older, his net wages had only fractionally improved. The correspondent concluded that, unless something was done, the spinners would be reduced to the level of the half-starved weavers, and believed that no project was better fitted to reverse that trend than the one proposed by the Regeneration Society. The last letter was in part a reply to an objection made to the regenerators by one employer, David Holt, that they threatened the 'mutual good understanding' between the employers and employed. It recalled the attempt of the work-men in 1831 to co-operate with the smaller mule owners in moderating the 1829 sliding scale, which was adversely affecting them both: their proposal had been contemptuously rejected by the large-mule masters,[132] and now the small-mule proprietors were coupling their machines and casting half their workmen adrift to want and misery. Which group really threatened the 'friendly feeling' in the factories—masters who practised daily acts of oppres-sion or the regenerators with their mutually beneficial plan?[133]

Despite these communications and a resolution of support for the regenera-tion scheme passed by the Manchester spinners on 23 April,[134] no action was taken to enforce their demand and there was only one minor and unconnected strike during the life of the Society—in April, in one mill, against the coup-ling of mules.[135] It is probable, however, that the connection with the Regeneration Society, as well as the spinners' realisation of their own impotence, caused them to listen once more to Doherty's further schemes for revival. At any rate, Doherty reappeared publicly as secretary of the Manchester spinners' society in June 1834, almost immediately after his editing duties on the *Herald* terminated. Despite the fact that he was now a bookseller and had not worked as a spinner for six years, he retained all the organising enthusiasm which he had shown during his previous period of office between 1828 and 1830. On 19 June 1834, a spinners' general meeting was convened, at which Doherty proposed a plan for reconstructing their union, and it was unanimously resolved that further consideration should take place three weeks later, while Doherty explained his propositions to the rank and file in the meantime. This he proceeded to do in a twelve-page pamphlet addressed to the Operative Spinners of Manchester and Salford and entitled *The Quinquarticular System of Organisation.*

Doherty began with an account of their proceedings over the previous quarter of a century, to show that the present despair was no new phenom-enon and had caused many of their misfortunes in the past. After their great efforts in the Stalybridge strike of 1810, their union was abandoned for a full eight years. Consequently the employers were able to make a considerable reduction in their wages in 1817 [*sic*], though they promised to restore it when trade picked up. Accordingly, in the following year, when the masters refused to fulfil their pledge, the operatives succeeded in reforming their union and staging a general strike lasting three months. They were again defeated and the union once more broke up, but on this occasion it was only five years before they managed to reconstitute it. In a third great strike in 1829, they were able to resist their employers for a full six months, with scarcely any support, and this time their union had continued to exist, despite their defeat, and they still had 700 good and regular payers,[136] even after five years of deplorable apathy. Now it was time to make a renewed effort and rekindle their former enthusiasm.

Doherty then went on to explain the new organisation he had proposed, which was intended to increase the responsibility of the officers and the participation of the membership. Every five men were to elect by ballot one of their number to be their 'Tithing-man', to receive their money, give them information, and communicate their wishes. Every five tithing-men were to select one from themselves to act similarly as 'Constable', and every five constables would likewise choose a 'Warden'. Given a membership of 1,500, the number of wardens would be twelve, and these would form a general committee, whose integrity would be guaranteed by the safeguard of three elections. Three wardens were to be changed each month, and the constables and tithing-men every three months, 'yet every one of them should be liable to be removed at the pleasure of their constituents'. This complex structure was to replace the present government by eight individuals, representing each of the Lodges, or groups of mills, that remained in the Union.[137]

He then proceeded to outline a new system of unemployment benefits, for all were agreed that the old method of 'Casual pay' was harmful. It had tied those thrown out of work to Manchester, thus increasing competition in the labour market, instead of dispersing them over the country in search of work, as other towns had always done, sending their unemployed 'to this town especially, where this very "casual pay" held out an additional inducement . . . to crowd here in the hope of sharing in the pittance which was thus allowed'. The committee now proposed to pay those made redundant a lump sum to assist them to look for work elsewhere, the amount to be fixed on a sliding scale according to the length of payment to the union; £1 was to be given to a payer of three months, rising by 5s for each extra month of membership to £4 10s after one year, and then advancing by £1 for every succeeding year.[138] Apart from unemployment pay, there was also to be a burial allowance for the funerals of members or their wives, defrayed by an additional subscription of 1d each; with 700 payers, the sum would be £2 18s, and from 1,500, a total of £6 5s, so it was 'the interest of every member to increase the number as much and as speedily as possible'. Finally, it was intended eventually to attach a sick fund to the system, with a penny weekly subscription providing 2s per week sick benefit, and proportionately more for those paying higher contributions; 'but as most men are either members of the Sick Clubs, or have established a Sick Fund in the mills, it would be improper at present to interfere with them'.

In conclusion, Doherty returned to the question of organisation. The committee's powers were to be purely administrative, while the legislative authority was to be vested entirely in the general meeting of members, to be held once a quarter. Grievances were no longer to be resolved by the committee, but by 'juries' selected by rotation from the rank and file; and a final and 'somewhat novel' suggestion was the appointment of 'a public officer' to watch the conduct of the officers, attend all meetings, and preside at all investigations of individuals, in short a 'tribune of the people'. But whatever arrangements were meticulously worked out and effected, they 'can only be rendered useful', Doherty reminded the operatives, 'by your individual exertions and co-operation. . . . We must support our own Union, or take the consequences of our own indolence upon ourselves.'

Doherty's comprehensive and ambitious proposals for a formal and closely structured organisation would require additional finance and he therefore recommended a weekly subscription of 4d to 6d, which would necessitate reversal of a recent reduction. A general meeting of payers and non-payers was convened at the 'Prince's Tavern' on 10 July for further consideration of the 'quinquarticular system' and, contrary to Smelser's belief that it 'never materialised', it does in fact seem to have been adopted, at least in part.[139]

The assembly also instructed Doherty as secretary to issue another appeal to those spinners in particular who had seceded from the union, and this second address was adopted at a further general meeting on 31 July. His opening words indicate that the Manchester spinners' society *had* incorporated some form of oath, despite his denials in 1829, but now like other unions it was abandoning the practice in view of recent events at Dorchester and Oldham.[140] Doherty asked those spinners who had withdrawn to remember that 'you have a vow registered in heaven, on behalf of your trade and your unfortunate brethren, and though your new brother members are not now required to give such a pledge, that circumstance, surely, cannot release you from the fulfilment of that most sacred and solemn vow'. It was both their duty and interest to rejoin their fellow-workmen, for the fewer there were in the union, the more they were in their masters' power.

> Come to us and help us, that you may the more effectually help yourselves; remember that you are rational and responsible beings. The great God of heaven has not placed you here merely that you may work, eat, sleep and die, there are other and higher objects which you are bound to attain, . . . and one of these objects is, that you may bequeath a nobler and happier inheritance to your children, than it was your own fortune to be born to, and one of . . . [your] duties is, that you should perform your share of the labour necessary to the attainment of so honourable, so patriotic an object.

If they had committed errors in their past movements, Doherty continued, they could learn from that experience. Their union had at least averted many evils which would sooner or more heavily have fallen upon them, and if they had failed to secure *all* their aims, it was not *because* of union but through *lack* of an extensive and universal union. And if they complained that the 'double-daggers' were in any case throwing half of them out of work, was not their best response to rejoin the union that they might be able to defend themselves against all their masters' attacks in future?

Over the following months a succession of notices was issued, convening meetings of the non-paying shops, and by the end of September the number of payers had increased to nearly 800, in forty-five mills. But this was still less than half the mills in the district,[141] and a copy of one of the notices, signed by Doherty, shows how much perseverance was needed to bring the men back into the union. This was addressed to the spinners at an unnamed mill, whom the committee earnestly entreated 'once more' to support their trade, despite the expense of repeated applications. 'The new system is now in full force, and promises important and novel benefits to its members, and as no arrears are to be charged to any man, there can be no solid objection to your becoming members.' The workmen were, therefore, invited to a shop-meeting at the 'Dog Tavern', Chorlton, 'where a deputation from the committee will be in attendance to meet you, among which your humble servant [Doherty] will have the honour to be one'.

It was the *Manchester Guardian* that first called public notice to these addresses by publishing copies on 4 October. Its motive was to point out to the spinners the real intention behind Doherty's 'high-flown exhortations', which was that they should 'Come and PAY! pay your money into the hands of myself and my friends, and you shall see what you will get for it . . . If you do not pay willingly, we will make you pay.' The spinners should remember that from their former combinations and struggles, from their large payments, and from the long turn-outs in Manchester and Ashton, all of which they engaged in under the advice of Doherty, they had derived not one advantage; in fact, these struggles had increased the number of spinners, leading to hundreds being permanently unemployed, and had speeded up the rate at which their labour had been superseded by improved machinery. The inducement to resort to the self-acting mule would be even greater in future, if Doherty revived hostile feelings against their employers.

> Mr Doherty, indeed, promises some advantages from some 'new system', which he says is in operation; but the spinners may rely upon it that his new systems will end like his old ones. *Somebody* may, no doubt, benefit by them; but the advantage will not be reaped by those who pay the money. Mr Doherty has had many new plans since he took an active part in managing the concerns of the working classes; but his turn-out schemes, his newspaper schemes, his national union scheme, and several others, have all terminated in the same manner,—in loss and suffering to those who joined them. One person, indeed, seems to have profited by them, and that person is Mr Doherty himself. A few years ago, he was a working spinner, he now appears to have a well-stocked shop, a well-furnished house, and to be in very comfortable circumstances. No doubt Mr Doherty knows very well what he is about, when he invites the spinners to 'join in the sacred bond of a renovated brotherhood'; but will they be such simpletons as to accept the invitation? We trust that former experience has not been entirely lost upon them.[142]

But neither Doherty's hopes nor the *Guardian*'s fears were fulfilled. During the whole of 1835 there were reports of only two small strikes in individual mills in Manchester. In March the spinners at Gaythorne mill turned out against the introduction of coupled mules, but the firm was easily able to procure new hands. One of these was assaulted on his way from work and two of the strikers were apprehended, but they denied their guilt and Doherty made a personal application to the millowner, Ferneley, to withdraw proceedings against them. 'That gentleman', however, declined to do so and the defendants were charged at the New Bailey on 25 March and eventually sent for trial at the subsequent sessions. At the same time, there was also a strike for an unspecified grievance at the Albion Mills, which led to a similar case of assault.[143]

It would appear, therefore, that Doherty was unable to bring much life back into the spinners' union, even at a time when trade was recovering and conditions favoured union activity.[144] Sometime early in the following year, he ceased for the second and last time to be the Manchester spinners' secretary. It is impossible to know if he resigned—his factory reform activities were extensive, and he had his shops to keep up—or was dismissed, but his relations with the operatives continued to be cordial. Perhaps the workmen desired their secretary to be more closely acquainted with their current problems in the workplace, for Doherty's successor, William Arrowsmith, combined his duties with continued employment as a coarse spinner. Doherty's salary between 1834 and 1836 was never specified, but Arrowsmith was recompensed with a weekly sum of 25s.[145]

What is certain is that early in the following year, dissatisfaction with Doherty's 'quinquarticular system' became widespread and a series of five general meetings was held to discuss amendments. A new constitution was finally adopted on 9 March 1837, which came into operation a fortnight later. A copy of these amended *Rules and Regulations to be observed by the Society of Friendly Associated Cotton Spinners of Manchester and its neighbourhood* was handed in by Doherty to the Select Committee on Combinations, when he was called to give evidence in June 1838. He explained that 'the present mode of government is different, I believe, from what it was'; but formerly, every five spinners elected one of their number as a 'constable' to represent them, every five of these 'constables' elected a 'warden', every five 'wardens' elected a councilman, and the councilmen, chosen by three elections, made up the committee; but 'I have not been connected with them very recently, and I understand there have been alterations lately'.[146]

The new constitution combined elements of Doherty's system with the previous method of organisation. Some of his cumbersomely democratic arrangements were altered, but extensive membership participation was retained in the election of the committee, every *twenty-five* members now appointing a warden, and every five wardens appointing a councilman; every officer served for three months, but could be dismissed at an earlier period if his constituents wished. The role of the independent 'public officer', supervising the conduct of the officers on behalf of the rank and file, was taken over by 'a president', elected monthly from the committee; but the supreme government was still in the hands of the quarterly general meeting, and all cases of disputes were still to be adjudicated by 'juries' selected by rotation from the ordinary membership. The regulations governing benefits were also slightly amended, a fixed sum being paid for funerals rather than from additional penny subscriptions, and the entitlement for the unemployed being heavily reduced, to half what the recipient had himself paid into the society, 'but not to exceed £4'. The weekly subscription was still to be at the discretion of the members, but appears to have been 7d at this time.[147]

Many features of the 'quinquarticular system' were thus retained. It was found necessary to abolish the intermediate post of 'constable' to reduce the complexity of the organisation; but the advantages of widening the area of responsibility must have been enough to prevent a complete return to the system of one representative from each mill. Doherty's scale of unemployment benefits had also been set too high at a time when redundancies were proliferating. And although the *principle* of lump sum payments for the out-of-work to go off and seek employment was retained in a revised form in 1837, even these amended regulations broke down under the weight of applicants and enforced a return to the system of small weekly doles.[148] Despite these difficulties, the union had managed to increase its membership from the 1834 level and comprised about 1,060 spinners by June 1838, at which time the society had funds of about £100. But the total number of spinners in Manchester was then between 1,400 and 1,500, and there were whole mills without a single member of the union.[149]

When Doherty was questioned by the Select Committee as to these facts, he could only estimate that 'there are as many out of the union as in it'; he estimated union membership to be about 1,000 out of a total of around 2,000 spinners in Manchester. But the latter figure was corrected by Arrowsmith, who pointed out that 'he [Doherty] has not been amongst us for two or three years, and the number of spinners has decreased . . . since his time, in consequence of the enlargement of machinery'.[150]

Nevertheless, even after finally surrendering his official position in the local spinners' society, Doherty still had links with them. He continued, as we shall see, to play a leading role in the factory reform movement. Moreover, the persistent appeal of his old policies was reflected in another attempt to combine the English spinning districts in a federal organisation, with the traditional aim of equalising piece prices. This occurred at the height of the trade boom in 1836, when conditions favoured movements for wage advances. The Manchester spinners held a meeting on 11 October 'to consider the propriety of organising . . . an union of the trade throughout the country, for protecting the price of labour'. Doherty was one of the speakers, together with Arrowsmith, McWilliams and others, and his views doubtless contributed to the final determination 'that an union of the cotton spinning districts . . . should be formed'. This proposal was immediately confirmed at a meeting in Bolton on 15 October, attended by delegates from the spinners of Manchester, Preston, Blackburn, Chorley, Warrington, Stockport, Wigan, Bolton and other towns, who decided on a combined movement to raise all their wages to the Bolton standard.[151]

As in the earlier federations, however, there was no strong central authority to control the constituent societies and soon there were reports of wages demands and stoppages in Oldham, Chorley, Stockport, Ashton, Blackburn, and Wigan.[152] The most serious situation, however, developed in Preston, where, in response to a demand for the Bolton list, the masters' association closed all their mills early in November, making a total of 15,000 workmen idle. An important motive behind this decision, according to the *Preston Chronicle*, was their determination 'to resist the general union existing throughout the trade amongst the workpeople', in which determination they apparently obtained financial backing from the Manchester and other millowners.[153] On their side, the operatives made vigorous and widespread efforts to mobilise support, issuing an address 'To the Working Men of England, particularly those connected with Trades' Unions', appealing for subscriptions to be sent not only through trade societies but also to radical publishers such as Henry Hetherington in London, John Doherty or Abel Heywood in Manchester, and others in Glasgow, Liverpool, Leeds, Sheffield and Birmingham, who would forward the money to Preston. In response to this appeal, numerous meetings were held in Lancashire towns, for the purpose of raising subscriptions.[154] In the placard summoning the Manchester meeting, early in January 1837, Doherty was among those billed to speak, but he does not appear to have done so.[155] Nor does he seem to have played any part in the subsequent struggle, which involved strikes not only in Preston but also in other towns, notably Oldham.[156] These ended in disastrous defeat by February–March 1837, the men being forced back to work on the masters' terms, while large numbers remained proscribed and unemployed, as the trade boom ended in crisis and recession.

The spinners' general union, of course, was involved in these defeats and soon disappeared. Doherty stated in June 1838 that the Manchester spinners' society had no organisational links outside the town,[157] and the next attempt to federate the different districts was not made until 1842. His part in these events was peripheral, however, offering support and encouragement, but not participating in the central direction. Nor does he appear to have been involved in the 'trades' union' or local trades federation which emerged in Manchester during 1837, initially for co-ordinating aid to unions engaged in strikes, but increasingly motivated by hostility to the new poor law and by radical political feeling.[158] This body was responsible for mobilising local support for the Glasgow cotton spinners' committee, arrested for organising violence, arson and even murder during a strike there in the autumn of 1837.[159] Although the Manchester spinners, led by Arrowsmith and McWilliams, were very active in this campaign, there is no reference to Doherty in the contemporary press reports, at the end of 1837 and early in 1838. But as the threat to trade unions became more general and more serious, Doherty came to resume an active role in their defence.

This threat came from the appointment in February 1838 of a Parliamentary Select Committee of enquiry into Combinations of Workmen, following evidence put forward by Daniel O'Connell on violence among trade unionists in Dublin, Glasgow and elsewhere. Believing this to be an attempt to secure reimposition of the Combination Laws, trade unionists immediately started to organise in self-defence, a trades' committee being established in London to co-operate with similar bodies in provincial towns.[160] And Francis Place set to work once more behind the scenes to prepare evidence and witnesses, as he had done in 1824–5. In mustering trade-union support, he wrote to the Manchester spinners requesting them immediately to select three reliable and respectable representatives to testify before the Select Committee; they should be able to give full evidence respecting their trade, particularly about the 1829 strike, and the union should provide them with financial support.[161]

In this dangerous situation, the Manchester spinners again recalled their old leader, Doherty, doubtless because of his long acquaintance with Place, with whom he had collaborated against the Combination Laws, and also because of his unrivalled experience in the trade-union and factory reform movements, including service on several previous London delegations. But Doherty, though willing to serve, was evidently not too happy at the prospect. Replying to Place on 5 April, he informed him that he had been appointed by the spinners as their delegate, 'although I have not had anything to do with them for now several years', and many circumstances, dates and figures relating to the spinners' strikes in various towns during the 'twenties and early 'thirties had escaped his memory and needed renewing. 'I pointed this out to the spinners in general meeting, the other evening, and asked them to send some efficient person to each of these places for the double purpose of collecting the facts, and ascertaining who are the most fit men to be summoned from each place, on the part of the workers. When it was shown, however, that the probable expense would be £10 or £15, they refused to go into it.' Doherty considered that it was essential for this to be done, but could not spare the time or money himself, especially as he would meanwhile have to pay a journeyman printer 30s per week to carry on his own work. He therefore asked Place if there was any fund which could be applied to for this purpose.

This lukewarm response infuriated Place. Replying to Doherty on 13 April he expressed angry disgust that, in this crisis, the spinners should have appointed only one delegate, and that one 'unacquainted with late proceedings'. This was a desertion both of 'their own interest and that of all other working men'. They must either 'become more manly, or . . . cowardly and weakly succumb to the enemy'. He emphasised that the Select Committee included men who were extremely hostile to trade unions, upon which they sought to reimpose legal restrictions; the cotton spinners were particularly threatened. If the Manchester spinners would not act under such circumstances, there were certainly no other funds available 'to encourage workmen to neglect themselves'. But it was urgent that Doherty at least should send to Lovett the names of reliable persons in Hyde, Ashton, and Bolton, who might be written to for details of the events there, as the workmen must be prepared to give an open and candid account of all their proceedings, or else a perverted version by the masters would be accepted.[162]

Place's letter, which he asked Doherty to 'read . . . to the assembled Cotton spinners', shook them out of their lethargy. On 21 April the *Manchester and Salford Advertiser* reported that they had joined the 'Manchester combination committee',[163] which had been established by the local 'Trades' Union', and they also delegated Arrowsmith and McWilliams to supplement Doherty's evidence to the Select Committee. In his testimony on 7 June, Doherty put up a stout defence of trade unions. He gave as far as he could an account of the present state of the Manchester spinners' union. It would not countenance violence or intimidation, although any squabble in the streets during a strike was falsely attributed to its influence, nor did it desire any oath-taking or secrecy, save in the amount of its funds. And it was managed by officers of great responsibility since they were elected by universal suffrage. He insisted, despite a long cross-examination by O'Connell, that a workman would be perfectly free in Manchester to accept spinning work at reduced prices and without joining the union, and still not be subject to acts of violence, although the union would make representations to the master concerned to end the practice, and 'of course' the spinners in the same room would not receive such a new worker as amicably as one who joined the union. But in fact the combination served to prevent violence in such cases, by giving workmen a chance of maintaining their position legally and 'allowing irritated feeling to evaporate . . . by some peaceable means'.

He then went on to give a long account of the Manchester spinners' strikes since the repeal of the Combination Laws. Almost all had been partial, against individual millowners, and these had often been supported by the other masters to bring up underpayers. The only 'general strike' in the town was in 1829 against a massive reduction imposed by their masters. The cause of this dispute was the masters' excessive greed, for the men recognised that Manchester wages were higher than in the neighbourhood and would have accepted a moderate abatement; the workmen's conduct throughout was entirely orderly, despite existing on 2s 2¼d per week; they had shown a continued conciliatory spirit, unlike the employers, by soliciting the adjudication of both churchwardens and magistrates; and far from 'agitators' stirring up the members, the strike-leaders had actually secured the return to work by falsifying the result of a vote by the rank and file.[164] Doherty asserted that generally the workmen only turned-out very unwillingly, for strikes meant loss of wages, probable loss of employment, and persecution and blacklisting of their leaders. Consequently their union often accepted reductions without opposition, and only engaged in strikes, as in 1829, if they believed reductions would be even more frequent and heavy without some check being placed upon them. Closely questioned by O'Connell, he had to admit that the 'general strike' of that year had not prevented several subsequent reductions, and that intelligent operatives well knew that such a strike was almost certain to fail, but nevertheless, 'notwithstanding that experience', he considered that circumstances could 'very likely' arise again that would lead to its repetition.

Doherty also adverted to the spinners' Grand General Union and the National Association, both of which had emerged from the workmen's recognition that individual and local trades could not withstand their combined employers. He asserted that the Association reached 'over 100,000' members, and was largely based on O'Connell's Catholic Association, adding that it failed not only because he had not 'the same materials but also not the same skill and ability to work them': thus he at least had not entirely lost his admiration for the Irish leader.[165] He firmly rejected any idea of legislation in regard to labour relations. When it was suggested that a law to prohibit masters reducing wages or men striking without a fortnight's notice might benefit both parties, Doherty agreed that it would prevent sudden and arbitrary reductions, without the men's knowledge, 'but I should certainly say (and I speak the sense of the great mass of operatives in Lancashire), that I would rather forego that good, than allow the present House of Commons to interfere with the subject at all. We believe, if they interfere at all, it will be to injure rather than benefit us.' In support of this belief he referred to the 1833 Factory Act, against the working of which the workmen had a large number of grievances, which Doherty detailed at length[166] before returning to his own part in trade-union affairs.

> For myself, I have had nothing to do with the combinations for some years; but I feel greatly interested that they should have fair play, and, I think, considering the influence of property, that the interests of the wealthy classes alone are represented in the House of Commons, the least you can do for the operatives is to let them alone. I can only add that, looking at the excitement which the history of the factory question has created, the reductions of wages, the increased labour, the increased use of machinery; all these irritating things taken together, as well as the defeats which have followed peaceable strikes, I would not undertake to conduct another strike to the same extent, for so long a period, for all the money the House of Commons could give me.

And he concluded with a warning. Although the Manchester spinners had never corresponded with continental workmen, they had often discussed the disturbances at Lyons in 1831 and deprecated them; but if the contemptuous treatment of the Lyons workmen by their employers was repeated in Manchester, as seemed possible from the recent refusal of one employer even to see a deputation from the union regarding a wages complaint, then 'I should certainly fear, if . . . they were to go on with the grievances they are labouring under at present, they might be provoked to do what I know in their sober judgements they dislike'.[167]

To support his statements, Doherty deposited with the Committee a copy of the report of the spinners' delegate conference on the Isle of Man as an example of the publicity given to their proceedings, a copy of the current rules of the Manchester society, and some statistics of 'Comparative Mortality' in manufacturing towns and agricultural counties revealing the worse conditions in the former. His testimony was also backed up by David McWilliams and William Arrowsmith, who both spoke from long experience of the spinning trade and spinners' unionism, emphasising the problems of technological change and the role of the union in trying to improve labour relations.[168] The only other witness from Lancashire was John Frederick Foster, the Manchester magistrate, who stubbornly resisted every pressure from the Committee to persuade him to condemn combinations as violent, and indeed spent most time denying that he had any intimate knowledge of their activities at all. He believed that unions were the 'natural result' of the circumstances in society, whereby the masters desired to pay the lowest, and the men to receive the highest, wages possible, and would not countenance any idea of reimposing the combination laws or forcing unions to be legally registered, which he feared would drive them back underground. He agreed, however, that it would be desirable to shift the burden of proof onto those who crowded around mills during strikes to show that they were innocent of intimidatory behaviour rather than for the prosecution to show them guilty.[169]

The Select Committee finished its first session of taking evidence in August, and although it later reassembled for further testimony on the state of Irish trade unions, it never in fact published a report. No anti-union legislation was introduced, and, indeed, the Glasgow cotton spinners, like the Tolpuddle martyrs before them, were pardoned in 1840 and given a heroes' reception on visiting Manchester on 27 July.[170] Quotations from Doherty's evidence were given in the *Northern Star* on 15 September 1838, along with condemnatory comments of O'Connell's behaviour.[171]

This was virtually Doherty's last official service for the Manchester spinners, and his contact with them thereafter was, with one exception, reserved for the factory reform question. In the late 'thirties and early 'forties, they were forced into quiescence by another severe trade depression, until heavy unemployment and wages reductions finally resulted in the 'Plug' riots of August 1842.[172] This situation brought Doherty briefly back into contact with the Manchester spinners' union, to propose a solution recalling part of the aims of the National Regeneration Society of 1833–4. Early in September 1842, as the last embers of the disturbances which had convulsed the town and district were dying down, meetings of unemployed cotton spinners were held to discuss measures of relief for their sufferings, which were said to be 'almost beyond endurance'. This distress resulted not only from the prolonged trade depression, but also from technological developments, for it was stated that one man was now performing as much work as four men did eight years before, because of improved machinery. The spinners' union, therefore, while not deprecating such improvements, considered that it was the duty of the government to provide for the maintenance of those made unemployed, 'either by locating them upon the waste lands which exist in such abundance, or by some other means compatible with the interests and welfare of an industrious, but at present a starving population'. The impetus behind the proposal seems to have come from Doherty, who made a long speech at a meeting on 13 September. He stated that he had addressed many spinners' meetings before, but had never spoken to so many totally without work.

> He was not a cotton spinner now, nor did he believe that he should ever enter a factory again; but he could not forget the struggles that he had made side by side with some of them to uphold their wages; and now for the last time perhaps that he should have the pleasure of addressing them, they had come together, not for the purpose of asking for the means of maintaining themselves from the hand of charity, or from the board of guardians, but they had come boldly before the country to ask for compensation for the injury that had been done to them.

It was digraceful, Doherty alleged, for the government to allow able-bodied men to stand idle after giving thirty years' service to the trade. The largest mules when he was a spinner had 696 spindles; now they had nearly 4,000, and did four men's work, yet wages were still 26–27s a week. The profits must all be going to the millowners, who should therefore be made to pay to relieve those who were harmed. And the workmen's claim was all the stronger because, although there had been extensive riots recently, he had been told by the local police superintendent that not a single unemployed spinner had been involved. Doherty stated they should never oppose machinery, but they did deserve justice. Hence each person present should submit his name, age and residence, the number of his children, the years of his employment, and his present circumstances, which information should be appended to a memorial to be drawn up by the committee and handed to the government by John Fielden, or directly to the Prime Minister, Peel, by a deputation of their number.

Doherty's suggestion was adopted and discussion then turned to a further motion, 'that a reduction of the number of hours to eight per day would still leave us far ahead of the quantity of work produced twenty-five years ago, . . . and could at once relieve the hands from the evil of over-exertion, and the masters from the evil of overproduction'. This was opposed by one John Wood, who ridiculed the idea of unemployed men demanding shorter hours and believed the whole thing was a scheme of Ashley's to strengthen the Tory government at a time when the manufacturers were about to start another campaign against the corn laws. But Doherty replied that they could not be thought idiots to desire that others do less and themselves more; while as to shorter hours, the meeting well knew that they had struggled for the same thing 'before Lord Ashley was known to them, and before the repeal of the corn laws was even heard'. So far as Doherty was concerned, Ashley knew no more of the present meeting than the man in the moon, and the only member who was aware of it was John Fielden, 'to whom he mentioned the subject about three weeks ago', and who considered it very desirable that the facts should be elicited. At the close of the proceedings, a committee of five, including Doherty, was appointed to draw up a memorial to the Queen asking for compensation.[173]

There is no evidence, however, that anything came of this appeal, which had the appearance of a somewhat hopeless proposal typical of a group of workers suffering under technological unemployment.[174] The number of hand-mule spinners in Manchester continued to decline, to an estimated 525 in 1844, and the remedy of employing redundant hands on the land—a panacea widely looked to in the decade of the Chartist land plan—was actually attempted in 1848 by the Oldham spinners' union, who purchased eight acres of land at the nearby village of Glodwick.[175] But from the end of 1842 onwards, the remaining hand-mule spinners were looking to a new federal union, which differed radically from its predecessors as it took in also the new self-actor minders and was centred in Bolton.[176] Doherty had no connection with it, except over the factory reform question, and the cotton spinners seem to have completely forgotten the greatest of their early leaders by the time of his death, almost unnoticed, in 1854.

Thus Doherty's participation in the Manchester cotton spinners' union spanned the years from his imprisonment as a raw youth for his activities during a strike in 1818 to his role as the old leader offering advice a quarter of a century later. He was also at the heart of the movement to form a general union of trades during the decade after repeal of the Combination Laws. And as a printer and bookseller after 1832, he continued to serve the movement, printing, for example, an undated address 'To the Leypayers of Salford' from the associated dyers and dressers of the town, asking them to condemn their overseers of the poor for refusing to grant relief to the workmen during a strike; he also printed the rules of the Manchester Fustian Cutters' Union in 1839.[177] Some years after his apparent retirement from public life, he briefly reappeared to second one of a number of resolutions passed at a meeting of Manchester workmen in October 1849, protesting against the sentencing of a young apprentice dyer to be flogged for participating in a strike, against the rules of his indenture.[178] This censure of injustice is the last public reference to Doherty before his death.

NOTES TO CHAPTER EIGHT

[1] Cole, *Attempts at General Union*, pp. 63–9; S. and B. Webb, *op. cit.*, pp. 124–33.
[2] *Times and Gazette*, 5 October 1833, quoting the *True Sun*.
[3] *Ibid.*, 31 August 1833.
[4] Cole, *Attempts at General Union*, p. 105.
[5] *Crisis*, 19 October, Supplement, 1833.
[6] Tufnell, *op. cit.*, p. 80. See above, p. 145.
[7] See above, pp. 142–5.
[8] See below, pp. 339–42.
[9] See below, Chapter x.
[10] *Voice*, 17 September 1831. See above, p. 145, and below, p. 367.
[11] *Advocate*, 23 June 1832.
[12] *Parl. Papers*, 1837–8, VIII, 3473.
[13] The invitation was sent through William Clegg, an Owenite manufacturer of Manchester, who referred in his letter to the working classes' 'attempts to establish a general union'. Owen Documents, Holyoake House, No. 623.
[14] *Crisis*, 23 November 1833.
[15] *Cobbett's Register*, 14 December 1833.
[16] *Catechism of the Society for Promoting National Regeneration* (Manchester, 1833).

[17] *Crisis,* 7 December; *Times and Gazette,* 30 November 1833.

[18] Owen Documents, Nos. 664, 668, 610 and 607.

[19] *Cobbett's Register,* 14 December 1833. His figures were based on the 1801 census and he included all dependants among the 'idlers'.

[20] *Advertiser,* 16 November 1833.

[21] *Ibid.,* 9 November 1833.

[22] *Chronicle,* 16 November 1833.

[23] J. P. Kay, *The Moral and Physical Condition of the Working-classes employed in the Cotton Manufacture in Manchester* (Manchester, 1832).

[24] *Times and Gazette,* 30 November; *Advertiser,* 30 November; *Guardian,* 30 November and 7 December; *Poor Man's Guardian,* 30 November 1833; and H.O. 40/31.

[25] *Guardian,* 7 December 1833, *inter alia.*

[26] *Ibid.; Chronicle,* 7 December; *Morning Chronicle,* quoted in *Cobbett's Register,* 14 December 1833.

[27] *Advertiser,* 18 January 1834. The solidarity of the Oldham radicals was, therefore, less complete than one recent commentator would have us believe. See J. Foster, 'Revolutionaries in Oldham', *Marxism Today,* Vol. 12, November 1968.

[28] *Advertiser,* 30 November–21 December 1833, and 18 and 25 January 1834.

[29] *Ibid.,* 28 December 1831, and the following editions.

[30] *Guardian,* 7 December; *Times and Gazette,* 14 December 1833; *Herald,* 22 February 1834. The missionaries appointed were Philip Grant, power-loom weaver, and Isaac Higginbottom, engraver, to visit towns north of Manchester; Sharrocks, mechanic, and Chamberlane, card-grinder and stripper, for those to the south; and James Turner, cotton yarn dresser, and James Rigby, plumber and glazier, to visit the Manchester trades.

[31] *Advertiser,* 21 December 1833; Clegg to Owen, 13 December 1833, Owen Documents, No. 603.

[32] *Advertiser,* 21 December 1833; Place Collection, Vol. 51, f. 48.

[33] Place Collection, Vol. 51, ff. 45 and 49.

[34] *Herald,* 22 February 1834.

[35] See below, p. 291.

[36] *Advertiser,* 28 December 1833, and 4 January 1834.

[37] *Crisis,* 14 December; *Agitator and Political Anatomist,* 7 December 1833, preserved in Place Collection, Vol. 51, f. 53.

[38] *Crisis,* 7 December 1833–1 February 1834; *Pioneer,* 7 December 1833; *Poor Man's Guardian,* 7 December 1833–4 January 1834.

[39] *Crisis,* 21 and 28 December 1833.

[40] *Ibid.,* 28 December 1833–18 January 1834.

[41] *Pioneer,* 11 January 1834.

[42] H.O. 40/32.

[43] *Chronicle,* 11 January; *Advertiser,* 1 February; *Chronicle,* 8 February 1834.

[44] *Herald,* 22 February 1834.

[45] *Chronicle,* 8 February; *Times and Gazette,* 1 February 1834.

[46] *Advertiser,* 1 and 8 February 1834.

[47] *Ibid.,* 8 February 1834.

[48] H.O. 40/32.

[49] *Herald,* 8 February–22 March 1834.

[50] *Chronicle,* 25 January 1834; Place Collection, Vol. 51, f. 58.

[51] For this contest, see J. T. Ward, *The Factory Movement, 1830–55* (1962). p. 116.

[52] Owen Documents, No. 674.

[53] A copy of this notice, printed at the *Advertiser* office, is in the Place Collection, Vol. 51, f. 29.

[54] *Guardian,* 22 February; *Herald,* 1 March 1834.

[55] *Herald,* 1 March; *Advertiser,* 1 March 1834. The *Guardian,* 1 March, quoted the date as 21 June! Some branches, especially Oldham, but also Chorlton-on-Medlock, Heywood, and Todmorden, had made some headway in interesting local trade societies and making applications to employers.

[56] H.O. 40/31.
[57] *Guardian*, 1 March 1834.
[58] *Herald*, 1 March 1834.
[59] *Ibid*, 8 March 1834.
[60] *Bradford Observer*, 6 and 27 February 1834; Ward, *The Factory Movement*, pp. 117–8; Owen Documents, No. 677.
[61] *Bradford Observer*, 27 February; *Herald*, 15 and 22 March, 19 April 1834. For Bull's attitude towards the Regeneration Society, see J. C. Gill, *The Ten Hours Parson* (1959), pp. 134–40.
[62] *Herald*, 15 and 29 March, and 5 April 1834.
[63] *Chronicle*, 22 March; *Advertiser* and *Herald*, 29 March 1834.
[64] See above, pp. 279 and 281.
[65] *Advertiser*, 25 January 1834. James Rigby, one of the Regeneration Society's missionaries and a prominent local co-operator, was secretary of the committee. In addition to meetings to help the Derby men, there were also lectures and discussions on the Regeneration Society. *Gauntlet*, 26 January 1834.
[66] *Poor Man's Guardian*, 15 February 1834.
[67] *Pioneer*, 15 and 29 March 1834.
[68] For the Derby strike, see Oliver, *op. cit.*, pp. 147–59.
[69] *Herald*, 26 April 1834.
[70] *Crisis*, 22 February 1834.
[71] Oliver, *op. cit.*, p. 231, quoting H.O. 52/54.
[72] See below, p. 294.
[73] *Herald*, 29 March 1834.
[74] See above, pp. 39–41.
[75] *Herald*, 5 April 1834. See above, pp. 23–7 and 249, however, for the earlier introduction of the idea. Doherty later used the phrase several times in evidence to the Select Committee on Combinations in 1838, in the sense of a general 'turn-out' by cotton spinners, as in Manchester in 1829. See also above, pp. 125–6.
[76] *Chronicle*, 12 April; *Advertiser*, 12 April; *Guardian*, 12 April 1834.
[77] *Herald*, 12 April 1834.
[78] Oliver, *op. cit.*, p. 278, quoting the *Leeds Mercury*.
[79] *Poor Man's Guardian*, 26 April 1834.
[80] *Chronicle*, 7, 21 and 28 December 1833, and 22 February 1834.
[81] *Stockport Advertiser*, 12 April 1834.
[82] Probably a reference to the local branch of the G.N.C.T.U., although the newspaper reports during these events did not make clear whether they were referring to this body, or to the local auxiliary of the National Regeneration Society, or to the local spinners' union. William Marcroft, writing in 1890, spoke of a 'Central Union Club', formed in the town in 1834, with central and district committees meeting at different inns, with an entrance fee of 1s 6d and many oaths and ceremonies. See W. Marcroft, *The Marcroft Family* (1890), pp. 103–6, quoted in Webb Collection, Vol. xxxiv, f. 52.
[83] *Guardian*, 19 and 26 April; *Chronicle*, 19 April; *Advertiser*, 26 April 1834.
[84] *Advertiser*, 19 April; *Herald*, 19 April 1834.
[85] Place Collection, Vol. 51, ff. 80–1.
[86] H.O. 40/32.
[87] *Advertiser*, 19 April; *Chronicle*, 19 April 1834.
[88] *Bolton Chronicle*, 3 and 17 May 1834.
[89] *Pioneer*, 26 April 1834.
[90] *Guardian*, 26 April 1834.
[91] *Bolton Chronicle*, 3 May; *Stockport Advertiser*, 3 and 16 May; *Times*, 17 May 1834.
[92] *Times*, 7 June; *Guardian*, 7 June 1834.
[93] *Bolton Chronicle*, 14 June and 5 July 1834.
[94] *Times*, 26 July and 23 August 1834. The sentences were later commuted.
[95] *Herald*, 12–26 April; *Times*, 19 April 1834. See above pp. 289–91. For Holt's letter, see also below, pp. 302–3.
[96] See above, p. 285. In addition to Doherty and Grant, there were delegates from Heywood, Todmorden, Ashton, Stockport, Blackburn, Oldham, Salford,

Bolton, Chorlton, Bury, and the Manchester spinners. Letters were received from Hyde, Stalybridge, Wigan, Liverpool, Congleton, Leeds, Hebden Bridge, Halifax, Barnsley, Huddersfield, Bradford, and Derby.

97 Doherty was in close agreement with James Mills, the Oldham spinners' secretary, with whom he had earlier associated.

98 *Herald*, 26 April 1834. For the May meeting in Oldham, see below, p. 297.

99 *Pioneer*, 19 April 1834.

100 H.O. 40/32, f. 180.

101 H.O. 40/32, letter from Foster to Melbourne, 23 April 1834.

102 *Ibid.*, letter from Joseph Adshead to Melbourne, 3 May 1834.

103 *Herald*, 3 May 1834.

104 *Ibid.*, 26 April 1834.

105 See above, p. 293.

106 *Poor Man's Guardian*, 19 April–10 May 1834.

107 *Herald*, 10 May 1834.

108 See above, p. 295.

109 *Herald*, 3 and 10 May 1834.

110 See above, p. 290.

111 Publicity was currently being given to a private member's bill, intended to be introduced by Rotch, the member for Knaresborough, 'to prevent the Combinations of Trades' Unions, as affecting the free trade in labour', by enforcing registration of their rules and officers' names and by tightening the law against secret oaths and intimidation.

112 *Times*, 10 May 1834; H.O. 40/32, letter from Joseph Adshead to Melbourne, 3 May, and letter from Lt. Col. Kennedy to Phillips, 5 May 1834.

113 *Guardian*, 10 May; *Poor Man's Guardian*, 10 May; *Manchester Herald*, 7 May; *Chronicle*, 10 May; *Advertiser*, 10 May 1834; H.O. 40/32, letter from Lt. Col. Kennedy quoted in previous note, and letter from Foster to Melbourne, 5 May 1834. These reports show the difficulties of estimating the size of crowds, but the figure 30,000 given by Morris, *op. cit.*, p. 243, is clearly based on a greatly exaggerated account.

114 *Herald*, 17 May 1834.

115 *Ibid.*, 24 May 1834.

116 *Ibid.*, 10–24 May 1834.

117 See above, pp. 293–4.

118 *Advertiser*, 7 June; *Chronicle*, 14 and 21 June 1834.

119 *Advertiser*, 21 June; *Guardian*, 21 June 1834.

120 *Advertiser*, 2 April 1835.

121 R. H. Greg, *The Factory Question Considered* (London, 1837), pp. 75–7; F. Place, *Essays for the People—No. 1 Mr Hanson's speech Examined* (London, 1834), p. 12; Parl. Papers, 1837–8, VIII, 3806.

122 J. T. Ward, 'The Factory Movement in Lancashire, 1830–55', *T.L.C.A.S.*, Vols. 75 and 76 (1965–6), p. 191, and *The Factory Movement, 1830–55*, p. 115; Smelser, *op. cit.*, pp. 242–3. See above, pp. 147–8.

123 J. Foster, *Class Struggle and the Industrial Revolution* (1974). This book was published after our typescript had gone to the printer's, so we have only been able to insert this brief reference to it. In general, we consider that the evidence has been selected and distorted so as to fit into a Marxist–Leninist ideological framework, demonstrating the alleged 'crisis of capitalism' and the growth of a violent, revolutionary, 'mass movement', without regard to the actual historical complexities.

124 *Ibid.*, pp. 108–114.

125 *Ibid.*, p. 110.

126 *Ibid.*, p. 101. Doherty had ceased to be secretary of any union by the end of 1830, the Grand General Union and National Association had collapsed in 1831–2, and the Manchester spinners' society was almost defunct.

127 See below, p. 310.

128 Musson, *British Trade Unions, 1800–1875*, p. 49.

129 See A. E. Musson, *Trade Union and Social History* (1974), Chapter 3.

130 *Ibid.*, Chapter 2, and *British Trade Unions, 1800–1875*, Chapter 6.

[131] See above, pp. 142–5.
[132] See above, p. 60.
[133] *Herald,* 15 and 22 February, and 17 May 1834.
[134] See above, p. 296.
[135] *Advertiser,* 3 May 1834.
[136] For membership of the union in 1829, see above, p. 55.
[137] For the number of lodges in 1829, see above, p. 55.
[138] Smelser, *op. cit.,* p. 335, wrongly describes this as an attempt to *abandon* tramping. It was quite the reverse.
[139] Smelser, *op. cit.,* p. 335. See below, p. 307.
[140] In 1838 he told the Combinations Committee that the Manchester spinners' society abolished oath-taking after the repeal of the Combination Laws, but the phraseology of the July address seems to fit a more recent abandonment of the practice. See Parl. Papers, 1837–8, VIII, 3359.
[141] There were 96 in 1832, according to Manchester Chamber of Commerce, *Proceedings,* 27 April 1833.
[142] *Guardian,* 4 October 1834. Doherty sent a long reply to this letter, but the editor would not insert it, making excuse that it was posted too late (*ibid.,* 25 October 1834). Doherty therefore printed it in the restarted *Poor Man's Advocate,* but unfortunately this number does not appear to have survived (see below, pp. 384–5).
[143] *Chronicle,* 28 March 1835.
[144] In that same year, the Oldham spinners' society was apparently broken up by the combined forces of the local masters' association and disillusionment among the operatives. *Chronicle,* 24 and 31 October 1835.
[145] Parl. Papers, 1837–8, VIII, 3808. Doherty stated that his salary was £1 13*s*, *ibid.,* 3504, but this may have referred only to his first term.
[146] *Ibid.,* 3369. Note that the terminology differed slightly from Doherty's original proposals (see above, pp. 303–4).
[147] 'Rules and Regulations', *ibid.,* Appendix 4, p. 303.
[148] *Ibid.,* 3795.
[149] *Ibid.,* 3358, 3784, 3785, and 3811.
[150] *Ibid.,* 3494, 3535, and 3785.
[151] *Advertiser,* 15 October; *Guardian,* 22 October 1836. The Bolton spinners had just obtained an advance of 7½ per cent.
[152] *Times,* 22 and 29 October; *Bolton Chronicle,* 22 and 29 October; *Chronicle,* 3 December 1836.
[153] *Guardian,* 2 November, quoting the *Preston Chronicle*; *Advertiser,* 12 November and 3 December; *Guardian,* 10 December 1836. For the causes and course of the Preston lock-out, see Turner, *op. cit.,* pp. 74–5, and H. Ashworth, *An Inquiry into the Origin, Progress and Results of the Strike of Operative Cotton Spinners of Preston, from October 1836 to February 1837* (Manchester, 1837); the latter, of course, is strongly anti-union.
[154] *Advertiser,* 19 November, 10 and 17 December 1836; Place Collection, Vol. 52, f. 71.
[155] *Guardian,* 7 January 1837.
[156] Reports are to be found in all the local papers from November 1836 to March 1837.
[157] Parl. Papers, 1837–8, VIII, 3356.
[158] It eventually became, in fact, the basis of the Chartist organisation in Manchester.
[159] See S. and B. Webb, *op. cit.,* pp. 170–3, for an account of the Glasgow spinners' case. Five of them were sentenced to seven years' transportation in January 1838.
[160] W. Lovett, *Life and Struggles* . . . (1967 edn.), pp. 131–2. The Manchester trades' union held several meetings in support of the measures taken by the metropolitan trades' committee. *Advertiser,* 10 and 17 March 1838.
[161] *Advertiser,* 24 February 1838.
[162] Place Collection, Vol. 52, f. 417. The cotton spinners had exasperated Place on several previous occasions, e.g. in refusing to accept his advice on the use.

lessness of strikes with an excess of hands in the trade; in supporting the National Regeneration Society; and in 'whining' about factory conditions, etc. (see above, pp. 67 and 279–80, and below, p. 411, n. 126). This exasperation was echoed in his present comments: 'When a foolish impracticable matter is proposed to them which admits of much loud talking and swaggering and threatening and pretending, they can appoint any number of delegates . . .' This is how Place regarded most of Doherty's earlier schemes.

163 *Advertiser*, 21 April 1838.

164 See above, p. 78.

165 O'Connell's earlier popularity with English radicals had been waning for some time, because of his association with the Whigs and his views on political economy, the new poor law and factory reform, as well as on trade unions. For Doherty's relations with him on Ireland, see below, pp. 448–55.

166 See below, pp. 395–6.

167 Parl. Papers, 1837–8, VIII, 3351–3641.

168 *Ibid.*, 3642–3815.

169 *Ibid.*, 3185–3350.

170 *Chronicle*, 1 August 1840.

171 *Northern Star*, 15 September 1838.

172 See A. G. Rose, 'The Plug Riots in Lancashire and Cheshire', *T.L.C.A.S.*, Vol. LXVII (1957).

173 *Chronicle*, 17 September 1842. On the conflict between factory reformers and free traders at this time, see below, pp. 398–403 and 441–2.

174 It was, in fact, part of the Tory-Radical reaction to the effects of industrialisation. The Tory-Radical, W. P. Ferrand, had put forward a similar proposal in the Commons three months previously. See R. L. Hill, *Toryism and the People 1832–1846* (1929), pp. 171–6.

175 *Northern Star*, 11 May 1844; *Times*, 8 March 1848.

176 For this body, see Turner, *op. cit.*, pp. 115–6.

177 Place Collection, Vol. 52, f. 55; *Regulations agreed to . . . 29 August 1839*, in Manchester Central Reference Library Collection of Broadsides.

178 *Northern Star*, 20 October 1849.

# IX     The new society:
## co-operation, education, and temperance

Labour historians, almost without exception, have regarded Doherty as a fervent apostle of Owenite Co-operation, primarily concerned with converting trade unionists and the working classes generally to belief in Utopian Socialism. The Webbs saw him as playing a leading role in the 'revolutionary period' of the late 1820s and early 1830s, characterised, in their view, by the conversion of trade unions to Owen's 'new view of society', culminating in the formation of the Grand National Consolidated Trades' Union and the attempt to overthrow capitalist competition by a kind of gild socialism or syndicalism.[1] G. D. H. Cole has described him as 'an ardent Owenite who believed the distinction between master and man was destined to be swept away by the advent of the Co-operative Commonwealth'.[2] This view has been followed by D. C. Morris, who depicts him as trying—though unsuccessfully —to get his 'idea of establishing a Co-operative Community' adopted by the spinners' union.[3] Earlier, indeed, S. J. Chapman considered that Doherty succeeded in this aim of converting the cotton spinners, thus causing 'their trade notions to be thoroughly undermined by Owenism'.[4] More recently, Rudé has asserted that Doherty and other leaders of the cotton spinners and the National Association, 'being Owenites, tended to indulge in the millenarial fantasy of rapidly transforming society into a co-operative commonwealth'.[5] E. P. Thompson has likewise declared that 'Doherty . . . rightly saw, in the growing popularity of Owenite ideas, a means of bringing the organised workers of the country into a common movement', that he converted first the cotton spinners and then the National Association to these ideas, and that 'thenceforward, the history of Owenism and of general unionism must be taken together'.[6] And J. F. C. Harrison has similarly depicted him as 'enthusiastic for the Owenite cause'.[7]

To a very large extent, however, these views are mistaken or distorted, based on inadequate historical research, but endlessly reiterated. In the first place, they greatly exaggerate the influence of Owenism itself, especially upon trade unions.[8] There is no doubt, of course, that the Co-operative movement did expand rapidly in this period, hundreds of societies being established, particularly in Lancashire and Yorkshire, but many working-class co-operators, while certainly influenced by Owenite ideas, did not become 'Owenites' in the strict sense.[9] In fact they often differed profoundly from Owen in his emphasis upon a classless movement—combining masters and men—and upon creating co-operative communities requiring large capital sums; they generally preferred more limited practical schemes for retail stores and co-operative production, and the majority of ordinary members appear never to have had much knowledge of or sympathy with the more high-flown Owenite ideas.[10]

Trade unionists certainly were not convinced by the Owenites: they could not accept the notion of class co-operation, when they were faced by the hostility of employers, wages reductions, etc., and by threats to their own existence through legal, police, and military repression; they placed trust first and foremost in their own established trade unions, as defensive organisations to maintain wages, apprenticeship regulations, and trade customs generally, and to provide mutual support in unemployment, sickness, and death; they could not accept the Owenite argument that such trade and benefit funds were useless and ought to be devoted to co-operative schemes, for they could not believe that a social revolution was just around the corner; they regarded co-operative communitarianism as largely visionary and impractical, while they themselves were immediately concerned with the down-to-earth realities of the present competitive industrial society; whilst, therefore, they agreed with the Owenite denunciations of existing social evils and expressed sympathy with Owenite endeavours to improve the lot of the labouring classes— the 'productive' and 'useful' sections of society who created the country's wealth—they could not generally accept the means proposed to remedy this situation, preferring to rely on their own trusted and traditional methods.

We have already seen that Doherty's attitude towards Co-operation coincided closely with the general trade-union view. He was certainly *not* a visionary idealist trying to lead trade unionists into a new co-operative–socialist world. Above all he was a trade unionist, convinced of the necessity for both sectional and general trade-union organisation, as the essential basis for all working-class improvement. As secretary of the Manchester spinners' union, as general secretary and to a large extent the creator of the cotton spinners' Grand General Union, in his similar role in the National Association, and even in the leadership of the Regeneration Society, he was primarily and continuously concerned with trade-union objectives such as extending membership, improving organisation, raising strike funds, resisting wages reductions, reducing working hours, restricting entry to the trade, trying to reduce unemployment, opposing harsh workshop regulations, fines, truck, etc., and fighting for factory legislation. Only for a brief period, early in the Regeneration Society, does he appear to have accepted the Owenite view of happy collaboration between masters and men to achieve social improvements such as an eight-hour day, and he soon became disillusioned with the attempt, reverting to militant trade-union strike pressure. On the other hand, although he frequently denounced capitalist class exploitation, he was not in general a rabid exponent of class war;[11] in fact he was a staunch advocate of peaceful collective bargaining and of co-operation with employers whenever possible, to secure improvements in wages and conditions of work, just as he collaborated with middle- and upper-class reformers to achieve factory legislation and political reform.[12] At the same time, however, he had a profound belief in independent working-class or trade-union action, in achieving things for themselves, and, in so far as they collaborated with the upper classes, doing so from a position of strength and from a standpoint of equality.

He was certainly not prepared to sacrifice or risk the hard-won position which trade unions had established for themselves and the concessions which they had gained, in favour of any utopian Owenite schemes. He did not, as we have seen, attempt to divert the cotton spinners' union from concern with its basic industrial objectives into Owenite fantasies; there is no evidence whatever for such a view. Nor did he make any such endeavour with the National Association, whose fundamental purpose, like that of the spinners' general union, was to raise a general strike fund for support of individual trade societies against wages reductions; only towards the end of the Association's existence, when it had been defeated in strikes and was disintegrating, did he clutch at Co-operation as a possible means of infusing it with new hope in an alternative project, and even then the idea did not originate with him but with the calico-printers, and it was in schemes of producers' co-operation, as a means of employing striking or unemployed members, not in Owenite communities, that he saw practical possibilities.

There is no doubt that Doherty shared the co-operators' dissatisfaction with the structure of society as it emerged from the first stages of the Industrial Revolution. He was obviously familiar with the writings of Owen, Thompson, Hodgskin and other critics of the existing competitive capitalist society, as well as of radicals such as Cobbett—in fact he became personally acquainted with some of these men. His various journals and pamphlets constantly expressed anti-capitalist views : that a relatively small number of landowners, millowners, merchants and financiers had succeeded in gaining socio-economic and political power and were robbing the working people of their right to the whole of what they produced, so that labour, the source of all wealth, was reduced to poverty and misery, whilst the capitalist expropriators, backed by the law, police and military forces, acquired the greater part of labour's product and thus amassed wealth and lived in affluence. On the other hand, there were also innumerable occasions when, as a practical trade unionist, he recognised the roles and 'rights' of employers, on which, he declared, trade unions had no wish to encroach—their ownership and managerial functions, their right to hire and dismiss labour (with due notice), and their commercial importance; he never seems to have seriously envisaged workers' control or a socialist revolution, although in his advocacy of producers' co-operation there were strands of gild-socialist or syndicalist ideas.

It was not, therefore, in the diagnosis of social ills that Doherty disagreed with Owenite co-operators, but in the remedies proposed. Whilst he certainly supported schemes for the establishment of co-operative stores and co-operative production—and also sympathised with the ideal of a socialist society based on co-operative communities—he never accepted Owenism as the sole, or even the main, solution. He placed far greater emphasis not only on trade-union organisation and objectives, but also on political agitation in order to achieve both parliamentary reform and legislative improvements such as factory acts. Co-operation would be simply a laudable auxiliary to these other movements; he would never accept the view of dedicated Owenites that trade unionism and political radicalism were futile and ought to be abandoned for co-operative socialism; on the contrary, he saw much greater possibilities of economic and social amelioration through these means than through co-operation. Eventually, in 1831, as we shall see, he did appear to be more completely converted to a belief in Co-operation, but this was when his schemes of general union were disintegrating and he thought that co-operative projects and the support of co-operative societies might be props to prevent total collapse; but even then he did not play an active part in the movement.

Doherty had evidently become interested in co-operative ideas at an early date, as evidenced by his later statements that in about 1822 he had proposed 'a plan of co-operation' to the Manchester cotton spinners, which, had it been adopted, he was convinced would have proved successful. 'But men's minds were not then prepared to receive it.'[13] There is no other evidence to illuminate these vague references, but they most probably relate to some scheme of co-operative production along the same lines as those he later favoured. At that time, however, as he stated, co-operative ideas had not spread among the working classes and it is not therefore surprising that Doherty appears to have taken no further interest in such schemes until their more widespread adoption from the late 'twenties onwards.

By 1830, however, they were beginning to spread rapidly in the Lancashire area and many societies were being founded both for retail trading and, less numerously, for co-operative production. But there is no evidence of either the Manchester spinners' society or the spinners' general union becoming involved in such schemes; the Ashton spinners, as we have seen, did, after their great defeat early in 1831, consider a plan of co-operative production for unemployed strike hands, but nothing seems to have come of it.[14] Contrary to the statements of Cole and others, the spinners did not reject Doherty's Owenite notions, because, in fact, he never tried to introduce them into the Grand General Union.[15] Moreover, he and other founders of the National Association refused to consider any diversion of their funds into co-operative schemes. When it was suggested by one speaker at the meeting of Manchester trade-union delegates on 30 September 1829, at which the Association was inaugurated, that the subscriptions might be better spent on co-operative production than in supporting strikes, the idea obtained no support and Doherty pointed out that the essential purpose of the general union was to provide financial aid for societies resisting wages reductions.[16]

The title of the Association's journal, however, the *United Trades' Co-operative Journal*, has often been taken as evidence of its support of co-operative principles and of the close links between the two movements. In fact, as we have shown, this title is misleading, in that the word 'co-operative' was here being used only in the sense of inter-union co-operation.[17] There is no doubt whatever that the predominant emphasis was upon the 'united trades'—on the necessity for general union in the National Association—and not upon co-operation in the Owenite sense. Nevertheless, the *Journal* certainly did demonstrate Doherty's considerable interest in and support of the co-operative movement. The first number contained an article extracted from the London *Co-operative Magazine*, which attributed the present extremes of wealth and poverty to the 'erroneous' economic and social system, whereby machinery competed against, rather than benefited, human labour. It went on to urge the working classes to become more educated, temperate and thrifty, 'purchasing all that you require for your consumption at co-operative stores', for not only were these goods cheaper and more wholesome, but 'by becoming members of trading associations you will eventually . . . be enabled to enjoy the . . . entire fruits of your labour and skill'.[18] Shortly afterwards Doherty inserted a long description of the 'extensive premises' recently opened by the Manchester dressers' and dyers' co-operative society at Pendleton—a scheme of producers' co-operation which he particularly commended.[19]

Very soon, however, the *Journal* also began to reflect the serious differences between trade unionists and co-operators, in which Doherty, while attempting to secure agreement, could not avoid expressing his own conviction of the prior importance of trade unionism. At the end of March 1830, William Pare, the Birmingham co-operative missionary, gave a series of lectures in Manchester (reported in the *Journal*), in which he attributed the wretched condition of the labouring classes to the introduction of machinery in a society organised competitively, and maintained that the only solution was co-operative production and exchange of goods, leading ultimately to a co-operative community. Whilst he sympathised with the object of trade unions in trying to keep up wages, he considered that they had inevitably failed to achieve this, because under the existing competitive system wages were determined by supply and demand, capitalists were obliged to pay as low wages as possible, and so it was futile to combine and strike against reductions; trade unions ought instead to put their funds into co-operative societies, which aimed at superseding the competitive system.[20] These sentiments provoked an editorial reply from Doherty, in which—whilst declaring that he was 'an ardent and zealous supporter' of the 'beautiful system' of co-operation, and agreeing that competition was the source of the evils afflicting the productive classes—he maintained that wages reductions were generally caused by the greed of a small number of masters seeking excessive profits, thus forcing others to follow suit, and therefore trade unions, or 'co-operative societies for the protection of labour', were a 'still more important and immediately useful measure' than co-operative trading societies. And because the basic evil was competition in *labour*, the source of all value, the only way to uphold wages and promote the interests of the working classes was to establish a grand 'National Association for the Protection of Labour'.[21]

In the following months, nevertheless, Doherty continued to give publicity to co-operation. For several weeks from 24 April he extracted from the *Associate*, a London co-operative journal, model rules for co-operative trading societies. On 8 May he published the resolutions passed at the delegate meeting establishing the Manchester and Salford Association for the Promotion of Co-operative Knowledge, and future meetings of that body were also reported. On 2 June, for example, Elijah Dixon and David McWilliams spoke on the evils resulting from the maldistribution of the products of machinery, and on 15 July Dixon again lectured on the practicality of communities like Owen's at New Harmony.[22]

The differences between trade unionists and co-operators, however, still continued. At the National Association's first general delegate meeting, in June 1830,[23] another proposal to link the two movements was again rejected. Lyster, a delegate from the calico printers, argued that merely depositing the funds in a bank would bring little profit and he therefore suggested using them to establish a co-operative store, to serve the trades. Doherty, however, opposed this plan as premature, for the distrust among workmen would have to be removed before they could think of subscribing to such a scheme, necessitating expenditure of huge sums on premises as big as the Rochdale canal warehouses; therefore 'it would be folly to talk of trading', and he joked that paying out relief in provisions might render them liable to prosecution for trucking.

This did not end the matter, however, and co-operators continued to urge the superiority of their schemes. On 31 July, for example, when Doherty and other representatives of the National Association visited Wigan for the purpose of establishing a branch there, an argument developed with William Carson, one of the most ardent and active co-operators in the north-west, who condemned the general union scheme and expressed his preference for the co-operative system of buying and selling provisions and dividing profits among the subscribers—thus co-operation would give them profits with every mouthful they ate. Doherty, in return, poured ridicule upon Carson's views: 'As to co-operation, he had always been inclined to look upon it favourably before that evening; but when he heard men talk about getting profit from every mouthful they eat, he confessed his opinion was somewhat changed. According to this doctrine all they had to do was to sit down and eat all before them in order to become completely happy. (Laughter.) The more they eat, the richer they would become. (Laughter.)'[24]

Similar, though less acrimonious, differences were apparent at Birmingham, where Doherty and other Association representatives spoke in late August and early September 1830.[25] He and William Pare obviously had considerable respect for each other, and Pare gave qualified approval to the Association, but he considered that it could only succeed if it adopted co-operative production during strikes, for otherwise it would be powerless against the forces of competition. Other Birmingham artisans also preferred Owenite co-operation, or collaboration with employers in the political union, rather than class-conscious trade unionism.[26]

Meanwhile, in Manchester, the wrangling between the two movements became more bitter, when Doherty convened a meeting on 23 August to discuss whether the National Association or the co-operative system was 'best calculated to promote the happiness and independence of the working classes'.[27] Thomas Oates detailed the benefits of general union, especially in maintaining wages, pointing out that co-operative societies were dependent upon the effectiveness of unions for continuance of their subscriptions. In reply, however, Elijah Dixon emphasised the rigidity of the economic laws governing wages, against which unions were ineffective, and contrasted their long history of failure with the success of co-operative schemes, both in retailing and production. He was met with vehement protests and contradictions: from James Turner, who gave examples of trade-union successes in advancing wages; from Oates, who accused co-operators of selfishly looking only to their own profits; and from Doherty, who 'did not like to oppose the co-operative system, but from the manner Mr Dixon had spoken of Trade Unions, feared he would be obliged'. Thereupon Dixon, who was defended only by David McWilliams, got up to leave, only to be charged by Doherty with lack of respect for opposing viewpoints. Fortunately, the meeting ultimately agreed to a suggestion by Doherty to adjourn for a week which allowed tempers to cool on both sides. Two further meetings were held, on 30 August and 6 September, in a better atmosphere, but no consensus emerged and Doherty could only wind up by saying that the meetings had at least demonstrated that the working classes could discuss their vital interests publicly with energy and moderation.[28]

Doherty still retained his basic trade-union position, but continued to show tolerance towards co-operators in the *Journal*. On 11 September he inserted a copy of a letter from John Finch, the Liverpool co-operator and temperance advocate, to local friendly societies, advising them to cease wasting money by meeting in public houses and to begin using their surplus capital for trading to their own advantage. Three weeks later he reported a meeting of Liverpool dock-labourers on 29 September, at which Finch persuaded them to adopt a scheme for co-operative dock labour.[29] He also inserted another long letter from William Pare, extolling the benefits of co-operation, but still maintaining an equivocal attitude towards the National Association, for though Pare 'highly approved' of its existence, he considered it folly for workmen to place their whole reliance on it and therefore urged them to follow the advice of the 'celebrated' William Thompson, of Cork, in case of strikes or lock-outs, by employing their funds 'in establishing trades' manufactories, and agricultural associations'; he concluded by calling for an end to quarrelling between co-operators and unionists, but only, it would appear, by recognition of the superiority of co-operative schemes.[30]

There are further signs of a rapprochement. On 26 October J. F. Foster, the Manchester magistrate, wrote to Home Secretary Peel, that 'the Union' had applied for the occupation of 'some considerable Print-works in the area', to carry on business on their own account and employ turn-outs, instead of paying allowances, and that they intended to pursue the system in other places.[31] Evidently the co-operators' arguments were beginning to bear fruit. At the same time, the Manchester dyers and dressers, who had left the Association because of the recent squabbles, decided to return to the fold after an appeal from Doherty and Hodgins. Doherty 'wished them success in that [co-operative] undertaking,[32] but still thought they ought to assist in supporting the general union. If they did not assist in preventing the reduction of wages their means of co-operating would be taken from them.' He blamed wages reductions not only on avaricious masters and the over-supply of hands, but also on the apathy of the workmen themselves, and he pointed out how the Association would remedy this situation.[33] Similarly, in his 'Address . . . to the Workmen of the United Kingdom' in early October, Doherty emphasised the fundamental importance of trade unionism both for maintenance of wages and for the success of co-operative schemes.[34]

Nevertheless, the disagreements between co-operators and unionists continued in the first half of 1831. On 16 March the familiar arguments were repeated by William Carson, Elijah Dixon, and Thomas Oates after a co-operative lecture given by Carson in the dyers' room, the co-operators still criticising the Association and extolling 'the superior advantages of the co-operative system above all other systems'.[35] On 14 May Doherty returned to the subject in a long editorial in the *Voice*. He had 'sometimes spoken disparagingly of the system of co-operation, not because of any hostility for the principles themselves, but from a belief that it could not be carried into complete and successful effect by the means proposed'. The main cause of his criticism was the absurd and extravagant claims made for it by its ill-judging admirers, but 'we confess . . . that we have some well-founded objections to the system proposed by Mr Owen, Mr Pare and others'. Since men were the 'creatures of circumstances', it was impossible that workmen from occupations as diverse as husbandry and cotton spinning, or letter-press printing and stable-keeping, could immediately agree on all points; hence community projects comprising all such workers were impracticable. But, Doherty continued, he enthusiastically supported 'co-operation by classes or trades', which was the true mode of applying co-operative principles. The present state of the Manchester dyers and dressers was a 'triumph of co-operation' : after having started co-operative production just over a year previously, in premises rented at Pendleton for £150 p.a., their business was now worth £150 per week; of their 1,100 members, 150 who would otherwise have been out of work were employed in the dye-works in two sets on alternate weeks for wages of 18s over the fortnight, while the weekly subscription had been halved because it was no longer necessary to pay redundancy benefits, and the employers had not reduced their wages as there were no surplus hands in the trade. To this form of co-operation, which not only applied the co-operative principle but also upheld wages, Doherty called the attention of every trade society in the country and urged them to open their own establishments, as he had heard more than one trade society already intended to do.

Thus, with the failure of strikes at Rochdale, Ashton, Derby and Nottingham, Doherty was now not only supporting producer co-operation in theory but advocating its practice as a supplementary form of trade-union 'association for the protection of labour'. But this change was insufficient to satisfy the co-operators, one of whom wrote to the *Voice* during the following week to complain that Doherty had not recommended the general adoption of co-operative principles, which would convert all profits into wages, reduce working hours, and increase the time for leisure and instruction. Doherty's reply revealed a further subtle shift of opinion. He denied that he had shown any reservations regarding co-operative principles at all, for 'we have been labouring in a thousand different ways to enforce them for the last ten years', and he referred to the 'plan of co-operation' which he had proposed, unsuccessfully, to the Manchester spinners 'some nine or ten years ago'. He did not condemn even '*indiscriminate*' co-operation, as proposed by Owen, but considered that it was not the best method in existing circumstances. Co-operating by trades would preserve the advantages of division of labour and avoid the inefficiencies of surplus tailors, smiths, sawyers, spinners, etc. all having to work in one particular area chosen for the first experiment, which would provoke jealousy and perhaps be fatally discouraging, 'because we know something of the difficulty of keeping any considerable portion of the working classes together, for any great length of time, in pursuit of any one common object, which does not promise an immediate and decided benefit'. Separately, the trades might at once produce all the articles required, which could then be assembled in a 'common stock'. Doherty concluded by re-asserting his anxiety for the success of this mode of co-operating, for 'any measure which seems to us likely to benefit the working classes shall, of course, have our most hearty concurrence'.

But this was still not enough for his correspondent, who wrote back stating that Doherty's caution and doubts about the fitness of the people for such a rewarding undertaking were themselves holding back the great changes. The fact was that if the labourers would combine not merely to protect wages, but to rearrange society so that they consumed all that they produced, they had the power immediately to supersede the capitalist, legislator, banker, churchman, landlord, etc. But only by knowledge would the progress be effected: hence they should form committees of the most intelligent workmen to buy cheap books and establish institutions to educate themselves and their children. In a third editorial on the subject, Doherty agreed on the necessity of the workmen combining to provide instruction for themselves unassisted,[36] especially as the 'pompous professions' of the middle-class Society for the Diffusion of Useful Knowledge had proved 'a complete failure'. He stressed that he looked forward to every trade society in the kingdom starting manufacturing 'as the natural and necessary result of the proper application of the [co-operative] principles', and believed if the people were but half convinced of their own power, they could better their condition 'in a single month'; but he could not see why men would be worse co-operators because they co-operated to uphold wages, on which everything depended, for they would thus begin at the roots, rather than the branches.[37]

Doherty's brief conversion to full support of co-operation occurred at the first national congress of co-operative societies, held at the 'Spread Eagle' inn, Salford, on 26 and 27 May, and attended by Robert Owen, William Thompson and most of the other leading figures in the movement. Over fifty societies were represented by a total of forty-six delegates, and two important decisions were made. Firstly they agreed to establish the North West of England United Co-operative Company, with John Dixon of Chester as president and John Finch of Liverpool as secretary; this was to open a wholesale warehouse in Liverpool, where retail societies could buy products at near to cost price, and goods manufactured co-operatively could be exchanged. Secondly, the proceeds of this business were to be used to establish a community, although the bulk of the capital was to be provided by 200 societies throughout the country subscribing £30 each; local trustees were appointed to collect these subscriptions, which were then to be forwarded to John Dixon, the treasurer. Doherty did not attend this congress, but immediately afterwards the *Voice* office published placards, advertising lectures to be given by Thompson in the theatre of the Mechanics' Institution on 1 and 6 June. These he did attend and reported at length. Thompson argued that the failures at Orbiston and New Harmony did not mean that they should delay, as Owen had asserted at the recent congress, although he had agreed to become a trustee; they indicated that another attempt should be made immediately, to prove that communities *were* practicable and the best mode of relieving pauperism by settling the poor on the land. It was also urgent to save the workmen from expensive losses in their brave, but misguided, attempts to set up their own manufactories, such as that of the Manchester dyers, which must inevitably fail because they could only employ a small minority of the hands in their trade, while they were perpetuating the competitive system and actually exacerbating the evils of over-production. Thompson's main theme was a comparison of Owen's plan for the organisation of communities with his own, which envisaged a far greater degree of communal living but had been criticised by Owen in their recent discussions. Both evenings terminated with 'conversation' and debate on the respective proposals, in which Doherty participated.[38]

Doherty's contact with the leading co-operators appears to have removed his previous reservations about their ideas, though this further shift of opinion must be seen in the context of the National Association's failure in supporting strikes and his consequent adoption of alternative schemes.[39] On 4 and 11 June he published a long 'Appeal to the Producers of Wealth, as to the best means of securing the Fruits of their own Industry', in which, while emphasising that workmen should first strive towards making the National Association a comprehensive union efficient at raising funds, he suggested that a portion of those funds might be applied to the purchase of land and erection of buildings for a co-operative community, which would be an important step 'towards the total renovation of the whole structure of society'. In fact on 11 June he expressed unqualified support for the community project, declaring that it was the most important measure ever brought before the public, and that he had not the slightest doubts of its prospering and introducing a new era in history. 'Co-operation, we firmly believe, is destined to change the whole face of society, as well as re-model its very form and structure. We owe it to the great cause of moral regeneration to acknowledge that, if we ever entertained any serious objections to the principles of co-operation, they are entirely removed. The more closely the system is examined, the more beautiful and striking its important advantages will appear.' The same number also carried an advertisement from the Manchester trustees, asking local co-operative societies for deposits towards shares in the community. Thereafter, however, there was no mention of the scheme until the next co-operative congress at Birmingham in October, save for a late and laudatory reference to the project's inception in the *Manchester and Salford Advertiser* of 9 July.[40]

Following Doherty's public announcement of his full acceptance of co-operative ideals, the volume of co-operative news in the *Voice* considerably increased. On 25 June there was a report of an address by Owen at his recently-opened lecture rooms in London, in which he explained how the evils in society arose from the great diversity in wealth and advocated change by peaceful and educative means rather than by violence. The next number carried an account of a co-operative sermon by Joseph Smith at Warrington the previous Sunday, and an advertisement from William Carson, president of the Lamberhead Green co-operative society near Wigan, of the sale of goods produced co-operatively by their own members and by societies in many other towns. This was followed by a report of a lecture by Carson in Salford on 5 July, describing the principles and progress of co-operation.[41]

Nevertheless, at this time the Council of the Manchester Association for the Promotion of Co-operative Knowledge decided that they required an organ exclusively in their interest, and the first edition of the *Lancashire Co-operator* was published on 11 June. But there was no rivalry between the two periodicals. Doherty welcomed the appearance of the new paper on 18 June, although he advised that it should not concentrate on the one subject alone but become a medium of general educational information for workmen, for only through the press could the people be made aware of their own strength, and until then they would continue to be plundered; all co-operative and trade societies should therefore petition parliament for the total abolition of those taxes which restricted 'the vital spread of political knowledge' by shackling the press. The *Voice* also printed extracts from the new publication on 18 June and 20 August, the first revealing the price reductions possible with co-operative trading and the advantages from limiting over-production by co-operative manufacturing, and the second on the importance of establishing schools. The latter number also included an address of the British Association for the Promotion of Co-operative Knowledge, announcing that subscriptions had been begun for Carpenter, Hetherington and other 'victims' of Whig prosecutions for evading the 'knowledge-gagging' taxes.[42]

During this period Doherty also continued to encourage individual trades to experiment in co-operative production, despite Thompson's warnings of failure. On 18 June and again on 2 July he wrote that it was essential for machinery to be co-operatively owned, so that its benefits might be fairly distributed instead of being kept by a few capitalists, the second article being in reply to a pamphlet on political economy by Thomas Hopkins, which preached the iron law of wages, but which Doherty believed was designed to dissuade workmen from strikes or any other action to protect their earnings.[43] The most outstanding example of such co-operative production at this time was that of the Lancashire calico-printers, who, as we have seen, responded to their employers' declaration of a general wages reduction in June by opening their own print-works at Birkacre near Chorley.[44] This scheme was, in fact, being formulated long before the strike began,[45] the committee of the Block Printers' Union announcing in the *Voice* of 16 July that they had finally agreed to start an establishment of their own; with a capital of £7,000 and weekly subscriptions from 3,000 workmen, extensive premises had been taken near Chorley, in which they would use the 'latest machinery'. In an editorial, Doherty exuded confidence, for, with about 700 co-operative societies already in existence and ready to become their customers, the printers could ignore the influence of the associated masters over merchants and drapers. And certainly there was soon evidence of practical progress to support this optimism. On 27 August Doherty reported that the calico printers were proceeding spiritedly in their undertaking and expected shortly to employ two or three hundred hands. Several trades had made them handsome donations and it was the duty of every trade in the kingdom to do so. Moreover, the principle could be extended, each trade being helped in turn to establish its own business, 'and so, by mutual assistance, the entire trade of the country would be brought into the hands of the workmen'.[46]

These highly exaggerated hopes—typical of Doherty's enthusiasm when he flung himself into another new venture—were soon deflated when the strike finally collapsed in early September. Nevertheless, the co-operative print-works was established, giving employment to three hundred members of the Block Printers' Union and being worked for about two years under the management of Ellis Pigot, their secretary and also one of the registered proprietors of the *Voice*.[47] Doherty therefore urged other trades to follow this example, and also that of the dyers, whose works were still in business, and on 13 August he revealed that the Manchester sawyers had opened a saw-yard, and were employing a number of men previously supported by the trade. This point was emphasised in an advertisement for the yard on 24 September, which stated that it had been opened 'to find employment for their members out of work'.[48] These schemes fitted into Doherty's revised strategy following the National Association's failure to prevent wages reductions: strikers could thus be employed productively, while employing surplus hands would help to keep up wages. His anxiety to ally the Association with this movement was demonstrated by the series of meetings organised in July and August 1831, to publicise 'the National Association and Co-operation' in several of the towns most affected by the calico printers' dispute, such as Great Harwood, Haslingden, Burnley and Blackburn.[49]

The suddenness of Doherty's conversion to unqualified support for co-operation did not pass unnoticed amongst his critics. On 9 July 'An Old Radical' wrote to the *Manchester Times and Gazette* to draw attention to the failure of Doherty's 'delegation scheme' and the approaching collapse of his 'grand National Association scheme'. The writer believed that Doherty recognised that these were lost causes, 'for now he is a convert to the co-operative system; which system, if successful, will knock his other system in the head, —the sooner it is knocked in the head the better for the pockets of the subscribers'. Doherty was now saying that the money spent on strikes, delegations and national associations would have been better expended on giving employment to redundant hands, as protecting wages was impossible because of excessive competition and an over-supply of hands. 'Not long since the co-operative plan was laughed at and ridiculed in his most ironical manner, by the same gentleman, who now appears to be one of its most enthusiastic admirers.' Clearly, therefore, Doherty was a man of 'no fixed principle', and workmen should regard his new and untried schemes to 'effect wonders in a short time' with the same caution as those of a quack doctor. The correspondent concluded by urging radicals to 'give up scheming' and work together for political reform, after which 'all else will follow as a matter of course'.[50]

Meanwhile, the co-operative projects instituted at the Manchester congress in May were not thriving. While the community plan made no progress, the North-West of England United Co-operative Company ran into immediate difficulties, for the amount of trade from co-operative societies proved far less than some of the more optimistic co-operators such as William Carson had anticipated. The consequent wrangle between Carson and Finch in the *Voice* provided an unedifying spectacle.[51] These matters therefore required the first consideration of the next co-operative congress, at Birmingham on 4 October. The notice convening this meeting was inserted in the *Voice* of 24 September, which also contained a letter suggesting that all the 700 co-operative societies in the kingdom should subscribe £1 each for the support and extension of that paper, 'as the accredited organ and medium of communication for producers throughout the United Kingdom'. Doherty believed that this would lead to very beneficial results, and although he could not attend the congress himself as he was in Yorkshire on Association business and about to travel to London to arrange for the transfer of the *Voice*,[52] the paper was represented by its reporter, Thomas Oates, whose views on co-operation had changed along with Doherty's. The delegates determined to continue the co-operative wholesale company at Liverpool, but to place the preparations for establishing a community in the hands of a special committee, to which, despite his absence, Doherty was appointed, along with Owen, Thompson, Vandaleur, Warden, Hamilton and others. The congress also agreed to a resolution recommending subsidies and support from all co-operators for the *Voice of the People*, which was henceforth to be officially recognised as one of the organs of the movement.[53]

Doherty's consultations with Owen and other leading co-operators in

London regarding the transfer of the paper, and his disagreement with Oates over whether the recognition of the paper was dependent upon the move, have already been described. In fact, however, the *Voice* did not survive to fulfil its new role and Doherty lost his official position in the Association.[54] The Manchester committee tried to maintain the connection between the two movements, especially in the *Union Pilot and Co-operative Intelligencer*, but this paper too ceased to appear after 5 May 1832, the Association slipped quickly into total obscurity, and Owen and the other co-operators looked in future to the other large unions that were developing for the proselytisation of their ideas.

There is no evidence that Doherty played any part in the committee established at Birmingham to forward the community scheme, if it ever functioned as such, nor did he participate in the 1832 congresses in April (London) and October (Liverpool). The National Association having collapsed by the end of 1831, Doherty's energies during the following year were devoted mainly to the establishment of his own printing and bookselling business and to the factory reform agitation. Nevertheless, his fourth periodical, the *Poor Man's Advocate*, continued to support co-operation. On 4 February he reported co-operative lectures by James Rigby at Bolton, and by members of the council of the Manchester and Salford Association for the Promotion of Co-operative Knowledge at Stockport. In the same edition he asserted that, while there had been a rapid increase in the number of co-operative societies in the manufacturing districts, nine out of every ten of them were in fact no more than 'joint-stock trading companies' and true knowledge of the real principles of co-operation were still very limited. To supply this deficiency, he printed occasional extracts over the following weeks from William Thompson's *Practical Directions for the Speedy and Economical Establishment of Communities, on the Principles of Mutual Co-operation, United Possessions and Equality of Exertions, and of the Means of Enjoyment* (1830). That he still had faith in co-operative principles was also demonstrated by his declaration on 21 April, in reference to certain oppressive acts of factory owners, that 'in no state of society, perhaps, short of full and complete co-operation, on the great and sublime principle of holding property in common, for the good of all, will it be possible to strip wealth of the pernicious influence which may be wielded, at pleasure, against the poor and the humble. Until the great principle be universally established, which we hope will be at no distant day, we shall have to deplore, we fear, many acts of oppression, which can only be punished by exposure, and prevented by fear.'[55]

On 19 May Doherty announced that he had become the Manchester agent for the sale of the *Crisis*, which Owen had recently begun for the explanation of the principles on which the 'new system of society' was to be founded; and on the same day, the *Crisis* contained an advertisement for the *Poor Man's Advocate*, headed 'Untaxed Knowledge' and stating that it fully exposed the 'workings of capital' and the lamentable effects of the present destructive system of individual competition, shown by the illegal fines and extortions practised, and the tyrannical regulations imposed, on the useful classes in large manufactories. On 17 November Doherty reported a speech by Owen at Birmingham about labour exchanges, adding that Owen was expected shortly in Manchester, when the working classes should pay heed to the principles which 'one of the most benevolent men perhaps that ever lived' had spent his life inculcating. And finally, in the following week, he copied an extract from 'An Important Address to the Trades' Unions', recommending co-operation to all workmen in the kingdom.[56]

Nevertheless, one must beware of exaggerating the extent to which Doherty had become Owenite. Basic divergencies, in fact, remained between his attitude as a trade unionist and that of leading co-operators towards employers and strikes. Even after his 'conversion' to co-operation, he still maintained that the first priority was the creation of an effective general union, though individual trades within it should be encouraged to produce co-operatively and part of the funds might ultimately be spent on a community. He still favoured independent trade-union action and supported strikes, a view quite different from that of John Finch, for example, who wrote an address, published in the *Voice* on 31 August and 14 September, 'To Manufacturers . . . and Shopkeepers; to the Labouring Classes of England; and particularly to the National Association for the Protection of Labour', in which he declared that good wages would not be obtained by strikes, violence, taxes on machinery, or meddling by government, but by using machines for their own advantage, which could be done by admitting masters to their managing committee and agreeing together to reduce hours by one-third, so as to limit production and keep up the same amount of wages.

When strikes failed and the Association disintegrated, and when, in their turn, the various trade-union schemes of co-operative production also ended in failure,[57] Doherty was briefly captivated by the National Regeneration Society of Fielden and Owen, towards the end of 1833, with proposals similar to those put forward earlier by Finch, that workmen should co-operate with employers to reduce hours of work. But, as we have seen, his basic distrust (even hatred) of employers soon re-emerged and by April 1834 he was again emphasising the need for trade-union solidarity and strikes.[58] It is therefore quite clear that, contrary to the general view of labour historians, Doherty never really became a convinced Owenite, that he always put trade-union objectives first, and that when he did turn to co-operative ventures this was only for tactical reasons, following strike failures and the threatened collapse of his general union scheme. Doherty's view of society was generally a class view, with emphasis on independent working-class action, especially through the trade unions. No doubt he did bring trade unionism and co-operation into closer relationship, preparing the way for adoption of co-operative ideas by the Builders' Union and the Grand National Consolidated Trades' Union; but the essential differences in outlook and tactics remained, as was to be amply demonstrated by the strikes of London tailors and cordwainers in breaking up the latter organisation, and by the disagreements between Owen and the editors of the *Pioneer* and *Crisis*, Morrison and Smith, in regard to the role of trade unions.[59]

But although Doherty was not an 'Owenite', he did share Owen's broader view that character is moulded by circumstances, that the social environment was to blame for the widespread ignorance, immorality, drunkenness, and vice, and that efforts must therefore be made to inculcate the benefits of education and knowledge and to demonstrate the evils of intemperance. But there was an aggressive element in the ideology of working-class co-operators: 'knowledge is power', they declared; the removal of ignorance and drunkenness would enable the working-class 'bees' to end exploitation by capitalist 'drones'.[60] Doherty certainly agreed also that one of the major evils in society was the mal-distribution of the benefits of machinery: 'the employment of machinery' should, he maintained, have brought additional comforts and leisure to every labourer, but was in danger of becoming a 'national curse' if the benefits continued to be confined to a relatively small number of machine-owners.[61] Education and knowledge would make the working classes aware of this situation and impel them to seek redress.

Doherty regretted his own lack of formal education, but was also aware of the great possibilities of 'self-education', for which he endeavoured to provide in his various publications. In the prospectus for the *Journal*, for example, he expressed the hope that this publication would serve as 'a medium of instruction',[62] and the first number contained an article on education, in which Doherty maintained that 'the people possess power, but they want the knowledge to use it. . . . Our chief aim shall be to diffuse such a knowledge. With that view we shall occasionally make extracts from such of the many valuable works extant, on Education, as may appear but calculated to promote so desirable an object.'[63] Thus by education he obviously did not mean simply reading, writing, and arithmetic: in fact, he saw the role of education primarily as fitting the working classes for the acquisition of their political and social rights. Thus when he replied on 18 September 1830 to a recent speech by Lord Wilton, who had lamented that the spread of education coincided with a reduction in the people's attachment to the country's laws, institutions and hereditary aristocracy, Doherty warned that 'the schoolmaster is abroad', and that if the aristocracy opposed this 'march of the mind', the irresistable power of accumulating knowledge would speedily overwhelm them and ultimately sweep their cherished 'order' from recollection.[64] In this educational process, radical journalism had a vital part to play: hence Doherty's insistence, in all the movements with which he was associated, upon the necessity for establishing a journal, not only to express particular views on trade unionism, factory reform, etc., but on all matters affecting the lives of the people. Hence, too, of course, his strong opposition to the 'taxes on knowledge' (the newspaper stamp, advertisement and paper duties), by means of which the labouring classes were kept in ignorance and the government was 'usurped' by a wealthy and influential minority; the very existence of these taxes, he declared, proved the need for 'a speedy, complete, and radical reform of the commons house of parliament'.[65]

At the same time, of course, Doherty supported the extension of formal education among the working classes. The ability to provide a good education for their children, he told a meeting of Manchester workmen, was one of the benefits to which they should be entitled with fair wages.[66] But the existing educational institutions were open to serious criticism because of the very limited instruction they provided for the working classes. Sunday schools, for example, were concerned only to teach the poor to work hard and obey their masters.[67] Some Sunday school governors even forbade lessons in reading and writing, like those at Macclesfield whom Doherty denounced as 'hypocrites, covering [their] enmity to our improvement . . . under the sacred mantle of religion'; not only should literacy be taught, he maintained, but also the subjects of society and government, and how wealth was distributed, so that an end would soon be put to such haughty oppression.[68]

Doherty's heaviest complaints, however, were against the managers of the Manchester Mechanics' Institution, which was founded in 1824. By its original constitution, the government was vested exclusively in the hands of the honorary members, who paid an annual subscription and comprised mainly manufacturers and merchants; no power was accorded to the ordinary subscribers. And because of the narrowly scientific and technical nature of the education provided, few working men attended its classes.[69] It is clear that Doherty did not approve of this kind of education, for he advised a meeting of Manchester workmen in 1827 'to obtain political knowledge, and to impart it to their children, observing that this would do more good than either Sunday Schools or Mechanics' Institutions'.[70] Later, in 1831, when Benjamin Heywood, a Lancashire member of parliament and leading director of the Institution, told a deputation of Manchester workmen that universal suffrage would be disastrous to their own interests, Doherty lamented that Heywood applied the same principles in the legislature as he had shown as a director of the Mechanics' Institution; for, although its government had been somewhat democratised by then, 'he has always resisted the repeatedly urged claims of the subscribers to possess the entire management of that institution', and preserved the nomination of half the directors for his 'little knot of aristocrats'.[71]

In February 1829 Rowland Detrosier, a frequent lecturer in Manchester in favour of education and radical reform, and himself an illustration of the prodigious efforts at self-instruction which some workmen were prepared to make, succeeded in forming the breakaway 'Useful Instruction' society, which in the following month took rooms in Poole Street under the name of the 'New Mechanics' Institution'. Governed democratically it soon attracted a hundred members away from the parent body.[72] Doherty was enthusiastic for this experiment which entailed the extension of independent action by the working classes into the educational field. In an editorial on 10 April 1830, he laid stress on the role of 'Mechanics' Institutions' in preparing the operatives' minds for the proper exercise of their political responsibilities. There were two such bodies in Manchester, he continued, both offering cheap instruction, ably conducted classes, and well-stocked libraries, but especially to be recommended was the New Mechanics' Institution, which was presided over by Detrosier, 'famed for his powerful eloquence and scientific acquirements', and was the result of a spontaneous effort by the workpeople unaided by 'patronage'.[73] In future months Doherty frequently referred to this Institution in the *Journal* and *Voice*, mentioning donations of books, lectures, etc.

On the second anniversary of the opening, Detrosier delivered an important lecture *On the Necessity of an Extension of Moral and Political Instruction among the Working Classes*, which was published in pamphlet form, and warmly commended by Doherty.[74] At the end of that year, Detrosier launched a scheme for moving the New Mechanics' Institution to a Mechanics' Hall of Science, to be financed by the workpeople purchasing shares. Doherty rejoiced that the Manchester artisans would soon have a building where every branch of human knowledge could be communicated, including political, which was 'most . . . essential to their social happiness and moral regeneration', and he revealed that 800 shares had already been taken up; this would show 'the huxtering owners of the misnamed Mechanics' Institution' that the day was gone when the millions would be satisfied 'with the puny morsel of mental food which aristocratic pride was willing to deal them'.[75] Detrosier was unable, however, to get sufficient support for this project, which lapsed after he moved to London (where he died in 1834), though it was to be successfully revived by the Manchester Owenites in 1839. Meanwhile, the New Mechanics' Institution itself closed down in September 1835, but the workmen's antipathy for the parent body remained, despite the introduction in 1834 of democratic election of all the directors. In March 1836, Doherty told a ten hours' bill meeting that, although the total membership of the Institution was over a thousand, only fifty-eight were employed in factories and many of these were overlookers. 'Did not this fact prove that the Mechanics' Institution was useless to factory people? They could not attend before 8.30 p.m.—the institution closed at 9.30 p.m., and after a long day's labour what could they learn? Why did not the Mechanics' Institution's promoters therefore join the factory reformers?'[76]

In his arguments for a ten hours' bill, Doherty often stressed the advantages of providing more leisure time for the working classes, but such time ought, he considered, to be spent in 'improving' ways, not in drinking and other idle and harmful debaucheries. His influence was evident in the arrangements made at the start of the long strike of Manchester spinners in 1829 for the workmen to have the opportunity of instruction in their room, while the very renting of that room in David Street marked a temporary break from the previous practice of assembling in public houses, with wasteful expenditure of wages on drink instead of on self-improving education or beneficial social activities.[77] Temperance and education were closely associated in Doherty's mind, a typically Owenite co-operative view. In the *Journal* of 3 April he condemned drinking as 'an expensive and demoralising habit', causing ignorance and immorality in the men and distress for their families, and urged instead that their money should be 'applied to the purchase of books'. On 26 June he published the prospectus of the Temperance Society of Manchester, of which he himself became a member, and he also devoted a full editorial to the subject. Drunkenness was reprobated as the worst of 'all vices which disgrace the age', and the habitual drunkard was attacked as a nuisance to society, a curse to his family, and a burden to himself. Doherty regretted that the Manchester society did not support total abstinence, he ridiculed the idea of grown men wishing to drink when not thirsty, and he also referred to the 'pleasures' of the *next morning*. But the greatest loss, he believed, was the waste of time that might have been spent in the pursuit of knowledge: thus were ignorance, poverty and dependence perpetuated. On 1 January 1831, the *Voice* carried an advertisement for the first number of Joseph Livesey's temperance and radical periodical, the *Moral Reformer*, as well as a report of a meeting of the Salford Temperance Society. A long account of a lecture to the Manchester Temperance Society on 8 June was also printed. On 9 July the 'Local Intelligence' column reported that seventy-three women and forty-five men had been seen entering one Manchester dram-shop in a fifteen-minute period on the previous Sunday, which provoked

Doherty to question how happiness or comfort could prevail in such a state of society. More directly, at meetings connected with National Association or *Voice* business at Birmingham in August 1830, and at London and Chesterfield in July and August 1831, Doherty stressed the benefits of temperance to his listeners, so forcefully on the first occasion that the owner of the inn where the meeting took place refused to allow Doherty to stay the night.[78]

Temperance continued to be a recurring theme in Doherty's later publications. On 14 January 1832, in the *Workman's Expositor*, and on 4 February in the *Poor Man's Advocate*, there were advertisements for the nightly meetings of the Manchester Temperance Society. The first number of the *Advocate* pointed out that circumstances made the poor drunkards, and that the temptations of taverns and dram-shops faced them on every street. If houses of instruction were as numerous as ale-houses, and if a similar amount was spent on making the workmen wise and virtuous as was now expended to barbarise them and perpetuate their ignorance, there would be no need for vice or temperance societies, less crime and fewer criminals.[79] Later, on 10 November, Doherty also revealed his 'deep-rooted aversion to filthy tobacco', which was enormously taxed, conveyed nothing nutritious to the body, and was merely an 'idle if not filthy habit'; but he approved of tea, 'this exhilarating yet sober beverage'.[80] In general, he warmly supported the provision by co-operative, friendly and trade societies of their own rooms, where non-alcoholic drinks were available and where education or harmless social pleasures could also be provided.

These improving moral influences were also evident in Doherty's later business ventures, when he opened his bookshop in Withy Grove, and in the following year his coffee and news-room, which he believed would encourage both temperance and education.[81] In October 1832, he initiated another series of weekly meetings of working men in the dyers' room, which were designed to 'improve their minds, enlarge their views, and increase their knowledge', and in the event were dominated entirely by political topics.[82] And on 29 October he delivered a lecture on the liberty of the press to the Salford Political Union of the working classes, and in his report of this meeting congratulated the workmen on their progress towards emancipating both mind and body, for instead of meeting in taverns amid filthy tobacco fumes and great uproar, they now had three rooms in the town where sober discussions of important political questions were held weekly. 'Something, then, has been done. The workmen have got knowledge enough, at least, to feel that they want more. . . . Their minds are in motion in pursuit of their just rights, and as well might government attempt to stop the sun in its course, as to check the progress of knowledge by stamp duties or imprisonments.'[83]

The close relationship between co-operation, temperance and education was, as we have seen, particularly visible in the National Regeneration Society, formed in October 1833. The Owenite influence was reflected in the emphasis on co-operation between masters and men and on ending over-production, while the necessity for general education and the abolition of vice, crime and drunkenness was stressed in the early literature and meetings. Doherty conformed to most of these attitudes in early numbers of the *Herald*, detailing the mutual interests of masters and men in adopting the regenerators' system, pointing out how gin-drinking damaged the imbiber and his family and helped to support the present political system through taxation, and backing the need for a national system of education in an article copied from the *Westminster Review*.

In the later phases of the Regeneration Society, however, Doherty's views diverged increasingly from those of Owen and other co-operators, from whom, indeed, he differed basically in his views not only on the role of trade unions, but even on that of education. Whilst co-operators looked for moral and social improvement by a peaceful, educative process, Doherty's attitude was much more aggressive: that education, like trade unionism, would make the working classes more conscious of, and more determined to fight for, their industrial and political rights.

It is not surprising, therefore, that Doherty did not participate in the later Owenite activities in Manchester, such as the formation of a branch of the Society of all Classes of all Nations in 1835 and the opening of a new Hall of Science in 1839. He continued, however, to denounce intemperance and promote education, just as, indeed, he had done at meetings totally un-connected with the co-operators during the earlier period. Twice, for example, on 8 March 1833, and 17 February 1834, Doherty, with other local radicals, frustrated meetings to support a more rigid observance of the Sabbath, and stated that the clergy would do better, if they really wanted to promote better behaviour, by agitating to close the gin-shops. He frequently found the patronising attitude of the 'respectable' classes intolerable. On 20 March 1833 many of the leading lay and clerical citizens of the town attended a meeting to form a Manchester and Salford Provident Society, similar to those successfully operating in Liverpool, London and Bristol, and designed to encourage thrift among the poor and cessation of their habit of squandering their wages in good times and relying on poor relief in depressions; the deserving poor, however, would be relieved by the Society, to encourage a 'closer union' between rich and poor. In the course of the proceedings, the ultra-conservative Rev Hugh Stowell asserted that the poor had been misled by 'dark, designing demagogues . . . who owed their short-lived distinction to keeping up the tempest of discord and exciting distrust amongst them'. Doherty was present and had not intended to speak, but an awareness that Stowell was referring to the events at the recent Sabbath observance meeting stung him to reply. He alleged that 'unmerited censure' had been cast upon the poor, whose improvidence was to be ascribed to the bad examples set before them by the rich, by the government, and by 'many learned, noble, aye and royal persons before them, whose improvidence was as great and more to be condemned than their own. The Duke of York had had his debts paid over and over again. . . . These men could wallow in and squander millions, but no one spoke of their improvidence. In the face of such facts to accuse the poor of improvidence, was most unmanly, base and calumniating.' At this point, he was prevented from speaking further by the chairman, and Stowell 'referred Mr Doherty to the ale-houses and gin-shops in Manchester on Satur-day night' to satisfy himself that the poor were by no means thrifty and frugal.[84]

Later that year Doherty was involved in a similar scene at the third annual meeting of the Manchester Temperance Society, when he maintained that such societies would be made almost unnecessary and the number of beer-shops reduced, if the antidote was applied of opening coffee-shops and reading-rooms on every street corner. Eventually, however, he must have found his presence in the same body as the Rev Stowell and others incompatible, for by May 1839, he was appearing as chairman at the annual meeting of the 'Roman Catholic Temperance Society', which was stated to be in a prosperous condition and had reformed many drunkards over the previous year.[85]

Doherty's disfavour did not, however, extend to beer, still regarded as a temperance drink and spoken of in the *Poor Man's Advocate* and the *Herald* as the 'beverage of their forefathers', the English yeomen, whose sturdy health was compared with the emaciated frames of those who drank wines and spirits. He believed that beer was an essential ingredient in the diet of the workman, his wife and children, attacked Poulett Thomson at a Manchester election meeting in January 1835 for his opposition to reducing the malt tax and thus affording the labourers cheap beer, and kept a beer barrel in his own cellar. It would seem that he lived up to his principles in his own private life, for at his inquest in 1854 the coroner stated that 'there was no appearance of death having been accelerated by intemperance'.[86]

Doherty's activities to promote education also continued after his connections with the Owenites lapsed. On 23 July 1834, when attending a meeting of Manchester leypayers to audit the constables' accounts, he asked if any application had been made to the churchwardens or town's authorities for means to erect or fit up any school to be attached to any mills, in conformity with the new Factory Act, or if they were aware of any such schools being established. He was told that no such application had been made and was referred for further information to Rickards, the factory inspector for the north-west district. In September 1837 he spoke at a meeting of the Catholic School Society, which had several schools in the Manchester area instructing a total of 1,500 children in 'reading, writing, arithmetic and the truths of the gospel', despite a shortage of funds because of the current trade depression. And in April 1843 he attended a meeting of Manchester dissenters to oppose the educational clauses in Graham's Factory Bill, and stated that he sympathised with their objects, but believed the reduction of working hours was more important.[87]

But Doherty's most important contribution to the spread of education during the 1830s was his small bookshop in the town. He took possession of new premises at 37 Withy Grove for publication of the *Poor Man's Advocate* in March 1832, and immediately advertised for sale there several of his own publications. Over the following month, he had joiners at work making alterations to the fittings and putting his name above the door, and on 28 April he gave notice that most of the London publications were now on hand or could be procured to order and that writing paper, quills, stationery, etc. were on sale. His family now moved their home to the shop and both he and his wife served behind the counter. By October 1832 the stock was advertised as 'The People's Library of Cheap and Entertaining Knowledge', including cheap pamphlets on political, educational, temperance and medical subjects, and a wide selection of popular works of romance and fiction sold in separate parts such as *Joseph Andrews* and the *Mysteries of Udolpho*.[88] At this time his financial position was desperate owing to his expenses over libel prosecutions,[89] but a public subscription enabled him to stay in business and on 2

March 1833, he announced the opening of 'The Manchester Coffee and News-Room' above his 'London Periodical Office'. A total of ninety-six newspapers and publications were taken, comprehending every shade of political opinion, although for some reason omitting the tory *Quarterly Review;* most could be bought at half-price when the succeeding number came out, 'except the *Manchester Guardian,* which may be had at any price'. All these, together with the *Mirror of Parliament,* the evidence given to parliamentary committees on child labour, the combination laws, and the poor laws, and a 'mass of other publications', could be seen for a charge of 1*d* between 6 a.m. and 10 p.m., or for nothing if the reader was also partaking of the coffee, tea, toast and eggs that were provided. According to Doherty, this establishment afforded advantages never before offered to the Manchester public,

> combining Economy, Health, Temperance, and Instruction, in having a wholesome and exhilarating beverage at a small expense, instead of the noxious and intoxicating stuff usually sold at the Alehouse and Dramshop, together with the privilege of perusing the most able and popular publications of the day, whether political, literary, or scientific, in a comfortable and genteel apartment, in the evening brilliantly lighted with gas.[90]

This advertisement was twice more repeated during March in the *Manchester and Salford Advertiser,* which also recommended the news-room to the attention of its readers. And it was also inserted, with the addition of a new heading, 'The Triumph of Temperance', in the *Manchester Times and Gazette* and the *Manchester and Salford Advertiser* in the following August, when the latter paper observed that 'the variety of publications taken, some of them of great value and interest, and the reasonableness of the charge, can hardly fail to secure an extensive patronage to Mr Doherty's establishment'. The tory *Wheeler's Manchester Chronicle* published a similar advertisement on 21 September, with the additional information that letterpress printing was 'neatly and expeditiously executed'. These notices also brought the establishment to the attention of Carlile in London, who remarked in the *Gauntlet* on 25 August that he was very glad to see the advertisement for 'Doherty's most useful reading establishment', where a man could peruse the best literature all day for 1*d*, or find half an hour's instruction over his breakfast or tea. 'This is better than the beer shops. We cannot have too many establishments of this kind. . . . A man of leisure can nowhere better spend his evening, in the absence of a school of free and fair discussion. Mr Doherty should, if convenient, add a discussion room to enliven the evening's entertainment. Sobriety and temperance will wear well.' In fact, the long hours of opening proved too much and in August they were reduced to 7 a.m. to 9 p.m. Moreover, the early patronage was perhaps not all that had been anticipated, for on 19 October Doherty publicly announced that whilst his bookselling, stationery and printing business would continue, 'the News Room is closed till the opening of parliament'.[91]

Nevertheless, according to schedule, Doherty notified the public of its reopening in the *Times* and *Advertiser* on 22 February 1834, both papers printing in addition an identical paragraph recommending such institutions to 'every real friend of temperance and sound morality'. On 8 March he again advertised the room in *Wheeler's Manchester Chronicle*, adding that while it encouraged temperance it was 'without the patronage of the Temperance Society'. By this time his bookselling business was prospering, so much so that he announced on 21 June that, because of the support received from the public since he commenced two years before as a bookseller, printer, stationer, and bookbinder, he was opening an additional shop at 109 Market Street. He appears to have overstretched himself, however, for soon after, on 23 August, he appended to an advertisement that he had become the Manchester agent for the *Dublin Satirist*, a notice that 'a small shop in Market Street [was] to be let'.[92]

Doherty's news-room was both a response and stimulus to the increasing literacy and interest in cheap knowledge among the northern operatives at this time. But there was no further mention of it after 1834. During the next two years, however, he inserted frequent advertisements in the local papers for his printing and bookselling activities; after April 1835 this business was carried on in new premises at 4 Withy Grove, referred to as 'Doherty's New and Cheap Printing Office . . . [where] Letter-press printing, Copper-plate, and Lithographic-printing [are] executed with neatness, elegance and dispatch, and on the lowest possible terms'. He employed an apprentice printer from May 1835, and the Manchester directories from the mid-1830s referred to Doherty as a 'stationer, bookseller and letter-press printer' at the above address. Between 1832 and 1840 he printed a series of placards and pamphlets on the subjects of factory reform, trade unions, radicalism, Irish questions, and local government reform, a Catholic prayer-book in 1836, and a portrait of Joseph Rayner Stephens in 1839. And in November 1837 he announced to the Catholics of the town that he had been appointed agent for the sale of the Catholic works of Messrs Simms & McIntyre of Belfast and could supply the whole of them at the publishers' prices; these works were, he added, equal in style to the best London works, and lower in price, and he appended a list of them as proof of his claim.[93] The shop was comparatively small, with a rateable assessment of only £16, but this was enough to qualify him for a vote in the election of the police commissioners until Manchester local government was reformed in 1837, and also in parliamentary elections between 1835 and 1840.[94]

From the time of his commencing business in 1832, Doherty's shop was, along with the older establishments of Abel Heywood and James Wroe, one of the leading centres in Manchester for the sale of the unstamped press. Towards the end of 1835 the Stamp Commissioners began a campaign in the capital and main provincial towns finally to eliminate that trade, prior to the government's reduction of the stamp duty in the following year. Numerous prosecutions were instituted, but typically it was Doherty's case that produced the most controversy in Manchester. On 19 December 1835, a man named Benson, an inspector of hawkers' and pedlars' licences, purchased a copy of *Cleave's Weekly Police Gazette* from Doherty at his shop. And on 21 January 1836, five informations were laid against him for vending that and other unstamped papers, which incurred liability to a total penalty of £100. But after Casson, the legal agent in Manchester for the Stamp Commissioners, had refused to entertain any compromise, Doherty's solicitor successfully pleaded that Benson and Hampson, in whose names the informations were laid, were not officially authorised as officers for the collection of stamp duties, and the magistrate, J. F. Foster, dismissed the cases on this tech-nicality.

At the end of this hearing Doherty pledged that he would abstain from selling unstamped papers in future, but Casson warned that similar informa-tions would be laid by persons properly qualified. For that purpose Casson secured a summons against Doherty ordering him to appear to answer the charges again at the New Bailey on 18 February. The execution of the summons was entrusted to Bianchi, the beadle, but he was unable to deliver it because Doherty was absent from Manchester. However, on the morning of 16 February Bianchi and Hughes, another officer, met Doherty in Water Street and the resulting angry fracas landed him in court two days early. Bianchi stated that he had taken Doherty into a nearby shop to avoid serving the summons in public, but the defendant had refused to take it; he therefore thrust the document towards Doherty, who shouted 'D—n you, I'll serve you out for this', and then struck him, for which he was taken into custody. Doherty testified that this version was only partially true. He had not absented himself from Manchester to avoid the summons, as had been insinuated, and moreover the officer had impertinently taken upon himself to search his house while he was away, even examining the beer-barrel in his cellar. He had had no chance to refuse to receive the summons, as Bianchi had crammed the paper into his breast without saying a word and dragged him into the shop by the collar. But Doherty admitted that, on coming out of the shop, he had told the officer that he had behaved like a ruffian, that he would certainly report his conduct to the authorities, and that 'he had never had a greater disposition to knock any man down than he had to knock him down at that moment'. Doherty's story was for the most part corroborated by the other officer, Hughes, so the magistrate ordered him to be set at liberty.

Two days later, Doherty appeared at the New Bailey again, stated his willingness to plead guilty to the first information, and repeated that he had given up selling unstamped papers and did not intend to resume the practice. Casson then agreed to proceed with that case alone, and Doherty was then convicted in the mitigated penalty of £5 plus 1 guinea costs, which he forth-with paid. The affair did not end there, however. On 26 February Doherty attended court for a fourth time to prefer a charge against Bianchi for using unnecessary violence in delivering the summons, but agreed to withdraw the charge on a public apology being made.[95]

Doherty's bookshop was mentioned with decreasing frequency towards the end of the 1830s, although he was still in business in October 1840, when he prosecuted an old man named John Machin, who had been in his employ-ment for the previous two months, for stealing books to the value of £10 during that time.[96] He was recorded as a 'letter-press printer' of Withy Grove in the 1841 census, but after that year his name disappeared from the Man-chester directories. It is reasonable to assume that his business was a victim of the terrible trade depression of that period, for in June 1842, a series of meetings of Manchester shopkeepers was held to discuss the state of trade in the course of which Abel Heywood informed his audience that 'he knew some in the same trade whose receipts were reduced by more than half [over the past twelve months], who might have to give up and enter the labour market'.[97]

NOTES TO CHAPTER NINE

[1] S. and B. Webb, *op. cit.*, Chapter III.

[2] Cole, *Attempts at General Union*, pp. 27–8.

[3] Morris, *op. cit.*, p. 53.

[4] Chapman, *op. cit.*, p. 220.

[5] Rudé, *op. cit.*, p. 92.

[6] Thompson, *op. cit.*, pp. 875–6.

[7] J. F. C. Harrison, *Robert Owen and the Owenites in Britain and America* (1969), p. 210. The pen-picture of Doherty's career on the same page contains factual errors relating to his date of birth, imprisonment, tenure of office as Manchester spinners' secretary, and venue of the 1829 strike.

[8] For a general criticism, see Musson, *British Trade Unions, 1800–1875*, Chapters 4 and 5.

[9] As Thompson has recognised, *op. cit.*, p. 868.

[10] For the local background, see Musson, 'The Ideology of Early Co-operation in Lancashire and Cheshire', *T.L.C.A.S.*, Vol. LXVIII (1958), reprinted in *Trade Union and Social History* (1974).

[11] There were certainly occasions, however, when he did adopt such an extremist attitude, as when the Tolpuddle labourers were convicted, at a time when strikes were widespread and there seemed to be a general threat to trade unionism (see above, pp. 289–90); but even then he opposed violence.

[12] See below, Chapters X and XI.

[13] *Journal*, 17 April 1830; *Voice*, 21 May 1831.

[14] *Voice*, 19 February 1831. See above, p. 137.

[15] See above, pp. 138–9.

[16] See above, p. 156.

[17] See above, p. 161.

[18] *Journal*, 6 March 1830.

[19] *Ibid.*, 27 March 1830. This scheme had been started at the end of 1829, according to Doherty, so that the dressers and dyers could avoid the fate of the Manchester spinners, in the event of striking against a general wages reduction. See also below, p. 326.

[20] *Ibid.*, 10 April 1830.

[21] *Ibid.*, 17 April 1830. Pare's letter in reply (*ibid.*, 19 June) largely repeated the opinions in his lectures.

[22] *Ibid.*, 24 April–8 May, 5 and 12 June, 24 July 1831. The participation of McWilliams and the co-operators' use of the spinners' room in David Street are indicative of cordial relations between the co-operators and the spinners' trade society.

[23] See above, pp. 167–71, for this meeting, reported in the *Journal*, July 1830.

[24] *Journal*, 7 August 1830. Carson's name was mistakenly reported as 'Castle'.

[25] *Ibid.*, 28 August, 25 September and 2 October 1830.

[26] See above, pp. 173–4, and 217.

[27] *Ibid.*, 21 August 1830.

[28] *Ibid.*, 4 and 11 September 1830.

[29] *Ibid.*, 11 September and 2 October 1830. For Finch and the short-lived Liverpool Dock Labourers' Society, see R. B. Rose, 'John Finch: a Liverpool Disciple of Robert Owen', *Lancs. and Chesh. Hist. Soc. Trans.*, Vol. 109 (1957).

[30] *Journal*, 23 September and 2 October 1830.

[31] H.O. 40/27, f. 312. He thought there was 'more to hope for here than fear'. 'The Union' was in this case the calico printers': see above, p. 228, and below, p. 330.

[32] See above, p. 323.

[33] *Times and Gazette*, 6 November 1830.

[34] See above, pp. 175–6.

[35] *Times and Gazette*, 19 March 1831. There was similar opposition to the National Association in Liverpool. See above, p. 239.

[36] See below, pp. 333–41, for his emphasis on the need for working-class education.

[37] *Voice*, 14–28 May 1831.

[38] *Guardian*, 28 May–11 June; *Voice*, 28 May and 11 June 1831; R. K. P. Pankhurst, *William Thompson 1775–1833* (1954); Musson, 'The Ideology of Early Co-operation', p. 129.

[39] See above, p. 236.

[40] *Voice*, 4 and 11 June; *Advertiser*, 9 July 1831.

[41] *Ibid.*, 25 June, 2 and 9 July 1831.

[42] *Ibid.*, 18 June and 20 August 1831. Doherty subsequently reported that a collection in the *Voice* office had produced £1 8s for Carpenter (*ibid.*, 10 September 1831).

[43] *Ibid.*, 18 June and 2 July 1831.

[44] See above, p. 228.

[45] See above, p. 326.

[46] *Voice*, 16 July and 27 August 1831.

[47] A forthcoming article by A. E. Musson will examine the Birkacre project in more detail.

[48] *Voice*, 13 August and 24 September 1831.

[49] See above, pp. 227–8.

[50] *Times and Gazette*, 9 July 1831.

[51] *Voice*, 9 and 30 July, 13 and 20 August 1831.

[52] See above, pp. 250–1.

[53] *Proceedings of the Second Co-operative Congress* (Birmingham, 1831); Pankhurst, *op. cit.*, p. 166.

[54] See above, pp. 250–2.

[55] *Advocate*, 4 February, 10 March, 21 April 1832.

[56] *Crisis*, 19 May; *Advocate and Operative Reporter*, 17 and 24 November 1832.

[57] The co-operative workshops of the dyers and calico-printers both came to an end in 1833; the co-operative wholesale company in Liverpool also collapsed.

[58] See above, Chapter VIII. Finch, like Owen and Fielden, belonged to the manufacturing–commercial middle class and therefore tended to be paternalist and to favour class-collaboration.

[59] Oliver, *op. cit.*, pp. 320–31.

[60] See Musson, 'The Ideology of Early Co-operation', for the importance of these aspects.

[61] *Voice*, 5 February 1831.

[62] See above, p. 160.

[63] *Journal*, 6 March 1830. In fact, extracts from Burdon's *Essay on Education* were regularly included in every number of the *Journal*.

[64] *Journal*, 18 September 1830.

[65] *Mercury*, 2 November 1830. The *Journal* had just been suppressed by the Stamp Commissioners. See above, pp. 187 and 330, and below, p. 421–2.

[66] *Guardian*, 23 May 1831.

[67] *Journal*, 26 June 1830, reporting a speech by John Knight, the Oldham radical.

[68] *Voice*, 25 June 1831.

[69] Tylecote, *op. cit.*, pp. 134–9.

[70] *Chronicle*, 1 September 1827.

[71] *Voice*, 16 July 1831.

[72] *Gazette*, 27 February 1829; Tylecote, *op. cit.*, pp. 136–7; G. A. Williams, 'Rowland Detrosier, a Working-Class Infidel', *Borthwick Papers*, No. 38. The 'New Mechanics' Institution' is dealt with by Dr. Kirby in D. S. L. Cardwell (ed.), *Artisan to Graduate* (Manchester, 1974).

[73] *Journal*, 10 April 1830.

[74] *Voice*, 9 April 1831.

[75] R. Detrosier, *An Address on the Advantages of the intended Mechanics' Hall of Science delivered at the Manchester New Mechanics' Institution, 31 December 1831* (Manchester, 1832); *Advocate*, 25 February 1832.

[76] Tylecote, *op. cit.*, p. 142; Manchester Mechanics' Institution, Minute Book, 1832–9, *Times and Gazette*, 5 March 1836.

[77] See above, p. 61.

78 *Journal*, 3 April, 26 June and 28 August 1830; *Voice*, 1 January, 11 June, 9 July and 20 August 1831; *Poor Man's Guardian*, 30 July 1831.
79 *Advocate*, 21 January 1832.
80 *Ibid.*, 10 November 1832.
81 See below, pp. 339–40.
82 See below, p. 434.
83 *Advocate and Operative Adviser*, 3 November 1832.
84 *Courier*, 16 March 1833; *Advertiser*, 22 February 1834; *Guardian*, 23 March 1833.
85 *Times and Gazette*, 7 December 1833; *Advertiser*, 1 June 1839.
86 *Advocate and Workman's Companion*, 29 December 1832; *Herald*, 24 May 1834; *Times*, 10 January 1835; *Advertiser*, 20 February 1836; *Guardian*, 22 April 1836, and 22 April 1854.
87 *Guardian*, 26 July 1834; *Times and Gazette*, 11 September 1837; *Guardian*, 29 April 1843. See below, p. 403.
88 *Advocate*, 24 March and 28 April; *Advocate and Operative Adviser*, 20 October 1832.
89 See below, pp. 435–8.
90 *Advertiser*, 2 March 1833. This advertisement contains a small engraving of the premises.
91 *Advertiser*, 9 and 23 March, 17 August and 29 October 1833; *Times and Gazette*, 10 August 1833; *Chronicle*, 21 September 1833; *Gauntlet*, 25 August 1833. The room in fact opened on 6 February.
92 *Advertiser*, 22 February; *Times and Gazette*, 22 February; *Chronicle*, 8 March; *Times*, 21 June; *Advertiser*, 23 August 1834.
93 *Advertiser*, 4 April; *Chronicle*, 30 May 1835, etc.; *Advertiser*, 14 March 1836; *Northern Star*, 20 April 1839; *Advertiser*, 11 November 1837; *Manchester Directory*, 1836.
94 *The Churchwardens' List of Voters, and Persons Eligible to serve as Commissioners of Police for Manchester, 1836* (Manchester, 1836); *Manchester: Register of Parliamentary Voters*, 1832–9, 1838–42.
95 *Guardian*, 23 January; *Advertiser*, 20 February; *Times*, 20 February; *Guardian*, 5 March 1836.
96 *Chronicle*, 28 October 1840. This account refers to the shop as being in Market Street, but this does not tally with the Manchester Directory for that year.
97 H.O. 107/53(2), Manchester Census Returns; *Chronicle*, 15 June 1842. See above, p. 5, however, for possible continuance of the family interest in printing.

# X    The factory reform movement

Historians of the factory reform movement have, as E. P. Thompson has rightly observed, tended to underestimate 'the part played in the agitation over twenty and more strenuous years, by such men as John Doherty and the workers' own Short-Time Committees'. This has resulted from an over-concentration, firstly on the more controversial figures in the Yorkshire agitation after 1830, such as Richard Oastler, Rev. George Bull, and later William Ferrand, compared with whom the only participant of comparable notoriety in Lancashire was Joseph Rayner Stephens, and secondly, on the parliamentary leaders, especially Michael Sadler and Lord Ashley and to a lesser extent John Fielden and Charles Hindley. This pattern was established by the first chroniclers of the movement, Samuel Kydd in 1857 and Philip Grant in 1866, in their understandable anxiety to praise those manufacturers and members of the ruling class who devoted so much time towards ameliorating working conditions in factories. In more recent times, almost all these humanitarians have had their biographers. On the other hand, the considerable activities of workmen and others in Lancashire for a decade and a half before 1830 have been largely overlooked. Turner believed that 'it was only with the appearance of the self-actor's threat to the spinners' employment that their campaign to limit factory working hours became really determined'; previously the rank and file had not supported shorter hours for fear of a reduction in their piece-rate earnings. Smelser similarly asserted that 'a large-scale "movement" did not begin among the cotton workers until the early 1830s', since it was only during this period that the break-up of the family working unit within the factory occurred, and hence according to his theory the spinners had no important motive for agitating before that decade, although their conditions were previously worse. And even J. T. Ward begins his major work on the factory movement in 1830 and has written elsewhere that it was 'really born in September 1830', when John Wood, the Tory worsted spinner from Bradford, converted Oastler to the cause.[1]

The origins of the movement should in fact be looked for in Lancashire, where the factory system itself first developed. The workers formed their first short-time committee in Manchester as early as 1814, John Lawton, a cotton spinner who was president of the spinners' club in 1825 and prominent in the local factory agitation until the 1840s, being a founder member.[2] It was financed by a benevolent local merchant, Nathaniel Gould, who was reputed to have spent £20,000 on the cause and left it £5,000 in his will. But donations were also made towards it by the working spinners, including a young spinner from Ireland who arrived in the city in 1816. Looking back over a quarter of a century's agitation, in a speech at Bolton in 1841, Doherty stated that, 'in November 1816, he had paid the first sixpence for the promotion of the object before them, and from that day to the time he stood before them, he had never ceased to forward it in one shape or another. From that day to the present moment, a short-time committee had always been in existence'. Confirmation of this early activity appeared in an editorial in the *Manchester and Salford Advertiser* in January 1842, stating that the Manchester cotton spinners had been active in the factory reform movement ever since the introduction of the elder Peel's bill in 1816; from that date they had devoted themselves to this cause 'with a perseverance never before manifested on any popular question'. Whatever agitations had occupied the public mind —the Charter, the emancipation of African slaves, the repeal of the Corn Laws, etc.—the abridgement of their own and their children's hours was never forgotten. And even Grant admitted that, before Oastler's dramatic intervention in 1830,

> the burden of the movement was principally borne by the operative fine spinners of Manchester, for although that body was united for the protection of their trade, yet, they were always ready and willing to stand by the advocates of a reduction of the hours of labour, and frequently supplied the sinews of war when all other sources lacked . . .; and it is worthy of note, that from the days of Thomas Foster and John Doherty to the present time, that body has been the mainstay of the short-time committee in Manchester.[3]

The Manchester short-time and spinners' union committees were thus closely related bodies, but they were not identical. In his evidence to the Combinations Committee in 1838, Doherty stated that although the union was broken up after the strike defeat in 1818,[4] the men continued to contribute regularly for the purpose of procuring a factory act and achieved their first success in 1819.[5] But from the beginning enemies of factory legislation alleged that the short-time agitation was organised by mischievous combination 'delegates' and that the workmen, aware that piecing and spinning were mutually dependent, were more interested in reducing their own hours than in humanitarian concern for their children's condition.

The movement really got under way in 1815, after Robert Owen's appeal on behalf of overworked factory children. Sir Robert Peel, seeing that his Act of 1802 was irrelevant to protect the 'free' labour of children in the steam-powered urban factories which were proliferating, introduced a new bill proposing to limit persons under eighteen to $10\frac{1}{2}$ hours' actual labour per day. A Select Committee of the Commons in the following year heard that children in Lancashire towns were working $13-14\frac{1}{2}$ hours daily and several doctors testified to the deleterious effects of this labour on health; but many employers opposed government intervention on economic grounds, asserting that more leisure would encourage the lower orders to vice, and after the progress of the bill was delayed by Peel's illness, the Manchester masters petitioned Parliament in February 1818 that the 'mischief had been occasioned by the combination of workmen, who had a kind of central Committee whose proceedings were calculated to promote the spirit of Luddism'. Peel was forced to amend his proposals considerably, and his amended bill passed the Commons, but the Lords merely referred it to a further Committee, which heard remarkable evidence of the invigorating results of labour in cotton factories from medical witnesses hired by a committee of Manchester masters.⁶

The Lancashire workers rallied to Peel's support. In January the Manchester spinners adopted a petition supporting the bill, detailing the 'extended labour' in 'ill-ventilated' rooms, and criticising the repeated parliamentary delays. They appointed John Hollis, a spinner retired due to ill-health, to take this petition up to London, where he remained for several months, receiving similar petitions from Ashton, Stalybridge, Glossop, Blackburn and Stockport, the last of which provoked an angry response from Sir James Graham that the signatories were 'idle, discontented, discarded, and good for nothing'. After Parliament was dissolved, Hollis visited several Lancashire towns at their request, giving them information about the progress of the bill and also receiving further details from them 'that might be useful when parliament reassembled'. When the Manchester spinners came out on strike in July on the wages issue, they also demanded a reduction in working hours and their propaganda frequently referred to factory conditions as evidence that they needed higher wages.

> We believe there is no species of labour so fraught with the want of natural comforts as that the spinners have to contend with, deprived of fresh air, and subjected to long confinement in the impure atmosphere of crowded rooms, continually inhaling the particles of metallic or vegetable dust, his physical powers become debilitated, his animal strength dwindles away, and few survive the meridian of life, and the grave is often the welcome asylum of his woes. His children!—but let us draw a veil over the scene!—our streets exhibit their cadavarous and decrepit forms, and any attempt to describe them would be impossible.⁷

The turn-out provided more ammunition for the opponents of factory reform. On 15 August *Wheeler's Manchester Chronicle* reprinted a letter denouncing 'the connection between Sir Robert Peel's Factory Bill and the present combination of spinners in Manchester', and James Norris, the magistrate, reported to the Home Office that Gould's agitation had caused 'great . . . apprehension of some mischief'. Nevertheless, at the end of the dispute, the master spinners held a general meeting and agreed to reduce working hours to twelve per day. Sidmouth, the Home Secretary, protested at this 'concession', but it was pointed out that, in fact, the best operatives preferred to work longer hours, to obtain higher piecework earnings, and had 'never expressed a wish to work a shorter time'. Indeed, Norris feared that if Peel's bill were passed it would perhaps result in another spinners' strike because of reduced wages.⁸ At the same time, the 'respectable' supporters of the measure sought to dissociate themselves from the workers' combinations, denying 'that the disturbances, or turn-out of the working spinners in Manchester, was connected with or encouraged by the moving of . . . the Bill'. The bill had, in fact, originated solely from humanitarian concern about the working hours of factory children, whereas the strikes were in regard to wages and were organised by 'unlawful combinations' of adults, with whose 'pernicious machinations' the promoters of the bill had no sympathy.⁹

In February 1819 a third parliamentary enquiry was instituted and several Manchester workmen gave evidence. The combined masters tried to discredit these witnesses, but 'the working spinners were on the alert' and made countervailing representations. Nevertheless, it was a considerably truncated measure that was eventually passed in July, prohibiting the employment of children under nine in cotton mills and limiting those under sixteen to a maximum of twelve hours' labour plus time for meals.[10]

This Act, however, proved completely ineffective, with only isolated efforts at enforcement. It was for this reason that William Smith, later editor of the *Bolton Chronicle* and leader of the factory reform movement in that town, together with John Brown, author of Robert Blincoe's famous *Memoir*, proposed, in November 1822, the establishment of a new journal in Manchester, to disclose the results of an exhaustive enquiry which had been undertaken into the evils of the factory system in different Lancashire towns, together with an explanation of how the master spinners' machinations and conspiracies with medical men between 1815 and 1819 had defeated the original hopes of the reformers; it was also proposed to publish Blincoe's *Memoir*. This project, however, was wholly independent of 'the organised bodies of complaining workpeople' and of 'the attempts that have been made in Lancashire . . . to enforce the clauses of the abortive law for the better regulation of Cotton Mills'—in fact the cruel and greedy overworking of children by the operative spinners was also condemned.[11] In reply, an anonymous correspondent asserted that the workmen were too frightened to apply to Parliament for Peel's Act to be strengthened, because of the 'dreaded example the combined masters have made of several of the witnesses of 1819'.[12] The proposed publication had to be postponed, however, and although there was another advertisement on 12 July 1823, announcing the forthcoming appearance of the *Manchester Examiner*, no copy of this work is extant, if it ever did come out.

During this period, however, the conditions of work in cotton factories were also kept before public attention by the strikes of spinners at Preston and Bolton, at both of which the workmen quoted the particular hardships of their employment to support their claims.[13] It was as a result of these disclosures that William Cobbett addressed a bitter public letter to Wilberforce in his *Register*, comparing the oppressions of half-starved 'free' British labourers with the 'fat, dancing frames' of 'lazy singing negroes'. But on the other hand, when the books of the Bolton spinners' union were seized by the authorities, Colonel Fletcher reported to the Home Office on 26 April 1823, that

> I have not found any direct contribution for regulating cotton factories, nor has it appeared that among the journeymen cotton spinners of this town and neighbourhood, any very lively interest is felt on that subject. Indeed, many of them, I fear, would prefer working at those mills where they work the greatest number of hours, and have the opportunity of making the most money. There may be, however, and doubtless are, many exceptions in this respect.[14]

There can be no doubt, in fact, that the operative cotton spinners were participating in the organisation of this early short-time agitation, although a substantial number of them were prepared to endure very long hours for higher earnings, and of course, as the employers frequently pointed out, it was the workmen themselves who generally employed the child piecers and who welcomed their small earnings to supplement the family income. As for Doherty's part in this first campaign, he was probably no more than a rank-and-file supporter between 1816 and 1818, and was in gaol for two years thereafter; but as he rose to prominence in the 'twenties he must have participated in the agitation conducted by the spinners' committee.

The formation of the spinners' federal union in 1824 was accompanied by a particularly active factory reform campaign, spearheaded by the Manchester spinners' union, but these efforts were completely ignored by Kydd, considered 'weak' by Smelser, and only briefly mentioned by Ward.[15] On 15 November the Manchester spinners' committee sent a circular to their masters, proposing occasional joint consultations between employers and workmen to regulate the trade, and seeking co-operation particularly in reducing the hours of labour, 'the greatest grievance under which we labour'.[16] It was hoped that this could be done by agreement rather than by parliamentary interference, which had proved so far ineffective, but the employers feared that such a voluntary system was not feasible and would only allow dishonourable masters to undersell the more humane by overworking their hands; hence they rejected an appeal by the operatives to meet to discuss the question on 25 November. The workmen, therefore, changed their tactics, hoping to persuade the employers to join them in petitioning Parliament for new legislation. They were already in touch with Francis Place over the campaign against re-enactment of the Combination Laws, and on 16 February 1825 Place wrote to suggest the propriety of another parliamentary investigation into factory labour, but this considerably alarmed the Manchester spinners, because it would 'raise the prejudices of our masters against us'. On 17 February they addressd another circular to the employers, regretting that nothing had transpired from their previous proposal, but setting forth for approval a series of resolutions agreed to by the men for petitioning Parliament in favour of an eleven-hour working day on five days, with 8½ hours on Saturday, for all persons under twenty-one years of age employed in water- and steam-powered cotton mills.[17] And on 20 February a petition to the House of Lords in these terms was sent to London, and D. Lee, the spinners' corresponding secretary, wrote to ask Place to request either Dr Law, Lord Kenyon, or any other 'ministerial man' to support its prayer. Lee also asserted that the petition 'embraces the views of many of our employers, nay we can assure you, that this petition has been drawn up at the instance and with the unqualified approbation of some of these gentlemen who have promised to support us so long as we don't go beyond the contents of this petition'.[18]

At the end of February, Thomas Foster and David McWilliams were deputed by the spinners to go to London to lobby members in favour of the petition. They were introduced to Place by a letter from Archibald Prentice, editor and proprietor of the *Manchester Gazette*, which was campaigning strongly for a new bill then being prepared by the radical-Whig member for Westminster, John Cam Hobhouse. Place, in turn, gave them a letter of introduction to Hobhouse on 8 March, asking the member to 'do all you can to assist them'. Their efforts were supplemented by petitions from other cotton-spinning towns such as Bury and Glasgow.[19] Place clearly played a key role in co-ordinating this agitation, as well as that on the Combination Laws—indeed he later claimed to have been the author of Hobhouse's bill.[20]

The Place Papers contain 'Some Observations on the nature and condition of children employed in Cotton Factories', made by McWilliams for Place's use and explaining the long hours and high temperatures from which the workers suffered and disposing of the argument that children were 'free' to leave the mills if they wanted. These remarks also formed the basis for a pamphlet published in London on 14 March by Foster and McWilliams, entitled *Observations on the State of Children in Cotton Mills*. This described the children's labour as requiring their whole attention and utmost exertion; in following the progress of the machinery as it travelled backwards and forwards, 'each child goes over twenty miles a day'. True to the moderate tone of this whole campaign, the delegates went on to state that 'we are far from desiring to impute blame, much less inhumanity, to the cotton manufacturers generally, the trade itself causing many unavoidable evils'; for instance, the artificial heat and lack of pure air were necessary for the productive process. Nevertheless, the legislature should take such factors into account in fixing the length of children's hours; and the effect of these conditions on health was explained by quotations from the Select Committees of 1816 and 1818, especially the comparisons made by Manchester medical men of the condition of factory children and others at Sunday schools. The pamphlet concluded by entreating that hours be reduced to the limit laid down in the spinners' petition of 20 February, though they were now prepared to accept that only children under sixteen could be included.[21]

When the deputies returned to Manchester, they arranged for £15 to be paid into a bank for Place's expenses while they were in London, 'in the name of John Lawton, president of our Committee'. On 30 March Foster, McWilliams and another spinner, Robert Hyde, addressed a meeting of the Manchester Chamber of Commerce in an effort to persuade them to agree to a limitation in the hours of work to sixty-six per week. Thus the workmen had further moderated their demands by abandoning the shorter working day on Saturdays; but George Phillips, the leading parliamentary spokesman against further legislation, and a local manufacturer, convinced the Chamber that it was not 'within its province' to decide the proper number of hours, and resolutions were passed that parliamentary interference was objectionable in principle, difficult to enforce, and gave the means to indulge spirits of revenge. The Chamber had 'no bias in favour of excessive labour, or against the comforts of the labouring classes', and admitted that the increased fixed capital in factories caused a stronger inclination to overwork, but if legislation was necessary, it should extend to all trades where machinery was used and to persons of all ages.[22] Despite this setback, the spinners' delegates continued to negotiate with individual masters, and in April, through the agency of manufacturers friendly to the cause like Joseph Brotherton and John Kennedy, thirty-two of the leading master cotton spinners in Manchester and Salford signed a public declaration in favour of the 66-hours limitation, an event which the *Manchester Gazette* hailed as a token of the more open and amicable relations in the trade since the repeal of the Combination Laws.[23]

From March onwards the operative spinners of Mossley, Ashton, Bolton, Burnley and Preston sent petitions to Parliament for a new factory bill, while groups of masters in Manchester and other Lancashire towns petitioned against such a measure. On 6 May Hobhouse finally moved for leave to

M*

introduce his bill, reducing children's hours from twelve to eleven per day, and improving the procedure for enforcement. Foster, McWilliams and Hyde were again deputed to London, together with Worsley from Stockport, and they resumed their arguments with Place who was still asserting the need for further enquiry. Such was their concern that co-operation with the favourable masters should not be threatened, that the spinners even agreed that their petition against the re-enactment of the Combination Laws should not be presented, much to the annoyance of the secretary of the Manchester Artisans' Committee, William Longson, who did not believe that such a change of plan was necessary.[24] Despite the operatives' conciliatory attitude, the opposition of the manufacturing interest in Parliament continued and ultimately forced Hobhouse to amend his bill to a limitation of sixty-nine hours per week, the only change in the existing regulation being the introduction of a nine hours' limit on Saturdays. By 22 June the bill had passed all its stages in its amended form and Foster wrote to the Manchester spinners that it would come into operation on 1 August. He inserted this letter in the *Manchester Gazette* to give it publicity, believing that even the amended bill would be 'productive of great good' and hoping that 'peace and goodwill' would always exist 'between masters and men'.[25]

Doherty's part in this campaign is again impossible to discern. He may have been a speaker at a meeting of Manchester spinners in January 1825 when a workman of his age bitterly attacked the evils of the factory system.[26] But there were clearly differences among the Manchester spinners at this time. Philip Grant, then a power-loom weaver, who joined the factory movement in 1825, urged 'a more extensive measure' at a meeting in Manchester. Many spinners also opposed the compromising tone adopted towards the masters, preferring an all-out assault against the threat of new Combination Laws. Doherty was probably among these, in view of the strong feelings which he expressed to Place, and he may also have been dubious about the spinners' dependence on Parliament rather than their own efforts to reduce hours. He did not speak at the public dinner of the Manchester spinners on 9 July to celebrate the successful mission of Foster and McWilliams, and among those who did there were signs of division.[27]

As in 1819, the 1825 Act was followed by a short-lived attempt by the workmen to enforce it. On 28 July David McWilliams issued a public address 'To the Cotton Masters of Manchester and its neighbourhood', praying that they would observe the new regulations 'as men, as Christians, as fathers', because it would give factory children a chance to cultivate their minds and rectify the shameful situation whereby adult workers found it impossible to partake of 'the benefits of Mechanics' Institutes'. When this appeal to humanity failed, the men resorted to action apparently with the aid of 'a Committee of respectable persons . . . formed in this town', according to a letter from a correspondent (probably John Brown) in the *Manchester Gazette* on 20 August, 'to adopt proper measures for bringing offenders . . . who are exceeding the number of hours specified in the act . . . to justice'.[28] In the next few years several prosecutions were reported in the local press, but they were not generally very successful.[29]

Hobhouse's Act proved as ineffective, in fact, as its predecessors, and interest in factory reform was at a low ebb during the next two years. There was a strong revival, however, in 1828. Early that year Carlile began the serialisation of Blincoe's life in the *Lion*, and also published findings of his own recent tour of the manufacturing areas. Although hours of work had been reduced to twelve in many factories, working conditions were so bad that the Lancashire cotton workers were in general a new race of people—'a degenerate, puny, crippled race of human beings'. At the same time, the *Bolton Chronicle* also reverted to the question, deploring long hours and night work in Oldham, Rochdale and Wigan, and urging the necessity of united efforts to prosecute law-breaking masters. At Stockport a committee was, in fact, formed for this purpose.[30] And in November Doherty, now secretary of the Manchester spinners' society, launched a concerted movement to secure enforcement of the existing legislation. The primary motive, no doubt, was humanitarian concern for the factory children, but since it was admitted that hours in Manchester mills were generally less than elsewhere, this agitation must also be seen as part of the strategy to prevent undercutting, in the form of longer hours as well as lower wages, in surrounding towns.

On 8 November 1828, Doherty published in several local papers an advertisement addressed 'To the Friends of Humanity' calling on them to attend a public meeting on 13 November at the theatre of the Mechanics' Institution to adopt measures best calculated to prevent the overworking of children in cotton factories, both 'to secure to the children that protection which the legislature designed for them' and 'to support the really . . . humane masters who honourably observe the law, against the unfair competition of those who violated it'. This meeting was chaired by Doherty and attended almost exclusively by workmen; most of the speakers were operative spinners except for Richard Potter and William Clegg. It was Potter who moved the first resolution regretting the frequent infractions of the law, both in overworking children under sixteen and employing children under nine, whose ages were fabricated by their poverty-stricken parents. He was supported by Thomas Foster, who could remember only two employers having been convicted in the nine years since Peel's Act. Parents were either too frightened or too poor to lay informations, and even when charges were brought, magistrates dismissed them for invalid reasons. After another spinner had given information on overworking in Oldham and Royton, Doherty gave examples from his own recent experiences in several other towns. He found when visiting Glossop the previous summer that between that town and Manchester there was not more than one manufacturer who obeyed the law. At Hayfield in Derbyshire he had observed children going to factories at 5 a.m. and not returning till 9 p.m., and they had told him that they were stopped 2d for every ten minutes they were late. At Hyde the hands were required to do a certain quantity of work each day, and to work through meal-times if necessary to make up arrears. And at Rochdale one mill was kept going permanently by employing two sets of workers.

After hearing all this evidence, the meeting agreed to establish a 'Society for the Protection of Children Employed in Cotton Factories', to enforce the existing law. A committee of twenty-one individuals was appointed to conduct the Society and to receive subscriptions of 1d or more per week from members; donors of a guinea would be competent to fill the offices, and those giving five guineas were to be honorary members for life. Three cheers were finally given for Potter, 'one of Manchester's leading citizens', for his conduct 'in always coming forward to protect the rights and interests of his fellow-townsmen, his poorer ones in particular'. Doherty was appointed secretary of the new Society, for which he inserted an advertisement in the *Manchester Gazette* on 29 November. He denied that they wished to interfere improperly in the management of manufacturers' concerns. But the legislature had wisely decreed that children should not labour more than a certain number of hours, and yet it was notorious that this law was widely disobeyed. The poor infants were thus doomed to incessant toil and ill health, and had no time for domestic, moral or intellectual education, merely 'to gratify the avarice of an unfeeling master'. The Society was determined that the law should be obeyed and had already been financially supported by several leading manu-facturers. Further subscriptions could be sent to the *Gazette* office, to Doherty, or to the Society's headquarters at the 'Prince's Tavern', where the committee held weekly meetings. On the same day Doherty announced in his own periodical, the *Conciliator*, that 'this benevolent and humane institu-tion' was meeting with cordial support from all classes of the community. Four out of five leading factory proprietors so far approached had expressed sympathy, a total of £18 5s 0½d had been subscribed, and letters had been received from various quarters, but particularly around Glossop, reporting a diminution in working hours.[31]

Thus, although it was the policy of the Society to bring law-breaking masters to justice, Doherty was anxious from the start to stress the mutual interests of fair employers and workmen in such action. Hence he began cautiously, attempting to secure observance by persuasion. Although the original committee was probably little more than the workers' short-time committee under a new name, Doherty was able to announce on 24 January 1829 that five gentlemen from the Manchester merchant and manufacturing class had been added—Richard Potter, Edward Baxter, G. W. Seed, Joseph Brotherton, and T. Townend—and in March he made a vain appeal to the Manchester master spinners to reduce hours rather than wages. Looking back on these proceedings in 1838, Doherty stated that he 'was the secretary of an association formed at Manchester, consisting of operatives and master manu-facturers, for the enforcement of the Factory Act'.[32] But with widespread spinners' strikes beginning in Stockport in January and Manchester in April, and with Doherty and Foster being the leading agents of the Society, the local press reports increasingly emphasised the close links between the Society and the spinners' union. The *Stockport Advertiser* was particularly hostile. On 6 February an editorial chastised the five respectable Manchester gentlemen who had allowed their names to be associated with a society whose heads were the same as those of the 'Combination Clubs' in that town. Did Potter and the others not realise that their new acquaintances were interested only in campaigning up and down the country, with good quarters, plenty of pay, nothing to do but make speeches, and laying informations against unsuspecting and respectable individuals after the fashion of 'bands of common informers'? Doherty published a defence of the Society in one of the Manchester papers, pointing out the masters' interest in halting the over-supply of goods on the market and consequent low prices, but this provoked the first of the vitriolic personal attacks upon him which were to become commonplace over the next five years.[33] On 19 February 1829, the *Stockport Advertiser* inserted an editorial on 'Manchester Clubs', rejoicing that the observations as to the way in which the money of honest work-people was daily preyed upon by 'certain scheming gentlemen' had alarmed the fears of such as 'Dogherty' (as the paper preferred to call him, with anti-Irish prejudice). Doherty had sent a letter to the editor, who declined, however, to answer a fellow of such 'low-bred ignorance and vulgarity', but went on to advise him to return to his former honest occupation and challenged him to publish the salaries and expenses of the officials and committee-men of his various clubs. The paper alleged that it supported factory legislation, but considered that enforcement should be left to 'respectable and responsible parties'. Committing such a charge to improper hands would lead to collisions and angry feelings because of the interference of workmen with masters, 'and the exasperation of the latter to find themselves threatened and domineered over by Combination or Protection Clubs (for the latter in its present shape is but the spawn of the former)'.[34]

During December 1828, Doherty travelled round the various spinning districts attempting to persuade the masters to regulate their works correctly. Only in Derbyshire did he resort to legal action, laying two informations against Messrs Sidebottom of Hayfield at the local petty sessions; eventually, after transfer of the cases to the Stockport bench, all but one of the masters promised to obey the law in future. At Blackburn, after waiting upon the different employers personally and being 'very cordially received by almost all', Doherty issued a notice on 25 December, on behalf of the Society, 'To the Master Spinners of Blackburn and its neighbourhood', informing them that most of their number had agreed to an immediate diminution of their hours to the prescribed limit, and that the Society would take measures to enforce the penalty if infractions persisted after 1 January 1829. This notice was succeeded by a similar general announcement on 26 December 'To the Master Cotton Spinners of Lancashire, Derbyshire, Cheshire and Yorkshire'. The main problem was evidently trade competition, especially from overworking mills 'in the more remote parts of the country'. But with co-operation from the honourable masters, following the Blackburn example, the law would be 'rigorously enforced' in the new year.[35]

These preliminary steps were accompanied by endeavours to form branch societies in surrounding towns. The first visit was to Wigan, where it was notorious, according to the *Bolton Chronicle*, that overworking was carried to greater lengths than in any other town in the manufacturing districts, and yet there was little chance of redress for the workmen because all the local magistrates were connected with the cotton trade, and hence excluded from judging factory cases, while the county magistrates had no power to act within the precincts of that 'immaculate borough'. At the end of November David McWilliams interviewed the Wigan masters, promising that the Society would overlook past transgressions if they would now decrease their hours to those worked in Manchester. This warning was ignored and so a fortnight later, on 10 December, Doherty, McWilliams and Foster returned to the town to inform the mayor that a master named Wood had recently worked from 6 a.m. to 12 p.m. with less than an hour for refreshment. They were received with great haughtiness by the town clerk and told to return next day. Then they were sent round to the back door and Doherty alone was allowed to enter while the others waited outside. The mayor told him that he could not interfere as he was a cotton manufacturer, nor might he call in the county magistrates because of their borough charter. And he subsequently tried to prevent a public meeting being held in the town on 11 December.

This meeting, nevertheless, was fairly well attended after the factories closed at 9 p.m., but few local workmen would speak in view of the fact that several had been discharged merely for appearing in the company of the Manchester delegates. McWilliams contended that their object was founded on religion, justice and humanity, while Foster castigated the hypocrisy of the Wigan magistrates pretending to administer the law with one hand while violating it with the other. He therefore proposed that the secretary of the Society should write to the Home Secretary, Robert Peel, to demand that he either appoint new magistrates for the borough of Wigan who would honestly perform their duty, or enable the county magistrates to interfere. And finally Doherty rejoiced, on behalf of every friend of humanity who had laboured to raise the working classes to their proper station in society and to a due sense of their own importance, that workmen were freely assembled that night to form a society to uphold the laws, whereas for so long they had been forced to meet in secret because of the odious combination laws, or else submit to greedy exploitation; but elements of slavish submission still persisted and he emphasised that if they were to achieve enforcement of the factory law, 'they must rely only on their own exertions. If their condition was to be improved, it must be done by themselves.'[36]

Whether a branch society was formed at Wigan was not specified, but in the new year Doherty proceeded with his instructions by writing to Peel on 12 February. Peel in turn directed his deputy to write to the Wigan magistrates on 17 February and enclose a copy of Doherty's communication. The under-secretary's letter also complained that a similar report respecting the factories of Wood and Darwell had been made early in 1828, when those gentlemen were warned as to their future conduct. 'I am now desired by Mr Peel to inform you that, if further breaches of the law are reported to him, he shall think it his duty to introduce a bill into Parliament for the purpose of giving to the Magistrates of the County a concurrent jurisdiction with the Magistrates of Wigan'. On the following day the under-secretary replied to Doherty, informing him 'that Mr Peel has made a communication to the Magistrates of Wigan upon the subject which he hopes will be effectual; at the same time he requests to be informed, in case the Society to which you are Secretary should have information of any repetition of the same offence'. This correspondence had the desired effect, for the Wigan masters were less inclined to shrug off a second warning from the government than they had been to sneer at Doherty's admonition. Early in March they held a general meeting and the result was an announcement in every factory that from 9 March they would begin to limit the working hours according to the law.[37]

The second town visited was Ashton, where a meeting of the 'friends of humanity' was held on 6 January to establish a branch society. The local spinners' secretary, Betts, took the chair, and the speakers included three delegates from Manchester, Foster, McWilliams and Clegg, and William Nicholson, a master spinner from Lees. Betts and Nicholson were appointed to form a committee, which was to hold weekly meetings to receive sub-scriptions. Finally, on 20 January, a meeting was held to establish a 'Bolton auxiliary society', addressed by several local leaders of the workmen and by delegates from Manchester including Foster, Doherty, Whittaker, Clegg and Lynch. After Foster had denounced the overworking masters and referred to plans for extending the existing legislation, Doherty gave a report of his recent mission to the different districts, many of which he had found to exceed the law by up to three hours, and detailed the varying reactions to his approaches at Glossop, Wigan and Blackburn, the Society having just insti-tuted its first successful conviction at the last-named town. He had found generally that abuses were worst in the small towns or remote places, where the masters often monopolised the supply of provisions and kept their hands in complete subservience; in the larger towns employers were kept partially in check by the force of public opinion. At the close of proceedings, it was agreed to form an auxiliary society, with William Smith as secretary.[38]

Doherty apparently hoped to make the *Conciliator* the organ of the Society after it had served its original purpose, but the expenses of publication were too great and it ceased to appear after 20 December.[39] Nevertheless, the Society set to work with a will after the expiration of its ultimatum on 1 January 1829. The procedure was for Doherty and Foster to file informations against law-breaking masters throughout the cotton-manufacturing district, either conducting the cases themselves or employing Edward Foulkes, a local solicitor, to do so. It was hoped to meet their own and the Society's expenses by securing convictions, for half the penalty was given to the informer. They were confronted with a bewildering variety of legal objections and techni-calities to frustrate them, a good deal of abuse both in court and in the press, and widespread intimidation of witnesses on whom they depended. This con-tinued unabated even after the passing of a minor factory act in May 1829 to facilitate prosecutions under Hobhouse's Act, the provisions of which had been 'defeated and set aside for want of form'. Many Manchester masters continued to support better enforcement of the Act, even though their participation in the Society virtually ceased after the start of the spinners' strike in April. On 30 May, for instance, J. B. Clarke wrote to Hobhouse of the necessity of securing compulsory observance of the law. 'None likes to be an informer', but whereas he abided by the legal 69-hour week, his neighbour worked two hours a day longer, employing children of forbidden age, and was thereby able to under-sell him. 'If you can include a clause to *compel* in all places observation of the law, you will confer great benefit on the honest master.'[40] Despite their manifold difficulties, Doherty and Foster laboured assiduously for almost two years to effect such a general compliance.

Doherty's first prosecutions were against Messrs Lunds & Foster, the only Blackburn firm not to abide by the undertaking desired by the Society. At the petty sessions at Whalley on 12 January 1829, he laid seven informations against them, although in view of the fact that the masters seemed unaware of the infractions Doherty agreed to give up six cases in return for a convic-tion in the mitigated penalty of £10 for employing a young boy in cleaning machinery during his dinner hour. But the firm did not learn its lesson, and on 13 March Doherty summoned them again for working the same boy from 5.30 a.m. to 9 p.m. on 2 February. A working spinner proved the truth of this charge, at which the firm's counsel 'submitted that no reliance could be placed on the evidence, for if servants were allowed to act as spies upon their masters, and turn against them as the occasion offered, there would be an end to the peace of society'. The magistrates disregarded this irrelevance, however, and convicted in the penalty of £10 plus costs. But Doherty was forced to withdraw other cases for lack of evidence. In the meantime, on 4 March he obtained a conviction in the full penalty of £20 against William Heginbottom, one of the few intransigent Ashton masters, for having worked a boy fourteen hours.[41]

On 2 April he laid eight informations against Messrs Garnett & Horsfall of Clitheroe for employing children during meal times, but they were all dismissed when the defence proved that the masters had previously ordered two men to clear the mill completely during these hours. Particularly bitter exchanges accompanied cases brought by Doherty against a number of Manchester firms during the fine spinners' strike. On 29 May he laid five informations against J. J. Parker for employing children during the night. His first case was confirmed in evidence, but the defending counsel asserted that several Manchester firms had been working at night for longer than his client, who had been singled out for attack by 'the society of turn-out spinners'. Doherty retorted that this was untrue and that he would be pleased to bring charges against the other firms, if their names were divulged. Finally he agreed to drop the other cases in return for a fine of £20 on the first, but the magistrate cut down the costs claimed for witnesses from £10 to £4.[42]

At this same time, Doherty also laid five informations against John Latham of Oxford Road Mill for employing children under nine, but all were dismissed when it was found that the proprietor was in fact Latham's son, William. Consequently, Doherty was forced to bring the informations forward again, under the correct name, on 25 June, when the defending counsel pleaded that the boy's work of scavenging was not employment in 'the preparation of cotton wool' as contemplated by the Act, and that Latham could not know the boy's real age as 'Mr Doherty, or any spinner, knows that many children in factories did not grow so tall as others'. But the magistrate, J. F. Foster, ignored both these excuses and convicted in the penalty of £10. The other informations, however, were all dismissed for lack of evidence, Doherty claiming that 'it was quite evident that the witnesses had been tampered with', which Latham indignantly denied.

On the same day Doherty brought five cases against Thomas Gough, but consented to accept one conviction in the full penalty of £20 plus £4 costs. He had to withdraw five other informations against William Derbyshire, however, because none of the witnesses whom he had summoned to attend turned up.[43] Doherty brought the cases forward again on 16 July, but this time Derbyshire himself did not appear, his solicitor claiming that his summons had not been correctly served; the charges were finally heard on 20 August on the information of Thomas Foster, but they all failed since 'his witnesses . . . denied every fact that he had summoned them to prove'. The New Bailey court was said to be excessively crowded with striking spinners on the former day, when Doherty also brought three informations against Robert Knott, the manager of Messrs Douglas. It was protested that less than the requisite notice of 48 hours had been given to the defendant, but Doherty argued that the summons had been served as late as possible 'to prevent the masters . . . from exerting that influence over the witnesses which it was found they had done'. Only one case could be heard, therefore, for working a boy during the breakfast period, for which Knott was convicted and fined £10; the other two charges against him were dealt with on 25 July, when both were dismissed as he had not 'knowingly' violated the act. Doherty also succeeded in exacting one penalty of £10 from James Ramsbottom on 26 July, but he withdrew another two informations against that employer on hearing that the overtime had been worked to give his hands the chance of a holiday during race week. The final prosecution brought by Doherty during 1829 was against Messrs Barker & Ainsworth of Warrington on 18 November for employing a girl under nine years of age, which resulted in the firm being fined £10.[44]

Thomas Foster's labours were equally indefatigable, but even less rewarded.[45] Towards the end of 1829, therefore, the Society reviewed its position, considering the numerous obstacles obstructing enforcement of the law. The Manchester committee, 'having been so repeatedly foiled in their attempts to convict the masters', determined to change their tactics and begin prosecutions instead under the 1819 Act, which had not been repealed. Moreover, the general spinners' conference on the Isle of Man early in December resolved that each district should discuss the necessity of an early application to Parliament for a completely new Act and for the existing provisions to be extended to all persons under 21 years; their opinions were to be sent to Doherty as soon as possible.[46]

Thus, after a year of active operations, the Society was even more closely identified with the cotton spinners' union. Reaction from the press still ranged from high praise to bitter hostility. The *Manchester Times and Gazette* reported on 12 December that Doherty and Foster were exerting themselves in different parts of the country to bring to justice those masters who daily violated the law.

> When the difficulty of getting their witnesses to prove the informations is taken into account, it is surprising that they can get the number of convictions which they do obtain; and if they were not men of more than ordinary nerve and ability, they would have long ago given up their task as a hopeless one. But we perceive that they are still on the alert, and we hope they will continue their praiseworthy exertions, which must in the end have a beneficial effect.

But the *Stockport Advertiser* on 1 January 1830, struck a somewhat different note, warning masters that 'during the present week five or six hirelings of the Manchester Committee have been in town making enquiries among the hands preparatory to laying informations'. Several cases were brought by Foster three weeks later, at which the *Advertiser* asserted that no town had less reason to complain of the infringement of Peel's Act than Stockport; if Foster really had the operatives' welfare in mind, he would turn his attention to those factories worked all day and night, rather than pick up a solitary case here and there, generally contrived on purpose by the workmen from motives of malice.[47]

The activities during 1830 differed in several respects from those of the previous year. Firstly, the cotton-spinning trade was deeply depressed, prices having declined steeply because of overproduction. To rectify this situation, the leading master spinners met together in Manchester on 26 January 1830, and agreed to restrict their works to the hours of daylight only until the crisis abated. Within a fortnight, more than 150 firms in the district had agreed to the new regulation and hence there were fewer examples of over-working for the Society to deal with. At the same time, however, a bill was brought before Parliament to prohibit the system of truck, and Doherty and Foster busied themselves in exposing cases of paying wages in goods before the courts. The Society also extended its operations to include a campaign for a new short-time bill, pursuant to the spinners' December resolution.

Doherty's first case in the new year was against Ellis Milne, the manager of an Ardwick mill, owned by Thomas Barton, at the New Bailey on 16 January, for overworking a boy, but no evidence was taken as Doherty had misspelt the defendant's name on the summons. The proceedings were resumed on 11 February, but the deputy-constable of Ardwick reported that neither the boy nor his father could now be found and the informations were set aside in consequence. Doherty asserted that he had no doubt 'that they had been directed to conceal themselves by someone who was likely to be affected by an investigation of the cases', an allegation vehemently denied by Barton. On the previous day Doherty had appeared at the Bolton petty sessions and obtained a conviction in £15 plus £4 15s 6d costs against Thomas Wilde, the same employer also being fined £10 for paying wages in goods. He was less successful in the same court on 15 February, when he summoned Messrs Ridgeway, bleachers of Horwich, for truck, but 'the only person who could prove the case had purposely absented himself'. The most important case on that day, however, was a truck prosecution brought by Doherty against Bollings, the Bolton spinners, for deducting the rent of their work-men's cottages from their wages. This was a test case, for such deductions were commonly practised by the proprietors of large concerns in the neigh-bourhood. Because of its significance, the defence applied for a postponement until 23 February to have more time to prepare the case, to which Doherty agreed on receiving 6s for his expenses. A large crowd assembled in court on the appointed day and the magistrate, Major Watkins, revealed his prejudice from the outset, when Doherty began to state the case and was promptly told 'that the bench would not be addressed by any person except he was in the profession of the law'. The defence claimed that the weekly rental payments were part of the workmen's contract and that all wages had been paid in 'lawful coin of the realm', the rent being technically a 'deduction' not a 'payment'. A cross-examination by Doherty was disallowed as 'irrelevant', and the bench ultimately dismissed the case 'without a moment's hesitation'. *Wheeler's Manchester Chronicle* rejoiced at the verdict, feeling assured that the 'paltry grounds' for the prosecution and the 'paltry quarter' from which it originated 'will speak more forcefully to the public than any comment from us. Repeatedly during the hearing, Mr Doherty was quietened by the Bench in a peremptory manner and we hope the outcome may produce a salutary effect on this individual.' But the *Bolton Chronicle* commented that 'several magistrates who were present declared that they would have convicted had they heard the case'. Finally, at the Bolton sessions on 12 April, Doherty was allowed to examine his witnesses and succeeded in exacting a fine of £10 for an unanswerable case of trucking from a firm which had already been summoned twice in the past for that offence and once for overworking.[48]

During this period Foster did not record a single success, though he brought prosecutions against firms in Stockport and Bolton.[49] Meanwhile Doherty, in his capacity as secretary, inserted in several local papers on 3 April an advertisement convening the first public meeting of members of the Society since its formation seventeen months earlier. It was to be held in the theatre of the Mechanics' Institution on 7 April for the purpose of discussing the best way to obtain an Act to regulate the hours of young persons not only in cotton but in all textile factories, as well as for confirming the accounts of the Society and hearing a report of the progress made in accomplishing its objects.[50] This meeting was attended by about 400 operatives, but the business commenced rather late due to Doherty's absence in Bolton on matters presumably connected with the strike there. When he finally arrived and presented his report, he began by describing the activities of Foster and himself against violations of the law. He found 'that nearly all the master spinners denied any infringement of the law in their own persons, but admitted that the evil was practised by almost everyone else'. He had visited Glossop, Hyde, Ashton, etc. in the course of his duties, and finally Wigan, where, after the Home Secretary's intervention, Doherty was pleased to state that 'the parties in question had been most exemplary in their adherence to the law'.[51] He then proceeded to comment upon the great difficulty of procuring evidence necessary to convict offenders, because potential witnesses dreaded to offend their masters. The result was that out of 187 cases which he and his colleague had brought, they had succeeded in obtaining convictions in only 24. Doherty concluded by reading a statement of the Society's accounts. These showed that the bulk of the subscriptions came from the Manchester spinners' society, with much smaller amounts from Wigan, Ashton, Bolton, and Blackburn; including also the proceeds from convictions and payment of legal costs, total receipts were £164 2s 1d, but after deducting all the legal and travelling expenses, payments to witnesses, printing bills, etc., there was only a balance of 10s 5d.[52]

The remainder of the meeting was taken up with the discussion and adoption of a petition to Parliament for a new factory bill, prohibiting the employment in any textile mill of persons under twenty-one for more than ten and a half hours per day during the week and eight hours on Saturdays, and rendering it easier to bring prosecutions by allowing evidence in court from persons not employed in the respective factories. Both Foster and Doherty condemned public apathy on this question, compared with the zeal for emancipation of black slaves; Doherty referred to children working fourteen–sixteen hours daily in Lancashire and Yorkshire textile mills, while adult felons and negro slaves in the West Indies were protected from working more than ten hours a day; night-working was denounced as a particularly serious evil. The meeting therefore appointed a new committee of twenty-one individuals to campaign for the bill and to continue prosecutions under the existing law. The members included Peter Maddocks, soon to succeed Doherty as secretary of the Manchester spinners' club, Elijah Dixon, John Hynes, James Turner, Thomas Daniel, Thomas Whittaker, Thomas Foster, John Lawton and Cornelius Lynch, with Doherty remaining as secretary of the Society.[53]

At this time it appeared that the operative spinners had a good chance of obtaining their employers' backing for their Isle of Man resolution to agitate for an extension of legislative protection. Early in the year, as we have seen, serious depression in the yarn market had caused a large number of firms to agree on reducing their working to the daytime hours.[54] Several members of the Manchester Chamber of Commerce had requested the Board to apply to Parliament for a law to prohibit altogether a cotton mill from being worked more than twelve hours daily, and although the Board refused on the grounds that it was unfair to restrict only one branch of textiles and that curtailing the freedom of labour was seldom beneficial, those individuals who believed such a measure would be of advantage were told to make the application themselves. At the same time, a memorial was sent to the Home Secretary, Peel, from the cotton and woollen manufacturers of Rochdale, blaming overproduction for low prices and wages and asking for legislation to forbid work in both trades between 9 p.m. and 5 a.m. These events were welcomed by Doherty on behalf of 'the friends of humanity' in an article in the first number of the *Journal* on 6 March. He was anxious to afford 'every assistance in our power towards obtaining a new and improved act', personal experience having shown him the difficulty under the present law of punishing offenders; with the opposition of the master spinners now removed, he believed that they might easily obtain the desired bill.[55]

Petitions in support of the bill were organised by the operatives in most of the Lancashire and Cheshire spinning towns, as well as from Glasgow,[56] and Thomas Foster, of Manchester, and William Smith, secretary of the Bolton auxiliary society, were deputed to London at the end of April to lobby M.P.s. In an editorial on 15 May Doherty asserted that the bill was about to be introduced. He condemned those unscrupulous employers who were prepared to amass extra profit at the expense of the health and morals of their infant workers and of the prosperity of their honourable competitors. He urged the power-loom, silk and woollen workers to give publicity to their hardships, 'such as was given by the operative spinners in 1819 and 1825', and concluded by quoting from O'Connell's speech of support on presenting the Manchester petition to the Commons.[57]

As late as July 1830 petitions were still being sent to Parliament in support of the bill, but all chance of obtaining legislation that year had by then passed. Towards the end of May the London delegates reported that a great proportion of the masters were willing to co-operate if the workmen would agree to raise the maximum limit to $11\frac{1}{2}$ hours, and according to the *Manchester Courier* the 'Committee of spinners' consented to this suggestion and were still expecting a bill to be passed. When Foster and Smith returned to Lancashire, however, they reported to a meeting of Bolton spinners on 8 June that 'it was doubtful whether the measure could be carried this session', although they hoped that the result of their exertions would be 'some material amelioration . . . [being] made in the present law during the next session'.[58]

While this agitation was proceeding, Doherty was also writing in the *Journal* in favour of a bill introduced by Littleton, a Staffordshire member, to prohibit the practice of truck. On 17 April he asserted that the 'abominable system' was very uncommon in Manchester, but the employers would ultimately have to introduce it or lower wages if their competitors in other towns continued to supplement their profits in such a way. He urged the workmen in every town, including Manchester, to call meetings to petition against 'the enslaving traffic'. And on 22 May, in his capacity as secretary to the Manchester spinners' club, he inserted a public denial, adopted at a general meeting two days earlier, that a petition presented to the Commons against that bill, 'from the cotton spinners of Manchester and the workmen in their employ', was genuine. Doherty alleged that the petition had been signed only by a few of the most oppressive masters like Hugh Birley and Thomas Ashton. These remarks considerably annoyed a correspondent in the *Stockport Advertiser* the following week, who explained that the petition had asked primarily for the practice of deducting rent from wages to be exempted from the bill, because of the difficulties of landlords in recovering arrears, and he accused Doherty of using 'every mean artifice to excite bad feelings among the labouring classes towards their employers'.[59]

The Protection Society continued to experience great difficulties in trying to secure enforcement of the existing factory legislation. Because of reduced working in the trade depression, and also through lack of funds, the number of informations which the Society was able to bring declined sharply. Apart from those cases that were left over from earlier postponements, Doherty's only prosecutions after that meeting were against John Sheldon of Bollington at the Macclesfield petty sessions on 21 June 1830. His first information broke down when he could not prove that the boy alleged to have been overworked was under sixteen, due to some confusion in the entries on the baptismal register; the second case was dismissed when the magistrates arbitrarily overturned a recent Oldham decision respecting employment of children to 'make up' time after 8 p.m.; and because of this last verdict, Doherty withdrew his third complaint. At the same time Foster had little more success in prosecutions against several Macclesfield and Stockport mill-owners.[60] Despite ill-health, however, he persisted in these endeavours almost up to his death in February 1831. Doherty paid a glowing tribute to his services in this cause:

> His favourite topic was the protection of children in cotton factories. On this he dwelt with delight; often with all the force and energy of natural eloquence. He is now gone, and his loss will be felt by none more than the helpless creatures who found in him both a friend and a protector.[61]

By this time Doherty also had been forced to abandon his efforts, but the work was taken over and continued during 1831 by two other spinners' leaders, John Lees of Oldham and Thomas Worsley of Stockport, who were reported as being agents of 'the operative spinners' society'. But their efforts were no more effectual than those of their predecessors, though they did succeed in forcing the Oldham magistrates into action in one case by taking them to the Court of King's Bench.[62] Their activities appear to have been independent of the 'Society for the Protection of Children Employed in Cotton

Factories', which had ceased to function by the autumn of 1830, although its committee continued to exist, reverting to the traditional role of the Manchester short-time committee, but now in co-operation with the new movement in Yorkshire.

Although Grant mistakenly stated that the Manchester short-time committee had been reformed in 1829, with four members—himself, Doherty, Turner, and Daniel—his assertion that the Manchester reformers had become 'disheartened and almost broken for want of support' and by 'delay upon delay' does appear to have some validity for the situation towards the end of 1830.[63] The Lancashire movement would doubtless have revived of its own accord, as it had done previously in 1825 and again in 1828, but as it transpired, the failure of the cotton spinners to induce the legislature to extend protection to all textile trades was soon followed by the start of a new agitation in Yorkshire in support of such an extension. Oastler's famous letters to the *Leeds Mercury* in the autumn of 1830 exposing the horrors of 'white slavery' in the worsted mills of Bradford soon led to the establishment of workers' short-time committees in the various West Riding towns similar to those that had existed in Lancashire, in Manchester especially, for well over a decade. The factory movement from this point has been meticulously detailed and analysed by J. T. Ward in his various publications on the subject. Hence it will only be necessary hereafter to describe Doherty's personal participation and importance in it.

In fact Doherty at first by no means welcomed the intervention of Oastler and other Tories in the factory question, believing it to be an attempt to divert the workers' attention away from the growing agitation for parliamentary reform.[64] At the same time, however, he himself became more deeply involved in trade-union affairs. He gave up his position of secretary to the Manchester short-time committee, being succeeded by Thomas Daniel. And the *Voice* contained surprisingly little on the subject of factory reform, despite its frequent references to the evils of capitalism and competition. True, Doherty published some interesting statistics on 29 January revealing how few spinners and stretchers working in the Ashton neighbourhood were over forty years of age due to the havoc wrought by employment in 'cotton hells'; but this was part of his propaganda in support of the current strike there. And on 19 February he accused W. R. G[reg]—who, ironically, published a pamphlet that year describing the labour of spinners and stretchers as 'amongst the most laborious that exists' and asserting the necessity of shorter hours[65]—of not allowing the lawful hour for dinner in his factories; but this was during a debate on the benefits of trade unions. Other early references to factory reform in the paper were mainly confined to the correspondence columns, Longson writing in on 2 February that legislation should control the hours of all factory workers and that the Stockport operatives were petitioning for a ten-hour day, while a Wigan correspondent on 30 April complained of continued overworking in that town.[66]

On 26 February, however, Doherty did refer to the bill being introduced by Hobhouse to reduce hours for young persons in all factories to $11\frac{1}{2}$ hours per day and $8\frac{1}{2}$ hours on Saturdays, urging workmen in every district to send in petitions to Parliament. And the following week he revealed that a delegate from Stockport had been sent to London to lobby in favour of the bill, and castigated the Stockport masters who had expressed their opposition to the measure. On 9 April an editorial in the *Voice* again censured the inhumanity of those masters who were organising resistance to Hobhouse's moderate measure, and asserted that the workmen should petition not only for this but for a ten-hour day; Doherty complained, however, that the delegates engaged on this business were not furnishing the paper with any information as to their activities. The question also came up for discussion at three consecutive meetings of the Manchester committee of the National Association. On 5 April Heywood, of Manchester, and Knight, of Oldham, spoke in favour of the short-time bill, but lamented that little had been done on its behalf in their district compared with Leeds and elsewhere. On 12 April Doherty stressed the necessity of all interested in the bill 'straining every nerve' to obtain it, for a masters' deputation was at that very time in London arguing against it; he desired petitions to be sent both from Manchester and from the committee. And on 19 April Fell again emphasised the urgency of action to frustrate the masters' designs and Doherty stated that he would have a petition prepared by the following week. Other workers, however, stressed the frequently long hours and heat in workshops where steam power was not used, and it was ultimately resolved 'that the petition apply to all trades'.[67]

Thereafter the *Voice* was silent on the issue until 18 June, when it reported a meeting of Manchester cotton-yarn dressers in support of new legislation, at which the speakers included Turner, Whittaker and Lawton. Two weeks later the advertisements included the annual report of the Manchester short-time committee, inserted by its secretary, Daniel. He complained that the existing law was a dead letter because of the difficulty of securing evidence. Only about forty convictions had been obtained out of 185 cases tried under it, and hence many country masters worked their mills fifteen hours daily to the great injury of both their workmen and the Manchester firms, who generally worked twelve. Daniel called upon the public to send subscriptions to the committee, which was still agitating for a 10½-hour restriction to apply to young persons under twenty-one years of age in all mills worked by machinery. Appended to this report was a statement of the committee's recent accounts, which revealed that its receipts came exclusively from the Manchester spinners and from dressers, power-loom weavers and overlookers at different mills in the town, and that co-operation continued with spinners in other towns such as Ashton and Bolton. No further allusion to the short-time question appeared in the *Voice*, though there was a forthright condemnation by Doherty on 6 August of the mill-regulations of a Stockport firm. It was with some justice, therefore, that a correspondent on 11 June regretted that there was 'one class which you [Doherty] have rather neglected since conducting the people's press—young children in cotton factories'; and he urged more vigorous support by Manchester workmen.[68]

Yorkshire, in fact, had become the main area of agitation, supporting Hobhouse's moderate measure, although there were already demands in the background for a ten-hours bill. In Lancashire the Bolton committee of the Protection Society, still apparently in being, petitioned in favour of the bill early in February, and the Stockport short-time committee deputed Thomas Worsley to go to London during March to lobby on its behalf, though he stated on his return that he still preferred restricting all under twenty-one years to 10½ hours daily.[69] This, as we have seen, continued to be the policy of the Manchester short-time committee, but they were rendered temporarily inactive by Doherty's withdrawal and Foster's death. A correspondent in the *Manchester Times* at the end of February stated that, despite unemployment caused by the coupling of mules—for which the only remedy was reduction of working hours—the Manchester men had made no move to petition in favour of Hobhouse's bill, in marked contrast to their earlier zeal. 'I suppose that Foster being dead, and the others who act for the operatives having their attention engaged by matters of less importance, occasion this surprising and otherwise unaccountable neglect.'[70]

Amid this disharmony the Yorkshire woollen masters succeeded in persuading Hobhouse to exclude their trade completely from his bill. The resulting Act of October 1831 applied only to cotton mills and even there proved ineffective. Nevertheless some masters continued to seek enforcement, although they had mostly withdrawn support from the Protection Society because of its connections with trade-union 'agitators', who, as a Blackburn employer complained, were only concerned with 'keeping up the irritation between masters and men' by means of spies and informers, and living on the contributions of the deluded workmen.[71] When Hobhouse's Act was passed, therefore, a group of Lancashire master spinners determined to enforce this measure themselves, for which purpose they formed a 'Cotton Factory Time Bill Association'. This was welcomed by the *Manchester Guardian*, which repeated the criticisms of Doherty's now discredited and defunct Protection Society.[72]

Nevertheless, the new Association continued to use the same methods as Doherty and Foster, and even secured the aid of some of the operatives, including Turner, Worsley and Downes as informers. Until August 1833 there were occasional reports of informations laid by one or other of these three, but they were repeatedly frustrated and outmanoeuvred as Doherty and Foster had previously been.[73] Turner testified to Sadler's Committee in June 1832, that a twelve-hour day was generally observed in Manchester, because the 'honourable employers' there had formed an association which 'looked very strictly after that matter'. But elsewhere Hobhouse's Act of 1831 was a completely dead letter, as Hindley admitted in March 1832, when he informed a meeting of factory reformers in Manchester that he knew of seventeen factories within a few miles of that town which worked children all through the night, and that the current Act seemed powerless to prevent it; though the Manchester masters' association had expended nearly £100, only five convictions had been obtained.[74] And the Cotton Factory Time Bill Association disappeared completely in the furore surrounding the passing of Althorp's Act in the summer of 1833.

Thus neither operatives nor masters had been very successful in their efforts at enforcing factory legislation. Nevertheless, the 'Society for the Protection of Children Employed in Cotton Factories' has been grossly underestimated by historians. Ward, for instance, devoted just one sentence to it in a book of over 400 pages, asserting that 'few ventured to support' Doherty's scheme.[75] It is true, as we have seen, that the proportion of convictions obtained was low, but many other informations were voluntarily given up in return for the imposition of one penalty or for a promise to observe the law in future. If its motive was to restrict adult hours as much as children's, there was no shame in that, and it does appear to have secured some improvement in several towns. Although the Society hoped for the masters' co-operation, it was in fact dominated by the spinners' union and was really a continuation of their earlier effort in this field. It provided the basis for the movement started in Yorkshire: none of the arguments used there, including Oastler's famous denunciation of 'white slavery', were new, while the Lancashire cotton spinners had long been participating in movements for legislation and grappling with the problems of enforcement.

The 1831 Act, still confining legislative control to cotton factories, outraged the Yorkshire reformers, who forthwith replaced Hobhouse with the Tory, Michael Sadler, as their parliamentary spokesman and began canvassing for candidates at the approaching elections who would commit themselves to supporting Sadler's ten-hours bill. Most of the Lancashire reformers also united behind the new rallying-cry and on 29 October the Manchester short-time committee demanded that the electors should return only members pledged to 'ten hours a day, with eight on Saturday, and a time-book'. But Doherty remained aloof. He was now giving his support to a policy determined at a meeting of Manchester spinners on 21 September, which had called on masters and operatives not to work more than *eight* hours per day.[76] Doherty believed that limiting production would end price and therefore wage decreases, while shorter hours would reduce unemployment; and he asserted that the regulation could easily be effected, even in defiance of the masters, and certainly without the irrelevance of parliamentary interference. It would seem that his experiences in the Protection Society had convinced him of the futility of statutory regulation and that he had now come round to advocacy of direct action by the trade unions—with the employers' co-operation if possible; if not, then presumably by strikes.

He explained his current position in a long letter to the *Manchester and Salford Advertiser* on 22 December 1831. He admitted that the niggardly protection afforded by previous enactments had been of some benefit to the unfortunate factory children, that it revealed 'some slight show of compassionate attention' to the labouring classes, indicating that they were 'not of less consequence to the state than the beasts of the field'. Indeed, it was a disgrace to the nation that nothing was done to preserve the memory of men like the late Nathaniel Gould, even by the group most benefited, the Manchester spinners, while monuments were erected to men like Canning and Huskisson who had amassed great fortunes by supporting 'borough-mongering tyranny'. But, Doherty asserted, 'legislative interference is at least but a negative good', a poor substitute for the workmen taking independent action themselves. 'To require an act of parliament to protect men from evils which they can . . . annihilate by their own exertions, is to endeavour to perpetuate that state of slavish dependence from which we are just emerging.' In Yorkshire, agitation for a ten-hours bill had reached such a pitch that it was almost a party question, candidates being asked to give pledges of support, but Doherty thought this mistaken, for the Tories would use it for party ends, while keeping the working classes in political servility. Moreover, it distracted attention from the real points on which, as Cobbett had shown, the workmen should demand pledges—an equitable adjustment of the national debt, a reduction of taxation and measures to leave the workman in possession of the fruits of his own industry. No law could govern workmen's hours; but if they united and determined to 'legislate for themselves', they could reduce their hours as they pleased within one day. 'Is it not, then, egregious folly to make the reducing of the hours of labour a parliamentary question, which can be settled better and speedier without its interference than with it?' And Doherty concluded by quoting from a recent address from the Glasgow spinners' committee announcing a decision to enforce a 58-hour week themselves. 'These are the sentiments of men who really feel their own dignity and are resolved to crouch no longer . . . Let the same sentiment be re-echoed through the country, and the thing is done.'[77]

Doherty's role in these activities was to encourage the operatives to action by publicising the oppressions under which they suffered. On 24 December 1831, only three months after the disappearance of the *Voice*, he gave notice that in the following week would be published the first number of the *Workman's Expositor*,

> in which will be exposed, the whole system of restrictions, extortions and oppression to which the Working classes are exposed, in all the various manufactories through the country. In every case the names of the masters, managers and overlookers will be given, without the least reserve, the object of the conductors . . . being to expose, if they cannot punish and prevent, the cruel system of injustice and of heartless oppression of the workman, which has gradually crept into almost all branches of our manufacturing industry.

Doherty invited well-authenticated examples of persecution to be sent to him for publication and promised to protect the names of his informants, though they would be expected to support their allegations should they be challenged. He fully recognised the risks of opposing 'the rich and worst men', especially as the libel laws did not accept the truth of particular statements as justification for their promulgation, but still he would not shrink from the responsibility. Reviews and extracts from popular works of literature, science and the arts would also be included, as well as a weekly list of forthcoming meetings of co-operative, benefit, trade and temperance societies, districts of the National Association, and Oddfellows' Lodges.[78]

The first edition of the *Workman's Expositor* appeared a week late on 7 January 1832. It comprised four quarto pages and was priced 2d. After only two numbers, however, Doherty reverted to his more regular format of eight octavo pages, halved the price, and altered the title to the *Poor Man's Advocate*. The papers were at first printed by Alexander Wilkinson in Market Street and sold by Abel Heywood, but the contents were so strong that they soon withdrew, and from March Doherty printed them himself, initially from temporary premises in Chorlton Row and later from his own shop in Withy Grove. From the end of June he was intermittently in gaol awaiting a libel prosecution by the Rev Gilpin, on which he was eventually found guilty on 25 August and sentenced to one month's imprisonment in November.[79] This provoked a further reorganisation of the paper in September, when it became a typical unstamped *political* publication, with a slightly amended title and a different publisher named each week to avoid being prosecuted under the stamp laws as a newspaper. Factory reform intelligence continued to be inserted, however, and James Turner and George Downes were at different times listed as the publisher. No figures for the circulation are available, but Doherty did have difficulty in distributing it. He had a London outlet through W. Strange of Paternoster Row, but by 28 April only four booksellers in Manchester were willing to sell the *Advocate* because of 'the threats and contrivances of the cotton lords, parsons, lawyers, and other "professional" men', and Doherty was forced to advertise for unemployed men to become street-sellers for a return of 9d per dozen.[80]

The bitter tone of the whole work was established in an article in the first number on 'The justice of exposing tyrannical employers'. To those who would decry his 'insolence' in interfering with the internal regulations of factories, Doherty asked if they believed that imprisoning thousands of industrious workmen in conditions of great heat, and regulating their conduct by arbitrary fines (thus also reducing their wages), was 'a mere matter of private business'. And to those who argued that the labourers had no complaint as they were free to quit such employment whenever they wished, Doherty replied that their only alternative was the workhouse whose inmates were even more closely confined and imprisoned more permanently than those in a 'Cotton-hell'. His basic principles were that masters and workmen were but two equal and contracting parties, with no question of a superior and a dependant, or of one party dictating terms; that no part of society and no individual members should benefit at the expense of others; and that human life and happiness were more important than inanimate property. If these standards were not accepted and factory abominations not exposed, Doherty reckoned that the whole fabric of society was in danger of being violently rent asunder. Hence in conclusion he asserted that his work would render 'an essential service to the government of the country', despite the legal restrictions hampering it.[81]

He then turned to individual cases. For five weeks he raved against James Patrick, manager in the factory of the late James Kennedy, the charges against whom included departing from the 1829 list of spinning prices without informing the men on what new scale they were to be paid, discharging operatives who had the temerity to ask for such information or to protest against the numerous fines exacted, refusing any exit from the mill during working hours, even for a drink of water, without a written certificate or 'jailor's warrant', and making deductions from spinners' wages for gas during summer when it was not even used. Yet the 'idle, ruffianly and pestilent police' did nothing to arrest this fellow, whose tyranny must therefore be overborne by the workmen themselves; 'our object is not only to expose the cruelty and injustice of the system, but at the same time to excite a spirit of discontent and of *resistance* to anything so grossly unjust and so destructive of that spirit of national independence, which is essential to the existence of institutions, bearing even the semblance of freedom'. The middle classes were reminded that misery and oppression would lead to revolt, as in the 'Swing' riots among agricultural labourers. Their welfare depended upon the prosperity of the working classes, and if they wished to avoid revolution they should help the workmen to overcome such evils.[82]

Patrick's offences were grievous, Doherty alleged, but only typical of the system. Over the following weeks, his attention was successively fixed on Thomas Harbottle, who 'in the teeth of humanity, public feeling and the law' worked his factory all night and regularly deducted 1*d* per yard of cloth from the wages of his dressers and thus added to his profits, yet had the audacity to condemn 'union pennies'; on Henry McConnell, for similar deductions from his spinners' wages and for the injury inflicted on domestic arrangements and moral habits by having set the precedent in 1810 for employing women as spinners to check the combinations of men; on Messrs Crompton and Ditchfield of Prestolee Mill near Bolton, who kept their young hands out of bed for sixteen hours at a stretch by complicated relays and employed two sets of spinners by night and day, deducting 10 per cent from the earnings of both if either failed to reach their output quota;[83] on Lawrence Rostron, who received public acclaim for subscribing £20 to the fund to fight cholera yet raised the money by reducing the wages of his fustian cutters and refusing to allow his dyers to join their union; on John Latham, who was the sole judge on the imposition of an enormous number of fines, had suspended a leaking water-tub above the 'Necessary' to encourage the user to haste, and would not even pay 10*s* for a door to preserve the modesty of females from the 'vulgar gaze'; on Thomas Barnes, who refused a character reference to a union man to prevent his getting new work; on Messrs Astley of Bollington, who employed an overlooker who delighted in beating child workers and in making obscene suggestions to those females whom the heat forced to remove part of their clothing; and finally on Benjamin Gray on 19 May, whose manager would not even allow the factory door—through which 'poor Brooks' was shot by Frost in 1818—to be opened for food to be brought in during the whole of Easter Monday.[84]

Doherty also inserted after 3 March 'A list of the Midnight Robbers of the Repose of the Poor, by working Factories in the night', amending the names slightly as particular firms were shamed into abandoning the practice or as others took it up. The whole tone of the work, in fact, reflected Doherty's anger at the extreme divisions in the new society which had developed over the past half-century, whereby the first master spinners, 'plain, industrious men' disposed to mingle socially with their workmen, had been transformed by massive profits into a 'new race' of haughty and forbidding 'cotton lords'. When the temporary violence of Doherty's political views were added,[85] it was an explosive mixture. He deplored that factory workers should submit to 'this infamous system of degradation' for the benefit of 'greedy and reckless speculators'. He wished their emancipation to be effected by other means than acts of violence, 'but if bolts and barriers are to be employed to shut them up to increasing . . . toil as a system . . ., as if they were the property of those who give them merely a nominal value for that toil, we have no hesitation in saying, that they would do infinitely more credit to themselves, and deserve, in a tenfold degree, the respect and admiration of posterity, by *breaking down* those illegal barriers to their personal freedom'. Certainly this bitterness can be partly accounted for by Doherty's own experience as a cotton spinner : he several times asserted that he had seen such evils 'with our own eyes' and, as we saw in Chapter One, his recollection of 'the petty tyranny and vulgar arrogance' was still strong.[86] However, he denied on 21 April that he wrote because of personal malice.

It has always been the highest point of our ambition to be able, and have the opportunity of exposing the vexatious annoyances and oppressions which have been so long practised upon the poor workman, whose misfortunes are rendered more intolerable from the prospect of their being perpetual; for they have no friend to complain to, and entertain no hope of redress. We now, thank God, have both the power and the means of exposing the authors and abettors of the system, and we promise them that we shall not spare them.

In such circumstances, it was remarkable that the first libel action came from none of these local employers whom he had so roundly condemned, but from a Stockport parson for a totally unconnected cause.[87]

By the time Doherty completed his survey of factory conditions on 19 May, however, his views on the need for legislative protection for workmen had completely reversed. This was partially because of an abrupt changeover by the Glasgow spinners from a determination to enforce a 58-hour week by unilateral action to a policy of seeking their employers' support for 'Mr Sadler's time bill now pending in Parliament'.[88] In addition, the Manchester spinners' union had lost much of its strength following the defeats of 1829–31 and was in no position to implement shorter hours unilaterally. From the other side, the attitude of the masters towards further legislation compelled Doherty to take notice. Sadler's bill, limiting all under eighteen years to a ten-hour day and forbidding night work for all under twenty-one years, was not introduced until 16 March, but the employers were already organising opposition beforehand. One group, led by Hindley and the 'Cotton Factory Time Bill Association', met in Manchester on 21 February to petition Parliament for a more effective enforcement of the present restrictions, by entirely prohibiting the motive power of factories being worked more than sixty-nine hours per week. They failed to secure the co-operation of the short-time committee, who were already collecting signatures for their own petition for Sadler's bill, but succeeded in convening a public meeting of clergy, professional men and manufacturers in Manchester on 8 March which sanctioned their proceedings. Other masters adopted a more extreme position. Preston employers petitioned against Sadler's bill on 2 March, asserting that only the most ignorant workpeople disagreed with them and they had been deluded 'by the persuasion of designing men' that their wages would not be reduced in proportion to their hours, which was of course 'impossible'. Stockport employers adopted similar petitions and dismissed workmen who would not sign them, as did Holland Hoole in Salford. Doherty condemned such injustices on 10 and 31 March. But Hoole retaliated by writing to Althorp on 12 March to defend conditions in the cotton industry and attack the leaders of the clamour for a ten-hours bill as ignorant philanthropists, inflammatory demagogues and operatives hoping to restore that monopoly power in the spinning departments which they had lost, an analysis which was supported by another local master in the silk trade, Vernon Royle. The *Guardian* lamented on 27 March that the employers' resistance to the threat of Sadler's bill was weak and divided, but when Parliament established another committee to consider the question, local reformers considered it a victory for the masters' delaying tactics and the necessity for such an enquiry was denied in the *Union Pilot* on 7 April.[89]

Doherty announced his conversion in an article on 25 February on cotton spinners' wages reductions. These could only be permanently avoided, he believed, by restricting the time of labour or reducing the quantity produced. 'This could be much more advantageously done by themselves than by parliament. But if they are not prepared to undertake the task, let them vigorously support Mr Sadler's bill for *ten hours a day*,' by which wages might even in the long run be advanced. He now rapidly became the bill's firmest supporter. Only their own indifference could prevent its passing, he asserted in the following number. Strenuous efforts were being made throughout Yorkshire; but Lancashire did not need to follow their example, only 'to pursue the same line of conduct now on this subject, which they have so often done before', and it would be obtained whatever opposition 'the Graspalls' might attempt. On 10 March he lamented that some Stockport operatives had acquiesced in signing the petitions against Sadler's bill, although a large majority of them were in fact opposed to it, which was a disgrace to their responsibilities as parents. If they feared for wages, they should recollect that making labour scarcer increased its value. But if they were anxious that the restriction be laid on the moving power, he answered that while an effective law *was* essential, the ten-hours' principle should first be recognised, for it would be difficult to persuade Parliament to amend an efficient twelve-hours' bill : they should stand out therefore for a 'ten-hours bill or no bill at all'. He repeated this rallying-call the following week. Labourers should support the bill from self-interest, as increasing labour had only increased their misery and privations, but more especially from humane considerations for their children. He reminded the Lancashire workers again of their former exertions in the cause and concluded by asking 'what are the operatives of Bolton, Preston, Blackburn, Chorley, Rochdale, Oldham, Ashton, Stockport and Macclesfield about?' And on 24 March he showed that his earlier scepticism of the new Tory supporters of factory reform had now completely disappeared. 'Mr Oastler is a tory in politics. But when . . . will any of your boasting "liberals", or professing whigs contribute a tithe of the service which Mr Oastler has . . . rendered to the cause of suffering humanity?'[90]

As usual, when Doherty altered his opinion on any subject, it did not pass without comment. As early as 28 January the Bolton spinners' committee had written to Francis Place, enclosing a petition in favour of Sadler's bill which they requested him to entrust to O'Connell for presentation. Over the next two months they spent £30 in the cause, sending up further petitions from Chorley, Tyldesley and Blackburn, supporting a delegate in London to confer with Sadler during March and corresponding with other northern towns and Glasgow. Doherty's accusations of indifference were therefore ill-received in that quarter and on 20 March their secretary wrote to Doherty to ask what Manchester had done in comparison and adding that 'the insinuation of negligence comes most ungraciously from one whose opinions on the propriety of applying for parliamentary interference have undergone such a sudden, indeed I may almost say, *miraculous* change'. Aware of the danger of reopening past differences with the Bolton men, Doherty replied in a conciliatory manner on 31 March. He admitted that he had at first suspected Oastler of being motivated by Tory party-political considerations, but, after acquiring 'a more intimate knowledge of that gentleman', recognised that he had done him an injustice: in fact he now lauded Oastler as 'the intrepid and uncompromising champion of the cause' and was convinced that there was 'nothing of party feeling' in Sadler's bill, but purely humanitarian concern. Hence, although he would still prefer independent action by the workmen themselves, partial protection by Parliament was better than nothing, and he urged all operatives, whether in Bolton, Manchester or elsewhere, to unite in support of Sadler's bill.[91]

Doherty's reappearance as an active factory reform campaigner was signalised at the last of a series of large Yorkshire meetings in preparation for the introduction of this bill, at Halifax on 6 March, when Oastler was among the speakers. Doherty seconded a resolution that the bill would also protect benevolent masters from unfair competition. He denied that Hobhouse's bill was efficient in Lancashire, expressed his pride at witnessing the enthusiasm prevailing in Yorkshire, and concluded by pledging to use every effort on his return to Manchester to stimulate the labouring population to support their efforts. He was warned by the chairman, however, for having 'diverged into political topics'.[92] Further to his promise, Doherty became active once more in the Manchester short-time committee, which had already during February raised 15,000 signatures for its petition for Sadler's bill plus a restriction on the moving power and imprisonment for witnesses who committed perjury. And at a meeting of Manchester clergymen and manufacturers on 8 March in favour of a more efficient 69-hour bill, Doherty seconded an unsuccessful amendment proposed by James Whittle for Sadler's proposals. He asserted that the proportion of children and females to adult males working the machinery in Manchester mills was five to one and that 'at this time there were hundreds of able-bodied workmen without a single occupation to turn their hands to, while their children were engaged in the factories, earning a livelihood for themselves and their parents'.[93]

The short-time committee considered that another meeting was necessary to express Manchester opinion, especially as, according to Doherty, many workmen were refused admission. A public meeting of the working classes took place at the Mechanics' Institution on 14 March, which passed resolutions in favour of Sadler's bill, against night-working, and in support of restraining the motive power of factories to the hours worked by 'convicted felons'. Thomas Brookes took the chair and the speakers included Whittle, Daniel, Lawton, Turner, Grant, and Pitkeithley from Huddersfield. Doherty moved two of the resolutions and advocated at great length the necessity for restriction on the moving power, for any enactment without it would inevitably be ineffectual, as demonstrated by the existence of several mills near Manchester working night and day by relays. Later in this speech, which was published in 1833 in a series of addresses on the factory reform question, Doherty attacked the Manchester clergy, not one of whom had come forward to oppose 'cotton mill slavery'. He had not expected any bishops or representatives of the established church to attend, but had thought ministers of other denominations would be present. And his suggestion that a vote of censure should be passed upon them all collectively was agreed amid shouts of 'down with the parsons'. The proceedings terminated with the appointment of a new committee of sixteen members and agreement to send two delegates to London to co-operate with Sadler.[94]

It had been hoped that Oastler might attend this gathering, but he was unable to do so because of business commitments. Instead he addressed an open letter to the chairman, which Doherty published in the *Advocate* on 24 March. Oastler regretted that he could not personally meet 'those who have been much longer in the field of benevolence than myself, who have for many years been endeavouring to remove the horrors of the factory system, before I was even aware of their existence'. He went on to describe in detail the immorality associated with 'white slavery', and also the network of committees based on Leeds now established in Yorkshire, and concluded by begging that they should not allow their enemies to divide them by introducing political or religious questions. Doherty also published an earlier letter of Oastler's, dated 5 March, in which he asserted that there was little chance of obtaining a ten-hours bill including a restriction on the moving power. This induced Doherty to make yet another change of policy, but most of the short-time committees in the district retained that demand, Stockport workmen, for instance, reasserting it at two meetings during April. And in view of the spinners' long history of frustrated efforts to enforce factory legislation, it was eventually to re-appear as part of their, and Doherty's, policy in 1835.[95]

Doherty now extended the scope of the *Advocate* to include reports of the factory agitation as well as denunciations of individual masters. On 7 April he welcomed the establishment of the metropolitan 'Society for the Improvement of the Condition of Factory Children', although as Ward shows this was to prove a disappointment. And the first two numbers in May were devoted almost entirely to an account copied from the *Leeds Patriot* of the county meeting at York on 23 April, after which Oastler was called 'the Factory King'. Meanwhile the new Manchester short-time committee, 'for support of Mr Sadler's Ten Hours' Bill and to lay all the restriction on the moving power', set vigorously to work. Still meeting at the 'Crown and Anchor' and with Daniel remaining secretary, they began to organise the collection of weekly subscriptions from local cotton factories and reports of their activities appeared in the *Advocate*.[96]

Although the reformers had at first been angry at the establishment of Sadler's Committee, they now made detailed plans to turn it to their own advantage. Doherty was closely involved in these preparations. In May he was forced to visit London twice on business connected with the Gilpin prosecution. On the first occasion he discussed progress with Sadler, and during the second he published an address 'To the Factory Operatives of Lancashire, Yorkshire, Derbyshire and Nottinghamshire' on 30 May. From his conversations with M.Ps, Doherty knew that the rich masters were making every effort to oppose the bill and had the ear of ministers, whereas Sadler was only supported by deputies from the poor operatives of Yorkshire, Glasgow and Stockport. In such circumstances it was essential to desist from requiring the moving power to be restricted, for scarcely a single member would countenance interfering with adult labour; if they persisted in that demand, 'I am fully persuaded that the bill cannot be possibly obtained this session except for twelve hours, and that, I do not hesitate to say, would be worse than no bill at all'. Therefore he urged the workmen in the four counties to petition for Sadler's bill alone, for once Parliament had accepted that principle, it would be forced to take steps eventually to make it effectual. Doherty's advice was followed in Manchester at least, for when Turner and Daniel were deputed to go to the capital early in June to lobby for the bill and give evidence to the Committee, they were instructed to abandon 'the very equivocal measure of moving power'. This, wrote Doherty on 16 June, was 'creditable to their understanding', and he again urged every factory and district in Lancashire to 'petition, petition, petition for a ten hours' bill, and PROMPTLY'. During the following week Sadler wrote to the Manchester short-time committee, requesting them to examine the condition of local Sunday-school children so that their delegates might testify to the effects of the 'accursed factory system'. And on 23 June Doherty reported that the investigation had proved factory children to be much smaller and lighter than their fellows. Two days later, however, Doherty was imprisoned because of his inability to meet the expense of a third trip to London to defend himself. His importance in the local organisation at this time can be gauged from the fact that his first action was to request the local magistrate for a quantity of writing-paper. 'I am induced to trouble you with this, chiefly on the ground that a committee of the house of commons are waiting for the names of several witnesses to be sent up, in order that they may be summoned for examination, and which names are in my possession alone.'[97]

Several of the Lancashire workmen who had been active in the short-time movement for a decade and more gave evidence to Sadler's Committee in June. From Manchester, James Turner gave the results of the survey of Sunday-school children, testified to the long hours and beatings of children as young as six years of age in silk mills like those of Vernon Royle and others, and stressed the strength of feeling among operatives in the town for the ten-hours bill, despite the fact that Hobhouse's Act was generally obeyed there; Thomas Daniel asserted that less than one in ten of Manchester factory children could write, though about two-thirds could read a little, and believed that protection should be extended to adults also; and Charles Aberdeen recounted his experience at the hands of Messrs Lambert, Hoole and Jackson following his refusal to sign their petition. From Ashton, George Downes bore witness to his own suffering as a child worker in Derbyshire and submitted Doherty's figures of January 1831 as to the ages of spinners and stretchers in his district to prove the necessity of a greater restriction of hours, now that machines were larger and faster. And from Stockport, William Longson detailed the masters' methods of blacklisting and fining to show that no factory labourers could be denominated 'free'. Meanwhile, Doherty published a horrendous series of illustrations in the *Advocate* to support these allegations. On 26 May he inserted, through the agency of Oastler, a copy of pictures of limbs deformed by factory labour exhibited by a Leeds surgeon at the York county meeting, asking if even Vernon Royle or Holland Hoole could defend such a system. Two weeks later he included an outline of the misshapen figure of Robert Blincoe, in anticipation of his republication later that month of Brown's account of that poor individual's early torments in country cotton mills at the turn of the century, quotations from which work were frequently used by factory reformers thereafter.[98] On 16 June his subject was John Mears, permanently crippled by beatings and hard labour in Wigan cotton factories and now in such desperate poverty

N

that Doherty sent off a petition to Sadler for presentation, praying for parliamentary compensation for Mears' injuries received in building up 'the riches of the country and the fortunes of the few'. And on 23 June he featured Henry Wooley, deformed by infant employment at Ashton. Later, on 28 July, the *Advocate* reprinted Oastler's speech on returning to Huddersfield from giving evidence in London, during which he boasted of his advocacy of flogging, the stocks or imprisonment to make employers obey a ten-hours bill. And on 9 August the spinners in the Manchester trades' procession to celebrate the passing of the Reform Bill carried representations of Sadler and Oastler, inscribed 'No White Slavery! Mr Sadler's Ten Hour Bill'.[99]

By the time Sadler's Committee finished hearing the evidence of the factory reformers on 7 August, Doherty had been in gaol for six weeks, the *Advocate* comprising in the meantime mainly letters from Doherty on prison conditions, other correspondence, and a large proportion of 'Miscellaneous' intelligence. His friends in the radical, trade union and short-time movements rallied to his support, establishing a committee which collected subscriptions on his behalf for the rest of the year.[100] On 27 July the Manchester short-time committee sent a deputation to a meeting of fine spinners, which agreed to advance money for Doherty's release; and Thomas Clayton, the acting secretary in Daniel's absence, wrote to Doherty the following day that the committee also passed a vote of thanks 'for your unwearied exertions in the cause which we have so much at heart, and for the able, fearless and independent manner in which you have advocated the cause of workingmen in general'. Doherty replied on 8 August that he was always gratified to receive the approval of his fellow men, in whose cause he had been 'a very inefficient, though very zealous labourer'. He had set out on his venture well aware that those who defended the 'poor, calumniated and despised workmen' from the 'unprincipled and arrogant . . . rich' were bound to meet furious vilification and persecution. What he had not expected was such a show of support for an '*advocate*' of the '*poor*', and this proved that the people had taken the first step towards their emancipation; 'and if my imprisonment should contribute anything . . . towards stirring the working classes to a determined resistance to oppression and insolence in every shape, I shall rejoice in that which was intended to crush me, as one of the happiest and proudest incidents of my life'.[101]

Doherty's release was in fact delayed until a few days before his trial on 25 August, when he was ordered to appear at the King's Bench in November for sentence, but released on bail in the meantime, one of his sureties being Robert Blincoe. His trial meant that he was forced to miss a great Manchester demonstration that day to welcome Oastler, Sadler, and John Wood to the town. He did, however, have time to prepare comments for the *Advocate* of 25 August. He urged the Manchester voters to remember the factory children and only support candidates pledged to the ten-hours bill. The English workmen had, he alleged, fewer and less powerful friends than the black slaves and hence 'must trust only to themselves to ameliorate their condition'; but it was their duty also to cherish those who did assist them and a rousing reception should be given to Sadler and Oastler on their arrival in the city. They were, in fact, escorted by a large procession, carrying banners on which Blincoe was pictured, to a meeting on Camp Field, attended by crowds estimated at between eight and twenty thousand and chaired by John Lawton; and during the speeches Sadler praised the London deputies, Turner and Daniel, for their zeal and ability, the assistance which they had given him, and their evidence to the Select Committee.[102]

For the remainder of 1832 the Manchester short-time committee was busy forming new committees at Chorlton and further afield, with great success according to Bull's short-lived journal on 16 November. But the principal preoccupation, as elsewhere, was with the approaching elections. Doherty rejoiced on 1 September that the Manchester short-time committee had resolved to address the Leeds electors on Sadler's behalf, as he believed the ten-hours bill would make little progress in the new reformed Parliament without Sadler's presence. And on 3 October a public meeting, chaired by George Higginbottom and addressed by Turner, Grant, Dixon and Daniel, adopted a vote of thanks to Sadler himself, which hoped that the Leeds electors would 'do their duty'. Over the succeeding two months other Lancashire towns adopted similar appeals at meetings frequently addressed by delegates from Manchester, as closer co-operation built up between the Lancashire committees once more and Manchester assumed the position of a Central Committee similar to that of Leeds in Yorkshire. The assembly on 3 October also recommended the Manchester workmen to bring their influence to bear on the election in that town by refusing to deal with any tradesman who would not vote for a candidate pledged to Sadler's bill. And later the short-time committee placarded the town with their views on the candidates. In the event, however, the new middle-class voters, representing that class most hostile to further legislation, swung heavily behind the Whigs who had enfranchised them and at the contests in December Sadler was defeated at Leeds and the two Whigs, Mark Philips and Poulett Thomson, were returned at Manchester. On the other hand, John Fielden, who had announced his support for the ten-hours bill in November in a speech printed in the *Advocate* at the request of the short-time committee, was elected at Oldham, together with William Cobbett, while the success of Joseph Brotherton at Salford was another important addition to the parliamentary friends of the cause.[103]

Doherty's role in these activities was chiefly as a publicist. On 24 October, however, he set out on a tour which was intended to take in all the manufacturing towns of the district, including Bolton, Chorley, Preston, Blackburn, Clitheroe, Burnley, Colne, Todmorden, Rochdale, Bury and Heywood. At each he was to ascertain and publish the facts of the workpeople's treatment by employers, for, although the Manchester mills had been shown to be tyrannically regulated, it was in 'secluded' places in the country that the 'cotton despots' reigned most completely and the workmen were the meanest slaves. Now Doherty hoped to expose them, while simultaneously infusing the operatives with a 'better, bolder and more restless spirit'. In addition, he intended to urge the workmen at each place to insist on Sadler's bill. He got as far as Burnley, from where he wrote on 25 October of his journey through the Rossendale valley, where brightly-lit factories met the eye on every side. The casual spectator might take these to be signs of 'prosperity', but to one who had experienced the heat, the smell of gas, and the vexatious restrictions, their appearance evinced only feelings of compassion for the labourers toiling inside. 'I could not but feel that those poor wretches . . . were wasting a life not only of misery, but of actual torture, to enrich the men who despised them; . . . and I confess that the wish involuntarily escaped me that [such places] had never been known.' At Burnley Doherty took the chair at a meeting in favour of Sadler's bill, urging the necessity of workmen throughout the kingdom uniting to obtain it, before introducing James Turner to the audience. And he concluded his letter by warning the Burnley employers, who were generally guilty of overworking and truck, that he had every intention of prosecuting them unless they began to treat their employees as equal contracting parties. Before he could proceed with that design or further with his tour, however, he was forced to return to Manchester by more serious legal entanglements.[104]

On 29 September Doherty had resumed his policy of exposing individual masters, by attacking the mill-regulations of Thomas Gough and the cruelties of Douglas whose factory had produced 'more idiots and cripples' than any other; and a communication was also printed from Lees detailing the extreme heights to which the fining system was carried on there by Messrs Ogden and Arrowsmith, which Doherty believed qualified the guilty parties for either throwing into the horsepond or tarring and feathering. On 2 October Ogden went to see Doherty and demanded to be given the names of his informants, which Doherty declined to do, offering instead to print a public retraction if any of the charges were untrue. But on 24 October the firm prosecuted Doherty for libel at the Salford Sessions and a true bill was found against him. On the following day their counsel applied for a bench warrant against Doherty on the ground that he had to report to London in the following month for judgement in the Gilpin case and might not appear for trial on the second charge at the Salford Sessions in December, but the chairman did not think Doherty was about to leave the country and therefore refused the application. On 7 November he attended at the New Bailey to submit further bail for the second libel and was now under total recognisances of £240. At first he put a bold face to his predicament, asserting in an article on Messrs Marsland of Manchester that for anyone to accuse them of unjustly fining their power-loom weavers would be a *'gross and scandalous libel* on their *fair fame'*. But when he was sentenced to a month's imprisonment in the King's Bench prison on 23 November, thus being unable to appear on the second prosecution, he wrote desperately to his Manchester friends on 4 December to get that postponed. Fortunately, they were able to do so and on 12 January 1833 the *Guardian* reported that the indictment for libel against Messrs Ogden and Arrowsmith had been removed to the next Lancaster Assizes. It appears, in fact, that the case never came to court, but one victim of Doherty's impoverishment was the *Advocate*, the last number of which appeared on 5 January 1833. And on 15 January, when the 'Lees Committee' addressed the operatives throughout Lancashire to continue support for Doherty, who had 'spent his time, his life in opposing' the system of 'white slavery' and was 'one of your oldest, truest and ablest advocates', they revealed that only half his expenses in the 'parson prosecution' had been raised and now the two 'cotton lords' threatened him with absolute ruin. No further reference to this appeal appeared, but nevertheless the response proved sufficient for him to open his coffee and newsroom in

February and for him to publish a complete set of the fifty numbers of the *Advocate* in one volume in the course of 1833. And he was therefore able to continue his factory reform activities unabated.[105]

The publication of the factory reformers' evidence to Sadler's Committee at the beginning of January 1833 caused a great sensation. Supporters of the ten-hours bill claimed that their policy was completely vindicated, but the manufacturers protested that only one side of the case had been presented and that much of the evidence related to conditions many years earlier.[106] The reformers therefore began preparing for a renewed ten-hours campaign when Parliament reassembled. On 11 January 1833 the first joint conference of Lancashire and Yorkshire short-time committees was convened at Bradford. Important decisions were made regarding the organisation of a subscribing membership, sending delegates to London, and forming new committees, Oastler was appointed as the 'centre of communication', and Bull was dispatched to the capital to select a new parliamentary leader. Doherty clearly played a significant role in these deliberations, for he seconded a motion to appoint William Halliwell, the Oldham delegate, to the chair, James Turner being nominated vice-chairman, and also moved that Bull be requested to act as the conference's secretary. The proceedings lasted three days and terminated with a large public meeting, at which Doherty was one of the speakers, denying that the ten-hours bill was 'tory trickery'. Bull's mission resulted in Lord Ashley being entrusted with the future conduct of Sadler's bill, and when the new spokesman gave notice on 5 February of his intention to reintroduce it, meetings were held throughout the north in his support. On 9 February Doherty's name was among a list of 863 signatories to a requisition to the borough-reeve and constables of Manchester to convene a public meeting of the 'Gentry, Clergy, Master Manufacturers, Tradesmen and other Electors' in support of the ten-hours bill. This meeting took place five days later and was addressed by Oastler, George Condy, Dixon and Hindley; a 'respectable' committee was appointed and the borough-reeve deputed to go to London with a petition in favour of the bill, but the attendance was generally considered disappointing and almost entirely of 'non-electors'. More successful were the meetings called by the short-time committee in other districts of the town. Doherty himself spoke at two of these gatherings. At Chorlton on 18 March he, Turner and Grant shared the platform with Oastler, then on a whirlwind Lancashire tour, and he moved a resolution deprecating night-work. His speech alluded to the progress which the factory movement had made since Peel's Bill was first introduced, answered objections to the principle of interference, and ended with a reassertion of his continuing belief, notwithstanding his anxiety for 'Sadler's bill' to pass, that 'excessive taxation' was one of the great causes of their hardships. And at Salford on 1 April he argued publicly with Holland Hoole, denouncing the employment of female spinners by the firm in which Hoole was a partner.[107]

Two days later, however, the manufacturing interest revealed the strength of their parliamentary influence, when Wilson Patten's motion for a further investigation of the question by a Royal Commission was carried by one vote. Reaction in the north was swift and passionate, in a series of protest meetings. At Manchester on 10 April, Doherty spoke along with most of the local leaders, asserting that a case had already been fully made out for the bill and that the Commission was merely an attempt at delay; he predicted that the millowners would conceal the worst evils of the factory system from the Commissioners and put on special displays for their visits. At a similar meeting at Chorlton on 16 April, he detailed several cases of extreme cruelty which he had witnessed.[108]

Meanwhile the Manchester Central Committee deputed George Condy to consult with the Yorkshire reformers regarding the adoption of uniform tactics to meet the new emergency. It was decided to call a second delegate conference at the Manchester headquarters in the 'Crown and Anchor'. After deliberating for three days, 22–24 April, they determined not to give any evidence to the Commission, but to demonstrate against the Commissioners wherever they went; and secret instructions were sent out to each local committee to prepare for their arrival. The *Guardian* commented that the refusal to recognise the Commission was due to the fact that the reformers knew that their allegations would not 'bear the test of honest investigation', but, unabashed, the delegates convened a public meeting in the Manor Court Room on 24 April to petition Parliament to pass the ten-hours bill 'without delay or waiting for the termination of that mockery of inquiry, the millowners' commission'. Oastler made a particularly violent speech, which was later published in pamphlet form in Huddersfield and advertised for sale at Doherty's shop, and Sadler defended the clause in the bill imposing personal punishment on offenders. The final speaker was Doherty, who brought up to the platform two deformed persons named Wilson and Wooley to state that their crookedness arose from factory labour.[109]

The northern towns carried out their instructions regarding the Commissioners to the letter. When Messrs Tufnell, Cowell and Hawkins arrived at the York Hotel in Manchester on 4 May, they were met by a procession of more than two thousand factory children, on behalf of whom Simeon Condy of the short-time committee handed in a memorial on the 'Evils of the Factory System'.[110] At the same time, the local short-time men adhered to the resolution to boycott the enquiry. On 18 May the Manchester Commissioners requested Thomas Daniel to give evidence, intending doubtless to question him on his testimony of the previous year. But Daniel replied on 22 May that he had already conveyed all the information at his disposal to the Select Committee, that ample evidence was already available to justify legislation, and that the only form of enquiry which could be of further use would be 'a commission to find out by practical experiment the evils of the system'.[111]

After the Manchester conference, Doherty and Turner were deputed to go to London to keep Ashley in touch with northern opinion. They installed themselves in lodgings in Covent Garden, where they stayed for almost three months, meeting frequently with Ashley, lobbying other members and seeing several ministers. After their arrival on 9 May, they were summoned to appear two days later at Whitehall before the Central Board of Commissioners. Doherty replied on 10 May that he must decline this request, since he had been sent by the Lancashire operatives with instructions only to forward the passing of Ashley's bill, 'without any reference whatever to the Commission'; hence his compliance might prejudice their right of reply to any evidence which might be procured from the millowners. He asserted that his constituents did not fear an investigation, indeed they courted it, but they believed that the evidence already before Parliament was sufficient. Moreover they could not consent 'to place themselves in the hands of men of whom they know nothing, and in whom they frankly avow that they have not the slightest reliance or hope of justice', and protested at the mode of procuring evidence by questionnaires and in secret, which would allow the millowners to suppress evidence more effectively. However, 'in obedience to and respect for the King's authority', Doherty disclosed that he had written to Manchester for instructions before he made a final refusal. The secretary of the Commission, John Wilson, waited a week for a further communication from Doherty and in the absence of such replied to the letter on 16 May. He reminded Doherty that 'no honest interest is likely to be compromised by the statement of the truth'; and even if a case for legislation had already been proved, the proper *mode* of interference was still the subject of controversy and required impartial investigation. He asked how Doherty could state on the one hand that the operatives knew nothing of the Commissioners and on the other that they had no hope of justice from them, and compared the manner of collecting evidence on the spot from gentlemen unconnected with any party and given on oath with the taking of depositions from 'picked witnesses procured from a distance to serve the cause of one of the parties interested'. He condemned Doherty's talk of the millowners' 'undue influence' without stating instances of such oppression and without reference to the Commission's explicit instructions regarding the protection of witnesses; and concluded by asserting that this sinister impression was not shared by the majority of workmen, for the Board had received a statement from the District Commissioners in the north that, 'we have met with every assistance in prosecuting our enquiries both from masters and operatives'.[112]

Even the sympathetic *Bolton Chronicle* commented that Wilson's letter had exposed 'the proneness to groundless suspicion' inherent in Doherty's communication; while the *Manchester Guardian* rejoiced that the reply had placed 'Mr John Doherty in a cleft stick, from which it is impossible he should extricate himself. The operatives in general, we hope, have too much discernment either to be misled by the sophistry of such reasoners as Doherty, who agitate for what they can get by it, or to be inflamed by the ravings of madmen.' Nevertheless, after communicating with Manchester, Doherty and Turner, as the 'deputies from the Operatives of Lancashire, in support of the Ten Hours' Bill', returned a joint answer to the Central Board on 24 May stating their determination 'formally and finally to decline taking any part in the proceedings of your commission'. They repelled the accusation that they showed a lack of respect for Parliament, for they did not believe the Commission emanated, other than formally, from the legislature. 'The simple truth is, that the commission is the millowners' commission'; it had been accepted by the House of Commons because the manufacturing interest could control fifty votes therein, whereas neither the poor children nor their parents had a single representative and the form of enquiry had never even been thought of by the government until it was chosen by 'the very parties who are now on their trial before the face of the country, on the charge of wholesale infanticide'. Could the operatives believe, moreover, that the members of that Commission had been impartially selected, when the responsibility of nomination lay with the Secretary of the Treasury, who well knew the mutual strengths of the conflicting parties in Parliament, and with Poulett Thomson, Vice-President of the Board of Trade, who was 'the representative of the millowners of Manchester . . . chosen that he might be retained in their service for such emergencies as the present'? An honest statement of the truth might not harm their case if the integrity of the judge and jury were unimpeachable, but even the honest man would hesitate before 'laying his case and his evidence before his adversary's attorney'. And they repeated that they could not trust the result of an enquiry when the witnesses were not even cross-examined and their evidence was to be abridged when printed rather than simply reproduced, and that there were many cases of workmen suffering for publicly disclosing 'the secrets of these prison houses'. Doherty and Turner concluded that they would let the Commission take its course, while protesting against Parliament taking further time to recognise that more than ten hours' labour destroyed the health and morals of white children, when they had just accepted the principle in the case of adult black slaves.[113]

The following weeks saw a series of rapid developments. On 29 May Doherty spoke at a meeting in favour of the ten-hours bill in the borough of Walworth. On 17 June Ashley introduced the bill for its second reading, though hinting at his own reservations respecting imprisonment for a third offence. On the following day, however, the delegate conference representing textile employers throughout the kingdom at the 'Palace Inn', London, issued their own proposals for limiting the hours of the youngest children, but working them in relays so as to preserve longer hours for adults. And on 25 June the Royal Commission issued its report, largely accepting the medical evidence on the effect of long hours on children but rejecting the reformers' allegations of the worst cruelties. They recommended an eight-hour limitation for children under thirteen, who should be worked in relays, with enforcement by inspectors, and provision of daily education. Ashley's bill was condemned as ineffective to protect children and concerned in reality with adult labour, and the ten-hours men were censured for obstructing the work of the Commission. 'The men who have placed themselves at the head of the agitation on this question are the same men who in every instance of rash or headlong strikes, have assumed the command of the discontented members of the operative body, and who have used the grossest means of intimidation to subjugate the quiet and content part of the workpeople.' They were not genuinely concerned to protect the children but had turned to this campaign to keep up the atmosphere of discontent from which they profited after their former techniques of fomenting strikes had failed. One of the District Commissioners. Tufnell, showed that he was not above using the same kind of smear of which he accused the witnesses to Sadler's Committee. While he wrote elsewhere that the ten-hours campaign was solely the product of the spinners' union's desire to limit adult hours and increase their wages, he referred in his *Supplementary Report* to the 'extraordinary' selection of the three witnesses from Manchester who appeared before Sadler.

> Not one was a medical man, a manufacturer, or a clergyman. The first was a dresser of yarn, and is now one of the two delegates sent by the Lancashire workpeople in London to forward the passing of the Ten Hours' Bill, and

whose colleague is a man named Doherty, who (it is right that the character of the leaders in this business should be known) originally came to Manchester with a forged character, and was subsequently imprisoned for two years for a gross assault on a woman; the second is the keeper of a small tavern in the purlieus of the town; the third is an atheist.

All had been invited to corroborate their former evidence. Turner and Daniel declined the invitation, but Aberdeen did attend, refused to take the oath, and had his thirty-year-old charges completely disproved.[114]

The reformers were outraged. Condy wrote in his paper that he was unaware that the Commissioners were appointed to collect evidence on 'former strikes'. Moreover, of the sixteen members of the Manchester short-time committee, only Turner and Doherty had led strikes and only the London delegates were paid for their time as well as their expenses, with the exception of two corresponding secretaries. These meagre sums contrasted with the high profits made by the Commissioners from the dinners and bribes of the rich manufacturers. Grant protested on 23 July that Cowell had white-washed factory conditions at Wigan and that he had *lost* money by his agitation. And the sense of betrayal increased when a District Commissioner named Stuart publicly accused the Central Board of suppressing his evidence relating to the impracticality of relays and of being influenced by the 'bit of a parliament' of millowners at the Palace Yard. In this atmosphere there was little hope that Ashley's desire for concession on the personal punishment clause would be accepted when the West Riding reformers assembled a mass meeting of 100,000 on Wibsey Low Moor on 1 July to demand the immediate passing of the ten-hours bill. Nonetheless, Doherty returned from London to represent Ashley's position. He explained that he was not himself inclined towards compromise. He had participated in the agitation since Nathaniel Gould obtained the twelve-hour limitation for cotton workers in 1819, and had been himself three times in prison and was therefore unlikely to wish to preserve the employers who put him there from the same fate. But having interviewed about two hundred M.Ps, he was convinced that to persist with the imprisonment clause would ensure the bill's defeat and lose support in the country. He concluded with a tribute to Lord Ashley : being himself an ultra-radical who had often denounced the peerage, he had gone to London with a natural suspicion against an ultra-tory peer, but after frequent intercourse with his Lordship he must say that in no walk of life had he found 'so honourable, so straightforward, kind and condescending, and at the same time talented and fearless a person as that young man'. Oastler's language was approaching the revolutionary at this stage, however, and the resolution advocating no concession was carried with only three dissentients.[115]

It was a final empty gesture. Ashley's bill was heavily defeated in the Commons on 18 July. Three weeks later Althorp's government measure was introduced, based on the Commission's recommendations, with an additional restriction of twelve hours on young persons under eighteen years, and rapidly passed through all its stages by 29 August. Employers resented the interference of inspectors and prepared to discharge protected children from their works. Workmen asserted that both the Act and the inspectors were the tools of the masters, and railed against the cost of the medical certificates now needed by the children and also against the effects on adult hours. But the

Act did for the first time apply to all textile mills and contained the potential for effective enforcement in the long run. And in a letter to the chairman of the Manchester short-time committee to acknowledge his indebtedness to the labours of Turner and Doherty, Ashley recognised that the Act at least provided for the protection of the youngest children and established the great principle that labour and education should be combined.[116]

Nevertheless, this was a serious setback to the ten-hours movement. In an attempt to resurrect the tory–radical alliance, Yorkshire delegates succeeded in forming the 'Factory Reformation Society', in support of a ten-hours bill and protection for all workers, at a meeting at Birstall on 28 October 1833, and on 19 November Oastler wrote hopefully 'that the Operatives of Manchester have warmly approved of the Resolutions of the Delegates and purpose to act upon them'.[117] But in reality a completely different venture was being hatched in Manchester. Disappointment with the 1833 Act revived Doherty's former distrust of legislation and caused a reversion to his policy of 1831. During his mission to London, he had interviewed Lord Althorp, who suggested that the workmen should try to reduce their own hours by industrial action.[118] Now, therefore, he flung himself into the schemes of the National Regeneration Society, developed by Owen and Fielden, with the idea of commencing an eight-hour day for all workers from 1 March 1834, when Althorp's Act was due to come into operation and children of eleven were to be subject to that limitation.[119] Doherty stressed once more the advantages of limiting production, sharing the work, raising the value of labour, and affording educational opportunities, but the Owenite influence caused him temporarily to hope for the scheme's implementation through co-operation with the masters. By April 1834, however, he was again advocating direct action by the workmen through their unions. Neither method was rewarded with success. After twice postponing the date of commencement for the intended eight-hour day, the somewhat hopeful project disappeared in the summer of 1834. Most of the short-time committees had transformed themselves into branch committees of the Regeneration Society and the failure left them considerably weakened, although it is doubtful if they broke up completely as Ward implies. Oastler's 'Factory Reformation Society' was, however, destroyed before it got off the ground.

Doherty's activities, nevertheless, continued unabated. In July 1834 at a meeting of Manchester leypayers he drew attention to the absence of attempts in the town to effect the education clauses of the 1833 Act.[120] And in October he was involved with Turner in an attempt to restart the *Poor Man's Advocate*, in which was to appear 'a faithful and fearless exposure and reprobation of insolent expressions, extortions, and heartless graspings of greedy and avaricious employers, of every class and degree'. No copies of this second volume are extant, but a further advertisement for the paper on 20 December in the *Poor Man's Guardian* revealed that five numbers had already appeared and that its price and contents were similar to the 1832 publication. The published list of articles included items on the factory bill, the factory inspectors, the 'workings of the New Poor Law Destruction Act', the state of the poor in Ireland, the newspaper stamp duty, the 'doings of the Cotton Lords', a letter from Place on the *Advocate* and the Malthusian Doctrine, the 'wickedness and cruelty of the Factory Act', and 'Mr Doherty's letter to the Editor of the *Manchester Guardian*, the deadly foe of the Working classes'.[121]

Meanwhile, the millowners were on their side no more satisfied with the 1833 Act in operation. The requirement of medical certificates of age caused endless controversy and doubts were soon felt about the practicability of operating the relay system, with different hours for children, young persons and adults. Before long the factory reformers were being blamed for the Act which they had so bitterly opposed.[122]

Peel's short-lived ministry of 1834–5, in which Lord Ashley held office, seemed to provide the ten-hours men with a favourable opportunity for another campaign. On 5 February, therefore, Higginbottom and Grant, as chairman and secretary respectively of the Manchester short-time committee, wrote to Ashley pledging their readiness to renew their efforts if he would use his position to introduce such a bill. Ashley replied on 11 February, however, that he would not advise a new appeal to Parliament before the present Act had come fully into operation and had been given a fair trial, but recommended the workmen to John Fielden for a second opinion as to their future course.[123]

Meanwhile Doherty, having again become secretary of the Manchester spinners' union, addressed a circular to the workmen of surrounding towns calling upon them to elect delegates to a district meeting in Manchester on 22 February to discuss the best means of obtaining a ten-hours bill, to be enforced by restriction upon the moving power. Six of the north-western towns were represented at this meeting, which authorised Doherty to make a second appeal to Ashley to reintroduce his bill. In his reply of 2 March, however, Ashley stated, 'I am at this period so much engaged that I cannot find time for the due and sufficient consideration of all that you have proposed to me'. He was still in favour of the ten-hours limitation, and had heard that Althorp's Act had altogether failed, 'but the house of commons may nevertheless require some longer time for the working of the measure before it consents to any further alteration'. Doherty thought this reply 'anything but satisfactory' and considered it essential to introduce their bill before their opponents made any move to amend the 1833 Act. He therefore wrote forthwith to John Fielden, 'who understood the question thoroughly' and 'of whose integrity there could be no manner of doubt'.[124]

It was decided to hold meetings in the various Lancashire towns, but a new situation was created in March when Hindley, who had been elected for Ashton in January, gave notice in the Commons of his intention to introduce a bill to restrict the moving power of machinery worked by persons under twenty-one to $11\frac{1}{2}$ hours per day, including $1\frac{1}{2}$ hours for meals, and to raise the minimum age to ten years with an additional entrance qualification of literacy. The Lancashire meetings were now, therefore, asked to pronounce on this proposal. At the first, at Ashton, on 10 March, despite Oastler's expression of distrust in Hindley as a millowner, a supporting petition was adopted. At Manchester on the following night, when Doherty read out his recent correspondence with Ashley, Oastler protested at the insinuation that 'his noble friend' had become lukewarm in the cause. Doherty therefore moved, and Oastler seconded, a vote of thanks to Ashley for his past exertions. Doherty also pointed out that, during his delegation to London with James Turner in 1833, he had told Lord Althorp that restricting different sets of workers to different hours would be totally impracticable. After Condy, Grant and Thomas Fielden had also spoken, it was agreed to petition Parliament for an 'effective ten-hours bill'. A similar meeting was held at Bolton on 13 March, when Doherty detailed the sufferings endured by factory children and moved a resolution laying the defects of the 1833 Act to their opponents' account. The campaign continued with meetings at Oldham the following night, at Stockport on 19 March, Wigan on 31 March, Todmorden on 8 May, and Chorley on 9 May, with growing support for Hindley's bill.[125]

It soon became evident, however, that this bill could make no progress in Parliament against all-party opposition, and that further public pressure would be necessary. A delegate conference of Lancashire spinners and factory workers was therefore convened at Preston on 23 August, which issued an address 'To the honest Labourers Producers of the United Kingdom', calling upon them to join in the agitation for the bill. The workpeople, it was emphasised, were kept ignorant by long hours, and were subject to divisions and intemperance largely because of that ignorance: hence they allowed the power in the land to be usurped by political economists and the 'monied interest', who coldly consigned them to 'coarser food, workhouses, gaols, or compulsory emigration'. All should therefore unite to protect the children from being overworked, and if the adults were ever to receive instruction and withstand wages reductions they deserved a similar limitation themselves. Were this appeal ignored, the address continued, 'the sequel . . . will be written in blood', although the delegates declared their opposition to 'confusion' and dissociated themselves entirely from extreme Socialist notions, in stating that 'we would spoil no man of his property—we dream not of perfect equality or Paradise below'. In conclusion it was disclosed that a further delegate meeting was intended shortly in Manchester for a final consideration of tactics.[126]

Bull represented Oastler at the Preston meeting, both continuing to suspect Hindley's constancy in the cause.[127] The Manchester conference, therefore, held in October and attended by delegates from Bradford, Preston, Chorley, Bury, Macclesfield, Oldham, Ashton and Manchester, urged the operatives to show 'union and determination' to win Hindley's bill themselves, although the support of parents, masters and clergy was also requested in their address to 'Friends and Fellow Labourers'. To finance these efforts, it was decided to open subscriptions in the districts, to be called the 'factory child's rent'— another example, perhaps, of Doherty copying O'Connell—with the Fieldens as grand treasurers; and it was also decided to remove the central committee from Bradford to Manchester, with James Turner as corresponding secretary, an indication of the leadership which the Lancashire reformers were again taking in the factory movement.[128]

In pursuit of this campaign, the Manchester committee issued a circular to all the Lancashire members of parliament, and a meeting took place at the 'Albion Hotel' on 1 December comprising Messrs Philips, Brotherton, Fielden, Hindley, Potter, Brocklehurst and Walker on the one side, and spinners from seven Lancashire towns on the other. Doherty and Turner acted as spokesmen for the workmen, the latter detailing the numerous evasions of the present Act and the inspectors' neglect of duty and Doherty entering into lengthy calculations to prove that because of the increased speed of machinery the distance travelled by each piecer per day had increased to twenty-five miles, a claim that was to be intermittently disputed for the next decade.[129] And when Philips and Potter asserted that labour had been lightened by improved machinery, the delegates informed them of the arduous nature of work on, and the unemployment caused by, the larger mules. At this meeting, Hindley also drew attention to evasions of the age regulations under the present Act and emphasised the first necessity of restricting the moving power, whatever number of hours were chosen. This statement, an apparent confirmation of Oastler's suspicions and an augmentation to Hindley's reputation for tergiversation which he had acquired among the spinners at the time of the Ashton strike,[130] induced the delegates to detain him after these proceedings had closed, and Doherty bluntly informed him 'that there is an opinion prevailing very generally among the operatives that you are not quite in earnest about insisting on ten hours . . . and there is . . . a strong and rather growing feeling of distrust of your sincerity in their respective districts'. Such doubts, Doherty asserted, 'tend greatly to retard the exertions that would otherwise be made for the cause, and if Mr Hindley can only remove these doubts, he will find things go on much better'. Hindley reminded Doherty of the tactics of O'Connell to ask for all one wants but to take care to secure at least something rather than lose all. But the parties eventually compromised upon the proposition of Grant, that if the ten-hours principle was defeated in the next session, Hindley would continue to propose it in the subsequent sessions until it was accepted.[131]

On 2 January 1836, another delegate meeting was convened at Manchester, attended by representatives from Manchester, Ashton, Oldham, Bury, Bolton, Macclesfield, and Preston, with Condy, Bull and Hindley present as visitors. Doherty took the chair and a lengthy discussion ensued, in which Hindley again showed signs of compromising, while Bull resolutely demanded a pledge for ten hours or nothing, but would agree to a clause restricting moving power if that principle were not abandoned. A resolution was ultimately adopted supporting Bull's position, but it was also agreed to give the fullest backing to Hindley's bill by sending petitions from every district and electing four delegates by universal suffrage of the members to lobby M.Ps in London.[132]

This conference was followed by another series of meetings in the surrounding towns, which were marked by two significant developments. Firstly, the agitations against the factory system and the new poor law became linked together, as the Lancashire workmen, already suffering under the oppressions of the former, now saw their power to resist threatened by the Poor Law Commissioners' attempt to put into effect the scheme of the Ashworths and R. H. Greg for transfer of southern agricultural labourers to the northern manufacturing districts.[133] Secondly, a new campaigner joined the movement in the Rev. J. R. Stephens, whose violent oratory soon matched even that of Oastler. Doherty spoke at two of the largest gatherings. At Ashton on 19 January he welcomed two new adherents to their cause—Stephens, whose 'powerful talents' would greatly enhance the claims of the factory children, and Charles Clay, who had announced his resignation from the office of surgical certifier under Althorp's Act because of his dissatisfaction with the situation that would arise when the eight hours' limitation was extended to children of thirteen on 1 March 1836. Doherty knew that the eight hours' clause was a cheat, intended in fact to raise adult hours to sixteen by working children in relays and making up the extra labour supply necessary from the agricultural counties, but now the trick had been exposed and the public undeceived. He then replied to the statements of writers like Ure that factory labour was 'a pleasant and gentle amusement'[134] by reasserting the distance travelled by piecers and entering on a second calculation to prove that the spinner expended more energy per day than a mail-coach horse. He hoped that the people would now agitate ceaselessly until an efficient ten-hours bill was procured, and afterwards eight and six hours bills. At Manchester on 2 March Doherty seconded a motion appointing a new committee to collect signatures for a petition for Hindley's bill and insisted that, though they were glad of the patronage of members of parliament, it was up to the workmen to 'work out their own emancipation', by demanding that the measure pass, as at the time of the Reform Bill. He recalled that the operatives had worked for nearly twenty years to obtain the same hours for their children as agricultural labourers or even felons; he censured the clergy of the established church in Manchester for not joining Bull in this campaign, referred to the low numbers of factory workers able to attend at the Mechanics' Institution, and revealed how he had recently disabused their 'kind, generous, and right-minded' member, Mark Philips, of the notion that improved machinery had lessened the labour or increased the prosperity of the operatives. Even the *Stockport Advertiser* commented that Doherty's speech 'embraced several interesting facts, whilst the tone and manner in which they were given were generally creditable to him', though his remarks on the national clergy were 'out of place and in bad taste', especially as the dissenting clergy could not even provide one representative.[135]

After this meeting, Grant, Turner, Gregson, McWilliams and James Mills proceeded to London as delegates from the central committee, along with Stephens representing Ashton and Nuttall representing Cheshire. They were faced by a new situation, however, early in March, when Poulett Thomson introduced a government bill to suspend introduction of the eight-hour clause for children up to thirteen, because of the employers' opposition. Thus thrown onto the defensive, they reacted vigorously : on 15 March they issued to all M.Ps a circular against the proposed amendments; two days later they determined that a ten-hours amendment of their own should be moved on the second reading of Thomson's bill; and on 28 March they decided to request Lord Ashley to take the lead in these proceedings in the Commons, while Hindley's bill stood temporarily in abeyance.[136] The government's submission to pressure from the employers and inspectors restored the earlier passions to the factory reform campaign and over the Easter recess a series of angry meetings was held in both Yorkshire and Lancashire to 'remonstrate' against the proposal, while Bull and Oastler both addressed printed letters to Hindley counselling steadfast adherence to the ten-hours principle. On the other side, the masters sent deputations to London in support of Thomson and saw Hindley in an attempt to get an agreed eleven-hour compromise, while Ure informed Hindley of his belief, founded upon an examination of the developing continental industry, that a ten-hours abridgement 'would prove a death-blow to British industry'. Amid great excitement, Thomson's amendment was carried by just two votes on 9 May, after a debate in which Fielden confirmed

Doherty's statement respecting piecers' distances after a trial in his own works. But the narrowness of this majority and the widespread popular opposition obliged the government to drop the measure a month later.[137]

The reformers celebrated their parliamentary victory by determining to press on immediately with the ten-hours bill. But Hindley, buffeted on all sides, agreed to drop his measure in June, on Russell's appointment of Leonard Horner to replace the ailing Rickards as factory inspector, with instructions to enforce the Act more stringently.[138] The short-time committees, however, were in no mood for compromise. At a delegate meeting at the 'Crown and Anchor' on 16 June, with Doherty again in the chair and with representatives from the Lancashire central committee, the Manchester spinners, Bradford, Ashton, Oldham, Bolton, Chorley, Hyde and Gorton, together with supporting letters from several other towns, it was agreed that the ten-hours bill should be tried without delay and a strongly-worded petition was adopted lamenting the persistent legislative neglect of the 'rights of industry' and imploring Parliament to pass an efficient ten-hours regulation for all factory workers above the age of nine, with restriction on the moving power, to come into immediate operation. It was resolved in addition that, should Parliament refuse such a measure, the delegates should reassemble within two weeks 'to consider the propriety of adult operatives throughout all the factories restricting their own labour to eight hours per day which the act prescribes for children under thirteen'. Finally, Doherty was instructed to sign as chairman the 'Address of the United Delegates', which he also printed and published, and which informed 'their operative friends' of the decisions taken, ridiculed the idea of ministers promising to enforce an Act which they knew to be impracticable, and urged the workmen to rally in support and victory was assured.[139]

The conference was reconvened on 9 July, to exert further pressure. Despite the brave talk, however, the delegates had not forgotten the fiasco of the 1834 strike threat and were in fact planning a new tactic, by which they would themselves ensure that the 1833 Act was properly enforced, and thus, by making relays impracticable, compel employers to accept the ten hours' principle. This conference was the most widely attended in the series, with delegates from fourteen towns in Lancashire, six in Yorkshire, and three in Cheshire, as well as Oastler, Condy, Gregory and Clegg; Doherty as usual took the chair, with Stephens acting as secretary. It was resolved that a list of competent persons should be submitted to Russell for him to choose an operative inspector for Lancashire and a second for Yorkshire, that an office be taken in Manchester, that a general secretary be appointed under the Manchester committee at a salary of 30s per week, and each committee was instructed to make vigorous efforts to obtain contributions. Meanwhile, the Bishop of Exeter was to be requested to introduce a ten-hours bill into the Lords immediately and extensive support was to be organised if he agreed.[140]

Another round of meetings ensued. Doherty attended at Dewsbury on 27 July, when he ridiculed the foreign competition arguments of Ure and moved a motion expressing their determination to achieve their purpose. And at Manchester on 15 August a resolution was adopted lamenting that the legislature still neglected their wishes, despite twenty years of agitation and the clear evidence of higher mortality rates in manufacturing areas presented to Sadler's Committee; the decisions at the July conference were also approved, and a new local committee of fifteen members was appointed including Gregory, Condy, Clegg, Doherty, Grant, Higginbottom, Turner, Arrowsmith, Dixon, Green and McWilliams. Most of these meetings were addressed by Stephens and Oastler, who were stimulated to new levels of violent language; at Blackburn, on 15 September, the latter made his notorious 'knitting-needle' threat, which so angered his opponents, lost him the sympathy of several colleagues, including Ashley, Bull, Hindley and Wood, and, as we shall see, adversely affected the efforts of Doherty's central committee.[141]

With Russell having declined to appoint operative inspectors, Doherty issued on 6 October a 'Caution to Millowners' that the central committee had themselves appointed James Turner for Lancashire and Mark Crabtree for Yorkshire, whose duty would be to deal with those parties violating the Act, to benefit both the children and the benevolent masters. Turner did, in fact, subsequently bring several informations against factory owners for breaches of the regulations regarding the ages and hours of children, for which small fines were imposed.[142] The central committee, however, was only able to indulge in these activities through the generosity of John Wood. During the summer the appeal for subscriptions met with a poor response from the factory workers, and on 20 September Doherty wrote to Wood to request assistance in clearing off their debts and financing the plan of inspection. He was rewarded with a gift of £50 by return of post, and the accounts for 8 October show a balance of £62 19s 11¼d mainly because of that donation and smaller sums from the Manchester spinners and other Lancashire towns, while Doherty himself was giving 1s per week. The secretary's salary had already been reduced to 6s 8d per week, but with £22 being paid out to Turner and Crabtree in the week ending 8 October alone, it was clear that a considerable income would be necessary to maintain the operation, for which purpose Doherty appended another appeal to the factory workers in the hope that 'this instance of generous liberality on the part of a millowner . . . [may] at last shame you into the performance of your duty to yourselves and your little ones—those whom heaven has given you to protect'.[143]

No such subscriptions were forthcoming, however, with the spinners occupied in a wave of strikes for increased wages, which they claimed to be necessary because of the advanced cost of piecing under the fully enforced 1833 Act, while no more help could be expected from John Wood after Oastler's outburst. In November the committee entertained Lord Ashley on his first visit to the manufacturing districts, recognising once more his parliamentary leadership, but at the local level the scheme of operative inspectors appears soon to have collapsed, no more informations being brought.[144] At the same time, a bitter dispute broke out concerning non-enforcement of the Act. The origin of this lay in the difficulty of ascertaining the true age of children before compulsory registration of births, and in September 1836 Horner issued a regulation to certifying surgeons for assessment of age according to height, children of 3ft 10in being allowed to work in factories as nine year olds, while those above 4ft 3½in were to be regarded as over thirteen. Already on 11 October Fielden had made a long protest, asserting from calculations made at his own works that the scale was set far too low and that it was introduced to produce the same effect as Thomson's amendment, which had been rejected by Parliament in the previous session.[145]

As chairman of the Manchester central committee, Doherty secured the republication of Fielden's letter on 29 October. Early in 1837 he went much farther by addressing a long memorial to the Home Secretary, Russell, condemning the laxity of the inspectors' administration of the law generally, which was giving the workmen the impression 'that justice, where the poor are concerned, is no longer even-handed, and that, in deference to the understood wishes of more opulent and therefore more influential parties, the law is in very numerous instances perverted or abused, and its more benevolent provisions trampled under foot'. Doherty first complained that no attempt had been made to enforce the clauses governing holidays and schooling, though the latter had been stressed so greatly by those who promoted the present law as against Ashley's bill; and indeed, even the principle had been broken by Horner's regulation that the twelve hours' education need not be distributed equally over the week but could be concentrated on Sundays. The memorialists also protested against allowing superintendents to act as certifying surgeons, instead of being disinterested and adequately paid public servants. But their most 'grievous complaint' was against Horner's standard of height, which they believed was intended to assist the millowners to employ under-age children for the full hours, contrary to the wishes of Parliament and to the intentions of the Act, according to a distiguished lawyer whom they had consulted. They demanded that no regulations should be issued in future until sanctioned by the law officers of the Crown and that inspectors and superintendents who joined in attempts to evade the Act should be dismissed. Despite Horner's regulation, however, the masters were still unable to find sufficient children, and the relay system had been proved to be impracticable, so that both masters and poor parents were encouraged to break the law. The remedy, Doherty concluded, was to adopt one uniform time of daily labour of ten hours for all under 21, but to raise the maximum entry-age to ten years to afford the youngest children more chance of education.[146]

Horner replied to these charges on 17 February 1837. He explained that complaints had to be made by the workers before action could be taken over holiday-working, and that his schooling regulations had enforced six days' attendance, but had allowed Sundays to be substituted for Saturdays when many schools were closed. Only one superintendent in his district was a medical man and he had been forbidden to grant certificates, while his height qualification was based upon the opinion of the Attorney-general that the 'declaration which the surgeon makes in his certificate has no reference to actual age'. Finally, Horner prayed for the Home Secretary's protection against such 'false and libellous' attacks upon his integrity.

There can be no doubt, however, that Horner had been exceeding his authority, and on 13 March Russell informed Ashley that he had told the inspector so. As a result, on 20 March Horner wrote to the superintendents that millowners were liable to be prosecuted for working protected persons during holidays unless they had distinctly stated their wish to do so. And on 3 April Horner's new instructions to certifying surgeons, having been submitted to Russell and the law officers for approval, asserted that they 'must never certify the strength and appearance of a child to be that of an age beyond what they know or have good reason to believe is its real age'. But the central committee remained dissatisfied with his conduct and Doherty submitted a second memorial to Russell on 13 July. While thanking Russell for his speedy response to the first communication, Doherty complained that Horner had taken no steps to have those children falsely certified re-examined and that his new regulations were equally vexatious, not having received prior approval nor comprising the only real standard, actual age. As a result, 'fully one half the number of children working under surgeons' certificates of thirteen are in fact not more than twelve, and many not more than eleven years of age'. as Horner himself had admitted in his recent letter to Nassau Senior.[147] The memorial concluded with an outspoken attack on Horner, who should be dismissed because of his misinterpretation and non-enforcement of the law and his disregard of his superior's instructions, in an effort to exercise 'in this free country, more than kingly power', and hinted that the millowners were his 'counsellors and abettors'. This attack, however, had less justification than the first. It was sent by Russell to Horner for comment, and the latter replied on 22 July that his new rules *had* been submitted for approval. He admitted that a legal register of baptism was the only proof of age, but since the law obviously did not intend to exclude all persons not so registered, the medical certificate which he had introduced for children over thirteen was 'the next best proof of age', especially as he had now ordered that the real age, if known, should never be ignored.

Whilst this controversy was proceeding, Doherty induced the central committee to make another short-lived attempt to obtain a ten-hours bill. On 14 January 1837, in his capacity as chairman, he issued an invitation to the owners of cotton, woollen, silk and flax mills to attend a meeting of factory delegates at the 'Ladyman's Hotel' in Manchester on 24 January, 'for the purpose of agreeing to the principles of a bill to be submitted to parliament . . . for the regulation of factories, in lieu of the present unsatisfactory act'. But despite the issue of 1,500 circulars, only eight employers attended at the appointed time—John and Thomas Fielden, Dugdale and Clegg from Manchester, Holliday and Halliwell from Oldham, and Taylor and Milne from Shaw—where they met ten delegates from the central committee including Doherty, McWilliams, Nuttall, Gregson and Pitkeithley. Doherty stated that the millowners had been approached because there was mounting bitterness among the operatives at the repeated refusal of their petitions, which might lead to outbreaks of violence; hence it was urgent that a ten-hours bill should soon pass. Both parties agreed to collect signatures from among their respective colleagues for a petition asserting that the increased speed of machinery had greatly increased productive capacity, that the labour of children and adults was inseparable, and that a ten-hours bill for all was essential. These consultations took place in the middle of a four-day conference of delegates from twenty-three districts at the 'Crown and Anchor', at the end of which the delegates agreed upon, and Doherty printed and published, their own 21-clause bill, many of the provisions of which reflected past and present difficulties with enforcement in Manchester. From 1 July 1837, all factory workers were to be employed no more than ten hours a day, with one and a half hours at set times for meals, the moving power to be completely stopped between 6 p.m. and 6 a.m., and no allowance whatever to be made for 'making-up'. No child was to be taken on until he was ten, and then only on production of a certificate that he was 'of the ordinary appearance and growth of a child of ten years and also a copy of its baptismal register'. No manufacturer or relative thereof could adjudicate in cases under the Act, the county magistrates were empowered to interfere where necessary, no informations or summonses should be quashed because of informality, persons refusing to testify should be committed, and penalties were to be set at £10–20 for a first offence, £20–50 for a second, and £50–100 plus one to three months in gaol for a third. Finally, one inspector was to be appointed for every 10,000 factory workers and they were to be elected by universal suffrage among the employers and workmen.[148]

As usual, the committee organised meetings in other towns to support the new campaign. At Stockport on 14 February resolutions were adopted in support of the operatives' bill and Edward Nuttall appointed as one of the delegates to go to London on its behalf. Turner and Doherty were among the speakers, both dismissing the 'bugbear of foreign competition' and asserting that wages of labour had been reduced as technological improvements had been made. Doherty pointed out that several workmen had addressed the meeting, which gave the lie to the assertions of manufacturers and M.Ps, such as G. W. Wood, that the labouring classes would be perfectly satisfied but for a set of hired demagogues making them discontented. He went on to show how easily they could obtain even an eight-hours bill by their own united action, as recommended by Althorp in 1833. 'It was true that for more and more the operatives now received less and less. They had the power in their own hands to alter it; and if they did not the surplus population would be starved to death according to the Malthusian Poor Law, which our present political economists lauded so much.' After similar meetings in other towns, Doherty, Nuttall, Mills (from Oldham) and five other delegates proceeded to London in time to hear Lord Ashley give notice in the Commons of his intention to reintroduce his own bill to limit all factory workers under eighteen to a 58-hour week.[149]

Doherty remained in London until 23 March and on the day after his return he was the chief speaker at a meeting of over two thousand workmen in Manchester to petition in support of the bill. He reported that from his interviews with 'our wise legislators' he believed that they could obtain the measure that session, if they could convince Parliament that they were in earnest—not because Parliament contained a dozen men who cared about them, but because they would yield to fear as with the Reform Bill. Tories, Whigs and Radicals alike had expressed shock at the deputation's desire to protect all workers—for it was intended to move amendments to include restrictions on adults and on the moving power as the bill was in progress. Hume and O'Connell had emphasised the dangers of foreign competition, especially from America, but Doherty had replied that British industry was perfectly capable of underselling any competitor and was only prevented from doing so by a 50 per cent tariff in America on imported cotton yarn, a 35 per cent tariff in some German states, and a complete prohibition in France. Hume and O'Connell did not answer these points, 'for the facts were unanswerable'. When Dr Lushington had also protested at including adults, Doherty enumerated the reduced numbers employed at Murray's mill in Manchester and the consequent saving in wages: 'forty-four adults had been thrown out to find new occupations as they could, or, as the Malthusian authors of the new poor law insisted upon, dying off if they could not help themselves, . . . in order to get gold to fill the pockets of the millowners'. Doherty then advised the people to raise money to send delegates to London : 1d per man from 30,000 would settle the question in a few weeks. And he concluded by detailing the provisions of Ashley's measure and the intended amendments according to the operatives' own bill, which included dispatching masters offending a third time 'for three months to the treadmill' and abolishing all the expensive paraphernalia of enforcement associated with the present Act. Grant then moved a resolution, seconded by Doherty, condemning Horner's standard of height, and the business terminated with the adoption of a petition to Parliament.[150]

But little enthusiasm was raised for the campaign and Ashley withdrew his intended bill early in April. Doherty explained the reason for the change of plan in a letter to the *Manchester and Salford Advertiser* on 21 April. The need for a defensive rather than offensive strategy had been recognised when it was learnt that the government intended to oppose the measure with their own bill; it would now be possible to move amendments to the latter. Nor could Ashley support the January resolution calling for a ten-hours restriction for all workers, which would allow the ministers to oppose it on the grounds of cruelty in increasing the labour of the youngest children, or would give them a pretext for removing some of the difficulties which the 1833 Act imposed on millowners by the impracticability of relays. In addition, the rapidly deteriorating trade situation gave uncommitted members an excuse for not interfering with manufacturing industry at such a time, although to some that depression 'furnishes a sufficient reason for limiting the hours of labour'. Finally, Ashley had to consider that few of his supporters had returned to town after the Easter recess, and it was 'only justice to add' that his course had been supported by Fielden, Brotherton, Hindley and most of the delegates.[151]

After this campaign, the proliferation of short-time working removed much of the stimulus behind the ten-hours movement and the factory reformers turned increasingly to the closely related topic of the new poor law, which the Commissioners were attempting to introduce into the north amid mounting unrest during 1837. Turner and Crabtree, for instance, investigated conditions in the poor law unions of the southern and midland agricultural counties towards the end of 1837 and reported to Fielden that if the people of the north suffered the 'infernal system' to be introduced among them, wages were bound to fall.[152] Doherty detested the law as strongly as his colleagues, but he did not play a prominent part in the new campaign. In May 1837 his shop was advertised as one of the places in Manchester where subscriptions would be received for defraying the expenses incurred by the operatives in supporting Oastler at the Huddersfield election, which was fought mainly on the new poor law issue. And in March 1838 he spoke at a Manchester meeting in support of R. J. Richardson and the Anti-Poor Law Association. But as this movement developed into Chartism, Doherty appears to have taken little active part in it.[153]

He did, however, help to keep the short-time movement alive for a last short campaign in 1838. In April of that year Fox Maule and Labouchere introduced a government bill to tighten enforcement of the 1833 Act by giving inspectors and superintendents additional powers and to make improvements in the educational clauses. On 19 April Holland Hoole, as chairman of the 'Central Committee of the General Association of Millowners' set up to watch the operation of the factory act, issued a circular urging employers to send deputations to London to oppose the introduction of regulations even more vexatious than the present provisions. A week later, Thomas Fielden, who had succeeded Doherty as chairman of the central short-time committee, issued a counter-appeal ridiculing the masters' opposition to their own Act, recommending the proceedings of the masters' oppressive 'combination' to the present parliamentary committee on trade unions, and urging workmen everywhere to send in 'remonstrances' for a ten-hours bill. On 2 May the Manchester factory operatives met at the 'Navigation Inn' to discuss the government bill. Doherty took the chair and opened the proceedings by reading its main clauses. Since the masters had deputations in London already, Doherty stated, the central committee had resolved to call the workpeople together to discuss tactics. Several speakers opined that the present depression and consequent distress could have been avoided if shorter hours had been introduced earlier, and it was ultimately resolved to petition for 'an efficient ten hours' bill for all ages'.[154]

As in the previous year, however, a desultory agitation followed and the government showed no enthusiasm for their own proposal. On 22 June Ashley himself moved the second reading of the bill, intending to move a ten-hours amendment in the committee stage, but he was opposed by Russell, Thomson, Peel and O'Connell and eventually defeated by eight votes. Doherty printed a pamphlet in Manchester giving a report of this debate, in which Ashley eloquently exposed the repeated delays of the government despite Russell's promises to promote the bill.[155] On 20 July Ashley again raised the question, denouncing the lenient penalties imposed by Lancashire magistrates and being supported by Brotherton and Fielden. O'Connell also denounced the impracticality of the relay system, quoting Doherty's recent evidence to the Select Committee on Combinations as proof of the connivance of surgeons, parents and employers to evade the eight hours' limitation. But O'Connell and Hume both opposed any interference with adult hours, which such a bill would entail, and maintained that the high price of food because of the corn laws was the real cause of overworking children; and Ashley was again defeated in the resulting division by fifteen votes.[156]

Doherty's evidence to the Combinations Committee in June 1838 contained the most detailed explanation of the operatives' discontent with the 1833 Act and their support for the ten-hours bill. Factory reform, he emphasised, had been pursued consistently by the Manchester spinners' union for the previous twenty years. He recalled that he had warned Althorp of the impracticality of assigning two periods of time to different workers, and that after the passing of the 1833 Act the spinners had attempted to implement Althorp's advice to shorten their own hours. He lamented that the proportion of females and young persons in factories was increasing, while the number of adult male spinners fell, and denied that the Manchester spinners supported the ten-hours bill because they thought their wages would be unaffected, although production and hence earnings on piece-rates certainly would not be reduced in proportion to the decline in hours. The spinners also wished the hours of all workers to be the same, since they had recently been forced either to employ older piecers at higher wages or else connive with surgeons and employers to procure false certificates for younger children; and they protested against the masters shifting the burden of responsibility for evasions onto the workpeople, a practice which Inspector Howell had also reprobated in December 1837. Doherty also complained of the low penalties enforced under Althorp's Act and of the conduct of the inspectors, who were the 'good friends' of the employers rather than the protectors of children, and asserted the necessity of reintroducing the right of laying private informations, as they had done under Hobhouse's Act between 1828 and 1831. O'Connell, as we have just seen, was strongly impressed by Doherty's evidence and also by his general intelligence.[157]

The three years after 1835 also saw an extensive literary controversy on the factory reform question and Doherty used his printing business to defend the views and activities of the ten-hours advocates. In 1835 Ure's *Philosophy of Manufactures* attributed the whole of the ten-hours campaign to the self-interest of the adult spinners, likened the children in factories to 'elves at play' whose only concern was at maltreatment by the workmen not by the masters, and repeated Tufnell's smears against Doherty and the Manchester witnesses before Sadler's Committee. In the following year Fielden replied with his *Curse of the Factory System*, which quoted from Blincoe's memoir as to early factory conditions, supported Doherty's estimate of piecers' distances, and stressed the evils of overproduction and home rather than foreign competition. Also in 1836, Doherty printed a number of *Letters* by Oastler violently denouncing those millowners who continued to break the act as 'lawbreakers, tyrants and murderers'. In 1837 Nassau Senior published his *Letters on the Factory Act*, containing his calculations that the cotton manufacturer derived all his profits from the last two hours of the day's labour,[158] and quoting the opinions of the Ashworths, Gregs and Thomas Ashton as to the vexations and meddling interference of inspectors in their concerns; to which Horner replied that not all millowners ran their factories as humanely as the gentlemen mentioned and quoted the frequency with which false certificates were granted to overwork young children. In the same year R. H. Greg published his *Factory Question Considered*, in which he gave yet further currency to Tufnell's allegations, reiterated that the operative spinners were the worst abusers of children, re-emphasised the threat of foreign competition, and mocked a letter which Doherty had apparently written to the employers earlier in 1837 asserting that young persons and even adults required the same protection as 'infantile labourers' because of their work 'in the impure and wasting atmosphere of a Factory'. Replies to Senior, Horner and Greg were contained in a pamphlet in 1838 entitled *Misrepresentations Exposed* and addressed to Lord Ashley, which was printed, published and probably written by Doherty. This contrasted the real conditions in cotton factories with Senior's picture based on the employers' biased information, while supporting his assertion that relays had failed. Horner was praised for overturning Senior's last-hour theory by pointing out the 'vast fortunes' made by cotton masters, though his deference to the three large firms referred to read strangely when they had been so often fined for breaking the Act and when the Manchester committee had so recently publicised the ill-treatment of the

Greg's parish apprentices. And the pamphlet concluded that the country had the superintendents and the short-time committees to thank for the law being even partially enforced. Finally, in June 1838, Doherty reprinted from the *London Standard* an account of a debate on infant labour in the French Chamber of Deputies, and asserted that

> it seems that France is not without her Gregs, and Ashworths and Ures, and Seniors, and, no doubt, all equally *disinterested* in their opinions of the factory system. It is gratifying, however, to find that, on the other hand, France has her Ashleys, and Sadlers, and Fieldens, and Woods, and that there, as here, truth and justice is on the side of the latter, and that therefore the great cause must ultimately prevail.[159]

But the 'great cause' made little progress during the next two years, in the course of which Stephens was imprisoned for sedition and Oastler for debt. Bull removed to Birmingham, and Chartism and the emergent Anti-Corn Law League held the centre of the northern stage. Doherty's reputation in the factory reform campaign was now such, however, that when Frances Trollope and her eldest son came to the north in January 1839, seeking information for a novel about factory conditions, Ashley recommended them to seek out Doherty along with Reuben Bullock of Macclesfield, who 'will show you the secrets of the place, as they showed them to me'. Doherty introduced his visitors to other factory reform leaders and took them to hear Stephens preach, although they found his oratory more restrained than usual, perhaps because he was then out on bail awaiting trial. Anthony Trollope later remembered that 'the little knot of apostles to whom Lord Shaftesbury's letters introduced us . . . [were] singularly new and strange'; most had been factory hands, but having succeeded in raising themselves slightly above that station devoted their lives to the relief of their former colleagues.

> One, I remember, a Mr Doherty, a very small bookseller, to whom we were specially recommended by Lord Shaftesbury. He was an Irishman, a Roman Catholic, and a furious Radical, but a *very* clever man. He was thoroughly acquainted with all that had been done, all that it was hoped to do, and with all the means that were being taken for the advancement of their hopes over the entire district. He came and dined with us at our hotel, but it was, I remember, with much difficulty that we persuaded him to do so, and when at table his excitement in talking was so great and continuous that he could eat next to nothing.

Mrs Trollope's novel, entitled *The Life and Adventures of Michael Armstrong* began to be serialised in twenty parts in February 1839 and was much praised by the *Northern Star* as being based on personal observation, but as Musson and Chaloner have pointed out, the narrative in fact bore a remarkable resemblance to Blincoe's memoir, about which Doherty must certainly have talked.[160]

Over the next year, even the Manchester short-time committee was not 'sitting periodically', and there seemed little interest in the question when Ashley secured a Select Committee in March 1840 to examine the working of the 1833 Act. The *Manchester and Salford Advertiser* reported on 30 May 1840 that 'all excitement on this once inflammable subject, both in and out of parliament, has subsided. The flame burned itself out by its own intensity. The Ten Hours' Bill is never mentioned. It is not expected that parliament will legislate on the measure this session.' But the publication in February 1841 of the report of Ashley's Committee, to which John Lawton had given evidence of the Manchester workmen's continued desire for a ten-hours bill, the appearance of William Dodd's account in March of factory sufferings to rival those of Blincoe, and the return of a Conservative government in July were all stimulants to a general revival in the summer of 1841. Already in May, Mark Crabtree had written to Ashley on behalf of the short-time committees of the West Riding hoping that he would not compromise their interests if he was offered a position in Peel's cabinet and was reassured by Ashley on 1 June. During the first week of August, Ashley paid his third visit to Lancashire to promote the renewed interest in factory reform and was accompanied at discussions with the 'intelligent operatives' of Manchester, Ashton and Bolton by Doherty and Turner, who now re-emerged as leading figures in the movement in that county. The *Guardian* alleged that the real motive of Ashley and 'those engaged with him in this scheme' was to divert the attention of the working classes away from the repeal of the Corn Laws— an accusation which was to become commonplace over the following years— but the paper could not see such tactics succeeding on this occasion, as the workmen had such bitter experience of compulsory short-time employment because of the trade depression. In fact there could be no doubting Ashley's sincerity, for in the following month, having failed to convince Peel of the need for social reform to keep the workmen loyal and pacified, he refused Peel's offer of a minor government post, communicating his decision to the grateful central committees of Yorkshire and Lancashire in letters to Crabtree and Turner, dated 4 September.[161]

Ashley's efforts were now backed by a resurgent agitation in the factory districts. Early in October Doherty was one of a deputation of workmen from the Lancashire central committee, who went to see Peel to inform him of the miserable condition of factory workers, its causes and their proposed remedies, pointing out their hostility to both the factory system and the new poor law, 'the latter being calculated to add to the sufferings of those engaged in the former'. The Premier received them 'with great courtesy' and complimented their proper and able mode of address, assuring them that 'he was deeply impressed with the great importance of their mission and of the facts which they had lain before him, and that he and his colleagues would devote their most serious attention to the question, with a view to the happiness and well-being of those concerned'. The deputies afterwards saw other Cabinet ministers, including Sir James Graham, Lord Ripon and the Duke of Buckingham, and also visited Oastler in the Fleet Prison, who rejoiced that the interviews would mark the end of a reign of lying Secretaries and Commissioners like Chadwick and Muggeridge and the re-emergence of concern for the operatives by the repeal of the new poor law and the passing of a ten-hours bill. The arguments were reinforced later in the month by a similar deputation of five Yorkshire workmen, who saw the same ministers and also Lords Wharncliffe and Lyndhurst and the young Gladstone.[162]

After September 1841 Dodd was engaged in his tour of the northern manufacturing districts, the condition of which he illustrated in a series of letters to Ashley, which were later to provide Bright with ammunition for accusations against his lordship of using 'hired evidence'. On 23 October Doherty visited the Ashworths at Turton along with a deputation of Bolton spinners, who were anxious to know why the firm abated 10 per cent from the Bolton prices and also their opinion of a ten-hours bill. According to Dodd, the Ashworths said they would not actively oppose such a bill and would even support an eleven-hours bill, although this seems unlikely in view of their well-known distaste for any legislative interference. The new agitation as it developed laid more stress on the particular necessity of reducing the hours of adult females, but there is no truth whatever in Smelser's assertion that it differed from the earlier 'disturbed' campaigns in laying more emphasis on morals, education, the woman's role in the home, and the higher aspirations of operatives, or that it was a more 'modern' movement in being less intense and better argued and organised. The first factors listed were, as we have seen, central in all the spinners' propaganda in the 1820s and 1830s, while the development and co-ordination of the Lancashire short-time committees was still largely dependent on Doherty's organising ability and experience, developed in the trade-union movement in the earlier period. And any agitation in which Doherty was involved was almost bound to become embroiled in heated controversy, as demonstrated by an argument which developed between Doherty and the 'liberal' press as soon as the campaign got under way.[163]

In the *Bolton Free Press* on 20 November a correspondent who called himself 'A Factory Worker' drew attention to the fact that although Doherty and James Dawson of Bolton had recently been in London interviewing ministers as the alleged representatives of the Lancashire factory operatives, they had in fact been elected by only a few select persons in the Manchester and Bolton short-time committees and at the request of Ashley, who was alleged to have paid all their expenses. Moreover, Ashley had agreed to pay Doherty £1 per day to agitate in the factory districts for a ten-hours bill, with the understanding that he would do all in his power to set the operatives against the corn law repealers. Doherty had since fulfilled his mission with regard to the Bolton spinners, to whom he had spoken for about five minutes on the ten-hours bill and for about twenty against those of their employers who favoured free trade. 'Factory workers', the correspondence concluded, 'beware of all such clap-trap and false friends!' This letter was copied into the *Guardian* on 27 November, which commented that it should show the operative spinners 'the real character of Lord Ashley and those other humanity-mongers, who have lately been railing so loudly against the factory system, with a view . . . to divert attention from the oppressive food monopoly, which produces . . . the worst evils connected with the manufacturing system'.[164]

On 25 and 26 November Peter Lyne, secretary of the Bolton short-time committee, and James Dawson addressed replies to the *Bolton Free Press*. The former stated that Dawson had been elected at a representative meeting of Bolton mill delegates, that the present movement could hardly be 'a scheme of the landowners' when the Bolton short-time committee had existed for twenty-four years and comprised conservatives, corn-law repealers, chartists and ten-hours agitators, and that Ashley had shown his sincerity in the cause by refusing office. And Dawson repeated that he had been fairly elected at a general meeting of spinners to inform Peel of their destitute condition because of the great mechanical improvements, while the allegation that Doherty was in Ashley's pay 'has not the semblance of truth, as not a word on the subject of the corn laws ever passed between Lord Ashley and ourselves, nor do I believe it was ever thought of'. Neither of these letters appeared in the paper on 27 November, however, and the reprint of the original charges in the *Guardian* sent Doherty hurrying to Bolton on 30 November to find out where they had originated. He called at the offices of the *Bolton Free Press* and secured the editor's promise that the two letters would be inserted in the next edition together with a statement of Doherty himself that

> the whole facts are either so grossly exaggerated or perverted or wholly unfounded as to justify the conclusion that the object of the writer is very different indeed, to that which he professes, namely the good of his fellow workmen. . . . I do not believe that Lord Ashley knows my opinions on the corn laws. He certainly never did say anything to me which led me to believe that he ever wished to know. And I never have been, and I hope never shall be, so impertinent and presumptuous as to obtrude my opinions on this or any other subject either upon his lordship, or anyone else, so entirely uncalled for.

However, although the paper on 4 December contained the communications of Lyne and Dawson, Doherty's statement did not appear.

On 8 December Doherty went once more to see the editor, but was told that the omission was 'a simple piece of neglect'. He therefore compiled an angry letter on 'The Editor of the *Bolton Free Press* and the Factory System', which was published in the rival *Bolton Chronicle* on 11 December. This detailed the paper's tardiness in printing retractions of the charges against him, despite having the firmest evidence that they were completely untrue, and asserted that the motive was to give 'a full fortnight for the *lie* to spread and take root'. And yet the editor made professions of 'liberality' and 'fair play'. Doherty denied that he was the 'tool' of anyone, but added that if he were to become so, 'I would prefer being the "tool" of any Tory I have ever yet known, to being the "tool" of such men as the Ashworths. *All* the Tories I have ever known are what my *liberal* friend of the *Manchester Guardian* would call "gentlemanly" men, and that is rather more than can be said for your patrons.' As for the Corn Laws, Doherty maintained that he had taken no part whatever in the current agitation and attended but few of the meetings. But he knew that the origin of the slander was the Anti-Corn Law League, whose real object was not the much-vaunted increase in the workpeople's welfare but to derive increased profits from their labour, hence their fear of the passing of the ten-hours bill. 'The people will not be deluded by such shallow and wicked devices. They will push for the attainment of a measure which they have been in constant pursuit of for a full quarter of a Century. But whether they obtain it or not, I believe they will have little to thank the Corn Law League for.'

On the same day, the *Bolton Free Press* finally inserted Doherty's original statement, explaining that it had not appeared before because of an 'oversight' and informing Doherty that the previous delays were 'unavoidable' and that the paper had not 'charged' him with anything but simply inserted correspondence. Finally, Doherty turned to the *Manchester Guardian*, sending in Dawson's, Lyne's and his own letters for inclusion on 11 December. But the edition on that day explained that these had only arrived on the previous evening and therefore too late for publication, hence Doherty's 'general contradiction . . . must suffice'.[165]

While these arguments still continued, Doherty was already engaged in a tour of Lancashire towns to report on the deputation to London and reconstitute committees where necessary. Early in November he addressed workers in Oldham, pointing out how ever-bigger and faster-running mules had increased the intensity of labour, whilst at the same time greatly reducing the number of operative spinners and creating more unemployment; between 1829 and 1841, he stated, the number of spinners in Manchester had fallen from two thousand to five hundred.[166] On 3 December he addressed a numerous meeting at the 'Bull's Head', Warrington, which agreed to petition for an efficient ten-hours bill. On 9 December 1,500 workmen crammed into Messrs Fieldens' weaving shed at Todmorden to hear Doherty's report, and when he was asked if they would have 'twelve hours' wages for ten hours' work', he referred to the case of the hatter who made too many hats and would have been better paid if he had made fewer. On 16 December he spoke for about an hour to Stockport operatives assembled in the Chartists' Association room, and a petition was adopted for a ten-hours bill. And on 30 December he appeared at a meeting of Bolton workmen, which agreed 'that a uniform system of ten hours a day would greatly ameliorate the condition of factory workers generally' and recommended a petition to Parliament 'praying for an act to that effect'. In view of the recent press controversy and the hostility of the local mill-owning members of the Anti-Corn Law League, Doherty pointed to his own long-continued involvement in the factory reform movement as proof that it was no new Tory trick,[167] and declared that it 'was not opposed to the agitation for the charter, to the repeal of the corn laws, or to any other'. And as for the rumour that the movement was financed from the Carlton Club, he revealed that, apart from small collections among factory workers, the money came from a Tory—John Wood, a Whig—Charles Hindley, and a radical—John Fielden. He concluded by declaring that the public would cease their apathy on the question if they once realised the true nature of factory employment, which he illustrated by repeating his calculations regarding piecers' distances.[168]

These meetings continued into the new year. The Chorlton workmen assembled at the Chartists' room on 14 January 1842, and four days later a similar gathering met in Manchester, at which Doherty was again the principal orator, speaking for an hour and a half. For the benefit of 'young men' in the audience, he rehearsed his old arguments for the ten-hours bill. He first attacked the 'foreign competition' objection which he deemed 'frivolous', by pointing to the high tariffs in America and France, quoting Fielden's 1833 tables exhibiting the low wages and profits which resulted from overproduction, and describing the experience of the previous four years when prices and wages had declined rapidly because of the overstocked market. It was home, not foreign, competition which caused this depression, yet the masters were determined to continue it and ruin themselves and their men. 'When the working men many years ago were agitating for a repeal of the corn laws, they were laughed at by the very men who now set up a cry of "repeal" as a cure for every evil, political and social, under which the country was labouring.' He went on to enumerate the greatly accelerated speed of machinery as proof that a ten-hours bill was even more necessary than in 1832, when medical evidence had shown it to be essential. And he ended by again mocking the idea that their agitation was a Tory trick, when the short-time movement was twenty years older than the League, and pointed out that they had more to fear from 'Whig trickery', as some recent editorial proceedings demonstrated. When Lawton moved the adoption of a petition, the leader of the local Operative Anti-Corn Law Society, Warren, proposed that additional prayers be inserted for Corn Law repeal and the Charter, in accordance with the policy of Sturge's Complete Suffrage Union; but Doherty countered by seeking a pledge that the ten-hours bill would be similarly included in all future anti-corn law petitions, and when Warren demurred the original motion was carried with only three dissentients. The final meeting in the campaign was held at Macclesfield on 10 February, when Doherty seconded Bullock's motion for a ten-hours bill for all under twenty-one and spoke of the mischievous effects of long hours on the trade itself, but more especially on the health and morals of children.[169]

By this time, however, Ashley had publicly announced Peel's hostility to the ten-hours bill in a letter addressed to the short-time committee on 2 February. Since his own persuasions, the workers' deputations, and Doherty's mass meetings had failed to convince Peel, Ashley realised that he could not obtain the ten-hours bill this session and concentrated instead on his mines bill. But Doherty did not immediately cease his exertions, as was clear from the fact that on 7 April he was summoned at the New Bailey by one Samuel Booth who claimed that he had not been paid his full wages by Doherty for collecting signatures for a petition in favour of a short-time bill; Booth explained that he had been employed by Doherty for eight days at 2s per day but had only received 8s, but the magistrate refused the application because 'the employment described could not be considered labour within the meaning of the act'. Whatever the methods employed, the Manchester short-time committee was enabled on 28 April to transmit a petition to Ashley for presentation with 62,773 signatures and nearly one mile in length, which, as the *Manchester and Salford Advertiser* observed, massively rebutted statements that the workpeople had grown indifferent to the ten-hours bill.[170]

Doherty continued his opposition to the Complete Suffrage Union during the violent summer which ensued, when chartists and free traders were making open threats and the trade depression grew so intense that there were widespread outbreaks of rioting in August. At the beginning of that month, the proprietor of the *Times*, John Walter, was elected on a Tory anti-poor-law platform at Nottingham after a particularly unruly contest with Joseph Sturge, during which both Doherty and Stephens were 'imported' into the town to speak for the Tory candidate.[171] And after the unrest had subsided in September, Doherty was, as we have seen, advocating a scheme for compensation from Parliament for the unemployment and distress caused among cotton spinners by machinery, a proposal which Ferrand had made in the Commons earlier in the year without gaining much support.[172] Doherty also spoke on that occasion in favour of an eight-hour day to share out the work and again asserted that support for such a measure long predated Ashley's interest in the question or the campaign against the Corn Laws. Meanwhile Ashley, who believed that Peel bore some responsibility for the August riots because of his rejection of social reform, travelled to Lancashire once more at the end of September to induce the operatives to return to legal methods of alleviating their condition. On 27 September Doherty presented him with an address from the Lancashire central short-time committee, in which they con-gratulated him on his success with the Mines Act and hoped that this would inspire him to reintroduce his bill in the next session to protect the factory children, who were forced to keep pace with the 'monstrous power' of the machinery, whether it travelled 'ten, twenty, thirty or even forty miles per day'. Ashley's reply urged the commitee to publicise how widely female labour was replacing male, and stressed the importance of the ten-hours bill as a preliminary to 'the great undertaking of domestic regeneration'. But the exchange failed to impress the *Guardian*, which copied an article from the *Globe* on 5 October asserting that conditions were worse in domestic industry and agriculture and that the alleged 'overproduction' was in reality under-consumption due to foreign markets being restricted because of the Corn Laws. The article concluded that the Lancashire committee had 'more honour in broad sheets than in its own country', and the *Guardian* agreed, describing Doherty, 'the old and well-known agitator', as 'its spokesman and chief representative', but maintaining that in Lancashire 'its honour is very little'.[173]

After 1842 Doherty remained on the short-time committee, but his public appearances became less numerous. The year 1843 was dominated by the non-conformist furore at the education proposals in Graham's factory bill, which drew attention away from the other provisions to allow employment at eight years but to reduce children's hours to six and a half.[174] On 27 April a meet-ing of Manchester dissenters was held to demand rejection of the education clauses, but Doherty interrupted the proceedings to ask if the workmen in the audience would signify their approval for the principle of shortening the hours of labour. He was assailed by cries of 'off!' and informed by the chairman that he was out of order, but he went on to explain that as a Roman Catholic he cordially approved of the resolutions adopted and merely wished to bring to their notice that while the present hours of labour were continued in factories it was utterly impossible that either the established or dissenting clergy could get at the children to educate them. At this point he was finally shouted down. It is likely that he attended the meeting of Lancashire delegates in May, which reaffirmed support for the ten-hours bill; but there was no chance of achieving the measure in the current session, while Graham abandoned his bill in June. The factory reformers' main activity during the next winter was to raise subscriptions for the release of Oastler, their efforts being rewarded with success in February 1844. Daniel was the organiser of the appeal in Manchester, but there is no reference to Doherty's participation, although he doubtless sympathised with the object, as the *Fleet Papers* had recorded his donations of two sets of books to Oastler in the summer of 1843.[175]

The year 1844 witnessed great efforts by the ten-hours men as they sought to amend Graham's new bill, which was introduced in February and largely

repeated the provisions of the previous year, except for omitting the controversial education clauses and extending the twelve hours' protection to adult
females. There was great excitement in the North when the ten-hours principle
was accepted in one division, but matching anger when the vote was soon
afterwards reversed due to government pressure. The parliamentary debates
were marked by great bitterness, Ashley provoking the manufacturers by his
statements relative to piecers' distances and Bright launching vitriolic personal
attacks upon Ashley with the aid of exposures made by William Dodd in his
letters to the Ashworths. Ashley's position was backed by a meeting of Lancashire mill delegates in Manchester on 11 April, which co-ordinated information brought from the districts regarding the hours worked, size of wheels,
number of females and children, and piecers' distances, and encouraged Ashley
to issue a public challenge to R. H. Greg and Henry Ashworth a few days later
to measure the distances in the company of Fielden; while the employers also
poured forth a constant stream of propaganda regarding the conditions of
agricultural labourers and the necessity of repealing the corn laws before
anything could be done about factory hours.

Doherty's name was not prominent in the reports of these activities, but
he was clearly still an influential figure in the Lancashire movement, for on
9 April Ashley wrote in his diary that 'the *Times* yesterday took Ashworth's
statement in hand, and treated both him and his document with suitable
contempt—Well does Doherty say that the manifesto from the Millowners
is worth more than £10,000 subscribed for the promotion of the factory bill'.
His continuing influence was also evident at a large Manchester meeting on
17 April, which adopted resolutions rejoicing that the ten hours' principle
had been accepted in one vote and petitioning that the ten-hours bill should
now pass without delay, thus benefiting 'both masters and men': the Rev
C. D. Wray, Vice-Dean of the Manchester Collegiate Church, took the chair
and the speakers included Oastler, Ferrand, Walter and Fielden, but it was
reported that the platform was also 'honoured with a full-muster of the "short-
time committee", of whom the only persons known to fame are John Doherty
(once editor of the long-defunct *Voice of the People*) and Philip Grant', and
that even among this high-powered company 'Mr Doherty stood at the chairman's side to instruct him'. But the upshot of this campaign was a further
defeat for Ashley's bill in the Commons in May, and the passing of Graham's
Act shortly afterwards. Lancashire delegates were again talking of enforcing
a ten-hours day by direct action at a conference on 25 May, but they were
persuaded by a letter from Ashley on 18 July to attempt to implement it
through voluntary agreements with their employers. In October Ashley was
again in Manchester, meeting the Lancashire central committee, who urged
him to persevere with his bill; and on 27 November he wrote to the secretary,
Henry Green, of his intention to renew the question in the next session and
urging a new campaign in its support. On the other side, when the Millowners'
Central Committee issued their annual report on 31 December, they also
counselled continued vigilance from their members and looked back on their
well-reasoned 'Statement of Facts' in the previous April which they contrasted
with the anonymous and questionable authorities used by Ashley. They
denounced the 'class of persons' who acted as the operatives' delegates to
Parliament; one of them was a cripple hired by Ashley to 'blacken the charac-

ters' of certain employers, and 'another . . . had first obtained employment in a mill in Manchester by means of a forged certificate of character, dated Belfast, . . . and had since been twice in prison'.[176]

Doherty's last public action for the factory movement was an attempt to arouse interest in the new campaign by addressing *A Letter to the Factory Operatives of Lancashire, on the necessity of Petitioning Parliament in favour of the Ten Hours' Bill*, which was published on 21 January 1845. He recalled that a quarter of a century's struggling had brought little practical relief to the children, but they should draw a moral from the sphere of religion.

> The pure and sublime and heavenly principles of Christianity have not yet been carried to half the human race, notwithstanding the thousands . . . of good and . . . learned men who have devoted their lives and fortunes to its propagation. But, thanks be to heaven, every . . . week adds to the number of those who acknowledge the meek and lowly JESUS as the great model for their imitation, and Christianity as the great system which is at once to enlighten and redeem the world!

Similarly, the 'holy cause' of factory reform had progressed from a defeat by 145 votes in 1833 to the securing of two majorities in 1844, and indeed the bill would have passed had not Sir Robert Peel betrayed the cause of his father and decided that 'bricks and mortar, . . . spindles and pulleys' were more important than 'morals, lives, blood and bones, as well as . . . immortal souls'. If one majority could be obtained, another was possible and Doherty urged the workmen to form new committees in every town, not only of factory hands but also 'of intelligent persons . . . altogether free from mill influences'; they should secure the support of the clergy and medical men for their petitions, while making it clear that 'you are far from objecting to [your children] working to earn their bread', which was 'the condition of existence', but denying that labour was 'the *sole end* of life'. Finally Doherty listed ten reasons why a ten-hours bill was essential for all workers. These included the facts that factory workers were not free agents and therefore needed outside protection, that other trades worked a similar period according to custom, that the selfish desires of masters needed to be restrained, that the size and speed of machinery had greatly increased, that employment on a steam engine 'which never tires or hungers' was especially fatiguing 'in an artificially, highly heated and impure atmosphere', that no time was allowed for religious exercises, domestic duties, the cultivation of the mind, recreation and repose, and that medical evidence had proved that to work children for twelve hours a day was nothing less than 'a system of *infanticide*'.[177]

Doherty's contact with the spinners in the factory movement remained close to the end. The spinners' federal union, which had been formed with its headquarters in Bolton in 1842 and largely financed the subsequent activities of the central short-time committee, adopted a resolution at its fortnightly delegate meeting at Manchester on 2 February, 'that the letter on the ten hours' bill by J. Doherty be paid for by the Central Committee and distributed throughout the district'. But his pamphlet was rather lukewarmly reviewed in the *Northern Star*, which agreed with its 'general tenor' but dissented strongly from his justification of infant labour: 'If Mr Doherty would proclaim [that no children should labour], he would be doing more to advance the truth and

406 The Voice of the People

the right than by putting slavish apologies into the mouths of parents for the working of their little ones.' Nevertheless, Doherty's pamphlet had the desired effect and at a meeting of factory delegates at Bolton on 2 March there were favourable reports of progress from numerous Lancashire and Cheshire towns.[178]

It would seem, however, that Doherty did not hold out much hope from petitioning. He acknowledged that Parliament paid 'little regard to the petitions of the people', and explained that 'we do not petition from any hope that the decisions of the members will be materially influenced by these petitions', but only to deprive their opponents of the argument that the work-people were indifferent to the ten-hours bill.[179] There are no further con-temporary references to him in the agitation of 1845, nor in the campaigns of the following two years, which culminated in final success for the ten-hours bill, introduced by Fielden in Ashley's temporary absence from Parlia-ment, on 1 June 1847. Nor does he figure in the reformers' protests at the employers' machinations to evade the Act over the subsequent years, or in the bitter divisions which split the movement when Ashley accepted the ten and a half hours' compromise in 1850.[180]

Whatever caused Doherty's withdrawal from the movement at the last, whether ill-health or sheer exhaustion, his contribution was not forgotten by his colleagues. In Grant's celebratory address in the *Ten Hours' Advocate* on 12 June 1847, in which tribute was paid to the efforts of all the leaders from Gould onwards, he asserted that 'there are also amongst the workmen many individuals whose early efforts should not be forgotten, and amongst that number we must not omit the names of Foster and Doherty, both of whom have in their day, done a lion's share of the good work'. And in his history of the movement the same writer asserted that, 'we are . . . greatly indebted to such men as the late Thomas Foster, John Doherty, James Turner, and a few others of the workpeople, who bravely fought the battle when it was dangerous to do so'. In addition, at the time of Doherty's death in 1854, Ashley wrote to Grant that, 'Poor Doherty was one of the most faithful to a cause that ever existed'.[181] As with so many of Doherty's concerns, his views on tactical procedures were liable to intermittent change, but he never varied in regard to the main objective of reducing working hours and improving factory conditions for both children and adults, and he certainly deserves to be recognised as one of the most important factory reform leaders, indeed his role in securing the ten-hours bill was perhaps the greatest of his practical achievements.

NOTES TO CHAPTER TEN

[1] Thompson, *op. cit.*, p. 384; Turner, *op. cit.*, p. 102; Smelser, *op. cit.*, p. 238; J. T. Ward, *The Factory Movement;* 'Matthew Balme, 1813–84: Factory Re-former', *Bradford Antiquary*, Vol. x (1962), pp. 217–28; 'The Factory Movement in Lancashire, 1830–55', *T.L.C.A.S.*, Vol. 75 and 76 (1965–6), pp. 186–210; 'Brad-ford and Factory Reform', *Journal of Bradford Textile Society*, 1960–1; 'Leeds and the Factory Reform Movement', *Thoresby Society Publications*, Vol. XLVI, 2 (1961); 'The Factory Reform Movement in Scotland', *Scottish Historical Review*, Vol. XLI, 132 (October 1962); 'Alfred' (S. Kydd), *The History of the Factory Movement* (1857); P. Grant, *The Ten Hours Bill* (Manchester, 1866). For Oastler, see C. Driver, *Tory Radical. The Life of Richard Oastler* (New York, 1946); for Sadler, see J. T. Ward, 'M. T. Sadler', *University of Leeds Review*, Vol. VII, 2

(December 1960); for Stephens, see J. T. Ward, 'Revolutionary Tory; Life of J. R. Stevens', in *T.L.C.A.S.*, Vol. LXVIII (1958); for Ashley, see E. Hodder, *The Life and Work of the Seventh Earl of Shaftesbury*, (1886, 3 vols.), J. L. and B. Hammond, *Lord Shaftesbury* (1923), and G. F. A. Best, *Shaftesbury* (1964); for Bull, see J. C. Gill, *The Ten Hours' Parson* (1959), and *Parson Bull of Byerley* (1963); and for Fielden, see introduction by J. T. Ward to J. Fielden, *The Curse of the Factory System* (2nd ed., 1969).

[2] Parl. Papers, 1840, x, 8475. The erroneous assertion of R. W. Cooke-Taylor, *The Factory System and the Factory Acts* (1894), p. 40, that this original committee comprised Doherty, Turner, Daniel and Grant is based upon a misunderstanding of P. Grant, *op. cit.*, p. 15, which referred, itself erroneously (see below, pp. 361–2), to the composition in 1829.

[3] *Bolton Free Press*, 31 December 1841; *Advertiser*, 22 January 1842; Grant, *op. cit.*, p. 22. Doherty does not appear to have played a leading role until late in the 1820s, but we have devoted some attention to the earlier period, in view of its previous neglect by historians and because of Doherty's undoubted (though obscure) participation: here are the origins of his later factory reform activities.

[4] In fact, subscriptions probably continued at individual mills: see above, p. 27.

[5] Parl. Papers, 1837–8, VIII, 3460.

[6] Ward, *The Factory Movement*, pp. 20–4; *Mercury*, 24 February 1818.

[7] *Chronicle*, 21 February; *Observer*, 21 February; *Mercury*, 7 and 21 April 1818; H.O. 42/182; *Black Dwarf*, 9 September 1818.

[8] *Chronicle*, 15 August 1818; H.O. 42/180, quoted in Aspinall, *op. cit.*, Nos. 294, 298 and 323. Grant, *op. cit.*, p. 15, stated that in the early days of the agitation, 'any meddling with the subject was unpopular, even amongst the masses', but, as we have seen, he elsewhere referred specifically to the Manchester spinners' importance in the first campaigns.

[9] H.O. 42/178 and 181; *Enquiry into the principle and tendency of the Bill now pending . . .* (1818); and *Answers to Certain Objections . . .* (Manchester, 1819).

[10] Ward, *The Factory Movement*, pp. 26–7; *William Hall's Vindication of the Chorley Spinners* (n.d.).

[11] *Gazette*, 2 and 30 November 1822. The advertisements for the proposed new journal were signed 'XYZ', but internal evidence indicates very strongly that Smith and Brown were behind it.

[12] *Ibid.*, 21 December 1822. That the masters *had* blacklisted witnesses is demonstrated by the case of Thomas Worsley: Parl. Papers, 1831–2, XV, 9488.

[13] See above, pp. 28–9.

[14] *Cobbett's Weekly Register*, 30 August 1823; H.O. 40/18, quoted in Aspinall, *op. cit.*, No. 393. The quotation from Cobbett demonstrates that Oastler's famous 'White Slavery' denunciation in 1830 was by no means original. An anonymous correspondent in the *Bolton Chronicle*, 7 June 1828, similarly denounced 'the Slave Trade in England', Doherty also used the same analogy. See below, p. 361

[15] Smelser, *op. cit.*, p. 238; Ward, *The Factory Movement*, pp. 28–9.

[16] *Stockport Advertiser*, 10 December 1824.

[17] Place Papers, Vol. XV, Add. MSS 27,803, Part I, f. 305.

[18] *Ibid.*, Vol. XIII, Add. MSS 27,801, ff. 268–9.

[19] *Gazette*, 23 and 30 April 1825; Place Papers, Vol. XV, Add. MSS 27,803, Part I, ff. 305, 318 and 449; Broughton Papers, Vol. VI, Add. MSS 36,461, f. 31.

[20] Place Collection, Vol. 54. This contains a copy of the evidence to the 1838 Combinations Committee, and Place's claim is made in a pencilled comment next to Doherty's answer to question 3626.

[21] Place Papers, Vol. XV, Add. MSS 27,803, Part I, f. 312; Place Collection, Vol. 61, Part II, f. 34.

[22] Place Papers, Vol. XV, Add. MSS 27,803, Part I, ff. 306–7; *Proceedings of the Manchester Chamber of Commerce*, 30 March 1825. The same volume of the Place Papers, ff. 310–11, contain some pen-written notes on the long hours, rigid discipline, and fines at Messrs Phillips & Lees' factory in Salford, presumably for use, if necessary, in the debates in the Commons.

[23] *Gazette,* 23 April and 14 May 1825.

[24] *Chronicle,* 26 March, 7 and 14 May, and 4 June 1825. Place Papers, Vol. xv, Add MSS 27,803, Part I, ff. 286 and 313. See above, pp. 33 and 49, n. 128.

[25] *Gazette,* 25 June 1825.

[26] See above, p. 30.

[27] Grant, *op. cit.,* p. 15; *Gazette,* 16 July 1825. See above, p. 33.

[28] *Gazette,* 30 July and 20 August 1825.

[29] See, for example, *Chronicle,* 10 September 1825, and 11 February 1826; *Mercury,* 13 March 1827; *Bolton Chronicle,* 8 September 1827.

[30] *Lion,* 18 January–29 February 1828; *Bolton Chronicle,* 2 February, 7 June and 13 September; *Stockport Advertiser,* 3 October 1828. The infractions at Wigan led to a complaint to the government and an ineffectual warning from the Home Secretary.

[31] *Guardian,* 8 and 15 November; *Times,* 15 November; *Courier,* 15 November; *Gazette,* 29 November; *Conciliator,* 29 November 1828.

[32] *Guardian,* 24 January 1829; Parl. Papers, 1837–8, VIII, 3502.

[33] Doherty's letter was probably in the *Manchester and Salford Advertiser,* which is not extant for this period.

[34] *Stockport Advertiser,* 19 February 1829. This was during the Stockport strike. See above, pp. 57–9.

[35] *Conciliator,* 20 December; *Stockport Advertiser,* 26 December; *Bolton Chronicle,* 27 December; *Gazette,* 27 December 1828.

[36] *Bolton Chronicle,* 20 December 1828 and 10 January 1829; *Conciliator,* 13 December 1828.

[37] H.O. 43/37, ff. 85–7; *Guardian,* 7 March 1829.

[38] *Times,* 10 January; *Bolton Chronicle,* 24 January 1829. Smith was a former operative spinner, now editor of the *Bolton Chronicle.*

[39] See above, p. 53.

[40] *Gazette,* 23 May 1829; Broughton Papers, Vol. x, Add. MSS 36,465, f. 168.

[41] *Guardian,* 24 January 1829; *Returns,* 17 January 1829, quoted in H.O. 40/23; *Chronicle,* 21 March; *Gazette,* 14 March 1829.

[42] *Mercury,* 14 April; *Chronicle,* 30 May 1829. Criticism appeared in the *Manchester Courier* at this time that Doherty was enriching himself by these activities, in addition to receiving a salary of 32s per week from the Society; but he immediately replied, pointing out that his services were completely gratuitous and that the receipts from penalties and costs went to the Society, not himself. *Courier,* 30 May and 6 June 1829. Doherty did, of course, receive a weekly salary of 33s as secretary of the spinners' society.

[43] *Mercury,* 30 June; *Times,* 27 June 1829.

[44] *Mercury,* 21 and 28 July, 25 August; *Times and Gazette,* 28 November 1829.

[45] Numerous reports of his prosecuting activities appeared, along with those of Doherty, in the Manchester, Stockport, Bolton and other local papers.

[46] *Mercury,* 24 November 1829; *Report of the Proceedings . . .* (December 1829).

[47] *Times and Gazette,* 12 December 1829; *Stockport Advertiser,* 1 and 22 January 1830.

[48] *Chronicle,* 30 January and 6 February; *Times and Gazette,* 16 January; *Chronicle,* 13 February; *Mercury,* 16 and 23 February; *Chronicle,* 27 February; *Bolton Chronicle,* 27 February; *Chronicle,* 17 April 1830.

[49] *Guardian,* 30 January; *Bolton Chronicle,* 20 March and 15 May 1830. Bollings, whose spinners were currently involved in a bitter strike against reduced piece prices (see above, pp. 100–3), were again involved, accused of overworking children employed in their mills, as well as of truck payments.

[50] The Protection Society's intention of forwarding a parliamentary petition for a new bill was previously announced by Doherty in the *Journal* on 27 March.

[51] But see the *Voice,* 30 April 1831, for a reported reversion of Wigan master spinners to their former malpractices.

[52] The accounts were audited by three masters, Messrs Harbottle, Harvey and Chappell.

[53] *Guardian,* 3 and 10 April; *Courier* and *Chronicle,* 10 April 1830.

54 See above, p. 360. Nightworking was blamed for unemployment and the overstocked market in the *Journal*, 3 April 1830.

55 *Times and Gazette*, 19 February; *Courier*, 13 February; *Journal*, 6 March 1830.

56 As reported in the various local papers and in the *Journal* during April and May 1830; see also Broughton Papers, Vol. XI, Add. MSS 36,466, f. 139.

57 *Journal*, 15 May 1830. O'Connell agreed to present the Protection Society's petition after Hobhouse had demurred, according to a letter from Foster (*ibid.*).

58 *Chronicle*, 10 July; *Courier*, 22 May; *Guardian*, 12 June 1830. In fact, no new legislation was passed in 1830.

59 *Journal*, 17 April and 22 May; *Stockport Advertiser*, 28 May 1830. Doherty had just previously been engaged in prosecuting Bollings, of Bolton, for such rent deductions (see above, pp. 360–1).

60 *Journal*, 26 June; *Times and Gazette*, 3 July; *Chronicle*, 9 October 1830. The Oldham decision had been on informations brought by Foster. *Bolton Chronicle*, 11 and 24 December; *Guardian*, 12 and 26 December 1829.

61 *Voice*, 19 February 1831.

62 *Times and Gazette*, 22 January, 7 May, 4 June 1831.

63 Grant, *op. cit.*, p. 13.

64 See below, pp. 367 and 372.

65 W. R. Greg, *Enquiry into the State of the Manufacturing Population* (1831), p. 12.

66 *Voice*, 29 January, 19 and 5 February and 30 April 1831.

67 *Ibid.*, 26 February, 3 March, 9–23 April 1831.

68 *Ibid.*, 11 and 18 June, 2 July and 6 August 1831.

69 *Chronicle*, 26 February and 9 April; *Voice*, 5 February and 9 April 1831.

70 *Times and Gazette*, 26 February 1831.

71 *Chronicle*, 27 November 1830.

72 *Guardian*, 29 October–19 November 1831. Charles Hindley and G. R. Chappell were the chief sponsors of this Association.

73 *Chronicle*, 28 April 1832 and 2 February 1833; *Advocate*, 2 June 1832.

74 Parl. Papers, 1831–2, XV, 7360; *Advertiser*, 10 March 1832.

75 Parl. Papers, 1833, XX, p. 67; Ward, *The Factory Movement*, p. 29.

76 *Times and Gazette*, 29 October; *Voice*, 24 September 1831.

77 *Advertiser*, 31 December 1831.

78 *Ibid.*, 24 December 1831 and 7 January 1832.

79 See below, pp. 435–8.

80 *Advocate*, 28 April 1832.

81 *Expositor*, 7 January 1832.

82 *Ibid.*, 14 January; *Advocate*, 21 January–4 February 1832.

83 A number of the firm's workmen contradicted these charges in the *Union Pilot*, but Doherty denied that their views were representative of the work force. See above, pp. 255–6.

84 *Advocate*, 28 January–19 May 1832. Two of the firms mentioned were among those summoned at this time by James Turner on behalf of the 'Cotton Factory Time Bill Association' formed by the masters. On 22 February the manager of Thomas Harbottle was fined £10 for employing a girl under age, but on 1 March James Patrick was acquitted of working a boy through the dinner hour—by the perjured evidence of three 'hired' under-managers, according to Doherty. See *Chronicle*, 24 February and 3 March, and *Advocate*, 10 March 1832.

85 See below, pp. 429–30.

86 See above, pp. 3–4.

87 *Advocate*, 3 March, 14 and 21 April, 19 May 1832. See below, pp. 435–8.

88 *Expositor*, 14 January; *Advocate*, 4 February 1832; Ward, 'The Factory Reform Movement in Scotland', *S.H.R.*, Vol. XLI (1962), p. 103.

89 *Times and Gazette*, 25 February and 10 March; *Advocate*, 10 and 31 March 1832; H. Hoole, *A Letter to the Rt. Hon. Lord Althorp* (Manchester, 1832); *Guardian*, 27 March; *Pilot*, 7 April 1832.

90 *Advocate*, 25 February–24 March 1832.

91 Place Collection, Vol. 16, Part II, f. 160; *Advocate*, 31 March 1832.

[92] *Mr Sadler's Factory Bill—Report of the Proceedings* . . ., in White Slavery Collection, Vol. 5, No. 2. This was presumably Doherty's first meeting with Oastler and caused him to change his mind about the tory–radical's sincerity.

[93] *Chronicle*, 24 February; *Advertiser*, 10 March 1832.

[94] *Advocate*, 10 March; *Advertiser*, 17 March 1832; *The Justice, Humanity and Policy of restricting the hours of children and young persons in the Mills and Factories of the United Kingdom, illustrated in the Letters, Speeches etc.* . . . (Leeds, 1833), in White Slavery Collection, Vol. 2, No. 9.

[95] *Advocate*, 10 and 24 March; *Advertiser*, 14 April; *Stockport Advertiser*, 17 April 1832. See below, p. 385.

[96] *Advocate*, 7 April, 28 April–12 May 1832; Ward, *The Factory Movement*, p. 63; *Report of the Committee* . . ., in University of London, Collection of Broadsides, 'Oastler and the Factory Movement', 547 (11).

[97] *Advocate*, 2, 16 and 23 June, 21 July 1832.

[98] See above, p. 10.

[99] Parl. Papers, 1831–2, xv, 7193–7638, 9372–9787; *Advocate*, 19 May–23 June, 28 July 1832; J. Brown, *A Memoir of Robert Blincoe* (Manchester, 1832); *Chronicle*, 11 August 1832.

[100] See below, pp. 435–8.

[101] *Advocate*, 11 August 1832.

[102] *Advocate*, 25 August; *Guardian*, 1 September 1832.

[103] *Advertiser*, 27 October; *British Labourer's Protector*, 16 November; *Advocate*, 1 September 1832; *Advertiser*, 13 October; poster headed 'White Slavery' in Place Collection, Vol. 52, Part i, f. 60; *Advocate and Operative Reporter*, 10 November; *Chronicle*, 15 December 1832.

[104] *Advocate and Operative's Adviser*, 27 October 1832.

[105] *A Penny Poor Man's Advocate*, 29 September; *Advocate and Political Adviser*, 6 October; *Guardian*, 27 October 1832; *Advocate and Operative Reporter*, 10 November; *Advocate or Oppressor's Castigator*, 8 December 1832; *Guardian*, 12 January; *Advertiser*, 26 January 1833.

[106] That there was some truth in the masters' allegations has been demonstrated by W. H. Hutt, 'The Factory System of the Early Nineteenth Century', *Economica*, March 1926, reprinted in F. A. Hayek (ed.), *Capitalism and the Historians* (1954).

[107] Ward, *The Factory Movement*, pp. 84–5; *Minutes, Resolutions etc.* . . ., in 'Oastler and the Factory Movement', 1830–3, No. 34; *Guardian*, 9 and 16 February; *Advertiser*, 23 March and 16 April 1833.

[108] *Advertiser*, 13 and 20 April 1833.

[109] *Tyranny's Last Shift* (Huddersfield, 11 April 1833), in Place Collection, Vol. 52, Part i, f. 25; *Guardian*, 27 April 1833; *Instructions to the Short Time Committees* . . . (1833), in 'Oastler and the Factory Movement', 1830–3; *A speech delivered by Richard Oastler* . . . (Huddersfield, 1833), in White Slavery Collection, Vol. i, No. 11.

[110] The *Guardian*, 11 May 1833, commented, however, that despite the carefully arranged ragged and dirty clothes, the lively spirits and healthy appearance of the children could not be disguised. Another observer pointed out, moreover, that the operative spinners were mainly responsible for the cruelties to factory children: *Observations on the Proposed Legislative Changes in Factory Labour* (Manchester, 1833). See also Greg, *op. cit.*, p. 31, for a similar comment.

[111] *Times and Gazette*, 25 May 1833.

[112] *Bolton Chronicle*, 25 May 1833.

[113] *Ibid.*; *Guardian*, 1 June; *Advertiser*, 1 June 1833.

[114] *Advertiser*, 8 June 1833; *Parl. Papers*, 1833, xx, and 1834, xix, D2, p. 210; Tufnell, *Character, Objects and Effects of Trades' Unions*, pp. 36–7, and *Supplementary Report of the Central Board of Factory Commissioners*, Parl. Papers, 1834, Vol. 19, D2, p. 210.

[115] *Advertiser*, 6 and 27 July 1833; *Factory Commission Correspondence* . . . in White Slavery Collection, Vol. 3, No. 19; *Great Meeting in the West Riding* . . . (Leeds, 1833), *ibid.*, Vol. 6, No. 7. Turner was also impressed by Ashley, for from that time onwards he acted as his 'confidential agent' in the north. In 1842 Ashley described him as 'a man much in the secret of all that passes in the

manufacturing districts, who enjoys the full confidence of the operatives, having for many years been one himself'. See Peel Papers, Vol. CCCIII, Add. MSS 404, 483, f. 42.

116 Ward, *The Factory Movement*, p. 110; Hodder, *op. cit.*, Vol. I, p. 167.
117 White Slavery Collection, Vol. 5, No. 19; Ward, *The Factory Movement*, p. 119.
118 See above, p. 273.
119 See above, Chapter VIII.
120 See above, p. 339.
121 *Advertiser*, 11 October; *Poor Man's Guardian*, 20 December 1834.
122 See, for example, the *Stockport Advertiser*, 10 November 1834.
123 *Advertiser*, 14 March 1835.
124 *Ibid.* The *Guardian*, 14 March 1835, suggested that the reason for Ashley's lack of ardour compared with 1833 was that, whereas he had then been intent on harassing the Whig government, 'the noble lord is [now] himself in office and wishes to escape from the factory bill and all other annoyances of the kind'. But Ashley's later record belies this suggestion.
125 *Bolton Chronicle*, 14 March; *Advertiser*, 21 March and 4 April; *Times*, 21 March; *Bolton Chronicle*, 16 May 1835.
126 *Let Labour Live . . .*, in Balme Collection, Bradford Central Reference Library. The wording of this appeal is strongly suggestive of Doherty's style and philosophy, but it was probably written by James Turner, long his close associate and very active in the factory reform movement. Turner sent a copy to Francis Place (enclosed in letter dated 21 September 1835, Place Collection, Vol. 52, Part I, f. 124), who responded with an open letter to the cotton spinners, advising them to stop 'whining' and to protect themselves by their own efforts. This, in turn, produced critical replies from Turner and from 'An Operative Spinner', pointing out the difficulties of forming an effective union under existing circumstances in the cotton trade. *Advertiser*, 10, 17, 31 October, 14 and 28 November 1835; Place Collection, Vol. 52, Part I, f. 87.
127 J. C. Gill, *Parson Bull of Byerley* (1963), p. 122.
128 *Advertiser*, 17 October 1835.
129 Grant claimed in a letter to the *Advertiser*, 26 December 1835, that this statement was made by him; but all other accounts attribute it to Doherty.
130 See above, pp. 104–7 and 120. Like many of the manufacturers who supported factory legislation, Hindley appears to have been primarily concerned with stopping competition from firms overworking cheap labour.
131 *Advertiser*, 12 December 1835.
132 *Ibid.*, 9 January 1836; Gill, *The Ten Hours' Parson*, p. 151. Hindley's fears about the possible effect of the bill on the export trade did not increase confidence in him; nor did the fact that his own firm had been fined for several infractions of the 1833 Act.
133 Redford, *op. cit.*, Chapter VI; Boyson, *op. cit.*, pp. 184–91.
134 See below, p. 396.
135 *Advertiser*, 23 January; *Times*, 5 March; *Stockport Advertiser*, 11 March 1836.
136 White Slavery Collection: Oastler's Letters and Cuttings, Vol. II, p. 182; *Advertiser*, 19 March 1836; *Manchester Times*, 21 October 1837.
137 Ward, *The Factory Movement*, pp. 151–3; *Times*, 9 April; *Guardian*, 14 May 1836.
138 *On the Factory Question* (Ashton, 1836), in White Slavery Collection, Vol. 15, No. 10.
139 *Advertiser*, 18 June 1836; *Address of the United Delegates . . .* (Manchester, 1836), in White Slavery Collection, Vol. 15, No. 9.
140 *Advertiser*, 9 and 16 July 1836.
141 *Ibid.*, 16 August; *Times*, 20 August 1836; Ward, *The Factory Movement*, pp. 160–2.
142 *Advertiser*, 8 and 15 October; *Bolton Chronicle*, 5 and 12 November 1836.
143 *Advertiser*, 8 October 1836. It has not been possible to discover who was appointed secretary by the Manchester Central Committee, in accordance with

the resolution of the delegate meeting on 9 July (see above, p. 389). Doherty was chairman, but appears to have conducted much of the correspondence.

[144] John Lawton claimed in 1840, however, that their appointment had led to a tightening up of factory inspection. Parl. Papers, 1840, x, 8473.

[145] *Advertiser*, 29 October 1836.

[146] The above paragraph and the two following are based on *H.O. Factory Inspectors' Reports* (Documents 5 and 7), Parl. Papers, 1837–8, xlv.

[147] See below, p. 396.

[148] *Advertiser*, 14 and 28 January 1837; *A Bill to regulate* . . . (Manchester, 1837).

[149] *Stockport Advertiser*, 17 February; *Times*, 18 February 1837.

[150] *Guardian*, 25 March 1837.

[151] *Advertiser*, 22 April 1837.

[152] *Northern Star*, 6 January 1838.

[153] *Advertiser*, 13 May 1837 and 31 March 1838. See below, p. 441.

[154] *Northern Star*, 28 April; *Advertiser*, 5 May 1838.

[155] *Debate on the Factory Question* . . ., in White Slavery Collection, Vol. 16, No. 8. During this year apparently, Doherty also printed a petition to the Commons from the Manchester central committee, stating that they were not demanding a ten-hours bill 'for the present Session', so that 'the existing Act may have such alterations in it, as that it may be a *bone fide* protection, and no longer be a mockery'. Manchester Central Ref. Library, Collection of Broadsides, f. 1836/5/B. The catalogue date 1836 is erroneous.

[156] *Hansard's Parl. Debates*, 3rd ser., Vol. 44 (9 July–16 August 1838).

[157] Parl. Papers, 1837–8, viii, 3351–3641. See above, pp. 1 and 395.

[158] Not the last hour, as commonly alleged: see N. Senior, *Letters on the Factory Act* (1837), and M. Bowley, *Nassau Senior and Classical Economics* (1937), pp. 255–8.

[159] A. Ure, *The Philosophy of Manufactures* (1835); Fielden, *op. cit.* (1836); R. Oastler, *The Factory Question and the Factory Agitation* . . ., and *A Letter to the Millowners* . . ., in White Slavery Collection, Vol. xi, Nos. 13 and 14; N. W. Senior, *Letters on the Factory Act* (1837); Greg, *op. cit.* (1837); *Misrepresentations Exposed* . . . (1838), in White Slavery Collection, Vol. 16, No. 11.

[160] Trollope, *op. cit.*, pp. 7–13; *Advertiser*, 16 February; *Northern Star*, 2 March; A. E. Musson, 'Robert Blincoe and the Early Factory System', *Derbyshire Miscellany*, February 1958, revised and reprinted in *Trade Union and Social History* (1974). W. H. Chaloner, 'Mrs Trollope and the Early Factory System', *Victorian Studies*, Vol. iv, No. 2 (December 1960), pp. 159–66.

[161] *Advertiser*, 30 May 1840; Parl. Papers, 1840, x, 8302–8621; *Northern Star*, 12 June; *Guardian*, 4 and 11 August 1841; Hodder, *op. cit.*, Vol. i, p. 359.

[162] *Advertiser*, 18 September and 9 October; *Fleet Papers*, 6 November and 23 October 1841; *Advertiser*, 8 and 15 January 1842.

[163] W. Dodd, *The Factory System Illustrated* (new edn., 1968); Smelser, *op. cit.*, pp. 299–302.

[164] *Bolton Free Press*, 20 November; *Guardian*, 27 November 1841.

[165] *Bolton Free Press*, 27 November, 4 and 11 December; *Bolton Chronicle*, 11 December; *Guardian*, 11 December 1841. This was a characteristic excuse of the *Guardian* for not printing letters revealing its own misrepresentations (cf. above, p. 318, n. 142).

[166] E. Butterworth's diary, Oldham, 3 November 1841, quoted in Foster, *op. cit.*, pp. 83, n. 15, 48 and 115.

[167] See above, p. 347.

[168] *Advertiser*, 11, 18 and 24 December 1841; *Chronicle*, 15 January 1842; *Bolton Free Press*, 31 December 1841.

[169] *Advertiser*, 22 January and 12 February 1842.

[170] *Ibid.*, 5 February; *Guardian*, 9 April; *Advertiser*, 30 April 1842.

[171] *Northern Star*, 6 August 1842. See below, p. 442.

[172] See above, pp. 312–4. Despite Doherty's denials, there seems little doubt that this scheme illustrates the links between working-class radicals and right-wing tory reactionaries in opposition to the effects of machinery and the factory system,

and to whig-liberal manufacturing and commercial interests. See Hill, *op. cit.*, Chapter v, especially pp. 171–6.

173 *Guardian*, 1 and 5 October 1842.

174 J. T. Ward and J. H. Treble, 'Religion and Education in 1843: Reaction to the Factory Education Bill', *Journal of Ecclesiastical History*, Vol. xx (1969).

175 *Guardian*, 19 April and 17 June; *Manchester Herald*, 27 May; *Advertiser*, 9 December 1843; *Fleet Papers*, 17 June and 15 July 1843.

176 W. Dodd, *op. cit.*, pp. vii–xii; *Guardian*, 17 April 1844; Diaries of Lord Ashley, Vol. ii (1843–5), quoted by permission of the Trustees of the Broadlands Archives; *Guardian*, 20 April; *Northern Star*, 1 June and 27 July; *Guardian*, 30 October and 7 December 1844; *Factory Legislation Report* . . . (Manchester, 1845).

177 J. Doherty, *A Letter* . . . (Manchester, 1845).

178 Webb Collection, Vol. xxxiv, f. 224; *Northern Star*, 25 January; *Guardian*, 8 March 1845.

179 Doherty, *A Letter* (1845).

180 For the last years of the campaign, see Ward, *The Factory Movement*, pp. 311–403.

181 *Ten Hours' Advocate*, 12 June 1847; Grant, *op. cit.*, p. 15; *Manchester Notes and Queries*, vii (1888), p. 229.

# XI    A political radical

It is well known that Doherty strongly supported the cause of radical reform in his publications, and particularly in the *Voice* during the crisis year of 1831. But it has not been realised that his involvement in radical activities began as early as, and matched in duration, his participation in trade unionism and factory reform. His basic belief in the dignity and importance of working men made him a radical rather than a moderate reformer—indeed at times of greatest excitement he was prone to use the threat of violence, though he generally supported peaceful constitutional change. He also made conflicting statements as to whether protecting wages, or abolishing competition, or acquiring political rights should be the *prime* object of the working classes. Nevertheless he always believed that it was a gross injustice for the producers of the nation's wealth to be excluded from participation in its government and that there was little chance of Parliament agreeing to the necessary social and economic reforms without a fundamental change in the interests represented therein.

Doherty's arrival in Manchester in 1816 coincided with a terrible post-war depression, which transformed the workers in the cotton industry, both hand-loom weavers and spinners, from the 'Church and King' rioters of the 1790s to enthusiastic supporters of radicals like Major Cartwright, Hunt and Cobbett, who could point to the unrepresentative Parliament, oppressive taxation, and the Corn Laws as exacerbating the suffering. The year 1817 witnessed the famous March of the Blanketeers by desperate hand-loom weavers and, although distress then abated somewhat, political excitement remained at a high level over the subsequent years culminating in ruthless official repression in 1819, the year of the Peterloo Massacre, widespread arrests and the Six Acts.[1] The tragedy of 16 August 1819, and the government's refusal to take action against the local magistrates and army officers responsible, was a constant topic in the speeches of radicals, including Doherty, for long afterwards. But Doherty himself was not present at this event, perhaps fortunately for his own personal safety in view of his fiery temper, for he had, as we have seen, been sentenced to two years' imprisonment in January 1819 for his part in the spinners' strike of the previous summer. By this time, however, Doherty was sufficiently well known in local radical circles for James Wroe, a book-seller prominent in the Manchester movement for the next two decades, to become one of his sureties, following his arrest, for his appearance at the trial. And not even imprisonment in Lancaster Castle could keep him completely quiet, for on 10 June 1820 he forwarded a petition from the Bridewell prisoners in the gaol complaining of their conditions to Robert Peel, asking him to present it to Parliament. When Peel had taken no action six weeks later, Doherty wrote to him again 'requesting him either to present it or return it, in order that it might be forwarded to some other member, who might feel himself more interested in the cause of Justice and Humanity'. Peel, who appears to have doubted the validity of the complaints, did return it, and on 12 August Doherty wrote to Hobhouse asking him to present it instead and explaining that the petitioners 'are ready and willing to prove, by affidavit, all the facts therein specified, if necessary'.[2]

During these years, financial support was organised for both political and trade-union prisoners and many towns established 'permanent relief funds' in the course of 1820. Such a fund was established by Manchester radicals, led by Evans, Candalet and Saxton, in the spring of 1820, and after reorganisation in January 1821 they aimed to provide each prisoner with 5s per week. On 7 April 1821, it was reported that £32 0s 7d had been collected over the previous quarter, and of the relief distributed £9 10s had gone to prisoners in Lancaster Castle.[3] Doherty was released at the end of January 1821, but had almost certainly been one of the recipients of this relief, as the spinners later claimed to have contributed towards a fund which relieved him with 5s weekly during his imprisonment.[4] And certainly relations between trade unionists and radicals were very close at this time, for on 23 February a public dinner was held in Bolton to celebrate the release of Robert Pilkington, Richard Kay, John Doherty and J. Shaw, 'the three first having been confined two years in Lancaster Castle for endeavouring to obtain an advance in wages, and the last one year in the same place for selling Sherwin's *Letter to the Soldiers*'. Toasts were drunk to the returned men, to 'fair profits for the manufacturer and reasonable wages to the workman', to 'the people—the only legitimate source of government', to Hunt, Wolseley and other victims, to Queen Caroline, and to the liberals in Europe.[5]

Doherty was soon closely involved in a new radical project. On 20 August 1821 the 'friends to radical reform' in Manchester met together in the Union Rooms, George Leigh Street, to discuss a letter from Henry Hunt, then imprisoned in Ilchester gaol for his part in Peterloo, in which he recommended the establishment of a 'Great Northern Union' among the radicals to amass by penny subscriptions a fund 'to secure the election of at least one honest representative' to Parliament—meaning, of course, himself. A committee of seven was appointed, including Candalet, Saxton, Cox and other prominent local radicals, who addressed a circular to northern towns requesting their opinions on the plan to be sent to a second meeting on 3 September. This assembly was attended by delegates from a number of towns in Lancashire, Cheshire and Yorkshire, while letters of support were received from others, and it was decided to establish the Union with a central committee in Manchester, strengthened by the addition of six more members, including Doherty, Pilkington and Eddy. An address 'To the Radical Reformers throughout the Empire' was adopted, urging them to support the Union because the election of Hunt 'would act as a talisman' for reform throughout the country.[6]

Over the following month, more details of Hunt's scheme emerged. Each county was to have its own central committee, Yorkshire's being organised at a Leeds meeting on 14 September. If 100,000 subscribers could be enrolled, they would raise £21,000 per year: of this, only a small amount would be needed to secure Hunt's return for Preston, where there was household

o*

suffrage, and the rest could be used to buy four nomination boroughs from their aristocratic owners for Wolseley, Cobbett, Cartwright and Wooler. Finally, at the district level, members were to be divided into groups of 100 led by 'Centurions' and sub-divided into classes of twenty led by 'Trusty Men', with subscriptions beginning after the celebrations to mark Hunt's birthday on 6 November. Enthusiastic support came from Wooler in both the *Manchester Observer* and the *Black Dwarf*, where he recalled that a similar scheme had been tried and failed in Manchester in 1819, but hoped that the examples of oppression in the meantime would encourage the reformers to greater efforts.[7]

Hunt did not publish the final particulars of his plan until 6 October, but meanwhile the Manchester central committee was very active. According to their report on 15 October, they decided that

> a Collector should be appointed to canvass the whole of the Manchester district, for enrolling the names and gathering the weekly subscriptions of those who were willing to join in aid of the projected Fund. Mr John Doherty was accordingly chosen Collector, with an allowance of 15s per week, in which office he has since been continued by the weekly voice of the Committee.

When Hunt's proposals were published in his *Memoirs*, a third general meeting of members was held in Manchester on 15 October, when Saxton reported that the committee were encouraged by progress so far and described the amount of funds raised by Doherty as being 'flattering and hopeful', considering the initial outlays of any 'infant institution'. The meeting authorised the committee to proceed along the lines recommended by Hunt and a number of collecting books were given out to 'Centurions' and 'Trusty Men'. On 30 October Cox was able to remit the first £10 from Manchester to the general funds, and by the time the committee finished its appointed half-yearly term on 21 January 1822 a total of £40 had been sent from the district; eighteen branches had also been established in other towns, although only one new central committee, at Taunton in Somerset.[8]

But, in fact, the Great Northern Union plan had caused serious divisions within the radicals. In Manchester the same individuals served upon the central committee and administered the prisoners' relief fund, and there was a similar unity at Birmingham, but on 21 January 1822 Saxton reported that in several other towns the organisers of these funds had shown a 'decided animosity' to the plan from fear of the contributions towards the 'incarcerated patriots' being reduced. Richard Carlile, himself a prisoner in Dorchester gaol, was especially hostile, declaring on 17 February that the funds of the Great Northern Union were to be applied to 'the worst of all purposes'—sending men into the present corrupt Parliament—and accusing those who sought seats in this way of doing so from 'personal vanity and ambition'. There was a particularly strong group of republican followers of Carlile at Leeds, who kept up a constant barrage of propaganda against the Union, and similar divisions eventually appeared among Manchester radicals.[9]

Although donations from Manchester and other towns continued throughout 1822, support gradually dwindled, especially with the return of more prosperous times, and there is no record of Doherty having participated in the later activities. By the end of August, Carlile was rejoicing at the Union's final failure. The original purpose can be said to have been officially abandoned in May 1823 when Cox announced that the Manchester district had donated £100 of its contributions to the Union for the cause of liberty in Spain. During the course of 1823, most of the relief funds were also wound up, as the beneficiaries were released from captivity. In December 1823 Wooler revealed that the *Black Dwarf* would in future become a work of general information, since the people had been betrayed by 'timid leaders' and 'the political character of the country is, for the present, almost at an end'. But in the following year, when he was forced to give up the publication altogether, he censured the people themselves: 'it is true that hundreds of thousands have petitioned and clamoured for reform; but the event has proved what their enemies asserted, and what the *Black Dwarf* treated as a calumny, that they only clamoured for bread'.[10]

The state of political quiescence around him did not soften Doherty's radical views and in 1825, when the Lords rejected Burdett's measure for Catholic Emancipation and the Commons passed the bill amending the repeal of the Combination Laws, Doherty wrote angrily to Francis Place on 1 July that,

> I never expected much from the Commons and my hopes are not more sanguine with respect to the Lords. Their habits, their thoughts, and feelings are too aristocratical to allow them to do much for the working classes. However, they shall have a trial. Perhaps a wish to regain public estimation, what they have so justly lost by rejecting the Catholic Relief Bill, may induce them to do us justice in this instance. The Bishops too will have an opportunity of canting about humanity, should the spirit so move them. The ministers it appears want to entangle us in the meshes of an unjust and arbitrary law, at the same time they wish us to believe that they are our best friends. The latter however they cannot do. Information is become too general among us . . . to be duped by their shallow artifices. If they will not do us justice, we shall detest them as heartily as we ever did while our increased and increasing information will enable us to prove a much greater annoyance to them than heretofore.

And he concluded, as we have seen, by threatening that workmen would form a general combination not only against their employers but also against the government if the amended bill was passed.[11]

With the onset of a renewed trade depression in 1826, intermittent meetings began to be held once more by Manchester workmen for a variety of radical causes and Doherty was almost always a participant. On 24 January 1826 about 1,500–2,000 met together in the Manor Court Room to petition Parliament for total repeal of the Corn Laws, when the main speakers were cotton spinners like Lawton, Foster, Hodgins, Doherty and Bradbury, but there were also addresses from two weavers, Rose and Longson, and from representatives of various other trades.[12] All the orators condemned the domination of the legislature by the landowning interest, by which they were enabled to preserve their corn monopoly, while foreign markets were lost to British manufactures and the suffering of working people was increased by dear bread. On this issue, it was emphasised, masters and men had a common interest. As an illustration of the distress, Doherty stated that he knew of three societies in Manchester which were raising money to emigrate to America, where they could get good wages and cheap food. The meeting adopted a petition and appointed a trades' committee to organise agitation against the Corn Laws.[13]

The spinners' leaders tried to keep up this political pressure, deploring the subsequent handloom weavers' riots against machinery in April. On 5 May, as we have seen, Doherty, Foster and Hodgins posted placards on the walls of the town, urging unemployed cotton spinners not to engage in such futile violence, but to join instead in petitioning Parliament for 'the total and immediate repeal of the Corn Laws', and also for measures to prevent irresponsible currency speculation and for retrenchment of government expenditure.[14] This agitation was rewarded by a minor relaxation in the Corn Laws when the government decided to release bonded corn from the warehouses, but distress continued unabated and on 26 October 1826 a further meeting of Manchester workmen was held to demand complete repeal, when Hodgins, Eddy, Foster, Detrosier, Brooks and Dixon were the principal figures. Doherty did not speak on this occasion, but he doubtless approved of the distinctly more bitter political tone reflected in resolutions passed not only against the Corn Laws but also against the high level of taxation generally, the wealth of the established church and the keeping of a standing army in peacetime, and in favour of retrenchment, of legislation to secure to the labourer the fruits of his industry and to the manufacturer fair profits, and above all of universal suffrage, annual parliaments and the ballot to give the people constitutional control over their legislators.[15]

An action by these legislators early in the following year considerably increased popular anger and resentment. Following the death of the Duke of York on 6 January 1827, the government proposed to increase the grant to the Duke of Clarence by £9,000 to £38,500 per annum since he now became heir to the throne. This was particularly provocative to workmen at a time when even the *Guardian* admitted that 'the labouring classes . . . are literally in a state of starvation', and on 21 February about 1,500 attended a protest meeting in the Manor Court Room. Thomas Foster took the chair and Hodgins, Brooks, Wheeler and Eddy severally pointed out that the grant originated from taxes paid by starving workmen, whose prayers for relief Parliament had ignored. But the most biting and eloquent condemnation came from Doherty, making what he himself regarded as the first major public speech of his career. He began by illustrating the melancholy state of the labouring classes with the recent case of a workman who had died in the streets of the town, literally of hunger, while fruitlessly searching for employment; and yet the *Guardian* had dared to accuse working families of improvidence for not saving something from their pittances for times like the present! What, Doherty asked, of the examples set by persons in 'higher' circles? He did not blame the Duke of Clarence who would probably spend as much as he was given, but it was the Ministers' responsibility and for it they deserved impeachment. With an honest Parliament freely elected by the people, Doherty went on, they would not have had £800 millions of debt, £60 millions of taxes, and £8 millions of tithes, nor have seen men imprisoned for poaching and boys for stealing an apple from the rich man's orchard, nor have witnessed their wives transported for stealing a few partridge eggs or taken to the tread-mill for begging, nor have experienced the 'bloody butcheries, in the presence of Parson Hay, in Peter's Field'. The chairman here asked Doherty to moderate his language, but Doherty refused to retract a syllable—'the language which he had used was not strong enough. Could they forget the butcheries of Peterloo? —when a drunken and infuriated set of wretches were turned with naked swords upon their wives and children?' And he concluded by pointing to his previous record of dissuading workmen from violence and asserting that his present advice to the government would likewise serve to keep the peace. Doherty then read out the intended petition to Parliament, protesting at the grant and again mentioning retrenchment and the Corn Laws, and sat down amidst thunderous applause. The petition was later presented and supported by Hume, but he received little backing and the grant passed through both houses virtually unhindered.[16]

With this speech Doherty began to acquire a reputation ranking him along with such men as Hodgins, Foster and Brooks as one of the leaders of radical opinion among Manchester workmen. And when the next important radical meetings were held in Manchester, later in 1827, Doherty was one of the chief organisers. At an assembly of the working classes of the town on 8 August, Dixon, Brooks, Hodgins, Foster and Oates spoke in favour of resolutions asserting that the labouring classes, though the source of all wealth, were impoverished by taxation, and therefore demanding strict government economy; declaring also that the House of Lords deserved censure for opposing the recent limited proposal for a sliding scale of corn duties, and that the 'king's prerogative was never more properly exercised' than in accepting the resignation of his late Tory ministers. The meeting was then adjourned for three weeks until 29 August, when Detrosier, Cox and Wyne supported motions for the application of the property of the established church to assist the poor, for the abolition of tithes, and against the over-issue of currency which had caused the financial crisis of 1825–6 and raised the cost of food for the hard-pressed labourer. Finally Doherty moved what he considered to be the most important resolution of all, proposing the basic remedy for all these grievances—universal suffrage, annual parliaments and the ballot. He then entered into a long description of the present constitution, theoretically a mixture of monarchy, aristocracy and democracy, but containing in reality the worst evils of all three—the expense of a monarch, who could declare war and force the people to fight and pay others to fight, the arrogance of an aristocracy, who had taken possession of all the land and claimed innumerable privileges including the right to make the nation's laws and spend the nation's money, and the most corrupt of democracies, where 474 of the 658 members of the lower house were sent there by 367 individuals, mostly peers, and the people's will was thwarted by a variety of devices which he detailed. It was because of this system of corruption that Parson Hay had been rewarded with a rich living for his actions at Peterloo rather than transported, and that the Six Acts had been passed, such as that preventing political pamphlets being published for less than 6d, which excluded the people from political knowledge.

> He would have every man a politician. No man could make a good member of society until he has been taught his rights. Politics were the peculiar science of the people and it was the duty of every man to make them his study. He was sorry to see politics excluded from mechanics' institutes— institutions peculiarly their own. The study of every other science was

permitted but this was excluded, on the plea that it would create squabbles. But this was not the fact. If a system were just it could not be too well known, and if bad, the sooner it were exploded the better.

Radical reform therefore was the only solution and not any piecemeal measures of alleviation, either in England or in Ireland.[17] And their tactics should no longer be limited to the petitioning of Parliament, which was as likely to reform itself as was a 'hungry ox' to leave 'a cloven field', but should include more decisive measures. 'He would recommend that meetings be held all over the country, to vote whether the present system should not be destroyed, and if the nation decided against it, the nation would enforce its command. To use the sublime saying of a French philosopher, 'For a nation to be free it was sufficient that she wills it.' Again, Doherty sat down amid loud applause, and it was finally agreed not to petition, but to send an address to the King, which comprehended the six resolutions adopted at the two meetings and which the organisers had composed with the help of Carlile, then on his northern tour.[18]

Despite the heat engendered at this meeting, Carlile commented on the 'contrast' and 'falling off' in the numbers attending compared with the support for radical reform in Manchester between 1817 and 1819. And it was not until 1830 that the radical reawakening occurred on anything like the former scale. Doherty, however, continued to propound his radical views. During his addresses to the public in the Manchester spinners' strike in 1829, for instance, he frequently alluded to political topics. On 27 June he admitted that the existence of £60 millions of taxes had restricted their employers' profits, but asserted that rather than wring compensation from the workmen they should instead co-operate with their men in demanding that the legislature abolish the odious Corn Laws and cut down public expenditure. And on 1 August he compared the earnings of a workmen from seventy-two hours' labour per week with a bishop's receipts of £20,000 per annum for reading an hour's discourse once a week. When he formed the National Association towards the end of that year, although he stressed that it was not a political body, he also maintained that its existence would assist the workmen to obtain their political rights, both directly in infusing them with a sense of their own importance and indirectly in forcing the employers to look for their salvation not in wages reductions but in economic reform, which a reformed Parliament alone could provide.[19] In November 1829 he told the hand-loom weavers of Bolton that, 'as regards our government, aristocracy, merchants and manufacturers, they will be indifferent to the conditions of the working classes, so long as they can procure the necessaries, comforts and luxuries of life. If unions take place the masters must come down, and when they do, they would join . . . [the men] to call upon the government to reduce taxation, remove the corn laws, the East India trade and all other monopolies'.[20]

The year 1830 saw a revival of radical activity, as parliamentary reform once more became the central issue. When, however, Doherty established the *Journal* in March 1830 as the organ of the National Association, he had to put up a pretence of excluding political news and comment so as to avoid the newspaper stamp duty. This duty, originally imposed in the early eighteenth century to restrict press criticism of the government, had been raised to 4*d* per copy by 1815, mainly to crush popular radical journals; and evasions of the duty by Cobbett, Carlile and others in the post-war political agitation had been stopped by the repressive legislation of 1819.[21] Any general newspaper, providing political and other intelligence, was now liable to this duty, which raised the price to 6*d* or 7*d*. Since this was prohibitive to working-class readers, the *Journal* had to pose as a purely trade periodical. Doherty, however, like other radicals, loathed these 'taxes on knowledge', on both general educational and political grounds.[22] Therefore, while paying lip-service to the law, he frequently expressed opposition to it. Thus, when 'A Weaver' wrote to the *Journal* on 28 April that the current strike in the silk smallware trade was partly the result of Huskisson's free-trade legislation, and went on to censure generally 'the cruel and unrelenting policies of alternate administrations of factions, called *whig* or *tory*', Doherty added a rider, begging this and future correspondents 'to abstain, as much as possible, from mixing political topics with his arguments. He must know that the law forbids us to discuss such subjects, and although we detest the law as heartily as our correspondent, we do not wish to come into contact with it.'[23]

Nevertheless, Doherty's own political views frequently found expression in the *Journal*. On 10 April he stressed the workmen's need for education to qualify them to send representatives to Parliament. On 5 June he justified the existence of the workmen's press by the necessity for publicising such bloody murders as had occurred at Peterloo. Two weeks later he printed an extract from the *Rights of Man*. And on 10 July he rejoiced that a new reign had commenced, which would witness recognition of the workman's true position in society and the abolition of the power of the contemptible Whigs and Tories. Moreover, the long reports of workmen's meetings could not avoid references to oppressions by their political as well as industrial masters. This was especially the case after the July revolution had rekindled the embers of radical fire in the hearts of workmen throughout the country.[24] On 7 August Doherty inserted an article, copied from another periodical, describing the events in France, with the excuse that these were now a matter of history rather than current political news and therefore the narrative was not illegal. But he again appended an emphatic protest against the press laws, 'these disgraceful and ignorance-creating laws', and asserted that the science of politics should be as open to discussion as any other subject of human knowledge, while it was of the greatest importance for people to know what their rulers were doing and how their taxes were expended; yet, 'such laws, however absurd they may appear, exist and although we may question their justice we must bow to their authority'. He went even further, however, on 4 September, with an editorial on 'The French Patriots'. A public meeting had been held in Manchester on 30 August, to open a subscription for the relief of the sufferers in the 'late glorious struggle', but the *Journal* was forbidden by law to advertise it previously. This prohibition, Doherty bitterly argued, was a disgrace to the age, and the working classes should petition immediately for its repeal when the new Parliament reassembled. Such censorship was even more unjust than that of the fallen Bourbons, which had applied to all alike and not just to the poor. Although aware that he was trespassing 'on dangerous ground', Doherty concluded by exhorting workmen to donate their pennies, to testify their gratitude to the noble Paris patriots for their 'unprecedented heroism in the cause of liberty', and thus to afford a 'practical refutation of the common slander that the "lower-orders", as the idiot Castlereagh insolently called them, were indifferent to, and incapable of appreciating, the blessings of freedom'.[25] Two weeks later a speech by Lord Wilton, lamenting the reduction of the people's attachment to the aristocracy, provoked a bitter riposte from Doherty against hereditary titles and the arrogance of that class which sought to keep the poor ignorant and lived off the labour of the toiling artisan, and yet had done nothing in return to compare with the inventions of Watt, Arkwright, or Bell, or the political writings of the 'unequalled and immortal Cobbett'.

These increasingly militant references to political events provided the government with justification for suppressing the *Journal* by using the Stamp Act. Early in October the Stamp Commissioners peremptorily informed the publishers that this work was a newspaper and must be registered as such, and demanded payment of duty on numbers previously published. With a threatened charge of between £400 and £500 over their heads, and the price of future numbers being inevitably prohibitive, the leaders of the National Association had no alternative but to cease publication.[26] Within a fortnight the last number of the *Journal* had appeared. Doherty, as editor, was no doubt mainly to blame, but some reference to political subjects was almost unavoidable at such a time, while the authorities, alarmed by growing trade-union radicalism, were ready to seize on any pretext to quash this outspoken periodical.

The suppression of the *Journal*, however, only further convinced Doherty of the need for an independent popular press, so from its ashes almost immediately arose the *Voice of the People*.[27] At the meeting of the Manchester district trades convened on 26 October to establish this new paper, bitter criticism was made of political oppression and of misrepresentation and bias in the stamped press. Doherty pointed out how the government—that is, the 'tax-makers, pensioners, placemen and tax-eaters in general' (following Cobbett's phraseology)—together with the employers, helped themselves to three-quarters of the product of agricultural and manufacturing labour, with the support of the 'hireling press', which depended upon these classes for sales and advertisements. The formation of an independent workmen's newspaper was therefore essential to end these iniquities and ensure the success of the National Association. A string of resolutions was unanimously carried, attributing the monopoly of legislative power by a few rich individuals to the want of knowledge among the people, asserting that the enormous taxation imposed on the press showed the necessity of radical reform, reprobating the official press, and especially the *Guardian*, for unscrupulously misrepresenting the character and actions of the operatives, and determining 'that a subscription be immediately entered into for the purpose of establishing a weekly newspaper, to be called *The Voice of the People*, devoted exclusively to the interests of the working classes'. It was finally agreed to send a petition to Parliament for the abolition of all restrictions on the press.[28] Writing to Place on 3 November, Doherty sought his support not only in the efforts being made to establish the *Voice*, but also in the campaign against 'the restrictions on the press'.[29] They were, he said, 'getting up petitions' and writing to leading members of both Houses of Parliament, seeking repeal of all laws interfering with the diffusion of knowledge. And he forwarded several parcels containing a few numbers of the *Journal*, which he asked Place to distribute to these members, 'as a sample of the work which has been suppressed' and to help persuade them to assist 'in getting the press freed from the disgraceful shackles with which it is bound'.

Doherty linked this struggle for press freedom with wider political agitation, for which he intended the *Voice* to provide outspoken expression. On 11 December, in his prospectus for the new paper, Doherty promised 'strenuous and undeviating' advocacy of universal suffrage, short parliaments, and 'above all, . . . that great security of independence, that antidote to perjury, corruption and crime—that sacred shield of freedom and key to every other political right—the VOTE BY BALLOT'.[30]

Doherty's radical activities, moreover, were not confined to journalistic forays. He also participated in local political meetings. As early as February we find him endeavouring to bring forward the subject of parliamentary reform at a public meeting in Manchester called by liberal and radical manufacturers to petition Parliament to remedy the current distress in the manufacturing districts by reducing taxes and the national debt, restricting the currency and decreasing government expenditure to the level of 1791. On this last point Doherty made a surprising speech from the floor, attacking such a measure as involving repudiation of the national debt—the burden of which he had frequently denounced; but his main aim was to turn the discussion to the necessity of 'decisive measures' to amend 'the great fault . . . the misrepresentation of the people'. When he did so, however, he was called to order by the chairman.[31]

At the same time, he continued to stress to working men the necessity for political action. In June 1830, for example, he told the Rochdale flannel weavers that whilst they should not meddle with political subjects as members of the National Association, they should most definitely consider them as individual members of society.

> He did not wish them to consider less of Radical Reform (of which he was an ardent advocate) than ever they did. Politics were the great science of Government, which every mother ought to teach her children: the object of that science was to manage the affairs of the nation—to administer the greatest quantity of happiness to the greatest number of people.

To this Benthamite dictum Doherty added another strong attack on the Corn Laws, 'which shut out the manufacturing produce of this country from foreign States which wished to exchange with us', and so prevented the prosperity and happiness of the people.[32]

The Tories were still opposed to the rising demands for parliamentary reform, but, divided and in disarray, they were at last swept from office at the elections in August 1830, following the death of George IV, and the Whigs were returned, pledged to a moderate measure of reform. Middle-class manufacturers and traders were as strongly discontented as working-class radicals at their continued exclusion from political power, and in November the Manchester Political Union was formally constituted with a council composed mainly of middle-class members like the Fieldens, Prentice and

Candalet, but also including workmen and shopkeepers usually associated with the more extreme radical cause like Detrosier, Dixon and McWilliams. In January 1831 the Union called a public meeting to welcome the government's declaration for reform and to petition in favour of an 'extended' franchise, 'shorter' parliaments, and the ballot, one of the places for signature being the *Voice* office. But even in anticipation of the ministerial measure there were deep divisions among Manchester reformers. At the November meeting, Nathan Broadhurst unfurled a tri-coloured flag among shouts of disapprobation, and on 26 January he wrote to the *Voice* that the followers of Hunt in the New Cross area, populated exclusively by workmen including many Irish weavers, had formed the Political Union of the Working Classes, determined only to accept full and radical reform.[33]

Hunt had stood for Preston in the elections of August 1830 and visited various Lancashire towns, in which supporting rallies were held. In Manchester on 16 August he chaired a Peterloo anniversary dinner in his honour, during which speeches were made by Candalet, Wroe, McWilliams, Foster and Dixon. An angry wrangle developed, however, over the theological tenets of Paine between Detrosier and Hodgins on one side and Prentice on the other, but Hunt cut short the latter by proposing another toast. Amid great tumult, the excitable Doherty, himself now a follower of Cobbett, jumped upon a table and shouted at the chairman:

> Is this the way Mr Hunt you intend to proceed? Are we to be dragooned into a compliance with your will and have toasts crammed down our throats whether we will or not? I can only say if this be the way in which you mean to prove your advocacy of the great cause of reform, the sooner you return to London the better, and the less you have to do in future with that cause the better for its success.[34]

Doherty and many other Manchester radicals were evidently more moderate reformers than the 'Huntites' and more inclined towards alliance with the middle-class Political Union. These divisions temporarily disappeared, however, at the end of the year amongst the excitement caused by Hunt's return to Parliament after a second contest with the Whig, Stanley, at Preston. On 28 December 'Mr Hunt's Friends' in Manchester met to discuss ways of contributing towards the Lancashire subscriptions being raised for the election expenses, and Doherty, who had spoken at the meeting, was requested along with Candalet and Whittle to appoint collectors. On New Year's Day 1831 Hunt made a triumphal entry into Manchester and attended another dinner, during which his Preston organiser, Mitchell, regretted the recent differences and Doherty 'apologised for having offended anyone at the last dinner . . .; and said that they had now got the man of the people, the *Voice of the People*, and would propose that they might have speedily—"The People's day"'. But the arguments were to re-emerge with increased asperity later in the year over the Reform Bill.[35]

In his first editorial in the *Voice*, Doherty declared that the cause of rational liberty was progressing throughout Europe, and the first blow on its behalf had been struck in England by the people of Preston in electing Henry Hunt to Parliament. Now was the most crucial time for the people's voice to be heard, that they might not be excluded from the important changes in the system of representation which were about to be made. Only by employing the moral force of a 'united people' could this be achieved, for 'no power could control it, no authority could crush it, and all usurped power trembled at it'.[36]

The early numbers of the *Voice* teemed with accounts of reform meetings throughout the country, and editorial comment ranged from condemnation of the Corn Laws and the established church to support for the French, Belgian and Polish patriots and onto the 'dangerous ground' of the Special Commissions to try the 'Swing' rioters, whose guilt, Doherty alleged, was infinitely less than that of the borough-mongers responsible for the prevailing distress. And his suspicion of the Whigs increased when, instead of abolishing the taxes on knowledge, they initiated prosecutions against Cobbett, Carlile and Carpenter, and when Althorp's first budget in February merely made a derisory reduction in the civil list, which proved to Doherty that no re-trenchment was possible until the commons was '*radically* reformed' and that the people should refuse to pay taxes until they were represented. Interest in reform was now at such fever pitch that when a meeting was convened at Oldham on 1 February in a room above an Independent Methodist chapel and addressed by Doherty, Knight, Fitton, Prentice and Hodgins, the roof threatened to collapse under the weight of numbers and the assembly had to be adjourned. But analysis could replace speculation after 1 March when the Whig measure of reform was finally introduced. Doherty was agreeably surprised. The bill admittedly contained no clause to benefit the wealth-producers, for none occupied a house at a rental of £10 per annum, nor would they have the security of the ballot or shorter parliaments; but at least the power of 168 borough-mongers would be abolished and above all 'the principle will be recognised and the way will thus be paved for other and more useful reforms'. Over the following weeks he urged the people to support 'the whole bill', although asserting they should demand radical reform if the bill was 'mutilated', and when the measure was defeated on 20 April Doherty angrily warned the ministers then considering their next move that 'the people's only alternative mode to petitioning was to fight'.[37]

On the other hand, Henry Hunt constantly asserted in the Commons that the bill was irrelevant to the needs of the working classes (although he voted in its favour), and in April he declared that Lancashire workpeople were universally hostile to the measure. Doherty, therefore, in an editorial on 9 April, while praising Hunt's past efforts in the people's cause, criticised his present ambivalent attitude. The working classes were quite aware, he stated, that the bill did nothing directly for them, but they were also convinced that, 'so long as the base borough-mongers—the traffickers in the most sacred rights of their countrymen—hold their present usurped and unconstitutional power, there can be neither amelioration of their condition, a reduction of their burdens, nor happiness to their country. They therefore rejoice at the adoption of anything which tends to strip them of their corruptly-obtained power. . . . The bill, then, should have the undivided support of every friend of the people.' On 19 April he persuaded the Manchester committee of the National Association to adopt a petition to Parliament that they supported the Reform Bill as a first step. And when during the following week handbills were posted on the walls of the town copying an article from the *Leeds Patriot* in which

John Foster asserted that Doherty's criticism of Hunt was a departure from his former professions to be a radical reformer, Doherty replied that he had merely pointed out that Hunt was in error and repeated that the operatives should 'look to no man or set of men. Rely only upon yourselves, and your cause must ultimately triumph.'[38]

To many Manchester workmen, however, Hunt was still an idol and the strength of his support was made clear when Hunt passed through the town once more on 1 May on his way to the Preston elections. The accompanying procession jeered as loudly when it passed the *Voice* offices as before those of other newspapers, and at an impromptu meeting on St Peter's Field Hunt secured the crowd's support for his statement that that paper had not for the last fortnight spoken 'the voice of the people' in its censure of him, and that the editor, who had acquired his situation with the money of the labourers, should now be replaced. Doherty then stood boldly forward in his own defence, asserting that he had been a lifelong supporter of Hunt and radical reform and should continue to be so, but repeated his opinion that the abolition of sixty rotten boroughs must bring some improvement and that the workmen must support the bill as a first step. He agreed that petitioning was useless, but the alternative of an appeal to arms was equally counterproductive.

> What I wish to see is a moral revolution, not a bloody and sanguinary one. We have seen revolutions, but even when successful, have we not seen them fail in producing their intended objects? Revolutions have been successful, but the leaders of them have become in turn themselves the most unprincipled tyrants, and crushed every man who had the honesty to oppose them. True, a glorious Revolution has lately been effected in France, but even that has been filched from the people. A few Paris bankers have succeeded in cheating them out of the revolution for which they fought, and wormed themselves into power.

Doherty went on that, to prove he was a radical, he was about to propose a scheme whereby the people might yet get the vote without opposing the bill; but before he could go on, Hunt asserted that they had heard enough and the crowd shouted Doherty down. Later Oates defended free press comment and criticised Hunt's treatment of 'a lifelong reformer, who had sacrificed his whole time and almost his health to his devotion to the interests of the working classes', but he too was howled down by cries of, 'Who kept us out of work three months longer than we should have been? Doherty! Who makes a living out of the pockets of the people? Doherty!' At the subsequent meeting of the Manchester committee of the Association on 10 May, there was some further criticism of Doherty, but he eventually secured a vote of confidence both for his conduct as editor and for his attitude to the Reform Bill. Nevertheless, with ministers having dissolved Parliament following their defeat and the subsequent elections having vindicated the cause of reform, Doherty was about to embark upon a new policy, as he hinted at the above meeting.[39]

Doherty's views on whether political reform was the basic improvement needed by the working classes were subject to fluctuation. Although he referred frequently to the significance of politics, he was inclined to put more

trust in the workers' own trade-union organisations and in their efforts at
co-operative production; in any case, union must come first. He told a meeting
of Manchester dyers on 3 November 1830, for example, that 'much might be
said about parliamentary reform and supporting their rights—fine speeches
might be made on that subject; but if they could not get a sufficiency of food
for themselves and [their] families, their political rights would not be worth
having—if wages sunk and were depreciated in value, their rights would be
gone'. And on 24 May 1831 he stated to the Manchester committee that 'if
reform passed tomorrow, the workman would be little bettered, for competition would still produce its evils'. But despite his conversion to co-operation
at this time, he continued to regard the acquisition of political rights as one
of the important benefits which would accrue to workmen from the establishment of a general union, as, for example, in his 'Appeal to the Producers
of the Wealth' on 4 and 11 June.[40] On 7 May, therefore, he proposed a scheme
whereby those rights might be procured then and there : meetings were to be
forthwith held in 300 of the largest towns in the kingdom to elect two delegates each to meet together in London on 14 June, the first day of the new
Parliament, to present loyal addresses to the King for dissolving the late
Parliament and to petition the government to extend the household male
suffrage as at Preston to the whole kingdom. Such an assembly would not be
illegal, but the presence of 600 determined delegates was bound to overawe
both ministers and borough-mongers, and it could be achieved if each workman would but subscribe 3d to 'the Operatives' Franchise Fund'. And on 9
May Doherty sent out a circular to leading workmen in the largest towns
of the north and midlands asserting the importance of his plan and the
urgency of acting upon it immediately. In a further editorial on 14 May he
urged the workmen to drop even their demands for short parliaments and the
ballot in a single effort for the franchise and denied that his plan could hurt
the Reform Bill.  He was certain that the enemies of the people would not
resist by force, but if they did, 'are we not in as good a condition to fight
them now as we shall be at any other period? If we are to have recourse to
force at all, it may as well be soon as late.'[41]

The project was greeted by the orthodox press with universal derision. The
*Sheffield Iris* and the *Manchester Guardian* attributed it to a desire of the
'faction of which Mr Hunt and Mr Doherty are the head and tail' to prevent
the Reform Bill from passing, since they knew that it would eliminate their
lucrative occupation of 'agitating'. The *Manchester Times and Gazette* likened
it to a 'wild goose chase'. *The Nottingham Review* believed it to be a 'new
stratagem of the Tories'. Even the *Manchester and Salford Advertiser* feared
that it would jeopardise the chances of the ministerial measure. And the
*Leeds Patriot* would support no plan that did not envisage universal suffrage.
In addition, there were strong protests from some trade unionists against
Doherty's raising this proposal at such a critical time for the Reform Bill, and
he quickly had to deny any intention to use the Association to forward the
scheme.[42] Nevertheless, Doherty claimed on 21 May that most of the north-
western towns were proceeding with alacrity and advised that each meeting
should pass a resolution approving of the Reform Bill '*as far as it goes*', to
remove any possible doubt.[43]

A series of meetings was now convened in towns surrounding Manchester.

Doherty spoke at Stockport, Preston, Bolton and Chorley during late May and early June, emphasising the necessity for independent political action by the working classes, but arguing against demanding universal suffrage because the Preston franchise was all they could realistically hope to obtain. Despite some differences of opinion, resolutions were passed in favour of his delegate scheme and delegates were appointed from these and several other Lancashire towns where meetings were held.[44]

Meanwhile, little headway was made in Manchester itself. Doherty claimed at Preston that his scheme had been sanctioned by the Political Union of the Working Classes, but at a delegate meeting called by that body on 27 May it was agreed that the London delegates should support universal suffrage, annual parliaments and the ballot. Nevertheless on 11 June a notice appeared in the *Voice*, signed by twenty-two individuals including representatives of the Political Union of the Working Classes like Edward Curran and William Brooks and some of the more radical members of the middle-class body including Elijah Dixon and James Cox, convening a public meeting of the productive classes for 13 June on St Peter's Field to discuss the election of delegates to address the King and petition for the Preston suffrage; and Doherty hoped that the workmen would come forward even 'at the eleventh hour', though he advised that no attempt be made at all unless it was general. In the event, however, the meeting did little to resolve the confusion of purpose. Brooks, Curran, Dixon and Ashmore all spoke in favour of the most radical reform, and Doherty made a bitter speech denouncing the middle classes for refusing to attend a meeting where the workmen's interests were involved and yet expecting them unselfishly to support a bill from which they were excluded. He advised the workmen not to demand the ballot under the present bill, for open voting would allow them to influence those shopkeepers who fancied themselves to be 'dirty little . . . aristocrats', by exclusive dealing. If the Preston suffrage were obtained, they would be enabled to ensure for themselves that men like G. W. Wood, 'a sly, crafty, creeping whig', or Hugh Birley, the villain of Peterloo, were never elected. He confessed that his opinions on the Reform Bill were 'a little changed' when he saw the indifferent attitude towards them of those that were to be enfranchised, and concluded with an appeal that the operatives should display the same spirit as their continental counterparts. Finally it was agreed that two delegates should be appointed to present the address and the petition, which contained a compromise formula demanding that the producers be granted 'a fair share in the representation of the country, shielded by the ballot and short parliaments'. The deliberations ended in more confusion, however, when Prentice asked why 'annual' parliaments should not be the policy, called the whole delegation plan absurd, and referred to the platform party as 'unfledged reformers', at which Doherty angrily recalled in refutation his imprisonment as long ago as 1819.[45]

Press opinion in Manchester declared this assembly a 'miserable failure'. Only 1,500 attended according to the *Guardian* and they displayed more interest in a dog-fight than in the speeches of Doherty, Dixon and Co., while *Wheeler's Manchester Chronicle* quoted the prayer of 'one old man' who heard the speeches that 'Lord help us and our country, if we are to be managed by poor ignorant drivelling quacks like these'. A week later, however, at another meeting called by the Political Union of the Working Classes, supporters of the plan elected Curran and Brooks as delegates, and they proceeded to London on 21 June along with Meikle from Blackburn. But Doherty apparently retained his opinion that a partial application of the project was worse than nothing and did not participate in these later proceedings. And on 30 June he announced his abandonment of the whole attempt. This took place at a meeting called by the middle-class Political Union to protest against a new clause in the Reform Bill to exclude from voting those who paid the requisite rent at less than half-yearly intervals. Richard Potter took the chair and Candalet, Whittle and Prentice spoke on behalf of a resolution condemning the new clause. But Dixon, Ashmore, Gilchrist and McLoughlin supported amendments for radical reform, and when Potter refused to put them they demanded his removal from the chair. Doherty opposed this step, asking the protesters if they believed that the workmen were prepared to make an effort for universal suffrage when their response to his delegation scheme had been so feeble. Only Manchester, Stockport and Blackburn, and perhaps shortly Preston and Leeds, had sent delegates, while the total subscriptions did not yet reach £12; he could not therefore in conscience press on with the plan. Doherty proposed a second amendment that 'this meeting regrets that the ministerial reform bill should have been so framed as to exclude from its engagements the producers of the nation's wealth. Believing, however, that the bill, as originally framed, was a step towards obtaining a better representation, they gave it their cordial support, but could not for a moment assent to the alteration introduced in the bill.' But Potter ruled this motion out of order also and amid the usual turbulent scenes the original resolution was carried by a substantial majority.[46]

Doherty's admission of failure provoked 'An Old Radical' to write to the *Manchester Times and Gazette* on 9 July that,

> though I give him credit for being a sincere reformer, I cannot give him credit for having one of the wisest heads on his shoulders. He calculated that about 600 delegates might be sent up to London by the opening of parliament and that these delegates would strike such awe into the souls of the borough-mongers, that they would almost instantly grant us all we asked. On reading the announcement of this scheme, I said, Mr ——— is scheming again—he is always scheming for the good of the working classes, but unfortunately none of his schemes produce any benefit. The delegation scheme was puffed, and puffed—and it has ended in smoke! Even the reviver of this scheme, for he is not the inventor, has acknowledged its complete failure, though he has attributed that failure to the working classes.[47]

Although Doherty was no longer officially connected with the delegates, he reported their activities in London, reacting with predictable anger when Hunt presented their petition on 8 July and Benjamin Heywood, the Lancashire member, asserted that radical reform would lead to 'the destruction and starvation of the working classes themselves', to which Doherty replied that to refuse any man a vote in the making of laws by which he was governed was an 'act of outlawry'. On 23 July he reported a statement by Benbow, in a lecture to the Manchester Political Union of the Working Classes during the week, that the deputies had not been favourably received by O'Connell or

Hume. And on 20 August he copied the congratulatory address sent by Curran, Brooks and Meikle to the 'Brave Parisians' and also the reply received. On 27 July, while in London, Doherty himself appeared with them at a meeting of the National Union of the Working Classes at the Rotunda, where he maintained that 'the day is not far distant when we shall assume our station in society . . . and no longer be called "the rabble" ', denounced the salary of the Queen as an insult to the wealth-producers, and predicted that if the government continued to ignore their desire, 'Swing' would commence again and 'his devastation will be still more terrible'.[48]

Despite the violence of his language, Doherty still supported the Reform Bill over the subsequent two months as a necessary first step, and when it passed the Commons early in September Doherty hoped that it would succeed also in the upper chamber, for he feared that an appeal to arms would be the 'inevitable consequence of the reform bill being rejected by the House of Lords'. On 24 September he censured the leaders of the 'Manchester Hunt party' for interrupting the meeting called by the middle-class Political Union two days earlier to petition the Lords to pass the bill, for only by the people presenting a united front would the reactionaries give way and there was no alternative to supporting the bill since the delegation plan 'was not answered as we expected'. Hence Doherty was particularly outraged when the Lords did reject the bill on 8 October and he later wrote that he regarded that day 'as being probably the start of a frightful and sanguinary revolution'. He was again in London at the time, trying to arrange the transfer of the Voice, and on 17 October he made a very violent speech to the National Union of the Working Classes, while supporting a resolution, moved by Watson and seconded by Benbow, recommending the government to proceed with a radical reform measure immediately. Doherty asserted that the power of Whigs or Tories would be as nothing if the people once united their numbers. He had hitherto advocated the bill to the best of his abilities, believing that 'more could not be had at the time without shedding some of the best blood in England; but now that the reform bill was rejected, he would, as far as his influence could extend, recommend the insisting upon a whole bill . . . that would give universal satisfaction, and he knew the country possessed the power, the means, aye and the inclination too of obtaining it. The lion of England was roused—the spirit was up, and it merely rested with the union prudently to direct it.' Doherty recalled the conduct of the Irish Catholics, which he recommended the workmen to follow by holding simultaneous meetings throughout the kingdom on 1 November; for such a display of moral force by one million men would render it immaterial whether the Whigs were the ministers or not. All that was necessary was for the capital to give the lead.[49]

Francis Place certainly believed that Doherty was making a serious proposition to the working people to come out and fight. From their correspondence in 1825 and 1829, Place already believed Doherty to be 'a very extraordinary man, . . . a rigid uncompromising intolerant Irish Catholic, altogether a wrong-headed, singularly obstinate man'. Now with Doherty acting in concert with a 'congenial spirit' in William Benbow, Place described him as 'one of the most narrow-minded of Irish bigoted roman catholics, one of the most malignant men I ever knew'. The two men met privately over the newspaper business and Doherty repeated the views expressed at the Rotunda. Place replied that it was absurd to expect the workmen to be able to defeat the army, that the workpeople had never accomplished any national movement without the aid of the middle classes, and that he was insane to suppose any change could be affected by force. According to Place, Doherty acknowledged that they had never formed a national union, but they were now organised and determined to have their rights, 'and . . . if it were possible they could fail it were better to be slain in the attempt than to go on as their enemies the wealth-accumulators now made them go, in misery unmitigable, and as they intended perpetually'.[50]

It is likely, in fact, that because of his personal dislike of Doherty, Place mistook violent language for violent intent. True, Doherty had recommended a general strike to workmen in September[51]—though it is impossible to discover whether this proposal originated with Doherty or Benbow—and the inflammatory tone was, as we have seen, fully maintained during 1832 in the *Poor Man's Advocate*. But he did not participate apparently in any of the proceedings organised by the 'Huntites' in Manchester during this period, for his name was not mentioned in connection with the 'simultaneous meetings' held in several Lancashire towns on 28 October 1831 to support the 'Declaration of Rights' adopted by the National Union of the Working Classes, nor with the so-called National Convention which met in Manchester during December, nor with the series of Sunday meetings held in January 1832 which were held on the Sabbath to allow factory workers, locked in their 'Bastilles' on all other days, to attend. The authorities retaliated by arresting the leaders of the Manchester Political Union of the Working Classes, and in March 1832 Gilchrist, Curran, Ashmore and Broadhurst were sentenced to one year's imprisonment for 'unlawful assembling'. Doherty's only connection with the 'Huntites' at this time ran counter to these activities. On 12 December he was one of an organising committee which convened a meeting of unemployed workmen in St George's Fields by the issue of a strongly-worded placard headed 'Bread! Bread! Bread!', which led the authorities to believe that an attack on the bakers' shops was intended and the military, special constables and police were called out in readiness. But Doherty cautioned those in attendance against saying anything that could lead spies to betray them, 'and observed that an unarmed multitude could do nothing against an armed force'. And when Broadhurst and Gilchrist moved a vote of censure on the 'venal Press', Doherty 'complained much of the introduction of this extraneous resolution'. Nevertheless he agreed that the unemployed should be advised not to deal with any tradesman who advertised in the *Guardian*, while a petition to Parliament 'demanding' relief was also adopted. Two days later his differences with this group were shown even more clearly when he seconded a motion at a meeting of the middle-class Manchester Political Union that Joseph Hume rather than Hunt should present their intended reform petition, for Doherty 'did not think that Mr Hunt represented him'.[52]

In fact Doherty's principal political activity over the next year was to prepare the local workmen to exert what influence they possessed to ensure a suitable candidate was returned when Manchester held its first election under the Reform Bill. He had begun to speculate as to who would be an adequate representative as early as March 1831, when the *Spectator* had published a list of eighteen possible candidates including G. W. Wood, a man whom Doherty claimed had gone to London in 1828 to demand that the qualification for voting in the new Manchester Police Bill should be twice as high as intended in the Reform Bill.[53] Doherty preferred the claims of 'real friends of the people' like Richard Potter or Dr John Bowring, and over the following months he published regular editorials in support of the latter, whom he described as the 'able' editor of the masterly *Westminster Review*. On 9 April he printed a letter in commendation of such a choice from Jeremy Bentham, 'a gentleman whose name is a sufficient passport to the confidence of every sincere friend of freedom in every part of the globe'. On 30 May Doherty wrote to Bowring stating that, 'if some of your friends, particularly Mr Bentham, would furnish me with some of the leading facts of your past exertions in the cause . . . of good government and happiness in this country and all others, it will be attended with a good deal of advantage. For the people . . . now ask . . . of every man who may be put forward in their representation—"Who is he?—What has he done?".' Two weeks later Bentham replied, describing Doherty's letter as 'a beautiful proof of the warmth of your zeal and of the judgement with which it is guided', and detailing Bowring's writings in the cause of liberty on the continent and in England, where he opposed the Corn Laws and corporation abuses and supported religious freedom, education and peace. At the same time, Doherty poured scorn on the candidate being brought forward in the Whig-liberal interest, Mark Philips, whose political abilities Doherty believed to be 'mediocre', while as a merchant and manufacturer he was not only the partner of G. W. Wood but more qualified for the role of a 'legal swindler' than a statesman.[54]

Although Bowring assisted the *Voice* by providing gratuitous copies of his periodical, Doherty's enthusiasm for him waned over the summer when he found that Bowring would give no pledge 'even for the reduction of the interest on the debt', and in the end he formally withdrew his support, sacrificing, according to James Whittle, 'all the ties of personal feeling to his sense of public duty'. Moreover, a new candidate was in the field in William Cobbett, whom Doherty unreservedly admired and could recommend to the Manchester voters without qualification. He reported with increasing optimism the results of the canvass undertaken by a committee for Cobbett in Manchester whose leading members were Whittle, Dixon and one James Howie, and on 17 September the *Voice* printed 'Mr Cobbett's Address to the Electors of Manchester' advocating rigid retrenchment, drastic cuts in taxation and the discharge of the debt within two years by selling off church and crown property. His return, Doherty argued, would rectify the evil consequences of the 'omissions' in the Reform Bill; and later he counselled the workmen to follow Cobbett's advice and obtain pledges on 'the great, the fundamental question of the debt' and that candidates should vote for an 'equitable adjustment' and for a reduction of 'the ruinous load of taxation' which the debt had imposed upon workmen.[55]

On 24 March 1832 he gave notice in the *Advocate* that he was to publish on 31 March the first number of a new monthly periodical, to be priced 1d and entitled the *Anti-Borough-monger* or *the Poor Man's Key to the Elections*. Its object would be 'to stimulate the working and middle-classes of society to unite their exertions, and make common cause, to elect only proper persons at the first election under the reform bill. The editor will endeavour to point out the means by which the working classes may greatly influence, if not wholly control, the issue of the elections.' A fearless investigation was promised into the merits of all the candidates in the manufacturing districts as well as the nature of the pledges that were to be required. And he concluded that 'the total and immediate annihilation of the debt will be the chief feature on which the strictures of this publication will be founded'. Publication had to be postponed for several weeks owing to the disruption caused by Doherty's removal to new premises in Withy Grove and the refusal of other printers to touch it, but the first number did appear on 1 May and was advertised for sale in the *Crisis* and the *Manchester and Salford Advertiser*. But no successor was possible amid Doherty's personal troubles with the Gilpin affair and even the first edition is not extant.[56]

At this juncture, planning for the future election was rudely shattered by a new crisis when the Lords again rejected the Reform Bill on 7 May. The middle-class reformers in Manchester thereupon succeeded in gaining the allegiance of the vast majority of workmen, save for a few who supported Brooks and the rump of the Political Union of the Working Classes, to a new Reform Association uniting all classes on a programme of 'no taxation without representation'. But the show of strength in the country and the threatened creation of new peers brought the Lords to their senses, the bill was reintroduced and rapidly passed all its stages by the beginning of June. Flushed with success, the Manchester middle classes then disgracefully betrayed their working-class allies and withdrew from the new Association, with the single exception of John Fielden. The society was continued by its more radical supporters, with Thomas Oates as secretary and Doherty's shop one of the places where it could be joined, and its principal activity comprised organising support for Cobbett in the forthcoming elections. Doherty was in gaol during July, but he resumed his political activities on his release towards the end of August. He was among the sellers of a reform sermon given by Rev. J. W. Morris on the anniversary of Peterloo, while in the *Advocate* on 11 August he copied an address from the Council of the Chorlton-upon-Medlock and Hulme Political Union recommending exclusive dealing, and two weeks later he printed a further letter from Cobbett to the Manchester electors critical of Philips' policy of repealing the Corn Laws without a commensurate reduction in all other taxes.[57]

From September, as we have seen, Doherty restyled the *Advocate* as a political paper, with a different title and publisher each week to avoid the stamp tax. Its main object, as in the *Anti-Borough-monger*, was to show the workmen how they could secure the return of Cobbett in the December elections, in which he was to be opposed by two liberal Whigs, Poulett Thomson and Mark Philips, and two Tories, Samuel Hope and James Loyd. On 8 September Doherty wrote that the forthcoming elections would decide whether the debt was to be abolished and public expenditure reduced to £5 millions per year, 'the very essence of the cure of all disasters and all our grievances', or if the Reform Bill was to prove 'a mere mockery' and they would have to gain 'these self-evident rights by the sword'. The workmen were to effect their object by refusing to deal with any tradesman who would not promise to vote for a candidate pledged to these improvements, and on 29 September he angrily attacked those who insulted the working classes by calling this tactic an 'intimidation of voters'. Meanwhile at the beginning of September, Cobbett himself gave a series of lectures in Manchester and was regularly interrupted by a Whig lecturer named Charles Wilkins imported into the town from Newark. Wilkins challenged Cobbett to a public debate on 12 September at the Exchange Dining Rooms, but Cobbett refused to appear and his reputation was defended instead by Doherty, who subsequently asserted in the *Advocate* of 22 September that Wilkins was in the pay of the government and accused him of moral and financial improprieties in his home town, but predicted that his 'machinations' could not prevent Cobbett from being elected. Wilkins replied in the *Times and Gazette* on 6 October that the charges made by Doherty, 'the Sancho Panza of the little Don Quixote', were libellous but he would not raise his publication from obscurity by prosecuting.

> I am sure that this sort of good-for-nothing Patlander was once a very serviceable character in his own country; and, as I do not choose to spoil a decent swine-herd, by raising him on the horn of a prosecution to a reputed patriot and martyr in the cause of liberty, I shall not honour him by an introduction to one of his majesty's justices, but content myself by assuring him that, clever as he may be in his original calling, on the present occasion he has got the wrong pig by the ear.[58]

On 10 October Doherty succeeded in forming a discussion society, which was to meet weekly in the dyers' room chiefly to debate how workmen could influence the elections. Doherty was appointed to the management committee of the society, whose motto declared that 'as the working classes are the great producers of all wealth, they ought . . . to be in possession of abundance of the comforts and conveniences of life'. Doherty took the chair at the first meeting on 16 October, when the subject was the Manchester election candidates, and not surprisingly it was agreed to recommend Cobbett. A fortnight later Philip Grant occupied the chair, while the company debated 'what are the most efficient means of securing the return of Mr Cobbett' and Doherty and Dixon strongly advocated exclusive dealing. Irish questions were discussed for the next three weeks, but on 27 November the question was, 'Is universal suffrage the right of every man unstained with crime?' and on 4 December the meeting considered, 'Whether the sending of members to parliament from Manchester would benefit it?'. Doherty was forced to miss these last two meetings as he was again in gaol, and with his inspiration removed no more assemblies were convened. Attendances were in any case very small, the numbers present at the first discussion—about a hundred—never being exceeded.[59]

Doherty was only once reported as taking a public part in any of the numerous election meetings in the two months before the actual contest. When Philips came to Shudehill on 17 October, he was asked a series of questions by an agent of Samuel Hope, who was interrupted by Doherty asking the audience whether they should allow 'questions to be put to a candidate who had chosen to come before them by the hired servant of . . . any other candidate who had not chosen to condescend to appear before them for the purpose of being interrogated'. Later Doherty himself asked if Philips would advocate the abolition of the financial qualification for members of parliament, and the candidate replied in the affirmative. Despite this friendly exchange, some hint of the basis for the future Tory–radical alliance in the city did appear in Doherty's abuse of Thomson and Philips in the *Advocate* of 6 October as supporters of the 'free trade schemes for the benefit of leading capitalists'. Nevertheless, L. S. Marshall has shown that this alliance was not numerically significant in the actual voting in December, 302 electors 'splitting' between Cobbett and Hope, 111 between Cobbett and Loyd; and in the event the two liberal candidates were returned with fairly substantial majorities.[60]

Doherty's activities during 1832 were hampered by a long-lasting legal entanglement, the ramifications of which stretched over the last nine months of the year and seemed at one time to threaten him with ruin. Towards the end of 1831, the body of a man named Perry was stolen from the graveyard of St Thomas's Church in Stockport and a strong rumour developed that the minister, the Rev Martin Gilpin, was implicated in the theft because his brother-in-law, a medical man, had two or three years before been discovered in possession of the body of an Irishman taken from another churchyard in the town. On 30 November 1831 Gilpin was forced to write to the *Stockport Advertiser* to deny the story and he began an action for damages against a rope manufacturer called Bates who repeated it. This case was settled by private arbitration and later in August 1832 Bates publicly acknowledged that the story was untrue; but in the meantime the whole proceeding had been narrated to Doherty as fact by Thomas Worsley. Anxious to expose what he considered to be the scandalous disregard for the feelings of the poor in the 'Sale of Dead Bodies Bill', and not inclined to overlook a chance to attack the abuses of the established church, and more especially a representative who was the minister at a government church built with taxpayers' money and also the chaplain of his local Orange Order, Doherty published the entire account, embellished with typically vitriolic prose, in an article headed 'Clerical Resurrectionism' in the *Advocate* on 31 March 1832. Shortly afterwards Gilpin came to Doherty's shop in the company of his attorney and threatened him with a libel prosecution if he did not make a public retraction and surrender his informant. Assured by Worsley that the allegations were correct, Doherty refused both demands, and indeed on 21 April warned that he would 'rake up the filthy stories and scandalous proceedings which have come to our ears' if Gilpin persisted. In retaliation Gilpin sent men round to all the booksellers in Manchester and Stockport demanding that they should cease to sell the *Advocate* and obtained a criminal information against Doherty in the King's Bench on 26 April. Doherty travelled to London on 8 May and, on complaining that he had insufficient time to prepare his evidence, succeeded in having the rule enlarged until the first day of the next legal term; but he had to promise to publish no more libels in the meantime. Nevertheless this did not prevent Doherty complaining in the *Advocate* on 19 May of the manner in which Gilpin was proceeding against him, by which he incurred the maximum expense and could not claim the truth of his assertions as a defence. These arguments he repeated in the King's Bench when the case came on once more on 26 May, but Gilpin's counsel declared that 'if a man was poor, he should take care not to write atrocious libels' and the Judge, believing that sufficient grounds had been shown to send the case to a jury, therefore made the rule absolute.[61]

These events aroused violently conflicting emotions in the press. The Tory *Stockport Advertiser* asserted that the charges were 'a tissue of falsehoods from beginning to end' and denounced the *Poor Man's Advocate* as a 'weekly vehicle of sedition and slander, professedly printed by *Mister* Doherty', who was one of that 'vile and unprincipled knot of infidel demagogues' who made daily attempts to 'overturn the established religion of this country'. The paper trusted that 'the highly respected and benevolent minister' would exact the 'utmost penalties of the law' from the 'vile miscreant' as an example to his breed. But the radical *Manchester and Salford Advertiser* maintained on 12 May that even in the present crisis of public affairs, the second Reform Bill having just been rejected, it was the duty of workmen to exert themselves to defend individuals who were persecuted for advocating the people's rights. It reported that a committee of workmen had been formed at a meeting on 7 May to collect donations towards Doherty's expenses; it sat each Saturday in the 'Royal Oak', Market Street, and subscriptions were also received at radical shops and inns at Stockport, Bolton, Leeds, Mansfield, Huddersfield, Nottingham and London. Moreover, Doherty showed continued defiance on 9 June by rashly printing a poem which became the subject of a second charge against him:

> Jesus and G–lp–n, so 'tis said,
> Both in their turn have rais'd the dead;
> One gave them back to light and life,
> The other to the surgeon's knife.

During the subsequent week he should have appeared in the King's Bench again to plead, but was unable to raise the necessary funds for a third journey to the capital and on 22 June a warrant was issued for his arrest. On 25 June he was taken into custody and lodged in the New Bailey, from where he wrote a succession of letters to the *Advocate* detailing the disgusting conditions and the brutal and oppressive treatment of the prisoners by the turnkeys, a state of affairs which he maintained cried out for reform. Nor was his temper improved when he complained to the governor of lice in his bed and was told that they 'might not have been there before I came', a proper reply to which would have been 'a solid argument between the eyes'. On 28 June he was transferred to Lancaster Castle where he found conditions more tolerable, but continued to rage against the injustice of a poor man being imprisoned without even being convicted of any offence.[62]

It was thought that Doherty would have to remain in gaol until judgement was given in November, unless bail could be raised of £80 for himself and two sureties in £40 each, and in these circumstances both trade unionists and reformers, whether radical or moderate, rallied to his support. On 30 June the *Advocate* copied an appeal for subscriptions 'To the operative cotton spinners of Glasgow' by Patrick McGowan, who declared that 'Mr Doherty's whole life has been devoted to promote the interests of that class to which he belongs', and in the following week the *Glasgow Trades' Advocate* recommended this appeal to the operatives of the town generally. On 25 July a public meeting was held at the 'Royal Oak', Manchester, to launch a special appeal amongst local factory workers. On 4 August Doherty's old adversary, Prentice, endorsed this subscription in a long editorial denouncing the libel laws. At the same time, as we have seen, the Manchester short-time committee was itself organising support. And on 1 August it was reported that trade unionists in Sutton-in-Ashfield were collecting for a 'man who has so strongly advocated our cause' in both the *Voice* and the *Advocate*. The first list of subscriptions was advertised on 4 August and continued for the rest of the year. During that time a total of £88 12s 0½d was donated, mainly by the Manchester spinners' union and by additional collections among spinners and dressers at individual factories, but smaller sums were also sent from Glasgow, Sutton and Warrington and the long list of individual subscribers included the Fieldens, the Potters, David Holt, Dixon, John Knight, Blincoe, Candalet, Brotherton, Daniel, Wroe, Rigby and the musician Paganini.[63]

These donations went towards Doherty's legal expenses, but the most pressing problem in August was to raise the money for his bail. This had been done by 11 August, with the Manchester spinners advancing the cash for Doherty and two sureties being found, one of whom was Robert Blincoe; but it was a further week before Doherty was released as Gilpin insisted that another £21 should be paid towards his own costs. Thus Doherty had only a week to prepare his case before it was heard at the Lancaster Assizes on 25 August amid great public interest. He made an eloquent speech lasting three hours in his own defence. He asserted that the story was well-known long before he printed it and referred to his duty as a public writer to publicise such stories, when Parliament had legalised the sale of the dead bodies of the poor and the horrific deeds of Burke and Hare were still fresh in recollection. He condemned the libel law which prevented him examining eight witnesses whom he could have produced to back his allegations and declared that the first act of the reformed Parliament should be to abolish it. He believed that Gilpin had dragged him through the mass of legal technicalities out of a spirit of revenge rather than to clear his reputation, which could not be vindicated by this method whatever the verdict. And he concluded by exhorting the jury not to perjure themselves by swearing his statements to be 'false' when they had heard no evidence to prove it. But Judge Bolland cautioned the jury that the only questions for their consideration was whether Doherty published the libel, and if so, whether it reflected upon the character of the prosecutor, and after three-quarters of an hour they returned a verdict of guilty. Doherty was ordered to appear at the King's Bench in November for sentence.

Doherty's address was widely praised in the press and he received unwonted editorial support, but over the succeeding months his situation rapidly deteriorated. Thomas Worsley had never consented to substantiate his original allegations in writing and finally his name was given up to Gilpin, but the latter refused to drop his case against Doherty, even when Doherty's wife was taken ill with cholera and seemed on the point of death and his departure for London entailed leaving his business in the care of his four young children. In court on 23 November he admitted that the statements which he had published on the authority of Worsley were untrue and was sentenced to one month's imprisonment, as well as to enter into recognisance to keep the peace and be of good behaviour for five years, himself in £100 and two sureties in

£10 each. This placed him in a desperate position, for as we have seen he was scheduled to appear at the New Bailey early in December to answer a second libel charge from Messrs Ogden and Arrowsmith.[64] For one of the few times in his life he seemed dispirited, swallowing his 'pride . . . patriotism and principles' and writing 'To the Working Classes and those friends who wish to secure their independence' on 4 December to beg that they take action to ensure that those who put up his bail on the second indictment did not suffer; and three days later he addressed a letter to his eldest son, Ambrose, to explain that he was not in prison for doing wrong, but for opposing, like Cobbett, Whittle and Candalet, those that did wrong, by whom he meant those few rich individuals descended from families given all the land and the exclusive right of making laws by the 'great public robber', William the Conqueror. With only just over half the money subscribed towards his legal expenses, which already amounted to £150, the *Advocate* ceased on 5 January 1833, the last two numbers containing a history of the Gilpin prosecution written by Doherty in the King's Bench prison on 13 December. He now blamed the whole sorry event on the despicable behaviour of Worsley, whose word, Doherty explained, he had trusted because of his factory reform activities, though he was aware of reports that Worsley had acted 'as a sort of spy for the government during Peel's days of power'.[65]

In the end, however, it was Worsley who suffered most from the sorry business, for he never again appeared as a leading figure among the workmen, while Doherty, resilient as ever, was soon participating once more in such radical activities as went on in Manchester after 1832. Fortunately his friends in the town had foreseen the danger in the second prosecution, and following a public meeting at St John's Tavern on 30 November to discuss a more effective organisation of the subscriptions, the committee had succeeded in having the hearing postponed until January, after which it seems to have been abandoned altogether. His financial embarrassments were also ameliorated by continued benefactions—a small donation from the Hyde and Newton Political Union was, for example, advertised in the *Poor Man's Guardian* on 23 February—and in February 1833 he opened his coffee and newsroom which served as a radical centre in the town for the short time it remained open. On 26 January his shop was advertised as one of the places to purchase a pamphlet entitled *The Elector's Guide*, which listed the names of all Manchester voters along with the candidate they had supported, and on 2 March Doherty was one of the sellers of a new and short-lived radical unstamped publication in the town entitled the *Salford Patriot*. He was soon working in concert with the 'Huntites' in the New Cross Political Union, with whom he had not co-operated since the failure of his delegation scheme in June 1831. Despite his recent experience, he joined with relish in the condemnation of the established clergy's neglect of the poor, when he, Broadhurst, Ashmore and Whittle disrupted a meeting to promote Sunday Observance in March 1833; and the same individuals adopted similar tactics with like effect when another meeting was attempted on the subject in February 1834. Doherty also served on the deputation of workmen organised by the New Cross Political Union in November 1833 to apprise Colonel Evans of the real state of distress in the country.[66] Nor did he cease to advocate the opinions of Cobbett, as he showed in the *Herald* in 1834, in which he continually stressed the hardships caused to the working classes by having to support vast numbers of pensioners, placemen and tax-eaters, and bitterly attacked the ruling classes for their repression of trade unions by use of the law, police and military. He was very bitter against the 'treachery' of the 'bloody-minded' Whigs, who, having betrayed the working classes over the Reform Bill, now so savagely oppressed them.[67]

Moreover, his activities continued to be a source of local publicity and excitement. During 1833 a strong movement developed against the assessed taxes, particularly those on houses and windows, and the radicals urged their replacement by direct property taxes. Associations were formed in various towns to organise their non-payment when the government refused to repeal them in its budget. In October Doherty refused to pay the sum of £1 2s 6d which he owed for the house and window duties, and the collector of taxes for the district seized a table from his shop in lieu of payment, which was deposited for sale in the 'New Boar's Head' public house, next door to Doherty's shop. Doherty immediately published a multitude of posters headed 'Whig Tyranny', stating that he should not pay taxes as a non-elector, that the government had broken its pledge to repeal the taxes, and that the table was in any case worth £4 5s; he invited Manchester inhabitants to attend the sale on the morning of 21 October to prevent the table being 'sacrificed'. A large crowd of radicals assembled at the appointed time, the auctioneer made no appearance, and when the time-limit for the sale expired, the table was paraded through the major streets with inscriptions chalked thereon proclaiming 'No votes, no taxes', and 'Seized for assessed taxes: bid who will, we will not'. The procession terminated in Withy Grove where the table was presented to Mrs Doherty as 'the gift of the people'. Broadhurst then urged the crowd to support Doherty's business, as well as all others who resisted the assessed taxes. The carnival events of the day concluded with an address by Doherty from his bedroom window. 'He said that in the step which he had just taken he was actuated by the purest motives of goodwill to his country and fellow men. The Whigs whom he had supported during the progress of the Reform Bill had betrayed the people, and in the deception practised by them originated his present resistance to the assessed taxes.' When calm was restored, Doherty discreetly returned the table, damaged as it then was, to the 'New Boar's Head' so as to avoid a charge of felony.[68]

This incident was symptomatic of the increasing disenchantment of radicals with the Whigs, as the memory of Tory oppression faded and the feeling grew that radicals and Tories shared a common hostility to the new 'liberalism' and the hated political economy. Dislike of the Whigs was exacerbated by repression in Ireland, the Factory Act, the Dorchester sentences, and the Poor Law Amendment Act. We have already seen Doherty's bitter reaction to the Whig government's policy in regard to factory reform and trade unions, and we shall shortly examine his equally strong views on Ireland. He also joined in the protest against the New Poor Law. As soon as the Poor Law Commissioners reported in 1834, in fact, Doherty declared that the Whigs were 'threatening to amend (to destroy) Elizabeth's poor law, which gives every labourer a better title to sustenance . . . than the landlord has to his rents . . . they will rob the poor man of his inheritance, and leave him to die by the roadside. The report of the Poor Law Commissioners proves that

P

they mean to do this. . . .'[69] And when this report was transformed into law later in 1834, Doherty condemned 'the New Poor Law Destruction Act' and the Malthusian doctrine underlying it.[70]

When, therefore, the King dismissed the government in November 1834 and sent for Wellington, and the Manchester Whigs and liberals convened a meeting to address the King 'on the present critical state of public affairs', their speakers, including Hindley, Wood, Philips and Thomas Potter, were swamped by angry radicals. Cobbett, Fielden, Wroe, Dixon and Doherty in turn denounced 'the base whigs'. Doherty denied that the Whigs could claim credit for the Reform Bill, which was the people's measure, and he instanced their 'swindling tricks' by pointing out that they had tried to raise the voting qualification from £10 to £20 but blamed the alteration on a clerical error when it was exposed. He ridiculed the idea that the government could not effect their pledges because of Tory opposition in the Lords; if this was so, they should have resigned as Cobbett had told them and the people would have carried them back as before. He believed that, if the Whigs were assisted to return to office now, they would continue to maltreat the people and that there was more chance of making the Tories into radicals than the Whigs into honest men; this was proved by the character of Whigs on the hustings such as G. W. Wood, whom 'he utterly despised', who was responsible for the present Police Act and who associated with the editor of the *Guardian*, and Mark Philips, also 'stained with Whiggery'. 'These men called upon the meeting to help them—would they go along with the meeting for universal suffrage? Not they. When the people asked for universal suffrage, these men called them a disaffected rabble, but now that their assistance was wanted, they were all wise men.' Ultimately an amended address was adopted, thanking His Majesty for dismissing such disgraceful ministers. Nevertheless, though so estranged from the Whigs, the radicals were not yet ready to join with the Tories and the meeting also adopted a resolution suggested by Prentice condemnatory of Tory support for the worst measures of the government. Doherty seconded this motion, remarking that 'this would show the tories that they must go along with the people if they expected support from them'.[71]

During the resulting elections, the radicals persuaded Sir Charles Wolseley to stand on a programme of radical reform, the ten-hours bill, separation of church and state, and opposition to the new poor law and malt tax. On 3 January 1835 Poulett Thomson put forward his election address in the Manchester Exchange, defending moderate reform against the extremes of the ultra-Tories and the 'destructives', and after he had finished he was catechised at length by Doherty, who wished to have certain actions explained 'in justice to himself and the class to which he belonged'. Doherty's questions related to specific votes. Why had Thomson voted for a Tory speaker if he considered them such 'frightful fellows'? Why had he opposed the clause in the Irish Church Temporalities Bill recognising the property of the church as under the control of the government? Why had he opposed the repeal of the malt tax? Why had he been absent during discussions on Grote's motion for the ballot? Why had he voted for the Irish Coercion Bill? Why had he opposed Attwood's motion for an enquiry into the condition of the labouring classes? And why, if the government had 'affection and regard for the working classes' as Thomson claimed, had it passed 'the poor law amendment bill'? But as a skilful politician Thomson was able to parry these questions, by claiming that the time was not right to introduce such measures as the ballot, by pointing to the turbulent state of the country to justify the Irish proceedings, and by arguing that all-party support was given to reforms like the new poor law. Even the *Manchester and Salford Advertiser* commented that 'Mr Thomson is too "cunning in fence" to be hit by so unpractised a swordsman as Mr Doherty, and therefore, his answers being very plausible, he lost nothing by the encounter'. At the polls there was more evidence of a Tory–radical coalition, Cobbett having issued a placard in favour of the Tory candidate, Benjamin Braidley, and 370 votes being split between Wolseley and Braidley, but the sitting members, Thomson and Philips, were easily returned. Doherty had moved into larger premises during the previous year and was thus able to vote for the first time; if and how he did so, however, is not recorded.[72]

On 31 January 1835 he was one of the advertised sellers of *Cobbett's Legacy to Labourers, or What is the Right which the Lords, Baronets and Squires have to the Lands of England*.[73] And for another year thereafter Doherty's shop remained one of the principal venues in Manchester for the sale of the unstamped, until he was compelled to desist through prosecution.[74] During the following years, however, he was mainly involved in the factory reform movement and his radical-political activities appear to have dwindled. In his evidence to the Combinations Committee in June 1838, he showed that his distrust for parliamentary interference with trade unions remained unabated, and in January 1839 he still struck Anthony Trollope as being a 'furious radical'.[75] But in fact he did not play a leading role in the radical resurgence which accompanied the profound trade depression of the later 1830s. He supported the aims of, but appeared only rarely in, the Anti-Poor Law campaign in the north during 1837–8. He evidently backed Oastler in that campaign, and in March 1838, spoke at a Manchester meeting in support of R. J. Richardson and the Anti-Poor Law Association.[76] But he was not a prominent figure in that movement, and when it merged into Chartism his connection was similarly intermittent. On 15 September 1838 his shop was advertised as one of the places where individuals could join the new and radical 'Manchester Political Union', but he was not a member of the council of that body, though it comprised forty-one persons including most of the local leaders in the agitations of the previous two decades. Later in the same month he was in the platform party at a great Chartist demonstration on Kersal Moor, but does not appear to have spoken.[77] In April 1839 he published a portrait of J. R. Stephens, which he had expressly commissioned from 'an eminent London artist', because of his martyrdom in the Anti-Poor Law and Chartist campaigns. The *Northern Star* was sold in Doherty's bookshop, but he was not on the official list of agents; and when he complained of lateness in deliveries, O'Connor replied that he could know nothing of the difficulties of running a newspaper office, a remark typical of O'Connor's ignorance of the exertions of others in the radical cause.[78] It is clear, however, that Doherty was not 'a prominent Chartist', as Hovell described him,[79] but only on the fringes of the movement.

In the other great socio-political movement of that time, the Anti-Corn Law agitation, Doherty's attitude also underwent a change. As we have seen, he had taken part in meetings against the Corn Laws from the mid-1820s, and continued to denounce them,[80] hence when the Anti-Corn Law League was formed in 1838 he apparently favoured its objective, despite his distrust of Manchester manufacturers and his opposition to the 'free trade' philosophy in general. On 28 December 1839 his shop was one of the places where tickets could be purchased for an 'Operative Anti-Corn Law Banquet' in Manchester the following month. On 13 March 1841 he was one of about 750 requisitionists who requested the Mayor, William Nield, to call a public meeting in the town to petition Parliament 'for the immediate abolition of the Corn and Provision Laws'. And on 15 May 1841 he was among about 1,270 requisitionists who requested Nield to convene another public meeting to support the reduction in the corn duties projected in the budget of the expiring Whig administration as a useful first step towards total repeal.[81] But Doherty's attitude had changed markedly, as we have seen, by the end of 1841, when manufacturers in the League spread rumours that he and Ashley were conspiring to whip up the ten-hours campaign as a 'tory trick' to divert the workmen's attention from the Corn Laws. This Doherty vehemently denied, pointing out his long record in the movements both for factory reform and repeal of the Corn Laws; at the same time, he revealed that he had taken little part in the current agitation of the League, that he strongly distrusted the manufacturers' motives, and that he found Tories such as Lord Ashley much more sympathetic towards the workmen's grievances.[82] During 1842 he asserted that he expected little benefit from the League's operations—certainly not to workmen, whose wages the employers were interested in reducing—and at the Nottingham by-election in August he supported the Tory anti-poor law candidate, Walter, against Sturge. It is clear that the middle-class free traders' opposition to factory reform, and their support of the new poor law, caused Doherty to oppose Sturge's Complete Suffrage Union and to find more hope in a Tory–Radical alliance.[83] He took no part, however, in the commotions in Manchester up to 1846 between supporters of the League and the Chartists, although when he was shouted down at a Dissenters' meeting to protest against the educational clauses of the Factory Bill in April 1843, the *Manchester Courier* blamed it on the 'League–Irish'.[84] His basic radicalism was still evident, however, in the factory reform movement, in which he continued to stress the importance of mobilising public opinion to bring pressure upon Parliament.[85]

Thus for more than a quarter-century Doherty had participated in radical political movements with the object of reforming Parliament and securing redress of social grievances. His views had sometimes been violently expressed, in bitter, almost revolutionary, class terms, especially in times of crisis, as in the Reform Bill struggle or when the Dorchester labourers were convicted. But his actual policies were usually moderate when compared with those of the more extreme radicals. Whilst emphasising the need for solidarity among the working people, he was usually prepared to collaborate with other classes, either with Whig–liberal manufacturers in agitating for corn-law repeal and parliamentary reform, or with Tory landowners in the factory and anti-poor law movements; and despite occasionally violent talk, verging on advocacy of physical force, he was generally realistic and pragmatic, fully aware of the strength of the police and military forces at the disposal of the authorities, warning against disorder and violence, and advocating peaceful, constitutional means of expressing popular opinion, in public meetings, petitions, delegations, and press publicity; his weapons were voice and pen, not torch and pike. He has been mistakenly contrasted with moderates such as Lovett— a contrast between the skilled, traditional craftsmen of the metropolis and the more turbulent factory workers of the north—but, in fact, he was very similar to Lovett in his political outlook and policies, with his belief in constitutional procedure, moderation, education, and forming public opinion. His mercurial Irish temperament occasionally caused outbursts of extremist, violent language, of the kind that alarmed Place, but in general there was little really 'revolutionary' about him.

It was not only on great national issues that Doherty was politically active. After 1832, when further parliamentary reform seemed remote, he began to participate in radical efforts to democratise local government in Manchester. These activities, too, though causing many angry scenes, could scarcely be called revolutionary, especially as his collaborators were mainly small shopkeepers, of which he himself was now one. Manchester was at this time still technically a manorial borough, with court-leet, borough-reeve and constables; in addition there was the parish administration of vestry meetings and churchwardens; but real power came increasingly into the hands of the Police Commissioners, established under a local improvement act, whose authority covered public health and other matters, as well as police functions. During the 1820s radicals exerted a growing influence over this body through election of men like Elijah Dixon and William Whitworth, but this was eliminated by an alliance of Whigs and Tories which gained a new Police Act in 1828 raising the qualification for voting in the elections for the Commissioners to householders paying rates of £16 per annum, while only those paying £28 per annum were eligible for election. Thus frustrated, the radicals tried a new policy of attending in strength at the quarterly meetings of leypayers to audit the constables' accounts and also at the annual meetings to elect new officers like the surveyors of highways. During 1831, for instance, the *Voice* reported on 22 January an unsuccessful effort led by Prentice to reduce the salary of Lavender, the unpopular deputy-constable, to £400 per annum, and on 13 August further opposition by Prentice, Candalet, Winder and Richard Potter to the donation of 15 per cent of the proceeds from the sale of stolen property to Lavender on top of his salary.[86] Radicals, of course, have always been particularly sensitive about the police and their functions in preserving order during mass meetings, demonstrations, and strikes. Doherty was certainly no exception in this respect, ever since his own arrest in 1818; he frequently attacked 'Bourbon police' methods and was personally involved in repeated incidents.[87] In this, as in other spheres of local government, therefore, he was a staunch advocate of democratic control. Moreover, just as he resented paying taxes to an unrepresentative central government, with its sinecures and corruption, backed by a standing army, so he also resented paying rates to a corrupt, oligarchic local government and police force.

To organise the attack on the local establishment, a meeting of radical ratepayers eventually agreed, on 2 May 1832, to form the Manchester Leypayers Association, with James Wroe as secretary, 'for mutual protection of rights and the redress of all local grievances' and to work for a new Police Act which would recognise the right of every leypayer to vote in the election of Commissioners. Its first trial of strength was at the annual parish meeting on 1 June when an amendment of Prentice's that the church rate for the next year should be $\frac{1}{2}d$ instead of 1d was carried, and by September it had over six hundred members. Meanwhile Doherty, who had resented Lavender's high-handed attitude when taking him to the New Bailey prison in June, printed a series of letters in the *Advocate* from an ex-police officer alleging that Lavender grossly overcharged on his expenses. Unwonted numbers turned up for the annual leypayers' meeting on 3 October, when a proposal that Lavender's salary be reduced to £400 per annum was carried by a massive majority. The borough-reeve, Benjamin Braidley, however, asserted that many persons were not leypayers and therefore determined that a poll should be held under Sturges Bourne's Select Vestry Act, by which votes were calculated according to the value of the property owned by the voter. At this juncture, Doherty, apparently a member of the Leypayers' Association, requested to have read that portion of the statute which bore upon the disputed point, but the law clerk, Milne, declined to do so. Nevertheless, in his report in the *Advocate*, Doherty admitted that the authorities' action was legal, if iniquitous. He therefore urged that leypayers should assert their rights, 'in the spirit of the reform bill', work towards the overthrow of that 'haughty faction', led by '*Bricks against Brains* Braidley', that had hitherto ruled the town and resisted any introduction of economy into the administration, and demand the abolition of 'that infamous act'. In the poll as arranged under the act, however, Braidley's own proposition that the salary should remain at £600 per annum was carried by a majority of more than four to one.[88]

Over the next two years, there was a series of angry wrangles between the authorities and the Association. At the parish meeting on 9 April 1833 Prentice and Wroe demanded the right to elect the new churchwardens and sidesmen, rather than their being simply nominated by the retiring officers. When a poll was ordered, they denied that Sturges Bourne's Act applied to townships covered by a local Police Act, and they advised the leypayers to boycott the poll while the validity of the proceeding was tested in the King's Bench. Next, at the leypayers' meeting to audit the constables' accounts on 1 August, attention was turned on Lavender's successor, Thomas, appointed in the previous month at the reduced salary of £400 per annum, but whose previous post had been in the capital—hence it was feared by Wroe and others that it was intended to introduce the London police system into Manchester with its attendant brutal methods of dealing with radical demonstrations. Thomas, however, found an unexpected defender in Doherty, who explained that he had recently stayed in the Covent Garden area for three months during his factory reform delegation, and being aware that Lavender was ill and that his successor was likely to be a Bow-street officer, he had taken pains to ascertain the characters of all the officers and made extensive enquiries among respectable householders and working people. He had found public feeling universally hostile to the new police, but had not heard a single complaint as to Thomas' conduct, and he predicted that within twelve months those disposed to oppose him would be his decided friends. *The Manchester and Salford Advertiser* asserted that 'our townsmen are indebted to Mr

Doherty for this instance of his vigilance', and the matter was dropped for the present, although suspicion that the metropolitan police system would be extended to the provinces to counter radicalism remained. In the following month, the Association was active at the annual vestry meeting demanding more say for the leypayers in the appointment of surveyors of highways for the township, with Doherty emphasising their rights of election, instead of nomination by the churchwardens. Later, in November, we find Doherty—himself recently involved in the contretemps over his arrears for assessed taxes—conveying a petition to the Police Commissioners from a poor old woman who had been roughly treated by their officers while they were seizing her property for arrears of rates.[89]

Another scandal blew up at the leypayers' meeting to audit the constables' quarterly accounts on 23 January 1834 when Wroe produced evidence of a police-officer being bribed by a local publican. Thomas promised an open investigation at which leypayers' representatives might be present, and Wroe and Doherty were appointed to attend—a sign of the increased respect which even a radical shopkeeper received compared with a trade-union leader—and the resulting enquiry having proved the story to be substantially true, action was taken against the officer involved. But there was a far less amicable settlement to a bitter dispute at the annual parish meeting on 1 April, when with a legal decision over the leypayers' right to elect churchwardens and sidesmen still pending from the previous year, Wroe again proposed a number of radical candidates; and he protested at the present mode of assessing rates by which a disproportionate burden was imposed upon poorer shopkeepers compared with the wealthier tradesmen and factory owners. But the chairman, the Rev. C. D. Wray, repeated his procedure of the previous year by simply reading out the nominations of the retiring churchwardens and proposing to adjourn the meeting for a poll at the Town Hall over the next five days, under Sturges Bourne's Act. Doherty made a vehement protest against this unjust and undemocratic exercise of power by the combined forces of the propertied and ecclesiastical establishments—as demonstrated also in the recent attacks on trade unions—in oppression of the poorer classes. But the poll was held regardless and with the radicals divided over boycotting, a heavy majority even in numbers was gained for the churchwardens' list. And on 6 May the Court of King's Bench decided in favour of the authorities' action at the 1833, and by implication the 1834 elections. Despite this double defeat, however, members of the Leypayers' Association were again present in strength at the meeting to audit the constables' quarterly accounts on 23 July, when Doherty, Wroe and Dixon all protested at lawless and drunken behaviour by soldiers stationed in the town, and it was ultimately agreed that the magistrates should deal with such offences in future under the civil law. This protest no doubt reflected Doherty's intense radical dislike of the 'standing army' as well as the 'Bourbon police'.[90]

Doherty's activities in these local parish meetings, involving clashes with the Rev. C. D. Wray and churchwardens, also revealed his detestation of the Anglican Establishment, both as a radical and as an Irish Catholic. He often recalled his sentence in 1819 by the 'reverend hypocrite', Parson Hay, and he criticised the Anglican clergy's exaction of tithes as well as church rates, their efforts to limit working-class education, their lukewarmness towards factory reform, their patronising attitude towards the poor, their hostility to trade unions, and their emphasis on strict Sabbath observance.[91] Their alliance with the local propertied classes in a corrupt and unrepresentative system of local government added to his angry disgust.

A new situation was created by the passage of the Municipal Corporations Act in 1835. The local Whigs were anxious to break what had been a virtual Tory stranglehold since 1828, and in 1836 a Whig committee enquired into the state of Manchester local government and recommended the amalgamation of the day and night police as the most urgent reform. But at a meeting of leypayers on 9 February 1837 the radicals succeeded in voting down this proposal, which they considered would entail the introduction of a police force strong enough to impose the new poor law on an unwilling people. The affair came to a head at the end of the year when William Nield refused to serve as borough-reeve and Richard Cobden composed his pamphlet, *Incorporate Your Borough*, pointing to the democratic nature of corporations elected by household suffrage compared with the inequalities of Sturges Bourne's Act. A meeting was convened for 9 February 1838 to discuss the propriety of petitioning the Queen for a charter of incorporation. Rapid preparations were made by Tories and Radicals to resist this measure, and shortly before it took place Doherty published a placard calling upon the people to attend the meeting to oppose this 'treachery' and disputing Cobden's arguments.

> The shabby dishonest Whigs are again at their *dirty work*, trying with all manner of lies to gull you into believing that the *Humbug Corporation Bill* . . . will do good to you all. Now every man who has read the Bill knows that this 'great Boon' to the people confers . . . more odious privileges to the wealthier classes than the present Police Act: for by this *Liberal* Corporation Act, those who are assessed at £100 have ten times the power in governing the town which they have who are assessed at £10 . . . What is this but making over the Poor to the tender mercies of the Rich, and those, too the pretended Liberals, the devilish Whigs! . . . Remember! The penalties for non-attendance are whig misrule, new and oppressive taxes, a Bourbon police and the premium for the bastard-begetting, infernal new poor law.[92]

A long and well-attended meeting took place, at which Cobden was the main supporter of incorporation, arguing that this would simplify local administration and denouncing the motives of its opponents, who professed to be radical reformers and yet opposed democratisation. But Wroe, Nightingale and Dixon strongly propounded the arguments set forth in Doherty's placard, and Doherty himself made a long speech. He censured Cobden's intemperate language and imputations, and asserted that he too favoured popular local government. The present Police Act had nothing liberal in it, yet its original supporters—G. W. Wood and J. E. Taylor—were the very men now clamouring against it and putting Cobden forward to propose incorporation, 'in the hope of hereafter assuming the dignity of the mayoralty, or of wrapping themselves up within the folds of the aldermanic gown'. A new Police Act including household suffrage could be obtained as an experiment for the cost of £500, a quarter of the town clerk's salary. If this proved efficient and incorporation was seen to work at Birmingham, then let them apply for a charter; but there was no urgency in the matter, for 'the town was peaceful; there was no insurrection; there were but few robberies. Their police could not be better managed.' Cobden replied that there was no need for delay—150 large towns had experienced incorporation for two years—and he suggested that Doherty had been hired to speak by the wealthy Tory opponents of the measure. And his original motion was carried by a large majority.[93]

An exchange of letters followed between Cobden and Doherty. Cobden withdrew his accusation of corrupt motives on Doherty's part, but repeated that it was at least 'ignorant' to oppose the replacement of a monopoly with a modified household suffrage qualification. Doherty replied that the present incorporators had procured that 'monopoly qualification—and are therefore to be suspected'—and challenged Cobden to prove his charge of ignorance. In fact there were hypocrites on both sides. Radicals *were* opposing a more democratic framework and Doherty's defence of the Police Commissioners reads strangely after his frequent brushes with them in the past; but as on such national questions as factory reform and poor relief, he was now prepared to join in a Tory-Radical alliance against the detested Whig manufacturers. On the other hand, as Barnes has shown, Whig assertions regarding the lawless state of the town overlooked the improvement in police efficiency made by the Commissioners' watch committee between 1830 and 1837, while their cant about democracy was shown up by their disregard of the fact that more signatures were obtained for a petition against incorporation after this meeting than for the petition in favour. In fact, the struggle was for local political power, and the Whigs with their friends in government won it, Manchester receiving its charter of incorporation by October 1838.[94]

But this far from settled the dispute. On 7 August 1839, Doherty—now defending the old 'establishment' which formerly he had so often criticised—was again present at a meeting of Tory and Radical leypayers in defence of the churchwardens and overseers, the legality of whose appointment and their right to levy poor rates was being challenged by the new Whig corporation. In response, the churchwardens and overseers were disputing the validity of the borough charter itself and the resulting court case lasted for several more years before the corporation gained sole control of the administration of the town.[95]

Meanwhile the radicals kept up a despairing campaign against the introduction of the new poor law in Manchester. But in December 1840 they were betrayed by the Tory churchwardens and overseers who, in the hope of avoiding the disturbances occasioned by its introduction in some other towns, determined to nominate as the first Poor Law Guardians in Manchester a compromise list half of Tories and half of Whigs, 'in order to save the great inconvenience and expense which a contested election would occasion'. This tactic was upset by Wroe, who forthwith presented his own list including himself, Doherty and several other Radicals for the consideration of the leypayers. At the resulting elections early in 1841, however, they were heavily defeated, supporters of the new poor law each receiving 3,000 or more votes, compared with 342 for Wroe, 240 for Thomas Fielden, 76 for John Whyatt, 59 for Doherty, and 21 for R. J. Richardson. On 26 February, nevertheless, 240 requisitionists including Doherty, Wroe, Thomas, Fielden and Dixon requested the mayor, borough-reeve and constables to call a public meeting to petition against Russell's bill to continue the operation of the new poor law, but the authorities declined to do so on the ground that the new organisation had not had sufficient trial in Manchester to warrant an opinion being expressed on behalf of the town. A meeting was eventually held on 8 March on the authority of the churchwardens, but Doherty did not speak nor did it have any positive result. And with this final defeat, the radical attempt to secure a substantial voice in Manchester local government virtually expired.[96]

As a Catholic Irishman, Doherty had strong concern for the interests of his co-religionists and fellow-countrymen. Place, as we have seen, referred to him as 'a rigid, uncompromising, intolerant Roman Catholic',[97] and Doherty certainly did, on numerous occasions, defend his own religious views and attack the Anglican establishment, especially, as we shall see, in the context of Irish affairs. But Place's opinions were prejudiced and, in this case, distorted, for in many ways Doherty's socio-radical views ran counter to those of the Roman Catholic hierarchy. In the 1830s the Catholic Church was strongly opposed to trade unions, especially on account of their subversive, secretive, oath-taking characteristics—supporting, instead, friendly societies and guilds under clerical control.[98] Doherty, however, clearly would not toe the clerical line in this respect: he was apparently a radical trade unionist first and a Catholic second—or, like trade unionists generally, he refused to mix religion with trade affairs. Moreover, as we have previously noted, the spinners' trade societies contained very few Irish Catholics, and the National Association did not have 'much impact upon the Irish communities in the northern counties'.[99] In politics, too, Doherty held independent views: he impressed Trollope, for instance, not only as 'an Irishman, a Roman Catholic', but also as 'a furious radical'.[100] At the same time, however, we find him actively supporting Catholic education and temperance societies.[101] Moreover, in opposing the Factory Education Bill in 1843, he was in agreement with official Catholic policy, reacting strongly against the threatened Anglican control of factory schools. But, as we have noticed, he appears to have been equally if not more concerned on that occasion with emphasising the paramount need for reducing children's working hours.[102] And it seems very probable that Doherty's long-continued campaign for factory reform contributed to the eventual change in the attitude of the Catholic Church, as it came to adopt a more sympathetic view of trade unionists' social demands, especially in Manchester, where the Rev D. Hearne was one of the first priests to support the Ten Hours' Bill and denounce the factory system.[103] Clearly, Doherty's trade-union and socio-political views were by no means determined by Irish-Catholic dogma; his broad radical working-class philosophy generally transcended religious opinions—indeed, he could hardly otherwise have achieved the leadership he did in proletarian movements.

Like most Irish immigrants, however, Doherty remained in close touch with his home country. This was the case on the personal level. In May 1825, when he wrote to Place asking if he would be required to give evidence to the Select Committee on the Combination Laws, he explained that he needed to know quickly in order to save any loss of time, 'because, at Whitsuntide, we have usually a holyday-week, and should it be your opinion that I shall not be wanted shortly, I intend visiting my Mother in Ireland, where I should stop, at least a week, perhaps a fortnight'. And it was equally true on a political level. Doherty remained a life-long admirer of Daniel O'Connell, despite fundamental differences in social policy for both England and Ireland; he consistently maintained that his National Association, with its penny subscriptions and policy of including all workmen in one union, was inspired by the success of the Catholic Association. And for more than a decade after 1824 there was scarcely a single major development in Ireland on which Doherty did not make some comment and attempt to elicit a sympathetic response from Irish and English radicals in Manchester.[104]

The most important question in the 1820s was, of course, Catholic Emancipation, and on this issue, as on many others, Doherty expressed conflicting views at different times. In July 1824 he wrote to O'Connell that the Manchester Catholics 'had it in contemplation to establish a Catholic newspaper in London' and hoped to engage W. E. Andrews, a well-known Catholic journalist, as its editor. Doherty believed that this step would be very advantageous to the Catholic cause and 'concluded by calling upon the Association to apportion a portion of the Catholic Rent towards establishing it'. O'Connell was highly enthusiastic for the project, which he believed would enable them to combat 'the slanders of the Orange Press', and he also welcomed the attack, contained in Doherty's letter, on the 'aristocratic' and 'superior' London Catholic Association. However, on 7 August O'Connell stated that from further information received 'he was exceedingly happy to find . . . that Mr Doherty's communication on behalf of the Catholics of Manchester, "that the English Catholic Board, intended to separate from the other Catholics of England and from the Irish Association", was totally unfounded'. And when the *Truth-Teller* was established in London in September 1824, with Andrews as its editor, O'Connell denied that any part of the Catholic Rent had been used to finance it.[105]

Doherty was still in favour of Emancipation in 1825, when he wrote angrily to Place criticising the rejection of Burdett's Catholic Relief Bill.[106] But he adopted a rather different position at a Manchester radical meeting in August, when he emphasised that first 'the whole [political] system must be changed'. His countrymen were greatly agitated on the subject of Catholic Emancipation to the neglect, he feared, of matters of higher importance. He was himself a Catholic, but not a friend to Emancipation. He believed that if Catholic Emancipation were obtained tomorrow, 'it would only strengthen the hands of our oppressors; and he hoped, if Ireland made a stand, it would be for principle, and not for such patch-work as these'. These views were presumably influenced by Cobbett, who supported Emancipation but believed parliamentary reform to be a more basic demand and therefore opposed the compromises of 1825 and 1829 as of benefit only to 'aristocrats and lawyers'. Doherty did not speak at a meeting in Manchester in July 1828, addressed by Richard Potter, Prentice and Hodgins, to raise a subscription towards O'Connell's election expenses in County Clare, but by the end of that year his opinions had apparently changed again. When a meeting was convened in the Manor Court Room on 24 November to oppose further political concessions to the Catholics as 'pregnant with danger to the constitution of these realms', Doherty gatecrashed it with about twenty other Catholic workmen, despite police being stationed at the door to prevent such an occurrence. He essayed continual interruptions, but was always forced to sit down by shouts from the audience and rulings from the chairman, whom Doherty censured for casting reflections 'upon the religion which I profess' and yet refusing him the right of reply. And when O'Connell accepted Emancipation along with disqualification of the 40s freeholders in 1829, Doherty later defended this action as a necessary compromise.[107]

With Emancipation obtained, Irish interest turned to agitation for the repeal of the Act of Union, while the most pressing problems were the extreme distress of the peasantry and the continuation of tithes to the Church of Ireland, both of which led to violence and counter-violence, and intermittently to Acts of Coercion when things threatened to get completely out of hand. Affairs were in this state at the beginning of 1831 when Doherty launched the *Voice*, and that paper contained a regular weekly column of Irish news as well as occasional editorial comment. On 22 January notice was given of a meeting of the friends of Ireland to be held on 25 January to petition Parliament for repeal of the Act of Union, 'as the general conviction is, that the cultivation of the waste lands and the employment of her people, are of much more intrinsic value than the cultivation of foreign colonies; besides the dire misfortune of the non-resident gentry, which tends to pauperise and degrade her injured people'. At the appointed time, over 1,200 persons attended to hear both Irish and English radicals support the motion that 'a free choice of government is the . . . inalienable right of every nation'. But Prentice maintained that radical reform must be the first priority and censured the Catholic leaders for bartering the rights of 300,000 freeholders for Emancipation, from which the only result had been the tyrannical Proclamation or Algerine Act extinguishing all civil liberties in Ireland. Doherty was the final speaker and he asserted that 'the emancipation bill was an equivalent for its attendant Algerine Act and the disfranchisement of the 40s freeholders'. Repeal would bring prosperity to Ireland, he went on, and also benefit English workmen who would no longer face competition from Irish immigrant labour. He condemned the government's restrictions on O'Connell's meetings, asserting that Manchester was prepared at any time to welcome his 'agitation', and concluding by proposing a vote of thanks for his 'spirited exertions'.[108]

The petition adopted by the meeting was eventually signed by 12,000 persons and presented in March, along with similar entreaties from towns throughout England and Ireland. Meanwhile the 'Old Radical', with whom Prentice regularly found himself in agreement, wrote to the *Manchester Times and Gazette* on 5 February to criticise the conduct of 'young reformers' like Oates, who forgot that Irish grievances existed before the Act of Union, as the 1798 rebellion proved. 'From John Doherty I expected better things. When he said that the emancipation bill was an equivalent for all that the Irish nation had paid for it, . . . I said to myself, "God help thee silly one, thou art a fine fellow to be at the head of a newspaper. I must not look up to thee as a political preceptor at any rate".'[109]

During that year conditions in Ireland grew close to famine and by April Doherty was writing in favour of the immediate introduction of poor laws there, to make the English absentee landlords responsible for the poverty they caused. If this was not done, he reasserted on 11 June, then the wretched

Irish poor could not be blamed for any consequent violence or deaths. And on 3 September he maintained that the Commons' lethargic response to Sadler's motion for Irish poor laws, compared with their haste to pass the Algerine Act or disenfranchise the 40s freeholders, showed the necessity of English and Irish workmen uniting to obtain radical reform or society would be 'torn up by the roots'. During the summer, resistance to the payment of tithes provoked dreadful retaliatory massacres at Castlepollard and Newtonbarry, yet when the County of Waterford petitioned for the total disarming of the yeomanry, Doherty wrote on 20 August, the government not only refused to do so but even to receive the petition. 'When the feelings and lives of the people are outraged, both factions in the house join against us.' Finally on 10 September, he condemned the 'modern teachers of state Christianity' who regarded tithes as 'a more sacred object of pious solicitude than the dying injunctions of the Divine Mother whom they profess to follow'; but he predicted that the 'insidious' alliance of church and state could not last much longer.[110]

There was little improvement in the situation, however, during 1832. On 23 January Irish and English radicals in Manchester, presumably including Doherty, formed the 'Friends of Ireland Society', aiming 'to aid the patriotic exertions of Daniel O'Connell for the freedom of Ireland'. Doherty had little space in the *Advocate* for Irish affairs until his imprisonment; then, on 7 July, he inserted a letter from 'Pauperrimus' urging that candidates pledged to vote for abolition of tithes should be supported in the elections; on 4 August O'Connell's 'Plan' for their extinction was copied, and two weeks later a lengthy article censured 'the cost of the Irish Church'. When the *Advocate* was transformed into a political periodical in September, this concentration on Irish affairs continued. A new tithe tragedy had occurred at Wallstown and the *Advocate* copied a series of letters from O'Connell 'To the Reformers of Great Britain', denouncing these 'murders', demanding the dismissal of the Irish ministers, Anglesey and Stanley, and proposing an alliance of English and Irish radicals to obtain radical reform and repeal. Doherty strongly favoured such an alliance, asking on 13 October if the British people would allow 'Whig perfidy and aristocratic domination' to wade through Irish blood in defence of 'accursed tithes' for an 'execrated church, which is not, and never was, in unison with even a tithe of the people'. At the same time, he also published as a separate pamphlet O'Connell's 'letter to the Members of the National Political Union' of Ireland, dated 24 September, proposing co-operation between men of all religions to demand repeal pledges at the forthcoming elections. And at the 'weekly meetings' of workmen which Doherty was organising in Manchester, the tithe question twice came up for discussion on 6 and 20 November and the injustice of forcing people to maintain a church from which they dissented was strongly proclaimed. Although Doherty was in a somewhat despondent mood in the King's Bench prison on 4 December, he could not resist saying that Gilpin was a member of 'the same church which is now drenching my unhappy country with blood, and which is benevolently employed in carrying away the last potato and the only blanket of the widow and the orphan, to gratify the rapacity and feed the profligate cormorants of an institution which is at once a disgrace to man, an insult to religion, and a blasphemy toward heaven'.[111]

In fact, Doherty's language on Irish affairs was fiery even by his own standards. In the new year the government introduced a new coercive measure, the Suppression of Disturbances Bill, and on 4 March a protest meeting was held in Camp Field, Manchester, at which Dixon, Curran, Adams, Candalet and others asserted that despotic powers were being taken up to compel the payment of tithes. Doherty believed that the bill was much more tyrannical and oppressive than the measures which drove France, America, Belgium and Poland to revolution, and the Irish people were therefore ten times more justified in resisting it. 'He hoped that the people of Ireland would not rashly fling themselves on the bayonets and bullets of the borough-mongering standing army; but first make a trial of their strength. He would just add what Lord Grey might not be acquainted with, . . . that within . . . six miles, including this town, there were, if the Irish people should be justified in resisting by means which are always justified by success (he meant physical force), . . . at the least 20,000 real, stout, determined Irishmen, prepared to assist them by every means within their power, and that feeling and spirit was not merely confined to Manchester or to this neighbourhood.' A petition was adopted praying for the withdrawal of the bill, the abolition of tithes, and the introduction of poor laws, and Doherty's shop was among the places where it could be signed. It gained the support of 14,000 names and was presented by Cobbett, but the bill had passed through all its stages by the end of the month.[112]

With the government reneging on their reparation for this bill, when Stanley persuaded the cabinet to drop the clause in the Irish Church Temporalities Bill proposing to create a fund to allow tenants on bishops' estates to buy land on short-term leases, O'Connell broke with the Whigs and initiated an extensive repeal agitation in Ireland. Doherty became secretary to the 'Manchester Repeal Association', with branches in the Irish districts of the town, and early in 1834 meetings were held in the different Lancashire towns in support of O'Connell's campaign. On 28 January Doherty, Oates and Condy spoke at a meeting in Stockport with several local workmen, and on 10 February Doherty and John Knight addressed a similar gathering at Oldham, when an association was formed for both radical reform and repeal to be supported by weekly penny subscriptions. But considerable difficulty was experienced by the Manchester repeal committee in organising a meeting in that town, for all applications for use of public rooms or Sunday schools were refused on the pretext that their purpose contravened the tenor of the King's speech. Finally they secured the Salford Old Cloth Hall for a meeting on 12 March, but despite having paid the rental found the door barred to them at the appointed time. Doherty addressed an angry crowd outside and stated that the meeting would now be held at St George's Fields on 17 March. Some of the committee had objected that this was St Patrick's day, but he was certain that 'if the saint could reappear on earth and be in Manchester on that day, he would attend the meeting himself. If there was a man who would not forgo the pleasure of a tawdry procession . . ., he was a rotten friend of the cause, and unworthy of the name of an Irishman'.[113]

Only about a thousand individuals, mainly Irish weavers, attended this assembly, which was addressed by Dixon, Lomax, West, Prentice and Wroe as well as Doherty, and passed motions deploring the present distress and bloodshed in Ireland, asserting that the Act of Union had been obtained by bribery and corruption, and adopting a petition to Parliament in favour of repeal, the abolition of tithes, and the establishment of poor laws, to be presented, on Doherty's recommendation, by Cobbett, the 'immortal author of *The Protestant Reformation'*. Doherty moved two of the main resolutions. He began by reading an account from Plowden's *History of Ireland* of the atrocities committed by the military about the time of the Union and of Earl Grey's condemnation of the Act as being obtained through 'influence' and giving Ireland too few representatives, which he contrasted with the Prime Minister's present opinion. The result of the Act had been the emigration of the landlords to England, where they spent their incomes; and they had been followed by shoals of Irish labourers, who bore down the wages of English workmen. Repeal would therefore be of advantage to both countries. Finally he referred to the absolute necessity of introducing a system of poor relief, in which opinion he 'certainly differed' from O'Connell, although 'in most things he should bow to the opinion of that great man'. Towards the end of the business, the St Patrick's day procession organised by the Manchester Hibernian Society passed within sight of the meeting, but they refused Doherty's invitation to join in and he expressed his deep disapproval of 'those Irishmen lured away by gaudy trappings and paraphernalia . . . from their important and patriotic duty'.[114]

Doherty's shop was again one of the places where the repeal petition could be signed, and by the time it was sent off on 14 April it had received over 26,000 signatures. On 26 April the Manchester Repeal Committee met at 'Hutton's Tavern' and resolved never to relax their exertions until a democratic Irish parliament was procured, for which purpose they established the Manchester and Salford Repeal Fund based on subscriptions of at least a penny per month. Two days later Doherty published on behalf of the Committee a twopenny pamphlet of twenty pages, containing O'Connell's 'celebrated' *Letter to the People of Ireland* on the repeal question written on 8 April of that year, O'Connell's speech in Parliament on the same subject on 22 April, and also his *Historical Sketch of the Rise, Progress and Triumph of the Catholic Association*. In a postscript, Doherty urged the readers, 'whatever country has given you birth', to further the cause of justice and liberty and to strengthen the union between English and Irish radicals, by circulating the pamphlet as widely as possible among their friends. On 17 May he inserted an advertisement in the *Poor Man's Guardian*, revealing that 20,000 copies of the pamphlet had been printed and a country-wide circulation was expected. The Manchester Repeal Association continued active in the cause for the rest of the year. In December placards printed by Doherty were posted upon the walls convening a meeting of the Association on 10 December to consider 'business deserving of the most anxious attention of every friend of liberty, and of Irishmen in particular'; new members were invited to attend, the subscription still being a penny per month, and the intention was to apply the money to support O'Connell's exertions. Oates and Doherty, their differences of 1831–2 presumably now forgotten, were the chief orators at the meeting. Oates desired that a declaration in favour of repeal be signed and sent over to Ireland by a deputation, recommending Doherty as a suitable person to lead it. But Doherty 'declined the honour' and urged the necessity of building up the funds of the Association so that the committee could continue to call meetings. According to the *Guardian*, however, only about half a dozen new members enrolled their names. At the Parliamentary elections in January 1835 Doherty as we have seen quizzed Poulett Thomson concerning Irish coercion and the rejection of the most important clause in the Irish Church Temporalities Bill.[115] But with O'Connell renewing his uneasy alliance with the Whig government shortly afterwards and hoping thereby to secure more attention to Irish reforms, interest in repeal lapsed until the revival in the 1840s.[116]

A new crisis occurred in 1836 when O'Connell was put to great expense in defending his own seat and those of his sons from Tory charges of irregularity in the elections, and subscriptions were begun on his behalf in almost every town in the kingdom. As an orthodox political economist, and hence supporter of the new poor law and opponent of restricting adult hours of labour, O'Connell's opinions on social reform differed radically from those of Doherty. But the latter could overlook even his hatred for the 'infernal science' in his admiration for O'Connell's work for Ireland, and Doherty played a leading part in the Manchester meeting to raise funds for the O'Connell subscription on 20 June. He proposed the first resolution and asserted that the action had been commenced against O'Connell by the united purses of the Carlton Club and the Orange Faction because they hated him for his great services to the cause of liberty and also desired to remove a supporter of the government. All must know that the Irish people had never united for one purpose before O'Connell's efforts for Catholic Emancipation and he had also set the example for English radicals. Some refused to recognise these services—Elijah Dixon, for instance, interrupted the proceedings to criticise O'Connell's attitudes towards the 40s freeholders, relief of the hand-loom weavers, factory reform and poor laws in England and Ireland—but Doherty stated that he had scrutinised all O'Connell's votes in Parliament and only disagreed with the vote on Poulett Thomson's amendment to the Factory Act. Certainly the Irish people appreciated the value of his efforts for they had already collected £15,000 for him. For this, 'hireling scribes' of the Tories called him the 'big beggarman', yet O'Connell had forsaken a lucrative professional career to serve the cause of Ireland for twenty-five years and the money had been donated freely, whereas the Tories liked nothing better than taking the people's money by compulsion. And with thanks also to Thomas Potter for bearing the whole cost of the recent petition from Manchester against the Lords' 'mutilations' of the Irish Municipal Corporations' Bill, Doherty concluded by moving the meeting's gratitude to O'Connell for his resistance to Tory corruption and Whig coercion; and he was later appointed to a committee of eleven individuals to superintend the subscriptions.[117]

Doherty continued to serve the Irish cause through his business activities. In August 1835 he had become the Manchester agent for the weekly *Dublin Satirist*, and in the autumn of 1836 he published in thirteen weekly parts at 1d each the *Life, Trial, and Conversations of Robert Emmett*, an Irish patriot executed in 1803 for leading an insurrection. Later, he became an official Catholic bookseller in Manchester, as well as participating in the activities of the Catholic Schools' and Temperance Societies.[118] Even during his evidence to the Commons' Combinations Committee in 1838, which O'Connell had been largely responsible for establishing, he showed continued regard for the Irish leader and indeed was complimented in return by O'Connell in the House of Commons.[119] But by the time the repeal agitation revived after 1841, Doherty's public efforts were mainly confined to factory reform and there is no record of his being involved in the increasingly turbulent movement in Manchester in support of the new campaign.

This survey of Doherty's political activities completes the account of his public career. Spanning twenty-eight hectic years between 1817 and 1845, it had comprehended trade unionism, factory reform, co-operation, political radicalism and journalism, Irish nationalism, temperance and education. Very rarely in that time did he use the term 'working class' in the singular, but his life was symbolic of the growing sense of solidarity among workmen which resulted in their support for all these various movements. Doherty never seriously attempted, however, to weld all these movements together: his 'Appeal to the Producers of Wealth', though a significant combination of current trade-union, co-operative and radical ideas, was not, as Beer asserted, a far-sighted plan for 'a political Labour Party' more than half a century ahead of its time.[120] Moreover, he never adopted a rigid 'class' outlook: for all his emphasis on independent action by the working classes, he tended to give uncritical support to individuals in 'superior' walks of life, even though many of their ideas were in direct opposition to elements of his own philosophy: to William Cobbett, a landowner and farmer, who frequently ridiculed the notion that labourers required 'heducashon' beyond their social and occupational status; to Daniel O'Connell, a lawyer, who supported the most rigid political economy in opposition to any interference with the supply and demand of labour; to Lord Ashley, an aristocrat whose principal reforming interest was in restricting children's working hours, but who was politically reactionary; and for a short period to Robert Owen, an erstwhile manufacturer, who regularly stressed the identity of interest of masters and workmen. Many of the inconsistencies and sudden changes of policy which have been pointed out perhaps arose from this anomaly.

Doherty borrowed and changed ideas like clothes. He switched his activities from one movement to another, according to success or failure, holding out great hopes first from one and then from another, and thus inevitably bringing criticism upon himself for inconsistency and lack of principle. It was not only anti-trade-union papers such as the *Guardian* and *Chronicle* in Manchester or the *Advertiser* in Stockport, but also trade unionists such as the spinners of Bolton and Ashton and other working-class critics who alleged that he was an unprincipled schemer, seeking personal power and prestige, profiting financially from the various movements which he puffed and inflated.[121] His exaggerations and instability were also commented on unfavourably by Place and Prentice. There is no doubt that he did often raise hopes that he was unable to fulfil, and that he slipped with remarkable adroitness from one movement to another as they rose and fell; or, with equal agility, trimmed his sails or altered tack, according to changing winds.

These shifts and inconsistencies, however, were largely forced upon him. He *had* to be flexible and pragmatic, because of the weakness of working-class organisations at that time, the strength of opposing forces, and the fluctuations of the trade cycle. Nor was he really a selfish, scheming agitator, trading on the gullibility and misfortunes of the working classes. There is certainly evidence to suggest that, like other prominent trade unionists and radicals, he became a marked man, proscribed by employers, and was therefore obliged to make a living, as it were, from the various working-class movements with which he became associated. But he was not just a trading agitator, driven into this kind of career: his own experiences and circumstances, his self-education, reading and widening contacts gradually shaped his philosophy, his consciousness of the ills of society, and his burning resolve to strive for working-class betterment, whilst his oratorical and literary abilities enabled him to play a leading role in different social movements with this general objective; his final resort to radical journalism, bookselling and printing was typical of many articulate working-class leaders in that period. He was certainly not, therefore, simply furthering his own interests, but was providing a voice for popular grievances. Nor did he, as enemies suggested, live in affluence at the expense of his dupes, but on a very modest scale, sometimes in financial hardship and with his family life perpetually disrupted. Moreover, despite his trimming and tacking, his general direction was steadily maintained, especially in trade unionism and factory reform; his faithfulness in the latter cause was particularly notable, as Lord Ashley affirmed,[122] while his trade-union loyalty and leadership were recognised by the subscriptions raised on his behalf during the Gilpin affair and by the reliance of the cotton spinners upon him in 1834–6 and 1838, after he had left the industry and become a bookseller.

Moreover, Doherty did bring something distinctive to the causes which he served. For radicalism, he provided the first example of cheap and well-written periodicals actually edited by a working man rather than by a middle-class sympathiser. For factory reform, he provided the most significant inspiration for efforts by the operatives themselves to reduce working hours and cheap child labour, sometimes by direct trade-union action, but most consistently by attempts to enforce and extend restrictive legislation, through agitation organised by the short-time committees. Most important, for trade unionism he provided the first experiment with any substance to give practical effect to that wider vision of society which the movement never entirely lost. Moreover, the multiplicity of his interests strengthened his contribution to individual causes by a cross-fertilisation of ideas. From his activities in the radical Great Northern Union and his support for the Irish Catholic Association, he brought the ideas of penny subscriptions and of organisations in the different towns controlled by a central committee, which he applied to the Grand General Union of Cotton Spinners and the National Association. And from his experience in general unionism, he brought a similar organisational network to the Lancashire short-time committees.

Despite his inconsistencies, Doherty did have a basic philosophy which underlay his participation in all these movements. He believed that the labour of working men provided the foundation for the strength and prosperity of the nation. Hence they deserved to receive in return for their efforts the whole of the resulting production, but were being robbed of that right by competitive capitalism. This robbery was sustained and aggravated by the workers' exclusion from political power, which they must obtain both because of natural justice and to assist their efforts to procure their economic rights. He supported any cause which he believed likely to fulfil these aims, his approach in each case being essentially pragmatic. His overriding ambition was for the material and spiritual well-being of his fellows. In 1831 he explained to an audience of Manchester workmen what he considered to be a fair reward for their labour—a definition which has been termed 'quaint' by a recent historian,[123] but which a more sympathetic observer of those harsh times might regard as almost touching:

> This ought, in his opinion, to be what would give the operative and his family four comfortable meals a day, with flesh meat at each, and a pint of beer for himself, and another for his wife and family at dinner, and the same at supper; a good suit of clothes for every day wear, and a better one for Sundays, a good bed to lie on; and sufficient means to give a good education to his children. Something of this sort the working-classes ought to consider as their due; and they should remember that while they are clothing everybody, they were themselves badly clothed and badly fed. If they were but properly alive to their own interests, they might be in possession of all these comforts in twelve months.[124]

But he also looked beyond this tangible objective to the formation of a more equitable society, wherein workmen would achieve their rightful position and be treated with the respect they deserved. Doherty's own words in August 1831 regarding this aspiration and his attempts to infuse the workmen with the spirit to attain it, again carry far more eloquence than those of writers looking back from a more comfortable existence almost a century and a half later:

> I want to better the condition of the people—to have them stand erect, and look boldly in the faces of their masters, and to tell them, 'We are not your slaves; we are your equals. We are one side of the bargain, you are only the other. We give you an equivalent for what we get from you, and are therefore entitled to, at least, equal respect'. Whoever opposes the present system will be the object of attacks. I will persevere to oppose it in whatever situation I may be placed. I am so convinced of its injustice, that the idea of those who create all receiving scarcely anything is so monstrous, that I can never be persuaded to remain quiet as long as the system exists.[125]

This resolute statement provides a fitting epitaph for John Doherty. He died unsung, but here, in his own words, still echoes 'the Voice of the People'.

NOTES TO CHAPTER ELEVEN

[1] D. Read, 'The Social and Economic Background to Peterloo', in *T.L.C.A.S.*, Vol. XIV (1954), pp. 1–18.
[2] Lancashire Quarter Sessions, Indictment Rolls, October 1818; Broughton Papers, Add. MSS 36,458, f. 427.
[3] *Observer*, 6 and 24 May 1820, 6 January 1821; *Black Dwarf*, 18 April 1821. See R. F. Wearmouth, *Methodism and the Working-Class Movements of England, 1800–50* (1937), pp. 106–7, which, however, misdates the formation of the fund to the meeting in January 1821.
[4] See above, pp. 27–8.

[5] *Observer,* 3 March 1821. Pilkington and Kay, of Bury, were two of the weavers' leaders who had been arrested and sentenced with Doherty. See above, p. 26.

[6] *Ibid.,* 25 August–8 September 1821.

[7] *Mercury,* 22 September; *Black Dwarf,* 19 September; *Observer,* 6 October 1821.

[8] *Observer,* 20 October 1821 and 26 January 1822; Wearmouth, *op. cit.,* pp. 108–12.

[9] *Observer,* 26 January; *Black Dwarf,* 20 February; *Republican,* 22 February; *Observer,* 8 June 1822.

[10] *Republican,* 30 August; *Black Dwarf,* 28 May 1823, and 1824 Preface.

[11] Place Papers, Vol. xv, Add MSS 27,803, f. 298. See also above, p. 40.

[12] See also above, p. 41.

[13] *Gazette,* 28 January; *Trades' Newspaper,* 29 January 1826.

[14] See above, pp. 41–2.

[15] *Gazette,* 29 April, 6 May and 28 October 1826.

[16] *Guardian,* 24 February; *Chronicle,* 24 February 1827.

[17] See below, pp. 637–48, for his attitude on Ireland.

[18] *Guardian,* 11 August and 1 September; *Gazette,* 1 September; *Chronicle,* 1 September 1827; *Lion,* 18 January 1828.

[19] 'Twelfth Week' and 'Seventeenth Week', in Place Collection, Vol. 16, Part II, ff. 66 and 73–4.

[20] *Courier,* 5 December 1829.

[21] For a general survey, see A. E. Musson, 'Parliament and the Press', *Parliamentary Affairs* (Hansard Society), 1956, revised in *Trade Union and Social History* (1974). For more detailed studies of the subject in this period, see W. H. Wickwar, *The Struggle for the Freedom of the Press, 1819–1832* (1928); P. Hollis, *The Pauper Press* (Oxford, 1970); J. H. Weiner, *The War of the Unstamped* (University of California Press, 1970).

[22] See above, p. 334.

[23] *Journal,* 1 May 1830.

[24] See above, pp. 105–6, 121, 123, 184, 185 for evidence of political feeling among cotton spinners during strikes at this time and the authorities' consequent alarm.

[25] *Journal,* 10 April, 5 and 19 June, 10 July, 7 August and 4 September 1830.

[26] *Times and Gazette,* 9 October 1830. See also above, p. 189.

[27] See above, pp. 188 *et seq.*

[28] *Times and Gazette,* 30 October; *Chronicle,* 30 October 1830. For the petition, see the *Prompter,* 11 December 1830.

[29] Place Papers, Add. MSS 37,950, ff. 96–7.

[30] *Times and Gazette,* 11 December 1830. It was to be a stamped paper, price 7*d.* See above, p. 206.

[31] *Guardian,* 27 February 1830.

[32] *Chronicle,* 26 June 1830.

[33] *Ibid.,* 4 December 1830; *Guardian,* 22 January; *Voice,* 29 January 1831.

[34] *Times and Gazette,* 14 August 1830.

[35] *Guardian,* 1 and 8 January 1831.

[36] *Voice,* 1 January 1831.

[37] *Ibid.,* 1 January–23 April 1831.

[38] *Ibid.,* 9, 23 and 30 April 1831.

[39] *Guardian,* 7 May; *Times and Gazette,* 7 May; *Voice,* 7 and 14 May 1831.

[40] See above, p. 234 and 235.

[41] *Times and Gazette,* 6 November 1830; *Voice,* 7, 14 and 28 May, 4 and 11 June; *Leeds Patriot,* 14 May 1831.

[42] See above, p. 237.

[43] *Sheffield Iris,* 28 May; *Times and Gazette,* 18 June; *Nottingham Review,* 20 May; *Advertiser,* 18 June; *Leeds Patriot,* 14 May; *Voice,* 21 May 1831.

[44] *Stockport Advertiser,* 7 June; *Voice,* 28 May; *Guardian,* 4 and 18 June; *Bolton Chronicle,* 25 June 1831.

[45] *Times and Gazette,* 28 May; *Voice,* 11 June; *Guardian,* 18 June 1831.

[46] *Guardian,* 18 June; *Chronicle,* 18 and 25 June; *Guardian,* 2 July 1831.

[47] The writer went on, as we have seen, to cast similar aspersions on Doherty's National Association and Co-operative projects. See above, p. 331.

[48] *Voice,* 16 and 23 July, 20 August; *Poor Man's Guardian,* 30 July 1831.

[49] *Voice,* 17 and 24 September; *A Letter to the Members* . . . (1832); *Poor Man's Guardian,* 22 October 1831.

[50] Place Papers, Vol. III, Add. MSS 27,791, ff. 270 and 304–6.

[51] See above, p. 249.

[52] *Voice,* 17 and 24 September; *Guardian,* 22 and 29 October and 26 November; *Times and Gazette,* 17 December; *Courier,* 17 December 1831.

[53] See below, p. 443.

[54] *Voice,* 26 March, 9 April, 18 June, 9 July 1831.

[55] *Advertiser,* 1 October; *Voice,* 9 July, 3 and 17 September; *Advertiser,* 31 December 1831.

[56] *Advocate,* 24 March, 7 April and 5 May; *Crisis,* 19 May; *Advertiser,* 19 May 1832.

[57] *Guardian,* 12 May–9 June 1832; *Advertiser,* 16 June; *Advocate,* 11 and 25 August; J. W. Morris, *Radical Reasons for Perseverance in Reform* . . . (Manchester, 1832).

[58] *A Pennyworth of Politics, by the Advocate,* 8 September; *A Penny Paper, by an Advocate,* 15 September; *A Poor Man's Advocate,* 22 September; *A Penny Advocate,* 29 September; *Guardian,* 15 September; *Times and Gazette,* 6 October 1832.

[59] *Advocate and Political Adviser,* 13 October; *Advocate or Tyrant's Chastiser,* 1 December 1832.

[60] *Chronicle,* 20 October; *Advocate and Pennyworth of Politics,* 6 October 1832; L. S. Marshall, 'The First Parliamentary Election in Manchester', *American Historical Review,* Vol. 47 (April 1942), pp. 518–38.

[61] *Stockport Advertiser,* 1 December 1831, 10 August 1832; *Advocate,* 31 March–21 April; *Advertiser,* 5 May; *Advocate,* 19 May and 9 June 1832.

[62] *Stockport Advertiser,* 5 April; *Advertiser,* 12 April; *Advocate,* 9 June–21 July 1832.

[63] *Advocate,* 30 June, 7 July; *Advertiser,* 28 July; *Times and Gazette,* 4 August; *Advocate,* 11 and 18 August 1832.

[64] See above, p. 378.

[65] *Advertiser,* 18 August; *Advocate,* 1 September; *Advocate and Tyrant's Chastiser,* 1 December 1832; *Advocate and Workman's Guide,* 5 January 1833.

[66] See above, pp. 276–7.

[67] *Advocate and Tyrant's Chastiser,* 1 December; *Guardian,* 12 January 1833; *Poor Man's Guardian,* 23 February and 2 March; *Advertiser,* 26 January 1833; *Guardian,* 16 March 1833 and 22 February 1834; *Herald,* 8 February and 5 April 1834. See also above, pp. 289–90.

[68] *Times and Gazette,* 26 October 1833.

[69] *Herald,* 5 April 1834.

[70] See above, pp. 384 and 393.

[71] *Courier,* 29 November 1834.

[72] *Times,* 10 January; *Advertiser,* 10 January 1835.

[73] *Advertiser,* 31 January 1835.

[74] See above, pp. 341–2.

[75] Parl. Papers, 1837–8, VIII, 3403; Trollope, *op. cit.,* p. 10.

[76] See above, p. 394.

[77] *Advertiser,* 15 September; *Guardian,* 28 September 1838.

[78] *Northern Star,* 20 April 1839.

[79] M. Hovell, *The Chartist Movement* (1918), p. 22.

[80] See above, pp. 417–8, 420, 425.

[81] *Chronicle,* 28 December 1839, 13 March and 15 May 1841.

[82] See above, pp. 399–401.

[83] See above, pp. 402–3.

[84] *Courier,* 29 April 1843. See above, p. 403.

[85] See above, pp. 405–6.

86 A. Redford, *The History of Local Government in Manchester* (1940), Vol. II, pp. 3–8; *Voice*, 22 January, 13 August 1831.

87 See above, pp. 21–2, 76, 77, 289–90, 292, 295, and 341–2.

88 *Times and Gazette*, 5 May and 9 June; *Advocate*, 16 June, 4 July, 28 July; *Chronicle*, 6 and 13 October; *Advocate and Pennyworth of Politics*, 6 October 1832.

89 *Advertiser*, 13 April, 3 August; *Chronicle*, 28 September; *Advertiser*, 16 November 1833.

90 *Times and Gazette*, 25 January, 1 February; *Guardian*, 5 April, 10 May; *Chronicle*, 26 July; *Herald*, 5 April 1834.

91 See above, pp. 88, 334–5, 338–9, and 373. The Gilpin affair also illustrates his hostility. See above, pp. 435–8.

92 *Chronicle*, 11 February 1837; Redford, *op. cit.*, pp. 12–16.

93 *Guardian*, 10 February; *Chronicle*, 10 February 1838.

94 *Advertiser*, 17 February 1839; M. J. Barnes, 'Policing Developments in Manchester in the Age of Reform', Unpub. B.A. thesis (Manchester, 1970).

95 *Guardian*, 10 August 1839.

96 *Advertiser*, 19 December 1840; *Guardian*, 6 January 1841; *Chronicle*, 6 and 10 March 1842.

97 See above, p. 430.

98 J. H. Treble, 'The Attitude of the Roman Catholic Church towards Trade Unionism in the North of England, 1833–42', *Northern History*, Vol. v (1970).

99 See above, p. 52; Treble, *op. cit.*, p. 97.

100 See above, p. 397.

101 See above, pp. 338–9.

102 See above, p. 403; Ward and Treble, *op. cit.*

103 Treble, *op. cit.*, p. 112.

104 Place Collection, Vol. xiv, Add. mss 27,802, f. 283. For the Catholic Association, see J. A. Reynolds, *The Catholic Emancipation Crisis in Ireland, 1823–9* (Yale, 1954).

105 A. Aspinall, *Politics and the Press, 1780–1850* (1949), pp. 319–20; *Proceedings of the Catholic Association in Dublin from May 1823 to 11 February 1825* (1825).

106 See above, p. 417.

107 *Guardian*, 11 August and 1 September; *Gazette*, 1 September 1827; Cassirer, *op. cit.*, p. 192; *Mercury*, 15 July; *Guardian*, 29 November 1828.

108 *Voice*, 22 January; *Times and Gazette*, 29 January 1831.

109 *Times and Gazette*, 5 February 1831.

110 *Voice*, 2 April, 11 June, 20 August, 3 and 10 September 1831.

111 *Times and Gazette*, 28 January; *Advocate*, 7 July, 4 and 18 August; *Advocate and Political Adviser*, 13 October; *Advocate or Oppressor's Castigator*, 8 December 1832; *Mr O'Connell's Letter* . . . (1832), in White Slavery Collection, Vol. 6, No. 5.

112 *Guardian*, 9 March and 6 April; *Advertiser*, 16 March 1833.

113 A. Macintyre, *The Liberator: Daniel O'Connell and the Irish Party, 1830–1847* (1965), pp. 36 and 41; *Stockport Advertiser*, 31 January; *Advertiser*, 15 February; *Guardian*, 15 March 1834.

114 *Guardian*, 22 March; *Chronicle*, 22 March 1834. This gave rise to an angry exchange of letters between the Hibernian Society (a non-political, charitable body established in 1821, mainly to promote Irish education) and Doherty, the latter continuing to emphasise the prime importance of political commitment on the repeal question and denouncing the Whigs' coercive measures, both in Ireland and England (e.g., against the Dorchester labourers). *Advertiser*, 29 March, 19 April 1834.

115 See above, pp. 440–1.

116 *O'Connell's Speeches in London* . . (Manchester, 1834); *Poor Man's Guardian*, 17 May; *Guardian*, 13 December 1834; *Times and Gazette*, 25 June 1836.

117 *Times and Gazette*, 25 June 1836.

[118] *Advertiser*, 23 August 1835; 17 September, 19 November 1836. See above, pp. 338, 339 and 341.

[119] See above, pp. 311 and 396.

[120] See above, pp. 234 and 237–8.

[121] See, for example, pp. 51–3, 90, 135, 185, 191–2, 211–3, 251–2, 306, 331, 429.

[122] See above, p. 406.

[123] Bythell, *op. cit.*, p. 128.

[124] *Guardian*, 21 May 1831.

[125] *Voice*, 27 August 1831.

# Appendix

## The Manchester List of Prices—For Spinning upon Mules of different Sizes

| Spindles Nos. | 300 s | 300 d | 312 s | 312 d | 324 s | 324 d | 336 s | 336 d | 348 s | 348 d | 360 s | 360 d | 372 s | 372 d | 384 s | 384 d | 396 s | 396 d | 408 s | 408 d | 420 s | 420 d | 432 s | 432 d | 444 s | 444 d | 456 s | 456 d | 468 s | 468 d |
|---|---|---|---|---|---|---|---|---|---|---|---|---|---|---|---|---|---|---|---|---|---|---|---|---|---|---|---|---|---|---|
| 80 | | 5 | | 5 | | 4¾ | | 4¾ | | 4¾ | | 4½ | | 4½ | | 4½ | | 4½ | | 4¼ | | 4¼ | | 4¼ | | 4 | | 4 | | 4 |
| 85 | | 5½ | | 5½ | | 5¼ | | 5¼ | | 5¼ | | 5 | | 5 | | 5 | | 4¾ | | 4¾ | | 4¾ | | 4½ | | 4½ | | 4½ | | 4½ |
| 90 | | 6 | | 6 | | 5¾ | | 5¾ | | 5¾ | | 5½ | | 5½ | | 5½ | | 5¼ | | 5¼ | | 5 | | 5 | | 5 | | 5 | | 5 |
| 95 | | 6¾ | | 6¾ | | 6½ | | 6¼ | | 6¼ | | 6¼ | | 6 | | 6 | | 5¾ | | 5¾ | | 5¾ | | 5½ | | 5½ | | 5½ | | 5½ |
| 100 | | 7½ | | 7½ | | 7¼ | | 7¼ | | 7 | | 7 | | 6¾ | | 6¾ | | 6½ | | 6½ | | 6¼ | | 6¼ | | 6¼ | | 6¼ | | 6¼ |
| 105 | | 8¼ | | 8¼ | | 8 | | 8 | | 7¾ | | 7¾ | | 7½ | | 7½ | | 7¼ | | 7¼ | | 7 | | 7 | | 6¾ | | 6¾ | | 6¾ |
| 110 | | 9¼ | | 9¼ | | 9 | | 8¾ | | 8¾ | | 8½ | | 8½ | | 8¼ | | 8 | | 8 | | 7¾ | | 7¾ | | 7½ | | 7½ | | 7½ |
| 115 | | 10¼ | | 10¼ | | 10 | | 9¾ | | 9¾ | | 9½ | | 9¼ | | 9¼ | | 8¾ | | 8¾ | | 8½ | | 8½ | | 8½ | | 8½ | | 8½ |
| 120 | | 11½ | | 11¼ | | 11 | | 11 | | 10¾ | | 10½ | | 10¼ | | 10¼ | | 10 | | 9¾ | | 9¾ | | 9¾ | | 9¾ | | 9¼ | | 9¼ |
| 125 | 1 | 0¾ | 1 | 0½ | 1 | 0¼ | 1 | 0¼ | 1 | 0 | 1 | 0 | | 11½ | | 11¼ | | 11¼ | | 11 | | 10¾ | | 10¾ | | 10¼ | | 10¼ | | 10¼ |
| 130 | 1 | 2¼ | 1 | 2 | 1 | 1¾ | 1 | 1½ | 1 | 1½ | 1 | 1¼ | 1 | 1 | 1 | 0¾ | 1 | 0¾ | 1 | 0¼ | 1 | 0 | 1 | 0 | | 11¾ | | 11¾ | | 11½ |
| 135 | 1 | 3½ | 1 | 3¼ | 1 | 3 | 1 | 2¾ | 1 | 2¾ | 1 | 2½ | 1 | 2¼ | 1 | 2 | 1 | 1¾ | 1 | 1½ | 1 | 1¼ | 1 | 1 | 1 | 0¾ | 1 | 0½ | 1 | 0¼ |
| 140 | 1 | 5 | 1 | 4¾ | 1 | 4½ | 1 | 4¼ | 1 | 4 | 1 | 3¾ | 1 | 3½ | 1 | 3¼ | 1 | 3 | 1 | 2¾ | 1 | 2½ | 1 | 2¼ | 1 | 2 | 1 | 1¾ | 1 | 1½ |
| 145 | 1 | 6½ | 1 | 6¼ | 1 | 6 | 1 | 5¾ | 1 | 5¼ | 1 | 5 | 1 | 4¾ | 1 | 4½ | 1 | 4¼ | 1 | 4 | 1 | 3¾ | 1 | 3½ | 1 | 3¼ | 1 | 3 | 1 | 2¾ |
| 150 | 1 | 8 | 1 | 7¾ | 1 | 7½ | 1 | 7¼ | 1 | 6¾ | 1 | 6½ | 1 | 6¼ | 1 | 6 | 1 | 5¾ | 1 | 5¼ | 1 | 5 | 1 | 4¾ | 1 | 4 | 1 | 4 | 1 | 3½ |
| 155 | 1 | 9½ | 1 | 9¼ | 1 | 8¾ | 1 | 8½ | 1 | 8 | 1 | 7¾ | 1 | 7½ | 1 | 7¼ | 1 | 7 | 1 | 6½ | 1 | 6¼ | 1 | 6 | 1 | 5¼ | 1 | 5 | 1 | 5 |
| 160 | 1 | 11 | 1 | 10½ | 1 | 10¼ | 1 | 10 | 1 | 9½ | 1 | 9¼ | 1 | 9 | 1 | 8½ | 1 | 8¼ | 1 | 7¾ | 1 | 7½ | 1 | 7¼ | 1 | 7 | 1 | 6¼ | 1 | 6 |
| 165 | 2 | 1 | 2 | 0¼ | 2 | 0¼ | 2 | 0 | 1 | 11½ | 1 | 11 | 1 | 10¾ | 1 | 10¼ | 1 | 10 | 1 | 9¾ | 1 | 9½ | 1 | 9 | 1 | 8¾ | 1 | 8¼ | 1 | 8 |

| Spindles | 300 | | 312 | | 324 | | 336 | | 348 | | 360 | | 372 | | 384 | | 396 | | 408 | | 420 | | 432 | | 444 | | 456 | | 468 | |
|---|---|---|---|---|---|---|---|---|---|---|---|---|---|---|---|---|---|---|---|---|---|---|---|---|---|---|---|---|---|---|
| Nos. | *s* | *d* | *s* | *d* | *s* | *d* | *s* | *d* | *s* | *d* | *s* | *d* | *s* | *d* | *s* | *d* | *s* | *d* | *s* | *d* | *s* | *d* | *s* | *d* | *s* | *d* | *s* | *d* | *s* | *d* |
| 170 | 2 | 3¼ | 2 | 3 | 2 | 2½ | 2 | 2 | 2 | 1½ | 2 | 1 | 2 | 0¾ | 2 | 0¼ | 2 | 0 | 1 | 11¾ | 1 | 11½ | 1 | 11 | 1 | 10½ | 1 | 10 | 1 | 9½ |
| 175 | 2 | 6 | 2 | 5½ | 2 | 5 | 2 | 4½ | 2 | 4 | 2 | 3½ | 2 | 3¼ | 2 | 2¾ | 2 | 2¼ | 2 | 2 | 2 | 1½ | 2 | 1 | 2 | 0¾ | 2 | 0¼ | 1 | 11½ |
| 180 | 2 | 8¾ | 2 | 8¼ | 2 | 7¾ | 2 | 7¼ | 2 | 6¾ | 2 | 6¼ | 2 | 6 | 2 | 5¼ | 2 | 4¾ | 2 | 4¼ | 2 | 3¾ | 2 | 3¼ | 2 | 3 | 2 | 2½ | 2 | 2 |
| 185 | 3 | 0¼ | 2 | 11¾ | 2 | 11¼ | 2 | 10½ | 2 | 10 | 2 | 9½ | 2 | 9¼ | 2 | 8½ | 2 | 8 | 2 | 7¼ | 2 | 6¾ | 2 | 6¼ | 2 | 5¾ | 2 | 5 | 2 | 4½ |
| 190 | 3 | 4 | 3 | 3¼ | 3 | 2¾ | 3 | 2 | 3 | 1½ | 3 | 1 | 3 | 0½ | 3 | 0 | 2 | 11¼ | 2 | 10½ | 2 | 10 | 2 | 9¼ | 2 | 8¾ | 2 | 8 | 2 | 7½ |
| 195 | 3 | 8½ | 3 | 7¾ | 3 | 7 | 3 | 6¼ | 3 | 5¾ | 3 | 5 | 3 | 4½ | 3 | 3¾ | 3 | 3 | 3 | 2½ | 3 | 1¾ | 3 | 1 | 3 | 0¼ | 2 | 11½ | 2 | 11 |
| 200 | 4 | 1 | 4 | 0¼ | 3 | 11½ | 3 | 10¾ | 3 | 10 | 3 | 9¼ | 3 | 8½ | 3 | 7¾ | 3 | 7 | 3 | 6¼ | 3 | 5¾ | 3 | 5 | 3 | 4 | 3 | 3¼ | 3 | 2½ |
| 205 | 4 | 5¾ | 4 | 4¾ | 4 | 4 | 4 | 3¼ | 4 | 2½ | 4 | 1½ | 4 | 0¾ | 4 | 0 | 3 | 11¼ | 3 | 10¼ | 3 | 9¾ | 3 | 9 | 3 | 8 | 3 | 7 | 3 | 6 |
| 210 | 4 | 10½ | 4 | 9½ | 4 | 8¾ | 4 | 8 | 4 | 7 | 4 | 6 | 4 | 5¼ | 4 | 4¼ | 4 | 3½ | 4 | 2½ | 4 | 1¾ | 4 | 1 | 4 | 0 | 3 | 11 | 3 | 10 |
| 215 | 5 | 4¼ | 5 | 3¼ | 5 | 2¼ | 5 | 1½ | 5 | 0½ | 4 | 11½ | 4 | 10½ | 4 | 9¼ | 4 | 8½ | 4 | 7½ | 4 | 6½ | 4 | 5½ | 4 | 4½ | 4 | 3½ | 4 | 3 |
| 220 | 5 | 10 | 5 | 9 | 5 | 8 | 5 | 7 | 5 | 6 | 5 | 5 | 5 | 3¾ | 5 | 2½ | 5 | 1½ | 5 | 0½ | 4 | 11½ | 4 | 10¼ | 4 | 9¼ | 4 | 8¼ | 4 | 7¼ |
| 225 | 6 | 5 | 6 | 3¾ | 6 | 2¾ | 6 | 1½ | 6 | 0½ | 5 | 11¼ | 5 | 10 | 5 | 8¾ | 5 | 7¾ | 5 | 6½ | 5 | 5½ | 5 | 4¼ | 5 | 3 | 5 | 2 | 5 | 1 |
| 230 | 7 | 0 | 6 | 10¾ | 6 | 9½ | 6 | 8¼ | 6 | 7 | 6 | 5¾ | 6 | 4½ | 6 | 3¼ | 6 | 2 | 6 | 0¼ | 5 | 11½ | 5 | 10¼ | 5 | 9 | 5 | 7½ | 5 | 6 |
| 235 | 7 | 8½ | 7 | 7 | 7 | 5¾ | 7 | 4¼ | 7 | 3 | 7 | 1½ | 7 | 0¼ | 6 | 10¾ | 6 | 9½ | 6 | 8 | 6 | 6½ | 6 | 5¼ | 6 | 4 | 6 | 2½ | 6 | 1 |
| 240 | 8 | 5 | 8 | 3½ | 8 | 2 | 8 | 0½ | 7 | 11 | 7 | 9½ | 7 | 8 | 7 | 6½ | 7 | 5 | 7 | 3¼ | 7 | 1¾ | 7 | 0¼ | 6 | 11 | 6 | 9½ | 6 | 7½ |
| 245 | 9 | 4 | 9 | 2¼ | 9 | 0¾ | 8 | 11 | 8 | 9½ | 8 | 7¾ | 8 | 6 | 8 | 4¼ | 8 | 2½ | 8 | 0¾ | 7 | 11 | 7 | 9½ | 7 | 8 | 7 | 6 | 7 | 4¼ |
| 250 | 10 | 3 | 10 | 1¼ | 9 | 11½ | 9 | 9¾ | 9 | 8 | 9 | 6 | 9 | 4 | 9 | 2 | 9 | 0 | 8 | 10¼ | 8 | 8½ | 8 | 6¾ | 8 | 5 | 8 | 3 | 8 | 1 |
| Per cent | | | 1½ | | 3 | | 4½ | | 6 | | 7½ | | 9 | | 10½ | | 12 | | 13½ | | 15 | | 16½ | | 18 | | 19½ | | 21 | |

20 March 1829. G. E. Aubrey.

*Note.* The numbers across the top of the table refer to the numbers of spindles per mule; those down the side to the numbers or counts of yarn. Prices fall with increasing numbers of spindles, but rise with rising (i.e. finer) numbers of yarn.

*Source.* Place Collection, Vol. 16, Part II, f. 62.

# Index

*Note.* We have not included in this index the names of the enormous number of employers and firms referred to in the text in connection with trade disputes, factory reform, etc. To have done so would have extended it to an inordinate length without a corresponding increase in its usefulness, though the book undoubtedly contains a great deal of interesting evidence concerning employers' attitudes and actions. We have, however, included the names of all trade unionists, co-operators and radicals with whom Doherty had relationships, including middle- and upper-class sympathisers and collaborators, since the main interest of readers is likely to be in these working-class movements and the socio-political aspects of the period. We have also included all references to particular towns and counties, for those wishing to trace local involvements. Of the many local magistrates concerned with the maintenance of law and order, we have included only the two most observant and objective, James Norris and J. F. Foster, both of Manchester, but others can be traced under that subject heading.

207, 217, 239, 241, 251, 281, 283, 287, 295, 308, 324, 325, 329, 331, 332, 337, 416
Bishop Auckland, 256
Blackburn, 10, 28, 33, 41, 42, 126, 164, 172, 188, 198, 225, 228, 241, 242, 251, 262, 282, 308, 316 (n. 96), 331, 348, 355, 357-8, 361, 372, 377, 380, 429
Blacklegs. *See* Non-unionists
Blacklisting. *See* Victimisation
Blackrod, 195, 198, 241, 262
Blacksmiths and farriers. *See* Metal workers
Blanketeers' march (1817), 12, 414
Bleachers (crofters), 26, 29, 101, 163, 165, 183, 199, 263
Blincoe, Robert, 5, 7 (n. 14), 10, 349, 353, 375, 376, 396, 397, 398, 437
Bollington, 55, 56, 198, 262, 362
Bolton, 10, 14, 15, 25, 28-9, 31, 32, 33, 35, 43, 52, 62, 85, 87 *et seq.*, 96, 98, 99, 100-3, 104, 107, 113, 114, 119, 125, 126, 134-5, 140, 153, 157-9, 163, 164, 165, 167, 168, 178, 181, 182, 184, 189, 190-3, 194, 195, 198, 207, 209, 211, 216, 221, 222, 223-4, 230, 232, 241, 242, 246, 251, 258, 261, 262, 282, 283, 299, 308, 310, 314, 316 (n. 96), 332, 346, 349, 351, 357, 360-1, 362, 365, 370, 372-3, 377, 386, 387, 389, 398, 399-401, 406, 420, 428, 436
Bonner, William, 242, 243
Bowring, Dr. John, 207, 432
Bradford, 40, 154, 185, 209, 232, 233, 250, 257, 262, 283, 286, 292, 316 (n. 96), 346, 364, 379, 386, 389
Braidley, Benjamin, 441, 444
Bricklayers. *See* Building workers
Bristol, 242, 338
Broadhurst, Nathan, 288, 424, 431, 438, 439
Bromsgrove, 243
Brooks, William, 418, 419, 428, 429, 430, 433
Brotherton, Joseph, 351, 354, 377, 386, 394, 395, 437
Brown, John, and factory reform, 349, 352, 375
Brough, John, 20-1
Building workers, 25, 29, 77, 96, 146, 155, 196, 199, 217, 220, 239, 259, 261, 263, 272, 275, 295, 297, 298, 302, 330, 333
Bull, Rev. G. S., 274, 277, 286, Chap. x (*passim*)
Bullock, H. N., 150 (n. 46), 216, 222, 225, 230, 235, 247, 250, 252, 255, 256, 257
Bullock, Reuben, 165, 258, 397, 402

Bulwell (Notts.), 262
Buncrana (Ireland), Doherty's birthplace, 2
Burnley, 228, 282, 331, 351, 377-8
Bury, 25, 26, 43, 154, 163-4, 168, 181, 183, 189, 198, 241, 257, 262, 271 (n. 264), 282, 287, 316 (n. 96), 350, 377, 386, 387
Bussey, Peter, 257, 286

Calico-printers, co-operative scheme among, 169, 218, 227-8, 239, 322, 324, 326, 330, 344 (n. 57)
trade unionism among, and strikes of, 25, 26, 29, 36, 101, 165, 167, 168, 171, 196, 199, 218, 220, 221, 225-8, 232, 239-40, 245, 258, 259, 263, 275
Candalet, P. T., 415, 424, 429, 437, 438, 443, 452
Capitalism, development of, and Doherty's views on, 3-4, 9-13, 36, 57-8, 64-5, 67, 70, 72, 86, 95, 109, 137, 171, 175-6, 179, 195, 208, 213, 217, 218, 234, 235, 275-6, 279, 282, 283-4, 289, 290, 294, 295-6, 320-34 (*passim*), 364, 369-70, 377-8, 393-4. *See also* Class-consciousness
Card grinders and strippers, 66, 77, 155, 196, 199, 263
Carlile, Richard, 10, 250, 340, 353, 416, 420, 421, 425
Carlisle, 31, 87 *et seq.*, 108, 113, 126, 153, 198, 262
Carpenter, William, 195, 243, 244, 245, 250, 330, 425
Carpenters. *See* Building workers
Carpet weavers, 154
Carson, William, 172, 239, 325, 326, 329, 331
Cartwright, Major, 414, 416
Catholic Association and Emancipation, and influence on Doherty's ideas, 122, 156, 162, 184, 238, 311, 386, 417, 430, 449-50, 456
Catholicism. *See* Roman Catholicism
Catterall (Lancs.), 262
Chartism, 217, 260, 314, 318 (n. 158), 347, 394, 397, 399, 401, 402, 441, 442
Cheetham, John, 138, 212, 229, 230, 233
Cheshire, trade unionism in. *See the various towns* (Bollington, Hyde, Macclesfield, Stalybridge, Stockport)
Chesterfield, 242, 243, 280, 337
Child and juvenile labour, 2, 9, 10, 15, 18, 19, 28, 73, 78, 90-1, 93-4, 100, 109, 110, 111, 114, 126, 142-3, 144, 145, 177, 273, Chap. x. *See also* Factory reform *and* Piecers

United Kingdom Alliance of Organised Trades (1866), 302
*United Trades' Co-operative Journal,* 98, 102, 107, 159–62, 166, 167, 170, 175–6, 177, 180–1, 182, 187–90, 236, 323–4, 420–2
Unskilled workers (labourers, dockers, quarrymen), 11, 199, 258, 263, 326
Unstamped press. *See* Press freedom
Ure, Andrew, 3, 147, 388, 389, 396, 397

Victimisation, 21, 27, 30, 31, 43, 78, 93, 137, 184, 213, 221, 231, 308, 311, 370, 375, 382, 456
Violence and intimidation by trade unions, 10, 12, 13, 14, 20–3, 24–5, 29, 30, 31, 33–4, 36, 37, 38, 40, 41–2, 43, 51, 52, 54–5, 56–7, 59, 68, 72, 76, 81 (n. 40), 97, 99, 101–4, 105–6, 111–2, 114, 115 (n. 11), 116 (n. 55), 121–4, 126, 128–32, 135–6, 143–4, 149 (n. 14 and 38), 158, 181, 183–4, 186, 192, 210–1, 219, 226, 231, 232, 238, 292–3, 306, 309, 310, 312, 317 (n. 111), 333, 382, 402, 418
Doherty's deprecation of, 32, 40, 41–2, 43, 51, 52, 58, 63, 66, 68, 70–1, 72, 76, 102, 104, 107, 112, 121–2, 128, 162, 171, 176, 202 (n. 130), 219, 227, 238, 261, 290, 310, 343 (n. 11), 370, 418, 419, 426, 442–3
*Voice of the People,* 6, 100, 103, 110, 126–7, 134–5, 136, 140, 141, 183, 188–96, 197, 206–8, 209, 216, 218–9, 222, 223, 224, 236–8, 239, 240, 241, 244, 247–8, 248–55, 258, 260, 326 *et seq.,* 331–2, 364–5, 414, 422 *et seq.,* 450

Wages and trade unions, in cotton industry, 4, 12, 13, 14, 15, Chaps. II–V (*passim*), 158–9, 181–2, 208–10, 225–8, 259–60, 276, 291–2, 302, 308, 310–1, 312–3, 321–2, 323, 348, 349, 353, 372, 382, 390, 395
in general, 11, 24–6, 36, 39, 40, 41, 77, 114, 146, Chaps. VI and VII (*passim*),

276, 278, 286, 321–2, 323, 324, 325, 327, 330, 427
Wakefield, 257
Wales, trade unionism in, 172, 178, 231, 232
Walter, John, of *The Times,* 402, 404, 442
Warrington, 87, 282, 308, 359, 401, 437
Water-frames. *See* Spinning machines
Water power, 9, 10
Watson, James, 26, 430
Weavers. *See* Handloom *and* Power-loom weavers
Whittaker, Thomas, 357, 362, 365
Whittle, James, 130, 249, 275, 373, 424, 429, 432, 438
Whitworth, William, 443
Wigan, 19, 87, 172, 178, 239, 262, 282, 308, 316 (n. 96), 325, 329, 353, 355–6, 357, 361, 364, 375, 383, 386
Wolseley, Sir Charles, 415, 416, 440–1
Wolverhampton, 217
Women workers. *See* Female labour
Wood, G. W., 393, 428, 432, 440, 446
Wood, John, 273, 277, 346, 376, 390, 397, 401
Woolcombers, 40, 195, 199, 232, 257
Wooler, T. J., 416, 417
Worcester, 277, 281
Working conditions. *See* Factories *and* Factory reform
*Workman's Expositor,* 254, 368
Worsley, Thomas, 38, 39, 48 (n. 113), 49 (n. 124), 107, 117 (n. 88), 155, 164, 165, 168, 172, 352, 363, 365, 366, 435–8
Wroe, James, 22, 27, 45 (n. 30), 46 (n. 60), 341, 414, 424, 437, 440, 443–7, 452

Yorkshire, vii, 26, 40, 185, 194, 196, 198, 209, 220, 231, 232–3, 246, 247, 249, 250, 257–8, 259, 262, 272, 274–5, 278, 284, 285, 286, 287, 289, 291, 292, 294, 295, 297, 346, 355, 364 *et seq.,* 415. *See also the entries for various Yorkshire towns*